EDMUND SPENSER

The Shorter Poems

Edited by RICHARD A. MCCABE

PENGUIN BOOKS

PENGUIN BOOKS

Published by the Penguin Group
Penguin Books Ltd, 27 Wrights Lane, London w8 5tz, England
Penguin Putnam Inc., 375 Hudson Street, New York, New York 10014, USA
Penguin Books Australia Ltd, Ringwood, Victoria, Australia
Penguin Books Canada Ltd, 10 Alcorn Avenue, Toronto, Ontario, Canada m4v 3b2
Penguin Books (NZ) Ltd, Private Bag 102902, NSMC, Auckland, New Zealand

Penguin Books Ltd, Registered Offices: Harmondsworth, Middlesex, England

Published in Penguin Books 1999
1 3 5 7 9 10 8 6 4 2

Set in 10/11.5 pt Monotype Ehrhardt
Typeset by Rowland Phototypesetting Ltd, Bury St Edmunds, Suffolk
Printed in England by Clays Ltd, St Ives plc

PENGUIN  CLASSICS

PENGUIN ENGLISH POETS
GENERAL EDITOR: CHRISTOPHER RICKS

EDMUND SPENSER: THE SHORTER POEMS

EDMUND SPENSER was born in London, probably in 1552, and was educated at the Merchant Taylors' School, from which he proceeded to Pembroke College, Cambridge. There he met Gabriel Harvey, scholar and University Orator, who exerted a considerable influence on his first important poem, *The Shepheardes Calender* (1579) and with whom he collaborated on a volume of familiar letters (1580). He graduated BA in 1573 and proceeded MA in 1576. By 1578 he was employed as secretary to John Young, Bishop of Rochester, formerly Master of Pembroke College. He may have also served briefly in the household of Robert Dudley, Earl of Leicester, where it is commonly assumed that he met the Earl's nephew, Sir Philip Sidney, to whom *The Shepheardes Calender* is dedicated. In 1580 he went to Ireland as Secretary to Lord Grey de Wilton, Lord Deputy of Ireland, and stayed there for much of the remainder of his life, eventually becoming an undertaker in the Plantation of Munster. While at Kilcolman, his estate in County Cork, he met or reacquainted himself with his neighbour, Sir Walter Ralegh, with whom he travelled to London in 1589 to present the first three books of *The Faerie Queene* (1590) to its dedicatee, Queen Elizabeth, who rewarded him with an annual pension of fifty pounds. 1591 saw the publication of *Complaints* and *Daphnaïda*, the former exciting political controversy owing to the criticism of Lord Burghley contained in *Mother Hubberds Tale*. Spenser's marriage to Elizabeth Boyle was celebrated in his *Amoretti and Epithalamion* (1595), and his pastoral eclogue, *Colin Clouts Come Home Againe*, appeared in the same year. In 1596 he brought out the second three books of *The Faerie Queene* as well as his *Fowre Hymnes* and *Prothalamion*. In 1598 his estate was burned during the Tyrone rebellion, and he fled to Cork and thence to London, where he died in 1599. He was buried in Westminster Abbey and posthumously celebrated as the 'Prince of Poets'. In 1609 a folio edition of *The Faerie Queene* appeared, including the previously unpublished 'Mutabilitie Cantos', followed, in 1611, by a folio edition of the complete poetical works. *A View of the Present State of Ireland*, written in 1596, was published by Sir James Ware in 1633.

RICHARD A. MCCABE is a Fellow of Merton College and Reader in English at Oxford University. He was formerly Drapers' Research Fellow at Pembroke College, Cambridge and a Fellow of Trinity College Dublin. His publications include, *Joseph Hall: A Study in Satire and Meditation* (1982), *The Pillars of Eternity: Time and Providence in 'The Faerie Queene'* (1989), *Incest, Drama and Nature's Law* (1993) and *Presenting Poetry: Composition, Publication, Reception* (1995), co-edited with Howard Erskine-Hill.

CONTENTS

ILLUSTRATIONS

All of the illustrations are by courtesy of the Bodleian Library with the exception of those from *Daphnaïda* and *Amoretti and Epithalamion* which are reproduced by permission of the British Library. Details of the editions used are supplied in the Textual Apparatus.

CHRONOLOGY

1583   Death of the Earl of Desmond.

1585   The Earl of Leicester campaigns in the Low Countries.

1586   Publication of the third quarto of *The Shepheardes Calender*. Death of Sir Philip Sidney at Zutphen.

1587   Execution of Mary Queen of Scots.

1588   Defeat of the Spanish Armada. Death of the Earl of Leicester.

1589   Spenser travels to England with Sir Walter Ralegh in October. Accession of Henry IV of France.

1590   Publication of *The Faerie Queene*, I–III. Spenser receives the royal grant of his estate at Kilcolman.

1591   Publication of *Complaints, Daphnaïda* and the fourth quarto of *The Shepheardes Calender*. Spenser is granted an annual pension of fifty pounds. He returns to Ireland.

1593   Henry IV of France converts to Roman Catholicism.

1594   Spenser marries Elizabeth Boyle on 11 June. Beginning of the Nine Years' War in Ireland.

1595   Publication of *Colin Clovts Come Home Againe* (with *Astrophel*) and *Amoretti and Epithalamion*.

1596   Publication of *The Faerie Queene*, IV–VI with the second edition of Books I–III. The work is banned in Scotland by James VI. Publication of *Fowre Hymnes* with the second edition of *Daphnaïda*. Publication of *Prothalamion*.

1597   Publication of the fifth quarto of *The Shepheardes Calender*.

1598   *A Vewe of the Present State of Ireland* is entered in the Stationers' Register. Kilcolman is sacked by Celtic forces. Spenser travels to London.

1599   Death of Spenser in London on 13 January.

1601   The Earl of Tyrone is defeated at the Battle of Kinsale. Execution of the Earl of Essex.

1603   Death of Elizabeth I. Accession of James I.

1607   The Flight of the Earls breaks Celtic power in Ulster.

1609   Publication of the first folio of *The Faerie Queene* containing the 'Mutabilitie Cantos'. The Plantation of Ulster begins.

1611   Publication of the first folio of Spenser's *Works*.

1617   Publication of the second folio of Spenser's *Works*.

1620   Monument erected to Spenser in Westminster Abbey by Anne Clifford, Countess of Dorset.

1633   Publication of *A Vewe of the Present State of Ireland*.

1679   Publication of the third folio of Spenser's *Works*.

INTRODUCTION:
'OPPOSD REFLEXION'

Spenser is most commonly celebrated as the author of *The Faerie Queene* yet had he written nothing other than the works collected in the present volume he would still rank amongst the foremost of English poets. His shorter poems are arguably as essential to the comprehension of his epic verse as are the *Eclogues* and *Georgics* to Virgil's *Aeneid* but, like their Virgilian counterparts, their primary importance lies in their intrinsic literary merit. They are no mere adjuncts to the epic project but integral components of a wider canon which acknowledges and explores both the strengths and limitations of the heroic outlook. Read in conjunction with, rather than in subordination to, *The Faerie Queene* they reveal the intellectual range and aesthetic diversity of a singularly complex and frequently dichotomous world view. To an even greater extent than the epic poetry they demonstrate Spenser's generic and stylistic versatility, his remarkable linguistic virtuosity and mastery of complex metrical forms. Here he adopted the conflicting, if oddly complementary, *personae* of satirist and eulogist, elegist and lover, polemicist and prophet and, in the process, radically transformed the classical and medieval genres he employed. The impact upon succeeding generations of poets from Shakespeare to Yeats was tremendous. Originality, bred by tradition, fostered the renewal of tradition. Long before the term 'Spenserian' passed into common critical usage the concept was well understood and the practice widely imitated.

The publication of *The Shepheardes Calender* in 1579 marked a crucial turning point in English literary history. The 'new Poete' introduced to, and concealed from, the reading public, by the mysterious 'E. K.' – a literary agent too ideal to be other than fictitious – issued a manifesto for a new poetics premised upon an aggressive confidence in the English language, 'which truely of it self is both ful enough for prose and stately enough for verse'. By appropriating to his yet anonymous cause the illustrious names of Virgil and Chaucer, he nominated himself as their successor, arrogantly proclaiming his talent even as he pretended to disclaim 'vaunted titles' and 'glorious showes'. For the contemporary reader the shock of the new entailed a startling accommodation with the old. The *Calender*'s archaic diction articulated its claims to kinship with Chaucer by lending 'great grace, and as one would say, auctoritie to the verse'. On behalf of the nation the new poet 'hath laboured to restore, as to theyr rightfull heritage such good and naturall English words, as haue ben long time out of vse and almost cleare disherited'. The matter was politically charged: at a time when 'fayre Elisa', the Queen whose unsullied virginity had come to symbolize the country's territorial and spiritual integrity, was preparing to wed the 'alien', Catholic and French-speaking Duc d'Alençon, the preface assailed those 'whose first shame is, that they are not ashamed, in their own mother tonge straungers to be counted and alienes'. 'Why a Gods name', Spenser asked the following year, 'may not we . . . haue the kingdome of our owne Language?' (cf. *Prose*, 16). From the outset linguistic and political sovereignty go hand in hand, and the political import of the *Calender* is most potently conveyed through the assurance of its wordplay. To write good English verse was to assert true English identity, to oppose the linguistic miscegenation of those who 'made our English tongue, a gallimaufray or hodgepodge of al other speches'. The play on 'gall' in 'gallimaufray' is a shrewd hit for as *The Faerie Queene* reminds us 'old *Gall* . . . now is cleeped *France*' (4. 11. 16). Apropos the French match we learn that, 'Of Hony and of Gaule in loue there is store: / The Honye is much, but the Gaule is more' (*March*, 122–3). Never had mere orthography been so politically loaded; Elizabeth's 'Gaule' was England's 'gall' and the 'natural speach' of all true Englishmen, 'which together with their Nources milk they sucked', proclaimed its antipathy to the proposed misalliance.

The *Shepheardes Calender* serves not merely as a precursor to *The Faerie Queene* but as a pre-emptive strike in defence of the beleaguered 'faery' mythology, which would later inform it. For this reason Spenserian pastoral is confrontational rather than escapist and more inclined to chart the landscape of wish-frustration than that of wish-fulfilment. As the 'envoy' indicates, the poetry is acutely responsive to the 'ieopardee' of the moment and draws nervous energy from the sense of peril. Just a few months previously John Stubbs had lost his right hand for penning the notorious anti-Alençon tract, *The Discoverie of a Gaping Gulf Whereinto England is like to be Swallowed* (1579). His printer was Hugh Singleton, the printer of the *Calender*, and Spenser took a considerable risk in echoing Stubbs's condemnation of those who 'gape for greedie governaunce / And match them selfe with mighty potentates' (*Februarie*, 121–2). The overt target is the pride of worldly prelates but the play on 'match', in such close conjunction with the Stubbsian 'gape', is unmistakable. Even in the *Aprill* eclogue, at the height of apparently seamless panegyric, the choice of Virgilian emblems pulls the ragged threads of discontent: 'O quam te memorem virgo? / O dea certe'. In the first book of the *Aeneid* Venus appears to her son disguised as a nymph of Diana. Both he, and the epic's subsequent Christian interpreters, are puzzled by her identity: does she represent chastity, or licence disguised as chastity? Is she really a virgin (*virgo*) or a goddess (*dea*)? Should the first emblem be translated as 'what shall I call you, maiden?' or 'shall I call you maiden?': the 'vision' is strongest at the point at which it threatens, like Virgil's Venus, to evaporate into thin air. The 'pastoral of power' feeds upon the anxieties of impotence.

In the aptly entitled collection of *Complaints* published in 1591 vision and satire coalesce. That the volume should have appeared shortly after the first instalment of *The Faerie Queene* should occasion little surprise since it illustrates the adverse circumstances in which Spenser's more idealized aspirations struggle for survival. The label of 'court' poet so often attached to him is grossly misleading for, as *Colin Clouts Come Home Againe* (1595) powerfully demonstrates, he was more of an outsider than a laureate. Consigned to the 'waste' landscape of Elizabethan Ireland with its 'griesly famine' and 'outlawes fell' (314–19), he wrote from the margins not the centre. While Virgil is frequently invoked as the model for his career, the despondent ghost of Ovid, driven into exile by Virgil's imperial patron, echoes in the subtextual background. Colin's voyage from Ireland to England is ironically replete with echoes of Ovid's *Tristia* thereby enforcing the ambiguity of the poem's title. Like Ovid, Spenser seldom played safe. *The Shepheardes Calender* risked prosecution, *Mother Hubberds Tale* was called in, the first instalment of *The Faerie Queene* gave offence to Lord Burghley, and the second was banned in Scotland by James VI. Spenser's famous assertions of epic weariness, so publicly canvassed in the *Amoretti* (sonnets 33 and 80), gesture towards the most poignant Ovidian expression of despair: 'think not all my work is trivial; oft have I set grand sails upon my bark. Six books of *Fasti* and as many more have I written ... This work did I recently compose Caesar, under thy name, dedicated to thee, but my fate has broken it off' (*Tristia*, 2. 547–52). Whereas Ovid suggests that all twelve books have at least been drafted, Spenser indefinitely defers the great project in honour of his 'dear dred' – an oxymoron which perfectly conveys the ambivalence of his attitude towards one of the primary sources of his inspiration.

In *Colin Clouts Come Home Againe* as in *The Shepheardes Calender* amorous complaint encodes political discontent. Both works, like most of the Spenserian canon, are relentlessly dialectical and self-reflexive. In the *Calender* even Colin's monologues give vent to the frustrated dialogues of a divided self, reflecting the *persona*'s own divided genesis in the garrulous, aggressive Colyn Cloute of John Skelton's court satires and the pensive, elegiac Colin of Clément Marot's plaintive pastorals. Writing his *Observations on the Faerie Queene* in 1754 Thomas Warton perceptively devoted a whole chapter to the unusual subject of 'Spenser's Imitations of Himself' in the belief that it would help to illustrate 'how variously he expresses the same thought'. But, as Warton himself demonstrates, the 'thought' is never quite the 'same'. The Spenserian imagination is obsessively dialogical, constantly interrogating, revising and redacting its material in a diversity of contexts, genres and styles. And yet, the very strategies which appear to offer an escape from solipsism often serve to compound it. E. K.'s identification of Spenser with Colin Clout, 'vnder which name this Poete secretly shadoweth himself', is richly disingenuous, designed to make the unwary forget that Spenser created, and speaks through, all of the *Calender*'s other *personae*, that he engineered all of their conflicts and disagreements, that he shunned dialectical closure in his pastoral verse as thoroughly as he avoided narrative closure in his epic – or, for that matter, emotional closure in his love poetry. The *Amoretti*, for example, is distinguished from other sonnet sequences by the repetition of sonnet 35 as sonnet 83 – an astonishingly bold act of self-quotation which also serves as a trenchant act of self-revision.

That it should be this sonnet and no other that is repeated is crucial: its subject is Narcissus and the repetition enacts the obsession. Self-quotation articulates, and effectively ironizes, self-love. The lady's eyes which ideally serve as a window to her soul may become no more than 'the myrrour' of the speaker's 'mazed hart' (sonnet 7). They may function as an avenue to emotional communion or an encouragement to solipsism. The delicate negotiation between two discrete selves, with which love is properly concerned, risks the imprisonment of both parties in their own self-images:

> Leaue lady in your glasse of christall clene,
>   Your goodly selfe for euermore to vew:
>   and in my selfe, my inward selfe I meane,
>   most liuely lyke behold your semblant trew.
>
> (*Amoretti*, sonnet 45)

The delicious paradox of 'semblant trew' encapsulates the psychological problem about which the *Amoretti* is constructed: the relation of image and self-image to reality, and the relevance, if any, of Plato's 'fayre Idea' of love to the selfish, and self-consuming, hunger of appetite. The lover's eyes are 'hungry eyes' and desire for another, bred in the 'inner part', consumes the self:

> Vnquiet thought, whom at the first I bred,
>   Of th'inward bale of my loue pined hart:
>   and sithens haue with sighes and sorrowes fed,
>   till greater then my wombe thou woxen art.
> Breake forth at length out of the inner part,
>   in which thou lurkest lyke to vipers brood:
>   and seeke some succour both to ease my smart
>   and also to sustayne thy selfe with food.
>
> (*Amoretti*, sonnet 2)

At the heart of Spenserian self-assertion is self-qualification: 'my selfe, my inward selfe I meane'. The startling imagery of a male 'wombe' threatens to confound the sexual distinction upon which the speaker's desire is premised. The 'art of eyes' which he is called upon to master is also the art of conflicting egos (sonnet 21). Spenser is acutely aware of the tendency for love poetry to degenerate into the poetry of self-love, just as elegiac verse finds us 'mourning in others, our owne miseries' (*Dolefull Lay of Clorinda*, 96). Hence the inevitable ambiguity of a line such as 'helpe me mine owne loues prayses to resound' even in a poem intended to celebrate the mutuality of marriage (*Epithalamion*, 14). In his comment upon the 'Emblem' to the *September* eclogue of *The Shepheardes Calender*, E. K. applies Narcissus' motto 'Inopem me copia fecit' (plenty has made me poor) to 'the author' – 'and to suche like effecte, as fyrste Narcissus spake it'. In *The Faerie Queene* Spenser speaks of reflecting Elizabeth Tudor 'In mirrours more then one' so that she may see 'her selfe' (3 Proem 5), but this is merely an extension of his preoccupation with anatomizing the whole notion of the 'selfe', with reflecting upon the chaotic emotional and intellectual fragmentation subsumed into the first person singular. The hope must be that, as *An Hymne in Honour of Beautie* asserts, 'two mirrors by opposd reflexion, / Doe both expresse the faces first impression' (181–2), but the very concept of 'opposd reflexion' betrays the multiple contradictions involved in the complex phenomenon of self-consciousness, in the desperate anxiety to objectify the subjective and 'see' the elusive 'inward selfe'. As a means to this end narrative *personae* proliferate in the shorter poems, and images of mirrors and echoes abound. Their close association is highly revealing. In classical mythology Echo was the maiden who died for unrequited love of a morbidly self-reflexive Narcissus: 'So I vnto my selfe alone will sing, / The woods shall to me answer and my Eccho ring' (*Epithalamion*, 17–18).

It has become common to speak of Spenserian 'self-fashioning' but his tendency to undermine his self-image by habits of 'opposd reflexion', or to multiply conflicting self-images 'in mirrours more then one', has been relatively neglected. Far more is involved in such manoeuvres than a courtly game of hide-and-seek. Even such a practical matter as the pursuit of a patron, one of the dominant concerns of the shorter poems, entails scrutiny of the speaker's fantastical *alter egos* which are constructed and deconstructed in 'expectation vayne / Of idle hopes, which still doe fly away, / Like empty shaddowes' (*Prothalamion*, 7–9). As Virgilian confidence struggles with Ovidian despair, the public poet often retreats, or represents himself as retreating, into the private man: 'I play to please my selfe, all be it ill' (*June*, 72). But this is a sentiment intended for publication and is 'spoken' not by Spenser but by Colin Clout. Though persistently auto-referential, the Spenserian 'I' is never truly autobiographical. Autobiography is the condition it never quite attains, auto-fabrication the condition it never quite escapes.

In works such as *The Shepheardes Calender* and *Colin Clouts Come Home Againe* images of circularity abound, pitting ideals of fulfilment against experiences of entrapment. And it is not only the speaker who is entrapped but also the objects of his attention. *Mother Hubberds Tale* was called in upon its publication in 1591 even though it is likely that large parts of it had been written some dozen years earlier. But this is the Elizabethan equivalent of *Animal Farm* and Spenser's analysis of the contemporary malaise proceeds beyond specific personalities to the very power structures of the Elizabethan regime. The sovereign lioness rejoices to see her favourite 'beast' romping about 'enchaste with chaine and circulet of golde ... buxome to his bands', yet she is offended by the 'late chayne' which has been laid about his neck. She would have him both 'wilde' and 'tame' simultaneously, wholly bound to her yet somehow also 'free' (624–30). Depending on the dating of the passage, the allusion may refer either to the Earl of Leicester's clandestine marriage to Lettice Knollys (1578) or to the Earl of Essex's clandestine marriage to Frances Walsingham (1590). On the deepest level, however, it matters little which we choose. Because of her unmarried state Elizabeth (whose personal motto was 'semper eadem', always the same) was fated to recurrent disappointments of this nature, and the political dynamics of the Elizabethan court, vulnerable as they were to the emotional vicissitudes of fruitless courtship, were correspondingly unstable. What the poem exposes is not an isolated incident but an endemic condition, a vicious circle of sexual jealousy and political disarray.

Given the force of such preoccupations, it is hardly surprising that the shorter poems so often gesture towards spiritual transcendence as a means of escape from the world's prevailing 'vanitie'. The *Fowre Hymnes* (1596) conclude with what might well be interpreted as a programme for the redemption of Narcissus:

> Ah then my hungry soule, which long hast fed
> On idle fancies of thy foolish thought,
> And with false beauties flattring bait misled,
> Hast after vaine deceiptfull shadowes sought,
> Which all are fled, and now haue left thee nought,
> But late repentance through thy follies prief;
> Ah ceasse to gaze on matter of thy grief.
>
> (*An Hymne of Heavenly Beautie*, 288–94)

The object may have changed but the 'hunger' survives. But has the object actually changed? Or, as the persistence of mirror imagery suggests, is the object still the subject? Is the love of God any less self-referential than the love of woman? The structure of the *Fowre Hymnes* is rigorously dialectical and the relationship between 'earthly' and 'heauenly' love cannot be explained solely, or even principally, in terms of ascent or renunciation. The process, as Spenser tells us, is not one of recantation but of 'retractation', a complex operation of revision or redaction. The two 'earthly' hymns are not suppressed but republished, like *Amoretti*'s repeated sonnet, in a new context. The structure of the volume expands to embrace, rather than to deny, its internal contradictions. Evident throughout the 'heavenly' pair is the struggle to sublimate earthly desire, a hallowing of Eros which inevitably entails a sexualizing of Agape. Even the God of the heavenly hymns, constructed in the image of the earthly speaker's 'hungry' desire, is a divine Narcissist who created man:

> In whom he might his mightie selfe behould:
> For loue doth loue the thing belou'd to see,
> That like it selfe in louely shape may bee.
>
> (*An Hymne of Heavenly Love*, 117–19)

God sees himself in creation and creation strives to glimpse his image by gazing upon reflections of itself. 'Rest' may be the word upon which the hymns close, but the poetry thrives upon the disquietude of complex metaphysical thought.

However fervent his aspirations towards perfection and stability, Spenser's imagination was complicit with the depredations of time, with emotional dislocation, with exile, and ultimately with the

'vanitie' he castigates. His music draws strength from the breaking
of Colin's pipe, from the fall of Rome, the fate of butterflies and
from the very corruption of Eliza's court. Even in the *Epithalamion*,
a rare poem of consummated desire, the speaker's Orphic power is
deliberately offset by darker resonances and echoes. The abrupt
ending may even suggest that personal fulfilment entails poetic loss.
E. K. divides the eclogues of *The Shepheardes Calender* into three
distinct groups, the 'plaintiue', the 'recreatiue' and the 'moral', but
the work itself challenges such distinctions. Plaintive 'undersongs'
resound in recreative verse, moral issues intrude into matters of
love, and a disturbingly 'doolful pleasaunce' is derived even from
elegy. All of the 'mirrours' are carefully angled to enhance the most
provocative effects of 'opposd reflexion'. The biographer's loss is
the reader's gain.

The present edition contains all of Spenser's shorter poetry including
the important Latin verse which appeared in the Spenser–Harvey
correspondence of 1580. A full translation from the Latin is supplied
in the commentary. The various works are arranged in the chrono-
logical order of publication thereby affording the reader a clear
overview of Spenser's public career. As the headnotes point out,
however, exact dates of composition are notoriously hard to deter-
mine and it is essential to bear this in mind when considering the
issue of Spenser's artistic development. The volume of *Complaints*
published in 1591, for example, contains revisions of material that
first appeared as early as 1569. The commentary is designed to alert
the reader to problems such as these while at the same time facilitating
immediate comprehension of difficult passages or terms. Because
Spenser is such an aggressively inter-textual writer, freely adapting,
and occasionally subverting, classical, biblical and contemporary
materials, I have endeavoured to supply concise references to all of
the most important sources and analogues. Comparison between
such passages and the Spenserian texts will generally be found to
throw considerable light upon the character of Spenser's poetic craft
and intellectual outlook. The headnotes are designed to examine
some of the more general problems of interpretation arising from
particular works, or collections of works, and to suggest various
avenues of critical approach.

As will be evident to those familiar with the history of Spenserian annotation, the commentary to the present edition is heavily reliant upon a wide range of scholarly authorities. So immensely rich is the editorial tradition that my contribution necessarily falls far short of my indebtedness, but this is very much in the nature of an exercise which seeks to consolidate past gains by a process of compilation, selection and synthesis. To edit Spenser is also to edit his editors. I acknowledge my obligations with gratitude; my errors are doubtless original. For the glossing of common nouns my single greatest debt is to the *OED*, valuably supplemented by C. G. Osgood, *A Concordance to Spenser* (1915). For classical allusions my principal sources are Natalis Comes, *Mythologiae* (1567), H. G. Lotspeich, *Classical Mythology in the Poetry of Edmund Spenser* (1942), N. G. L. Hammond and H. H. Scullard (eds.), *The Oxford Classical Dictionary* (1970) and Pierre Grimal, *The Dictionary of Classical Mythology* (1986). For plants and herbs I have drawn upon John Gerard, *The Herbal or General Historie of Plantes* (1597) and Nicholas Culpeper, *The Complete Herbal* (1653). For political, historical and miscellaneous allusions (particularly in *Complaints*) my work is greatly indebted, as are all recent editions of Spenser, to the editors of *The Works of Edmund Spenser. A Variorum Edition* (1932–58). Classical sources have generally been cited from the relevant Loeb editions, and Shakespeare's works from the Arden editions. The Bible has been consulted in both the Genevan and King James's versions.

Severe restrictions of space generally preclude the recording of specific attributions in the course of the commentary, but I have drawn with profit upon all of the following sources (listed in chronological order): John Jortin, *Remarks on Spenser's Poems* (1734); Thomas Warton, *Observations on the Faerie Queene of Spenser* (1754); the collected editions of Spenser's *Works* by H. J. Todd (1805); F. J. Child (1864) and A. B. Grosart (1882–4); C. H. Herford (ed.), *The Shepheards Calendar* (1895); L. Winstanley (ed.), *The Fowre Hymnes* (1907); F. I. Carpenter, *A Reference Guide to Edmund Spenser* (1923); W. L. Renwick (ed.), *Complaints* (1928), *Daphnaïda and Other Poems* (1929) and *The Shepheardes Calender* (1930); H. S. V. Jones, *A Spenser Handbook* (1930); F. R. Johnson, *A Critical Bibliography of the Works of Edmund Spenser Printed before 1700* (1933); E. Welsford, *Spenser: 'Fowre Hymnes', 'Epithalamion': A Study of Edmund Spenser's Doctrine of Love* (1967); C. G. Smith, *Spenser's Proverb Lore* (1970); A. C. Hamilton (ed.), *The Faerie Queene* (1977);

T. P. Roche, Jr (ed.), *The Faerie Queene* (Penguin English Poets, 1978); W. A. Oram, E. Bjorvand, R. Bond, T. H. Cain, A. Dunlop and R. Schell (eds.), *The Yale Edition of the Shorter Poems of Edmund Spenser* (1989); A. C. Hamilton et al. (eds.), *The Spenser Encyclopedia* (1990); H. Maclean and A. L. Prescott (eds.), *Edmund Spenser's Poetry* (3rd edn, 1993); D. Brooks-Davies (ed.), *Edmund Spenser: Selected Shorter Poems* (1995). I am also immensely grateful to the following scholars for their generous assistance with particular problems of interpretation: Mr Thomas Braun, Dr Susie Clark, Mr Sam Eidinow, Dr Steve Gunn, Dr Nicholas Richardson and Mr Colin Wilcockson.

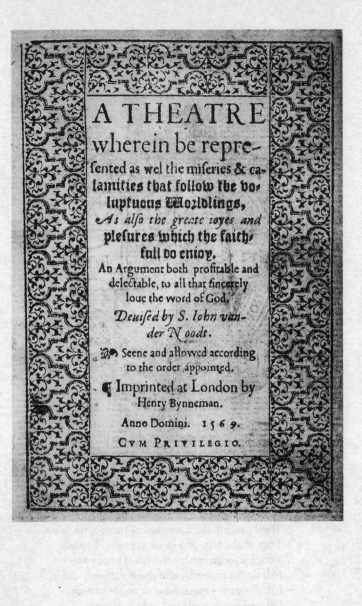

A THEATRE

wherein be repre-
sented as wel the miseries & ca-
lamities that follow the vo-
luptuous Worldlings,

As also the greate ioyes and
plesures which the faith-
full do enioy.

An Argument both profitable and
delectable, to all that sincerely
loue the word of God.

Deuised by S. Iohn van-
der Noodt.

Seene and allowed according
to the order appointed.

¶ Imprinted at London by
Henry Bynneman.

Anno Domini. 1569.

CVM PRIVILEGIO.

Epigrams.

[1]

Being one day at my window all alone,
So many strange things hapned me to see,
As much it grieueth me to thinke thereon.
At my right hande, a Hinde appearde to me,
So faire as mought the greatest God delite:
Two egre Dogs dyd hir pursue in chace,
Of whiche the one was black, the other white.
With deadly force so in their cruell race
They pinchte the haunches of this gentle beast,
That at the last, and in shorte time, I spied,
Vnder a rocke, where she (alas) opprest,
Fell to the grounde, and there vntimely dide.
Cruell death vanquishing so noble beautie,
Oft makes me waile so harde a destinie.

[2]

After at Sea a tall Ship dyd appere,
Made all of Heben and white Iuorie,
The sailes of Golde, of Silke the tackle were:
Milde was the winde, calme seemed the sea to be:
The Skie eche where did shew full bright and faire.   5
With riche treasures this gay ship fraighted was.
But sodaine storme did so turmoyle the aire,
And tombled vp the sea, that she, alas,
Strake on a rocke that vnder water lay.
O great misfortune, O great griefe, I say,   10
Thus in one moment to see lost and drownde
So great riches, as lyke can not be founde.

[3]

Then heauenly branches did I see arise,
Out of a fresh and lusty Laurell tree
Amidde the yong grene wood. Of Paradise
Some noble plant I thought my selfe to see,
5   Suche store of birdes therein yshrouded were,
Chaunting in shade their sundry melodie.
My sprites were rauisht with these pleasures there.
While on this Laurell fixed was mine eye,
The Skie gan euery where to ouercast,
10   And darkned was the welkin all aboute,
When sodaine flash of heauens fire outbrast,
And rent this royall tree quite by the roote.
Which makes me much and euer to complaine,
For no such shadow shal be had againe.

[4]

Within this wood, out of the rocke did rise
A Spring of water mildely romblyng downe,
Whereto approched not in any wise
The homely Shepherde, nor the ruder cloune,
But many Muses, and the Nymphes withall,   5
That sweetely in accorde did tune their voice
Vnto the gentle sounding of the waters fall.
The sight wherof dyd make my heart reioyce.
But while I toke herein my chiefe delight,
I sawe (alas) the gaping earth deuoure   10
The Spring, the place, and all cleane out of sight.
Whiche yet agreues my heart euen to this houre.

[5]

I saw a Phœnix in the wood alone,
With purple wings and crest of golden hew,
Straunge birde he was, wherby I thought anone,
That of some heauenly wight I had the vew:
Vntill he came vnto the broken tree
And to the spring that late deuoured was.
What say I more? Eche thing at length we see
Doth passe away: the Phœnix there, alas,
Spying the tree destroyde, the water dride,
Himselfe smote with his beake, as in disdaine,
And so forthwith in great despite he dide.
For pitie and loue my heart yet burnes in paine.

[6]

At last so faire a Ladie did I spie,
That in thinking on hir I burne and quake,
On herbes and floures she walked pensiuely.
Milde, but yet loue she proudely did forsake.
White seemed hir robes, yet wouen so they were,   5
As snowe and golde together had bene wrought.
Aboue the waste a darke cloude shrouded hir,
A stinging Serpent by the heele hir caught,
Wherewith she languisht as the gathered floure:
And well assurde she mounted vp to ioy.   10
Alas in earth so nothing doth endure
But bitter griefe that dothe our hearts anoy.

[7]

My Song thus now in thy Conclusions,
Say boldly that these same six visions
Do yelde vnto thy lorde a sweete request,
Ere it be long within the earth to rest.

Sonets.

[1]

It was the time when rest the gift of Gods
Sweetely sliding into the eyes of men,
Doth drowne in the forgetfulnesse of slepe,
The carefull trauailes of the painefull day:
5   Then did a ghost appeare before mine eyes
On that great riuers banke that runnes by Rome,
And calling me then by my propre name,
He bade me vpwarde vnto heauen looke.
He cride to me, and loe (quod he) beholde,
10   What vnder this great Temple is containde,
Loe all is nought but flying vanitie.
So I knowing the worldes vnstedfastnesse,
Sith onely God surmountes the force of tyme,
In God alone do stay my confidence.

[2]

On hill, a frame an hundred cubites hie
I sawe, an hundred pillers eke about,
All of fine Diamant decking the front,
And fashiond were they all in Dorike wise.
Of bricke, ne yet of marble was the wall,   5
But shining Christall, which from top to base
Out of deepe vaute threw forth a thousand rayes
Vpon an hundred steps of purest golde.
Golde was the parget: and the sielyng eke
Did shine all scaly with fine golden plates.   10
The floore was Iaspis, and of Emeraude.
O worldes vainenesse. A sodein earthquake loe,
Shaking the hill euen from the bottome deepe,
Threwe downe this building to the lowest stone.

[3]

Then did appeare to me a sharped spire
Of diamant, ten feete eche way in square,
Iustly proportionde vp vnto his height,
So hie as mought an Archer reache with sight.
5   Vpon the top therof was set a pot
Made of the mettall that we honour most.
And in this golden vessell couched were
The ashes of a mightie Emperour.
Vpon foure corners of the base there lay
10   To beare the frame, foure great Lions of golde.
A worthie tombe for such a worthie corps.
Alas, nought in this worlde but griefe endures.
A sodaine tempest from the heauen, I saw,
With flushe stroke downe this noble monument.

[4]

I saw raisde vp on pillers of Iuorie,
Whereof the bases were of richest golde,
The chapters Alabaster, Christall frises,
The double front of a triumphall arke.
On eche side portraide was a victorie.   5
With golden wings in habite of a Nymph.
And set on hie vpon triumphing chaire,
The auncient glorie of the Romane lordes.
The worke did shewe it selfe not wrought by man,
But rather made by his owne skilfull hande   10
That forgeth thunder dartes for Ioue his sire.
Let me no more see faire thing vnder heauen,
Sith I haue seene so faire a thing as this,
With sodaine falling broken all to dust.

[5]

Then I behelde the faire Dodonian tree,
Vpon seuen hilles throw forth his gladsome shade,
And Conquerers bedecked with his leaues
Along the bankes of the Italian streame.
5   There many auncient Trophees were erect,
Many a spoile, and many goodly signes,
To shewe the greatnesse of the stately race,
That erst descended from the Troian bloud.
Rauisht I was to see so rare a thing,
10   When barbarous villaines in disordred heape,
Outraged the honour of these noble bowes.
I hearde the tronke to grone vnder the wedge.
And since I saw the roote in hie disdaine
Sende forth againe a twinne of forked trees.

[6]

I saw the birde that dares beholde the Sunne,
With feeble flight venture to mount to heauen,
By more and more she gan to trust hir wings,
Still folowing th'example of hir damme:
I saw hir rise, and with a larger flight   5
Surmount the toppes euen of the hiest hilles,
And pierce the cloudes, and with hir wings to reache
The place where is the temple of the Gods,
There was she lost, and sodenly I saw
Where tombling through the aire in lompe of fire, 10
All flaming downe she fell vpon the plaine.
I saw hir bodie turned all to dust,
And saw the foule that shunnes the cherefull light
Out of hir ashes as a worme arise.

[7]

Then all astonned with this nightly ghost,
I saw an hideous body big and strong,
Long was his beard, and side did hang his hair,
A grisly forehed and Saturnelike face.
5   Leaning against the belly of a pot
He shed a water, whose outgushing streame
Ran flowing all along the creekie shoare
Where once the Troyan Duke with Turnus fought.
And at his feete a bitch Wolfe did giue sucke
10   To two yong babes. In his right hand he bare
The tree of peace, in left the conquering Palme,
His head was garnisht with the Laurel bow.
Then sodenly the Palme and Oliue fell,
And faire greene Laurel witherd vp and dide.

[8]

Hard by a riuers side, a wailing Nimphe,
Folding hir armes with thousand sighs to heauen
Did tune hir plaint to falling riuers sound,
Renting hir faire visage and golden haire,
Where is (quod she) this whilome honored face?   5
Where is thy glory and the auncient praise,
Where all worldes hap was reposed,
When erst of Gods and man I worshipt was?
Alas, suffisde it not that ciuile bate
Made me the spoile and bootie of the world,   10
But this new Hydra mete to be assailde
Euen by an hundred such as Hercules,
With seuen springing heds of monstrous crimes,
So many Neroes and Caligulaes
Must still bring forth to rule this croked shore.   15

[9]

Vpon a hill I saw a kindled flame,
Mounting like waues with triple point to heauen,
Which of incense of precious Ceder tree
With Balmelike odor did perfume the aire.
5   A bird all white, well fetherd on hir winges
Hereout did flie vp to the throne of Gods,
And singing with most plesant melodie
She climbed vp to heauen in the smoke.
Of this faire fire the faire dispersed rayes
10   Threw forth abrode a thousand shining leames,
When sodain dropping of a golden shoure
Gan quench the glystering flame. O greuous chaunge!
That which erstwhile so pleasaunt scent did yelde,
Of Sulphure now did breathe corrupted smel.

[10]

I saw a fresh spring rise out of a rocke,
Clere as Christall against the Sunny beames,
The bottome yellow like the shining land,
That golden Pactol driues vpon the plaine.
It seemed that arte and nature striued to ioyne   5
There in one place all pleasures of the eye.
There was to heare a noise alluring slepe
Of many accordes more swete than Mermaids song,
The seates and benches shone as Iuorie,
An hundred Nymphes sate side by side about,   10
When from nie hilles a naked rout of Faunes
With hideous cry assembled on the place,
Which with their feete vncleane the water fouled,
Threw down the seats, and droue the Nimphs to flight.

[11]

At length, euen at the time when Morpheus
Most truely doth appeare vnto our eyes,
Wearie to see th'inconstance of the heauens:
I saw the great Typhæus sister come,
5   Hir head full brauely with a morian armed,
In maiestie she seemde to matche the Gods.
And on the shore, harde by a violent streame,
She raisde a Trophee ouer all the worlde.
An hundred vanquisht kings gronde at hir feete,
10   Their armes in shamefull wise bounde at their backes.
While I was with so dreadfull sight afrayde,
I saw the heauens warre against hir tho,
And seing hir striken fall with clap of thunder,
With so great noyse I start in sodaine wonder.

[12]

I saw an vgly beast come from the sea,
That seuen heads, ten crounes, ten hornes did beare,
Hauing theron the vile blaspheming name.
The cruell Leopard she resembled much:
Feete of a beare, a Lions throte she had. 5
The mightie Dragon gaue to hir his power.
One of hir heads yet there I did espie,
Still freshly bleeding of a grieuous wounde.
One cride aloude. What one is like (quod he)
This honoured Dragon, or may him withstande? 10
And then came from the sea a sauage beast,
With Dragons speche, and shewde his force by fire,
With wondrous signes to make all wights adore
The beast, in setting of hir image vp.

[13]

  I saw a Woman sitting on a beast
  Before mine eyes, of Orenge colour hew:
  Horrour and dreadfull name of blasphemie
  Filde hir with pride. And seuen heads I saw,
5 Ten hornes also the stately beast did beare.
  She seemde with glorie of the scarlet faire,
  And with fine perle and golde puft vp in heart.
  The wine of hooredome in a cup she bare.
  The name of Mysterie writ in hir face.
10 The bloud of Martyrs dere were hir delite.
  Most fierce and fell this woman seemde to me.
  An Angell then descending downe from Heauen,
  With thondring voice cride out aloude, and sayd,
  Now for a truth great Babylon is fallen.

[14]

Then might I see vpon a white horse set
The faithfull man with flaming countenaunce,
His head did shine with crounes set therupon.
The worde of God made him a noble name.
His precious robe I saw embrued with bloud.   5
Then saw I from the heauen on horses white,
A puissant armie come the selfe same way.
Then cried a shining Angell as me thought,
That birdes from aire descending downe on earth
Should warre vpon the kings, and eate their flesh.   10
Then did I see the beast and Kings also
Ioinyng their force to slea the faithfull man.
But this fierce hatefull beast and all hir traine,
Is pitilesse throwne downe in pit of fire.

[15]

I saw new Earth, new Heauen, sayde Saint Iohn.
And loe, the sea (quod he) is now no more.
The holy Citie of the Lorde, from hye
Descendeth garnisht as a loued spouse.
5   A voice then sayde, beholde the bright abode
Of God and men. For he shall be their God,
And all their teares he shall wipe cleane away.
Hir brightnesse greater was than can be founde,
Square was this Citie, and twelue gates it had.
10   Eche gate was of an orient perfect pearle,
The houses golde, the pauement precious stone.
A liuely streame, more cleere than Christall is,
Ranne through the mid, sprong from triumphant seat.
There growes lifes fruite vnto the Churches good.

THE
Shepheardes Calender

Conteyning twelue Æglogues proportionable
to the twelue monethes.

by E. K.

Entitled
TO THE NOBLE AND VERTV-
ous Gentleman most worthy of all titles
both of learning and cheualrie M.
Philip. Sidney.

(.·)

AT LONDON.
Printed by Hugh Singleton, dwelling in
Creede Lane neere vnto Ludgate at the
signe of the golden Tunne, and
are there to be solde.
1579.

TO HIS BOOKE.

Goe little booke: thy selfe present,
As child whose parent is vnkent:
To him that is the president
Of noblesse and of cheualree,
5 *And if that Enuie barke at thee,*
As sure it will, for succoure flee
   Vnder the shadow of his wing,
And asked, who thee forth did bring,
A shepheards swaine saye did thee sing,
10 *All as his straying flocke he fedde:*
And when his honor has thee redde,
Craue pardon for my hardyhedde.
   But if that any aske thy name,
Say thou wert base begot with blame:
15 *For thy thereof thou takest shame.*
And when thou art past ieopardee,
Come tell me, what was sayd of mee:
And I will send more after thee.
                           Immeritô.

¶ *To the most excellent and learned both*
Orator and Poete, Mayster Gabriell Haruey, his
verie special and singular good frend E. K. commen-
deth the good lyking of this his labour,
and the patronage of the
new Poete.
(∵)

VNCOVTHE VNKISTE, Sayde the olde famous Poete
Chaucer: whom for his excellencie and wonderfull skil in
making, his scholler Lidgate, a worthy scholler of so excellent
a maister, calleth the Loadestarre of our Language: and whom
our Colin clout in his Æglogue called Tityrus the God of   5
shepheards, comparing hym to the worthines of the Roman
Tityrus Virgile. Which prouerbe, myne owne good friend
Ma. Haruey, as in that good old Poete it serued well Pandares
purpose, for the bolstering of his baudy brocage, so very well
taketh place in this our new Poete, who for that he is vncouthe   10
(as said Chaucer) is vnkist, and vnknown to most men, is
regarded but of few. But I dout not, so soone as his name
shall come into the knowledg of men, and his worthines be
sounded in the tromp of fame, but that he shall be not onely
kiste, but also beloued of all, embraced of the most, and   15
wondred at of the best. No lesse I thinke, deserueth his
wittinesse in deuising, his pithinesse in vttering, his com-
plaints of loue so louely, his discourses of pleasure so pleas-
antly, his pastorall rudenesse, his morall wisenesse, his dewe
obseruing of Decorum euerye where, in personages, in seasons,   20
in matter, in speach, and generally in al seemely simplycitie
of handeling his matter, and framing his words: the which of
many thinges which in him be straunge, I know will seeme
the straungest, the words them selues being so auncient, the
knitting of them so short and intricate, and the whole Periode   25
and compasse of speache so delightsome for the roundnesse,
and so graue for the straungenesse. And firste of the wordes
to speake, I graunt they be something hard, and of most men
vnused, yet both English, and also vsed of most excellent

30   Authors and most famous Poetes. In whom whenas this our
Poet hath bene much traueiled and throughly redd, how could
it be, (as that worthy Oratour sayde) but that walking in the
sonne although for other cause he walked, yet needes he
mought be sunburnt; and hauing the sound of those auncient
35   Poetes still ringing in his eares, he mought needes in singing
hit out some of theyr tunes. But whether he vseth them by
such casualtye and custome, or of set purpose and choyse, as
thinking them fittest for such rusticall rudenesse of
shepheards, eyther for that theyr rough sounde would make
40   his rymes more ragged and rustical, or els because such olde
and obsolete wordes are most vsed of country folke, sure I
think, and think I think not amisse, that they bring great grace
and, as one would say, auctoritie to the verse. For albe amongst
many other faultes it specially be obiected of Valla against
45   Liuie, and of other against Saluste, that with ouer much studie
they affect antiquitie, as coueting thereby credence and honor
of elder yeeres, yet I am of opinion, and eke the best learned
are of the lyke, that those auncient solemne wordes are a great
ornament both in the one and in the other; the one labouring
50   to set forth in hys worke an eternall image of antiquitie,
and the other carefully discoursing matters of grauitie and
importaunce. For if my memory fayle not, Tullie in that
booke, wherein he endeuoureth to set forth the paterne of a
perfect Oratour, sayth that ofttimes an auncient worde maketh
55   the style seeme graue, and as it were reuerend: no otherwise
then we honour and reuerence gray heares for a certein
religious regard, which we haue of old age. yet nether euery
where must old words be stuffed in, nor the commen Dialecte
and maner of speaking so corrupted therby, that as in old
60   buildings it seme disorderly and ruinous. But all as in most
exquisite pictures they vse to blaze and portraict not onely
the daintie lineaments of beautye, but also rounde about it
to shadow the rude thickets and craggy clifts, that by the
basenesse of such parts, more excellency may accrew to the
65   principall; for oftimes we fynde ourselues, I knowe not how,
singularly delighted with the shewe of such naturall rudenesse,
and take great pleasure in that disorderly order. Euen so doe
those rough and harsh termes enlumine and make more clearly

to appeare the brightnesse of braue and glorious words. So
ofentimes a dischorde in Musick maketh a comely con-   70
cordaunce: so great delight tooke the worthy Poete Alceus to
behold a blemish in the ioynt of a wel shaped body. But if
any will rashly blame such his purpose in choyse of old and
vnwonted words, him may I more iustly blame and condemne,
or of witlesse headinesse in iudging, or of heedelesse hardinesse   75
in condemning. for not marking the compasse of hys bent, he
wil iudge of the length of his cast. for in my opinion it is one
special prayse, of many whych are dew to this Poete, that he
hath laboured to restore, as to theyr rightfull heritage such
good and naturall English words, as haue ben long time out   80
of vse and almost cleare disherited. Which is the onely cause,
that our Mother tonge, which truely of it self is both ful
enough for prose and stately enough for verse, hath long time
ben counted most bare and barrein of both. which default
when as some endeuoured to salue and recure, they patched   85
vp the holes with peces and rags of other languages, borrowing
here of the french, there of the Italian, euery where of the
Latine, not weighing how il, those tongues accorde with
themselues, but much worse with ours: So now they haue
made our English tongue, a gallimaufray or hodgepodge of al   90
other speches. Other some not so wel seene in the English
tonge as perhaps in other languages, if them happen to here
an olde word albeit very naturall and significant, crye out
streight way, that we speak no English, but gibbrish, or rather
such, as in old time Euanders mother spake. whose first shame   95
is, that they are not ashamed, in their own mother tonge
straungers to be counted and alienes. The second shame no
lesse then the first, that what so they vnderstand not, they
streight way deeme to be sencelesse, and not at al to be
vnderstode. Much like to the Mole in Æsopes fable, that being   100
blynd her selfe, would in no wise be perswaded, that any beast
could see. The last more shameful then both, that of their
owne country and natural speach, which together with their
Nources milk they sucked, they haue so base regard and
bastard iudgement, that they will not onely themselues not   105
labor to garnish and beautifie it, but also repine, that of other
it shold be embellished. Like to the dogge in the maunger,

that him selfe can eate no hay, and yet barketh at the hungry
bullock, that so faine would feede: whose currish kind though
cannot be kept from barking, yet I conne them thanke that
they refrain from byting.

Now for the knitting of sentences, whych they call the
ioynts and members therof, and for al the compasse of the
speach, it is round without roughnesse, and learned wythout
hardnes, such indeede as may be perceiued of the leaste,
vnderstoode of the moste, but iudged onely of the learned.
For what in most English wryters vseth to be loose, and as it
were vngyrt, in this Authour is well grounded, finely framed,
and strongly trussed vp together. In regard wherof, I scorne
and spue out the rakehellye route of our ragged rymers (for
so themselues vse to hunt the letter) which without learning
boste, without iudgement iangle, without reason rage and
fome, as if some instinct of Poeticall spirite had newly rauished
them aboue the meanenesse of commen capacitie. And being
in the middest of all theyr brauery, sodenly eyther for want
of matter, or of ryme, or hauing forgotten theyr former
conceipt, they seeme to be so pained and traueiled in theyr
remembrance, as it were a woman in childebirth or as that
same Pythia, when the traunce came vpon her.

Os rabidum fera corda domans &c.

Nethelesse let them a Gods name feede on theyr owne
folly, so they seeke not to darken the beames of others glory.
As for Colin, vnder whose person the Authour selfe is
shadowed, how furre he is from such vaunted titles and
glorious showes, both him selfe sheweth, where he sayth.

Of Muses Hobbin. I conne no skill.   And,
Enough is me to paint out my vnrest, &c.

And also appeareth by the basenesse of the name, wherein,
it semeth, he chose rather to vnfold great matter of argument
couertly, then professing it, not suffice thereto accordingly.
which moued him rather in Æglogues, then other wise to
write, doubting perhaps his habilitie, which he little needed,

or mynding to furnish our tongue with this kinde, wherein it
faulteth, or following the example of the best and most auncient
Poetes, which deuised this kind of wryting, being both so base   145
for the matter, and homely for the manner, at the first to trye
theyr habilities: and as young birdes, that be newly crept out
of the nest, by little first to proue theyr tender wyngs, before
they make a greater flyght. So flew Theocritus, as you may
perceiue he was all ready full fledged. So flew Virgile, as not   150
yet well feeling his winges. So flew Mantuane, as being not
full somd. So Petrarque. So Boccace; So Marot, Sanazarus,
and also diuers other excellent both Italian and French Poetes,
whose foting this Author euery where followeth, yet so as
few, but they be wel sented can trace him out. So finally flyeth   155
this our new Poete, as a bird, whose principals be scarce
growen out, but yet as that in time shall be hable to keepe
wing with the best.

    Now as touching the generall dryft and purpose of his
Æglogues, I mind not to say much, him selfe labouring to   160
conceale it. Onely this appeareth, that his vnstayed yougth
had long wandred in the common Labyrinth of Loue, in which
time to mitigate and allay the heate of his passion, or els to
warne (as he sayth) the young shepheards .s. his equalls and
companions of his vnfortunate folly, he compiled these xij.   165
Æglogues, which for that they be proportioned to the state
of the xij. monethes, he termeth the SHEPHEARDS CAL-
ENDAR, applying an olde name to a new worke. Hereunto
haue I added a certain Glosse or scholion for thexposition of
old wordes and harder phrases: which maner of glosing and   170
commenting, well I wote, wil seeme straunge and rare in our
tongue: yet for somuch as I knew many excellent and proper
deuises both in wordes and matter would passe in the speedy
course of reading, either as vnknowen, or as not marked, and
that in this kind, as in other we might be equal to the learned   175
of other nations, I thought good to take the paines vpon me,
the rather for that by meanes of some familiar acquaintaunce
I was made priuie to his counsell and secret meaning in them,
as also in sundry other works of his. which albeit I know he
nothing so much hateth, as to promulgate, yet thus much   180
haue I aduentured vpon his frendship, him selfe being for

long time furre estraunged, hoping that this will the rather
occasion him, to put forth diuers other excellent works of his,
which slepe in silence, as his Dreames, his Legendes, his
185   Court of Cupide, and sondry others; whose commendations
to set out, were verye vayne; the thinges though worthy of
many, yet being knowen to few. These my present paynes if
to any they be pleasurable or profitable, be you iudge, mine
own good Maister Haruey, to whom I haue both in respect
190   of your worthinesse generally, and otherwyse vpon some par-
ticular and special considerations voued this my labour, and
the maydenhead of this our commen frends Poetrie, himselfe
hauing already in the beginning dedicated it to the Noble and
worthy Gentleman, the right worshipfull Ma. Phi. Sidney, a
195   special fauourer and maintainer of all kind of learning. Whose
cause I pray you Sir, yf Enuie shall stur vp any wrongful
accusasion, defend with your mighty Rhetorick and other
your rare gifts of learning, as you can, and shield with your
good wil, as you ought, against the malice and outrage of so
200   many enemies, as I know wilbe set on fire with the sparks of
his kindled glory. And thus recommending the Author vnto
you, as vnto his most special good frend, and my selfe vnto
you both, as one making singuler account of two so very good
and so choise frends, I bid you both most hartely farwel, and
205   commit you and your most commendable studies to the tuicion
of the greatest.

Your owne assuredly to
be commaunded E. K.

Post scr

210   Now I trust M. Haruey, that vpon sight of your speciall frends
and fellow Poets doings, or els for enuie of so many vnworthy
Quidams, which catch at the garlond, which to you alone is
dewe, you will be perswaded to pluck out of the hateful
darknesse, those so many excellent English poemes of yours,
215   which lye hid, and bring them forth to eternall light. Trust
me you doe both them great wrong, in depriuing them of
the desired sonne, and also your selfe, in smoothering your
deserued prayses, and all men generally, in withholding from
them so diuine pleasures, which they might conceiue of your

gallant English verses, as they haue already doen of your   220
Latine Poemes, which in my opinion both for inuention and
Elocution are very delicate, and superexcellent. And thus
againe, I take my leaue of my good Mayster Haruey. from
my lodging at London thys 10. of Aprill. 1579.

The generall argument of
the whole booke.

Little I hope, needeth me at large to discourse the first Originall
of Æglogues, hauing alreadie touched the same. But for the
word Æglogues I know is vnknowen to most, and also mistaken
of some the best learned (as they think) I wyll say somewhat
thereof, being not at all impertinent to my present purpose.

They were first of the Greekes the inuentours of them
called Æglogaj as it were αἴγον or αἰγονόμων. λόγοι. that is
Goteheards tales. For although in Virgile and others thespeak-
ers be more shepheards, then Goteheards, yet Theocritus
in whom is more ground of authoritie, then in Virgile, this
specially from that deriuing, as from the first head and wel-
spring the whole Inuencion of his Æglogues, maketh Gote-
heards the persons and authors of his tales. This being, who
seeth not the grossenesse of such as by colour of learning would
make vs beleeue that they are more rightly termed Eclogai,
as they would say, extraordinary discourses of vnnecessarie
matter, which difinition albe in substaunce and meaning it
agree with the nature of the thing, yet nowhit answereth with
the ἀνάλυσις and interpretation of the word. For they be not
termed Eclogues, but Æglogues. which sentence this authour
very well obseruing, vpon good iudgement, though indeede
few Goteheards haue to doe herein, nethelesse doubteth not
to cal them by the vsed and best knowen name. Other curious
discourses hereof I reserue to greater occasion. These xij.
Æclogues euery where answering to the seasons of the
twelue monthes may be well deuided into three formes or
ranckes. For eyther they be Plaintiue, as the first, the sixt,
the eleuenth, and the twelfth, or recreatiue, such as al those
be, which conceiue matter of loue, or commendation of special
personages, or Moral: which for the most part be mixed with
some Satyrical bitternesse, namely the second of reuerence
dewe to old age, the fift of coloured deceipt, the seuenth
and ninth of dissolute shepheards and pastours, the tenth of
contempt of Poetrie and pleasaunt wits. And to this diuision
may euery thing herein be reasonably applyed: A few onely

except, whose speciall purpose and meaning I am not priuie
to. And thus much generally of these xij. Æclogues. Now will
we speake particularly of all, and first of the first. which he
calleth by the first monethes name Ianuarie: wherein to some
he may seeme fowly to haue faulted, in that he erroniously   40
beginneth with that moneth, which beginneth not the yeare.
For it is wel known, and stoutely maynteyned with stronge
reasons of the learned, that the yeare beginneth in March. for
then the sonne reneweth his finished course, and the seasonable
spring refresheth the earth, and the plesaunce thereof being   45
buried in the sadnesse of the dead winter now worne away,
reliueth. This opinion maynteine the olde Astrologers and
Philosophers, namely the reuerend Andalo, and Macrobius
in his holydayes of Saturne, which accoumpt also was generally
obserued both of Grecians and Romans. But sauing the leaue   50
of such learned heads, we mayntaine a custome of coumpting
the seasons from the moneth Ianuary, vpon a more speciall
cause, then the heathen Philosophers euer coulde conceiue,
that is, for the incarnation of our mighty Sauiour and eternall
redeemer the L. Christ, who as then renewing the state of the   55
decayed world, and returning the compasse of expired yeres
to theyr former date and first commencement, left to vs his
heires a memoriall of his birth in the ende of the last yeere and
beginning of the next. which reckoning, beside that eternall
monument of our saluation, leaneth also vppon good proofe   60
of special iudgement. For albeit that in elder times, when as
yet the coumpt of the yere was not perfected, as afterwarde
it was by Iulius Cæsar, they began to tel the monethes from
Marches beginning, and according to the same God (as is
sayd in Scripture) comaunded the people of the Iewes to   65
count the moneth Abib, that which we call March, for the
first moneth, in remembraunce that in that moneth he brought
them out of the land of Ægipt: yet according to tradition of
latter times it hath bene otherwise obserued, both in gouern-
ment of the church, and rule of Mightiest Realmes. For from   70
Iulius Cæsar who first obserued the leape yeere which he
called Bissextilem Annum, and brought in to a more certain
course the odde wandring dayes which of the Greekes were
called ὑπερβαίνοντες. of the Romanes intercalares (for in

75 such matter of learning I am forced to vse the termes of the learned) the monethes haue bene nombred xij. which in the first ordinaunce of Romulus were but tenne, counting but CCCiiij. dayes in euery yeare, and beginning with March. But Numa Pompilius, who was the father of al the Romain

80 ceremonies and religion, seeing that reckoning to agree neither with the course of the sonne, nor of the Moone, therevnto added two monethes, Ianuary and February: wherin it seemeth, that wise king minded vpon good reason to begin the yeare at Ianuarie, of him therefore so called tanquam Ianua

85 anni the gate and entraunce of the yere, or of the name of the god Ianus, to which god for that the old Paynims attributed the byrth and beginning of all creatures new comming into the worlde, it seemeth that he therfor to him assigned the beginning and first entraunce of the yeare. which account for

90 the most part hath hetherto continued. Notwithstanding that the Ægiptians beginne theyr yeare at September, for that according to the opinion of the best Rabbins, and very purpose of the scripture selfe, God made the worlde in that Moneth, that is called of them Tisri. And therefore he commaunded

95 them, to keepe the feast of Pauilions in the end of the yeare, in the xv. day of the seuenth moneth, which before that time was the first.

But our Authour respecting nether the subtiltie of thone parte, nor the antiquitie of thother, thinketh it fittest according

100 to the simplicitie of commen vnderstanding, to begin with Ianuarie, wening it perhaps no decorum, that Shepheard should be seene in matter of so deepe insight, or canuase a case of so doubtful iudgment. So therefore beginneth he, and so continueth he throughout.

Januarye.

Ægloga prima.

ARGVMENT.

In this fyrst Æglogue Colin cloute *a shepheardes boy complaineth him of his vnfortunate loue, being but newly (as semeth) enamoured of a countrie lasse called* Rosalinde: *with which strong affection being very sore traueled, he compareth his carefull case to the sadde season of the yeare, to the frostie ground, to the frosen trees, and to his owne winterbeaten flocke. And lastlye, fynding himselfe robbed of all former pleasaunce and delights, hee breaketh his Pipe in peeces, and casteth him selfe to the ground.*

COLIN Clovte.

A shepheards boye (no better doe him call)
when Winters wastful spight was almost spent,
All in a sunneshine day, as did befall,
Led forth his flock, that had bene long ypent.
So faynt they woxe, and feeble in the folde,   5
That now vnnethes their feete could them vphold.

All as the Sheepe, such was the shepeheards looke,
For pale and wanne he was, (alas the while,)
May seeme he lovd, or els some care he tooke:
10   Well couth he tune his pipe, and frame his stile.
Tho to a hill his faynting flocke he ledde,
And thus him playnd, the while his shepe there fedde.

Ye Gods of loue, that pitie louers payne,
(If any gods the paine of louers pitie:)
15   Looke from aboue, where you in ioyes remaine,
And bowe your eares vnto my dolefull dittie.
And *Pan* thou shepheards God, that once didst loue,
Pitie the paines, that thou thy selfe didst proue.

Thou barrein ground, whome winters wrath hath wasted,
20   Art made a myrrhour, to behold my plight:
Whilome thy fresh spring flowrd, and after hasted
Thy sommer prowde with Daffadillies dight.
And now is come thy wynters stormy state,
Thy mantle mard, wherein thou maskedst late.

25   Such rage as winters, reigneth in my heart,
My life bloud friesing with vnkindly cold:
Such stormy stoures do breede my balefull smart,
As if my yeare were wast, and woxen old.
And yet alas, but now my spring begonne,
30   And yet alas, yt is already donne.

You naked trees, whose shady leaues are lost,
Wherein the byrds were wont to build their bowre:
And now are clothd with mosse and hoary frost,
Instede of bloosmes, wherwith your buds did flowre:
35   I see your teares, that from your boughes doe raine,
Whose drops in drery ysicles remaine.

All so my lustfull leafe is drye and sere,
My timely buds with wayling all are wasted:
The blossome, which my braunch of youth did beare,

With breathed sighes is blowne away, and blasted,   40
And from mine eyes the drizling teares descend,
As on your boughes the ysicles depend.

Thou feeble flocke, whose fleece is rough and rent,
Whose knees are weake through fast and euill fare:
Mayst witnesse well by thy ill gouernement,   45
Thy maysters mind is ouercome with care.
Thou weake, I wanne: thou leane, I quite forlorne:
With mourning pyne I, you with pyning mourne.

A thousand sithes I curse that carefull hower,
Wherein I longd the neighbour towne to see: 50
And eke tenne thousand sithes I blesse the stoure,
Wherein I sawe so fayre a sight, as shee.
Yet all for naught: such sight hath bred my bane.
Ah God, that loue should breede both ioy and payne.

It is not *Hobbinol*, wherefore I plaine,   55
Albee my loue he seeke with dayly suit:
His clownish gifts and curtsies I disdaine,
His kiddes, his cracknelles, and his early fruit.
Ah foolish *Hobbinol*, thy gyfts bene vayne:
Colin them giues to *Rosalind* againe.   60

I loue thilke lasse, (alas why doe I loue?)
And am forlorne, (alas why am I lorne?)
Shee deignes not my good will, but doth reproue,
And of my rurall musick holdeth scorne.
Shepheards deuise she hateth as the snake,   65
And laughes the songes, that *Colin Clout* doth make.

Wherefore my pype, albee rude *Pan* thou please,
Yet for thou pleasest not, where most I would:
And thou vnlucky Muse, that wontst to ease
My musing mynd, yet canst not, when thou should: 70
Both pype and Muse, shall sore the while abye.
So broke his oaten pype, and downe dyd lye.

By that, the welked *Phœbus* gan availe,
His weary waine, and nowe the frosty *Night*
75   Her mantle black through heauen gan ouerhaile.
Which seene, the pensife boy halfe in despight
Arose, and homeward droue his sonned sheepe,
Whose hanging heads did seeme his carefull case to weepe.

Colins Embleme.
80   *Anchôra speme.*

GLOSSE.

[1] COLIN Cloute) is a name not greatly vsed, and yet haue I sene
a Poesie of M. Skeltons vnder that title. But indeede the word
Colin is Frenche, and vsed of the French Poete Marot (if he be
worthy of the name of a Poete) in a certein Æglogue. Vnder
which name this Poete secretly shadoweth himself, as sometime
did Virgil vnder the name of Tityrus, thinking it much fitter,
then such Latine names, for the great vnlikelyhoode of the
language.

[6] vnnethes) scarcely.

[10] couthe) commeth of the verbe Conne, that is, to know or to
haue skill. As well interpreteth the same the worthy Sir Tho.
Smitth in his booke of gouerment: wherof I haue a perfect copie
in wryting, lent me by his kinseman, and my verye singular good
freend, M. Gabriel Haruey: as also of some other his most graue
and excellent wrytings.

[49] Sythe) time.   [50] Neighbour towne) the next towne:
expressing the Latine Vicina.

[51] Stoure) a fitt.   [37] Sere) withered.

[57] His clownish gyfts) imitateth Virgils verse,

Rusticus es Corydon, nec munera curat Alexis.

[59] Hobbinol) is a fained country name, whereby, it being so
commune and vsuall, seemeth to be hidden the person of some
his very speciall and most familiar freend, whom he entirely and
extraordinarily beloued, as peraduenture shall be more largely
declared hereafter. In thys place seemeth to be some sauour of

disorderly loue, which the learned call pæderastice: but it is
gathered beside his meaning. For who that hath red Plato his
dialogue called Alcybiades, Xenophon and Maximus Tyrius of
Socrates opinions, may easily perceiue, that such loue is muche
to be alowed and liked of, specially so meant, as Socrates vsed it:
who sayth, that in deede he loued Alcybiades extremely, yet not
Alcybiades person, but hys soule, which is Alcybiades owne selfe.
And so is pæderastice much to be præferred before gynerastice,
that is the loue whiche enflameth men with lust toward woman
kind. But yet let no man thinke, that herein I stand with Lucian
or hys deuelish disciple Vnico Aretino, in defence of execrable
and horrible sinnes of forbidden and vnlawful fleshlinesse. Whose
abominable errour is fully confuted of Perionius, and others.

[61] I loue) a prety Epanorthosis in these two verses, and withall a
Paronomasia or playing with the word, where he sayth (I loue
thilke lasse (alas &c.

[60] Rosalinde) is also a feigned name, which being wel ordered, wil
bewray the very name of hys loue and mistresse, whom by that
name he coloureth. So as Ouide shadoweth hys loue vnder the
name of Corynna, which of some is supposed to be Iulia, themp-
eror Augustus his daughter, and wyfe to Agryppa. So doth
Aruntius Stella euery where call his Lady Asteris and Ianthis,
albe it is wel knowen that her right name was Violantilla: as
witnesseth Statius in his Epithalamium. And so the famous
Paragone of Italy, Madonna Cœlia in her letters enuelopeth her
selfe vnder the name of Zima: and Petrona vnder the name of
Bellochia. And this generally hath bene a common custome of
counterfeicting the names of secret Personages.

[73] Auail) bring downe.
[75] Ouerhaile) drawe ouer.

Embleme.

His Embleme or Poesye is here vnder added in Italian, Anchóra
speme: the meaning wherof is, that notwithstande his extreme
passion and lucklesse loue, yet leaning on hope, he is some what
recomforted.

Februarie.

Ægloga Secunda.

ARGVMENT.

This Æglogue is rather morall and generall, then bent to any secrete or particular purpose. It specially conteyneth a discourse of old age, in the persone of Thenot *an olde Shepheard, who for his crookednesse and vnlustinesse, is scorned of* Cuddie *an vnhappy Heardmans boye. The matter very well accordeth with the season of the moneth, the yeare now drouping, and as it were, drawing to his last age. For as in this time of yeare, so then in our bodies there is a dry and withering cold, which congealeth the crudled blood, and frieseth the wetherbeaten flesh, with stormes of Fortune, and hoare frosts of Care. To which purpose the olde man telleth a tale of the Oake and the Bryer, so liuely and so feelingly, as if the thing were set forth in some Picture before our eyes, more plainly could not appeare.*

CVDDIE.   THENOT.

Ah for pittie, wil rancke Winters rage,
These bitter blasts neuer ginne tasswage?
The kene cold blowes through my beaten hyde,
All as I were through the body gryde.

My ragged rontes all shiver and shake,   5
As doen high Towers in an earthquake:
They wont in the wind wagge their wrigle tailes,
Perke as Peacock: but nowe it auales.

THENOT.

  Lewdly complainest thou laesie ladde,
Of Winters wracke, for making thee sadde.   10
Must not the world wend in his commun course
From good to badd, and from badde to worse,
From worse vnto that is worst of all,
And then returne to his former fall?
Who will not suffer the stormy time,   15
Where will he liue tyll the lusty prime?
Selfe haue I worne out thrise threttie yeares,
Some in much ioy, many in many teares:
Yet neuer complained of cold nor heate,
Of Sommers flame, nor of Winters threat: 20
Ne euer was to Fortune foeman,
But gently tooke, that vngently came.
And euer my flocke was my chiefe care,
Winter or Sommer they mought well fare.

CVDDIE.

  No marueile *Thenot*, if thou can beare   25
Cherefully the Winters wrathfull cheare:
For Age and Winter accord full nie,
This chill, that cold, this crooked, that wrye.
And as the lowring Wether lookes downe,
So semest thou like good fryday to frowne.   30
But my flowring youth is foe to frost,
My shippe vnwont in stormes to be tost.

THENOT.

  The soueraigne of seas he blames in vaine,
That once seabeate, will to sea againe.
So loytring liue you little heardgroomes,   35
Keeping your beastes in the budded broomes:

And when the shining sunne laugheth once,
You deemen, the Spring is come attonce.
Tho gynne you, fond flyes, the cold to scorne,
And crowing in pypes made of greene corne,
You thinken to be Lords of the yeare.
But eft, when ye count you freed from feare,
Comes the breme winter with chamfred browes,
Full of wrinckles and frostie furrowes:
Drerily shooting his stormy darte,
Which cruddles the blood, and pricks the harte.
Then is your carelesse corage accoied,
Your carefull heards with cold bene annoied.
Then paye you the price of your surquedrie,
With weeping, and wayling, and misery.

CVDDIE.

Ah foolish old man, I scorne thy skill,
That wouldest me, my springing youngth to spil.
I deeme, thy braine emperished bee
Through rusty elde, that hath rotted thee:
Or sicker thy head veray tottie is,
So on thy corbe shoulder it leanes amisse.
Now thy selfe hast lost both lopp and topp,
Als my budding braunch thou wouldest cropp:
But were thy yeares greene, as now bene myne,
To other delights they would encline.
Tho wouldest thou learne to caroll of Loue,
And hery with hymnes thy lasses gloue.
Tho wouldest thou pype of *Phyllis* prayse:
But *Phyllis* is myne for many dayes:
I wonne her with a gyrdle of gelt,
Embost with buegle about the belt.
Such an one shepeheards woulde make full faine:
Such an one would make thee younge againe.

40

45

50

55

60

65

THENOT.

Thou art a fon, of thy loue to boste,
All that is lent to loue, wyll be lost.   70

CVDDIE.

Seest, howe brag yond Bullocke beares,
So smirke, so smoothe, his pricked eares?
His hornes bene as broade, as Rainebowe bent,
His dewelap as lythe, as lasse of Kent.
See howe he venteth into the wynd.   75
Weenest of loue is not his mynd?
Seemeth thy flocke thy counsell can,
So lustlesse bene they, so weake so wan,
Clothed with cold, and hoary wyth frost.
Thy flocks father his corage hath lost: 80
Thy Ewes, that wont to haue blowen bags,
Like wailefull widdowes hangen their crags:
The rather Lambes bene starued with cold,
All for their Maister is lustlesse and old.

THENOT.

Cuddie, I wote thou kenst little good,   85
So vainely taduaunce thy headlesse hood.
For Youngth is a bubble blown vp with breath,
Whose witt is weakenesse, whose wage is death,
Whose way is wildernesse, whose ynne Penaunce,
And stoopegallaunt Age the hoste of Greeuaunce.   90
But shall I tel thee a tale of truth,
Which I cond of *Tityrus* in my youth,
Keeping his sheepe on the hils of Kent?

CVDDIE.

To nought more *Thenot*, my mind is bent,
Then to heare nouells of his deuise: 95
They bene so well thewed, and so wise,
What euer that good old man bespake.

THENOT.

Many meete tales of youth did he make,
And some of loue, and some of cheualrie:
100   But none fitter then this to applie.
Now listen a while, and hearken the end.

There grewe an aged Tree on the greene,
A goodly Oake sometime had it bene,
With armes full strong and largely displayd,
105   But of their leaues they were disarayde:
The bodie bigge, and mightely pight,
Throughly rooted, and of wonderous hight:
Whilome had bene the King of the field,
And mochell mast to the husband did yielde,
115   And with his nuts larded many swine.
But now the gray mosse marred his rine,
His bared boughes were beaten with stormes,
His toppe was bald, and wasted with wormes,
His honor decayed, his braunches sere.

115   Hard by his side grewe a bragging brere,
Which proudly thrust into Thelement,
And seemed to threat the Firmament.
Yt was embellisht with blossomes fayre,
And thereto aye wonned to repayre
120   The shepheards daughters, to gather flowres,
To peinct their girlonds with his colowres.
And in his small bushes vsed to shrowde
The sweete Nightingale singing so lowde:
Which made this foolish Brere wexe so bold,
125   That on a time he cast him to scold,
And snebbe the good Oake, for he was old.

Why standst there (quoth he) thou brutish blocke?
Nor for fruict, nor for shadowe serues thy stocke:
Seest, how fresh my flowers bene spredde,
130   Dyed in Lilly white, and Cremsin redde,
With Leaues engrained in lusty greene,
Colours meete to clothe a mayden Queene.
Thy wast bignes but combers the grownd,
And dirks the beauty of my blossomes rownd.

The mouldie mosse, which thee accloieth,   135
My Sinamon smell too much annoieth.
Wherefore soone I rede thee, hence remoue,
Least thou the price of my displeasure proue.
So spake this bold brere with great disdaine:
Little him answered the Oake againe,   140
But yielded, with shame and greefe adawed,
That of a weede he was ouerawed.

   Yt chaunced after vpon a day,
The Hus-bandman selfe to come that way,
Of custome for to seruewe his grownd,   145
And his trees of state in compasse rownd.
Him when the spitefull brere had espyed,
Causlesse complained, and lowdly cryed
Vnto his Lord, stirring vp sterne strife:
O my liege Lord, the God of my life,   150
Pleaseth you ponder your Suppliants plaint,
Caused of wrong, and cruell constraint,
Which I your poore Vassall dayly endure:
And but your goodnes the same recure,
Am like for desperate doole to dye,   155
Through felonous force of mine enemie.

   Greatly aghast with this piteous plea,
Him rested the goodman on the lea,
And badde the Brere in his plaint proceede.
With painted words tho gan this proude weede,   160
(As most vsen Ambitious folke:)
His colowred crime with craft to cloke.

   Ah my soueraigne, Lord of creatures all,
Thou placer of plants both humble and tall,
Was not I planted of thine owne hand,   165
To be the primrose of all thy land,
With flowring blossomes, to furnish the prime,
And scarlot berries in Sommer time?
How falls it then, that this faded Oake,
Whose bodie is sere, whose braunches broke,   170
Whose naked Armes stretch vnto the fyre,
Vnto such tyrannie doth aspire:

Hindering with his shade my louely light,
And robbing me of the swete sonnes sight?
175   So beate his old boughes my tender side,
That oft the bloud springeth from wounds wyde:
Vntimely my flowres forced to fall,
That bene the honor of your Coronall.
And oft he lets his cancker wormes light
180   Vpon my braunches, to worke me more spight:
And oft his hoarie locks downe doth cast,
Where with my fresh flowretts bene defast.
For this, and many more such outrage,
Crauing your goodlihead to aswage
185   The ranckorous rigour of his might,
Nought aske I, but onely to hold my right:
Submitting me to your good sufferance,
And praying to be garded from greeuance.
    To this the Oake cast him to replie
190   Well as he couth: but his enemie
Had kindled such coles of displeasure,
That the good man noulde stay his leasure,
But home him hasted with furious heate,
Encreasing his wrath with many a threate.
195   His harmefull Hatchet he hent in hand,
(Alas, that it so ready should stand)
And to the field alone he speedeth.
(Ay little helpe to harme there needeth)
Anger nould let him speake to the tree,
200   Enaunter his rage mought cooled bee:
But to the roote bent his sturdy stroke,
And made many wounds in the wast Oake.
The Axes edge did oft turne againe,
As halfe vnwilling to cutte the graine:
205   Semed, the sencelesse yron dyd feare,
Or to wrong holy eld did forbeare.
For it had bene an auncient tree,
Sacred with many a mysteree,
And often crost with the priestes crewe,
210   And often halowed with holy water dewe.

But sike fancies weren foolerie,
And broughten this Oake to this miserye.
For nought mought they quitten him from decay:
For fiercely the good man at him did laye.
The blocke oft groned vnder the blow,   215
And sighed to see his neare ouerthrow.
In fine the steele had pierced his pitth,
Tho downe to the earth he fell forthwith:
His wonderous weight made the grounde to quake,
Thearth shronke vnder him, and seemed to shake.   220
There lyeth the Oake, pitied of none.
    Now stands the Brere like a Lord alone,
Puffed vp with pryde and vaine pleasaunce:
But all this glee had no continuaunce.
For eftsones Winter gan to approche,   225
The blustring Boreas did encroche,
And beate vpon the solitarie Brere:
For nowe no succoure was seene him nere.
Now gan he repent his pryde to late:
For naked left and disconsolate,   230
The byting frost nipt his stalke dead,
The watrie wette weighed downe his head,
And heaped snowe burdned him so sore,
That nowe vpright he can stand no more:
And being downe, is trodde in the durt   235
Of cattell, and brouzed, and sorely hurt.
Such was thend of this Ambitious brere,
For scorning Eld

CVDDIE.

    Now I pray thee shepheard, tel it not forth:
Here is a long tale, and little worth.   240
So longe haue I listened to thy speche,
That graffed to the ground is my breche:
My hartblood is welnigh frorne I feele,
And my galage growne fast to my heele:
But little ease of thy lewd tale I tasted.   245
Hye thee home shepheard, the day is nigh wasted.

Thenots Embleme.
Iddio perche è vecchio,
Fa suoi al suo essempio.

250   Cuddies Embleme.
Niuno vecchio,
Spaventa Iddio.

GLOSSE.

[3] Kene) sharpe.

[4] Gride) perced: an olde word much vsed of Lidgate, but not found
(that I know of) in Chaucer.

[5] Ronts) young bullockes.

[10] Wracke) ruine or Violence, whence commeth shipwracke: and
not wreake, that is vengeaunce or wrath.

[21] Foeman) a foe.

[25] Thenot) the name of a shepheard in Marot his Æglogues.

[33] The soueraigne of Seas) is Neptune the God of the seas. The
saying is borowed of Mimus Publianus, which vsed this prouerb
in a verse.

Improbè Neptunum accusat, qui iterum naufragium facit.

[35] Heardgromes) Chaucers verse almost whole.

[39] Fond Flyes) He compareth carelesse sluggardes or ill hus-
bandmen to flyes, that so soone as the sunne shineth, or yt wexeth
any thing warme, begin to flye abroade, when sodeinly they be
ouertaken with cold.

[42] But eft when) A verye excellent and liuely description of Winter,
so as may bee indifferently taken, eyther for old Age, or for
Winter season.

[43] Breme) chill, bitter.   [43] Chamfred) chapt, or wrinckled.

[47] Accoied) plucked downe and daunted.   [49] Surquedrie)
pryde.

[54] Elde) olde age.   [55] Sicker) sure.   [55] Tottie)
wauering.

[56] Corbe) crooked.   [62] Herie) worshippe.

[63] Phyllis) the name of some mayde vnknowen, whom Cuddie,

whose person is secrete, loued. The name is vsuall in Theocritus, Virgile, and Mantuane.

[66] Belte) a girdle or wast band.   [69] A fon) a foole.

[74] lythe) soft and gentile.

[75] Venteth) snuffeth in the wind.   [80] Thy flocks Father) the Ramme.   [82] Crags) neckes.

[83] Rather Lambes) that be ewed early in the beginning of the yeare.

[87] Youth is) A verye moral and pitthy Allegorie of youth, and the lustes thereof, compared to a wearie wayfaring man.

[92] Tityrus) I suppose he meane Chaucer, whose prayse for pleasaunt tales cannot dye, so long as the memorie of hys name shal liue, and the name of Poetrie shal endure.

[96] Well thewed) that is, Bene moratæ, full of morall wisenesse.

[102] There grew) This tale of the Oake and the Brere, he telleth as learned of Chaucer, but it is cleane in another kind, and rather like to Æsopes fables. It is very excellente for pleasaunt descriptions, being altogether a certaine Icon or Hypotyposis of disdainfull younkers.

[118] Embellisht) beautified and adorned.   [119] To wonne) to haunt or frequent.   [126] Sneb) checke.

[127] Why standst) The speach is scorneful and very presumptuous.   [131] Engrained) dyed in grain.

[135] Accloieth) encombreth.   [141] Adawed) daunted and confounded.

[146] Trees of state) taller trees fitte for timber wood.

[149] Sterne strife) said Chaucer .s. fell and sturdy.   [150] O my liege) A maner of supplication, wherein is kindly coloured the affection and speache of Ambitious men.

[178] Coronall) Garlande.   [182] Flourets) young blossomes.

[166] The Primrose) The chiefe and worthiest.

[171] Naked armes) metaphorically ment of the bare boughes, spoyled of leaues. This colourably he speaketh, as adiudging hym to the fyre.

[176] The blood) spoken of a blocke, as it were of a liuing creature, figuratiuely, and (as they saye) κατ' εἰκασμόν.

[181] Hoarie lockes) metaphorically for withered leaues.

[195] Hent) caught.   [199] Nould) for would not.

[198] Ay) euermore.   [202] Wounds) gashes.

[200] Enaunter) least that.

[209] The priestes crewe) holy water pott, wherewith the popishe
     priest vsed to sprinckle and hallowe the trees from mischaunce.
     Such blindnesse was in those times, which the Poete supposeth,
     to haue bene the finall decay of this auncient Oake.
[215] The blocke oft groned) A liuelye figure, whiche geueth sence
     and feeling to vnsensible creatures, as Virgile also sayeth: Saxa
     gemunt grauido &c.
[226] Boreas) The Northerne wynd, that bringeth the moste stormie
     weather.
[224] Glee) chere and iollitie.
[238] For scorning Eld) And minding (as shoulde seme) to haue
     made ryme to the former verse, he is conningly cutte of by
     Cuddye, as disdayning to here any more.
[244] Galage) a startuppe or clownish shoe.

Embleme.

This embleme is spoken of Thenot, as a moral of his former tale:
namelye, that God, which is himselfe most aged, being before al
ages, and without beginninge, maketh those, whom he loueth
like to himselfe, in heaping yeares vnto theyre dayes, and blessing
them wyth longe lyfe. For the blessing of age is not giuen to all,
but vnto those, whome God will so blesse: and albeit that many
euil men reache vnto such fulnesse of yeares, and some also wexe
olde in myserie and thraldome, yet therefore is not age euer the
lesse blessing. For euen to such euill men such number of yeares
is added, that they may in their last dayes repent, and come to
their first home. So the old man checketh the rashheaded boy,
for despysing his gray and frostye heares.
Whom Cuddye doth counterbuff with a byting and bitter prouerbe,
spoken indeede at the first in contempt of old age generally. for
it was an old opinion, and yet is continued in some mens conceipt,
that men of yeares haue no feare of god at al, or not so much as
younger folke. For that being rypened with long experience, and
hauing passed many bitter brunts and blastes of vengeaunce, they
dread no stormes of Fortune, nor wrathe of Gods, nor daunger
of menne, as being eyther by longe and ripe wisedome armed
against all mischaunces and aduersitie, or with much trouble

hardened against all troublesome tydes: lyke vnto the Ape, of
which is sayd in Æsops fables, that oftentimes meeting the Lyon,
he was at first sore aghast and dismayed at the grimnes and
austeritie of hys countenance, but at last being acquainted with
his lookes, he was so furre from fearing him, that he would
familiarly gybe and iest with him: Suche longe experience breed-
eth in some men securitie. Although it please Erasmus a great
clerke and good old father, more fatherly and fauourablye to
construe it in his Adages for his own behoofe, That by the
prouerbe Nemo Senex metuit Iouem, is not meant, that old men
haue no feare of God at al, but that they be furre from superstition
and Idolatrous regard of false Gods, as is Iupiter. But his greate
learning notwithstanding, it is to plaine, to be gainsayd, that olde
men are muche more enclined to such fond fooleries, then younger
heades.

March.

Ægloga Tertia.

ARGVMENT.

In this Æglogue two shepheards boyes taking occasion of the season, beginne to make purpose of loue and other plesaunce, which to springtime is most agreeable. The speciall meaning hereof is, to giue certaine markes and tokens, to know Cupide the Poets God of Loue. But more particularlye I thinke, in the person of Thomalin is meant some secrete freend, who scorned Loue and his knights so long, till at length him selfe was entangled, and vnwares wounded with the dart of some beautifull regard, which is Cupides arrowe.

WILLYE   THOMALIN.

Thomalin, why sytten we soe,
As weren ouerwent with woe,
    Vpon so fayre a morow?
The ioyous time now nigheth fast,
That shall alegge this bitter blast,
    And slake the winters sorowe.

5

THOMALIN.
Sicker Willye, thou warnest well:
For Winters wrath beginnes to quell,
   And pleasant spring appeareth.
The grasse nowe ginnes to be refresht,   10
The Swallow peepes out of her nest,
   And clowdie Welkin cleareth.

WILLYE.
Seest not thilke same Hawthorne studde,
How bragly it beginnes to budde,
   And vtter his tender head?   15
Flora now calleth forth eche flower,
And bids make ready *Maias* bowre,
   That newe is vpryst from bedde.
Tho shall we sporten in delight,
And learne with Lettice to wexe light,   20
   That scornefully lookes askaunce,
Tho will we little Loue awake,
That nowe sleepeth in *Lethe* lake,
   And pray him leaden our daunce.

THOMALIN.
Willye, I wene thou bee assott: 25
For lustie Loue still sleepeth not,
   But is abroad at his game.

WILLYE.
How kenst thou, that he is awoke?
Or hast thy selfe his slomber broke?
   Or made preuie to the same?   30

THOMALIN.
No, but happely I hym spyde,
Where in a bush he did him hide,
   With winges of purple and blewe.
And were not, that my sheepe would stray,
The preuie marks I would bewray,   35
   Whereby by chaunce I him knewe.

WILLYE.

Thomalin, haue no care for thy,
My selfe will haue a double eye,
   Ylike to my flocke and thine:
For als at home I haue a syre,
A stepdame eke as whott as fyre,
   That dewly adayes counts mine.

THOMALIN.

Nay, but thy seeing will not serue,
My sheepe for that may chaunce to swerue,
   And fall into some mischiefe.
For sithens is but the third morowe,
That I chaunst to fall a sleepe with sorowe,
   And waked againe with griefe:
The while thilke same vnhappye Ewe,
Whose clouted legge her hurt doth shewe,
   Fell headlong into a dell,
And there vnioynted both her bones:
Mought her necke bene ioynted attones,
   She shoulde haue neede no more spell.
Thelf was so wanton and so wood,
(But now I trowe can better good)
   She mought ne gang on the greene.

WILLYE.

Let be, as may be, that is past:
That is to come, let be forecast.
   Now tell vs, what thou hast seene.

THOMALIN.

It was vpon a holiday,
When shepheardes groomes han leaue to playe,
   I cast to goe a shooting.
Long wandring vp and downe the land,
With bowe and bolts in either hand,
   For birds in bushes tooting:
At length within an Yuie todde
(There shrouded was the little God)

I heard a busie bustling.
I bent my bolt against the bush,   70
Listening if any thing did rushe,
　　But then heard no more rustling.
Tho peeping close into the thicke,
Might see the mouing of some quicke,
　　Whose shape appeared not: 75
But were it faerie, feend, or snake,
My courage earnd it to awake,
　　And manfully thereat shotte.
With that sprong forth a naked swayne,
With spotted winges like Peacocks trayne,   80
　　And laughing lope to a tree.
His gylden quiuer at his backe,
And siluer bowe, which was but slacke,
　　Which lightly he bent at me.
That seeing I, leuelde againe,   85
And shott at him with might and maine,
　　As thicke, as it had hayled.
So long I shott, that al was spent:
Tho pumie stones I hastly hent,
　　And threwe: but nought availed: 90
He was so wimble, and so wight,
From bough to bough he lepped light,
　　And oft the pumies latched.
Therewith affrayd I ranne away:
But he, that earst seemd but to playe,   95
　　A shaft in earnest snatched,
And hit me running in the heele:
For then I little smart did feele:
　　But soone it sore encreased.
And now it ranckleth more and more,   100
And inwardly it festreth sore,
　　Ne wote I, how to cease it.

WILLYE.

Thomalin, I pittie thy plight.
Perdie with loue thou diddest fight:
    I know him by a token.
For once I heard my father say,
How he him caught vpon a day,
    (Whereof he wilbe wroken)
Entangled in a fowling net,
Which he for carrion Crowes had set,
    That in our Peeretree haunted.
Tho sayd, he was a winged lad,
But bowe and shafts as then none had:
    Els had he sore be daunted.
But see the Welkin thicks apace,
And stouping *Phebus* steepes his face:
    Yts time to hast vs homeward.

Willyes Embleme.
To be wise and eke to loue,
Is graunted scarce to God aboue.

Thomalins Embleme.
Of Hony and of Gaule in loue there is store:
The Honye is much, but the Gaule is more.

GLOSS.

This Æglogue seemeth somewhat to resemble that same of Theo-
    critus, wherein the boy likewise telling the old man, that he had
    shot at a winged boy in a tree, was by hym warned, to beware of
    mischiefe to come.
[2] Ouer went) ouergone.   [5] Alegge) to lessen or aswage.
[8] To quell) to abate.   [12] Welkin) the skie.
[11] The swallow) which bird vseth to be counted the messenger,
    and as it were, the fore runner of springe.
[16] Flora) the Goddesse of flowres, but indede (as saith Tacitus) a
    famous harlot, which with the abuse of her body hauing gotten
    great riches, made the people of Rome her heyre: who in remem-

braunce of so great beneficence, appointed a yearely feste for the
memoriall of her, calling her, not as she was, nor as some doe
think, Andronica, but Flora: making her the Goddesse of all
floures, and doing yerely to her solemne sacrifice.

[17] Maias bowre) that is the pleasaunt fielde, or rather the Maye
bushes. Maia is a Goddes and the mother of Mercurie, in honour
of whome the moneth of Maye is of her name so called, as sayth
Macrobius.

[20] Lettice) the name of some country lasse.

[21] Ascaunce) askewe or asquint.   [37] For thy) therefore.

[23] Lethe) is a lake in hell, which the Poetes call the lake of
forgetfulnes. For Lethe signifieth forgetfulnes. Wherein the
soules being dipped, did forget the cares of their former lyfe. So
that by loue sleeping in Lethe lake, he meaneth he was almost
forgotten and out of knowledge, by reason of winters hardnesse,
when al pleasures as it were, sleepe and weare oute of mynde.

[25] Assotte) to dote.

[29] His slomber) To breake Loues slomber, is to exercise the
delightes of Loue and wanton pleasures.

[33] Winges of purple) so is he feyned of the Poetes.

[40] For als) he imitateth Virgils verse.

Est mihi namque domi pater, est iniusta nouerca &c.

[51] A dell) a hole in the ground.

[54] Spell) is a kinde of verse or charme, that in elder tymes they
vsed often to say ouer euery thing, that they would haue preserued,
as the Nightspel for theeues, and the woodspell. And herehence
I thinke is named the gospell, as it were Gods spell or worde.
And so sayth Chaucer, Listeneth Lordings to my spell.

[57] Gange) goe.   [67] An Yuie todde) a thicke bushe.

[79] Swaine) a boye: For so is he described of the Poetes, to be a
boye .s. alwayes freshe and lustie: blindfolded, because he maketh
no difference of Personages: wyth diuers coloured winges, .s. ful
of flying fancies: with bowe and arrow, that is with glaunce of
beautye, which prycketh as a forked arrowe. He is sayd also to
haue shafts, some leaden, some golden: that is, both pleasure for
the gracious and loued, and sorow for the louer that is disdayned
or forsaken. But who liste more at large to behold Cupids colours
and furniture, let him reade ether Propertius, or Moschus his

Idyllion of wandring loue, being now most excellently translated into Latine by the singuler learned man Angelus Politianus: whych worke I haue seene amongst other of thys Poets doings, very wel translated also into Englishe Rymes.

[91] Wimble and wighte) Quicke and deliuer.

[97] In the heele) is very Poetically spoken, and not without speciall iudgement. For I remember, that in Homer it is sayd of Thetis, that shee tooke her young babe Achilles being newely borne, and holding him by the heele, dipped him in the Riuer of Styx. The vertue whereof is, to defend and keepe the bodyes washed therein from any mortall wound. So Achilles being washed al ouer, saue onely his hele, by which his mother held, was in the rest inuulnerable: therfore by Paris was feyned to bee shotte with a poysoned arrowe in the heele, whiles he was busie about the marying of Polyxena in the temple of Apollo. which mysticall fable Eustathius vnfolding, sayth: that by wounding in the hele, is meant lustfull loue. For from the heele (as say the best Phisitions) to the preuie partes there passe certaine veines and slender synnewes, as also the like come from the head, and are carryed lyke little pypes behynd the eares: so that (as sayth Hipocrates) yf those veynes there be cut a sonder, the partie straighte becommeth cold and vnfruiteful. which reason our Poete wel weighing, maketh this shepheards boye of purpose to be wounded by Loue in the heele.

[93] Latched) caught.   [108] Wroken) reuenged.

[106] For once) In this tale is sette out the simplicitye of shepheards opinion of Loue.

[116] Stouping Phæbus) Is a Periphrasis of the sunne setting.

Embleme.

Hereby is meant, that all the delights of Loue, wherein wanton youth walloweth, be but follye mixt with bitternesse, and sorow sawced with repentaunce. For besides that the very affection of Loue it selfe tormenteth the mynde, and vexeth the body many wayes, with vnrestfulnesse all night, and wearines all day, seeking for that we can not haue, and fynding that we would not haue: euen the selfe things which best before vs lyked, in course of time and

chaung of ryper yeares, whiche also therewithall chaungeth our
wonted lyking and former fantasies, will then seeme lothsome
and breede vs annoyaunce, when yougthes flowre is withered,
and we fynde our bodyes and wits aunswere not to suche vayne
iollitie and lustfull pleasaunce.

Aprill.

Ægloga Quarta.

ARGVMENT.

This Æglogue is purposely intended to the honor and prayse of our most gracious souereigne, Queene Elizabeth. The speakers herein be Hobbinoll and Thenott, two shepheardes: the which Hobbinoll being before mentioned, greatly to haue loued Colin, is here set forth more largely, complayning him of that boyes great misaduenture in Loue, whereby his mynd was alienate and with drawen not onely from him, who moste loued him, but also from all former delightes and studies, aswell in pleasaunt pyping, as conning ryming and singing, and other his laudable exercises. Whereby he taketh occasion, for proofe of his more excellencie and skill in poetrie, to recorde a songe, which the sayd Colin sometime made in honor of her Maiestie, whom abruptely he termeth Elysa.

THENOT.   HOBBINOLL.

Tell me good Hobbinoll, what garres thee greete?
What? hath some Wolfe thy tender Lambes ytorne?
Or is thy Bagpype broke, that soundes so sweete?
Or art thou of thy loued lasse forlorne?

Or bene thine eyes attempred to the yeare,   5
Quenching the gasping furrowes thirst with rayne?
Like April shoure, so stremes the trickling teares
Adowne thy cheeke, to quenche thy thristye payne.

HOBBINOLL.

Nor thys, nor that, so muche doeth make me mourne,
But for the ladde, whome long I lovd so deare,   10
Nowe loues a lasse, that all his loue doth scorne:
He plongd in payne, his tressed locks dooth teare.

Shepheards delights he dooth them all forsweare,
Hys pleasaunt Pipe, whych made vs meriment,
Hy wylfully hath broke, and doth forbeare   15
His wonted songs, wherein he all outwent.

THENOT.

What is he for a Ladde, you so lament?
Ys loue such pinching payne to them, that proue?
And hath he skill to make so excellent,
Yet hath so little skill to brydle loue?   20

HOBBINOLL.

Colin thou kenst, the Southerne shepheardes boye:
Him Loue hath wounded with a deadly darte.
Whilome on him was all my care and ioye,
Forcing with gyfts to winne his wanton heart.

But now from me hys madding mynd is starte,   25
And woes the Widdowes daughter of the glenne:
So nowe fayre *Rosalind* hath bredde hys smart,
So now his frend is chaunged for a frenne.

THENOT.

But if hys ditties bene so trimly dight,
I pray thee *Hobbinoll*, recorde some one: 30
The whiles our flockes doe graze about in sight,
And we close shrowded in thys shade alone.

HOBBINOL.

Contented I: then will I singe his laye
Of fayre *Elisa*, Queene of shepheardes all:
35 Which once he made, as by a spring he laye,
And tuned it vnto the Waters fall.

Ye dayntye Nymphs, that in this blessed Brooke
        doe bathe your brest,
For sake your watry bowres, and hether looke,
40   at my request:
And eke you Virgins, that on *Parnasse* dwell,
Whence floweth *Helicon* the learned well,
        Helpe me to blaze
        Her worthy praise,
45 Which in her sexe doth all excell.

Of fayre *Elisa* be your siluer song,
        that blessed wight:
The flowre of Virgins, may shee florish long,
        In princely plight.
50 For shee is *Syrinx* daughter without spotte,
Which *Pan* the shepheards God of her begot:
        So sprong her grace
        Of heauenly race,
No mortall blemishe may her blotte.

55 See, where she sits vpon the grassie greene,
        (O seemely sight)
Yclad in Scarlot like a mayden Queene,
        And Ermines white.
Vpon her head a Cremosin coronet,
60 With Damaske roses and Daffadillies set:
        Bayleaues betweene,
        And Primroses greene
Embellish the sweete Violet.

Tell me, haue ye seene her angelick face,
    Like *Phœbe* fayre?   65
Her heauenly haueour, her princely grace
    can you well compare?
The Redde rose medled with the White yfere,
In either cheeke depeincten liuely chere.
    Her modest eye,   70
    Her Maiestie,
Where haue you seene the like, but there?

I sawe *Phœbus* thrust out his golden hedde,
    vpon her to gaze:
But when he sawe, how broade her beames did spredde,   75
    it did him amaze.
He blusht to see another Sunne belowe,
Ne durst againe his fyrye face out showe:
    Let him, if he dare,
    His brightnesse compare   80
With hers, to haue the ouerthrowe.

Shewe thy selfe *Cynthia* with thy siluer rayes,
    and be not abasht:
When shee the beames of her beauty displayes,
    O how art thou dasht?   85
But I will not match her with *Latonaes* seede,
Such follie great sorow to *Niobe* did breede.
    Now she is a stone,
    And makes dayly mone,
Warning all other to take heede.   90

Pan may be proud, that euer he begot
    such a Bellibone,
And *Syrinx* reioyse, that euer was her lot
    to beare such an one.
Soone as my younglings cryen for the dam,   95
To her will I offer a milkwhite Lamb:
    Shee is my goddesse plaine,
    And I her shepherds swayne,
Albee forswonck and forswatt I am.

100   I see *Calliope* speede her to the place,
               where my Goddesse shines:
         And after her the other Muses trace,
               with their Violines.
         Bene they not Bay braunches, which they doe beare,
105   All for *Elisa* in her hand to weare?
               So sweetely they play,
               And sing all the way,
         That it a heauen is to heare.

         Lo how finely the graces can it foote
110   to the Instrument:
         They dauncen deffly, and singen soote,
               in their meriment.
         Wants not a fourth grace, to make the daunce euen?
         Let that rowme to my Lady be yeuen:
115   She shalbe a grace,
               To fyll the fourth place,
         And reigne with the rest in heauen.

         And whither rennes this beuie of Ladies bright,
               raunged in a rowe?
120   They bene all Ladyes of the lake behight,
               that vnto her goe.
         Chloris, that is the chiefest Nymph of al,
         Of Oliue braunches beares a Coronall:
               Oliues bene for peace,
125   When wars doe surcease:
         Such for a Princesse bene principall.

         Ye shepheards daughters, that dwell on the greene,
               hye you there apace:
         Let none come there, but that Virgins bene,
130   to adorne her grace.
         And when you come, whereas shee is in place,
         See, that your rudenesse doe not you disgrace:
               Binde your fillets faste,
               And gird in your waste,
135   For more finesse, with a tawdrie lace.

Bring hether the Pincke and purple Cullambine,
    With Gelliflowres:
Bring Coronations, and Sops in wine,
    worne of Paramoures.
Strowe me the ground with Daffadowndillies,   140
And Cowslips, and Kingcups, and loued Lillies:
    The pretie Pawnce,
      And the Cheuisaunce,
Shall match with the fayre flowre Delice.

Now ryse vp *Elisa*, decked as thou art,   145
    in royall aray:
And now ye daintie Damsells may depart
    echeone her way,
I feare, I haue troubled your troupes to longe:
Let dame *Eliza* thanke you for her song.   150
    And if you come hether,
      When Damsines I gether,
I will part them all you among.

THENOT.
And was thilk same song of *Colins* owne making?
Ah foolish boy, that is with loue yblent: 155
Great pittie is, he be in such taking,
For naught caren, that bene so lewdly bent.

HOBBINOL.
Sicker I hold him, for a greater fon,
That loues the thing, he cannot purchase.
But let vs homeward: for night draweth on,   160
And twincling starres the daylight hence chase.

Thenots Embleme.
O quam te memorem virgo?

Hobbinols Embleme.
O dea certe.   165

GLOSSE.

[1] Gars thee greete) causeth thee weepe and complain.

   [4] Forlorne) left and forsaken.

[5] Attempred to the yeare) agreeable to the season of the yeare, that
   is Aprill, which moneth is most bent to shoures and seasonable
   rayne: to quench, that is, to delaye the drought, caused through
   drynesse of March wyndes.

[10] The Ladde) Colin Clout.   [11] The Lasse) Rosalinda.

   [12] Tressed locks) wrethed and curled.

[17] Is he for a ladde) A straunge manner of speaking .s. what maner
   of Ladde is he?

[19] To make) to rime and versifye. For in this word making, our
   olde Englishe Poetes were wont to comprehend all the skil of
   Poetrye, according to the Greeke woorde ποιεῖν, to make, whence
   commeth the name of Poetes.

[21] Colin thou kenst) knowest. Seemeth hereby that Colin pertey-
   neth to some Southern noble man, and perhaps in Surrye or
   Kent, the rather bicause he so often nameth the Kentish downes,
   and before, As lythe as lasse of Kent.

[26] The Widowes) He calleth Rosalind the Widowes daughter of
   the glenne, that is, of a country Hamlet or borough, which I
   thinke is rather sayde to coloure and concele the person, then
   simply spoken. For it is well knowen, euen in spighte of Colin
   and Hobbinoll, that shee is a Gentle woman of no meane house,
   nor endewed with anye vulgare and common gifts both of nature
   and manners: but suche indeede, as neede nether Colin be
   ashamed to haue her made knowne by his verses, nor Hobbinol
   be greued, that so she should be commended to immortalitie for
   her rare and singular Vertues: Specially deseruing it no lesse, then
   eyther Myrto the most excellent Poete Theocritus his dearling, or
   Lauretta the diuine Petrarches Goddesse, or Himera the worthye
   Poete Stesichorus hys Idole: Vpon whom he is sayd so much to
   haue doted, that in regard of her excellencie, he scorned and
   wrote against the beauty of Helena. For which his præsumptuous
   and vnheedie hardinesse, he is sayde by vengeaunce of the Gods,
   thereat being offended, to haue lost both his eyes.

[28] Frenne) a straunger. The word I thinke was first poetically

put, and afterwarde vsed in commen custome of speach for forenne.

[29] Dight) adorned.   [33] Laye) a songe. As Roundelayes and Virelayes. In all this songe is not to be respected, what the worthinesse of her Maiestie deserueth, nor what to the highnes of a Prince is agreeable, but what is moste comely for the meanesse of a shepheards witte, or to conceiue, or to vtter. And therefore he calleth her Elysa, as through rudenesse tripping in her name: and a shepheards daughter, it being very vnfit, that a shepheards boy brought vp in the shepefold, should know, or euer seme to haue heard of a Queenes roialty.

[37] Ye daintie) is, as it were an Exordium ad preparandos animos.

[41] Virgins) the nine Muses, daughters of Apollo and Memorie, whose abode the Poets faine to be on Parnassus, a hill in Grece, for that in that countrye specially florished the honor of all excellent studies.

[42] Helicon) is both the name of a fountaine at the foote of Parnassus, and also of a mounteine in Bæotia, out of which floweth the famous Spring Castalius, dedicate also to the Muses: of which spring it is sayd, that when Pegasus the winged horse of Perseus (whereby is meant fame and flying renowme) strooke the grownde with his hoofe, sodenly thereout sprange a wel of moste cleare and pleasaunte water, which fro thence forth was consecrate to the Muses and Ladies of learning.

[46] Your siluer song) seemeth to imitate the lyke in Hesiodus ἀργυρέον μέλος.

[50] Syrinx) is the name of a Nymphe of Arcadie, whom when Pan being in loue pursued, she flying from him, of the Gods was turned into a reede. So that Pan catching at the Reedes in stede of the Damosell, and puffing hard (for he was almost out of wind) with hys breath made the Reedes to pype: which he seeing, tooke of them, and in remembraunce of his lost loue, made him a pype thereof. But here by Pan and Syrinx is not to bee thoughte, that the shephearde simplye meante those Poetical Gods: but rather supposing (as seemeth) her graces progenie to be diuine and immortall (so as the Paynims were wont to iudge of all Kinges and Princes, according to Homeres saying.

> Θυμὸς δὴ μέγας ἐστὶ διοτρεφέως βασιλήως
> τιμὴ δ' ἐκ διός ἐστι, φιλεῖ δε ὁ μητίετα Ζεύς.)

could deuise no parents in his iudgement so worthy for her, as Pan the shepeheards God, and his best beloued Syrinx. So that by Pan is here meant the most famous and victorious King, her highnesse Father, late of worthy memorye K. Henry the eyght. And by that name, oftymes (as hereafter appeareth) be noted kings and mighty Potentates: And in some place Christ himselfe, who is the verye Pan and god of Shepheardes.

[59] Cremosin coronet) he deuiseth her crowne to be of the finest and most delicate flowers, instede of perles and precious stones, wherewith Princes Diademes vse to bee adorned and embost.

[63] Embellish) beautifye and set out.

[65] Phebe) the Moone, whom the Poets faine to be sister vnto Phæbus, that is the Sunne.

[68] Medled) mingled.

[68] Yfere) together. By the mingling of the Redde rose and the White, is meant the vniting of the two principall houses of Lancaster and of Yorke: by whose longe discord and deadly debate, this realm many yeares was sore traueiled, and almost cleane decayed. Til the famous Henry the seuenth, of the line of Lancaster, taking to wife the most vertuous Princesse Elisabeth, daughter to the fourth Edward of the house of Yorke, begat the most royal Henry the eyght aforesayde, in whom was the firste vnion of the Whyte Rose and the Redde.

[100] Calliope) one of the nine Muses: to whome they assigne the honor of all Poetical Inuention, and the firste glorye of the Heroicall verse. other say, that shee is the Goddesse of Rhetorick: but by Virgile it is manifeste, that they mystake the thyng. For there in hys Epigrams, that arte semeth to be attributed to Polymnia, saying:

Signat cuncta manu, loquiturque Polymnia gestu.

which seemeth specially to be meant of Action and elocution, both special partes of Rhetorick: besyde that her name, which (as some construe it) importeth great remembraunce, conteineth another part. but I holde rather with them, which call her Polymnia or Polyhymnia of her good singing.

[104] Bay branches) be the signe of honor and victory, and therfore of myghty Conquerors worn in theyr triumphes, and eke of famous Poets, as saith Petrarch in hys Sonets.

Arbor vittoriosa triomphale,
Honor d' Imperadori & di Poëti, &c.

[109] The Graces) be three sisters, the daughters of Iupiter, (whose
names are Aglaia, Thalia, Euphrosyne, and Homer onely addeth
a fourth .s. Pasithea) otherwise called Charites, that is thanks.
whom the Poetes feyned to be the Goddesses of al bountie and
comelines, which therefore (as sayth Theodontius) they make
three, to wete, that men first ought to be gracious and bountiful
to other freely, then to receiue benefits at other mens hands
curteously, and thirdly to requite them thankfully: which are
three sundry Actions in liberalitye. And Boccace saith, that they
be painted naked, (as they were indeede on the tombe of C.
Iulius Cæsar) the one hauing her backe toward vs, and her face
fromwarde, as proceeding from vs: the other two toward vs,
noting double thanke to be due to vs for the benefit, we haue
done.

[111] Deaffly) Finelye and nimbly.   [111] Soote) Sweete.
[112] Meriment) Mirth.

[118] Beuie) A beauie of Ladyes, is spoken figuratiuely for a company
or troupe. the terme is taken of Larkes. For they say a Beuie of
Larkes, euen as a Couey of Partridge, or an eye of Pheasaunts.

[120] Ladyes of the lake) be Nymphes. For it was an olde opinion
amongste the Auncient Heathen, that of euery spring and foun-
taine was a goddesse the Soueraigne. Whiche opinion stucke in
the myndes of men not manye yeares sithence, by meanes of
certain fine fablers and lowd lyers, such as were the Authors of
King Arthure the great and such like, who tell many an vnlawfull
leasing of the Ladyes of the Lake, that is, the Nymphes. For the
word Nymphe in Greeke signifieth Well water, or otherwise a
Spouse or Bryde.

[120] Behight) called or named.

[122] Cloris) the name of a Nymph, and signifieth greenesse, of
whome is sayd, that Zephyrus the Westerne wind being in loue
with her, and coueting her to wyfe, gaue her for a dowrie, the
chiefedome and soueraigntye of al flowres and greene herbes,
growing on earth.

[124] Oliues bene) The Oliue was wont to be the ensigne of Peace
and quietnesse, eyther for that it cannot be planted and pruned,

and so carefully looked to, as it ought, but in time of peace: or els for that the Oliue tree, they say, will not growe neare the Firre tree, which is dedicate to Mars the God of battaile, and vsed most for speares and other instruments of warre. Whereupon is finely feigned, that when Neptune and Minerua stroue for the naming of the citie of Athens, Neptune striking the ground with his mace, caused a horse to come forth, that importeth warre, but at Mineruaes stroke sprong out an Oliue, to note that it should be a nurse of learning, and such peaceable studies.

[133] Binde your) Spoken rudely, and according to shepheardes simplicitye.

[136] Bring) all these be names of flowers. Sops in wine a flowre in colour much like to a Coronation, but differing in smel and quantitye. Flowre delice, that which they vse to misterme, Flowre de luce, being in Latine called Flos delitiarum.

[92] A Bellibone) or a Bonibell. homely spoken for a fayre mayde or Bonilasse.

[99] Forswonck and forswatt) ouerlaboured and sunneburnt.

[73] I saw Phæbus) the sunne. A sensible Narration, and present view of the thing mentioned, which they call παρουσία.

[82] Cynthia) the Moone so called of Cynthus a hyll, where she was honoured.

[86–7] Latonaes seede) Was Apollo and Diana. Whom when as Niobe the wife of Amphion scorned, in respect of the noble fruict of her wombe, namely her seuen sonnes, and so many daughters, Latona being therewith displeased, commaunded her sonne Phœbus to slea al the sonnes, and Diana all the daughters: whereat the vnfortunate Niobe being sore dismayed, and lamenting out of measure, was feigned of the Poetes, to be turned into a stone vpon the sepulchre of her children. for which cause the shepheard sayth, he will not compare her to them, for feare of like mysfortune.

[145] Now rise) is the conclusion. For hauing so decked her with prayses and comparisons, he returneth all the thanck of hys laboure to the excellencie of her Maiestie.

[152] When Damsins) A base reward of a clownish giuer.

[155] Yblent) Y, is a poeticall addition. blent blinded.

Embleme.

This Poesye is taken out of Virgile, and there of him vsed in the person of Æneas to his mother Venus, appearing to him in likenesse of one of Dianaes damosells: being there most diuinely set forth. To which similitude of diuinitie Hobbinoll comparing the excelency of Elisa, and being through the worthynes of Colins song, as it were, ouercome with the hugenesse of his imagination, brusteth out in great admiration, (O quam te memorem virgo?) being otherwise vnhable, then by soddein silence, to expresse the worthinesse of his conceipt. Whom Thenot answereth with another part of the like verse, as confirming by his graunt and approuaunce, that Elisa is no whit inferiour to the Maiestie of her, of whome that Poete so boldly pronounced, O dea certe.

Maye.

Ægloga Quinta.

ARGVMENT.

In this fift Æglogue, vnder the persons of two shepheards Piers and Palinodie, be represented two formes of pastoures or Ministers, or the protestant and the Catholique: whose chiefe talke standeth in reasoning, whether the life of the one must be like the other. with whom hauing shewed, that it is daungerous to mainteine any felowship, or giue too much credit to their colourable and feyned goodwill, he telleth him a tale of the foxe, that by such a counterpoynt of craftines deceiued and deuoured the credulous kidde.

PALINODE.   PIERS.

Is not thilke the mery moneth of May,
When loue lads masken in fresh aray?
How falles it then, we no merrier bene,
Ylike as others, girt in gawdy greene?
Our bloncket liueryes bene all to sadde,
For thilke same season, when all is ycladd
With pleasaunce: the grownd with grasse, the Wods
With greene leaues, the bushes with bloosming Buds.

Yougthes folke now flocken in euery where,
To gather may buskets and smelling brere: 10
And home they hasten the postes to dight,
And all the Kirke pillours eare day light,
With Hawthorne buds, and swete Eglantine,
And girlonds of roses and Sopps in wine.
Such merimake holy Saints doth queme,   15
But we here sytten as drownd in a dreme.

PIERS.

For Younkers *Palinode* such follies fitte,
But we tway bene men of elder witt.

PALINODE.

Sicker this morrowe, ne lenger agoe,
I sawe a shole of shepeheardes outgoe,   20
With singing, and shouting, and iolly chere:
Before them yode a lusty Tabrere,
That to the many a Horne pype playd,
Whereto they dauncen eche one with his mayd.
To see those folkes make such iouysaunce,   25
Made my heart after the pype to daunce.
Tho to the greene Wood they speeden hem all,
To fetchen home May with their musicall:
And home they bringen in a royall throne,
Crowned as king: and his Queene attone   30
Was Lady Flora, on whom did attend
A fayre flocke of Faeries, and a fresh bend
Of louely Nymphs. (O that I were there,
To helpen the Ladyes their Maybush beare)
Ah *Piers*, bene not thy teeth on edge, to thinke,   35
How great sport they gaynen with little swinck?

PIERS.

Perdie so farre am I from enuie,
That their fondnesse inly I pitie.
Those faytours little regarden their charge,
While they letting their sheepe runne at large,   40

Passen their time, that should be sparely spent,
In lustihede and wanton meryment.
Thilke same bene shepeheards for the Deuils stedde,
That playen, while their flockes be vnfedde.
45   Well is it seene, theyr sheepe bene not their owne,
That letten them runne at randon alone.
But they bene hyred for little pay
Of other, that caren as little as they,
What fallen the flocke, so they han the fleece,
50   And get all the gayne, paying but a peece.
I muse, what account both these will make,
The one for the hire, which he doth take,
And thother for leauing his Lords taske,
When great *Pan* account of shepeherdes shall aske.

PALINODE.

55   Sicker now I see thou speakest of spight,
All for thou lackest somedele their delight.
I (as I am) had rather be enuied,
All were it of my foe, then fonly pitied:
And yet if neede were, pitied would be,
60   Rather, then other should scorne at me:
For pittied is mishappe, that nas remedie,
But scorned bene dedes of fond foolerie.
What shoulden shepheards other things tend,
Then sith their God his good does them send,
65   Reapen the fruite thereof, that is pleasure,
The while they here liuen, at ease and leasure?
For when they bene dead, their good is ygoe,
They sleepen in rest, well as other moe.
Tho with them wends, what they spent in cost,
70   But what they left behind them, is lost.
Good is no good, but if it be spend:
God giueth good for none other end.

PIERS.

Ah *Palinodie*, thou art a worldes childe:
Who touches Pitch mought needes be defilde.
But shepheards (as Algrind vsed to say,)   75
Mought not liue ylike, as men of the laye:
With them it sits to care for their heire,
Enaunter their heritage doe impaire:
They must prouide for meanes of maintenaunce,
And to continue their wont countenaunce.   80
But shepheard must walke another way,
Sike worldly souenance he must foresay.
The sonne of his loines why should he regard
To leaue enriched with that he hath spard?
Should not thilke God, that gaue him that good,   85
Eke cherish his child, if in his wayes he stood?
For if he misliue in leudnes and lust,
Little bootes all the welth and the trust,
That his father left by inheritaunce:
All will be soone wasted with misgouernaunce.   90
But through this, and other their miscreaunce,
They maken many a wrong cheuisaunce,
Heaping vp waues of welth and woe,
The floddes whereof shall them ouerflowe.
Sike mens follie I cannot compare   95
Better, then to the Apes folish care,
That is so enamoured of her young one,
(And yet God wote, such cause hath she none)
That with her hard hold, and straight embracing,
She stoppeth the breath of her youngling.   100
So often times, when as good is meant,
Euil ensueth of wrong entent.
   The time was once, and may againe retorne,
(For ought may happen, that hath bene beforne)
When shepeheards had none inheritaunce,   105
Ne of land, nor fee in sufferaunce:
But what might arise of the bare sheepe,
(Were it more or lesse) which they did keepe.
Well ywis was it with shepheards thoe:
Nought hauing, nought feared they to forgoe.   110

For *Pan* himselfe was their inheritaunce,
And little them serued for their mayntenaunce.
The shepheards God so wel them guided,
That of nought they were vnprouided,
115   Butter enough, honye, milke, and whay,
And their flockes fleeces, them to araye.
But tract of time, and long prosperitie:
That nource of vice, this of insolencie,
Lulled the shepheards in such securitie,
120   That not content with loyall obeysaunce,
Some gan to gape for greedie gouernaunce,
And match them selfe with mighty potentates,
Louers of Lordship and troublers of states:
Tho gan shepheards swaines to looke a loft,
125   And leaue to liue hard, and learne to ligge soft:
Tho vnder colour of shepeheards, somewhile
There crept in Wolues, ful of fraude and guile,
That often deuoured their owne sheepe,
And often the shepheards, that did hem keepe.
130   This was the first sourse of shepheards sorowe,
That now nill be quitt with baile, nor borrowe.

PALINODE.
Three thinges to beare, bene very burdenous,
But the fourth to forbeare, is outragious.
Wemen that of Loues longing once lust,
135   Hardly forbearen, but haue it they must:
So when choler is inflamed with rage,
Wanting reuenge, is hard to asswage:
And who can counsell a thristie soule,
With patience to forbeare the offred bowle?
140   But of all burdens, that a man can beare,
Moste is, a fooles talke to beare and to heare.
I wene the Geaunt has not such a weight,
That beares on his shoulders the heauens height.
Thou findest faulte, where nys to be found,
145   And buildest strong warke vpon a weake ground:
Thou raylest on right withouten reason,
And blamest hem much, for small encheason.

How shoulden shepheardes liue, if not so?
What? should they pynen in payne and woe?
Nay sayd I thereto, by my deare borrowe,   150
If I may rest, I nill liue in sorrowe.
    Sorrowe ne neede be hastened on:
For he will come without calling anone.
While times enduren of tranquillitie,
Usen we freely our felicitie.   155
For when approchen the stormie stowres,
We mought with our shoulders beare of the sharpe
        showres.
And sooth to sayne, nought seemeth sike strife,
That shepheardes so witen ech others life,
And layen her faults the world beforne,   160
The while their foes done eache of hem scorne.
Let none mislike of that may not be mended:
So conteck soone by concord mought be ended.

PIERS.

Shepheard, I list none accordaunce make
With shepheard, that does the right way forsake.   165
And of the twaine, if choice were to me,
Had leuer my foe, then my freend he be.
For what concord han light and darke sam?
Or what peace has the Lion with the Lambe?
Such faitors, when their false harts bene hidde,   170
Will doe, as did the Foxe by the Kidde.

PALINODE.

Now *Piers*, of felowship, tell vs that saying:
For the Ladde can keepe both our flocks from straying.

PIERS.

Thilke same Kidde (as I can well deuise)
Was too very foolish and vnwise.   175
For on a tyme in Sommer season,
The Gate her dame, that had good reason,
Yode forth abroade vnto the greene wood,
To brouze, or play, or what shee thought good.

180   But for she had a motherly care
Of her young sonne, and wit to beware,
Shee set her youngling before her knee,
That was both fresh and louely to see,
And full of fauour, as kidde mought be:
185   His Vellet head began to shoote out,
And his wreathed hornes gan newly sprout:
The blossomes of lust to bud did beginne,
And spring forth ranckly vnder his chinne.
    My sonne (quoth she) (and with that gan weepe:
190   For carefull thoughts in her heart did creepe)
God blesse thee poore Orphane, as he mought me,
And send thee ioy of thy iollitee.
Thy father (that word she spake with payne:
For a sigh had nigh rent her heart in twaine)
195   Thy father, had he liued this day,
To see the braunche of his body displaie,
How would he haue ioyed at this sweete sight?
But ah false Fortune such ioy did him spight,
And cutte of hys dayes with vntimely woe,
200   Betraying him into the traines of hys foe.
Now I a waylfull widdowe behight,
Of my old age haue this one delight,
To see thee succeede in thy fathers steade,
And florish in flowres of lusty head.
205   For euen so thy father his head vpheld,
And so his hauty hornes did he weld.
    Tho marking him with melting eyes,
A thrilling throbbe from her hart did aryse,
And interrupted all her other speache,
210   With some old sorowe, that made a newe breache:
Seemed shee sawe in the younglings face
The old lineaments of his fathers grace.
At last her solein silence she broke,
And gan his newe budded beard to stroke.
215   Kiddie (quoth shee) thou kenst the great care,
I haue of thy health and thy welfare,
Which many wyld beastes liggen in waite,
For to entrap in thy tender state:

But most the Foxe, maister of collusion:
For he has voued thy last confusion.   220
For thy my Kiddie be ruld by mee,
And neuer giue trust to his trecheree.
And if he chaunce come, when I am abroade,
Sperre the yate fast for feare of fraude:
Ne for all his worst, nor for his best,   225
Open the dore at his request.

    So schooled the Gate her wanton sonne,
That answerd his mother, all should be done,
Tho went the pensife Damme out of dore,
And chaunst to stomble at the threshold flore: 230
Her stombling steppe some what her amazed,
(For such, as signes of ill luck bene dispraised)
Yet forth shee yode thereat halfe aghast:
And Kiddie the dore sperred after her fast.
It was not long, after shee was gone,   235
But the false Foxe came to the dore anone:
Not as a Foxe, for then he had be kend,
But all as a poore pedler he did wend,
Bearing a trusse of tryfles at hys backe,
As bells, and babes, and glasses in hys packe.   240
A Biggen he had got about his brayne,
For in his headpeace he felt a sore payne.
His hinder heele was wrapt in a clout,
For with great cold he had gotte the gout.
There at the dore he cast me downe hys pack,   245
And layd him downe, and groned, Alack, Alack.
Ah deare Lord, and sweete Saint Charitee,
That some good body woulde once pitie mee.

    Well heard Kiddie al this sore constraint,
And lengd to know the cause of his complaint: 250
Tho creeping close behind the Wickets clinck,
Preuelie he peeped out through a chinck:
Yet not so preuilie, but the Foxe him spyed:
For deceitfull meaning is double eyed.

    Ah good young maister (then gan he crye)   255
Iesus blesse that sweete face, I espye,

And keepe your corpse from the carefull stounds,
That in my carrion carcas abounds.
The Kidd pittying hys heauinesse,
260   Asked the cause of his great distresse,
And also who, and whence that he were.
Tho he, that had well ycond his lere,
Thus medled his talke with many a teare,
Sicke, sicke, alas, and little lack of dead,
265   But I be relieued by your beastlyhead.
I am a poore Sheepe, albe my coloure donne:
For with long traueile I am brent in the sonne.
And if that my Grandsire me sayd, be true,
Sicker I am very sybbe to you:
270   So be your goodlihead doe not disdayne
The base kinred of so simple swaine.
Of mercye and fauour then I you pray,
With your ayd to forstall my neere decay.
      Tho out of his packe a glasse he tooke:
275   Wherein while kiddie vnwares did looke,
He was so enamored with the newell,
That nought he deemed deare for the iewell.
Tho opened he the dore, and in came
The false Foxe, as he were starke lame.
280   His tayle he clapt betwixt his legs twayne,
Lest he should be descried by his trayne.
      Being within, the Kidde made him good glee,
All for the loue of the glasse he did see.
After his chere the Pedler can chat,
285   And tell many lesings of this, and that:
And how he could shewe many a fine knack.
Tho shewed his ware, and opened his packe,
All saue a bell, which he left behind
In the bas-ket for the Kidde to fynd.
290   Which when the Kidde stooped downe to catch,
He popt him in, and his basket did latch,
Ne stayed he once, the dore to make fast,
But ranne awaye with him in all hast.
Home when the doubtfull Damme had her hyde,
295   She mought see the dore stand open wyde.

All agast, lowdly she gan to call
Her Kidde: but he nould answere at all.
Tho on the flore she sawe the merchandise,
Of which her sonne had sette to dere a prise.
What helpe? her Kidde shee knewe well was gone: 300
Shee weeped, and wayled, and made great mone.
Such end had the Kidde, for he nould warned be
Of craft, coloured with simplicitie:
And such end perdie does all hem remayne,
That of such falsers freendship bene fayne.   305

PALINODIE.

Truly *Piers*, thou art beside thy wit,
Furthest fro the marke, weening it to hit,
Now I pray thee, lette me thy tale borrowe
For our sir Iohn, to say to morrowe
At the Kerke, when it is holliday: 310
For well he meanes, but little can say.
But and if Foxes bene so crafty, as so,
Much needeth all shepheards hem to knowe.

PIERS.

Of their falshode more could I recount.
But now the bright Sunne gynneth to dismount: 315
And for the deawie night now doth nye,
I hold it best for vs, home to hye.

Palinodes Embleme.
Πὰς μὲν ἄπιστος ἀπιστεῖ.

Piers his Embleme.   320
Τὶς δ' ἄρα πίστις ἀπίστω;

GLOSSE.

[1] Thilke) this same moneth. It is applyed to the season of the
moneth, when all menne delight them selues with pleasaunce of
fieldes, and gardens, and garments.

[5] Bloncket liueries) gray coates.   [6] Yclad) arrayed, Y,
redoundeth, as before.

[9] In euery where) a straunge, yet proper kind of speaking.

[10] Buskets) a Diminutiue .s. little bushes of hauthorne.

[12] Kirke) church.   [15] Queme) please.

[20] A shole) a multitude; taken of fishe, whereof some going in
great companies, are sayde to swimme in a shole.

[22] Yode) went.   [25] Iouyssance) ioye.   [36] Swinck)
labour.   [38] Inly) entirely.   [39] Faytours) vagabonds.

[54] Great pan) is Christ, the very God of all shepheards, which
calleth himselfe the greate and good shepherd. The name is most
rightly (me thinkes) applyed to him, for Pan signifieth all or
omnipotent, which is onely the Lord Iesus. And by that name
(as I remember) he is called of Eusebius in his fifte booke de
Preparat. Euang; who thereof telleth a proper storye to that
purpose. Which story is first recorded of Plutarch, in his booke
of the ceasing of oracles, and of Lauetere translated, in his booke
of walking sprightes. who sayth, that about the same time, that
our Lord suffered his most bitter passion for the redemtion of
man, certein passengers sayling from Italy to Cyprus and passing
by certain Iles called Paxæ, heard a voyce calling alowde Thamus,
Thamus, (now Thamus was the name of an Ægyptian, which
was Pilote of the ship,) who giuing eare to the cry, was bidden,
when he came to Palodes, to tel, that the great Pan was dead:
which he doubting to doe, yet for that when he came to Palodes,
there sodeinly was such a calme of winde, that the shippe stoode
still in the sea vnmoued, he was forced to cry alowd, that Pan
was dead: wherewithall there was heard suche piteous outcryes
and dreadfull shriking, as hath not bene the like. By whych
Pan, though of some be vnderstoode the great Satanas, whose
kingdome at that time was by Christ conquered, the gates of hell
broken vp, and death by death deliuered to eternall death, (for
at that time, as he sayth, all Oracles surceased, and enchaunted
spirits, that were wont to delude the people, thenceforth held
theyr peace) and also at the demaund of the Emperoure Tiberius,
who that Pan should be, answere was made him by the wisest
and best learned, that it was the sonne of Mercurie and Penelope,
yet I think it more properly meant of the death of Christ, the
onely and very Pan, then suffering for his flock.

[57] I as I am) seemeth to imitate the commen prouerb, Malim
Inuidere mihi omnes quam miserescere.

[61] Nas) is a syncope, for ne has, or has not: as nould, for would
not.

[69] Tho with them) doth imitate the Epitaphe of the ryotous king
Sardanapalus, whych caused to be written on his tombe in Greeke:
which verses be thus translated by Tullie.

,, Hæc habui quæ edi, quæque exaturata libido
,, Hausit, at illa manent multa ac præclara relicta.

which may thus be turned into English.

,, All that I eate did I ioye, and all that I greedily gorged:
,, As for those many goodly matters left I for others.

Much like the Epitaph of a good olde Erle of Deuonshire, which
though much more wisedome bewraieth, then Sardanapalus, yet
hath a smacke of his sensuall delights and beastlinesse. the rymes
be these.

,, Ho, Ho, who lies here?
,, I the good Erle of Deuonshere,
,, And Maulde my wife, that was ful deare,
,, We liued together lv. yeare.
,,   That we spent, we had:
,,   That we gaue, we haue:
,,   That we lefte, we lost.

[75] Algrind) the name of a shepheard.   [76] Men of the Lay)
Lay men.   [78] Enaunter) least that.

[82] Souenaunce) remembraunce.   [91] Miscreaunce) despeire
or misbeliefe.

[92] Cheuisaunce) sometime of Chaucer vsed for gaine: sometime
of other for spoyle, or bootie, or enterprise, and sometime for
chiefdome.

[111] Pan himselfe) God. according as is sayd in Deuteronomie,
That in diuision of the lande of Canaan, to the tribe of Leuie no
portion of heritage should bee allotted, for GOD himselfe was
their inheritaunce.

[121] Some gan) meant of the Pope, and his Antichristian prelates,
which vsurpe a tyrannicall dominion in the Churche, and with

Peters counterfet keyes, open a wide gate to al wickednesse and insolent gouernment. Nought here spoken, as of purpose to deny fatherly rule and godly gouernaunce (as some malitiously of late haue done to the great vnreste and hinderaunce of the Churche) but to displaye the pride and disorder of such, as in steede of feeding their sheepe, indeede feede of theyr sheepe.

[130] Sourse) welspring and originall.   [131] Borrowe) pledge or suertie.

[142] The Geaunte) is the greate Atlas, whom the poetes feign to be a huge geaunt, that beareth Heauen on his shoulders: being in deede a merueilous highe mountaine in Mauritania, that now is Barbarie, which to mans seeming perceth the cloudes, and seemeth to touch the heauens. Other thinke, and they not amisse, that this fable was meant of one Atlas king of the same countrye, (of whome may bee, that that hil had his denomination) brother to Prometheus who (as the Grekes say) did first fynd out the hidden courses of the starres, by an excellent imagination, wherefore the poetes feigned, that he susteyned the firmament on hys shoulders. Many other coniectures needelesse be told hereof.

[145] Warke) worke.   [147] Encheason) cause, occasion.

[150] Deare borow) that is our sauiour, the commen pledge of all mens debts to death.

[159] Wyten) blame.   [158] Nought seemeth) is vnseemely. [163] Conteck) strife contention.

[160] Her) theyr, as vseth Chaucer.   [168] Han) for haue. [168] Sam) together.

[174] This tale is much like to that in Æsops fables, but the Catastrophe and end is farre different. By the Kidde may be vnderstoode the simple sorte of the faythfull and true Christians. By hys dame Christe, that hath alreadie with carefull watchewords (as heere doth the gote) warned his little ones, to beware of such doubling deceit. By the Foxe, the false and faithlesse Papistes, to whom is no credit to be giuen, nor felowshippe to be vsed.

[177] The gate) the Gote: Northernely spoken to turne O into A. [178] Yode) went. afforesayd.

[182] She set) A figure called Fictio. which vseth to attribute reasonable actions and speaches to vnreasonable creatures.

[187] The bloosmes of lust) be the young and mossie heares, which

then beginne to sproute and shoote foorth, when lustfull heate
beginneth to kindle.

[189] And with) A very Poeticall πάθος.

[191] Orphane) A youngling or pupill, that needeth a Tutour and
gouernour.

[193] That word) A patheticall parenthesis, to encrease a carefull
Hyperbaton.

[196] The braunch) of the fathers body, is the child.

[205] For euen so) Alluded to the saying of Andromache to Ascanius
in Virgile.

> Sic oculos, sic ille manus, sic ora ferebat.

[208] A thrilling throb) a percing sighe.   [217] Liggen) lye.

[219] Maister of collusion) .s. coloured guile, because the Foxe of al
beasts is most wily and crafty.

[224] Sperre the yate) shut the dore.

[232] For such) The gotes stombling is here noted as an euill signe.
The like to be marked in all histories: and that not the leaste of
the Lorde Hastingues in king Rycharde the third his dayes. For
beside his daungerous dreame (whiche was a shrewde prophecie
of his mishap, that folowed) it is sayd that in the morning ryding
toward the tower of London, there to sitte vppon matters of
counsell, his horse stombled twise or thrise by the way: which of
some, that ryding with hym in his company, were priuie to his
neere destenie, was secretly marked, and afterward noted for
memorie of his great mishap, that ensewed. For being then as
merye, as man might be, and least doubting any mortall daunger,
he was within two howres after, of the Tyranne put to a shamefull
deathe.

[240] As belles) by such trifles are noted, the reliques and ragges of
popish superstition, which put no smal religion in Belles: and
Babies .s. Idoles: and glasses .s. Paxes, and such lyke trumperies.

[244] Great cold.) For they boast much of their outward patience, and
voluntarye sufferaunce as a worke of merite and holy humblenesse.

[247] Sweete S. Charitie.) The Catholiques comen othe, and onely
speache, to haue charitye alwayes in their mouth, and sometime
in their outward Actions, but neuer inwardly in fayth and godly
zeale.

[251] Clincke.) a key hole. Whose diminutiue is clicket, vsed of Chaucer for a Key.

[257] Stoundes) fittes: aforesayde.   [262] His lere) his les-son.   [263] Medled) mingled.

[265] Bestlihead.) agreeing to the person of a beast.

[269] Sibbe.) of kynne.

[276] Newell) a newe thing.   [273] To forestall) to præu-ent.   [282] Glee) chere, afforesayde.

[299] Deare a price.) his lyfe, which he lost for those toyes.

[304] Such ende) is an Epiphonèma, or rather the morall of the whole tale, whose purpose is to warne the protestaunt beware, howe he geueth credit to the vnfaythfull Catholique: whereof we haue dayly proofes sufficient, but one moste famous of all, practised of Late yeares in Fraunce by Charles the nynth.

[305] Fayne) gladde or desyrous.

[309] Our sir Iohn) a Popishe priest. A saying fit for the grosenesse of a shepheard, but spoken to taunte vnlearned Priestes.

[315] Dismount) descende or set.   [316] Nye) draweth nere.

Embleme.

Both these Emblemes make one whole Hexametre. The first spoken of Palinodie, as in reproche of them, that be distrustfull, is a peece of Theognis verse, intending, that who doth most mistrust is most false. For such experience in falsehod breedeth mistrust in the mynd, thinking nolesse guile to lurke in others, then in hymselfe. But Piers thereto strongly replyeth with another peece of the same verse, saying as in his former fable, what fayth then is there in the faythlesse. For if fayth be the ground of religion, which fayth they dayly false, what hold then is there of theyr religion. And thys is all that they saye.

June.

Ægloga sexta.

ARGVMENT.

*This Æglogue is wholly vowed to the complayning of Colins ill successe
in his loue. For being (as is aforesaid) enamoured of a Country lasse
Rosalind, and hauing (as seemeth) founde place in her heart, he lamenteth
to his deare frend Hobbinoll, that he is nowe forsaken vnfaithfully, and
in his steede Menalcas, another shepheard receiued disloyally. And this
is the whole Argument of this Æglogue.*

HOBBINOL.   COLIN CLOVTE.

Lo *Colin,* here the place, whose pleasaunt syte
From other shades hath weand my wandring mynde.
Tell me, what wants me here, to worke delyte?
The simple ayre, the gentle warbling wynde,
So calme, so coole, as no where else I fynde: 5
The grassye ground with daintye Daysies dight,
The Bramble bush, where Byrds of euery kynde
To the waters fall their tunes attemper right.

COLLIN.

O happy *Hobbinoll*, I blesse thy state,
10 That Paradise hast found, whych *Adam* lost.
Here wander may thy flock early or late,
Withouten dreade of Wolues to bene ytost:
Thy louely layes here mayst thou freely boste.
But I vnhappy man, whom cruell fate,
15 And angry Gods pursue from coste to coste,
Can nowhere fynd, to shroude my lucklesse pate.

HOBBINOLL.

Then if by me thou list aduised be,
Forsake the soyle, that so doth thee bewitch:
Leaue me those hilles, where harbrough nis to see,
20 Nor holybush, nor brere, nor winding witche:
And to the dales resort, where shepheards ritch,
And fruictfull flocks bene euery where to see.
Here no night Rauens lodge more black then pitche,
Nor eluish ghosts, nor gastly owles doe flee.

25 But frendly Faeries, met with many Graces,
And lightfote Nymphes can chace the lingring night,
With Heydeguyes, and trimly trodden traces,
Whilst systers nyne, which dwell on *Parnasse* hight,
Doe make them musick, for their more delight:
30 And *Pan* himselfe to kisse their christall faces,
Will pype and daunce, when *Phœbe* shineth bright:
Such pierlesse pleasures haue we in these places.

COLLIN.

And I, whylst youth, and course of carelesse yeeres
Did let me walke withouten lincks of loue,
35 In such delights did ioy amongst my peeres:
But ryper age such pleasures doth reproue,
My fancye eke from former follies moue
To stayed steps: for time in passing weares
(As garments doen, which wexen old aboue)
40 And draweth newe delightes with hoary heares.

Tho couth I sing of loue, and tune my pype
Vnto my plaintiue pleas in verses made:
Tho would I seeke for Queene apples vnrype,
To giue my *Rosalind*, and in Sommer shade
Dight gaudy Girlonds, was my comen trade,   45
To crowne her golden locks, but yeeres more rype,
And losse of her, whose loue as lyfe I wayd,
Those weary wanton toyes away dyd wype.

HOBBINOLL.

Colin, to heare thy rymes and roundelayes,
Which thou were wont on wastfull hylls to singe,   50
I more delight, then larke in Sommer dayes:
Whose Echo made the neyghbour groues to ring,
And taught the byrds, which in the lower spring
Did shroude in shady leaues from sonny rayes,
Frame to thy songe their chereful cheriping,   55
Or hold theyr peace, for shame of thy swete layes.

I sawe *Calliope* wyth Muses moe,
Soone as thy oaten pype began to sound,
Theyr yuory Luyts and Tamburins forgoe:
And from the fountaine, where they sat around,   60
Renne after hastely thy siluer sound.
But when they came, where thou thy skill didst showe,
They drewe abacke, as halfe with shame confound,
Shepheard to see, them in theyr art outgoe.

COLLIN.

Of Muses *Hobbinol*, I conne no skill: 65
For they bene daughters of the hyghest *Ioue*,
And holden scorne of homely shepheards quill.
For sith I heard, that *Pan* with *Phœbus* stroue,
Which him to much rebuke and Daunger droue:
I neuer lyst presume to *Parnasse* hyll,   70
But pyping lowe in shade of lowly groue,
I play to please my selfe, all be it ill.

Nought weigh I, who my song doth prayse or blame,
Ne striue to winne renowne, or passe the rest:
75   With shepheard sittes not, followe flying fame:
But feede his flocke in fields, where falls hem best.
I wote my rymes bene rough, and rudely drest:
The fytter they, my carefull case to frame:
Enough is me to paint out my vnrest,
80   And poore my piteous plaints out in the same.

The God of shepheards *Tityrus* is dead,
Who taught me homely, as I can, to make.
He, whilst he liued, was the soueraigne head
Of shepheards all, that bene with loue ytake:
85   Well couth he wayle hys Woes, and lightly slake
The flames, which loue within his heart had bredd,
And tell vs mery tales, to keepe vs wake,
The while our sheepe about vs safely fedde.

Nowe dead he is, and lyeth wrapt in lead,
90   (O why should death on hym such outrage showe?)
And all hys passing skil with him is fledde,
The fame whereof doth dayly greater growe.
But if on me some little drops would flowe,
Of that the spring was in his learned hedde,
95   I soone would learne these woods, to wayle my woe,
And teache the trees, their trickling teares to shedde.

Then should my plaints, causd of discurtesee,
As messengers of all my painfull plight,
Flye to my loue, where euer that she bee,
100   And pierce her heart with poynt of worthy wight:
As shee deserues, that wrought so deadly spight.
And thou *Menalcas*, that by trecheree
Didst vnderfong my lasse, to wexe so light,
Shouldest well be knowne for such thy villanee.

105   But since I am not, as I wish I were,
Ye gentle shepheards, which your flocks do feede,
Whether on hylls, or dales, or other where,

Beare witnesse all of thys so wicked deede:
And tell the lasse, whose flowre is woxe a weede,
And faultlesse fayth, is turned to faithlesse fere,   110
That she the truest shepheards hart made bleede,
That lyues on earth, and loued her most dere.

HOBBINOL.

O carefull *Colin*, I lament thy case,
Thy teares would make the hardest flint to flowe.
Ah faithlesse Rosalind, and voide of grace,   115
That art the roote of all this ruthfull woe.
But now is time, I gesse, homeward to goe:
Then ryse ye blessed flocks, and home apace,
Least night with stealing steppes doe you forsloe,
And wett your tender Lambes, that by you trace.   120

Colins Embleme.
Gia speme spenta.

GLOSSE.

[1] Syte) situation and place.
[10] Paradise) A Paradise in Greeke signifieth a Garden of pleasure,
or place of delights. So he compareth the soile, wherin Hobbinoll
made his abode, to that earthly Paradise, in scripture called Eden;
wherein Adam in his first creation was placed. Which of the most
learned is thought to be in Mesopotamia, the most fertile and
pleasaunte country in the world (as may appeare by Diodorus
Syculus description of it, in the hystorie of Alexanders conquest
thereof.) Lying betweene the two famous Ryuers (which are sayd
in scripture to flowe out of Paradise) Tygris and Euphrates,
whereof it is so denominate.
[18] Forsake the soyle) This is no poetical fiction, but vnfeynedly
spoken of the Poete selfe, who for speciall occasion of priuate
affayres (as I haue bene partly of himselfe informed) and for his
more preferment remouing out of the Northparts came into the
South, as Hobbinoll indeede aduised him priuately.

[19] Those hylles) that is the North countrye, where he dwelt.

[19] N'is) is not.

[21] The Dales) The Southpartes, where he nowe abydeth, which
thoughe they be full of hylles and woodes (for Kent is very hyllye
and woodye; and therefore so called: for Kantsh in the Saxons
tongue signifieth woodie) yet in respecte of the Northpartes they
be called dales. For indede the North is counted the higher
countrye.

[23] Night Rauens &c.) by such hatefull byrdes, hee meaneth all
misfortunes (Whereof they be tokens) flying euery where.

[25] Frendly faeries) the opinion of Faeries and elfes is very old, and
yet sticketh very religiously in the myndes of some. But to roote
that rancke opinion of Elfes oute of mens hearts, the truth is,
that there be no such thinges, nor yet the shadowes of the things,
but onely by a sort of bald Friers and knauish shauelings so
feigned; which as in all other things, so in that, soughte to nousell
the comen people in ignorounce, least being once acquainted
with the truth of things, they woulde in tyme smell out the
vntruth of theyr packed pelfe and Massepenie religion. But the
sooth is, that when all Italy was distraicte into the Factions of
the Guelfes and the Gibelins, being two famous houses in Flor-
ence, the name began through their great mischiefes and many
outrages, to be so odious or rather dreadfull in the peoples eares,
that if theyr children at any time were frowarde and wanton, they
would say to them that the Guelfe or the Gibeline came. Which
words nowe from them (as many thinge els) be come into our
vsage, and for Guelfes and Gibelines, we say Elfes and Goblins.
No otherwise then the Frenchmen vsed to say of that valiaunt
captain, the very scourge of Fraunce, the Lord Thalbot, afterward
Erle of Shrewsbury; whose noblesse bred such a terrour in the
hearts of the French, that oft times euen great armies were
defaicted and put to flyght at the onely hearing of hys name. In
somuch that the French wemen, to affray theyr chyldren, would
tell them that the Talbot commeth.

[25] Many Graces) though there be indeede but three Graces or
Charites (as afore is sayd) or at the vtmost but foure, yet in
respect of many gyftes of bounty, there may be sayde more. And
so Musæus sayth, that in Heroes eyther eye there satte a hundred

graces. And by that authoritye, thys same Poete in his Pageaunts sayth.

> An hundred Graces on her eyeledde satte. &c.

[27] Haydeguies) A country daunce or rownd. The conceipt is, that the Graces and Nymphes doe daunce vnto the Muses, and Pan his musicke all night by Moonelight. To signifie the pleasauntnesse of the soyle.

[35] Peeres) Equalles and felow shepheards.   [43] Queneapples vnripe) imitating Virgils verse.

> Ipse ego cana legam tenera lanugine mala.

[52] Neighbour groues) a straunge phrase in English, but word for word expressing the Latine vicina nemora.

[53] Spring) not of water, but of young trees springing.

[57] Calliope) afforesayde. Thys staffe is full of verie poetical inuention.   [59] Tamburines) an olde kind of instrument, which of some is supposed to be the Clarion.

[68] Pan with Phæbus) the tale is well knowne, howe that Pan and Apollo striuing for excellencye in musicke, chose Midas for their iudge. Who being corrupted wyth partiall affection, gaue the victorye to Pan vndeserued: for which Phœbus sette a payre of Asses eares vpon hys head &c.

[81] Tityrus) That by Tityrus is meant Chaucer, hath bene already sufficiently sayde, and by thys more playne appeareth, that he sayth, he tolde merye tales. Such as be hys Canterburie tales. whom he calleth the God of Poetes for hys excellencie, so as Tullie calleth Lentulus, Deum vitæ suæ .s. the God of hys lyfe.

[82] To make) to versifie.   [90] O why) A pretye Epanorthosis or correction.

[97] Discurtesie) he meaneth the falsenesse of his louer Rosalinde, who forsaking hym, hadde chosen another.

[100] Poynte of worthy wite) the pricke of deserued blame.

[102] Menalcas) the name of a shephearde in Virgile; but here is meant a person vnknowne and secrete, agaynst whome he often bitterly inuayeth.

[103] vnderfonge) vndermyne and deceiue by false suggestion.

Embleme.

You remember, that in the fyrst Æglogue, Colins Poesie was Anchora
    speme: for that as then there was hope of fauour to be found in
    tyme. But nowe being cleane forlorne and reiected of her, as
    whose hope, that was, is cleane extinguished and turned into
    despeyre, he renounceth all comfort and hope of goodnesse to
    come. which is all the meaning of thys Embleme.

Julye.

Ægloga septima.

ARGVMENT.

*This Æglogue is made in the honour and commendation of good
shepeheardes, and to the shame and disprayse of proude and ambitious
Pastours. Such as Morrell is here imagined to bee.*

THOMALIN.   MORRELL.

Is not thilke same a goteheard prowde,
    that sittes on yonder bancke,
Whose straying heard them selfe doth shrowde
    emong the bushes rancke?

MORRELL.

What ho, thou iollye shepheards swayne,
    come vp the hyll to me:
Better is, then the lowly playne,
    als for thy flocke, and thee.

5

THOMALIN.

Ah God shield, man, that I should clime,
    and learne to looke alofte,
This reede is ryfe, that oftentime
    great clymbers fall vnsoft.
In humble dales is footing fast,
    the trode is not so tickle:
And though one fall through heedlesse hast,
    yet is his misse not mickle.
And now the Sonne hath reared vp
    his fyriefooted teme,
Making his way betweene the Cuppe,
    and golden Diademe:
The rampant Lyon hunts he fast,
    with Dogge of noysome breath,
Whose balefull barking bringes in hast
    pyne, plagues, and dreery death.
Agaynst his cruell scortching heate
    where hast thou couerture?
The wastefull hylls vnto his threate
    is a playne ouerture.
But if thee lust, to holden chat
    with seely shepherds swayne,
Come downe, and learne the little what,
    that Thomalin can sayne.

MORRELL.

Syker, thous but a laesie loord,
    and rekes much of thy swinck,
That with fond termes, and weetlesse words
    to blere myne eyes doest thinke.
In euill houre thou hentest in hond
    thus holy hylles to blame,
For sacred vnto saints they stond,
    and of them han theyr name.
S. Michels mount who does not know,
    that wardes the Westerne coste?
And of S. Brigets bowre I trow,
    all Kent can rightly boaste:

And they that con of Muses skill,   45
   sayne most what, that they dwell
(As goteheards wont) vpon a hill,
   beside a learned well.
And wonned not the great God *Pan*,
   vpon mount *Oliuet*:   50
Feeding the blessed flocke of *Dan*,
   which dyd himselfe beget?

THOMALIN.

O blessed sheepe, O shepheard great,
   that bought his flocke so deare,
And them did saue with bloudy sweat   55
   from Wolues, that would them teare.

MORREL.

Besyde, as holy fathers sayne,
   there is a hyllye place,
Where *Titan* ryseth from the mayne,
   to renne hys dayly race.   60
Vpon whose toppe the starres bene stayed,
   and all the skie doth leane,
There is the caue, where *Phebe* layed,
   the shepheard long to dreame.
Whilome there vsed shepheards all   65
   to feede theyr flocks at will,
Till by his foly one did fall,
   that all the rest did spill.
And sithens shepheardes bene foresayd
   from places of delight: 70
For thy I weene thou be affrayd,
   to clime this hilles height.
Of *Synah* can I tell thee more,
   and of our Ladyes bowre:
But little needes to strow my store,   75
   suffice this hill of our.

Here han the holy *Faunes* resourse,
    and *Syluanes* haunten rathe.
Here has the salt Medway his sourse,
80   wherein the Nymphes doe bathe.
The salt Medway, that trickling stremis
    adowne the dales of Kent:
Till with his elder brother Themis
    his brackish waues be meynt.
85 Here growes *Melampode* euery where,
    and *Teribinth* good for Gotes:
The one, my madding kiddes to smere,
    the next, to heale theyr throtes.
Hereto, the hills bene nigher heuen,
90   and thence the passage ethe.
As well can proue the piercing leuin,
    that seeldome falls bynethe.

THOMALIN.

Syker thou speakes lyke a lewde lorrell,
    of Heauen to demen so:
95 How be I am but rude and borrell,
    yet nearer wayes I knowe.
To Kerke the narre, from God more farre,
    has bene an old sayd sawe.
And he that striues to touch the starres,
100   oft stombles at a strawe.
Alsoone may shepheard clymbe to skye,
    that leades in lowly dales,
As Goteherd prowd that sitting hye,
    vpon the Mountaine sayles.
105 My seely sheepe like well belowe,
    they neede not *Melampode*:
For they bene hale enough, I trowe,
    and liken theyr abode.
But if they with thy Gotes should yede,
110   they soone myght be corrupted:
Or like not of the frowie fede,
    or with the weedes be glutted.

The hylls, where dwelled holy saints,
   I reuerence and adore:
Not for themselfe, but for the sayncts,   115
   which han be dead of yore.
And nowe they bene to heauen forewent,
   theyr good is with them goe:
Theyr sample onely to vs lent,
   that als we mought doe soe.   120
Shepheards they weren of the best,
   and liued in lowlye leas:
And sith theyr soules bene now at rest,
   why done we them disease?
Such one he was, (as I haue heard   125
   old Algrind often sayne)
That whilome was the first shepheard,
   and liued with little gayne:
As meeke he was, as meeke mought be,
   simple, as simple sheepe,   130
Humble, and like in eche degree
   the flocke, which he did keepe.
Often he vsed of hys keepe
   a sacrifice to bring,
Nowe with a Kidde, now with a sheepe   135
   the Altars hallowing.
So lowted he vnto hys Lord,
   such fauour couth he fynd,
That sithens neuer was abhord,
   the simple shepheards kynd.   140
And such I weene the brethren were,
   that came from *Canaan*:
The brethren twelue, that kept yfere
   the flockes of mighty *Pan*.
But nothing such thilk shephearde was,   145
   whom *Ida* hyll dyd beare,
That left hys flocke, to fetch a lasse,
   whose loue he bought to deare:

For he was proude, that ill was payd,
    (no such mought shepheards bee)
And with lewde lust was ouerlayd:
    tway things doen ill agree:
But shepheard mought be meeke and mylde,
    well eyed, as *Argus* was,
With fleshly follyes vndefyled,
    and stoute as steede of brasse.

Sike one (sayd *Algrin*) *Moses* was,
    that sawe hys makers face,
His face more cleare, then Christall glasse,
    and spake to him in place.

This had a brother, (his name I knewe)
    the first of all his cote,
A shepheard trewe, yet not so true,
    as he that earst I hote.

Whilome all these were lowe, and lief,
    and loued their flocks to feede,
They neuer strouen to be chiefe,
    and simple was theyr weede.

But now (thanked be God therefore)
    the world is well amend,
Their weedes bene not so nighly wore,
    such simplesse mought them shend:
They bene yclad in purple and pall,
    so hath theyr god them blist,
They reigne and rulen ouer all,
    and lord it, as they list:
Ygyrt with belts of glitterand gold,
    (mought they good sheepeheards bene)
Theyr Pan theyr sheepe to them has sold,
    I saye as some haue seene.

For Palinode (if thou him ken)
    yode late on Pilgrimage
To Rome, (if such be Rome) and then
    he sawe thilke misusage.

For shepeheards (sayd he) there doen leade,   185
    as Lordes done other where,
Theyr sheepe han crustes, and they the bread:
    the chippes, and they the chere:
They han the fleece, and eke the flesh,
    (O seely sheepe the while)   190
The corne is theyrs, let other thresh,
    their hands they may not file.
They han great stores, and thriftye stockes,
    great freendes and feeble foes:
What neede hem caren for their flocks?   195
    theyr boyes can looke to those.
These wisards weltre in welths waues,
    pampred in pleasures deepe,
They han fatte kernes, and leany knaues,
    their fasting flockes to keepe.   200
Sike mister men bene all misgone,
    they heapen hylles of wrath:
Sike syrlye shepheards han we none,
    they keepen all the path.

MORRELL.

Here is a great deale of good matter,   205
    lost for lacke of telling,
Now sicker I see, thou doest but clatter:
    harme may come of melling.
Thou medlest more, then shall haue thanke,
    to wyten shepheards welth: 210
When folke bene fat, and riches rancke,
    it is a signe of helth.
But say me, what is *Algrin* he,
    that is so oft bynempt.

THOMALIN.

He is a shepheard great in gree,   215
    but hath bene long ypent.

One daye he sat vpon a hyll,
   (as now thou wouldest me:
But I am taught by *Algrins* ill,
220   to loue the lowe degree.)
For sitting so with bared scalpe,
   An Eagle sored hye,
That weening hys whyte head was chalke,
   a shell fish downe let flye:
225   She weend the shell fishe to haue broake,
   but therewith bruzd his brayne,
So now astonied with the stroke,
   he lyes in lingring payne.

MORRELL.

Ah good *Algrin*, his hap was ill,
230   but shall be bett in time.
Now farwell shepheard, sith thys hyll
   thou hast such doubt to climbe.

Thomalins Embleme.
In medio virtus.

235   *Morrells Embleme.*
In summo fœlicitas.

GLOSSE.

[1] A Goteheard) By Gotes in scrypture be represented the wicked
and reprobate, whose pastour also must needes be such.

[2] Banck) is the seate of honor.   [3] Straying heard) which
wander out of the waye of truth.

[8] Als) for also.   [9] Clymbe) spoken of Ambition.

[12] Great clymbers) according to Seneca his verse, Decidunt
celsa grauiore lapsu.   [16] Mickle) much.

[17] The sonne) A reason, why he refuseth to dwell on Mountaines,
because there is no shelter against the scortching sunne. according
to the time of the yeare, whiche is the whotest moneth of all.

[19–20] The Cupp and Diademe) Be two signes in the Firmament, through which the sonne maketh his course in the moneth of Iuly.

[21] Lion) Thys is Poetically spoken, as if the Sunne did hunt a Lion with one Dogge. The meaning whereof is, that in Iuly the sonne is in Leo. At which tyme the Dogge starre, which is called Syrius or Canicula reigneth, with immoderate heate causing Pestilence, drougth, and many diseases.

[28] Ouerture) an open place. The word is borrowed of the French, and vsed in good writers.

[29] To holden chatt) to talke and prate.

[33] A loorde) was wont among the old Britons to signifie a Lorde. And therefore the Danes, that long time vsurped theyr Tyrannie here in Brytanie, were called for more dread then dignitie, Lurd-anes .s. Lord Danes. At which time it is sayd, that the insolencie and pryde of that nation was so outragious in thys Realme, that if it fortuned a Briton to be going ouer a bridge, and sawe the Dane set foote vpon the same, he muste retorne back, till the Dane were cleane ouer, or els abyde the pryce of his displeasure, which was no lesse, then present death. But being afterwarde expelled that name of Lurdane became so odious vnto the people, whom they had long oppressed, that euen at this daye they vse for more reproche, to call the Quartane ague the Feuer Lurdane.

[34] Recks much of thy swinck) counts much of thy paynes.

[35] Weetelesse) not vnderstoode.

[41] S. Michels mount) is a promontorie in the West part of England.

[47] A hill) Parnassus afforesayd.   [49] Pan) Christ.

[51] Dan) One trybe is put for the whole nation per Synecdochen.

[59] Where Titan) the Sonne. Which story is to be redde in Diodorus Syc. of the hyl Ida; from whence he sayth, all night time is to bee seene a mightye fire, as if the skye burned, which toward morning beginneth to gather into a rownd forme, and thereof ryseth the sonne, whome the Poetes call Titan.

[64] The Shepheard) is Endymion, whom the Poets fayne, to haue bene so beloued of Phœbe .s. the Moone, that he was by her kept a sleepe in a caue by the space of xxx. yeares, for to enioye his companye.

[63] There) that is in Paradise, where through errour of shepheards vnderstanding, he sayth, that all shepheards did vse to feede theyr flocks, till one, (that is Adam) by hys follye and disobedience,

made all the rest of hys ofspring be debarred and shutte out from thence.

[73] Synah) a hill in Arabia, where God appeared.

[74] Our Ladyes bowre) a place of pleasure so called.

[77–8] Faunes or Syluanes) be of Poetes feigned to be Gods of the Woode.

[79] Medway) the name of a Ryuer in Kent, which running by Rochester, meeteth with Thames; whom he calleth his elder brother, both because he is greater, and also falleth sooner into the Sea.

[84] Meynt) mingled.   [85–6] Melampode and Terebinth) be hearbes good to cure diseased Gotes. of thone speaketh Mantuane, and of thother Theocritus.

τερμίνθου τράγων ἔσχατον ἀκρέμονα.

[89] Nigher heauen) Note the shepheards simplenesse, which supposeth that from the hylls is nearer waye to heauen.

[91] Leuin) Lightning; which he taketh for an argument, to proue the nighnes to heauen, because the lightning doth comenly light on hygh mountaynes, according to the saying of the Poete. Feriuntque summos fulmina montes.

[93] Lorrell) A losell.   [95] A borell.) a playne fellowe.

[97] Narre) nearer.

[107] Hale) for hole.   [109] Yede) goe.   [111] Frowye) mustye or mossie.

[116] Of yore) long agoe.   [117] Forewente) gone afore.

[127] The firste shepheard) was Abell the righteous, who (as scripture sayth) bent hys mind to keeping of sheepe, as did hys brother Cain to tilling the grownde.

[133] His keepe) hys charge s. his flocke.   [137] Lowted) did honour and reuerence.

[143] The brethren) the twelue sonnes of Iacob, whych were shepemaisters, and lyued onelye thereupon.

[146] Whom Ida) Paris, which being the sonne of Priamus king of Troy, for his mother Hecubas dreame, which being with child of hym, dreamed shee broughte forth a firebrand, that set all the towre of Ilium on fire, was cast forth on the hyll Ida; where being fostered of shepheards, he eke in time became a shepheard, and lastly came to knowledge of his parentage.

[147] A lasse) Helena the wyfe of Menelaus king of Lacedemonia, was by Venus for the golden Aple to her geuen, then promised to Paris, who thereupon with a sorte of lustye Troyanes, stole her out of Lacedemonia, and kept her in Troye. which was the cause of the tenne yeares warre in Troye, and the moste famous citye of all Asia most lamentably sacked and defaced.

[154] Argus) was of the Poets deuised to be full of eyes, and therefore to hym was committed the keeping of the transformed Cow Io: So called because that in the print of a Cowes foote, there is figured an I in the middest of an O.

[161] His name) he meaneth Aaron: whose name for more Decorum, the shephearde sayth he hath forgot, lest his remembraunce and skill in antiquities of holy writ should seeme to exceede the meanenesse of the Person.

[163] Not so true) for Aaron in the absence of Moses started aside, and committed Idolatry.

[173] In purple) Spoken of the Popes and Cardinalles, which vse such tyrannical colours and pompous paynting.   [177] Belts) Girdles.

[177] Glitterand) Glittering. a Participle vsed sometime in Chaucer, but altogether in I. Goore.

[179] Theyr Pan) that is the Pope, whom they count theyr God and greatest shepheard.

[181] Palinode) A shephearde, of whose report he seemeth to speake all thys.

[197] Wisards) greate learned heads.   [197] Welter) wallowe.   [199] Kerne) a Churle or Farmer.

[201] Sike mister men) such kinde of men.   [203] Surly) stately and prowde.   [208] Melling) medling.

[230] Bett) better.   [214] Bynempte) named.   [215] Gree) for degree.

[213] Algrin) the name of a shepheard afforesayde, whose myshap he alludeth to the chaunce, that happened to the Poet Æschylus, that was brayned with a shellfishe.

Embleme.

By thys poesye Thomalin confirmeth that, which in hys former
speach by sondrye reasons he had proued. for being both hymselfe
sequestred from all ambition and also abhorring it in others of
hys cote, he taketh occasion to prayse the meane and lowly state,
as that wherein is safetie without feare, and quiet without danger,
according to the saying of olde Philosophers, that vertue dwelleth
in the middest, being enuironed with two contrary vices: whereto
Morrell replieth with continuaunce of the same Philosophers
opinion, that albeit all bountye dwelleth in mediocritie, yet perfect
felicitye dwelleth in supremacie. for they say, and most true it
is, that happinesse is placed in the highest degree, so as if any
thing be higher or better, then that streight way ceaseth to be
perfect happines. Much like to that, which once I heard alleaged
in defence of humilitye out of a great doctour, Suorum Christus
humillimus: which saying a gentle man in the company taking at
the rebownd, beate backe again with lyke saying of another
Doctoure, as he sayde. Suorum deus altissimus.

August.

Ægloga octaua.

ARGVMENT.

In this Æglogue is set forth a delectable controuersie, made in imitation of that in Theocritus: whereto also Virgile fashioned his third and seuenth Æglogue. They choose for vmpere of their strife, Cuddie a neatheards boye, who hauing ended their cause, reciteth also himselfe a proper song, whereof Colin he sayth was Authour.

WILLYE.   PERIGOT.   CVDDIE.

Tell me *Perigot*, what shalbe the game,
Wherefore with myne thou dare thy musick matche?
Or bene thy Bagpypes renne farre out of frame?
Or hath the Crampe thy ioynts benomd with ache?

PERIGOT.

Ah *Willye*, when the hart is ill assayde,
How can Bagpipe, or ioynts be well apayd?

5

WILLYE.

What the foule euill hath thee so bestadde?
Whilom thou was peregall to the best,
And wont to make the iolly shepeheards gladde
10   With pyping and dauncing, didst passe the rest.

PERIGOT.

Ah *Willye* now I haue learnd a newe daunce:
My old musick mard by a newe mischaunce.

WILLYE.

Mischiefe mought to that newe mischaunce befall,
That so hath raft vs of our meriment.
15   But reede me, what payne doth thee so appall?
Or louest thou, or bene thy younglings miswent?

PERIGOT.

Loue hath misled both my younglings, and mee:
I pyne for payne, and they my payne to see.

WILLYE.

Perdie and wellawaye: ill may they thriue:
20   Neuer knewe I louers sheepe in good plight.
But and if in rymes with me thou dare striue,
Such fond fantsies shall soone be put to flight.

PERIGOT.

That shall I doe, though mochell worse I fared:
Neuer shall be sayde that *Perigot* was dared.

WILLYE.

25   Then loe *Perigot* the Pledge, which I plight:
A mazer ywrought of the Maple warre:
Wherein is enchased many a fayre sight
Of Beres and Tygres, that maken fiers warre:
And ouer them spred a goodly wild vine,
30   Entrailed with a wanton Yuie twine.

Thereby is a Lambe in the Wolues iawes:
But see, how fast renneth the shepheard swayne,
To saue the innocent from the beastes pawes:
And here with his shepehooke hath him slayne.
Tell me, such a cup hast thou euer sene?   35
Well mought it beseme any haruest Queene.

PERIGOT.
Thereto will I pawne yonder spotted Lambe,
Of all my flocke there nis sike another:
For I brought him vp without the Dambe.
But *Colin Clout* rafte me of his brother,   40
That he purchast of me in the playne field:
Sore against my will was I forst to yield.

WILLYE.
Sicker make like account of his brother.
But who shall iudge the wager wonne or lost?

PERIGOT.
That shall yonder heardgrome, and none other,   45
Which ouer the pousse hetherward doth post.

WILLYE.
But for the Sunnebeame so sore doth vs beate,
Were not better, to shunne the scortching heate?

PERIGOT.
Well agreed *Willy:* then sitte thee downe swayne:
Sike a song neuer heardest thou, but *Colin* sing.   50

CUDDIE.
Gynne, when ye lyst, ye iolly shepheards twayne:
Sike a iudge, as *Cuddie*, were for a king.

> *Perigot.*   It fell vpon a holly eue,
> *Willye.*   hey ho hollidaye,
> *Per.*   When holly fathers wont to shrieue: 55
> *Wil.*   now gynneth this roundelay.

	Per.	Sitting vpon a hill so hye
	Wil.	hey ho the high hyll,
	Per.	The while my flocke did feede thereby,
60	*Wil.*	the while the shepheard selfe did spill:
	Per.	I saw the bouncing Bellibone,
	Wil.	hey ho Bonibell,
	Per.	Tripping ouer the dale alone,
	Wil.	she can trippe it very well:
65	*Per.*	Well decked in a frocke of gray,
	Wil.	hey ho gray is greete,
	Per.	And in a Kirtle of greene saye,
	Wil.	the greene is for maydens meete:
	Per.	A chapelet on her head she wore,
70	*Wil.*	hey ho chapelet,
	Per.	Of sweete Violets therein was store,
	Wil.	she sweeter then the Violet.
	Per.	My sheepe did leaue theyr wonted foode,
	Wil.	hey ho seely sheepe,
75	*Per.*	And gazd on her, as they were wood,
	Wil.	woode as he, that did them keepe.
	Per.	As the bonilasse passed bye,
	Wil.	hey ho bonilasse,
	Per.	She roude at me with glauncing eye,
80	*Wil.*	as cleare as the christall glasse:
	Per.	All as the Sunnye beame so bright,
	Wil.	hey ho the Sunne beame,
	Per.	Glaunceth from *Phœbus* face forthright,
	Wil.	so loue into thy hart did streame:
85	*Per.*	Or as the thonder cleaues the cloudes,
	Wil.	hey ho the Thonder,
	Per.	Wherein the lightsome leuin shroudes,
	Wil.	so cleaues thy soule a sonder:
	Per.	Or as Dame *Cynthias* siluer raye
90	*Wil.*	hey ho the Moonelight,
	Per.	Vpon the glyttering waue doth playe:
	Wil.	such play is a pitteous plight.

Per. The glaunce into my heart did glide,
Wil.   hey ho the glyder,
Per. Therewith my soule was sharply gryde,   95
Wil.   such woundes soone wexen wider.
Per. Hasting to raunch the arrow out,
Wil.   hey ho Perigot.
Per. I left the head in my hart roote:
Wil.   it was a desperate shot.   100
Per. There it ranckleth ay more and more,
Wil.   hey ho the arrowe,
Per. Ne can I find salue for my sore:
Wil.   loue is a curelesse sorrowe.
Per. And though my bale with death I bought,   105
Wil.   hey ho heauie cheere,
Per. Yet should thilk lasse not from my thought:
Wil.   so you may buye gold to deare.
Per. But whether in paynefull loue I pyne,
Wil.   hey ho pinching payne,   110
Per. Or thriue in welth, she shalbe mine.
Wil.   but if thou can her obteine.
Per. And if for gracelesse greefe I dye,
Wil.   hey ho gracelesse griefe,
Per. Witnesse, shee slewe me with her eye: 115
Wil.   let thy follye be the priefe.
Per. And you, that sawe it, simple shepe,
Wil.   hey ho the fayre flocke,
Per. For priefe thereof, my death shall weepe,
Wil.   and mone with many a mocke.   120
Per. So learnd I loue on a hollye eue,
Wil.   hey ho holidaye,
Per. That euer since my hart did greue.
Wil.   now endeth our roundelay.

CUDDYE.

Sicker sike a roundle neuer heard I none.   125
Little lacketh *Perigot* of the best.
And *Willye* is not greatly ouergone,
So weren his vndersongs well addrest.

WILLYE.

Herdgrome, I feare me, thou haue a squint eye:
130   Areede vprightly, who has the victorye?

CUDDIE.

Fayth of my soule, I deeme ech haue gayned.
For thy let the Lambe be *Willye* his owne:
And for *Perigot* so well hath hym payned,
To him be the wroughten mazer alone.

PERIGOT.

135   *Perigot* is well pleased with the doome:
Ne can *Willye* wite the witelesse herdgroome.

WILLYE.

Neuer dempt more right of beautye I weene,
The shepheard of *Ida*, that iudged beauties Queene.

CUDDIE.

But tell me shepherds, should it not yshend
140   Your roundels fresh, to heare a doolefull verse
Of Rosalend (who knowes not Rosalend?)
That Colin made, ylke can I you rehearse.

PERIGOT.

Now say it *Cuddie*, as thou art a ladde:
With mery thing its good to medle sadde.

WILLY.

145   Fayth of my soule, thou shalt ycrouned be
In *Colins* stede, if thou this song areede:
For neuer thing on earth so pleaseth me,
As him to heare, or matter of his deede.

CUDDIE.

Then listneth ech vnto my heauy laye,
150   And tune your pypes as ruthful, as ye may.

Ye wastefull woodes beare witnesse of my woe,
   Wherein my plaints did oftentimes resound:
   Ye carelesse byrds are priuie to my cryes,
   Which in your songs were wont to make a part:
   Thou pleasaunt spring hast luld me oft a sleepe,   155
   Whose streames my tricklinge teares did ofte augment.
Resort of people doth my greefs augment,
   The walled townes do worke my greater woe:
   The forest wide is fitter to resound
   The hollow Echo of my carefull cryes,   160
   I hate the house, since thence my loue did part,
   Whose waylefull want debarres myne eyes from sleepe.
Let stremes of teares supply the place of sleepe:
   Let all that sweete is, voyd: and all that may augment
   My doole, drawe neare. More meete to wayle my woe,   165
   Bene the wild woddes my sorrowes to resound,
   Then bedde, or bowre, both which I fill with cryes,
   When I them see so waist, and fynd no part
Of pleasure past. Here will I dwell apart
   In gastfull groue therefore, till my last sleepe   170
   Doe close mine eyes: so shall I not augment
   With sight of such a chaunge my restlesse woe:
   Helpe me, ye banefull byrds, whose shrieking sound
   Ys signe of dreery death, my deadly cryes
Most ruthfully to tune. And as my cryes   175
   (Which of my woe cannot bewray least part)
   You heare all night, when nature craueth sleepe,
   Increase, so let your yrksome yells augment.
   Thus all the night in plaints, the daye in woe
   I vowed haue to wayst, till safe and sound   180
She home returne, whose voyces siluer sound
   To cheerefull songs can chaunge my cherelesse cryes.
   Hence with the Nightingale will I take part,
   That blessed byrd, that spends her time of sleepe
   In songs and plaintiue pleas, the more taugment   185
   The memory of hys misdeede, that bred her woe:
And you that feele no woe, | when as the sound
   Of these my nightly cryes | ye heare apart,
   Let breake your sounder sleepe | and pitie augment.

PERIGOT.

190   O *Colin, Colin,* the shepheards ioye,
    How I admire ech turning of thy verse:
    And *Cuddie,* fresh *Cuddie* the liefest boye,
    How dolefully his doole thou didst rehearse.

CUDDIE.

    Then blowe your pypes shepheards, til you be at home:
195   The night nigheth fast, yts time to be gone.

Perigot his Embleme.
Vincenti gloria victi.

Willyes Embleme.
Vinto non vitto.

200   Cuddies Embleme.
Felice chi puo.

GLOSSE.

[7] Bestadde) disposed, ordered.   [8] Peregall) equall.
    [8] Whilome) once.
[14] Rafte) bereft, depriued.   [16] Miswent) gon a straye.
    [19] Ill may) according to Virgile.

Infelix o semper ouis pecus.

[26] A mazer) So also do Theocritus and Virgile feigne pledges of
    their strife.
[27] Enchased) engrauen. Such pretie descriptions euery where vseth
    Theocritus, to bring in his Idyllia. For which speciall cause indede
    he by that name termeth his Æglogues: for Idyllion in Greke
    signifieth the shape or picture of any thyng, wherof his booke is
    ful. And not, as I haue heard some fondly guesse, that they be
    called not Idyllia, but Hædilia, of the Goteheards in them.
[30] Entrailed) wrought betwene.
[36] Haruest Queene) The manner of country folke in haruest
    tyme.   [46] Pousse.) Pease.

[53] It fell vpon) Perigot maketh hys song in prayse of his loue, to
whom Willy answereth euery vnder verse. By Perigot who is
meant, I can not vprightly say: but if it be, who is supposed, his
love deserueth no lesse prayse, then he giueth her.
[66] Greete) weeping and complaint.   [69] Chaplet) a kind of
Garlond lyke a crowne.
[87] Leuen) Lightning.   [89] Cynthia) was sayd to be the
Moone.   [95] Gryde) perced.
[112] But if) not vnlesse.   [129] Squint eye) partiall iudge-
ment.   [131] Ech haue) so saith Virgile.

Et vitula tu dignus, et hic &c.

So by enterchaunge of gyfts Cuddie pleaseth both partes.
[135] Doome) iudgement.   [137] Dempt) for deemed, iudged.
[136] Wite the witelesse) blame the blamelesse.   [138] The
shepherd of Ida) was sayd to be Paris.
[138] Beauties Queene) Venus, to whome Paris adiudged the golden
Apple, as the pryce of her beautie.

Embleme.

The meaning hereof is very ambiguous: for Perigot by his poesie
claming the conquest, and Willye not yeelding, Cuddie the arbiter
of theyr cause, and Patron of his own, semeth to chalenge it, as
his dew, saying, that he, is happy which can, so abruptly ending
but hee meaneth eyther him, that can win the beste, or moderate
him selfe being best, and leaue of with the best.

September.

Ægloga Nona.

ARGVMENT.

Herein Diggon Dauie is deuised to be a shepheard, that in hope of more gayne, droue his sheepe into a farre countrye. The abuses whereof, and loose liuing of Popish prelates, by occasion of Hobbinols demaund, he discourseth at large.

HOBBINOL.   DIGGON DAUIE.
Diggon Dauie, I bidde her god day:
Or Diggon her is, or I missaye.

DIGGON.
Her was her, while it was daye light,
But now her is a most wretched wight.
For day, that was, is wightly past,
And now at earst the dirke night doth hast.

5

HOBBINOLL.

Diggon areede, who has thee so dight?
Neuer I wist thee in so poore a plight.
Where is the fayre flocke, thou was wont to leade?
Or bene they chaffred? or at mischiefe dead?   10

DIGGON.

Ah for loue of that, is to thee moste leefe,
Hobbinol, I pray thee gall not my old griefe:
Sike question ripeth vp cause of newe woe,
For one opened mote vnfolde many moe.

HOBBINOLL.

Nay, but sorrow close shrouded in hart   15
I know, to kepe, is a burdenous smart.
Eche thing imparted is more eath to beare:
When the rayne is faln, the cloudes wexen cleare.
And nowe sithence I sawe thy head last,
Thrise three Moones bene fully spent and past: 20
Since when thou hast measured much grownd,
And wandred I wene about the world rounde,
So as thou can many thinges relate:
But tell me first of thy flocks astate.

DIGGON.

My sheepe bene wasted, (wae is me therefore)   25
The iolly shepheard that was of yore,
Is nowe nor iollye, nor shepehearde more.
In forrein costes, men sayd, was plentye:
And so there is, but all of miserye.
I dempt there much to haue eeked my store,   30
But such eeking hath made my hart sore.
In tho countryes, whereas I haue bene,
No being for those, that truely mene,
But for such, as of guile maken gayne,
No such countrye, as there to remaine.   35
They setten to sale their shops of shame,
And maken a Mart of theyr good name.

The shepheards there robben one another,
And layen baytes to beguile her brother.
40 Or they will buy his sheepe out of the cote,
Or they will caruen the shepheards throte.
The shepheards swayne you cannot wel ken,
But it be by his pryde, from other men:
They looken bigge as Bulls, that bene bate,
45 And bearen the cragge so stiffe and so state,
As cocke on his dunghill, crowing cranck.

HOBBINOLL.

Diggon, I am so stiffe, and so stanck,
That vneth may I stand any more:
And nowe the Westerne wind bloweth sore,
50 That nowe is in his chiefe souereigntee,
Beating the withered leafe from the tree.
Sitte we downe here vnder the hill:
Tho may we talke, and tellen our fill,
And make a mocke at the blustring blast.
55 Now say on Diggon, what euer thou hast.

DIGGON.

Hobbin, ah Hobbin, I curse the stounde,
That euer I cast to haue lorne this grounde.
Wel-away the while I was so fonde,
To leaue the good, that I had in hande,
60 In hope of better, that was vncouth:
So lost the Dogge the flesh in his mouth.
My seely sheepe (ah seely sheepe)
That here by there I whilome vsd to keepe,
All were they lustye, as thou didst see,
65 Bene all sterued with pyne and penuree.
Hardly my selfe escaped thilke payne,
Driuen for neede to come home agayne.

HOBBINOLL.

Ah fon, now by thy losse art taught,
That seeldome chaunge the better brought.
Content who liues with tryed state,   70
Neede feare no chaunge of frowning fate:
But who will seeke for vnknowne gayne,
Oft liues by losse, and leaues with payne.

DIGGON.

I wote ne Hobbin how I was bewitcht
With vayne desyre, and hope to be enricht.   75
But sicker so it is, as the bright starre
Seemeth ay greater, when it is farre:
I thought the soyle would haue made me rich:
But nowe I wote, it is nothing sich.
For eyther the shepeheards bene ydle and still,   80
And ledde of theyr sheepe, what way they wyll:
Or they bene false, and full of couetise,
And casten to compasse many wrong emprise.
But the more bene fraight with fraud and spight,
Ne in good nor goodnes taken delight: 85
But kindle coales of conteck and yre,
Wherewith they sette all the world on fire:
Which when they thinken agayne to quench
With holy water, they doen hem all drench.
They saye they con to heauen the high way,   90
But by my soule I dare vndersaye,
They neuer sette foote in that same troade,
But balk the right way, and strayen abroad.
They boast they han the deuill at commaund:
But aske hem therefore, what they han paund.   95
Marrie that great *Pan* bought with deare borrow,
To quite it from the blacke bowre of sorrowe.
But they han sold thilk same long agoe:
For thy woulden drawe with hem many moe.
But let hem gange alone a Gods name: 100
As they han brewed, so let hem beare blame.

HOBBINOLL.

Diggon, I praye thee speake not so dirke.
Such myster saying me seemeth to mirke.

DIGGON.

Then playnely to speake of shepheards most what,
105   Badde is the best (this english is flatt.)
Their ill hauiour garres men missay,
Both of their doctrine, and of their faye.
They sayne the world is much war then it wont,
All for her shepheards bene beastly and blont.
110   Other sayne, but how truely I note,
All for they holden shame of theyr cote.
Some sticke not to say, (whote cole on her tongue)
That sike mischiefe graseth hem emong,
All for they casten too much of worlds care,
115   To deck her Dame, and enrich her heyre:
For such encheason, If you goe nye,
Fewe chymneis reeking you shall espye:
The fatte Oxe, that wont ligge in the stal,
Is nowe fast stalled in her crumenall.
120   Thus chatten the people in theyr steads,
Ylike as a Monster of many heads.
But they that shooten neerest the pricke,
Sayne, other the fat from their beards doen lick.
For bigge Bulles *of Basan* brace hem about,
125   That with theyr hornes butten the more stoute:
But the leane soules treaden vnder foote.
And to seeke redresse mought little boote:
For liker bene they to pluck away more,
Then ought of the gotten good to restore.
130   For they bene like foule wagmoires ouergrast,
That if thy galage once sticketh fast,
The more to wind it out thou doest swinck,
Thou mought ay deeper and deeper sinck.
Yet better leaue of with a little losse,
135   Then by much wrestling to leese the grosse.

HOBBINOLL.

Nowe Diggon, I see thou speakest to plaine:
Better it were, a little to feyne,
And cleanly couer, that cannot be cured.
Such il, as is forced, mought nedes be endured.
But of sike pastoures howe done the flocks creepe?   140

DIGGON.

Sike as the shepheards, sike bene her sheepe,
For they nill listen to the shepheards voyce,
But if he call hem at theyr good choyce,
They wander at wil, and stray at pleasure,
And to theyr foldes yead at their owne leasure.   145
But they had be better come at their cal:
For many han into mischiefe fall,
And bene of rauenous Wolues yrent,
All for they nould be buxome and bent.

HOBBINOLL.

Fye on thee Diggon, and all thy foule leasing,   150
Well is knowne that sith the Saxon king,
Neuer was Woolfe seene many nor some,
Nor in all Kent, nor in Christendome:
But the fewer Woolues (the soth to sayne,)
The more bene the Foxes that here remaine.   155

DIGGON.

Yes, but they gang in more secrete wise,
And with sheepes clothing doen hem disguise,
They walke not widely as they were wont
For feare of raungers, and the great hunt:
But priuely prolling two and froe,   160
Enaunter they mought be inly knowe.

HOBBINOL.

Or priue or pert yf any bene,
We han great Bandogs will teare their skinne.

DIGGON.

Indeede thy ball is a bold bigge curre,
165   And could make a iolly hole in theyr furre.
But not good Dogges hem needeth to chace,
But heedy shepheards to discerne their face.
For all their craft is in their countenaunce,
They bene so graue and full of mayntenaunce.
170   But shall I tell thee what my selfe knowe,
Chaunced to Roffynn not long ygoe?

HOBBINOL.

Say it out Diggon, what euer it hight,
For not but well mought him betight,
He is so meeke, wise, and merciable,
175   And with his word his worke is conuenable. ⸱
Colin clout I wene be his selfe boye,
(Ah for Colin he whilome my ioye)
Shepheards sich, God mought vs many send,
That doen so carefully theyr flocks tend.

DIGGON.

180   Thilk same shepheard mought I well marke:
He has a Dogge to byte or to barke,
Neuer had shepheard so kene a kurre,
That waketh, and if but a leafe sturre.
Whilome there wonned a wicked Wolfe,
185   That with many a Lambe had glutted his gulfe.
And euer at night wont to repayre
Vnto the flocke, when the Welkin shone faire,
Ycladde in clothing of seely sheepe,
When the good old man vsed to sleepe.
190   Tho at midnight he would barke and ball,
(For he had eft learned a curres call.)
As if a Woolfe were emong the sheepe.
With that the shepheard would breake his sleepe,
And send out Lowder (for so his dog hote)
195   To raunge the fields with wide open throte.
Tho when as Lowder was farre awaye,
This Woluish sheepe would catchen his pray,

A Lambe, or a Kidde, or a weanell wast:
With that to the wood would he speede him fast.
Long time he vsed this slippery pranck,   200
Ere Roffy could for his laboure him thanck.
At end the shepheard his practise spyed,
(For Roffy is wise, and as Argus eyed)
And when at euen he came to the flocke,
Fast in theyr folds he did them locke,   205
And tooke out the Woolfe in his counterfect cote,
And let out the sheepes bloud at his throte.

HOBBINOLL.

Marry Diggon, what should him affraye,
To take his owne where euer it laye?
For had his wesand bene a little widder,   210
He would haue deuoured both hidder and shidder.

DIGGON.

Mischiefe light on him, and Gods great curse,
Too good for him had bene a great deale worse:
For it was a perilous beast aboue all,
And eke had he cond the shepherds call.   215
And oft in the night came to the shepecote,
And called Lowder, with a hollow throte,
As if it the old man selfe had bene.
The dog his maisters voice did it weene,
Yet halfe in doubt, he opened the dore,   220
And ranne out, as he was wont of yore.
No sooner was out, but swifter then thought,
Fast by the hyde the Wolfe lowder caught:
And had not Roffy renne to the steuen,
Lowder had be slaine thilke same euen.   225

HOBBINOLL.

God shield man, he should so ill haue thriue,
All for he did his deuoyr beliue.
If sike bene Wolues, as thou hast told,
How mought we Diggon, hem be-hold.

DIGGON.

230   How, but with heede and watchfulnesse,
Forstallen hem of their wilinesse?
For thy with shepheard sittes not playe,
Or sleepe, as some doen, all the long day:
But euer liggen in watch and ward,
235   From soddein force theyr flocks for to gard.

HOBBINOLL.

Ah Diggon, thilke same rule were too straight,
All the cold season to wach and waite.
We bene of fleshe, men as other bee.
Why should we be bound to such miseree?
240   What euer thing lacketh chaungeable rest,
Mought needes decay, when it is at best.

DIGGON.

Ah but Hobbinol, all this long tale,
Nought easeth the care, that doth me forhaile.
What shall I doe? what way shall I wend,
245   My piteous plight and losse to amend?
Ah good Hobbinol, mought I thee praye,
Of ayde or counsell in my decaye.

HOBBINOLL.

Now by my soule Diggon, I lament
The haplesse mischief, that has thee hent,
250   Nethelesse thou seest my lowly saile,
That froward fortune doth euer auaile.
But were Hobbinoll, as God mought please,
Diggon should soone find fauour and ease.
But if to my cotage thou wilt resort,
255   So as I can, I wil thee comfort:
There mayst thou ligge in a vetchy bed,
Till fayrer Fortune shewe forth her head.

DIGGON.

Ah Hobbinol, God mought it thee requite.
Diggon on fewe such freends did euer lite.

Diggons Embleme.
Inopem me copia fecit.

GLOSSE.

The Dialecte and phrase of speache in this Dialogue, seemeth some-
what to differ from the comen. The cause whereof is supposed
to be, by occasion of the party herein meant, who being very
freend to the Author hereof, had bene long in forraine countryes,
and there seene many disorders, which he here recounteth to
Hobbinoll.

[1] Bidde her) Bidde good morrow. For to bidde, is to praye, whereof
commeth beades for prayers, and so they say, To bidde his beades.
s. to saye his prayers.

[5] Wightly) quicklye, or sodenlye.   [10] Chaffred) solde.
[10] Dead at mischiefe) an vnusuall speache, but much vsurped
of Lidgate, and sometime of Chaucer.

[11] Leefe) deare.   [17] Ethe) easie.   [20] Thrise thre
moones) nine monethes.   [21] Measured) for traueled.

[25] Wae) woe Northernly.   [30] Eeked) encreased.
[41] Caruen) cutte.   [42] Kenne) know.

[45] Cragge) neck.   [45] State) stoutely.   [47] Stanck) wea-
rie or fainte.

[49] And nowe) He applieth it to the tyme of the yeare, which is in
thend of haruest, which they call the fall of the leafe: at which
tyme the Westerne wynde beareth most swaye.

[54] A mocke) Imitating Horace, Debes ludibrium ventis.
[57] Lorne) lefte.   Soote) swete.

[60] Vncouthe) vnknowen.   [63] Hereby there) here and there.
[76] As the brighte) Translated out of Mantuane.
[83] Emprise) for enterprise. Per Syncopen.   [86] Contek)
strife.

[92] Trode) path.   [96] Marrie that) that is, their soules, which
by popish Exorcismes and practises they damme to hell.

[97] Blacke) hell.   [100] Gange) goe.   [103] Mister) maner.
[103] Mirke) obscure.   [108] Warre) worse.

[119] Crumenall) purse.   [124] Brace) compasse.
[116] Encheson) occasion.   [130] Ouergrast) ouergrowen

with grasse.   [131] Galage) shoe.   [135] The grosse) the whole.

[149] Buxome and bent) meeke and obedient.

[151] Saxon king) K. Edgare, that reigned here in Brytanye in the yeare of our Lorde.   which king caused all the Wolues, whereof then was store in thys countrye, by a proper policie to be destroyed. So as neuer since that time, there haue ben Wolues here founde, vnlesse they were brought from other countryes. And therefore Hobbinoll rebuketh him of vntruth, for saying there be Wolues in England.

[153] Nor in Christendome) This saying seemeth to be strange and vnreasonable: but indede it was wont to be an olde prouerbe and comen phrase. The original whereof was, for that most part of England in the reigne of king Ethelbert was christened, Kent onely except, which remayned long after in mysbeliefe and vnchristened, So that Kent was counted no part of Christendome.

[159] Great hunt) Executing of lawes and iustice.

    [161] Enaunter) least that.

[161] Inly) inwardly. afforesayde.   [162] Priue or pert) openly sayth Chaucer.

[171] Roffy) The name of a shepehearde in Marot his Æglogue of Robin and the Kinge. whome he here commendeth for greate care and wise gouernance of his flock.

[176] Colin cloute) Nowe I thinke no man doubteth but by Colin is euer meante the Authour selfe. Whose especiall good freend Hobbinoll sayth he is, or more rightly Mayster Gabriel Haruey: of whose speciall commendation, aswell in Poetrye as Rhetorike and other choyce learning, we haue lately had a sufficient tryall in diuerse his workes, but specially in his Musarum Lachrymæ, and his late Gratulationum Valdinensium which boke in the progresse at Audley in Essex, he dedicated in writing to her Maiestie. afterward presenting the same in print vnto her High-nesse at the worshipfull Maister Capells in Hertfordshire. Beside other his sundrye most rare and very notable writings, partely vnder vnknown Tytles, and partly vnder counterfayt names, as hys Tyrannomastix, his Ode Natalitia, his Rameidos, and esspecially that parte of Philomusus, his diuine Anticosmopolita, and diuers other of lyke importance. As also by the names of

other shepheardes, he couereth the persons of diuers other his
familiar freendes and best acquayntaunce.

[180–225] This tale of Roffy seemeth to coloure some particular
Action of his. But what, I certeinlye know not.

[184] Wonned) haunted.   [187] Welkin) skie. afforesaid.

[198] A Weanell waste) a weaned youngling.   [211] Hidder and
shidder) He and she. Male and Female.   [224] Steuen)
Noyse.   [227] Beliue) quickly.   [240] What euer)
Ouids verse translated.

Quod caret alterna requie, durabile non est.

[243] Forehaile) drawe or distresse.   [256] Vetchie) of Pease
strawe.

Embleme.

This is the saying of Narcissus in Ouid. For when the foolishe boye
by beholding hys face in the brooke, fell in loue with his owne
likenesse: and not hable to content him selfe with much looking
thereon, he cryed out, that plentye made him poore. meaning
that much gazing had bereft him of sence. But our Diggon vseth
it to other purpose, as who that by tryall of many wayes had
founde the worst, and through greate plentye was fallen into
great penurie. This poesie I knowe, to haue bene much vsed of
the author, and to suche like effecte, as fyrste Narcissus spake it.

October.

Ægloga decima.

ARGVMENT.

*In Cuddie is set out the perfecte paterne of a Poete, which finding no main-
tenaunce of his state and studies, complayneth of the contempte of Poetrie,
and the causes thereof: Specially hauing bene in all ages, and euen amongst
the most barbarous always of singular accounpt and honor, and being
indede so worthy and commendable an arte: or rather no arte, but a diuine
gift and heauenly instinct not to bee gotten by laboure and learning, but
adorned with both: and poured into the witte by a certaine ἐνθουσιασμὸς.
and celestiall inspiration, as the Author hereof els where at large discourseth,
in his booke called the English Poete, which booke being lately come to my
hands, I mynde also by Gods grace vpon further aduisement to publish.*

PIERCE.　　　CUDDIE.

Cvddie, for shame hold vp thy heauye head,
And let vs cast with what delight to chace,
And weary thys long lingring *Phœbus* race.
Whilome thou wont the shepheards laddes to leade,
In rymes, in ridles, and in bydding base:
Now they in thee, and thou in sleepe art dead.

5

CUDDYE.

Piers, I haue pyped erst so long with payne,
That all mine Oten reedes bene rent and wore:
And my poore Muse hath spent her spared store,
Yet little good hath got, and much lesse gayne.   10
Such pleasaunce makes the Grashopper so poore,
And ligge so layd, when Winter doth her straine:

The dapper ditties, that I wont deuise,
To feede youthes fancie, and the flocking fry,
Delighten much: what I the bett for thy?   15
They han the pleasure, I a sclender prise.
I beate the bush, the byrds to them doe flye:
What good thereof to Cuddie can arise?

PIERS.

Cuddie, the prayse is better, then the price,
The glory eke much greater then the gayne: 20
O what an honor is it, to restraine
The lust of lawlesse youth with good aduice:
Or pricke them forth with pleasaunce of thy vaine,
Whereto thou list their trayned willes entice.

Soone as thou gynst to sette thy notes in frame,   25
O how the rurall routes to thee doe cleaue:
Seemeth thou dost their soule of sence bereaue,
All as the shepheard, that did fetch his dame
From *Plutoes* balefull bowre withouten leaue:
His musicks might the hellish hound did tame.   30

CUDDIE.

So praysen babes the Peacoks spotted traine,
And wondren at bright *Argus* blazing eye:
But who rewards him ere the more for thy?
Or feedes him once the fuller by a graine?
Sike prayse is smoke, that sheddeth in the skye,   35
Sike words bene wynd, and wasten soone in vayne.

PIERS.

Abandon then the base and viler clowne,
Lyft vp thy selfe out of the lowly dust:
And sing of bloody Mars, of wars, of giusts.
Turne thee to those, that weld the awful crowne,
To doubted Knights, whose woundlesse armour rusts,
And helmes vnbruzed wexen dayly browne.

There may thy Muse display her fluttryng wing,
And stretch her selfe at large from East to West:
Whither thou list in fayre *Elisa* rest,
Or if thee please in bigger notes to sing,
Aduaunce the worthy whome shee loueth best,
That first the white beare to the stake did bring.

And when the stubborne stroke of stronger stounds,
Has somewhat slackt the tenor of thy string:
Of loue and lustihead tho mayst thou sing,
And carrol lowde, and leade the Myllers rownde,
All were *Elisa* one of thilke same ring.
So mought our *Cuddies* name to Heauen sownde.

CUDDYE.

Indeede the Romish *Tityrus*, I heare,
Through his *Mecænas* left his Oaten reede,
Whereon his earst had taught his flocks to feede,
And laboured lands to yield the timely eare,
And eft did sing of warres and deadly drede,
So as the Heauens did quake his verse to here.

But ah *Mecænas* is yclad in claye,
And great *Augustus* long ygoe is dead:
And all the worthies liggen wrapt in leade,
That matter made for Poets on to play:
For euer, who in derring doe were dreade,
The loftie verse of hem was loued aye.

But after vertue gan for age to stoupe,
And mighty manhode brought a bedde of ease:
The vaunting Poets found nought worth a pease,
To put in preace among the learned troupe.   70
Tho gan the streames of flowing wittes to cease,
And sonnebright honour pend in shamefull coupe.

And if that any buddes of Poesie,
Yet of the old stocke gan to shoote agayne:
Or it mens follies mote be forst to fayne,   75
And rolle with rest in rymes of rybaudrye:
Or as it sprong, it wither must agayne:
Tom Piper makes vs better melodie.

PIERS.

O pierlesse Poesye, where is then thy place?
If nor in Princes pallace thou doe sitt: 80
(And yet is Princes pallace the most fitt)
Ne brest of baser birth doth thee embrace.
Then make thee winges of thine aspyring wit,
And, whence thou camst, flye backe to heauen apace.

CUDDIE.

Ah *Percy* it is all to weake and wanne,   85
So high to sore, and make so large a flight:
Her peeced pyneons bene not so in plight,
For *Colin* fittes such famous flight to scanne:
He, were he not with loue so ill bedight,
Would mount as high, and sing as soote as Swanne.   90

PIERS.

Ah fon, for loue does teach him climbe so hie,
And lyftes him vp out of the loathsome myre:
Such immortall mirrhor, as he doth admire,
Would rayse ones mynd aboue the starry skie.
And cause a caytiue corage to aspire,   95
For lofty loue doth loath a lowly eye.

CUDDIE.

All otherwise the state of Poet stands,
For lordly loue is such a Tyranne fell:
That where he rules, all power he doth expell.
100   The vaunted verse a vacant head demaundes,
Ne wont with crabbed care the Muses dwell:
Vnwisely weaues, that takes two webbes in hand.

Who euer casts to compasse weightye prise,
And thinks to throwe out thondring words of threate:
105   Let powre in lauish cups and thriftie bitts of meate,
For *Bacchus* fruite is frend to *Phœbus* wise.
And when with Wine the braine begins to sweate,
The nombers flowe as fast as spring doth ryse.

Thou kenst not *Percie* howe the ryme should rage.
110   O if my temples were distaind with wine,
And girt in girlonds of wild Yuie twine,
How I could reare the Muse on stately stage,
And teache her tread aloft in buskin fine,
With queint *Bellona* in her equipage.

115   But ah my corage cooles ere it be warme,
For thy, content vs in thys humble shade:
Where no such troublous tydes han vs assayde,
Here we our slender pipes may safely charme.

PIERS.

And when my Gates shall han their bellies layd:
120   *Cuddie* shall haue a Kidde to store his farme.

Cuddies Embleme.
Agitante calescimus illo &c.

GLOSSE.

This Æglogue is made in imitation of Theocritus his xvi. Idilion,
wherein hee reproued the Tyranne Hiero of Syracuse for his

nigardise towarde Poetes, in whome is the power to make men immortal for theyr good dedes, or shameful for their naughty lyfe. And the lyke also is in Mantuane, The style hereof as also that in Theocritus, is more loftye then the rest, and applyed to the heighte of Poeticall witte.

[1] Cuddie) I doubte whether by Cuddie be specified the authour selfe, or some other. For in the eyght Æglogue the same person was brought in, singing a Cantion of Colins making, as he sayth. So that some doubt, that the persons be different.

[4] Whilome) sometime.   [8] Oaten reedes) Auena.

[12] Ligge so layde) lye so faynt and vnlustye.   [13] Dapper) pretye.

[14] Frye) is a bold Metaphore, forced from the spawning fishes. for the multitude of young fish be called the frye.

[21] To restraine.) This place seemeth to conspyre with Plato, who in his first booke de Legibus sayth, that the first inuention of Poetry was of very vertuous intent. For at what time an infinite number of youth vsually came to theyr great solemne feastes called Panegyrica, which they vsed euery fiue yeere to hold, some learned man being more hable then the rest, for speciall gyftes of wytte and Musicke, would take vpon him to sing fine verses to the people, in prayse eyther of vertue or of victory or of immortality or such like. At whose wonderful gyft al men being astonied and as it were rauished, with delight, thinking (as it was indeed) that he was inspired from aboue, called him vatem: which kinde of men afterwarde framing their verses to lighter musick (as of musick be many kinds, some sadder, some lighter, some martiall, some heroical: and so diuersely eke affect the mynds of men) found out lighter matter of Poesie also, some playing wyth loue, some scorning at mens fashions, some powred out in pleasures, and so were called Poetes or makers.

[27] Sence bereaue) what the secrete working of Musick is in the myndes of men, aswell appeareth, hereby, that some of the auncient Philosophers, and those the moste wise, as Plato and Pythagoras held for opinion, that the mynd was made of a certaine harmonie and musicall nombers, for the great compassion and likenes of affection in thone and in the other as also by that memorable history of Alexander: to whom when as Timotheus the great Musitian playd the Phrygian melodie, it is said, that he

was distraught with such vnwonted fury, that streight way rysing from the table in great rage, he caused himselfe to be armed, as ready to goe to warre (for that musick is very war like:) And immediatly whenas the Musitian chaunged his stroke into the Lydian and Ionique harmony, he was so furr from warring, that he sat as styl, as if he had bene in matters of counsell. Such might is in musick. wherefore Plato and Aristotle forbid the Arabian Melodie from children and youth. for that being altogither on the fyft and vii. tone, it is of great force to molifie and quench the kindly courage, which vseth to burne in yong brests. So that it is not incredible which the Poete here sayth, that Musick can bereaue the soule of sence.

[28] The shepheard that) Orpheus: of whom is sayd, that by his excellent skil in Musick and Poetry, he recouered his wife Eurydice from hell.

[32] Argus eyes) of Argus is before said, that Iuno to him committed hir husband Iupiter his Paragon Iô, bicause he had an hundred eyes: but afterwarde Mercury wyth hys Musick lulling Argus aslepe, slew him and brought Iô away, whose eyes it is sayd that Iuno for his eternall memory placed in her byrd the Peacocks tayle. for those coloured spots indeede resemble eyes.

[41] Woundlesse armour) vnwounded in warre, doe rust through long peace.

[43] Display) A poeticall metaphore: whereof the meaning is, that if the Poet list showe his skill in matter of more dignitie, then is the homely Æglogue, good occasion is him offered of higher veyne and more Heroicall argument, in the person of our most gratious soueraign, whom (as before) he calleth Elisa. Or if mater of knighthoode and cheualrie please him better, that there be many Noble and valiaunt men, that are both worthy of his payne in theyr deserued prayses, and also fauourers of hys skil and faculty.

[47] The worthy) he meaneth (as I guesse) the most honorable and renowmed the Erle of Leycester, whom by his cognisance (although the same be also proper to other) rather then by his name he bewrayeth, being not likely, that the names of noble princes be known to country clowne.

[50] Slack) that is when thou chaungest thy verse from stately discourse, to matter of more pleasaunce and delight.

[52] The Millers) a kind of daunce.   [53] Ring) company of
dauncers.

[55] The Romish Tityrus) wel knowen to be Virgile, who by Mecænas
means was brought into the fauour of the Emperor Augustus,
and by him moued to write in loftier kinde, then he erst had
doen.

[57] Whereon) in these three verses are the three seuerall workes of
Virgile intended. For in teaching his flocks to feede, is meant his
Æglogues. In labouring of lands, is hys Georgiques. In singing
of wars and deadly dreade, is his diuine Æneis figured.

[65] In derring doe) In manhoode and cheualrie.

[65] For euer) He sheweth the cause, why Poetes were wont be had
in such honor of noble men; that is, that by them their worthines
and valor shold through theyr famous Posies be commended to
al posterities. wherfore it is sayd, that Achilles had neuer bene
so famous, as he is, but for Homeres immortal verses. which is
the only aduantage, which he had of Hector. And also that
Alexander the great comming to his tombe in Sigeus, with naturall
teares blessed him, that euer was his hap to be honoured with so
excellent a Poets work: as so renowmed and ennobled onely by
hys meanes. which being declared in a most eloquent Oration of
Tullies, is of Petrarch no lesse worthely sette forth in a sonet

> Giunto Alexandro a la famosa tomba
> Del fero Achille sospirando disse
> O fortunato che si chiara tromba.   Trouasti &c.

And that such account hath bene alwayes made of Poetes, aswell
sheweth this that the worthy Scipio in all his warres against
Carthage and Numantia had euermore in his company, and that
in a most familiar sort the good olde Poet Ennius: as also that
Alexander destroying Thebes, when he was enformed that the
famous Lyrick Poet Pindarus was borne in that citie, not onely
commaunded streightly, that no man should vpon payne of death
do any violence to that house by fire or otherwise: but also
specially spared most, and some highly rewarded, that were of
hys kinne. So fauoured he the only name of a Poete. whych prayse
otherwise was in the same man no lesse famous, that when he
came to ransacking of king Darius coffers, whom he lately had
ouerthrowen, he founde in a little coffer of siluer the two bookes

of Homers works, as layd vp there for speciall iewells and richesse, which he taking thence, put one of them dayly in his bosome, and thother euery night layde vnder his pillowe. Such honor haue Poetes alwayes found in the sight of princes and noble men. which this author here very well sheweth, as els where more notably.

[67] But after) he sheweth the cause of contempt of Poetry to be idlenesse and basenesse of mynd.   [72] Pent) shut vp in slouth, as in a coope or cage.

[78] Tom piper) An Ironicall Sarcasmus, spoken in derision of these rude wits, whych make more account of a ryming rybaud, then of skill grounded vpon learning and iudgment.

[82] Ne brest) the meaner sort of men.   [87] Her peeced pineons) vnperfect skil. Spoken wyth humble modestie.

[90] As soote as Swanne) The comparison seemeth to be strange: for the swanne hath euer wonne small commendation for her swete singing: but it is sayd of the learned that the swan a little before hir death, singeth most pleasantly, as prophecying by a secrete instinct her neere destinie. As wel sayth the Poete elswhere in one of his sonetts.

> The siluer swanne doth sing before her dying day
> As shee that feeles the deepe delight that is in death &c.

[93] Immortall myrrhour) Beauty, which is an excellent obiect of Poeticall spirites, as appeareth by the worthy Petrachs saying.

> Fiorir faceua il mio debile ingegno
> A la sua ombra, et crescer ne gli affanni.

[95] A caytiue corage) a base and abiect minde.

[96] For lofty loue) I think this playing with the letter to be rather a fault then a figure, aswel in our English tongue, as it hath bene alwayes in the Latine, called Cacozelon.

[100] A vacant) imitateth Mantuanes saying. vacuum curis diuína cerebrum Poscit.

[105] Lauish cups) Resembleth that comen verse Fæcundi calices quem non fecere disertum.

[110] O if my) He seemeth here to be rauished with a Poetical furie. For (if one rightly mark) the numbers rise so ful, and the verse

groweth so big, that it seemeth he hath forgot the meanenesse of shepheards state and stile.

[111] Wild yuie) for it is dedicated to Bacchus and therefore it is sayd that the Mænades (that is Bacchus franticke priestes) vsed in theyr sacrifice to carry Thyrsos, which were pointed staues or Iauelins, wrapped about with yuie.

[113] In buskin) it was the maner of Poetes and plaiers in tragedies to were buskins, as also in Comedies to vse stockes and light shoes. So that the buskin in Poetry is vsed for tragical matter, as it said in Virgile. Sola sophocleo tua carmina digna cothurno. And the like in Horace, Magnum loqui, nitique cothurno.

[114] Queint) strange Bellona; the goddesse of battaile, that is Pallas, which may therefore wel be called queint for that (as Lucian saith) when Iupiter hir father was in traueile of her, he caused his sonne Vulcane with his axe to hew his head. Out of which leaped forth lustely a valiant damsell armed at all poyntes, whom seeing Vulcane so faire and comely, lightly leaping to her, proferred her some cortesie, which the Lady disdeigning, shaked her speare at him, and threatned his saucinesse. Therefore such straungenesse is well applyed to her.

[114] Æquipage.) order.   [117] Tydes) seasons.

[118] Charme) temper and order. for Charmes were wont to be made by verses as Ouid sayth.   Aut si carminibus.

Embleme.

Hereby is meant, as also in the whole course of this Æglogue, that Poetry is a diuine instinct and vnnatural rage passing the reache of comen reason. Whom Piers answereth Epiphonematicos as admiring the excellencye of the skyll whereof in Cuddie hee hadde alreadye hadde a taste.

Nouember.

Ægloga vndecima.

ARGVMENT.

*In this xi. Æglogue he bewayleth the death of some mayden of greate
bloud, whom he calleth Dido. The personage is secrete, and to me altogether
vnknowne, albe of him selfe I often required the same. This Æglogue is
made in imitation of Marot his song, which he made vpon the death of
Loys the frenche Queene. But farre passing his reache, and in myne
opinion all other the Eglogues of this booke.*

THENOT.   COLIN.

Colin my deare, when shall it please thee sing,
As thou were wont songs of some iouisaunce?
Thy Muse to long slombreth in sorrowing,
Lulled a sleepe through loues misgouernaunce
5   Now somewhat sing, whose endles souenaunce,.
Emong the shepeheards swaines may aye remaine,
Whether thee list thy loued lasse aduaunce,
Or honor *Pan* with hymnes of higher vaine.

COLIN.

Thenot, now nis the time of merimake.
Nor *Pan* to herye, nor with loue to playe: 10
Sike myrth in May is meetest for to make,
Or summer shade vnder the cocked haye.
But nowe sadde Winter welked hath the day,
And *Phœbus* weary of his yerely taske,
Ystabled hath his steedes in lowlye laye,   15
And taken vp his ynne in *Fishes* haske.
Thilke sollein season sadder plight doth aske:
And loatheth sike delightes, as thou doest prayse:
The mornefull Muse in myrth now list ne maske,
As shee was wont in youngth and sommer dayes.   20
But if thou algate lust light virelayes,
And looser songs of loue to vnderfong
Who but thy selfe deserues sike Poetes prayse?
Relieue thy Oaten pypes, that sleepen long.

THENOT.

The Nightingale is souereigne of song,   25
Before him sits the Titmose silent bee:
And I vnfitte to thrust in skilfull thronge,
Should *Colin* make iudge of my fooleree.
Nay, better learne of hem, that learned bee,
And han be watered at the Muses well: 30
The kindlye dewe drops from the higher tree,
And wets the little plants that lowly dwell.
But if sadde winters wrathe and season chill,
Accorde not with thy Muses meriment:
To sadder times thou mayst attune thy quill,   35
And sing of sorrowe and deathes dreeriment.
For deade is Dido, dead alas and drent,
Dido the greate shepehearde his daughter sheene:
The fayrest May she was that euer went,
Her like shee has not left behinde I weene.   40
And if thou wilt bewayle my wofull tene:
I shall thee giue yond Cosset for thy payne:
And if thy rymes as rownd and rufull bene,
As those that did thy *Rosalind* complayne,

45   Much greater gyfts for guerdon thou shalt gayne,
        Then Kidde or Cosset, which I thee bynempt:
        Then vp I say, thou iolly shepeheard swayne,
        Let not my small demaund be so contempt.

COLIN.

        Thenot to that I choose, thou doest me tempt,
50   But ah to well I wote my humble vaine,
        And howe my rymes bene rugged and vnkempt:
        Yet as I conne, my conning I will strayne.

        Vp then *Melpomene* thou mournefulst Muse of nyne,
        Such cause of mourning neuer hadst afore:
55   Vp grieslie ghostes and vp my rufull ryme,
        Matter of myrth now shalt thou haue no more.
        For dead shee is, that myrth thee made of yore.
            Dido my deare alas is dead,
            Dead and lyeth wrapt in lead:
60   O heauie herse,
        Let streaming teares be poured out in store:
                O carefull verse.

        Shepheards, that by your flocks on Kentish downes abyde,
        Waile ye this wofull waste of natures warke:
65   Waile we the wight, whose presence was our pryde:
        Waile we the wight, whose absence is our carke.
        The sonne of all the world is dimme and darke:
            The earth now lacks her wonted light,
            And all we dwell in deadly night,
70   O heauie herse.
        Breake we our pypes, that shrild as lowde as Larke,
                O carefull verse.

        Why doe we longer liue, (ah why liue we so long)
        Whose better dayes death hath shut vp in woe?
75   The fayrest floure our gyrlond all emong,
        Is faded quite and into dust ygoe.

Sing now ye shepheards daughters, sing no moe
  The songs that *Colin* made in her prayse,
  But into weeping turne your wanton layes,
    O heauie herse,   80
Now is time to dye. Nay time was long ygoe,
    O carefull verse.

Whence is it, that the flouret of the field doth fade,
And lyeth buryed long in Winters bale:
Yet soone as spring his mantle doth displaye,   85
It floureth fresh, as it should neuer fayle?
But thing on earth that is of most availe,
  As vertues braunch and beauties budde,
  Reliuen not for any good.
    O heauie herse,   90
The braunch once dead, the budde eke needes must quaile,
    O carefull verse.

She while she was, (that was, a woful word to sayne)
For beauties prayse and plesaunce had no pere:
So well she couth the shepherds entertayne,   95
With cakes and cracknells and such country chere.
Ne would she scorne the simple shepheards swaine,
  For she would cal hem often heme
  And giue hem curds and clouted Creame.
    O heauie herse,   100
Als *Colin cloute* she would not once disdayne.
    O carefull verse.

But nowe sike happy cheere is turnd to heauie chaunce,
Such pleasaunce now displast by dolors dint:
All Musick sleepes, where death doth leade the daunce,   105
And shepherds wonted solace is extinct.
The blew in black, the greene in gray is tinct,
  The gaudie girlonds deck her graue,
  The faded flowres her corse embraue.
    O heauie herse,   110
Morne nowe my Muse, now morne with teares besprint.
    O carefull verse.

O thou greate shepheard *Lobbin*, how great is thy griefe,
Where bene the nosegayes that she dight for thee:
115   The colourd chaplets wrought with a chiefe,
The knotted rushrings, and gilte Rosemaree?
For shee deemed nothing too deere for thee.
    Ah they bene all yclad in clay,
    One bitter blast blewe all away.
120   O heauie herse,
Thereof nought remaynes but the memoree.
       O carefull verse.

Ay me that dreerie death should strike so mortall stroke,
That can vndoe Dame natures kindly course:
125   The faded lockes fall from the loftie oke,
The flouds do gaspe, for dryed is theyr sourse,
And flouds of teares flowe in theyr stead perforse.
    The mantled medowes mourne,
    Theyr sondry colours tourne.
130   O heauie herse,
The heauens doe melt in teares without remorse.
       O carefull verse.

The feeble flocks in field refuse their former foode,
And hang theyr heads, as they would learne to weepe:
135   The beastes in forest wayle as they were woode,
Except the Wolues, that chase the wandring sheepe:
Now she is gon that safely did hem keepe,
    The Turtle on the bared braunch,
    Laments the wound, that death did launch.
140   O heauie herse,
And *Philomele* her song with teares doth steepe.
       O carefull verse.

The water Nymphs, that wont with her to sing and daunce,
And for her girlond Oliue braunches beare,
145   Now balefull boughes of Cypres doen aduaunce:
The Muses, that were wont greene bayes to weare,

Now bringen bitter Eldre braunches seare:
  The fatall sisters eke repent,
  Her vitall threde so soone was spent.
    O heauie herse,   150
Morne now my Muse, now morne with heauie cheare.
    O carefull verse.

O trustlesse state of earthly things, and slipper hope
Of mortal men, that swincke and sweate for nought,
And shooting wide, doe misse the marked scope: 155
Now haue I learnd (a lesson derely bought)
That nys on earth assuraunce to be sought:
  For what might be in earthlie mould,
  That did her buried body hould.
    O heauie herse,   160
Yet saw I on the beare when it was brought
    O carefull verse.

But maugre death, and dreaded sisters deadly spight,
And gates of hel, and fyrie furies forse:
She hath the bonds broke of eternall night,   165
Her soule vnbodied of the burdenous corpse.
Why then weepes Lobbin so without remorse?
  O Lobb, thy losse no longer lament,
  Dido nis dead, but into heauen hent.
    O happye herse,   170
Cease now my Muse, now cease thy sorrowes sourse,
    O ioyfull verse.

Why wayle we then? why weary we the Gods with playnts,
As if some euill were to her betight?
She raignes a goddesse now emong the saintes,   175
That whilome was the saynt of shepheards light:
And is enstalled nowe in heauens hight.
  I see thee blessed soule, I see,
  Walke in *Elisian* fieldes so free.
    O happy herse,   180
Might I once come to thee (O that I might)
    O ioyfull verse.

Vnwise and wretched men to weete whats good or ill,
We deeme of Death as doome of ill desert:
185　But knewe we fooles, what it vs bringes vntil,
Dye would we dayly, once it to expert.
No daunger there the shepheard can astert:
　　Fayre fieldes and pleasaunt layes there bene,
　　The fieldes ay fresh, the grasse ay greene:
190　　　　O happy herse,
Make hast ye shepheards, thether to reuert,
　　　　O ioyfull verse.

Dido is gone afore (whose turne shall be the next?)
There liues shee with the blessed Gods in blisse,
195　There drincks she *Nectar* with *Ambrosia* mixt,
And ioyes enioyes, that mortall men doe misse.
The honor now of highest gods she is,
　　That whilome was poore shepheards pryde,
　　While here on earth she did abyde.
200　　　　O happy herse,
Ceasse now my song, my woe now wasted is.
　　　　O ioyfull verse.

THENOT.

Ay francke shepheard, how bene thy verses meint
With doolful pleasaunce, so as I ne wotte,
205　Whether reioyce or weepe for great constrainte?
Thyne be the cossette, well hast thow it gotte.
Vp *Colin* vp, ynough thou morned hast,
Now gynnes to mizzle, hye we homeward fast.

Colins Embleme.
210　*La mort ny mord.*

GLOSSE.

[2] Iouisaunce) myrth.　　　[5] Souenaunce) remembraunce.
　[10] Herie) honour.

[13] Welked) shortned or empayred. As the Moone being in the waine is sayde of Lidgate to welk.

[15] In lowly lay) according to the season of the moneth Nouember, when the sonne draweth low in the South toward his Tropick or returne.

[16] In fishes haske) the sonne, reigneth that is, in the signe Pisces all Nouember. a haske is a wicker pad, wherein they vse to cary fish.

[21] Virelaies) a light kind of song.

[30] Bee watred) For it is a saying of Poetes, that they haue dronk of the Muses well Castalias, whereof was before sufficiently sayd.

[36] Dreriment) dreery and heauy cheere.

[38] The great shepheard) is some man of high degree, and not as some vainely suppose God Pan. The person both of the shephearde and of Dido is vnknowen and closely buried in the Authors conceipt. But out of doubt I am, that it is not Rosalind, as some imagin: for he speaketh soone after of her also.

[38] Shene) fayre and shining.   [39] May) for mayde.

[41] Tene) sorrow.

[45] Guerdon) reward.   [46] Bynempt) bequethed.

[46] Cosset) a lambe brought vp without the dam.

[51] Vnkempt) Incompti Not comed, that is rude and vnhansome.

[53] Melpomene) The sadde and waylefull Muse vsed of Poets in honor of Tragedies: as saith Virgile Melpomene Tragico proclamat mæsta boatu.

[55] Vp griesly gosts) The maner of Tragicall Poetes, to call for helpe of Furies and damned ghostes: so is Hecuba of Euripides, and Tantalus brought in of Seneca. And the rest of the rest.   [60] Herse) is the solemne obsequie in funeralles.

[64] Wast of) decay of so beautifull a peece.   [66] Carke) care.

[73] Ah why) an elegant Epanorthosis. as also soone after. nay time was long ago.

[83] Flouret) a diminutiue for a little floure. This is a notable and sententious comparison A minore ad maius.

[89] Reliuen not) liue not againe .s. not in theyr earthly bodies: for in heauen they enioy their due reward.

[91] The braunch) He meaneth Dido, who being, as it were the

mayne braunch now withered the buddes that is beautie (as he sayd afore) can nomore flourish.

[96] With cakes) fit for shepheards bankets.   [98] Heame) for home. after the northerne pronouncing.   [107] Tinct) deyed or stayned.

[108] The gaudie) the meaning is, that the things, which were the ornaments of her lyfe, are made the honor of her funerall, as is vsed in burialls.

[113] Lobbin) the name of a shepherd, which seemeth to haue bene the louer and deere frende of Dido.   [116] Rushrings) agreeable for such base gyftes.

[125] Faded lockes) dryed leaues. As if Nature her selfe bewayled the death of the Mayde.

[126] Sourse) spring.   [128] Mantled medowes) for the sondry flowres are like a Mantle or couerlet wrought with many colours.

[141] Philomele) the Nightingale. whome the Poetes faine once to haue bene a Ladye of great beauty, till being rauished by hir sisters husbande, she desired to be turned into a byrd of her name. whose complaintes be very well set forth of Ma. George Gaskin a wittie gentleman, and the very chefe of our late rymers, who and if some partes of learning wanted not (albee it is well knowen he altogyther wanted not learning) no doubt would haue attayned to the excellencye of those famous Poets. For gifts of wit and naturall promptnesse appeare in hym aboundantly.

[145] Cypresse) vsed of the old Paynims in the furnishing of their funerall Pompe. and properly the signe of all sorow and heauinesse.

[148] The fatall sisters) Clotho Lachesis and Atropos, daughters of Herebus and the Nighte, whom the Poetes fayne to spinne the life of man, as it were a long threde, which they drawe out in length, till his fatal howre and timely death be come; but if by other casualtie his dayes be abridged, then one of them, that is Atropos, is sayde to haue cut the threde in twain. Hereof commeth a common verse.

Clotho colum baiulat, lachesis trahit, Atropos occat.

[153] O trustlesse) a gallant exclamation moralized with great wisedom and passionate wyth great affection.   [161] Beare) a frame, wheron they vse to lay the dead corse.

[164] Furies) of Poetes be feyned to be three, Persephone Alecto and Megera, which are sayd to be the Authours of all euill and mischiefe.

[165] Eternall night) Is death or darknesse of hell.

[174] Betight) happened.

[178] I see) A liuely Icon, or representation as if he saw her in heauen present.

[179] Elysian fieldes) be deuised of Poetes to be a place of pleasure like Paradise, where the happye soules doe rest in peace and eternal happynesse.

[186] Dye would) The very expresse saying of Plato in Phædone.

[187] Astert) befall vnwares.

[195] Nectar and Ambrosia) be feigned to be the drink and foode of the gods: Ambrosia they liken to Manna in scripture and Nectar to be white like Creme, whereof is a proper tale of Hebe, that spilt a cup of it, and stayned the heauens, as yet appeareth. But I haue already discoursed that at large in my Commentarye vpon the dreames of the same Authour.   [203] Meynt) Mingled.

Embleme.

Which is as much to say, as death biteth not. For although by course of nature we be borne to dye, and being ripened with age, as with a timely haruest, we must be gathered in time, or els of our selues we fall like rotted ripe fruite fro the tree: yet death is not to be counted for euil, nor (as the Poete sayd a little before) as doome of ill desert. For though the trespasse of the first man brought death into the world, as the guerdon of sinne, yet being ouercome by the death of one, that dyed for al, it is now made (as Chaucer sayth) the grene path way to lyfe. So that it agreeth well with that was sayd, that Death byteth not (that is) hurteth not at all.

December.

Ægloga Duodecima.

ARGVMENT.

*This Æglogue (euen as the first beganne) is ended with a complaynte of
Colin to God Pan. wherein as weary of his former wayes, he proportioneth
his life to the foure seasons of the yeare, comparing hys youthe to the
spring time, when he was fresh and free from loues follye. His manhoode
to the sommer, which he sayth, was consumed with greate heate and
excessiue drouth caused throughe a Comet or blasinge starre, by which
hee meaneth loue, which passion is comenly compared to such flames and
immoderate heate. His riper yeares hee resembleth to an vnseasonable
harueste wherein the fruites fall ere they be rype. His latter age to winters
chyll and frostie season, now drawing neare to his last ende.*

> The gentle shepheard satte beside a springe,
> All in the shadowe of a bushye brere,
> That *Colin* hight, which wel could pype and singe,
> For he of *Tityrus* his songs did lere.
> There as he satte in secreate shade alone,
> Thus gan he make of loue his piteous mone.

5

O soueraigne *Pan* thou God of shepheards all,
Which of our tender Lambkins takest keepe:
And when our flocks into mischaunce mought fall,
Doest saue from mischiefe the vnwary sheepe: 10
    Als of their maisters hast no lesse regarde,
    Then of the flocks, which thou doest watch and ward:

I thee beseche (so be thou deigne to heare,
Rude ditties tund to shepheards Oaten reede,
Or if I euer sonet song so cleare,   15
As it with pleasaunce mought thy fancie feede)
    Hearken awhile from thy greene cabinet,
    The rurall song of carefull Colinet.

Whilome in youth, when flowrd my ioyfull spring,
Like Swallow swift I wandred here and there: 20
For heate of heedlesse lust me so did sting,
That I of doubted daunger had no feare.
    I went the wastefull woodes and forest wyde,
    Withouten dreade of Wolues to bene espyed.

I wont to raunge amydde the mazie thickette,   25
And gather nuttes to make me Christmas game:
And ioyed oft to chace the trembling Pricket,
Or hunt the hartlesse hare, til shee were tame.
    What wreaked I of wintrye ages waste,
    Tho deemed I, my spring would euer laste.   30

How often haue I scaled the craggie Oke,
All to dislodge the Rauen of her neste:
Howe haue I wearied with many a stroke,
The stately Walnut tree, the while the rest
    Vnder the tree fell all for nuts at strife: 35
    For ylike to me was libertee and lyfe.

And for I was in thilke same looser yeares,
(Whether the Muse, so wrought me from my birth,
Or I tomuch beleeued my shepherd peres)
Somedele ybent to song and musicks mirth,   40

A good olde shephearde, *Wrenock* was his name,
Made me by arte more cunning in the same.

Fro thence I durst in derring doe compare
With shepheards swayne, what euer fedde in field:
45 And if that *Hobbinol* right iudgement bare,
To *Pan* his owne selfe pype I neede not yield.
    For if the flocking Nymphes did folow *Pan*,
    The wiser Muses after *Colin* ranne.

But ah such pryde at length was ill repayde,
50 The shepheards God (perdie God was he none)
My hurtlesse pleasaunce did me ill vpbraide,
My freedome lorne, my life he lefte to mone.
    Loue they him called, that gaue me checkmate,
    But better mought they haue behote him Hate.

55 Tho gan my louely Spring bid me farewel,
And Sommer season sped him to display
(For loue then in the Lyons house did dwell)
The raging fyre, that kindled at his ray.
    A comett stird vp that vnkindly heate,
60   That reigned (as men sayd) in *Venus* seate.

Forth was I ledde, not as I wont afore,
When choise I had to choose my wandring waye:
But whether luck and loues vnbridled lore
Would leade me forth on Fancies bitte to playe:
65   The bush my bedde, the bramble was my bowre,
    The Woodes can witnesse many a wofull stowre.

Where I was wont to seeke the honey Bee,
Working her formall rowmes in Wexen frame:
The grieslie Todestoole growne there mought I see
70 And loathed Paddocks lording on the same.
    And where the chaunting birds luld me a sleepe,
    The ghastlie Owle her grieuous ynne doth keepe.

Then as the springe giues place to elder time,
And bringeth forth the fruite of sommers pryde:
Also my age now passed youngthly pryme,   75
To thinges of ryper reason selfe applyed.
   And learnd of lighter timber cotes to frame,
   Such as might saue my sheepe and me fro shame.

To make fine cages for the Nightingale,
And Baskets of bulrushes was my wont: 80
Who to entrappe the fish in winding sale
Was better seene, or hurtful beastes to hont?
   I learned als the signes of heauen to ken,
   How *Phœbe* fayles, where *Venus* sittes and when.

And tryed time yet taught me greater thinges,   85
The sodain rysing of the raging seas:
The soothe of byrds by beating of their wings,
The power of herbs, both which can hurt and ease:
   And which be wont tenrage the restlesse sheepe,
   And which be wont to worke eternall sleepe.   90

But ah vnwise and witlesse *Colin cloute*,
That kydst the hidden kinds of many a wede:
Yet kydst not ene to cure thy sore hart roote,
Whose ranckling wound as yet does rifelye bleede.
   Why liuest thou stil, and yet hast thy deathes wound? 95
   Why dyest thou stil, and yet aliue art founde?

Thus is my sommer worne away and wasted,
Thus is my haruest hastened all to rathe:
The eare that budded faire, is burnt and blasted,
And all my hoped gaine is turnd to scathe.   100
   Of all the seede, that in my youth was sowne,
   Was nought but brakes and brambles to be mowne.

My boughes with bloosmes that crowned were at firste,
And promised of timely fruite such store,
Are left both bare and barrein now at erst: 105
The flattring fruite is fallen to grownd before,

And rotted, ere they were halfe mellow ripe:
My haruest wast, my hope away dyd wipe.

The fragrant flowres, that in my garden grewe,
110   Bene withered, as they had bene gathered long.
Theyr rootes bene dryed vp for lacke of dewe,
Yet dewed with teares they han be euer among.
    Ah who has wrought my *Rosalind* this spight
    To spil the flowres, that should her girlond dight?

115   And I, that whilome wont to frame my pype,
Vnto the shifting of the shepheards foote:
Sike follies nowe haue gathered as too ripe,
And cast hem out, as rotten and vnsoote.
    The loser Lasse I cast to please nomore,
120   One if I please, enough is me therefore.

And thus of all my haruest hope I haue
Nought reaped but a weedye crop of care:
Which, when I thought haue thresht in swelling sheaue,
Cockel for corne, and chaffe for barley bare.
125   Soone as the chaffe should in the fan be fynd,
    All was blowne away of the wauering wynd.

So now my yeare drawes to his latter terme,
My spring is spent, my sommer burnt vp quite:
My harueste hasts to stirre vp winter sterne,
130   And bids him clayme with rigorous rage hys right.
    So nowe he stormes with many a sturdy stoure,
    So now his blustring blast eche coste doth scoure.

The carefull cold hath nypt my rugged rynde,
And in my face deepe furrowes eld hath pight:
135   My head besprent with hoary frost I fynd,
And by myne eie the Crow his clawe dooth wright.
    Delight is layd abedde, and pleasure past,
    No sonne now shines, cloudes han all ouercast.

Now leaue ye shepheards boyes your merry glee,
My Muse is hoarse and weary of thys stounde: 140
Here will I hang my pype vpon this tree,
Was neuer pype of reede did better sounde.
    Winter is come, that blowes the bitter blaste,
    And after Winter dreerie death does hast.

Gather ye together my little flocke,   145
My little flock, that was to me so liefe:
Let me, ah lette me in your folds ye lock,
Ere the breme Winter breede you greater griefe.
    Winter is come, that blowes the balefull breath,
    And after Winter commeth timely death.   150

Adieu delightes, that lulled me asleepe,
Adieu my deare, whose loue I bought so deare:
Adieu my little Lambes and loued sheepe,
Adieu ye Woodes that oft my witnesse were:
    Adieu good *Hobbinol*, that was so true,   155
    Tell *Rosalind*, her *Colin* bids her adieu.

Colins Embleme.

GLOSSE.

[4] Tityrus) Chaucer: as hath bene oft sayd.   [8] Lambkins)
    young lambes.

[11] Als of their) Semeth to expresse Virgils verse

Pan curat oues ouiumque magistros.

[13] Deigne) voutchsafe.   [17–18] Cabinet) Colinet) dimi-
    nutiues.

[25] Mazie) For they be like to a maze whence it is hard to get out
    agayne.

[39] Peres) felowes and companions.

[40] Musick) that is Poetry as Terence sayth Qui artem tractant
    musicam, speking of Poetes.

[43] Derring doe) aforesayd.

[57] Lions house) He imagineth simply that Cupid, which is loue, had his abode in the whote signe Leo, which is in middest of somer; a pretie allegory, whereof the meaning is, that loue in him wrought an extraordinarie heate of lust.

[58] His ray) which is Cupides beame or flames of Loue.

[59] A Comete) a blasing starre, meant of beautie, which was the cause of his whote loue.

[60] Venus) the goddesse of beauty or pleasure. Also a signe in heauen, as it is here taken. So he meaneth that beautie, which hath alwayes aspect to Venus, was the cause of all his vnquietnes in loue.

[67] Where I was) a fine discription of the chaunge of hys lyfe and liking; for all things nowe seemed to hym to haue altered their kindly course.

[70] Lording) Spoken after the maner of Paddocks and Frogges sitting which is indeed Lordly, not remouing nor looking once a side, vnlesse they be sturred.

[73] Then as) The second part. That is his manhoode.

[77] Cotes) sheepecotes. for such be the exercises of shepheards.

[81] Sale) or Salow a kind of woodde like Wyllow, fit to wreath and bynde in leapes to catch fish withall.

[84] Phæbe fayles) The Eclipse of the Moone, which is alwayes in Cauda or Capite Draconis, signes in heauen.

[84] Venus) .s. Venus starre otherwise called Hesperus and Vesper and Lucifer, both because he seemeth to be one of the brightest starres, and also first ryseth and setteth last. All which skill in starres being conuenient for shepheardes to knowe as Theocritus and the rest vse.

[86] Raging seaes) The cause of the swelling and ebbing of the sea commeth of the course of the Moone, sometime encreasing, sometime wayning and decreasing.

[87] Sooth of byrdes) A kind of sooth saying vsed in elder tymes, which they gathered by the flying of byrds; First (as is sayd) inuented by the Thuscanes, and from them deriued to the Romanes, who (as is sayd in Liuie) were so supersticiously rooted in the same, that they agreed that euery Noble man should put his sonne to the Thuscanes, by them to be brought vp in that knowledge.

[88] Of herbes) That wonderous thinges be wrought by herbes,

aswell appeareth by the common working of them in our bodies, as also by the wonderful enchauntments and sorceries that haue bene wrought by them; insomuch that it is sayde that Circe a famous sorceresse turned men into sondry kinds of beastes and Monsters, and onely by herbes: as the Poete sayth Dea sæua potentibus herbis &c.

[92] Kidst) knewest.   [99] Eare) of corne.   [100] Scathe) losse hinderaunce.

[112] Euer among) Euer and anone.

[97–8] Thus is my) The thyrde parte wherein is set forth his ripe yeres as an vntimely haruest, that bringeth little fruite.

[109] The fragrant flowres) sundry studies and laudable partes of learning, wherein how our Poete is seene, be they witnesse which are priuie to his study.

[127] So now my yeere) The last part, wherein is described his age by comparison of wyntrye stormes.

[133] Carefull cold) for care is sayd to coole the blood.
    [139] Glee) mirth.

[135] Hoary frost) A metaphore of hoary heares scattred lyke to a gray frost.

[148] Breeme) sharpe and bitter.

[151] Adiew delights) is a conclusion of all. where in sixe verses he comprehendeth briefly all that was touched in this booke. In the first verse his delights of youth generally. in the second, the loue of Rosalind, in the thyrd, the keeping of sheepe, which is the argument of all Æglogues. In the fourth his complaints. And in the last two his professed frendship and good will to his good friend Hobbinoll.

Embleme.

The meaning wherof is that all thinges perish and come to theyr last end, but workes of learned wits and monuments of Poetry abide for euer. And therefore Horace of his Odes a work though ful indede of great wit and learning, yet of no so great weight and importaunce boldly sayth.

> Exegi monimentum ære perennius,
> Quod nec imber nec aquilo vorax &c.

Therefore let not be enuied, that this Poete in his Epilogue sayth
he hath made a Calendar, that shall endure as long as time &c.
folowing the ensample of Horace and Ouid in the like.

> Grande opus exegi quod nec Iouis ira nec ignis,
> Nec ferrum poterit nec edax abolere vetustas &c.

> *Loe I haue made a Calender for euery yeare,*
> *That steele in strength, and time in durance shall outweare:*
> *And if I marked well the starres reuolution,*
> *It shall continewe till the worlds dissolution.*
5   *To teach the ruder shepheard how to feede his sheepe,*
> *And from the falsers fraud his folded flocke to keepe.*
> *Goe lyttle Calender, thou hast a free passeporte,*
> *Goe but a lowly gate emongste the meaner sorte.*
> *Dare not to match thy pype with Tityrus hys style,*
10   *Nor with the Pilgrim that the Ploughman playde a whyle:*
> *But followe them farre off, and their high steppes adore,*
> *The better please, the worse despise, I aske nomore.*

> *Merce non mercede.*

¶THREE PROPER,
and wittie, familiar Letters:
lately paſſed betvvene tvvo V-
niuerſitie men: touching the Earth-
quake in Aprill laſt, and our Engliſh
refourned Verſifying.

With the Preface of a wellwiller
to them both.

IMPRINTED AT LON-
don, by H.Bynneman, dvvelling
in Thames ſtreate, neere vnto
Baynardes Caſtell.
Anno Domini. 1580.

Cum gratia & priuⁱegio Regiæ Maieſtatis.

From *Letter to Harvey, Oct. 16, 1579.*

Iambicum Trimetrum

Vnhappie Verse, the witnesse of my vnhappie state,
    Make thy selfe fluttring wings of thy fast flying thought,
    And fly forth vnto my Loue, whersoeuer she be:
Whether lying reastlesse in heauy bedde, or else
5   Sitting so cheerelesse at the cheerfull boorde, or else
    Playing alone carelesse on hir heauenlie Virginals.
If in Bed, tell hir, that my eyes can take no reste:
    If at Boorde, tel hir, that my mouth can eate no meate:
    If at hir Virginals, tel hir, I can heare no mirth.
10 Asked why? say: Waking Loue suffereth no sleepe:
    Say, that raging Loue dothe appall the weake stomacke:
    Say, that lamenting Loue marreth the Musicall.
Tell hir, that hir pleasures were wonte to lull me asleepe:
    Tell hir, that hir beautie was wonte to feede mine eyes:
    Tel hir, that hir sweete Tongue was wonte to make me
15   mirth.
Nowe doe I nightly waste, wanting my kindely reste:
    Nowe doe I dayly starue, wanting my liuely foode:
    Nowe doe I alwayes dye, wanting thy timely mirth.
And if I waste, who will bewaile my heauy chaunce?
20   And if I starue, who will record my cursed end?
    And if I dye, who will saye: *this was, Immerito?*

Ad Ornatissimum virum, multis iamdiu
nominibus clarissimum, G. H. Immerito
sui, mox in Gallias nauigaturi,
εὐτυχεῖν.

Sic malus egregium, sic non inimicus Amicum:
Sicque nouus veterem iubet ipse Poëta Poëtam,
Saluere, ac caelo post secula multa secundo
Iam reducem, caelo mage, quàm nunc ipse, secundo
Vtier. Ecce Deus, (modò sit Deus ille, renixum   5
Qui vocet in scelus, et iuratos perdat amores)
Ecce Deus mihi clara dedit modò signa Marinus,
Et sua veligero lenis parat Æquora Ligno,
Mox sulcanda, suas etiam pater Æolus Iras
Ponit, et ingentes animos Aquilonis—   10
Cuncta vijs sic apta meis: ego solus ineptus.
Nam mihi nescio quo mens saucia vulnere, dudum
Fluctuat ancipiti Pelago, dum Nauita proram
Inualidam validus rapit huc Amor, et rapit illuc.
Consilijs Ratio melioribus vsa, decusque   15
Immortale leui diffissa Cupidinis Arcu.
Angimur hoc dubio, et portu vexamur in ipso.
Magne pharetrati nunc tu contemptor Amoris,
(Id tibi Dij nomen precor haud impune remittant)
Hos nodos exsolue, et eris mihi magnus Apollo.   20
Spiritus ad summos, scio, te generosus Honores
Exstimulat, maiusque docet spirare Poëtam,
Quàm leuis est Amor, et tamen haud leuis est Amor omnis.
Ergo nihil laudi reputas aequale perenni,
Praeque sacrosancta splendoris imagine tanti,   25
Caetera, quae vecors, vti Numina, vulgus adorat,
Praedia, Amicitias, vrbana peculia, Nummos,
Quaeque placent oculis, formas, spectacula, Amores
Conculcare soles, vt humum, et ludibria sensus.
Digna meo certè Haruejo sententia, digna   30
Oratore amplo, et generoso pectore, quam non
Stoica formidet veterum Sapientia vinclis
Sancire aeternis: sapor haud tamen omnibus idem.

Dicitur effaeti proles facunda Laërtae,
35   Quamlibet ignoti iactata per aequora Caeli,
Inque procelloso longùm exsul gurgite ponto,
Prae tamen amplexu lachrymosae Coniugis, Ortus
Caelestes Diuûmque thoros spreuisse beatos.
Tantùm Amor, et Mulier, vel Amore potentior. Illum
40   Tu tamen illudis: tua Magnificentia tanta est:
Praeque subumbrata Splendoris Imagine tanti,
Praeque illo Meritis famosis nomine parto,
Caetera, quae Vecors, vti Numina, vulgus adorat,
Praedia, Amicitias, armenta, peculia, nummos.
45   Quaeque placent oculis, formas, spectacula, Amores,
Quaeque placent ori, quaeque auribus, omnia temnis.
Nae tu grande sapis, Sapor at sapientia non est:
Omnis et in paruis benè qui scit desipuisse,
Saepe supercilijs palmam sapientibus aufert.
50   Ludit Aristippum modò tetrica Turba Sophorum,
Mitia purpureo moderantem verba Tyranno
Ludit Aristippus dictamina vana Sophorum,
Quos leuis emensi male torquet Culicis vmbra:
Et quisquis placuisse Studet Heroibus altis,
55   Desipuisse studet, sic gratia crescit ineptis.
Denique Laurigeris quisquis sua tempora vittis,
Insignire volet, Populoque placere fauenti,
Desipere insanus discit, turpemque pudendae
Stultitiae laudem quaerit. Pater Ennius vnus
60   Dictus in innumeris sapiens: laudatur at ipse
Carmina vesano fudisse liquentia vino.
Nec tu pace tua, nostri Cato Maxime saecli,
Nomen honorati sacrum mereare Poëtae,
Quantamuis illustre canas, et nobile Carmen,
65   Ni *stultire* velis, sic Stultorum omnia plena.
Tuta sed in medio superest via gurgite, nam Qui
Nec reliquis nimiùm vult desipuisse videri,
Nec sapuisse nimis, Sapientem dixeris vnum.
Hinc te merserit vnda, illinc combusserit Ignis.
70   Nec tu delicias nimis aspernare fluentes,
Nec serò Dominam, venientem in vota, nec Aurum
Si sapis, oblatum, (Curijs ea, Fabricijsque

Linque viris miseris miseranda Sophismata: quondam
Grande sui decus ij, nostri sed dedecus aeui:)
Nec sectare nimis. Res vtraque crimine plena.   75
Hoc bene qui callet, (si quis tamen hoc bene callet)
Scribe, vel invito sapientem hunc Socrate solum.
Vis facit vna pios: Iustos facit altera: et altra
Egregiè cordata, ac fortia pectora: verùm
Omne tulit punctum, *qui miscuit vtile dulci*.   80
Dij mihi, dulce diu dederant: verùm vtile nunquam:
Vtile nunc etiam, ô vtinam quoque dulce dedissent.
Dij mihi, (quippe Dijs aequiualia maxima paruis)
Ni nimis inuideant mortalibus esse beatis,
Dulce simul tribuisse queant, simul vtile: tanta   85
Sed Fortuna tua est: pariter quaeque vtile, quaeque
Dulce dat ad placitum: saeuo nos sydere nati
Quaesitum imus eam per inhospita Caucasa longè,
Perque Pyrenaeos montes, Babilonaque turpem,
Quòd si quaesitum nec ibi invenerimus, ingens   90
Æquor inexhaustis permensi erroribus, vltrâ
Fluctibus in medijs socij quaeremus Vlyssis.
Passibus inde Deam fessis comitabimur aegram,
Nobile cui furtum quaerenti defuit orbis.
Namque sinu pudet in patrio, tenebrisque pudendis   95
Non nimis ingenio Iuuenem infoelice, virentes,
Officijs frustra deperdere vilibus Annos,
Frugibus et vacuas speratis cernere spicas.
Ibimus ergo statim: (quis eunti fausta precetur?)
Et pede Clivosas fesso calcabimus Alpes.   100
Quis dabit interea conditas rore Britanno,
Quis tibi Litterulas? quis carmen amore petulcum?
Musa sub Oebalij desueta cacumine montis,
Flebit inexhausto tam longa silentia planctu,
Lugebitque sacrum lachrymis Helicona tacentem.   105
Harueiusque bonus, (charus licet omnibus idem,
Idque suo merito, prope suauior omnibus vnus,)
Angelus et Gabriel, (quamuis comitatus amicis
Innumeris, geniûmque choro stipatus amaeno)
Immerito tamen vnum absentem saepe requiret,   110
Optabitque, Vtinam meus hîc *Edmundus* adesset,

Qui noua scripsisset, nec Amores conticuisset,
Ipse suos, et saepe animo, verbisque benignis
Fausta precaretur: Deus illum aliquando reducat. etc.
115 Plura vellem per Charites, sed non licet per Musas.
Vale, Vale plurimùm, Mi amabilissime Harueie, meo
cordi, meorum omnium longè charissime.

From *Letter to Harvey, April 10, 1580*.

[1]

See yee the blindefoulded pretie God, that feathered
      Archer,
   Of Louers Miseries which maketh his bloodie Game?
Wote ye why, his Moother with a Veale hath coouered his
      Face?
   Trust me, least he my Looue happely chaunce to
      beholde.

[2]

That which I eate, did I ioy, and that which I greedily
      gorged,
   As for those many goodly matters leaft I for others.

Complaints.

Containing sundrie
small Poemes of the
Worlds Va-
nitie.

VVhereof the next Page
maketh menti-
on.

By Ed. Sp.

LONDON.
Imprinted for VVilliam
Ponsonbie, dwelling in Paules
Churchyard at the signe of
the Bishops head.

1591.

A note of the sundrie Poemes contained
in this Volume.

The Printer to the
Gentle Reader.

SINCE my late setting foorth of the *Faerie Queene*, finding
that it hath found a fauourable passage amongst you; I haue
sithence endeuoured by all good meanes (for the better
encrease and accomplishment of your delights,) to get into
my handes such smale Poemes of the same Authors; as I heard   5
were disperst abroad in sundrie hands, and not easie to bee
come by, by himselfe; some of them hauing bene diuerslie
imbeziled and purloyned from him, since his departure ouer
Sea. Of the which I haue by good meanes gathered togeather
these fewe parcels present, which I haue caused to bee   10
imprinted altogeather, for that they al seeme to containe
like matter of argument in them: being all complaints and
meditations of the worlds vanitie; verie graue and profitable.
To which effect I vnderstand that he besides wrote sundrie
others, namelie *Ecclesiastes*, and *Canticum canticorum* trans-   15
lated, *A senights slumber, The hell of louers, his Purgatorie*, being
all dedicated to Ladies; so as it may seeme he ment them all to
one volume. Besides some other Pamphlets looselie scattered
abroad: as *The dying Pellican, The howers of the Lord, The
sacrifice of a sinner, The seuen Psalmes, &c.* which when I can   20
either by himselfe, or otherwise attaine too, I meane likewise
for your fauour sake to set foorth. In the meane time praying
you gentlie to accept of these, and graciouslie to entertaine
the new Poet. *I take leaue.*

Dedicated
To the right Noble and beauti-
full Ladie, the La. Marie
Countesse of Pembrooke.

*MOST Honourable and bountifull Ladie, there bee long sithens
deepe sowed in my brest, the seede of most entire loue and humble
affection vnto that most braue Knight your noble brother deceased;
which taking roote began in his life time somewhat to bud forth:*
5 *and to shew themselues to him, as then in the weakenes of their
first spring: And would in their riper strength (had it pleased high
God till then to drawe out his daies) spired forth fruit of more
perfection. But since God hath disdeigned the world of that most
noble Spirit, which was the hope of all learned men, and the*
10 *Patron of my young* Muses; *togeather with him both their hope
of anie further fruit was cut off: and also the tender delight of
those their first blossoms nipped and quite dead. Yet sithens my
late cumming into* England, *some frends of mine (which might
much preuaile with me, and indeede commaund me) knowing with*
15 *howe straight bandes of duetie I was tied to him: as also bound
vnto that noble house, (of which the chiefe hope then rested in him)-
haue sought to reuiue them by vpbraiding me: for that I haue not
shewed anie thankefull remembrance towards him or any of them;
but suffer their names to sleep in silence and forgetfulnesse. Whome*
20 *chieflie to satisfie, or els to auoide that fowle blot of vnthankefulnesse,
I haue conceiued this small Poeme, intituled by a generall name of
the* worlds Ruines: *yet speciallie intended to the renowming of
that noble race, from which both you and he sprong, and to the
eternizing of some of the chiefe of them late deceased. The which*
25 *I dedicate vnto your La. as whome it most speciallie concerneth:
and to whome I acknowledge my selfe bounden, by manie
singular fauours and great graces. I pray for
your Honourable happinesse: and
so humblie kisse your*
30 *handes.*

Your Ladiships euer

humblie at commaund.

E. S.

The Ruines of Time.

It chaunced me on day beside the shore
Of siluer streaming *Thamesis* to bee,
Nigh where the goodly *Verlame* stood of yore,
Of which there now remaines no memorie,
Nor anie little moniment to see,   5
By which the trauailer, that fares that way,
This once was she, may warned be to say.

There on the other side, I did behold
A Woman sitting sorrowfullie wailing,
Rending her yeolow locks, like wyrie golde,   10
About her shoulders careleslie downe trailing,
And streames of teares from her faire eyes forth railing.
In her right hand a broken rod she held,
Which towards heauen shee seemd on high to weld.

Whether she were one of that Riuers Nymphes,   15
Which did the losse of some dere loue lament,
I doubt; or one of those three fatall Impes,
Which draw the dayes of men forth in extent;
Or th'auncient *Genius* of that Citie brent:
But seeing her so piteouslie perplexed,   20
I (to her calling) askt what her so vexed.

Ah what delight (quoth she) in earthlie thing,
Or comfort can I wretched creature haue?
Whose happines the heauens enuying,
From highest staire to lowest step me draue,   25
And haue in mine owne bowels made my graue,
That of all Nations now I am forlorne,
The worlds sad spectacle, and fortunes scorne.

Much was I mooued at her piteous plaint,
And felt my heart nigh riuen in my brest   30
With tender ruth to see her sore constraint,
That shedding teares a while I still did rest,

And after did her name of her request.
Name haue I none (quoth she) nor anie being,
35   Bereft of both by Fates vniust decreeing.

I was that Citie, which the garland wore
Of *Britaines* pride, deliuered vnto me
By *Romane* Victors, which it wonne of yore;
Though nought at all but ruines now I bee,
40   And lye in mine owne ashes, as ye see:
Verlame I was; what bootes it that I was,
Sith now I am but weedes and wastfull gras?

O vaine worlds glorie, and vnstedfast state
Of all that liues, on face of sinfull earth,
45   Which from their first vntill their vtmost date
Tast no one hower of happines or merth,
But like as at the ingate of their berth,
They crying creep out of their mothers woomb,
So wailing backe go to their wofull toomb.

50   Why then dooth flesh, a bubble glas of breath,
Hunt after honour and aduauncement vaine,
And reare a trophee for deuouring death,
With so great labour and long lasting paine,
As if his daies for euer should remaine?
55   Sith all that in this world is great or gaie,
Doth as a vapour vanish, and decaie.

Looke backe, who list, vnto the former ages,
And call to count, what is of them become:
Where be those learned wits and antique Sages,
60   Which of all wisedome knew the perfect somme:
Where those great warriors, which did ouercomme
The world with conquest of their might and maine,
And made one meare of th'earth and of their raine?

What nowe is of th'*Assyrian* Lyonesse,
Of whome no footing now on earth appeares? 65
What of the *Persian* Beares outragiousnesse,
Whose memorie is quite worne out with yeares?
Who of the *Grecian* Libbard now ought heares,
That ouerran the East with greedie powre,
And left his whelps their kingdomes to deuoure? 70

And where is that same great seuen headded beast,
That made all nations vassals of her pride,
To fall before her feete at her beheast,
And in the necke of all the world did ride?
Where doth she all that wondrous welth nowe hide? 75
With her own weight down pressed now shee lies,
And by her heaps her hugenesse testifies.

O *Rome* thy ruine I lament and rue,
And in thy fall my fatall ouerthrowe,
That whilom was, whilst heauens with equall vewe 80
Deignd to behold me, and their gifts bestowe,
The picture of thy pride in pompous shew:
And of the whole world as thou wast the Empresse,
So I of this small Northerne world was Princesse.

To tell the beawtie of my buildings fayre, 85
Adornd with purest golde, and precious stone;
To tell my riches, and endowments rare
That by my foes are now all spent and gone:
To tell my forces matchable to none,
Were but lost labour, that few would beleeue, 90
And with rehearsing would me more agreeue.

High towers, faire temples, goodly theaters,
Strong walls, rich porches, princelie pallaces,
Large streetes, braue houses, sacred sepulchers,
Sure gates, sweete gardens, stately galleries, 95
Wrought with faire pillours, and fine imageries,
All those (O pitie) now are turnd to dust,
And ouergrowen with blacke obliuions rust.

Theretoo for warlike power, and peoples store,
In *Britannie* was none to match with mee,
That manie often did abie full sore:
Ne *Troynouant*, though elder sister shee,
With my great forces might compared bee;
That stout *Pendragon* to his perill felt,
Who in a siege seauen yeres about me dwelt.

But long ere this *Bunduca* Britonnesse
Her mightie hoast against my bulwarkes brought,
Bunduca, that victorious conqueresse,
That lifting vp her braue heroick thought
Boue womens weaknes, with the *Romanes* fought,
Fought, and in field against them thrice preuailed:
Yet was she foyld, when as she me assailed.

And though at last by force I conquered were
Of hardie *Saxons*, and became their thrall;
Yet was I with much bloodshed bought full deere,
And prizde with slaughter of their Generall:
The moniment of whose sad funerall,
For wonder of the world, long in me lasted;
But now to nought through spoyle of time is wasted.

Wasted it is, as if it neuer were,
And all the rest that me so honord made,
And of the world admired eu'rie where,
Is turnd to smoake, that doth to nothing fade;
And of that brightnes now appeares no shade,
But greislie shades, such as doo haunt in hell
With fearfull fiends, that in deep darknes dwell.

Where my high steeples whilom vsde to stand,
On which the lordly Faulcon wont to towre,
There now is but an heap of lyme and sand,
For the Shriche-owle to build her balefull bowre:
And where the Nightingale wont forth to powre
Her restles plaints, to comfort wakefull Louers,
There now haunt yelling Mewes and whining Plouers.

And where the christall *Thamis* wont to slide
In siluer channell, downe along the Lee,   135
About whose flowrie bankes on either side
A thousand Nymphes, with mirthfull iollitee
Were wont to play, from all annoyance free;
There now no riuers course is to be seene,
But moorish fennes, and marshes euer greene.   140

Seemes, that that gentle Riuer for great griefe
Of my mishaps, which oft I to him plained;
Or for to shunne the horrible mischiefe,
With which he saw my cruell foes me pained,
And his pure streames with guiltles blood oft stained,   145
From my vnhappie neighborhood farre fled,
And his sweete waters away with him led.

There also where the winged ships were seene
In liquid waues to cut their fomie waie,
And thousand Fishers numbred to haue been,   150
In that wide lake looking for plenteous praie
Of fish, which they with baits vsde to betraie,
Is now no lake, nor anie fishers store,
Nor euer ship shall saile there anie more.

They all are gone, and all with them is gone,   155
Ne ought to me remaines, but to lament
My long decay, which no man els doth mone,
And mourne my fall with dolefull dreriment.
Yet it is comfort in great languishment,
To be bemoned with compassion kinde,   160
And mitigates the anguish of the minde.

But me no man bewaileth, but in game,
Ne sheddeth teares from lamentable eie:
Nor anie liues that mentioneth my name
To be remembred of posteritie,   165
Saue One that maugre fortunes iniurie,
And times decay, and enuies cruell tort,
Hath writ my record in true-seeming sort.

Cambden the nourice of antiquitie,
170 And lanterne vnto late succeeding age,
To see the light of simple veritie,
Buried in ruines, through the great outrage
Of her owne people, led with warlike rage,
Cambden, though time all moniments obscure,
175 Yet thy iust labours euer shall endure.

But whie (vnhappie wight) doo I thus crie,
And grieue that my remembrance quite is raced
Out of the knowledge of posteritie,
And all my antique moniments defaced?
180 Sith I doo dailie see things highest placed,
So soone as fates their vitall thred haue shorne,
Forgotten quite as they were neuer borne.

It is not long, since these two eyes beheld
A mightie Prince, of most renowmed race,
185 Whom *England* high in count of honour held,
And greatest ones did sue to gaine his grace;
Of greatest ones he greatest in his place,
Sate in the bosome of his Soueraine,
And *Right and loyall* did his word maintaine.

190 I saw him die, I saw him die, as one
Of the meane people, and brought foorth on beare,
I saw him die, and no man left to mone
His dolefull fate, that late him loued deare:
Scarse anie left to close his eylids neare;
195 Scarse anie left vpon his lips to laie
The sacred sod, or *Requiem* to saie.

O trustlesse state of miserable men,
That builde your blis on hope of earthly thing,
And vainly thinke your selues halfe happie then,
200 When painted faces with smooth flattering
Doo fawne on you, and your wide praises sing,
And when the courting masker louteth lowe,
Him true in heart and trustie to you trow.

All is but fained, and with oaker dide,
That euerie shower will wash and wipe away,   205
All things doo change that vnder heauen abide,
And after death all friendship doth decaie.
Therefore what euer man bearst worldlie sway,
Liuing, on God, and on thy selfe relie;
For when thou diest, all shall with thee die.   210

He now is dead, and all is with him dead,
Saue what in heauens storehouse he vplaid:
His hope is faild, and come to passe his dread,
And euill men now dead, his deeds vpbraid:
Spite bites the dead, that liuing neuer baid.   215
He now is gone, the whiles the Foxe is crept
Into the hole, the which the Badger swept.

He now is dead, and all his glorie gone,
And all his greatnes vapoured to nought,
That as a glasse vpon the water shone,   220
Which vanisht quite, so soone as it was sought:
His name is worne alreadie out of thought,
Ne anie Poet seekes him to reuiue;
Yet manie Poets honourd him aliue.

Ne doth his *Colin*, carelesse *Colin Cloute*,   225
Care now his idle bagpipe vp to raise,
Ne tell his sorrow to the listning rout
Of shepherd groomes, which wont his songs to praise:
Praise who so list, yet I will him dispraise,
Vntill he quite him of this guiltie blame: 230
Wake shepheards boy, at length awake for shame.

And who so els did goodnes by him gaine,
And who so els his bounteous minde did trie,
Whether he shepheard be, or shepheards swaine,
(For manie did, which doo it now denie)   235
Awake, and to his Song a part applie:
And I, the whilest you mourne for his decease,
Will with my mourning plaints your plaint increase.

He dyde, and after him his brother dyde,
240 His brother Prince, his brother noble Peere,
That whilste he liued, was of none enuyde,
And dead is now, as liuing, counted deare,
Deare vnto all that true affection beare:
But vnto thee most deare, O dearest Dame,
245 His noble Spouse, and Paragon of fame.

He whilest he liued, happie was through thee,
And being dead is happie now much more;
Liuing, that lincked chaunst with thee to bee,
And dead, because him dead thou dost adore
250 As liuing, and thy lost deare loue deplore.
So whilst that thou, faire flower of chastitie,
Dost liue, by thee thy Lord shall neuer die.

Thy Lord shall neuer die, the whiles this verse
Shall liue, and surely it shall liue for euer:
255 For euer it shall liue, and shall rehearse
His worthie praise, and vertues dying neuer,
Though death his soule doo from his bodie seuer.
And thou thy selfe herein shalt also liue;
Such grace the heauens doo to my verses giue.

260 Ne shall his sister, ne thy father die,
Thy father, that good Earle of rare renowne,
And noble Patrone of weake pouertie;
Whose great good deeds in countrey and in towne
Haue purchast him in heauen an happie crowne;
265 Where he now liueth in eternall blis,
And left his sonne t'ensue those steps of his.

He noble bud, his Grandsires liuelie hayre,
Vnder the shadow of thy countenaunce
Now ginnes to shoote vp fast, and flourish fayre
270 In learned artes and goodlie gouernaunce,
That him to highest honour shall aduaunce.
Braue Impe of *Bedford*, grow apace in bountie,
And count of wisedome more than of thy Countie.

Ne may I let thy husbands sister die,
That goodly Ladie, sith she eke did spring   275
Out of this stocke, and famous familie,
Whose praises I to future age doo sing,
And foorth out of her happie womb did bring
The sacred brood of learning and all honour;
In whom the heauens powrde all their gifts vpon her.   280

Most gentle spirite breathed from aboue,
Out of the bosome of the makers blis,
In whom all bountie and all vertuous loue
Appeared in their natiue propertis,
And did enrich that noble breast of his,   285
With treasure passing all this worldes worth,
Worthie of heauen it selfe, which brought it forth.

His blessed spirite full of power diuine
And influence of all celestiall grace,
Loathing this sinfull earth and earthlie slime,   290
Fled backe too soone vnto his natiue place,
Too soone for all that did his loue embrace,
Too soone for all this wretched world, whom he
Robd of all right and true nobilitie.

Yet ere his happie soule to heauen went   295
Out of this fleshlie goale, he did deuise
Vnto his heauenlie maker to present
His bodie, as a spotles sacrifise;
And chose, that guiltie hands of enemies
Should powre forth th'offring of his guiltles blood: 300
So life exchanging for his countries good.

O noble spirite, liue there euer blessed,
The worlds late wonder, and the heauens new ioy,
Liue euer there, and leaue me here distressed
With mortall cares, and cumbrous worlds anoy.   305
But where thou dost that happines enioy,
Bid me, O bid me quicklie come to thee,
That happie there I maie thee alwaies see.

Yet whilest the fates affoord me vitall breath,
310   I will it spend in speaking of thy praise,
And sing to thee, vntill that timelie death
By heauens doome doo ende my earthlie daies:
Thereto doo thou my humble spirite raise,
And into me that sacred breath inspire,
315   Which thou there breathest perfect and entire.

Then will I sing, but who can better sing,
Than thine owne sister, peerles Ladie bright,
Which to thee sings with deep harts sorrowing,
Sorrowing tempered with deare delight,
320   That her to heare I feele my feeble spright
Robbed of sense, and rauished with ioy,
O sad ioy made of mourning and anoy.

Yet will I sing, but who can better sing,
Than thou thy selfe, thine owne selfes valiance,
325   That whilest thou liuedst, madest the forrests ring,
And fields resownd, and flockes to leap and daunce,
And shepheards leaue their lambs vnto mischaunce,
To runne thy shrill *Arcadian* Pipe to heare:
O happie were those dayes, thrice happie were.

330   But now more happie thou, and wretched wee,
Which want the wonted sweetnes of thy voice,
Whiles thou now in *Elisian* fields so free,
With *Orpheus*, and with *Linus*, and the choice
Of all that euer did in rimes reioyce,
335   Conuersest, and doost heare their heauenlie layes,
And they heare thine, and thine doo better praise.

So there thou liuest, singing euermore,
And here thou liuest, being euer song
Of vs, which liuing loued thee afore,
340   And now thee worship, mongst that blessed throng
Of heauenlie Poets and Heroes strong.
So thou both here and there immortall art,
And euerie where through excellent desart.

But such as neither of themselues can sing,
Nor yet are sung of others for reward,   345
Die in obscure obliuion, as the thing
Which neuer was, ne euer with regard
Their names shall of the later age be heard,
But shall in rustie darknes euer lie,
Vnles they mentiond be with infamie.   350

What booteth it to haue been rich aliue?
What to be great? what to be gracious?
When after death no token doth suruiue,
Of former being in this mortall hous,
But sleepes in dust dead and inglorious,   355
Like beast, whose breath but in his nostrels is,
And hath no hope of happinesse or blis.

How manie great ones may remembred be,
Which in their daies most famouslie did florish;
Of whome no word we heare, nor signe now see,   360
But as things wipt out with a sponge do perishe,
Because they liuing, cared not to cherishe
No gentle wits, through pride or couetize,
Which might their names for euer memorize.

Prouide therefore (ye Princes) whilst ye liue,   365
That of the *Muses* ye may friended bee,
Which vnto men eternitie do giue;
For they be daughters of Dame memorie,
And *Ioue* the father of eternitie,
And do those men in golden thrones repose,   370
Whose merits they to glorifie do chose.

The seuen fold yron gates of grislie Hell,
And horrid house of sad *Proserpina*,
They able are with power of mightie spell
To breake, and thence the soules to bring awaie   375
Out of dread darkenesse, to eternall day,
And them immortall make, which els would die
In foule forgetfulnesse, and nameles lie.

So whilome raised they the puissant brood
380 Of golden girt *Alcmena*, for great merite,
Out of the dust, to which the *Oetæan* wood
Had him consum'd, and spent his vitall spirite:
To highest heauen, where now he doth inherite
All happinesse in *Hebes* siluer bowre,
385 Chosen to be her dearest Paramoure.

So raisde they eke faire *Ledaes* warlick twinnes,
And interchanged life vnto them lent,
That when th'one dies, th'other then beginnes
To shew in Heauen his brightnes orient;
390 And they, for pittie of the sad wayment,
Which *Orpheus* for *Eurydice* did make,
Her back againe to life sent for his sake.

So happie are they, and so fortunate,
Whom the *Pierian* sacred sisters loue,
395 That freed from bands of impacable fate,
And power of death, they liue for aye aboue,
Where mortall wreakes their blis may not remoue:
But with the Gods, for former vertues meede,
On *Nectar* and *Ambrosia* do feede.

400 For deeds doe die, how euer noblie donne,
And thoughts of men do as themselues decay,
But wise wordes taught in numbers for to runne,
Recorded by the Muses, liue for ay;
Ne may with storming showers be washt away,
405 Ne bitter breathing windes with harmfull blast,
Nor age, nor enuie shall them euer wast.

In vaine doo earthly Princes then, in vaine
Seeke with Pyramides, to heauen aspired;
Or huge Colosses, built with costlie paine;
410 Or brasen Pillours, neuer to be fired,
Or Shrines, made of the mettall most desired;
To make their memories for euer liue:
For how can mortall immortalitie giue?

Such one *Mausolus* made, the worlds great wonder,
But now no remnant doth thereof remaine: 415
Such one *Marcellus*, but was torne with thunder:
Such one *Lisippus*, but is worne with raine:
Such one King *Edmond*, but was rent for gaine.
All such vaine moniments of earthlie masse,
Deuour'd of Time, in time to nought doo passe.   420

But fame with golden wings aloft doth flie,
Aboue the reach of ruinous decay,
And with braue plumes doth beate the azure skie,
Admir'd of base-borne men from farre away:
Then who so will with vertuous deeds assay   425
To mount to heauen, on *Pegasus* must ride,
And with sweete Poets verse be glorifide.

For not to haue been dipt in *Lethe* lake,
Could saue the sonne of *Thetis* from to die;
But that blinde bard did him immortall make   430
With verses, dipt in deaw of *Castalie*:
Which made the Easterne Conquerour to crie,
O fortunate yong-man, whose vertue found
So braue a Trompe, thy noble acts to sound.

Therefore in this halfe happie I doo read   435
Good *Melibæ*, that hath a Poet got,
To sing his liuing praises being dead,
Deseruing neuer here to be forgot,
In spight of enuie, that his deeds would spot:
Since whose decease, learning lies vnregarded,   440
And men of armes doo wander vnrewarded.

Those two be those two great calamities,
That long agoe did grieue the noble spright
Of *Salomon* with great indignities;
Who whilome was aliue the wisest wight.   445
But now his wisedome is disprooued quite;
For he that now welds all things at his will,
Scorns th'one and th'other in his deeper skill.

O griefe of griefes, O gall of all good heartes,
450   To see that vertue should dispised bee
Of him, that first was raisde for vertuous parts,
And now broad spreading like an aged tree,
Lets none shoot vp, that nigh him planted bee:
O let the man, of whom the Muse is scorned,
455   Nor aliue, nor dead be of the Muse adorned.

O vile worlds trust, that with such vaine illusion
Hath so wise men bewitcht, and ouerkest,
That they see not the way of their confusion,
O vainesse to be added to the rest,
460   That do my soule with inward griefe infest:
Let them behold the piteous fall of mee:
And in my case their owne ensample see.

And who so els that sits in highest seate
Of this worlds glorie, worshipped of all,
465   Ne feareth change of time, nor fortunes threate,
Let him behold the horror of my fall,
And his owne end vnto remembrance call;
That of like ruine he may warned bee,
And in himselfe be moou'd to pittie mee.

470   Thus hauing ended all her piteous plaint,
With dolefull shrikes shee vanished away,
That I through inward sorrowe wexen faint,
And all astonished with deepe dismay,
For her departure, had no word to say:
475   But sate long time in sencelesse sad affright,
Looking still, if I might of her haue sight.

Which when I missed, hauing looked long,
My thought returned greeued home againe,
Renewing her complaint with passion strong,
480   For ruth of that same womans piteous paine;
Whose wordes recording in my troubled braine,
I felt such anguish wound my feeble heart,
That frosen horror ran through euerie part.

So inlie greeuing in my groning brest,
And deepelie muzing at her doubtfull speach,   485
Whose meaning much I labored foorth to wreste,
Being aboue my slender reasons reach;
At length by demonstration me to teach,
Before mine eies strange sights presented were,
Like tragicke Pageants seeming to appeare.   490

                            1

I saw an Image, all of massie gold,
Placed on high vpon an Altare faire,
That all, which did the same from farre beholde,
Might worship it, and fall on lowest staire.
Not that great Idoll might with this compaire,   495
To which th'*Assyrian* tyrant would haue made
The holie brethren, falslie to haue praid.

But th'Altare, on the which this Image staid,
Was (O great pitie) built of brickle clay,
That shortly the foundation decaid,   500
With showres of heauen and tempests worne away,
Then downe it fell, and low in ashes lay,
Scorned of euerie one, which by it went;
That I it seing, dearelie did lament.

                            2

Next vnto this a statelie Towre appeared,   505
Built all of richest stone, that might bee found,
And nigh vnto the Heauens in height vpreared,
But placed on a plot of sandie ground:
Not that great Towre, which is so much renownd
For tongues confusion in holie writ,   510
King *Ninus* worke might be compar'd to it.

But O vaine labours of terrestriall wit,
That buildes so stronglie on so frayle a soyle,
As with each storme does fall away, and flit,
515   And giues the fruit of all your trauailes toyle,
To be the pray of Tyme, and Fortunes spoyle:
I saw this Towre fall sodainlie to dust,
That nigh with griefe thereof my heart was brust.

3

Then did I see a pleasant Paradize,
520   Full of sweete flowres and daintiest delights,
Such as on earth man could not more deuize,
With pleasures choyce to feed his cheerefull sprights;
Not that, which *Merlin* by his Magicke flights
Made for the gentle squire, to entertaine
525   His fayre *Belphœbe*, could this gardine staine.

But O short pleasure bought with lasting paine,
Why will hereafter anie flesh delight
In earthlie blis, and ioy in pleasures vaine,
Since that I sawe this gardine wasted quite,
530   That where it was scarce seemed anie sight?
That I, which once that beautie did beholde,
Could not from teares my melting eyes with-holde.

4

Soone after this a Giaunt came in place,
Of wondrous power, and of exceeding stature,
535   That none durst vewe the horror of his face,
Yet was he milde of speach, and meeke of nature.
Not he, which in despight of his Creatour
With railing tearmes defied the Iewish hoast,
Might with this mightie one in hugenes boast.

For from the one he could to th'other coast,   540
Stretch his strong thighes, and th'Occæan ouerstride,
And reatch his hand into his enemies hoast.
But see the end of pompe and fleshlie pride;
One of his feete vnwares from him did slide,
That downe hee fell into the deepe Abisse,   545
Where drownd with him is all his earthlie blisse.

5

Then did I see a Bridge, made all of golde,
Ouer the Sea from one to other side,
Withouten prop or pillour it t'vpholde,
But like the coulored Rainbowe arched wide: 550
Not that great Arche, which *Traian* edifide,
To be a wonder to all age ensuing,
Was matchable to this in equall vewing.

But (ah) what bootes it to see earthlie thing
In glorie, or in greatnes to excell,   555
Sith time doth greatest things to ruine bring?
This goodlie bridge, one foote not fastned well,
Gan faile, and all the rest downe shortlie fell,
Ne of so braue a building ought remained,
That griefe thereof my spirite greatly pained.   560

6

I saw two Beares, as white as anie milke,
Lying together in a mightie caue,
Of milde aspect, and haire as soft as silke,
That saluage nature seemed not to haue,
Nor after greedie spoyle of blood to craue: 565
Two fairer beasts might not elswhere be found,
Although the compast world were sought around.

But what can long abide aboue this ground
In state of blis, or stedfast happinesse?
The Caue, in which these Beares lay sleeping sound,   570

Was but earth, and with her owne weightinesse
Vpon them fell, and did vnwares oppresse,
That for great sorrow of their sudden fate,
Henceforth all worlds felicitie I hate.

575 ¶ Much was I troubled in my heauie spright,
At sight of these sad spectacles forepast,
That all my senses were bereaued quight,
And I in minde remained sore agast,
Distraught twixt feare and pitie; when at last
580 I heard a voyce, which loudly to me called,
That with the suddein shrill I was appalled.

Behold (said it) and by ensample see,
That all is vanitie and griefe of minde,
Ne other comfort in this world can be,
585 But hope of heauen, and heart to God inclinde;
For all the rest must needs be left behinde:
With that it bad me, to the other side
To cast mine eye, where other sights I spide.

I

¶ Vpon that famous Riuers further shore,
590 There stood a snowie Swan of heauenly hiew,
And gentle kinde, as euer Fowle afore;
A fairer one in all the goodlie criew
Of white *Strimonian* brood might no man view:
There he most sweetly sung the prophecie
595 Of his owne death in dolefull Elegie.

At last, when all his mourning melodie
He ended had, that both the shores resounded,
Feeling the fit that him forewarnd to die,
With loftie flight aboue the earth he bounded,
600 And out of sight to highest heauen mounted:
Where now he is become an heauenly signe;
There now the ioy is his, here sorrow mine.

2

Whilest thus I looked, loe adowne the *Lee*,
I sawe an Harpe stroong all with siluer twyne,
And made of golde and costlie yuorie,   605
Swimming, that whilome seemed to haue been
The harpe, on which *Dan Orpheus* was seene
Wylde beasts and forrests after him to lead,
But was th'Harpe of *Philisides* now dead.

At length out of the Riuer it was reard   610
And borne aboue the cloudes to be diuin'd,
Whilst all the way most heauenly noyse was heard
Of the strings, stirred with the warbling wind,
That wrought both ioy and sorrow in my mind:
So now in heauen a signe it doth appeare,   615
The Harpe well knowne beside the Northern Beare.

3

Soone after this I saw on th'other side,
A curious Coffer made of *Heben* wood,
That in it did most precious treasure hide,
Exceeding all this baser worldes good: 620
Yet through the ouerflowing of the flood
It almost drowned was, and done to nought,
That sight thereof much grieu'd my pensiue thought.

At length when most in perill it was brought,
Two Angels downe descending with swift flight,   625
Out of the swelling streame it lightly caught,
And twixt their blessed armes it carried quight
Aboue the reach of anie liuing sight:
So now it is transform'd into that starre,
In which all heauenly treasures locked are.   630

4

Looking aside I saw a stately Bed,
Adorned all with costly cloth of gold,
That might for anie Princes couche be red,
And deckt with daintie flowres, as if it shold
635   Be for some bride, her ioyous night to hold:
Therein a goodly Virgine sleeping lay;
A fairer wight saw neuer summers day.

I heard a voyce that called farre away
And her awaking bad her quickly dight,
640   For lo her Bridegrome was in readie ray
To come to her, and seeke her loues delight:
With that she started vp with cherefull sight,
When suddeinly both bed and all was gone,
And I in languor left there all alone.

5

645   Still as I gazed, I beheld where stood
A Knight all arm'd, vpon a winged steed,
The same that was bred of *Medusaes* blood,
On which *Dan Perseus* borne of heauenly seed,
The faire *Andromeda* from perill freed:
650   Full mortally this Knight ywounded was,
That streames of blood foorth flowed on the gras.

Yet was he deckt (small ioy to him alas)
With manie garlands for his victories,
And with rich spoyles, which late he did purchas
655   Through braue atcheiuements from his enemies:
Fainting at last through long infirmities,
He smote his steed, that straight to heauen him bore,
And left me here his losse for to deplore.

6

Lastly I saw an Arke of purest golde
Vpon a brazen pillour standing hie,⠀⠀⠀⠀⠀⠀⠀⠀660
Which th'ashes seem'd of some great Prince to hold,
Enclosde therein for endles memorie
Of him, whom all the world did glorifie:
Seemed the heauens with the earth did disagree,
Whether should of those ashes keeper bee.⠀⠀⠀⠀⠀665

At last me seem'd wing footed *Mercurie*,
From heauen descending to appease their strife,
The Arke did beare with him aboue the skie,
And to those ashes gaue a second life,
To liue in heauen, where happines is rife:⠀⠀⠀⠀670
At which the earth did grieue exceedingly,
And I for dole was almost like to die.

L:Envoy.

⠀Immortall spirite of *Philisides*,
Which now art made the heauens ornament,
That whilome wast the worlds chiefst riches;⠀⠀⠀675
Giue leaue to him that lou'de thee to lament
His losse, by lacke of thee to heauen hent,
And with last duties of this broken verse,
Broken with sighes, to decke thy sable Herse.

⠀And ye faire Ladie th'honor of your daies,⠀⠀⠀680
And glorie of the world, your high thoughts scorne;
Vouchsafe this moniment of his last praise,
With some few siluer dropping teares t'adorne:
And as ye be of heauenlie off-spring borne,
So vnto heauen let your high minde aspire,⠀⠀⠀685
And loath this drosse of sinfull worlds desire.

FINIS.

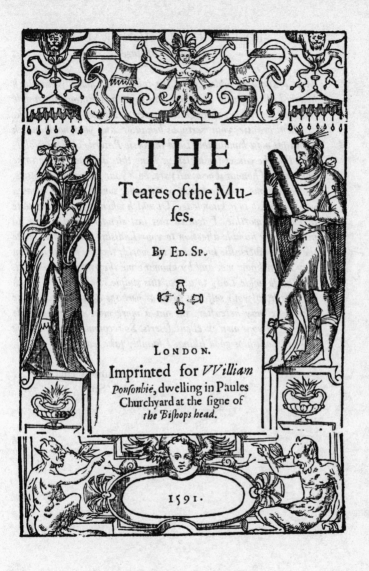

THE
Teares of the Muses.

By Ed. Sp.

LONDON.

Imprinted for *William
Ponsonbie*, dwelling in Paules
Churchyard at the signe of
the Bishops head.

1591.

TO THE RIGHT HONORABLE
the Ladie *Strange*.

Most braue and noble Ladie, the things that make ye so much
honored of the world as ye bee, are such, as (without my simple
lines testimonie) are throughlie knowen to all men; namely, your
excellent beautie, your vertuous behauior, and your noble match
5 *with that most honourable Lord the verie Paterne of right Nobil-*
itie: But the causes for which ye haue thus deserued of me to be
honoured (if honour it be at all) are, both your particular bounties,
and also some priuate bands of affinitie, which it hath pleased
your Ladiship to acknowledge. Of which whenas I found my selfe
10 *in no part worthie, I deuised this last slender meanes, both to*
intimate my humble affection to your Ladiship and also to make
the same vniuersallie knowen to the world; that by honouring you
they might know me, and by knowing me they might honor you.
Vouchsafe noble Lady to accept this simple remembrance, thogh
15 *not worthy of your self, yet such, as perhaps by good acceptance*
therof, ye may hereafter cull out a more meet and memorable
euidence of your own excellent deserts. So recommending the same
to your Ladiships good liking, I humbly take leaue.

Your La: humbly euer.
20   Ed. Sp.

The Teares of the Muses.

Rehearse to me ye sacred Sisters nine,
The golden brood of great *Apolloes* wit,
Those piteous plaints and sorowfull sad tine,
Which late ye powred forth as ye did sit
Beside the siluer Springs of *Helicone*,   5
Making your musick of hart-breaking mone.

For since the time that *Phœbus* foolish sonne
Ythundered through *Ioues* auengefull wrath,
For trauersing the charret of the Sunne
Beyond the compasse of his pointed path,   10
Of you his mournfull Sisters was lamented,
Such mournfull tunes were neuer since inuented.

Nor since that faire *Calliope* did lose
Her loued Twinnes, the dearlings of her ioy,
Her *Palici*, whom her vnkindly foes   15
The fatall Sisters, did for spight destroy,
Whom all the Muses did bewaile long space;
Was euer heard such wayling in this place.

For all their groues, which with the heauenly noyses
Of their sweete instruments were wont to sound,   20
And th'hollow hills, from which their siluer voyces
Were wont redoubled Echoes to rebound,
Did now rebound with nought but rufull cries,
And yelling shrieks throwne vp into the skies.

The trembling streames which wont in chanels cleare   25
To romble gently downe with murmur soft,
And were by them right tunefull taught to beare
A Bases part amongst their consorts oft;
Now forst to ouerflowe with brackish teares,
With troublous noyse did dull their daintie eares.   30

The ioyous Nymphes and lightfoote Faeries
Which thether came to heare their musick sweet,
And to the measure of their melodies
Did learne to moue their nimble shifting feete;
35   Now hearing them so heauily lament,
Like heauily lamenting from them went.

And all that els was wont to worke delight
Through the diuine infusion of their skill,
And all that els seemd faire and fresh in sight,
40   So made by nature for to serue their will,
Was turned now to dismall heauinesse,
Was turned now to dreadfull vglinesse.

Ay me, what thing on earth that all thing breeds,
Might be the cause of so impatient plight?
45   What furie, or what feend with felon deeds
Hath stirred vp so mischieuous despight?
Can griefe then enter into heauenly harts,
And pierce immortall breasts with mortall smarts?

Vouchsafe ye then, whom onely it concernes,
50   To me those secret causes to display;
For none but you, or who of you it learnes
Can rightfully aread so dolefull lay.
Begin thou eldest Sister of the crew,
And let the rest in order thee ensew.

Clio.

55   Heare thou great Father of the Gods on hie
That most art dreaded for thy thunder darts:
And thou our Syre that raignst in *Castalie*
And mount *Parnasse*, the God of goodly Arts:
Heare and behold the miserable state
60   Of vs thy daughters, dolefull desolate.

Behold the fowle reproach and open shame,
The which is day by day vnto vs wrought
By such as hate the honour of our name,
The foes of learning, and each gentle thought;
They not contented vs themselues to scorne,   65
Doo seeke to make vs of the world forlorne.

Ne onely they that dwell in lowly dust,
The sonnes of darknes and of ignoraunce;
But they, whom thou great *Ioue* by doome vniust
Didst to the type of honour earst aduaunce;   70
They now puft vp with sdeignfull insolence,
Despise the brood of blessed Sapience.

The sectaries of my celestiall skill,
That wont to be the worlds chiefe ornament,
And learned Impes that wont to shoote vp still,   75
And grow to hight of kingdomes gouernment
They vnderkeep, and with their spredding armes
Doo beat their buds, that perish through their harmes.

It most behoues the honorable race
Of mightie Peeres, true wisedome to sustaine,   80
And with their noble countenaunce to grace
The learned forheads, without gifts or gaine:
Or rather learnd themselues behoues to bee;
That is the girlond of Nobilitie.

But (ah) all otherwise they doo esteeme   85
Of th'heauenly gift of wisdomes influence,
And to be learned it a base thing deeme;
Base minded they that want intelligence:
For God himselfe for wisedome most is praised,
And men to God thereby are nighest raised.   90

But they doo onely striue themselues to raise
Through pompous pride, and foolish vanitie;
In th'eyes of people they put all their praise,
And onely boast of Armes and Auncestrie:

95 But vertuous deeds, which did those Armes first giue
  To their Grandsyres, they care not to atchiue.

  So I, that doo all noble feates professe
  To register, and sound in trump of gold;
  Through their bad dooings, or base slothfulnesse,
100 Finde nothing worthie to be writ, or told:
  For better farre it were to hide their names,
  Than telling them to blazon out their blames.

  So shall succeeding ages haue no light
  Of things forepast, nor moniments of time,
105 And all that in this world is worthie hight
  Shall die in darknesse, and lie hid in slime:
  Therefore I mourne with deep harts sorrowing,
  Because I nothing noble haue to sing.

  With that she raynd such store of streaming teares,
110 That could haue made a stonie heart to weep,
  And all her Sisters rent their golden heares,
  And their faire faces with salt humour steep.
  So ended shee: and then the next anew,
  Began her grieuous plaint as doth ensew.

Melpomene.

115 O who shall powre into my swollen eyes
  A sea of teares that neuer may be dryde,
  A brasen voice that may with shrilling cryes
  Pierce the dull heauens and fill the ayer wide,
  And yron sides that sighing may endure,
120 To waile the wretchednes of world impure?

  Ah wretched world the den of wickednesse,
  Deformd with filth and fowle iniquitie;
  Ah wretched world the house of heauinesse,
  Fild with the wreaks of mortall miserie;
125 Ah wretched world, and all that is therein
  The vassals of Gods wrath, and slaues of sin.

Most miserable creature vnder sky
Man without vnderstanding doth appeare;
For all this worlds affliction he thereby,
And Fortunes freakes is wisely taught to beare: 130
Of wretched life the onely ioy shee is,
And th'only comfort in calamities.

She armes the brest with constant patience,
Against the bitter throwes of dolours darts,
She solaceth with rules of Sapience   135
The gentle mind, in midst of worldlie smarts:
When he is sad, shee seeks to make him merie,
And doth refresh his sprights when they be werie.

But he that is of reasons skill bereft,
And wants the staffe of wisedome him to stay,   140
Is like a ship in midst of tempest left
Withouten helme or Pilot her to sway,
Full sad and dreadfull is that ships euent:
So is the man that wants intendiment.

Whie then doo foolish men so much despize   145
The precious store of this celestiall riches?
Why doo they banish vs, that patronize
The name of learning? Most vnhappie wretches,
The which lie drowned in deep wretchednes,
Yet doo not see their owne vnhappines.   150

My part it is and my professed skill
The Stage with Tragick buskin to adorne,
And fill the Scene with plaint and outcries shrill
Of wretched persons, to misfortune borne:
But none more tragick matter I can finde   155
Than this, of men depriu'd of sense and minde.

For all mans life me seemes a Tragedy,
Full of sad sights and sore Catastrophees;
First comming to the world with weeping eye,
Where all his dayes like dolorous Trophees,   160

Are heapt with spoyles of fortune and of feare,
And he at last laid forth on balefull beare.

So all with rufull spectacles is fild
Fit for *Megera* or *Persephone*;
165   But I that in true Tragedies am skild,
The flowre of wit, finde nought to busie me:
Therefore I mourne, and pitifully mone,
Because that mourning matter I haue none.

Then gan she wofully to waile, and wring
170   Her wretched hands in lamentable wise;
And all her Sisters thereto answering,
Threw forth lowd shrieks and drerie dolefull cries.
So rested she: and then the next in rew,
Began her grieuous plaint as doth ensew.

Thalia.

175   Where be the sweete delights of learnings treasure,
That wont with Comick sock to beautefie
The painted Theaters, and fill with pleasure
The listners eyes, and eares with melodie;
In which I late was wont to raine as Queene,
180   And maske in mirth with Graces well beseene?

O all is gone, and all that goodly glee,
Which wont to be the glorie of gay wits,
Is layd abed, and no where now to see;
And in her roome vnseemly Sorrow sits,
185   With hollow browes and greisly countenaunce,
Marring my ioyous gentle dalliaunce.

And him beside sits vgly Barbarisme,
And brutish Ignorance, ycrept of late
Out of dredd darknes of the deep Abysme,
190   Where being bredd, he light and heauen does hate:
They in the mindes of men now tyrannize,
And the faire Scene with rudenes foule disguize.

All places they with follie haue possest,
And with vaine toyes the vulgare entertaine;
But me haue banished, with all the rest   195
That whilome wont to wait vpon my traine,
Fine Counterfesaunce and vnhurtfull Sport,
Delight and Laughter deckt in seemly sort.

All these, and all that els the Comick Stage
With seasoned wit and goodly pleasance graced;   200
By which mans life in his likest image
Was limned forth, are wholly now defaced;
And those sweete wits which wont the like to frame,
Are now despizd, and made a laughing game.

And he the man, whom Nature selfe had made   205
To mock her selfe, and Truth to imitate,
With kindly counter vnder Mimick shade,
Our pleasant *Willy*, ah is dead of late:
With whom all ioy and iolly meriment
Is also deaded, and in dolour drent.   210

In stead thereof scoffing Scurrilitie,
And scornfull Follie with Contempt is crept,
Rolling in rymes of shameles ribaudrie
Without regard, or due Decorum kept,
Each idle wit at will presumes to make,   215
And doth the Learneds taske vpon him take.

But that same gentle Spirit, from whose pen
Large streames of honnie and sweete Nectar flowe,
Scorning the boldnes of such base-borne men,
Which dare their follies forth so rashlie throwe;   220
Doth rather choose to sit in idle Cell,
Than so himselfe to mockerie to sell.

So am I made the seruant of the manie,
And laughing stocke of all that list to scorne,
Not honored nor cared for of anie;   225
But loath'd of losels as a thing forlorne:

Therefore I mourne and sorrow with the rest,
Vntill my cause of sorrow be redrest.

Therewith she lowdly did lament and shrike,
230 Pouring forth streames of teares abundantly,
And all her Sisters with compassion like,
The breaches of her singulfs did supply.
So rested shee: and then the next in rew
Began her grieuous plaint, as doth ensew.

Euterpe.

235 Like as the dearling of the Summers pryde,
Faire *Philomele*, when winters stormie wrath
The goodly fields, that earst so gay were dyde
In colours diuers, quite despoyled hath,
All comfortlesse doth hide her chearlesse head
240 During the time of that her widowhead:

So we, that earst were wont in sweet accord
All places with our pleasant notes to fill,
Whilest fauourable times did vs afford
Free libertie to chaunt our charmes at will:
245 All comfortlesse vpon the bared bow,
Like wofull Culuers doo sit wayling now.

For far more bitter storme than winters stowre
The beautie of the world hath lately wasted,
And those fresh buds, which wont so faire to flowre,
250 Hath marred quite, and all their blossoms blasted:
And those yong plants, which wont with fruit t'abound,
Now without fruite or leaues are to be found.

A stonie coldnesse hath benumbd the sence
And liuelie spirits of each liuing wight,
255 And dimd with darknesse their intelligence,
Darknesse more than *Cymerians* daylie night:
And monstrous error flying in the ayre,
Hath mard the face of all that semed fayre.

Image of hellish horrour Ignorance,
Borne in the bosome of the black *Abysse*,   260
And fed with furies milke, for sustenaunce
Of his weake infancie, begot amisse
By yawning Sloth on his owne mother Night;
So hee his sonnes both Syre and brother hight.

He armd with blindnesse and with boldnes stout,   265
(For blind is bold) hath our fayre light defaced;
And gathering vnto him a ragged rout
Of *Faunes* and *Satyres*, hath our dwellings raced
And our chast bowers, in which all vertue rained,
With brutishnesse and beastlie filth hath stained.   270

The sacred springs of horsefoot *Helicon*,
So oft bedeawed with our learned layes,
And speaking streames of pure *Castalion*,
The famous witnesse of our wonted praise,
They trampled haue with their fowle footings trade,   275
And like to troubled puddles haue them made.

Our pleasant groues, which planted were with paines,
That with our musick wont so oft to ring,
And arbors sweet, in which the Shepheards swaines
Were wont so oft their Pastoralls to sing,   280
They haue cut downe and all their pleasaunce mard,
That now no pastorall is to bee hard.

In stead of them fowle Goblins and Shriekowles,
With fearfull howling do all places fill;
And feeble *Eccho* now laments and howles,   285
The dreadfull accents of their outcries shrill.
So all is turned into wildernesse,
Whilest ignorance the Muses doth oppresse.

And I whose ioy was earst with Spirit full
To teach the warbling pipe to sound aloft,   290
My spirits now dismayd with sorrow dull,
Doo mone my miserie in silence soft.

Therefore I mourne and waile incessantly,
Till please the heauens affoord me remedy.

295   Therewith shee wayled with exceeding woe
And pitious lamentation did make,
And all her sisters seeing her doo soe,
With equall plaints her sorrowe did partake.
So rested shee: and then the next in rew,
300   Began her grieuous plaint as doth ensew.

Terpsichore.

Who so hath in the lap of soft delight
Beene long time luld, and fed with pleasures sweet,
Feareles through his own fault or Fortunes spight,
To tumble into sorrow and regreet,
305   Yf chaunce him fall into calamitie,
Findes greater burthen of his miserie.

So wee that earst in ioyance did abound
And in the bosome of all blis did sit,
Like virgin Queenes with laurell garlands cround,
310   For vertues meed and ornament of wit;
Sith ignorance our kingdome did confound,
Bee now become most wretched wightes on ground:

And in our royall thrones which lately stood
In th'hearts of men to rule them carefully,
315   He now hath placed his accursed brood,
By him begotten of fowle infamy;
Blind Error, scornefull Follie, and base Spight,
Who hold by wrong, that wee should haue by right.

They to the vulgar sort now pipe and sing,
320   And make them merrie with their fooleries,
They cherelie chaunt and rymes at randon fling,
The fruitfull spawne of their ranke fantasies:
They feede the eares of fooles with flattery,
And good men blame, and losels magnify:

All places they doo with their toyes possesse,   325
And raigne in liking of the multitude,
The schooles they fill with fond newfanglenesse,
And sway in Court with pride and rashnes rude;
Mongst simple shepheards they do boast their skill,
And say their musicke matcheth *Phœbus* quill.   330

The noble hearts to pleasures they allure,
And tell their Prince that learning is but vaine,
Faire Ladies loues they spot with thoughts impure,
And gentle mindes with lewd delights distaine:
Clerks they to loathly idlenes entice,   335
And fill their bookes with discipline of vice.

So euery where they rule and tyrannize,
For their vsurped kingdomes maintenaunce,
The whiles we silly Maides, whom they dispize,
And with reprochfull scorne discountenaunce,   340
From our owne natiue heritage exilde,
Walk through the world of euery one reuilde.

Nor anie one doth care to call vs in,
Or once vouchsafeth vs to entertaine,
Vnlesse some one perhaps of gentle kin,   345
For pitties sake compassion our paine,
And yeeld vs some reliefe in this distresse:
Yet to be so relieu'd is wretchednesse.

So wander we all carefull comfortlesse,
Yet none doth care to comfort vs at all;   350
So seeke we helpe our sorrow to redresse,
Yet none vouchsafes to answere to our call:
Therefore we mourne and pittilesse complaine,
Because none liuing pittieth our paine.

With that she wept and wofullie waymented,   355
That naught on earth her griefe might pacifie;
And all the rest her dolefull din augmented,
With shrikes and groanes and grieuous agonie.

So ended shee: and then the next in rew,
360   Began her piteous plaint as doth ensew.

Erato

Ye gentle Spirits breathing from aboue,
Where ye in *Venus* siluer bowre were bred,
Thoughts halfe deuine full of the fire of loue,
With beawtie kindled and with pleasure fed,
365   Which ye now in securitie possesse,
Forgetfull of your former heauinesse:

Now change the tenor of your ioyous layes,
With which ye vse your loues to deifie,
And blazon foorth an earthlie beauties praise,
370   Aboue the compasse of the arched skie:
Now change your praises into piteous cries,
And Eulogies turne into Elegies.

Such as ye wont whenas those bitter stounds
Of raging loue first gan you to torment,
375   And launch your hearts with lamentable wounds
Of secret sorrow and sad languishment,
Before your Loues did take you vnto grace;
Those now renew as fitter for this place.

For I that rule in measure moderate
380   The tempest of that stormie passion,
And vse to paint in rimes the troublous state
Of Louers life in likest fashion,
Am put from practise of my kindlie skill,
Banisht by those that Loue with leawdnes fill.

385   Loue wont to be schoolmaster of my skill,
And the deuicefull matter of my song;
Sweete Loue deuoyd of villanie or ill,
But pure and spotles, as at first he sprong
Out of th'Almighties bosome, where he nests;
390   From thence infused into mortall brests.

Such high conceipt of that celestiall fire,
The base-borne brood of blindnes cannot gesse,
Ne euer dare their dunghill thoughts aspire
Vnto so loftie pitch of perfectnesse,
But rime at riot, and doo rage in loue; 395
Yet little wote what doth thereto behoue.

Faire *Cytheree* the Mother of delight,
And Queene of beautie, now thou maist go pack;
For lo thy Kingdome is defaced quight,
Thy scepter rent, and power put to wrack; 400
And thy gay Sonne, that winged God of Loue,
May now goe prune his plumes like ruffed Doue.

And ye three Twins to light by *Venus* brought,
The sweete companions of the Muses late,
From whom what euer thing is goodly thought 405
Doth borrow grace, the fancie to aggrate;
Go beg with vs, and be companions still
As heretofore of good, so now of ill.

For neither you nor we shall anie more
Finde entertainment, or in Court or Schoole: 410
For that which was accounted heretofore
The learneds meed, is now lent to the foole;
He sings of loue, and maketh louing layes,
And they him heare, and they him highly prayse.

With that she powred foorth a brackish flood 415
Of bitter teares, and made exceeding mone;
And all her Sisters seeing her sad mood,
With lowd laments her answered all at one.
So ended she: and then the next in rew
Began her grieuous plaint, as doth ensew. 420

Calliope

To whom shall I my euill case complaine,
Or tell the anguish of my inward smart,
Sith none is left to remedie my paine,
Or deignes to pitie a perplexed hart;
425   But rather seekes my sorrow to augment
With fowle reproach, and cruell banishment.

For they to whom I vsed to applie
The faithfull seruice of my learned skill,
The goodly off-spring of *Ioues* progenie,
430   That wont the world with famous acts to fill;
Whose liuing praises in heroïck style,
It is my chiefe profession to compyle.

They all corrupted through the rust of time,
That doth all fairest things on earth deface,
435   Or through vnnoble sloth, or sinfull crime,
That doth degenerate the noble race;
Haue both desire of worthie deeds forlorne,
And name of learning vtterly doo scorne.

Ne doo they care to haue the auncestrie
440   Of th'old Heroës memorizde anew,
Ne doo they care that late posteritie
Should know their names, or speak their praises dew:
But die forgot from whence at first they sprong,
As they themselues shalbe forgot ere long.

445   What bootes it then to come from glorious
Forefathers, or to haue been nobly bredd?
What oddes twixt *Irus* and old *Inachus*,
Twixt best and worst, when both alike are dedd;
If none of neither mention should make,
450   Nor out of dust their memories awake?

Or who would euer care to doo braue deed,
Or striue in vertue others to excell;
If none should yeeld him his deserued meed,
Due praise, that is the spur of dooing well?
For if good were not praised more than ill,   455
None would choose goodnes of his owne freewill.

Therefore the nurse of vertue I am hight,
And golden Trompet of eternitie,
That lowly thoughts lift vp to heauens hight,
And mortall men haue powre to deifie: 460
Bacchus and *Hercules* I raisd to heauen,
And *Charlemaine*, amongst the Starris seauen.

But now I will my golden Clarion rend,
And will henceforth immortalize no more:
Sith I no more finde worthie to commend   465
For prize of value, or for learned lore:
For noble Peeres whom I was wont to raise,
Now onely seeke for pleasure, nought for praise.

Their great reuenues all in sumptuous pride
They spend, that nought to learning they may spare;   470
And the rich fee which Poets wont diuide,
Now Parasites and Sycophants doo share:
Therefore I mourne and endlesse sorrow make,
Both for my selfe and for my Sisters sake.

With that she lowdly gan to waile and shrike,   475
And from her eyes a sea of teares did powre,
And all her sisters with compassion like,
Did more increase the sharpnes of her showre.
So ended she: and then the next in rew
Began her plaint, as doth herein ensew.   480

Vrania.

What wrath of Gods, or wicked influence
Of Starres conspiring wretched men t'afflict,
Hath powrd on earth this noyous pestilence,
That mortall mindes doth inwardly infect
485　　With loue of blindnesse and of ignorance,
To dwell in darkenesse without souenance?

What difference twixt man and beast is left,
When th'heauenlie light of knowledge is put out,
And th'ornaments of wisdome are bereft?
490　　Then wandreth he in error and in doubt,
Vnweeting of the danger hee is in,
Through fleshes frailtie and deceipt of sin.

In this wide world in which they wretches stray,
It is the onelie comfort which they haue,
495　　It is their light, their loadstarre and their day;
But hell and darkenesse and the grislie graue
Is ignorance, the enemie of grace,
That mindes of men borne heauenlie doth debace.

Through knowledge we behold the worlds creation,
500　　How in his cradle first he fostred was;
And iudge of Natures cunning operation,
How things she formed of a formelesse mas:
By knowledge wee do learne our selues to knowe,
And what to man, and what to God wee owe.

505　　From hence wee mount aloft vnto the skie,
And looke into the Christall firmament,
There we behold the heauens great *Hierarchie*,
The Starres pure light, the Spheres swift mouement,
The Spirites and Intelligences fayre,
510　　And Angels waighting on th'Almighties chayre.

And there with humble minde and high insight,
Th'eternall Makers maiestie wee viewe,
His loue, his truth, his glorie, and his might,
And mercie more than mortall men can vew.
O soueraigne Lord, O soueraigne happinesse   515
To see thee, and thy mercie measurelesse:

Such happines haue they, that doo embrace
The precepts of my heauenlie discipline;
But shame and sorrow and accursed case
Haue they, that scorne the schoole of arts diuine,   520
And banish me, which do professe the skill
To make men heauenly wise, through humbled will.

How euer yet they mee despise and spight,
I feede on sweet contentment of my thought,
And please my selfe with mine owne selfe-delight,   525
In contemplation of things heauenlie wrought:
So loathing earth, I looke vp to the sky,
And being driuen hence I thether fly.

Thence I behold the miserie of men,
Which want the blis that wisedom would them breed,   530
And like brute beasts doo lie in loathsome den,
Of ghostly darkenes, and of gastlie dreed:
For whom I mourne and for my selfe complaine,
And for my Sisters eake whom they disdaine.

With that shee wept and waild so pityouslie,   535
As if her eyes had beene two springing wells:
And all the rest her sorrow to supplie,
Did throw forth shrieks and cries and dreery yells.
So ended shee, and then the next in rew,
Began her mournfull plaint as doth ensew.   540

Polyhymnia.

A dolefull case desires a dolefull song,
Without vaine art or curious complements,
And squallid Fortune into basenes flong,
Doth scorne the pride of wonted ornaments.
545   Then fittest are these ragged rimes for mee,
To tell my sorrowes that exceeding bee:

For the sweet numbers and melodious measures,
With which I wont the winged words to tie,
And make a tunefull Diapase of pleasures,
550   Now being let to runne at libertie
By those which haue no skill to rule them right,
Haue now quite lost their naturall delight.

Heapes of huge words vphoorded hideously,
With horrid sound though hauing little sence,
555   They thinke to be chiefe praise of Poëtry;
And thereby wanting due intelligence,
Haue mard the face of goodly Poësie,
And made a monster of their fantasie:

Whilom in ages past none might professe
560   But Princes and high Priests that secret skill,
The sacred lawes therein they wont expresse,
And with deepe Oracles their verses fill:
Then was shee held in soueraigne dignitie,
And made the noursling of Nobilitie.

565   But now nor Prince nor Priest doth her maintayne,
But suffer her prophaned for to bee
Of the base vulgar, that with hands vncleane
Dares to pollute her hidden mysterie;
And treadeth vnder foote hir holie things,
570   Which was the care of Kesars and of Kings.

One onelie liues, her ages ornament,
And myrrour of her Makers maiestie;
That with rich bountie and deare cherishment,
Supports the praise of noble Poësie:
Ne onelie fauours them which it professe,   575
But is her selfe a peereles Poëtresse.

Most peereles Prince, most peereles Poëtresse,
The true *Pandora* of all heauenly graces,
Diuine *Elisa*, sacred Emperesse:
Liue she for euer, and her royall P'laces   580
Be fild with praises of diuinest wits,
That her eternize with their heauenlie writs.

Some few beside, this sacred skill esteme,
Admirers of her glorious excellence,
Which being lightned with her beawties beme,   585
Are thereby fild with happie influence:
And lifted vp aboue the worldes gaze,
To sing with Angels her immortall praize.

But all the rest as borne of saluage brood,
And hauing beene with Acorns alwaies fed,   590
Can no whit sauour this celestiall food;
But with base thoughts are into blindnesse led,
And kept from looking on the lightsome day:
For whome I waile and weepe all that I may.

Eftsoones such store of teares shee forth did powre,   595
As if shee all to water would haue gone;
And all her sisters seeing her sad stowre,
Did weep and waile and made exceeding mone,
And all their learned instruments did breake.
The rest vntold no louing tongue can speake.   600

FINIS.

Virgils Gnat.

Long since dedicated
To the most noble and excellent Lord,
the Earle of Leicester, late
deceased.

Wrong'd, yet not daring to expresse my paine,
To you (great Lord) the causer of my care,
In clowdie teares my case I thus complaine
Vnto your selfe, that onely priuie are:
5   *But if that any* Oedipus *vnware*
Shall chaunce, through power of some diuining spright,
To reade the secrete of this riddle rare,
And know the purporte of my euill plight,
     Let him rest pleased with his owne insight,
10   *Ne further seeke to glose vpon the text:*
For griefe enough it is to grieued wight
To feele his fault, and not be further vext.
     But what so by my selfe may not be showen,
May by this Gnatts complaint be easily knowen.

Virgils Gnat.

We now haue playde (*Augustus*) wantonly,
Tuning our song vnto a tender Muse,
And like a cobweb weauing slenderly,
Haue onely playde: let thus much then excuse
This Gnats small Poeme, that th'whole history   5
Is but a iest, though enuie it abuse:
But who such sports and sweet delights doth blame,
Shall lighter seeme than this Gnats idle name.

Hereafter, when as season more secure
Shall bring forth fruit, this Muse shall speak to thee   10
In bigger notes, that may thy sense allure,
And for thy worth frame some fit Poesie,
The golden offspring of *Latona* pure,
And ornament of great *Ioues* progenie,
Phœbus shall be the author of my song,   15
Playing on yuorie harp with siluer strong.

He shall inspire my verse with gentle mood
Of Poets Prince, whether he woon beside
Faire *Xanthus* sprincled with *Chimæras* blood;
Or in the woods of *Astery* abide;   20
Or whereas mount *Parnasse*, the Muses brood,
Doth his broad forhead like two hornes diuide,
And the sweete waues of sounding *Castaly*
With liquid foote doth slide downe easily.

Wherefore ye Sisters which the glorie bee   25
Of the *Pierian* streames, fayre *Naiades*,
Go too, and dauncing all in companie,
Adorne that God: and thou holie *Pales*,
To whome the honest care of husbandrie
Returneth by continuall successe,   30
Haue care for to pursue his footing light;
Throgh the wide woods, and groues, with green leaues dight.

Professing thee I lifted am aloft
Betwixt the forrest wide and starrie sky:
And thou most dread (*Octauius*) which oft
To learned wits giuest courage worthily,
O come (thou sacred childe) come sliding soft,
And fauour my beginnings graciously:
For not these leaues do sing that dreadfull stound,
When Giants bloud did staine *Phlegræan* ground.

Nor how th'halfe horsy people, *Centaures* hight,
Fought with the bloudie *Lapithaes* at bord,
Nor how the East with tyranous despight
Burnt th'*Attick* towres, and people slew with sword;
Nor how mount *Athos* through exceeding might
Was digged downe, nor yron bands abord
The *Pontick* sea by their huge Nauy cast,
My volume shall renowne, so long since past.

Nor *Hellespont* trampled with horses feete,
When flocking *Persians* did the *Greeks* affray;
But my soft Muse, as for her power more meete,
Delights (with *Phœbus* friendly leaue) to play
An easie running verse with tender feete.
And thou (dread sacred child) to thee alway,
Let euerlasting lightsome glory striue,
Through the worlds endles ages to suruiue.

And let an happie roome remaine for thee
Mongst heauenly ranks, where blessed soules do rest;
And let long lasting life with ioyous glee,
As thy due meede that thou deseruest best,
Hereafter many yeares remembred be
Amongst good men, of whom thou oft are blest;
Liue thou for euer in all happinesse:
But let vs turne to our first businesse.

The fiery Sun was mounted now on hight   65
Vp to the heauenly towers, and shot each where
Out of his golden Charet glistering light;
And fayre *Aurora* with her rosie heare,
The hatefull darknes now had put to flight,
When as the shepheard seeing day appeare,   70
His little Goats gan driue out of their stalls,
To feede abroad, where pasture best befalls.

To an high mountaines top he with them went,
Where thickest grasse did cloath the open hills:
They now amongst the woods and thickets ment,   75
Now in the valleies wandring at their wills,
Spread themselues farre abroad through each descent;
Some on the soft greene grasse feeding their fills;
Some clambring through the hollow cliffes on hy,
Nibble the bushie shrubs, which growe thereby.   80

Others the vtmost boughs of trees doe crop,
And brouze the woodbine twigges, that freshly bud;
This with full bit doth catch the vtmost top
Of some soft Willow, or new growen stud;
This with sharpe teeth the bramble leaues doth lop,   85
And chaw the tender prickles in her Cud;
The whiles another high doth ouerlooke
Her owne like image in a christall brooke.

O the great happines, which shepheards haue,
Who so loathes not too much the poore estate,   90
With minde that ill vse doth before depraue,
Ne measures all things by the costly rate
Of riotise, and semblants outward braue;
No such sad cares, as wont to macerate
And rend the greedie mindes of couetous men,   95
Do euer creepe into the shepheards den.

Ne cares he if the fleece, which him arayes,
Be not twice steeped in Assyrian dye,
Ne glistering of golde, which vnderlayes
100   The summer beames, doe blinde his gazing eye.
Ne pictures beautie, nor the glauncing rayes
Of precious stones, whence no good commeth by;
Ne yet his cup embost with Imagery
Of *Bætus* or of *Alcons* vanity.

105   Ne ought the whelky pearles esteemeth hee,
Which are from Indian seas brought far away:
But with pure brest from carefull sorrow free,
On the soft grasse his limbs doth oft display,
In sweete spring time, when flowres varietie
110   With sundrie colours paints the sprincled lay;
There lying all at ease, from guile or spight,
With pype of fennie reedes doth him delight.

There he, Lord of himselfe, with palme bedight,
His looser locks doth wrap in wreath of vine:
115   There his milk dropping Goats be his delight,
And fruitefull *Pales*, and the forrest greene,
And darkesome caues in pleasaunt vallies pight,
Wheras continuall shade is to be seene,
And where fresh springing wells, as christall neate,
120   Do alwayes flow, to quench his thirstie heate.

O who can lead then a more happie life,
Than he, that with cleane minde and heart sincere,
No greedy riches knowes nor bloudie strife,
No deadly fight of warlick fleete doth feare,
125   Ne runs in perill of foes cruell knife,
That in the sacred temples he may reare
A trophee of his glittering spoyles and treasure,
Or may abound in riches aboue measure.

Of him his God is worshipt with his sythe,
And not with skill of craftsman polished: 130
He ioyes in groues, and makes himselfe full blythe,
With sundrie flowers in wilde fieldes gathered;
Ne frankincens he from *Panchæa* buyth,
Sweete quiet harbours in his harmeles head,
And perfect pleasure buildes her ioyous bowre,   135
Free from sad cares, that rich mens hearts deuowre.

This all his care, this all his whole indeuour,
To this his minde and senses he doth bend,
How he may flow in quiets matchles treasour,
Content with any food that God doth send;   140
And how his limbs, resolu'd through idle leisour,
Vnto sweete sleepe he may securely lend,
In some coole shadow from the scorching heat,
The whiles his flock their chawed cuds do eate.

O flocks, O Faunes, and O ye pleasaunt springs   145
Of *Tempe*, where the countrey Nymphs are rife,
Through whose not costly care each shepheard sings
As merrie notes vpon his rusticke Fife,
As that *Ascræan* bard, whose fame now rings
Through the wide world, and leads as ioyfull life;   150
Free from all troubles and from worldly toyle,
In which fond men doe all their dayes turmoyle.

In such delights whilst thus his carelesse time
This shepheard driues, vpleaning on his batt,
And on shrill reedes chaunting his rustick rime,   155
Hyperion throwing foorth his beames full hott,
Into the highest top of heauen gan clime,
And the world parting by an equall lott,
Did shed his whirling flames on either side,
As the great *Ocean* doth himselfe diuide.   160

Then gan the shepheard gather into one
His stragling Goates, and draue them to a foord,
Whose cærule streame, rombling in Pible stone,
Crept vnder mosse as greene as any goord.
165   Now had the Sun halfe heauen ouergone,
When he his heard back from that water foord,
Draue from the force of *Phœbus* boyling ray,
Into thick shadowes, there themselues to lay.

Soone as he them plac'd in thy sacred wood
170   (O *Delian* Goddesse) saw, to which of yore
Came the bad daughter of old *Cadmus* brood,
Cruell *Agaue*, flying vengeance sore
Of king *Nictileus* for the guiltie blood,
Which she with cursed hands had shed before;
175   There she halfe frantick hauing slaine her sonne,
Did shrowd her selfe like punishment to shonne.

Here also playing on the grassy greene,
Woodgods, and Satyres, and swift Dryades,
With many Fairies oft were dauncing seene.
180   Not so much did Dan *Orpheus* represse,
The streames of *Hebrus* with his songs I weene,
As that faire troupe of woodie Goddesses
Staied thee, (O *Peneus*) powring foorth to thee,
From cheerefull lookes great mirth and gladsome glee.

185   The verie nature of the place, resounding
With gentle murmure of the breathing ayre,
A pleasant bowre with all delight abounding
In the fresh shadowe did for them prepayre,
To rest their limbs with wearines redounding.
190   For first the high Palme trees with braunches faire,
Out of the lowly vallies did arise,
And high shoote vp their heads into the skyes.

And them amongst the wicked Lotos grew,
Wicked, for holding guilefully away
Vlysses men, whom rapt with sweetenes new,   195
Taking to hoste, it quite from him did stay,
And eke those trees, in whose transformed hew
The Sunnes sad daughters waylde the rash decay
Of *Phaeton*, whose limbs with lightening rent,
They gathering vp, with sweete teares did lament.   200

And that same tree, in which *Demophoon*,
By his disloyalty lamented sore,
Eternall hurte left vnto many one:
Whom als accompanied the Oke, of yore
Through fatall charmes transformd to such an one: 205
The Oke, whose Acornes were our foode, before
That *Ceres* seede of mortall men were knowne,
Which first *Triptoleme* taught how to be sowne.

Here also grew the rougher rinded Pine,
The great *Argoan* ships braue ornament   210
Whom golden Fleece did make an heauenly signe;
Which coueting, with his high tops extent,
To make the mountaines touch the starres diuine,
Decks all the forrest with embellishment,
And the blacke Holme that loues the watrie vale,   215
And the sweete Cypresse signe of deadly bale.

Emongst the rest the clambring Yuie grew,
Knitting his wanton armes with grasping hold,
Least that the Poplar happely should rew
Her brothers strokes, whose boughes she doth enfold   220
With her lythe twigs, till they the top survew,
And paint with pallid greene her buds of gold.
Next did the Myrtle tree to her approach,
Not yet vnmindfull of her olde reproach.

225   But the small Birds in their wide boughs embowring,
Chaunted their sundrie tunes with sweete consent,
And vnder them a siluer Spring forth powring
His trickling streames, a gentle murmure sent;
Thereto the frogs, bred in the slimie scowring
230   Of the moist moores, their iarring voyces bent;
And shrill grashoppers chirped them around:
All which the ayrie Echo did resound.

In this so pleasant place this Shepheards flocke
Lay euerie where, their wearie limbs to rest,
235   On euerie bush, and euerie hollow rocke
Where breathe on them the whistling wind mote best;
The whiles the Shepheard self tending his stocke,
Sate by the fountaine side, in shade to rest,
Where gentle slumbring sleep oppressed him,
240   Displaid on ground, and seized euerie lim.

Of trecherie or traines nought tooke he keep,
But looslie on the grassie greene dispredd,
His dearest life did trust to careles sleep;
Which weighing down his drouping drowsie hedd,
245   In quiet rest his molten heart did steep,
Deuoid of care, and feare of all falshedd:
Had not inconstant fortune, bent to ill,
Bid strange mischance his quietnes to spill.

For at his wonted time in that same place
250   An huge great Serpent all with speckles pide,
To drench himselfe in moorish slime did trace,
There from the boyling heate himselfe to hide:
He passing by with rolling wreathed pace,
With brandisht tongue the emptie aire did gride,
255   And wrapt his scalie boughts with fell despight,
That all things seem'd appalled at his sight.

Now more and more hauing himselfe enrolde,
His glittering breast he lifteth vp on hie,
And with proud vaunt his head aloft doth holde;
His creste aboue spotted with purple die,   260
On euerie side did shine like scalie golde,
And his bright eyes glauncing full dreadfullie,
Did seeme to flame out flakes of flashing fyre,
And with sterne lookes to threaten kindled yre.

Thus wise long time he did himselfe dispace   265
There round about, when as at last he spide
Lying along before him in that place,
That flocks grand Captaine, and most trustie guide:
Eftsoones more fierce in visage, and in pace,
Throwing his firie eyes on euerie side,   270
He commeth on, and all things in his way
Full stearnly rends, that might his passage stay.

Much he disdaines, that anie one should dare
To come vnto his haunt; for which intent
He inly burns, and gins straight to prepare   275
The weapons, which Nature to him hath lent;
Fellie he hisseth, and doth fiercely stare,
And hath his iawes with angrie spirits rent,
That all his tract with bloudie drops is stained,
And all his foldes are now in length outstrained.   280

Whom thus at point prepared, to preuent,
A litle ncoursling of the humid ayre,
A Gnat vnto the sleepie Shepheard went,
And marking where his ey-lids twinckling rare,
Shewd the two pearles, which sight vnto him lent,   285
Through their thin couerings appearing fayre,
His little needle there infixing deep,
Warnd him awake, from death himselfe to keep.

Wherewith enrag'd, he fiercely gan vpstart,
290   And with his hand him rashly bruzing, slewe
As in auengement of his heedles smart,
That streight the spirite out of his senses flew,
And life out of his members did depart:
When suddenly casting aside his vew,
295   He spide his foe with felonous intent,
And feruent eyes to his destruction bent.

All suddenly dismaid, and hartles quight,
He fled abacke, and catching hastie holde
Of a yong alder hard beside him pight,
300   It rent, and streight about him gan beholde,
What God or Fortune would assist his might.
But whether God or Fortune made him bold
Its hard to read: yet hardie will he had
To ouercome, that made him lesse adrad.

305   The scalie backe of that most hideous snake
Enwrapped round, oft faining to retire,
And oft him to assaile, he fiercely strake
Whereas his temples did his creast-front tyre;
And for he was but slowe, did slowth off shake,
310   And gazing ghastly on (for feare and yre
Had blent so much his sense, that lesse he feard;)
Yet when he saw him slaine, himselfe he cheard.

By this the night forth from the darksome bowre
Of *Herebus* her teemed steedes gan call,
315   And laesie *Vesper* in his timely howre
From golden *Oeta* gan proceede withall;
Whenas the Shepheard after this sharpe stowre,
Seing the doubled shadowes low to fall,
Gathering his straying flocke, does homeward fare,
320   And vnto rest his wearie ioynts prepare.

Into whose sense so soone as lighter sleepe
Was entered, and now loosing euerie lim,
Sweete slumbring deaw in carelesnesse did steepe,
The Image of that Gnat appeard to him,
And in sad tearmes gan sorrowfully weepe,   325
With greislie countenaunce and visage grim,
Wailing the wrong which he had done of late,
In steed of good hastning his cruell fate.

Said he, what haue I wretch deseru'd, that thus
Into this bitter bale I am outcast,   330
Whilest that thy life more deare and precious
Was than mine owne, so long as it did last?
I now in lieu of paines so gracious,
Am tost in th'ayre with euerie windie blast:
Thou safe deliuered from sad decay,   335
Thy careles limbs in loose sleep dost display.

So liuest thou, but my poore wretched ghost
Is forst to ferrie ouer *Lethes* Riuer,
And spoyld of *Charon* too and fro am tost.
Seest thou, how all places quake and quiuer   340
Lightned with deadly lamps on euerie post?
Tisiphone each where doth shake and shiuer
Her flaming fire brond, encountring me,
Whose lockes vncombed cruell adders be.

And *Cerberus*, whose many mouthes doo bay,   345
And barke out flames, as if on fire he fed;
Adowne whose necke in terrible array,
Ten thousand snakes cralling about his hed
Doo hang in heapes, that horribly affray,
And bloodie eyes doo glister firie red;   350
He oftentimes me dreadfullie doth threaten,
With painfull torments to be sorely beaten.

Ay me, that thankes so much should faile of meed,
For that I thee restor'd to life againe,
Euen from the doore of death and deadlie dreed.
Where then is now the guerdon of my paine?
Where the reward of my so piteous deed?
The praise of pitie vanisht is in vaine,
And th'antique faith of Iustice long agone
Out of the land is fled away and gone.

I saw anothers fate approaching fast,
And left mine owne his safetie to tender;
Into the same mishap I now am cast,
And shun'd destruction doth destruction render:
Not vnto him that neuer hath trespast,
But punishment is due to the offender.
Yet let destruction be the punishment,
So long as thankfull will may it relent.

I carried am into waste wildernesse,
Waste wildernes, amongst *Cymerian* shades,
Where endles paines and hideous heauinesse
Is round about me heapt in darksome glades.
For there huge *Othos* sits in sad distresse,
Fast bound with serpents that him oft inuades;
Far of beholding *Ephialtes* tide,
Which once assai'd to burne this world so wide.

And there is mournfull *Tityus* mindefull yet
Of thy displeasure, O *Latona* faire;
Displeasure too implacable was it,
That made him meat for wild foules of the ayre:
Much do I feare among such fiends to sit;
Much do I feare back to them to repayre,
To the black shadowes of the *Stygian* shore,
Where wretched ghosts sit wailing euermore.

There next the vtmost brinck doth he abide,   385
That did the bankets of the Gods bewray,
Whose throat through thirst to nought nigh being dride
His sense to seeke for ease turnes euery way:
And he that in auengement of his pride,
For scorning to the sacred Gods to pray,   390
Against a mountaine rolls a mightie stone,
Calling in vaine for rest, and can haue none.

Go ye with them, go cursed damosells,
Whose bridale torches foule *Erynnis* tynde,
And *Hymen* at your Spousalls sad, foretells   395
Tydings of death and massacre vnkinde:
With them that cruell *Colchid* mother dwells,
The which conceiu'd in her reuengefull minde,
With bitter woundes her owne deere babes to slay,
And murdred troupes vpon great heapes to lay.   400

There also those two *Pandionian* maides,
Calling on *Itis*, *Itis* euermore,
Whom wretched boy they slew with guiltie blades;
For whome the *Thracian* king lamenting sore,
Turn'd to a Lapwing, fowlie them vpbraydes,   405
And fluttering round about them still does sore;
There now they all eternally complaine
Of others wrong, and suffer endles paine.

But the two brethren borne of *Cadmus* blood,
Whilst each does for the Soueraignty contend,   410
Blinde through ambition, and with vengeance wood
Each doth against the others bodie bend
His cursed steele, of neither well withstood,
And with wide wounds their carcases doth rend;
That yet they both doe mortall foes remaine,   415
Sith each with brothers bloudie hand was slaine.

Ah (waladay) there is no end of paine,
Nor chaunge of labour may intreated bee:
Yet I beyond all these am carried faine,
420   Where other powers farre different I see,
And must passe ouer to th'*Elisian* plaine:
There grim *Persephone* encountring mee,
Doth vrge her fellow Furies earnestlie,
With their bright firebronds me to terrifie.

425   There chast *Alceste* liues inuiolate,
Free from all care, for that her husbands daies
She did prolong by changing fate for fate,
Lo there liues also the immortall praise
Of womankinde, most faithfull to her mate,
430   *Penelope:* and from her farre awayes
A rulesse rout of yongmen, which her woo'd
All slaine with darts, lie wallowed in their blood.

And sad *Eurydice* thence now no more
Must turne to life, but there detained bee,
435   For looking back, being forbid before:
Yet was the guilt thereof, *Orpheus*, in thee.
Bold sure he was, and worthie spirite bore,
That durst those lowest shadowes goe to see,
And could beleeue that anie thing could please
440   Fell *Cerberus*, or Stygian powres appease.

Ne feard the burning waues of *Phlegeton*,
Nor those same mournfull kingdomes, compassed
With rustie horrour and fowle fashion,
And deep digd vawtes, and Tartar couered
445   With bloodie night, and darke confusion,
And iudgement seates, whose Iudge is deadlie dred,
A iudge, that after death doth punish sore
The faults, which life hath trespassed before.

But valiant fortune made *Dan Orpheus* bolde:
For the swift running riuers still did stand,   450
And the wilde beasts their furie did withhold,
To follow *Orpheus* musicke through the land:
And th'Okes deep grounded in the earthly molde
Did moue, as if they could him vnderstand;
And the shrill woods, which were of sense bereau'd,   455
Through their hard barke his siluer sound receau'd.

And eke the Moone her hastie steedes did stay,
Drawing in teemes along the starrie skie,
And didst (O monthly Virgin) thou delay
Thy nightly course, to heare his melodie?   460
The same was able with like louely lay
The Queene of hell to moue as easily,
To yeeld *Eurydice* vnto her fere,
Backe to be borne, though it vnlawfull were.

She (Ladie) hauing well before approoued,   465
The feends to be too cruell and seuere,
Obseru'd th'appointed way, as her behooued,
Ne euer did her ey-sight turne arere,
Ne euer spake, ne cause of speaking mooued:
But cruell *Orpheus*, thou much crueller,   470
Seeking to kisse her, brok'st the Gods decree,
And thereby mad'st her euer damn'd to be.

Ah but sweete loue of pardon worthie is,
And doth deserue to haue small faults remitted;
If Hell at least things lightly done amis   475
Knew how to pardon, when ought is omitted:
Yet are ye both receiued into blis,
And to the seates of happie soules admitted.
And you, beside the honourable band
Of great Heroës doo in order stand.   480

There be the two stout sonnes of *Aeacus*,
Fierce *Peleus*, and the hardie *Telamon*,
Both seeming now full glad and ioyeous
Through their Syres dreadfull iurisdiction,
485 Being the Iudge of all that horrid hous:
And both of them by strange occasion,
Renown'd in choyce of happie marriage
Through *Venus* grace, and vertues cariage.

For th'one was rauisht of his owne bondmaide,
490 The faire *Hesione* captiu'd from *Troy:*
But th'other was with *Thetis* loue assaid,
Great *Nereus* his daughter, and his ioy.
On this side them there is a yongman layd,
Their match in glorie, mightie, fierce and coy;
495 That from th'*Argolick* ships, with furious yre,
Bett back the furie of the Troian fyre.

O who would not recount the strong diuorces
Of that great warre, which Troianes oft behelde,
And oft beheld the warlike Greekish forces,
500 When *Teucrian* soyle with bloodie riuers swelde,
And wide *Sigæan* shores were spred with corses,
And *Simois* and *Xanthus* blood outwelde,
Whilst *Hector* raged with outragious minde,
Flames, weapons, wounds in *Greeks* fleete to haue
      tynde.

505 For *Ida* selfe, in ayde of that fierce fight,
Out of her mountaines ministred supplies,
And like a kindly nourse, did yeeld (for spight)
Store of firebronds out of her nourseries,
Vnto her foster children, that they might
510 Inflame the Nauie of their enemies,
And all the *Rhetæan* shore to ashes turne,
Where lay the ships, which they did seeke to burne.

Gainst which the noble sonne of *Telamon*
Opposd' himselfe, and thwarting his huge shield,
Them battell bad, gainst whom appeard anon   515
Hector, the glorie of the *Troian* field:
Both fierce and furious in contention
Encountred, that their mightie strokes so shrild,
As the great clap of thunder, which doth ryue
The ratling heauens, and cloudes asunder dryue.   520

So th'one with fire and weapons did contend
To cut the ships, from turning home againe
To *Argos*, th'other stroue for to defend
The force of *Vulcane* with his might and maine.
Thus th'one *Aeacide* did his fame extend: 525
But th'other ioy'd, that on the *Phrygian* playne
Hauing the blood of vanquisht *Hector* shedd,
He compast *Troy* thrice with his bodie dedd.

Againe great dole on either partie grewe,
That him to death vnfaithfull *Paris* sent,   530
And also him that false *Vlysses* slewe,
Drawne into danger through close ambushment:
Therefore from him *Laërtes* sonne his vewe
Doth turne aside, and boasts his good euent
In working of *Strymonian Rhæsus* fall,   535
And efte in *Dolons* slye surprysall.

Againe the dreadfull *Cycones* him dismay,
And blacke *Læstrigones*, a people stout:
Then greedie *Scilla*, vnder whom there bay
Manie great bandogs, which her gird about: 540
Then doo the *Aetnean* Cyclops him affray,
And deep *Charybdis* gulphing in and out:
Lastly the squalid lakes of *Tartarie*,
And griesly Feends of hell him terrifie.

545   There also goodly *Agamemnon* bosts,
    The glorie of the stock of *Tantalus*,
    And famous light of all the Greekish hosts,
    Vnder whose conduct most victorious,
    The *Dorick* flames consum'd the *Iliack* posts.
550   Ah but the *Greekes* themselues more dolorous,
    To thee, O *Troy*, paid penaunce for thy fall,
    In th'*Hellespont* being nigh drowned all.

    Well may appeare by proofe of their mischaunce,
    The chaungfull turning of mens slipperie state,
555   That none, whom fortune freely doth aduaunce,
    Himselfe therefore to heauen should eleuate:
    For loftie type of honour through the glaunce
    Of enuies dart, is downe in dust prostrate;
    And all that vaunts in worldly vanitie,
560   Shall fall through fortunes mutabilitie.

    Th'*Argolicke* power returning home againe,
    Enricht with spoyles of th'*Ericthonian* towre,
    Did happie winde and weather entertaine,
    And with good speed the fomie billowes scowre:
565   No signe of storme, no feare of future paine,
    Which soone ensued them with heauie stowre.
    Nereïs to the Seas a token gaue,
    The whiles their crooked keeles the surges claue.

    Suddenly, whether through the Gods decree,
570   Or haplesse rising of some froward starre,
    The heauens on euerie side enclowded bee:
    Black stormes and fogs are blowen vp from farre,
    That now the Pylote can no loadstarre see,
    But skies and seas doo make most dreadfull warre;
575   The billowes striuing to the heauens to reach,
    And th'heauens striuing them for to impeach.

And in auengement of their bold attempt,
Both Sun and starres and all the heauenly powres
Conspire in one to wreake their rash contempt,
And downe on them to fall from highest towres: 580
The skie in pieces seeming to be rent,
Throwes lightning forth, and haile, and harmful showres
That death on euerie side to them appeares
In thousand formes, to worke more ghastly feares.

Some in the greedie flouds are sunke and drent,   585
Some on the rocks of *Caphareus* are throwne;
Some on th'*Euboick* Cliffs in pieces rent;
Some scattred on the *Hercæan* shores vnknowne;
And manie lost, of whom no moniment
Remaines, nor memorie is to be showne: 590
Whilst all the purchase of the *Phrigian* pray
Tost on salt billowes, round about doth stray.

Here manie other like Heroës bee,
Equall in honour to the former crue,
Whom ye in goodly seates may placed see,   595
Descended all from *Rome* by linage due,
From *Rome*, that holds the world in souereigntie,
And doth all Nations vnto her subdue:
Here *Fabij* and *Decij* doo dwell,
Horatij that in vertue did excell.   600

And here the antique fame of stout *Camill*
Doth euer liue, and constant *Curtius*,
Who stifly bent his vowed life to spill
For Countreyes health, a gulph most hideous
Amidst the Towne with his owne corps did fill,   605
T'appease the powers; and prudent *Mutius*,
Who in his flesh endur'd the scorching flame,
To daunt his foe by ensample of the same.

And here wise *Curius*, companion
610 Of noble vertues, liues in endles rest;
And stout *Flaminius*, whose deuotion
Taught him the fires scorn'd furie to detest;
And here the praise of either *Scipion*
Abides in highest place aboue the best,
615 To whom the ruin'd walls of *Carthage* vow'd,
Trembling their forces, sound their praises lowd.

Liue they for euer through their lasting praise:
But I poore wretch am forced to retourne
To the sad lakes, that *Phœbus* sunnie rayes
620 Doo neuer see, where soules doo alwaies mourne,
And by the wayling shores to waste my dayes,
Where *Phlegeton* with quenchles flames doth burne;
By which iust *Minos* righteous soules doth seuer
From wicked ones, to liue in blisse for euer.

625 Me therefore thus the cruell fiends of hell
Girt with long snakes, and thousand yron chaynes,
Through doome of that their cruell Iudge, compell
With bitter torture and impatient paines,
Cause of my death, and iust complaint to tell.
630 For thou art he, whom my poore ghost complaines
To be the author of her ill vnwares,
That careles hear'st my intollerable cares.

Them therefore as bequeathing to the winde,
I now depart, returning to thee neuer,
635 And leaue this lamentable plaint behinde.
But doo thou haunt the soft downe rolling riuer,
And wilde greene woods, and fruitful pastures minde,
And let the flitting aire my vaine words seuer.
Thus hauing said, he heauily departed
640 With piteous crie, that anie would haue smarted.

Now, when the sloathfull fit of lifes sweete rest
Had left the heauie Shepheard, wondrous cares
His inly grieued minde full sore opprest;
That balefull sorrow he no longer beares,
For that Gnats death, which deeply was imprest: 645
But bends what euer power his aged yeares
Him lent, yet being such, as through their might
He lately slue his dreadfull foe in fight.

By that same Riuer lurking vnder greene,
Eftsoones he gins to fashion forth a place,   650
And squaring it in compasse well beseene,
There plotteth out a tombe by measured space:
His yron headed spade tho making cleene,
To dig vp sods out of the flowrie grasse,
His worke he shortly to good purpose brought,   655
Like as he had conceiu'd it in his thought.

An heape of earth he hoorded vp on hie,
Enclosing it with banks on euerie side,
And thereupon did raise full busily
A little mount, of greene turffs edifide;   660
And on the top of all, that passers by
Might it behold, the toomb he did prouide
Of smoothest marble stone in order set,
That neuer might his luckie scape forget.

And round about he taught sweete flowres to growe,   665
The Rose engrained in pure scarlet die,
The Lilly fresh, and Violet belowe,
The Marigolde, and cherefull Rosemarie,
The *Spartan* Mirtle, whence sweet gumb does flowe,
The purple Hyacinthe, and fresh Costmarie,   670
And Saffron sought for in *Cilician* soyle,
And Lawrell th'ornament of *Phœbus* toyle.

Fresh *Rhododaphne*, and the *Sabine* flowre
Matching the wealth of th'auncient Frankincence,
675 And pallid Yuie building his owne bowre,
And Box yet mindfull of his olde offence,
Red *Amaranthus*, lucklesse Paramour,
Oxeye still greene, and bitter Patience;
Ne wants there pale *Narcisse*, that in a well
680 Seeing his beautie, in loue with it fell,

And whatsoeuer other flowre of worth,
And whatso other hearb of louely hew
The ioyous Spring out of the ground brings forth,
To cloath her selfe in colours fresh and new;
685 He planted there, and reard a mount of earth,
In whose high front was writ as doth ensue.

To thee, small Gnat, in lieu of his life saued,
    The Shepheard hath thy deaths record engraued.

FINIS.

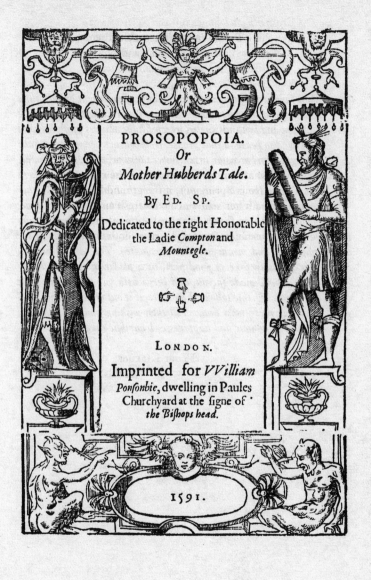

PROSOPOPOIA.
Or
Mother Hubberds Tale.

By Ed. Sp.

Dedicated to the right Honorable
the Ladie *Compton* and
Mountegle.

LONDON.

Imprinted for *VVilliam*
Ponsonbie, dwelling in Paules
Churchyard at the signe of
the Bishops head.

1591.

To the right Honourable, the
Ladie *Compton* and
Mountegle.

Most faire and vertuous Ladie; hauing often sought opportunitie
by some good meanes to make knowen to your Ladiship, the humble
affection and faithfull duetie, which I haue alwaies professed, and
am bound to beare to that House, from whence yee spring, I haue
5 *at length found occasion to remember the same, by making a simple*
present to you of these my idle labours; which hauing long sithens
composed in the raw conceipt of my youth, I lately amongst other
papers lighted vpon, and was by others, which liked the same,
mooued to set them foorth. Simple is the deuice, and the composition
10 *meane, yet carrieth some delight, euen the rather because of the*
simplicitie and meannesse thus personated. The same I beseech
your Ladiship take in good part, as a pledge of that profession
which I haue made to you, and keepe with you vntill with some
other more worthie labour, I do redeeme it out of your hands, and
15 *discharge my vtmost dutie. Till then wishing your Ladiship all*
increase of honour and happinesse, I humblie take leaue.

Your La: euer
humbly;
Ed. Sp.

Prosopopoia: or
Mother Hubberds Tale.

It was the month, in which the righteous Maide,
That for disdaine of sinfull worlds vpbraide,
Fled back to heauen, whence she was first conceiued,
Into her siluer bowre the Sunne receiued;
And the hot *Syrian* Dog on him awayting,   5
After the chafed Lyons cruell bayting,
Corrupted had th'ayre with his noysome breath,
And powr'd on th'earth plague, pestilence, and death.
Emongst the rest a wicked maladie
Raign'd emongst men, that manie did to die,   10
Depriu'd of sense and ordinarie reason;
That it to Leaches seemed strange and geason.
My fortune was mongst manie others moe,
To be partaker of their common woe;
And my weake bodie set on fire with griefe,   15
Was rob'd of rest, and naturall reliefe.
In this ill plight, there came to visite mee
Some friends, who sorie my sad case to see,
Began to comfort me in chearfull wise,
And meanes of gladsome solace to deuise.   20
But seeing kindly sleep refuse to doe
His office, and my feeble eyes forgoe,
They sought my troubled sense how to deceaue
With talke, that might vnquiet fancies reaue;
And sitting all in seates about me round,   25
With pleasant tales (fit for that idle stound)
They cast in course to waste the wearie howres:
Some tolde of Ladies, and their Paramoures;
Some of braue Knights, and their renowned Squires;
Some of the Faeries and their strange attires;   30
And some of Giaunts hard to be beleeued,
That the delight thereof me much releeued.
Amongst the rest a good old woman was,
Hight Mother *Hubberd*, who did farre surpas

35   The rest in honest mirth, that seem'd her well:
      She when her turne was come her tale to tell,
      Tolde of a strange aduenture, that betided
      Betwixt the Foxe and th'Ape by him misguided;
      The which for that my sense it greatly pleased,
40   All were my spirite heauie and diseased,
      Ile write in termes, as she the same did say,
      So well as I her words remember may.
      No Muses aide me needes heretoo to call;
      Base is the style, and matter meane withall.
45   ¶ Whilome (said she) before the world was ciuill,
      The Foxe and th'Ape disliking of their euill
      And hard estate, determined to seeke
      Their fortunes farre abroad, lyeke with his lyeke:
      For both were craftie and vnhappie witted;
50   Two fellowes might no where be better fitted.
      The Foxe, that first this cause of griefe did finde,
      Gan first thus plaine his case with words vnkinde.
      Neighbour Ape, and my Gossip eke beside,
      (Both two sure bands in friendship to be tide,)
55   To whom may I more trustely complaine
      The euill plight, that doth me sore constraine,
      And hope thereof to finde due remedie?
      Heare then my paine and inward agonie.
      Thus manie yeares I now haue spent and worne,
60   In meane regard, and basest fortunes scorne,
      Dooing my Countrey seruice as I might,
      No lesse I dare saie than the prowdest wight;
      And still I hoped to be vp aduaunced,
      For my good parts; but still it hath mischaunced.
65   Now therefore that no lenger hope I see,
      But froward fortune still to follow mee,
      And losels lifted vp on high, where I did looke,
      I meane to turne the next leafe of the booke.
      Yet ere that anie way I doo betake,
70   I meane my Gossip priuie first to make.
      Ah my deare Gossip, (answer'd then the Ape,)
      Deeply doo your sad words my wits awhape,

Both for because your griefe doth great appeare,
And eke because my selfe am touched neare:
For I likewise haue wasted much good time,   75
Still wayting to preferment vp to clime,
Whilest others alwayes haue before me stept,
And from my beard the fat away haue swept;
That now vnto despaire I gin to growe
And meane for better winde about to throwe.   80
Therefore to me, my trustie friend, aread
Thy councell: two is better than one head.
Certes (said he) I meane me to disguize
In some straunge habit, after vncouth wize,
Or like a Pilgrime, or a Lymiter,   85
Or like a *Gipsen*, or a Iuggeler,
And so to wander to the worlds ende,
To seeke my fortune, where I may it mend:
For worse than that I haue, I cannot meete.
Wide is the world I wote, and euerie streete   90
Is full of fortunes, and aduentures straunge,
Continuallie subiect vnto chaunge.
Say my faire brother now, if this deuice
Doth like you, or may you to like entice.
Surely (said th'Ape) it likes me wondrous well;   95
And would ye not poore fellowship expell,
My selfe would offer you t'accompanie
In this aduentures chauncefull ieopardie.
For to wexe olde at home in idlenesse,
Is disaduentrous, and quite fortunelesse: 100
Abroad where change is, good may gotten bee.
The Foxe was glad, and quickly did agree:
So both resolu'd, the morrow next ensuing,
So soone as day appeard to peoples vewing,
On their intended iourney to proceede;   105
And ouer night, whatso theretoo did neede,
Each did prepare, in readines to bee.
The morrow next, so soone as one might see
Light out of heauens windowes forth to looke,
Both their habiliments vnto them tooke,   110

And put themselues (a Gods name) on their way.
Whenas the Ape beginning well to wey
This hard aduenture, thus began t'aduise;
Now read Sir Reynold, as ye be right wise,
What course ye weene is best for vs to take,   115
That for our selues we may a liuing make.
Whether shall we professe some trade or skill?
Or shall we varie our deuice at will,
Euen as new occasion appeares?
Or shall we tie our selues for certaine yeares   120
To anie seruice, or to anie place?
For it behoues ere that into the race
We enter, to resolue first herevpon.
Now surely brother (said the Foxe anon)
Ye haue this matter motioned in season: 125
For euerie thing that is begun with reason
Will come by readie meanes vnto his end;
But things miscounselled must needs miswend.
Thus therefore I aduize vpon the case,
That not to anie certaine trade or place,   130
Nor anie man we should our selues applie;
For why should he that is at libertie
Make himselfe bond? sith then we are free borne,
Let vs all seruile base subiection scorne;
And as we bee sonnes of the world so wide,   135
Let vs our fathers heritage diuide,
And chalenge to our selues our portions dew
Of all the patrimonie, which a few
Now hold in hugger mugger in their hand,
And all the rest doo rob of good and land.   140
For now a few haue all and all haue nought,
Yet all be brethren ylike dearly bought:
There is no right in this partition,
Ne was it so by institution
Ordained first, ne by the law of Nature,   145
But that she gaue like blessing to each creture
As well of worldly liuelode as of life,
That there might be no difference nor strife,

Nor ought cald mine or thine: thrice happie then
Was the condition of mortall men.   150
That was the golden age of *Saturne* old,
But this might better be the world of gold:
For without golde now nothing wilbe got.
Therefore (if please you) this shalbe our plot,
We will not be of anie occupation,   155
Let such vile vassalls borne to base vocation
Drudge in the world, and for their liuing droyle
Which haue no wit to liue withouten toyle.
But we will walke about the world at pleasure
Like two free men, and make our ease a treasure.   160
Free men some beggers call, but they be free,
And they which call them so more beggers bee:
For they doo swinke and sweate to feed the other,
Who liue like Lords of that which they doo gather,
And yet doo neuer thanke them for the same,   165
But as their due by Nature doo it clame.
Such will we fashion both our selues to bee,
Lords of the world, and so will wander free
Where so vs listeth, vncontrol'd of anie.
Hard is our hap, if we (emongst so manie)   170
Light not on some that may our state amend;
Sildome but some good commeth ere the end.
Well seemd the Ape to like this ordinaunce:
Yet well considering of the circumstaunce,
As pausing in great doubt, awhile he staid,   175
And afterwards with graue aduizement said;
I cannot, my lief brother, like but well
The purpose of the complot which ye tell:
For well I wot (compar'd to all the rest
Of each degree) that Beggers life is best: 180
And they that thinke themselues the best of all,
Oft-times to begging are content to fall.
But this I wot withall that we shall ronne
Into great daunger like to bee vndonne,
Thus wildly to wander in the worlds eye,   185
Without pasport or good warrantie,

For feare least we like rogues should be reputed,
And for eare marked beasts abroad be bruted:
Therefore I read, that we our counsells call,
190   How to preuent this mischiefe ere it fall,
And how we may with most securitie,
Beg amongst those that beggers doo defie.
Right well deere Gossip ye aduized haue,
(Said then the Foxe) but I this doubt will saue:
195   For ere we farther passe, I will deuise
A pasport for vs both in fittest wize,
And by the names of Souldiers vs protect;
That now is thought a ciuile begging sect.
Be you the Souldier, for you likest are
200   For manly semblance, and small skill in warre:
I will but wayte on you, and as occasion
Falls out, my selfe fit for the same will fashion.
The Pasport ended, both they forward went,
The Ape clad Souldierlike, fit for th'intent,
205   In a blew iacket with a crosse of redd
And manie slits, as if that he had shedd
Much blood throgh many wounds therein receaued,
Which had the vse of his right arme bereaued;
Vpon his head an old Scotch cap he wore,
210   With a plume feather all to peeces tore:
His breeches were made after the new cut,
Al Portugese, loose like an emptie gut;
And his hose broken high aboue the heeling,
And his shooes beaten out with traueling.
215   But neither sword nor dagger he did beare,
Seemes that no foes reuengement he did feare;
In stead of them a handsome bat he held,
On which he leaned, as one farre in elde.
Shame light on him, that through so false illusion,
220   Doth turne the name of Souldiers to abusion,
And that, which is the noblest mysterie,
Brings to reproach and common infamie.
Long they thus trauailed, yet neuer met
Aduenture, which might them a working set:

Yet manie waies they sought, and manie tryed;   225
Yet for their purposes none fit espyed.
At last they chaunst to meete vpon the way
A simple husbandman in garments gray;
Yet though his vesture were but meane and bace,
A good yeoman he was of honest place,   230
And more for thrift did care than for gay clothing:
Gay without good, is good hearts greatest loathing.
The Foxe him spying, bad the Ape him dight
To play his part, for loe he was in sight,
That (if he er'd not) should them entertaine,   235
And yeeld them timely profite for their paine.
Eftsoones the Ape himselfe gan vp to reare,
And on his shoulders high his bat to beare,
As if good seruice he were fit to doo;
But little thrift for him he did it too: 240
And stoutly forward he his steps did straine,
That like a handsome swaine it him became:
When as they nigh approached, that good man
Seeing them wander loosly, first began
T'enquire of custome, what and whence they were?   245
To whom the Ape, I am a Souldiere,
That late in warres haue spent my deerest blood,
And in long seruice lost both limbs and good,
And now constrain'd that trade to ouergiue,
I driuen am to seeke some meanes to liue: 250
Which might it you in pitie please t'afford,
I would be readie both in deed and word,
To doo you faithfull seruice all my dayes.
This yron world (that same he weeping sayes)
Brings downe the stowtest hearts to lowest state: 255
For miserie doth brauest mindes abate,
And make them seeke for that they wont to scorne,
Of fortune and of hope at once forlorne.
The honest man, that heard him thus complaine,
Was grieu'd, as he had felt part of his paine;   260
And well disposd' him some reliefe to showe,
Askt if in husbandrie he ought did knowe,

To plough, to plant, to reap, to rake, to sowe,
To hedge, to ditch, to thrash, to thetch, to mowe;
265   Or to what labour els he was prepar'd?
For husbands life is labourous and hard.
Whenas the Ape him hard so much to talke
Of labour, that did from his liking balke,
He would haue slipt the coller handsomly,
270   And to him said; good Sir, full glad am I,
To take what paines may anie liuing wight:
But my late maymed limbs lack wonted might
To doo their kindly seruices, as needeth:
Scarce this right hand the mouth with diet feedeth,
275   So that it may no painfull worke endure,
Ne to strong labour can it selfe enure.
But if that anie other place you haue,
Which askes small paines, but thriftines to saue,
Or care to ouerlooke, or trust to gather,
280   Ye may me trust as your owne ghostly father.
With that the husbandman gan him auize
That it for him were fittest exercise
Cattell to keep, or grounds to ouersee;
And asked him, if he could willing bee
285   To keep his sheep, or to attend his swyne,
Or watch his mares, or take his charge of kyne?
Gladly (said he) what euer such like paine
Ye put on me, I will the same sustaine:
But gladliest I of your fleecie sheepe
290   (Might it you please) would take on me the keep.
For ere that vnto armes I me betooke,
Vnto my fathers sheepe I vsde to looke,
That yet the skill thereof I haue not loste:
Thereto right well this Curdog by my coste
295   (Meaning the Foxe) will serue, my sheepe to gather,
And driue to follow after their Belwether.
The Husbandman was meanly well content,
Triall to make of his endeuourment,
And home him leading, lent to him the charge
300   Of all his flocke, with libertie full large,

Giuing accompt of th'annuall increce
Both of their lambes, and of their woolly fleece.
Thus is this Ape become a shepheard swaine
And the false Foxe his dog. (God giue them paine)
For ere the yeare haue halfe his course out-run,   305
And doo returne from whence he first begun,
They shall him make an ill accompt of thrift.
Now whenas Time flying with winges swift,
Expired had the terme, that these two iauels
Should render vp a reckning of their trauels   310
Vnto their master, which it of them sought,
Exceedingly they troubled were in thought,
Ne wist what answere vnto him to frame,
Ne how to scape great punishment, or shame,
For their false treason and vile theeuerie.   315
For not a lambe of all their flockes supply
Had they to shew: but euer as they bred,
They slue them, and vpon their fleshes fed:
For that disguised Dog lou'd blood to spill,
And drew the wicked Shepheard to his will.   320
So twixt them both they not a lambkin left,
And when lambes fail'd, the old sheepes liues they reft;
That how t'acquite themselues vnto their Lord,
They were in doubt, and flatly set abord.
The Foxe then counsel'd th'Ape, for to require   325
Respite till morrow, t'answere his desire:
For times delay new hope of helpe still breeds.
The goodman granted, doubting nought their deeds,
And bad, next day that all should readie be.
But they more subtill meaning had than he: 330
For the next morrowes meed they closely ment,
For feare of afterclaps for to preuent.
And that same euening, when all shrowded were
In careles sleep, they without care or feare,
Cruelly fell vpon their flock in folde,   335
And of them slew at pleasure what they wolde:
Of which whenas they feasted had their fill,
For a full complement of all their ill,

They stole away, and tooke their hastie flight,
340 Carried in clowdes of all-concealing night.
So was the husbandman left to his losse,
And they vnto their fortunes change to tosse.
After which sort they wandered long while,
Abusing manie through their cloaked guile;
345 That at the last they gan to be descryed
Of euerie one, and all their sleights espyed.
So as their begging now them failed quyte;
For none would giue, but all men would them wyte:
Yet would they take no paines to get their liuing,
350 But seeke some other way to gaine by giuing,
Much like to begging but much better named;
For manie beg, which are thereof ashamed.
And now the Foxe had gotten him a gowne,
And th'Ape a cassocke sidelong hanging downe;
355 For they their occupation meant to change,
And now in other state abroad to range:
For since their souldiers pas no better spedd,
They forg'd another, as for Clerkes booke-redd.
Who passing foorth, as their aduentures fell,
360 Through manie haps, which needs not here to tell;
At length chaunst with a formall Priest to meete,
Whom they in ciuill manner first did greete,
And after askt an almes for Gods deare loue.
The man straight way his choler vp did moue,
365 And with reproachfull tearmes gan them reuile,
For following that trade so base and vile;
And askt what license, or what Pas they had?
Ah (said the Ape as sighing wondrous sad)
Its an hard case, when men of good deseruing
370 Must either driuen be perforce to steruing,
Or asked for their pas by euerie squib,
That list at will them to reuile or snib:
And yet (God wote) small oddes I often see
Twixt them that aske, and them that asked bee.
375 Natheles because you shall not vs misdeeme,
But that we are as honest as we seeme,

Yee shall our pasport at your pleasure see,
And then ye will (I hope) well mooued bee.
Which when the Priest beheld, he vew'd it nere,
As if therein some text he studying were,   380
But little els (God wote) could thereof skill:
For read he could not euidence, nor will,
Ne tell a written word, ne write a letter,
Ne make one title worse, ne make one better:
Of such deep learning little had he neede,   385
Ne yet of Latine, ne of Greeke, that breede
Doubts mongst Diuines, and difference of texts,
From whence arise diuersitie of sects,
And hatefull heresies, of God abhor'd:
But this good Sir did follow the plaine word,   390
Ne medled with their controuersies vaine.
All his care was, his seruice well to saine,
And to read Homelies vpon holidayes:
When that was done, he might attend his playes;
An easie life, and fit high God to please.   395
He hauing ouerlookt their pas at ease,
Gan at the length them to rebuke againe,
That no good trade of life did entertaine,
But lost their time in wandring loose abroad,
Seeing the world, in which they bootles boad,   400
Had wayes enough for all therein to liue;
Such grace did God vnto his creatures giue.
Said then the Foxe; who hath the world not tride,
From the right way full eath may wander wide.
We are but Nouices, new come abroad,   405
We haue not yet the tract of anie troad,
Nor on vs taken anie state of life,
But readie are of anie to make preife.
Therefore might please you, which the world haue proued,
Vs to aduise, which forth but lately moued,   410
Of some good course, that we might vndertake;
Ye shall for euer vs your bondmen make.
The Priest gan wexe halfe proud to be so praide,
And thereby willing to affoord them aide;

415 It seemes (said he) right well that ye be Clerks,
Both by your wittie words, and by your werks.
Is not that name enough to make a liuing
To him that hath a whit of Natures giuing?
How manie honest men see ye arize
420 Daylie thereby, and grow to goodly prize?
To Deanes, to Archdeacons, to Commissaries,
To Lords, to Principalls, to Prebendaries;
All iolly Prelates, worthie rule to beare,
Who euer them enuie: yet spite bites neare.
425 Why should ye doubt then, but that ye likewise
Might vnto some of those in time arise?
In the meane time to liue in good estate,
Louing that loue, and hating those that hate;
Being some honest Curate, or some Vicker
430 Content with little in condition sicker.
Ah but (said th'Ape) the charge is wondrous great,
To feed mens soules, and hath an heauie threat.
To feede mens soules (quoth he) is not in man:
For they must feed themselues, doo what we can.
435 We are but charg'd to lay the meate before:
Eate they that list, we need to doo no more.
But God it is that feedes them with his grace,
The bread of life powr'd downe from heauenly place.
Therefore said he, that with the budding rod
440 Did rule the Iewes, *All shalbe taught of God*.
That same hath Iesus Christ now to him raught,
By whom the flock is rightly fed, and taught:
He is the Shepheard, and the Priest is hee;
We but his shepheard swaines ordain'd to bee.
445 Therefore herewith doo not your selfe dismay;
Ne is the paines so great, but beare ye may;
For not so great as it was wont of yore,
It's now a dayes, ne halfe so streight and sore:
They whilome vsed duly euerie day
450 Their seruice and their holie things to say,
At morne and euen, besides their Anthemes sweete,
Their penie Masses, and their Complynes meete,

Their Dirges, their Trentals, and their shrifts,
Their memories, their singings, and their gifts.
Now all those needlesse works are laid away;   455
Now once a weeke vpon the Sabbath day,
It is enough to doo our small deuotion,
And then to follow any merrie motion.
Ne are we tyde to fast, but when we list,
Ne to weare garments base of wollen twist,   460
But with the finest silkes vs to aray,
That before God we may appeare more gay,
Resembling *Aarons* glorie in his place:
For farre vnfit it is, that person bace
Should with vile cloaths approach Gods maiestie,   465
Whom no vncleannes may approachen nie:
Or that all men, which anie master serue,
Good garments for their seruice should deserue;
But he that serues the Lord of hoasts most high,
And that in highest place, t'approach him nigh,   470
And all the peoples prayers to present
Before his throne, as on ambassage sent
Both too and fro, should not deserue to weare
A garment better, than of wooll or heare.
Beside we may haue lying by our sides   475
Our louely Lasses, or bright shining Brides:
We be not tyde to wilfull chastitie,
But haue the Gospell of free libertie.
By that he ended had his ghostly sermon,
The Foxe was well induc'd to be a Parson;   480
And of the Priest eftsoones gan to enquire,
How to a Benefice he might aspire.
Marie there (said the Priest) is arte indeed.
Much good deep learning one thereout may reed,
For that the ground-worke is, and end of all,   485
How to obtaine a Beneficiall.
First therefore, when ye haue in handsome wise
Your selfe attyred, as you can deuise,
Then to some Noble man your selfe applye,
Or other great one in the worldes eye,   490

That hath a zealous disposition
To God, and so to his religion:
There must thou fashion eke a godly zeale,
Such as no carpers may contrayre reueale:
495　For each thing fained, ought more warie bee.
There thou must walke in sober grauitee,
And seeme as Saintlike as Saint *Radegund*:
Fast much, pray oft, looke lowly on the ground,
And vnto euerie one doo curtesie meeke:
500　These lookes (nought saying) doo a benefice seeke,
And be thou sure one not to lacke or long.
But if thee list vnto the Court to throng,
And there to hunt after the hoped pray,
Then must thou thee dispose another way:
505　For there thou needs must learne, to laugh, to lie,
To face, to forge, to scoffe, to companie,
To crouche, to please, to be a beetle stock
Of thy great Masters will, to scorne, or mock:
So maist thou chaunce mock out a Benefice,
510　Vnlesse thou canst one coniure by deuice,
Or cast a figure for a Bishoprick:
And if one could, it were but a schoole-trick.
These be the wayes, by which without reward
Liuings in Court be gotten, though full hard.
515　For nothing there is done without a fee:
The Courtier needes must recompenced bee
With a Beneuolence, or haue in gage
The *Primitias* of your Parsonage:
Scarse can a Bishoprick forpas them by,
520　But that it must be gelt in priuitie.
Doo not thou therefore seeke a liuing there,
But of more priuate persons seeke elswhere,
Whereas thou maist compound a better penie,
Ne let thy learning question'd be of anie.
525　For some good Gentleman that hath the right
Vnto his Church for to present a wight,
Will cope with thee in reasonable wise;
That if the liuing yerely doo arise

To fortie pound, that then his yongest sonne
Shall twentie haue, and twentie thou hast wonne: 530
Thou hast it wonne, for it is of franke gift,
And he will care for all the rest to shift;
Both that the Bishop may admit of thee,
And that therein thou maist maintained bee.
This is the way for one that is vnlern'd   535
Liuing to get, and not to be discern'd.
But they that are great Clerkes, haue nearer wayes,
For learning sake to liuing them to raise:
Yet manie eke of them (God wote) are driuen,
T'accept a Benefice in peeces riuen.   540
How saist thou (friend) haue I not well discourst
Vpon this Common place (though plaine, not wourst)?
Better a short tale, than a bad long shriuing.
Needes anie more to learne to get a liuing?
Now sure and by my hallidome (quoth he)   545
Ye a great master are in your degree:
Great thankes I yeeld you for your discipline,
And doo not doubt, but duly to encline
My wits theretoo, as ye shall shortly heare.
The Priest him wisht good speed, and well to fare.   550
So parted they, as eithers way them led.
But th'Ape and Foxe ere long so well them sped,
Through the Priests holesome counsell lately tought,
And throgh their own faire handling wisely wroght,
That they a Benefice twixt them obtained;   555
And craftie Reynold was a Priest ordained;
And th'Ape his Parish Clarke procur'd to bee.
Then made they reuell route and goodly glee.
But ere long time had passed, they so ill
Did order their affaires, that th'euill will   560
Of all their Parishners they had constraind;
Who to the Ordinarie of them complain'd,
How fowlie they their offices abusd',
And them of crimes and heresies accusd';
That Pursiuants he often for them sent: 565
But they neglected his commaundement.

So long persisted obstinate and bolde,
Till at the length he published to holde
A Visitation, and them cyted thether:
570 Then was high time their wits about to geather;
What did they then, but made a composition
With their next neighbor Priest for light condition,
To whom their liuing they resigned quight
For a few pence, and ran away by night.
575 So passing through the Countrey in disguize,
They fled farre off, where none might them surprize,
And after that long straied here and there,
Through euerie field and forrest farre and nere;
Yet neuer found occasion for their tourne,
580 But almost steru'd, did much lament and mourne.
At last they chaunst to meete vpon the way
The Mule, all deckt in goodly rich aray,
With bells and bosses, that full lowdly rung,
And costly trappings, that to ground downe hung.
585 Lowly they him saluted in meeke wise,
But he through pride and fatnes gan despise
Their meanesse; scarce vouchsafte them to requite.
Whereat the Foxe deep groning in his sprite,
Said, Ah sir Mule, now blessed be the day,
590 That I see you so goodly and so gay
In your attyres, and eke your silken hyde
Fil'd with round flesh, that euerie bone doth hide.
Seemes that in fruitfull pastures ye doo liue,
Or fortune doth you secret fauour giue.
595 Foolish Foxe (said the Mule) thy wretched need
Praiseth the thing that doth thy sorrow breed.
For well I weene, thou canst not but enuie
My wealth, compar'd to thine owne miserie,
That art so leane and meagre waxen late,
600 That scarse thy legs vphold thy feeble gate.
Ay me (said then the Foxe) whom euill hap
Vnworthy in such wretchednes doth wrap,
And makes the scorne of other beasts to bee:
But read (faire Sir, of grace) from whence come yee?

Or what of tidings you abroad doo heare?   605
Newes may perhaps some good vnweeting beare.
From royall Court I lately came (said he)
Where all the brauerie that eye may see,
And all the happinesse that heart desire,
Is to be found; he nothing can admire,   610
That hath not seene that heauens portracture:
But tidings there is none I you assure,
Saue that which common is, and knowne to all,
That Courtiers as the tide doo rise and fall.
But tell vs (said the Ape) we doo you pray,   615
Who now in Court doth beare the greatest sway.
That if such fortune doo to vs befall,
We may seeke fauour of the best of all.
Marie (said he) the highest now in grace,
Be the wilde beasts, that swiftest are in chace;   620
For in their speedie course and nimble flight
The Lyon now doth take the most delight:
But chieflie, ioyes on foote them to beholde,
Enchaste with chaine and circulet of golde:
So wilde a beast so tame ytaught to bee,   625
And buxome to his bands is ioy to see.
So well his golden Circlet him beseemeth:
But his late chayne his Liege vnmeete esteemeth;
For so braue beasts she loueth best to see,
In the wilde forrest raunging fresh and free.   630
Therefore if fortune thee in Court to liue,
In case thou euer there wilt hope to thriue,
To some of these thou must thy selfe apply:
Els as a thistle-downe in th'ayre doth flie,
So vainly shalt thou too and fro be tost,   635
And loose thy labour and thy fruitles cost.
And yet full few, which follow them I see,
For vertues bare regard aduaunced bee,
But either for some gainfull benefit,
Or that they may for their owne turnes be fit.   640
Nath'les perhaps ye things may handle soe,
That ye may better thriue than thousands moe.

But (said the Ape) how shall we first come in,
That after we may fauour seeke to win?
645   How els (said he) but with a good bold face,
And with big words, and with a stately pace,
That men may thinke of you in generall,
That to be in you, which is not at all:
For not by that which is, the world now deemeth,
650   (As it was wont) but by that same that seemeth.
Ne do I doubt, but that ye well can fashion
Your selues theretoo, according to occasion:
So fare ye well, good Courtiers may ye bee;
So proudlie neighing from them parted hee.
655   Then gan this craftie couple to deuize,
How for the Court themselues they might aguize:
For thither they themselues meant to addresse,
In hope to finde there happier successe,
So well they shifted, that the Ape anon
660   Himselfe had cloathed like a Gentleman,
And the slie Foxe, as like to be his groome,
That to the Court in seemly sort they come.
Where the fond Ape himselfe vprearing hy
Vpon his tiptoes, stalketh stately by,
665   As if he were some great *Magnifico*,
And boldlie doth amongst the boldest go.
And his man Reynold with fine counterfesaunce
Supports his credite and his countenaunce.
Then gan the Courtiers gaze on euerie side,
670   And stare on him, with big lookes basen wide,
Wondring what mister wight he was, and whence:
For he was clad in strange accoustrements,
Fashion'd with queint deuises neuer seene
In Court before, yet there all fashions beene:
675   Yet he them in newfanglenesse did pas:
But his behauiour altogether was
Alla Turchesca, much the more admyr'd,
And his lookes loftie, as if he aspyr'd
To dignitie, and sdeign'd the low degree;
680   That all which did such strangenesse in him see,

By secrete meanes gan of his state enquire,
And priuily his seruant thereto hire:
Who throughly arm'd against such couerture,
Reported vnto all, that he was sure
A noble Gentleman of high regard,   685
Which through the world had with long trauel far'd,
And seene the manners of all beasts on ground;
Now here arriu'd, to see if like he found.
Thus did the Ape at first him credit gaine,
Which afterwards he wisely did maintaine   690
With gallant showe, and daylie more augment
Through his fine feates and Courtly complement;
For he could play, and daunce, and vaute, and spring,
And all that els pertaines to reueling,
Onely through kindly aptnes of his ioynts.   695
Besides he could doo manie other poynts,
The which in Court him serued to good stead:
For he mongst Ladies could their fortunes read
Out of their hands, and merie leasings tell,
And iuggle finely, that became him well: 700
But he so light was at legier demaine,
That what he toucht, came not to light againe;
Yet would he laugh it out, and proudly looke,
And tell them, that they greatly him mistooke.
So would he scoffe them out with mockerie,   705
For he therein had great felicitie;
And with sharp quips ioy'd others to deface,
Thinking that their disgracing did him grace:
So whilst that other like vaine wits he pleased,
And made to laugh, his heart was greatly eased.   710
But the right gentle minde would bite his lip,
To heare the Iauell so good men to nip:
For though the vulgar yeeld an open eare,
And common Courtiers loue to gybe and fleare
At euerie thing, which they heare spoken ill,   715
And the best speaches with ill meaning spill;
Yet the braue Courtier, in whose beauteous thought
Regard of honour harbours more than ought,

Doth loath such base condition, to backbite

720   Anies good name for enuie or despite:
He stands on tearmes of honourable minde,
Ne will be carried with the common winde
Of Courts inconstant mutabilitie,
Ne after euerie tattling fable flie;

725   But heares, and sees the follies of the rest,
And thereof gathers for himselfe the best:
He will not creepe, nor crouche with fained face,
But walkes vpright with comely stedfast pace,
And vnto all doth yeeld due curtesie;

730   But not with kissed hand belowe the knee,
As that same Apish crue is wont to doo:
For he disdaines himselfe t'embase theretoo.
He hates fowle leasings, and vile flatterie,
Two filthie blots in noble Gentrie;

735   And lothefull idlenes he doth detest,
The canker worme of euerie gentle brest;
The which to banish with faire exercise
Of knightly feates, he daylie doth deuise:
Now menaging the mouthes of stubborne steedes,

740   Now practising the proofe of warlike deedes,
Now his bright armes assaying, now his speare,
Now the nigh aymed ring away to beare;
At other times he casts to sew the chace
Of swift wilde beasts, or runne on foote a race,

745   T'enlarge his breath (large breath in armes most needfull)
Or els by wrestling to wex strong and heedfull,
Or his stiffe armes to stretch with Eughen bowe,
And manly legs, still passing too and fro,
Without a gowned beast him fast beside;

750   A vaine ensample of the *Persian* pride,
Who after he had wonne th'*Assyrian* foe,
Did euer after scorne on foote to goe.
Thus when this Courtly Gentleman with toyle
Himselfe hath wearied, he doth recoyle

755   Vnto his rest, and there with sweete delight
Of Musicks skill reuiues his toyled spright,

Or els with Loues, and Ladies gentle sports,
The ioy of youth, himselfe he recomforts:
Or lastly, when the bodie list to pause,
His minde vnto the Muses he withdrawes;   760
Sweete Ladie Muses, Ladies of delight,
Delights of life, and ornaments of light:
With whom he close confers with wise discourse,
Of Natures workes, of heauens continuall course,
Of forreine lands, of people different,   765
Of kingdomes change, of diuers gouernment,
Of dreadfull battailes of renowmed Knights;
With which he kindleth his ambitious sprights
To like desire and praise of noble fame,
The onely vpshot whereto he doth ayme: 770
For all his minde on honour fixed is,
To which he leuels all his purposis,
And in his Princes seruice spends his dayes,
Not so much for to gaine, or for to raise
Himselfe to high degree, as for his grace,   775
And in his liking to winne worthie place;
Through due deserts and comely carriage,
In whatso please employ his personage,
That may be matter meete to gaine him praise;
For he is fit to vse in all assayes,   780
Whether for Armes and warlike amenaunce,
Or else for wise and ciuill gouernaunce.
For he is practiz'd well in policie,
And thereto doth his Courting most applie:
To learne the enterdeale of Princes strange,   785
To marke th'intent of Counsells, and the change
Of states, and eke of priuate men somewhile,
Supplanted by fine falshood and faire guile;
Of all the which he gathereth, what is fit
T'enrich the storehouse of his powerfull wit,   790
Which through wise speaches, and graue conference
He daylie eekes, and brings to excellence.
Such is the rightfull Courtier in his kinde:
But vnto such the Ape lent not his minde;

795 Such were for him no fit companions,
Such would descrie his lewd conditions:
But the yong lustie gallants he did chose
To follow, meete to whom he might disclose
His witlesse pleasance, and ill pleasing vaine.
800 A thousand wayes he them could entertaine,
With all the thriftles games, that may be found
With mumming and with masking all around,
With dice, with cards, with balliards farre vnfit,
With shuttelcocks, misseeming manlie wit,
805 With courtizans, and costly riotize,
Whereof still somewhat to his share did rize:
Ne, them to pleasure, would he sometimes scorne
A Pandares coate (so basely was he borne);
Thereto he could fine louing verses frame,
810 And play the Poet oft. But ah, for shame
Let not sweete Poets praise, whose onely pride
Is vertue to aduaunce, and vice deride,
Be with the worke of losels wit defamed,
Ne let such verses Poetrie be named:
815 Yet he the name on him would rashly take,
Maugre the sacred Muses, and it make
A seruant to the vile affection
Of such, as he depended most vpon,
And with the sugrie sweete thereof allure
820 Chast Ladies eares to fantasies impure.
To such delights the noble wits he led
Which him relieu'd, and their vaine humours fed
With fruitles follies, and vnsound delights.
But if perhaps into their noble sprights
825 Desire of honor, or braue thought of armes
Did euer creepe, then with his wicked charmes
And strong conceipts he would it driue away,
Ne suffer it to house there halfe a day.
And whenso loue of letters did inspire
830 Their gentle wits, and kindly wise desire,
That chieflie doth each noble minde adorne,
Then he would scoffe at learning, and eke scorne

The Sectaries thereof, as people base
And simple men, which neuer came in place
Of worlds affaires, but in darke corners mewd,   835
Muttred of matters, as their bookes them shewd,
Ne other knowledge euer did attaine,
But with their gownes their grauitie maintaine.
From them he would his impudent lewde speach
Against Gods holie Ministers oft reach,   840
And mocke Diuines and their profession:
What else then did he by progression,
But mocke high God himselfe, whom they professe?
But what car'd he for God, or godlinesse?
All his care was himselfe how to aduaunce,   845
And to vphold his courtly countenaunce
By all the cunning meanes he could deuise;
Were it by honest wayes, or otherwise,
He made small choyce: yet sure his honestie
Got him small gaines, but shameles flatterie,   850
And filthie brocage, and vnseemly shifts,
And borowe base, and some good Ladies gifts:
But the best helpe, which chiefly him sustain'd,
Was his man Raynolds purchase which he gain'd.
For he was school'd by kinde in all the skill   855
Of close conueyance, and each practise ill
Of coosinage and cleanly knauerie,
Which oft maintain'd his masters brauerie.
Besides he vsde another slipprie slight,
In taking on himselfe in common sight,   860
False personages fit for euerie sted,
With which he thousands cleanly coosined:
Now like a Merchant, Merchants to deceaue,
With whom his credite he did often leaue
In gage, for his gay Masters hopelesse dett: 865
Now like a Lawyer, when he land would lett,
Or sell fee-simples in his Masters name,
Which he had neuer, nor ought like the same:
Then would he be a Broker, and draw in
Both wares and money, by exchange to win: 870

Then would he seeme a Farmer, that would sell
Bargaines of woods, which he did lately fell,
Or corne, or cattle, or such other ware,
Thereby to coosin men not well aware;
875   Of all the which there came a secret fee
To th'Ape, that he his countenaunce might bee.
Besides all this, he vsd' oft to beguile
Poore suters, that in Court did haunt some while:
For he would learne their busines secretly,
880   And then informe his Master hastely,
That he by meanes might cast them to preuent,
And beg the sute, the which the other ment.
Or otherwise false Reynold would abuse
The simple Suter, and wish him to chuse
885   His Master, being one of great regard
In Court, to compas anie sute not hard,
In case his paines were recompenst with reason:
So would he worke the silly man by treason
To buy his Masters friuolous good will,
890   That had not power to doo him good or ill.
So pitifull a thing is Suters state.
Most miserable man, whom wicked fate
Hath brought to Court, to sue for had ywist,
That few haue found, and manie one hath mist;
895   Full little knowest thou that hast not tride,
What hell it is, in suing long to bide:
To loose good dayes, that might be better spent;
To wast long nights in pensiue discontent;
To speed to day, to be put back to morrow;
900   To feed on hope, to pine with feare and sorrow;
To haue thy Princes grace, yet want her Peeres;
To haue thy asking, yet waite manie yeeres;
To fret thy soule with crosses and with cares;
To eate thy heart through comfortlesse dispaires;
905   To fawne, to crowche, to waite, to ride, to ronne,
To spend, to giue, to want, to be vndonne.
Vnhappie wight, borne to desastrous end,
That doth his life in so long tendance spend.

Who euer leaues sweete home, where meane estate
In safe assurance, without strife or hate,   910
Findes all things needfull for contentment meeke;
And will to Court for shadowes vaine to seeke,
Or hope to gaine, himselfe will a daw trie:
That curse God send vnto mine enemie.
For none but such as this bold Ape vnblest,   915
Can euer thriue in that vnluckie quest;
Or such as hath a Reynold to his man,
That by his shifts his Master furnish can.
But yet this Foxe could not so closely hide
His craftie feates, but that they were descride   920
At length, by such as sate in iustice seate,
Who for the same him fowlie did entreate;
And hauing worthily him punished,
Out of the Court for euer banished.
And now the Ape wanting his huckster man,   925
That wont prouide his necessaries, gan
To growe into great lacke, ne could vpholde
His countenaunce in those his garments olde:
Ne new ones could he easily prouide,
Though all men him vncased gan deride,   930
Like as a Puppit placed in a play,
Whose part once past all men bid take away:
So that he driuen was to great distresse,
And shortly brought to hopelesse wretchednesse.
Then closely as he might he cast to leaue   935
The Court, not asking any passe or leaue;
But ran away in his rent rags by night,
Ne euer stayd in place, ne spake to wight,
Till that the Foxe his copesmate he had found,
To whome complayning his vnhappy stound,   940
At last againe with him in trauell ioynd,
And with him far'd some better chaunce to fynde.
So in the world long time they wandered,
And mickle want and hardnesse suffered;
That them repented much so foolishly   945
To come so farre to seeke for misery,

And leaue the sweetnes of contented home,
Though eating hipps, and drinking watry fome.
Thus as they them complayned too and fro,
950   Whilst through the forest rechlesse they did goe,
Lo where they spide, how in a gloomy glade,
The Lyon sleeping lay in secret shade,
His Crowne and Scepter lying him beside,
And hauing doft for heate his dreadfull hide:
955   Which when they sawe, the Ape was sore afrayde,
And would haue fled with terror all dismayde.
But him the Foxe with hardy words did stay,
And bad him put all cowardize away:
For now was time (if euer they would hope)
960   To ayme their counsels to the fairest scope,
And them for euer highly to aduaunce,
In case the good which their owne happie chaunce
Them freely offred, they would wisely take.
Scarse could the Ape yet speake, so did he quake,
965   Yet as he could, he askt how good might growe,
Where nought but dread and death do seeme in show.
Now (sayd he) whiles the Lyon sleepeth sound,
May we his Crowne and Mace take from the ground,
And eke his skinne the terror of the wood,
970   Wherewith we may our selues (if we thinke good)
Make Kings of Beasts, and Lords of forests all,
Subiect vnto that powre imperiall.
Ah but (sayd the Ape) who is so bold a wretch,
That dare his hardy hand to those outstretch:
975   When as he knowes his meede, if he be spide,
To be a thousand deathes, and shame beside?
Fond Ape (sayd then the Foxe) into whose brest
Neuer crept thought of honor, nor braue gest,
Who will not venture life a King to be,
980   And rather rule and raigne in soueraign see,
Than dwell in dust inglorious and bace,
Where none shall name the number of his place?
One ioyous houre in blisfull happines,
I chose before a life of wretchednes.

Be therefore counselled herein by me, 985
And shake off this vile harted cowardree.
If he awake, yet is not death the next,
For we may coulor it with some pretext
Of this, or that, that may excuse the cryme:
Else we may flye; thou to a tree mayst clyme, 990
And I creepe vnder ground; both from his reach:
Therefore be rul'd to doo as I doo teach.

The Ape, that earst did nought but chill and quake,
Now gan some courage vnto him to take,
And was content to attempt that enterprise, 995
Tickled with glorie and rash couetise.
But first gan question, whether should assay
Those royall ornaments to steale away?
Marie that shall your selfe (quoth he theretoo)
For ye be fine and nimble it to doo; 1000
Of all the beasts which in the forrests bee,
Is not a fitter for this turne than yee:
Therefore, mine owne deare brother take good hart,
And euer thinke a Kingdome is your part.

Loath was the Ape, though praised, to aduenter, 1005
Yet faintly gan into his worke to enter,
Afraid of euerie leafe, that stir'd him by,
And euerie stick, that vnderneath did ly;
Vpon his tiptoes nicely he vp went,
For making noyse, and still his eare he lent 1010
To euerie sound, that vnder heauen blew,
Now went, now stept, now crept, now backward drew,
That it good sport had been him to haue eyde:
Yet at the last (so well he him applyde,)
Through his fine handling, and cleanly play, 1015
He all those royall signes had stolne away,
And with the Foxes helpe them borne aside,
Into a secret corner vnespide.
Whither whenas they came, they fell at words,
Whether of them should be the Lord of Lords: 1020
For th'Ape was stryfull, and ambicious;
And the Foxe guilefull, and most couetous,

That neither pleased was, to haue the rayne
Twixt them diuided into euen twaine,
1025 But either (algates) would be Lords alone:
For Loue and Lordship bide no paragone.
I am most worthie (said the Ape) sith I
For it did put my life in ieopardie:
Thereto I am in person, and in stature
1030 Most like a man, the Lord of euerie creature,
So that it seemeth I was made to raigne,
And borne to be a Kingly soueraigne.
Nay (said the Foxe) Sir Ape you are astray:
For though to steale the Diademe away
1035 Were the worke of your nimble hand, yet I
Did first deuise the plot by pollicie;
So that it wholly springeth from my wit:
For which also I claime my selfe more fit
Than you, to rule: for gouernment of state
1040 Will without wisedome soone be ruinate.
And where ye claime your selfe for outward shape
Most like a man, Man is not like an Ape
In his chiefe parts, that is, in wit and spirite;
But I therein most like to him doo merite
1045 For my slie wyles and subtill craftinesse,
The title of the Kingdome to possesse.
Nath'les (my brother) since we passed are
Vnto this point, we will appease our iarre,
And I with reason meete will rest content,
1050 That ye shall haue both crowne and gouernment,
Vpon condition, that ye ruled bee
In all affaires, and counselled by mee;
And that ye let none other euer drawe
Your minde from me, but keepe this as a lawe:
1055 And herevpon an oath vnto me plight.
The Ape was glad to end the strife so light,
And thereto swore: for who would not oft sweare,
And oft vnsweare a Diademe to beare?
Then freely vp those royall spoyles he tooke,
1060 Yet at the Lyons skin he inly quooke;

But it dissembled, and vpon his head
The Crowne, and on his backe the skin he did,
And the false Foxe him helped to array.
Then when he was all dight he tooke his way
Into the forest, that he might be seene   1065
Of the wilde beasts in his new glory sheene.
There the two first, whome he encountred, were
The Sheepe and th'Asse, who striken both with feare
At sight of him, gan fast away to flye,
But vnto them the Foxe alowd did cry,   1070
And in the Kings name bad them both to stay,
Vpon the payne that thereof follow may.
Hardly naythles were they restrayned so,
Till that the Foxe forth toward them did goe,
And there disswaded them from needlesse feare,   1075
For that the King did fauour to them beare;
And therefore dreadles bad them come to Corte:
For no wild beasts should do them any torte
There or abroad, ne would his maiestye
Vse them but well, with gracious clemencye,   1080
As whome he knew to him both fast and true;
So he perswaded them, with homage due
Themselues to humble to the Ape prostrate,
Who gently to them bowing in his gate,
Receyued them with chearefull entertayne.   1085
Thenceforth proceeding with his princely trayne,
He shortly met the Tygre, and the Bore,
Which with the simple Camell raged sore
In bitter words, seeking to take occasion,
Vpon his fleshly corpse to make inuasion: 1090
But soone as they this mock-King did espy,
Their troublous strife they stinted by and by,
Thinking indeed that it the Lyon was:
He then to proue, whether his powre would pas
As currant, sent the Foxe to them streight way,   1095
Commaunding them their cause of strife bewray;
And if that wrong on eyther side there were,
That he should warne the wronger to appeare

The morrow next at Court, it to defend;
1100   In the meane time vpon the King t'attend.
The subtile Foxe so well his message sayd,
That the proud beasts him readily obayd:
Whereby the Ape in wondrous stomack woxe,
Strongly encorag'd by the crafty Foxe;
1105   That King indeed himselfe he shortly thought,
And all the Beasts him feared as they ought:
And followed vnto his palaice hye,
Where taking Conge, each one by and by
Departed to his home in dreadfull awe,
1110   Full of the feared sight, which late they sawe.
The Ape thus seized of the Regall throne,
Eftsones by counsell of the Foxe alone,
Gan to prouide for all things in assurance,
That so his rule might lenger haue endurance.
1115   First to his Gate he pointed a strong gard,
That none might enter but with issue hard:
Then for the safegard of his personage,
He did appoint a warlike equipage
Of forreine beasts, not in the forest bred,
1120   But part by land, and part by water fed;
For tyrannie is with strange ayde supported.
Then vnto him all monstrous beasts resorted
Bred of two kindes, as Griffons, Minotaures,
Crocodiles, Dragons, Beauers, and Centaures:
1125   With those himselfe he strengthned mightelie,
That feare he neede no force of enemie.
Then gan he rule and tyrannize at will,
Like as the Foxe did guide his graceles skill,
And all wylde beasts made vassals of his pleasures,
1130   And with their spoyles enlarg'd his priuate treasures.
No care of iustice, nor no rule of reason,
No temperance, nor no regard of season
Did thenceforth euer enter in his minde,
But crueltie, the signe of currish kinde,
1135   And sdeignfull pride, and wilfull arrogaunce;
Such followes those whom fortune doth aduaunce.

But the false Foxe most kindly plaid his part:
For whatsoeuer mother wit, or arte
Could worke, he put in proofe: no practise slie,
No counterpoint of cunning policie,   1140
No reach, no breach, that might him profit bring,
But he the same did to his purpose wring.
Nought suffered he the Ape to giue or graunt,
But through his hand must passe the Fiaunt.
All offices, all leases by him lept,   1145
And of them all whatso he likte, he kept.
Iustice he solde iniustice for to buy,
And for to purchase for his progeny.
Ill might it prosper, that ill gotten was,
But so he got it, little did he pas.   1150
He fed his cubs with fat of all the soyle,
And with the sweete of others sweating toyle,
He crammed them with crumbs of Benefices,
And fild their mouthes with meeds of malefices,
He cloathed them with all colours saue white,   1155
And loded them with lordships and with might,
So much as they were able well to beare,
That with the weight their backs nigh broken were;
He chaffred Chayres in which Churchmen were set,
And breach of lawes to priuie ferme did let;   1160
No statute so established might bee,
Nor ordinaunce so needfull, but that hee
Would violate, though not with violence,
Yet vnder colour of the confidence
The which the Ape reposd' in him alone,   1165
And reckned him the kingdomes corner stone.
And euer when he ought would bring to pas,
His long experience the platforme was:
And when he ought not pleasing would put by,
The cloke was care of thrift, and husbandry,   1170
For to encrease the common treasures store;
But his owne treasure he encreased more
And lifted vp his loftie towres thereby,
That they began to threat the neighbour sky;

1175 The whiles the Princes pallaces fell fast
      To ruine: (for what thing can euer last?)
      And whilest the other Peeres, for pouertie
      Were forst their auncient houses to let lie,
      And their olde Castles to the ground to fall,
1180 Which their forefathers famous ouer all
      Had founded for the Kingdomes ornament,
      And for their memories long moniment.
      But he no count made of Nobilitie,
      Nor the wilde beasts whom armes did glorifie,
1185 The Realmes chiefe strength and girlond of the crowne.
      All these through fained crimes he thrust adowne,
      Or made them dwell in darknes of disgrace:
      For none, but whom he list might come in place.
      Of men of armes he had but small regard,
1190 But kept them lowe, and streigned verie hard.
      For men of learning little he esteemed;
      His wisedome he aboue their learning deemed.
      As for the rascall Commons least he cared;
      For not so common was his bountie shared;
1195 Let God (said he) if please, care for the manie,
      I for my selfe must care before els anie:
      So did he good to none, to manie ill,
      So did he all the kingdome rob and pill,
      Yet none durst speake, ne none durst of him plaine;
1200 So great he was in grace, and rich through gaine.
      Ne would he anie let to haue accesse
      Vnto the Prince, but by his owne addresse:
      For all that els did come, were sure to faile,
      Yet would he further none but for auaile.
1205 For on a time the Sheepe, to whom of yore
      The Foxe had promised of friendship store,
      What time the Ape the kingdome first did gaine,
      Came to the Court, her case there to complaine,
      How that the Wolfe her mortall enemie
1210 Had sithence slaine her Lambe most cruellie;
      And therefore crau'd to come vnto the King,
      To let him knowe the order of the thing.

Soft Gooddie Sheepe (then said the Foxe) not soe:
Vnto the King so rash ye may not goe,
He is with greater matter busied,   1215
Than a Lambe, or the Lambes owne mothers hed.
Ne certes may I take it well in part,
That ye my cousin Wolfe so fowly thwart,
And seeke with slaunder his good name to blot:
For there was cause, els doo it he would not.   1220
Therefore surcease good Dame, and hence depart.
So went the Sheepe away with heauie hart.
So manie moe, so euerie one was vsed,
That to giue largely to the boxe refused.
Now when high *Ioue*, in whose almightie hand   1225
The care of Kings, and power of Empires stand,
Sitting one day within his turret hye,
From whence he vewes with his blacklidded eye,
Whatso the heauen in his wide vawte containes,
And all that in the deepest earth remaines,   1230
The troubled kingdome of wilde beasts behelde,
Whom not their kindly Souereigne did welde,
But an vsurping Ape with guile suborn'd,
Had all subuerst, he sdeignfully it scorn'd
In his great heart, and hardly did refraine,   1235
But that with thunder bolts he had him slaine,
And driuen downe to hell, his dewest meed:
But him auizing, he that dreadfull deed
Forbore, and rather chose with scornfull shame
Him to auenge, and blot his brutish name   1240
Vnto the world, that neuer after anie
Should of his race be voyd of infamie:
And his false counsellor, the cause of all,
To damne to death, or dole perpetuall,
From whence he neuer should be quit, nor stal'd.   1245
Forthwith he *Mercurie* vnto him cal'd,
And bad him flie with neuer resting speed
Vnto the forrest, where wilde beasts doo breed,
And there enquiring priuily, to learne,
What did of late chaunce to the Lyon stearne,   1250

That he rul'd not the Empire, as he ought;
And whence were all those plaints vnto him brought
Of wrongs and spoyles, by saluage beasts committed;
Which done, he bad the Lyon be remitted
1255 Into his seate, and those same treachours vile
Be punished for their presumptuous guile.
The Sonne of *Maia* soone as he receiu'd
That word, streight with his azure wings he cleau'd
The liquid clowdes, and lucid firmament;
1260 Ne staid, till that he came with steep descent
Vnto the place, where his prescript did showe.
There stouping like an arrowe from a bowe,
He soft arriued on the grassie plaine,
And fairly paced forth with easie paine,
1265 Till that vnto the Pallace nigh he came.
Then gan he to himselfe new shape to frame,
And that faire face, and that Ambrosiall hew,
Which wonts to decke the Gods immortall crew,
And beautefie the shinie firmament,
1270 He doft, vnfit for that rude rabblement.
So standing by the gates in strange disguize,
He gan enquire of some in secret wize,
Both of the King, and of his gouernment,
And of the Foxe, and his false blandishment:
1275 And euermore he heard each one complaine
Of foule abuses both in realme and raine.
Which yet to proue more true, he meant to see,
And an ey-witnes of each thing to bee.
Tho on his head his dreadfull hat he dight,
1280 Which maketh him inuisible in sight,
And mocketh th'eyes of all the lookers on,
Making them thinke it but a vision.
Through power of that, he runnes through enemies swerds;
Through power of that, he passeth through the herds
1285 Of rauenous wilde beasts, and doth beguile
Their greedie mouthes of the expected spoyle;
Through power of that, his cunning theeueries
He wonts to worke, that none the same espies;

And through the power of that, he putteth on
What shape he list in apparition.   1290
That on his head he wore, and in his hand
He tooke *Caduceus* his snakie wand,
With which the damned ghosts he gouerneth,
And furies rules, and Tartare tempereth.
With that he causeth sleep to seize the eyes,   1295
And feare the harts of all his enemyes;
And when him list, an vniuersall night
Throughout the world he makes on euerie wight;
As when his Syre with *Alcumena* lay.
Thus dight, into the Court he tooke his way,   1300
Both through the gard, which neuer him descride,
And through the watchmen, who him neuer spide:
Thenceforth he past into each secrete part,
Whereas he saw, that sorely grieu'd his hart;
Each place abounding with fowle iniuries,   1305
And fild with treasure rackt with robberies:
Each place defilde with blood of guiltles beasts,
Which had been slaine, to serue the Apes beheasts;
Gluttonie, malice, pride, and couetize,
And lawlesnes raigning with riotize;   1310
Besides the infinite extortions,
Done through the Foxes great oppressions,
That the complaints thereof could not be tolde.
Which when he did with lothfull eyes beholde,
He would no more endure, but came his way,   1315
And cast to seeke the Lion, where he may,
That he might worke the auengement for this shame,
On those two caytiues, which had bred him blame.
And seeking all the forrest busily,
At last he found, where sleeping he did ly: 1320
The wicked weed, which there the Foxe did lay,
From vnderneath his head he tooke away,
And then him waking, forced vp to rize.
The Lion looking vp gan him auize,
As one late in a traunce, what had of long   1325
Become of him: for fantasie is strong.

Arise (said *Mercurie*) thou sluggish beast,
That here liest senseles, like the corpse deceast,
The whilste thy kingdome from thy head is rent,
1330   And thy throne royall with dishonour blent:
Arise, and doo thy selfe redeeme from shame,
And be aueng'd on those that breed thy blame.
Thereat enraged, soone he gan vpstart,
Grinding his teeth, and grating his great hart,
1335   And rouzing vp himselfe, for his rough hide
He gan to reach; but no where it espide.
Therewith he gan full terribly to rore,
And chafte at that indignitie right sore.
But when his Crowne and scepter both he wanted,
1340   Lord how he fum'd, and sweld, and rag'd, and panted;
And threatned death, and thousand deadly dolours
To them that had purloyn'd his Princely honours.
With that in hast, disroabed as he was,
He toward his owne Pallace forth did pas;
1345   And all the way he roared as he went,
That all the forrest with astonishment
Thereof did tremble, and the beasts therein
Fled fast away from that so dreadfull din.
At last he came vnto his mansion,
1350   Where all the gates he found fast lockt anon,
And manie warders round about them stood:
With that he roar'd alowd, as he were wood,
That all the Pallace quaked at the stound,
As if it quite were riuen from the ground,
1355   And all within were dead and hartles left;
And th'Ape himselfe, as one whose wits were reft,
Fled here and there, and euerie corner sought,
To hide himselfe from his owne feared thought.
But the false Foxe when he the Lion heard,
1360   Fled closely forth, streightway of death afeard,
And to the Lion came, full lowly creeping,
With fained face, and watrie eyne halfe weeping,
T'excuse his former treason and abusion,
And turning all vnto the Apes confusion:

Nath'les the royall Beast forbore beleeuing,   1365
But bad him stay at ease till further preeuing.
Then when he saw no entrance to him graunted,
Roaring yet lowder that all harts it daunted,
Vpon those gates with force he fiercely flewe,
And rending them in pieces, felly slewe   1370
Those warders strange, and all that els he met.
But th'Ape still flying, he no where might get:
From rowme to rowme, from beame to beame he fled
All breathles, and for feare now almost ded:
Yet him at last the Lyon spide, and caught,   1375
And forth with shame vnto his iudgement brought.
Then all the beasts he causd' assembled bee,
To heare their doome, and sad ensample see:
The Foxe, first Author of that treacherie,
He did vncase, and then away let flie.   1380
But th'Apes long taile (which then he had) he quight
Cut off, and both eares pared of their hight;
Since which, all Apes but halfe their eares haue left,
And of their tailes are vtterlie bereft.

So Mother *Hubberd* her discourse did end: 1385
Which pardon me, if I amisse haue pend,
For weake was my remembrance it to hold,
And bad her tongue that it so bluntly tolde.

FINIS.

Ruines of Rome: by Bellay.

1

Ye heauenly spirites, whose ashie cinders lie
Vnder deep ruines, with huge walls opprest,
But not your praise, the which shall neuer die
Through your faire verses, ne in ashes rest;
5   If so be shrilling voyce of wight aliue
May reach from hence to depth of darkest hell,
Then let those deep Abysses open riue,
That ye may vnderstand my shreiking yell.
    Thrice hauing seene vnder the heauens veale
10   Your toombs deuoted compasse ouer all,
Thrice vnto you with lowd voyce I appeale,
And for your antique furie here doo call,
      The whiles that I with sacred horror sing
      Your glorie, fairest of all earthly thing.

2

15   Great *Babylon* her haughtie walls will praise,
And sharped steeples high shot vp in ayre;
Greece will the olde *Ephesian* buildings blaze;
And *Nylus* nurslings their Pyramides faire;
    The same yet vaunting *Greece* will tell the storie
20   Of *Ioues* great Image in *Olympus* placed,
Mausolus worke will be the *Carians* glorie,
And *Crete* will boast the Labyrinth, now raced;
    The antique *Rhodian* will likewise set forth
The great Colosse, erect to Memorie;
25   And what els in the world is of like worth,
Some greater learned wit will magnifie.
      But I will sing aboue all moniments
      Seuen *Romane* Hils, the worlds seuen wonderments.

3

Thou stranger, which for *Rome* in *Rome* here seekest,
And nought of *Rome* in *Rome* perceiu'st at all,   30
These same olde walls, olde arches, which thou seest,
Olde Palaces, is that which *Rome* men call.
   Behold what wreake, what ruine, and what wast,
And how that she, which with her mightie powre
Tam'd all the world, hath tam'd herselfe at last,   35
The pray of time, which all things doth deuowre.
   Rome now of *Rome* is th'onely funerall,
And onely *Rome* of *Rome* hath victorie;
Ne ought saue *Tyber* hastning to his fall
Remaines of all: O worlds inconstancie.   40
     That which is firme doth flit and fall away,
     And that is flitting, doth abide and stay.

4

She, whose high top aboue the starres did sore,
One foote on *Thetis*, th'other on the Morning,
One hand on *Scythia*, th'other on the *More*,   45
Both heauen and earth in roundnesse compassing,
   Ioue fearing, least if she should greater growe,
The old Giants should once againe vprise,
Her whelm'd with hills, these seuen hils, which be nowe
Tombes of her greatnes, which did threate the skies: 50
   Vpon her head he heapt Mount *Saturnal*,
Vpon her bellie th'antique *Palatine*,
Vpon her stomacke laid Mount *Quirinal*,
On her left hand the noysome *Esquiline*,
     And *Cælian* on the right; but both her feete   55
     Mount *Viminal* and *Auentine* doo meete.

5

Who lists to see, what euer nature, arte,
And heauen could doo, O *Rome*, thee let him see,
In case thy greatnes he can gesse in harte,
By that which but the picture is of thee.
    Rome is no more: but if the shade of *Rome*
May of the bodie yeeld a seeming sight,
It's like a corse drawne forth out of the tombe
By Magicke skill out of eternall night:
    The corpes of *Rome* in ashes is entombed,
And her great spirite reioyned to the spirite
Of this great masse, is in the same enwombed;
But her braue writings, which her famous merite
    In spight of time, out of the dust doth reare,
    Doo make her Idole through the world appeare.

6

Such as the *Berecynthian* Goddesse bright
In her swift charret with high turrets crownde,
Proud that so manie Gods she brought to light;
Such was this Citie in her good daies fownd:
    This Citie, more than that great *Phrygian* mother
Renowm'd for fruite of famous progenie,
Whose greatnes by the greatnes of none other,
But by her selfe her equall match could see:
    Rome onely might to *Rome* compared bee,
And onely *Rome* could make great *Rome* to tremble:
So did the Gods by heauenly doome decree,
That other earthlie power should not resemble
    Her that did match the whole earths puissaunce,
    And did her courage to the heauens aduaunce.

7

Ye sacred ruines, and ye tragick sights,   85
Which onely doo the name of *Rome* retaine,
Olde moniments, which of so famous sprights
The honour yet in ashes doo maintaine:
    Triumphant Arcks, spyres neighbours to the skie,
That you to see doth th'heauen it selfe appall,   90
Alas, by little ye to nothing flie,
The peoples fable, and the spoyle of all:
    And though your frames do for a time make warre
Gainst time, yet time in time shall ruinate
Your workes and names, and your last reliques marre.   95
My sad desires, rest therefore moderate:
      For if that time make ende of things so sure,
      It als will end the paine, which I endure.

8

Through armes and vassals *Rome* the world subdu'd,
That one would weene, that one sole Cities strength   100
Both land and sea in roundnes had suruew'd,
To be the measure of her bredth and length:
    This peoples vertue yet so fruitfull was
Of vertuous nephewes, that posteritie
Striuing in power their grandfathers to passe,   105
The lowest earth, ioin'd to the heauen hie;
    To th'end that hauing all parts in their power,
Nought from the Romane Empire might be quight,
And that though time doth Commonwealths deuowre,
Yet no time should so low embase their hight,   110
      That her head earth'd in her foundations deep,
      Should not her name and endles honour keep.

9

Ye cruell starres, and eke ye Gods vnkinde,
Heauen enuious, and bitter stepdame Nature,
115 Be it by fortune, or by course of kinde
That ye doo weld th'affaires of earthlie creature;
 Why haue your hands long sithence traueiled
To frame this world, that doth endure so long?
Or why were not these Romane palaces
120 Made of some matter no lesse firme and strong?
 I say not, as the common voyce doth say,
That all things which beneath the Moone haue being
Are temporall, and subiect to decay:
But I say rather, though not all agreeing
125 With some, that weene the contrarie in thought;
  That all this whole shall one day come to nought.

10

As that braue sonne of *Aeson*, which by charmes
Atcheiu'd the golden Fleece in *Colchid* land,
Out of the earth engendred men of armes
130 Of Dragons teeth, sowne in the sacred sand;
 So this braue Towne, that in her youthlie daies
An *Hydra* was of warriours glorious,
Did fill with her renowmed nourslings praise
The firie sunnes both one and other hous:
135 But they at last, there being then not liuing
An *Hercules*, so ranke seed to represse;
Emongst themselues with cruell furie striuing,
Mow'd downe themselues with slaughter mercilesse;
 Renewing in themselues that rage vnkinde,
140 Which whilom did those earthborn brethren blinde.

11

Mars shaming to haue giuen so great head
To his off-spring, that mortall puissaunce
Puft vp with pride of Romane hardie head,
Seem'd aboue heauens powre it selfe to aduaunce;
　　Cooling againe his former kindled heate,   145
With which he had those Romane spirits fild,
Did blowe new fire, and with enflamed breath,
Into the Gothicke colde hot rage instil'd:
　　Then gan that Nation, th'earths new Giant brood,
To dart abroad the thunder bolts of warre,   150
And beating downe these walls with furious mood
Into her mothers bosome, all did marre;
　　To th'end that none, all were it *Ioue* his sire
　　Should boast himselfe of the Romane Empire.

12

　　Like as whilome the children of the earth   155
Heapt hils on hils, to scale the starrie skie,
And fight against the Gods of heauenly berth,
Whiles *Ioue* at them his thunderbolts let flie;
　　All suddenly with lightning ouerthrowne,
The furious squadrons downe to ground did fall,   160
That th'earth vnder her childrens weight did grone,
And th'heauens in glorie triumpht ouer all:
　　So did that haughtie front which heaped was
On these seuen Romane hils, it selfe vpreare
Ouer the world, and lift her loftie face   165
Against the heauen, that gan her force to feare.
　　But now these scorned fields bemone her fall,
　　And Gods secure feare not her force at all.

13

Nor the swift furie of the flames aspiring,
170   Nor the deep wounds of victours raging blade,
Nor ruthlesse spoyle of souldiers blood-desiring,
The which so oft thee (*Rome*) their conquest made;
Ne stroke on stroke of fortune variable,
Ne rust of age hating continuance,
175   Nor wrath of Gods, nor spight of men vnstable,
Nor thou opposd' against thine owne puissance;
Nor th'horrible vprore of windes high blowing,
Nor swelling streames of that God snakie-paced,
Which hath so often with his overflowing
180   Thee drenched, haue thy pride so much abaced;
But that this nothing, which they haue thee left,
Makes the world wonder, what they from thee reft.

14

As men in Summer fearles passe the foord,
Which is in Winter lord of all the plaine,
185   And with his tumbling streames doth beare aboord
The ploughmans hope, and shepheards labour vaine:
And as the coward beasts vse to despise
The noble Lion after his liues end,
Whetting their teeth, and with vaine foolhardise
190   Daring the foe, that cannot him defend:
And as at *Troy* most dastards of the Greekes
Did braue about the corpes of *Hector* colde;
So those which whilome wont with pallid cheekes
The Romane triumphs glorie to behold,
195   Now on these ashie tombes shew boldnesse vaine,
And conquer'd dare the Conquerour disdaine.

15

Ye pallid spirits, and ye ashie ghoasts,
Which ioying in the brightnes of your day,
Brought foorth those signes of your presumptuous boasts
Which now their dusty reliques do bewray;   200
    Tell me ye spirits (sith the darksome riuer
Of *Styx*, not passable to soules returning,
Enclosing you in thrice three wards for euer,
Doo not restraine your images still mourning)
    Tell me then (for perhaps some one of you   205
Yet here aboue him secretly doth hide)
Doo ye not feele your torments to accrewe,
When ye sometimes behold the ruin'd pride
    Of these old *Romane* works built with your hands,
    Now to become nought els, but heaped sands?   210

16

Like as ye see the wrathfull Sea from farre,
In a great mountaine heap't with hideous noyse,
Eftsoones of thousand billowes shouldred narre,
Against a Rocke to breake with dreadfull poyse:
    Like as ye see fell *Boreas* with sharpe blast,   215
Tossing huge tempests through the troubled skie,
Eftsoones hauing his wide wings spent in wast,
To stop his wearie cariere suddenly:
    And as ye see huge flames spred diuerslie,
Gathered in one vp to the heauens to spyre,   220
Eftsoones consum'd to fall downe feebily:
So whilom did this Monarchie aspyre
    As waues, as winde, as fire spred ouer all,
    Till it by fatall doome adowne did fall.

17

225 So long as *Ioues* great Bird did make his flight,
Bearing the fire with which heauen doth vs fray,
Heauen had not feare of that presumptuous might,
With which the Giaunts did the Gods assay.
But all so soone, as scortching Sunne had brent
230 His wings, which wont the earth to ouerspredd,
The earth out of her massie wombe forth sent
That antique horror, which made heauen adredd.
Then was the Germane Rauen in disguise
That Romane Eagle seene to cleaue asunder,
235 And towards heauen freshly to arise
Out of these mountaines, now consum'd to pouder.
In which the foule that serues to beare the lightning,
Is now no more seen flying, nor alighting.

18

These heapes of stones, these old wals which ye see,
240 Were first enclosures but of saluage soyle;
And these braue Pallaces which maystred bee
Of time, were shepheards cottages somewhile.
Then tooke the shepheards Kingly ornaments
And the stout hynde arm'd his right hand with steele:
245 Eftsoones their rule of yearely Presidents
Grew great, and six months greater a great deele;
Which made perpetuall, rose to so great might,
That thence th'Imperiall Eagle rooting tooke,
Till th'heauen it selfe opposing gainst her might,
250 Her power to *Peters* successor betooke;
Who shepheardlike, (as fates the same foreseeing)
Doth shew, that all things turne to their first being.

19

All that is perfect, which th'heauen beautefies;
All that's imperfect, borne belowe the Moone;
All that doth feede our spirits and our eies;   255
And all that doth consume our pleasures soone;
   All the mishap, the which our daies outweares,
All the good hap of th'oldest times afore,
Rome in the time of her great ancesters,
Like a *Pandora*, locked long in store.   260
   But destinie this huge *Chaos* turmoyling,
In which all good and euill was enclosed,
Their heauenly vertues from these woes assoyling,
Caried to heauen, from sinfull bondage losed:
      But their great sinnes, the causers of their paine,   265
      Vnder these antique ruines yet remaine.

20

   No otherwise than raynie cloud, first fed
With earthly vapours gathered in the ayre,
Eftsoones in compas arch't, to steepe his hed,
Doth plonge himselfe in *Tethys* bosome faire;   270
   And mounting vp againe, from whence he came,
With his great bellie spreds the dimmed world,
Till at the last dissoluing his moist frame,
In raine, or snowe, or haile he forth is horld;
   This Citie, which was first but shepheards shade,   275
Vprising by degrees, grewe to such height,
That Queene of land and sea her selfe she made.
At last not able to beare so great weight,
      Her power disperst, through all the world did vade;
      To shew that all in th'end to nought shall fade.   280

21

The same which *Pyrrhus*, and the puissaunce
Of *Afrike* could not tame, that same braue Citie,
Which with stout courage arm'd against mischaunce,
Sustein'd the shocke of common enmitie;
285   Long as her ship tost with so manie freakes,
Had all the world in armes against her bent,
Was neuer seene, that anie fortunes wreakes
Could breake her course begun with braue intent.
    But when the obiect of her vertue failed,
290 Her power it selfe against it selfe did arme;
As he that hauing long in tempest sailed,
Faine would ariue, but cannot for the storme,
      If too great winde against the port him driue,
      Doth in the port it selfe his vessell riue.

22

295   When that braue honour of the Latine name,
Which mear'd her rule with *Africa*, and *Byze*,
With *Thames* inhabitants of noble fame,
And they which see the dawning day arize;
    Her nourslings did with mutinous vprore
300 Harten against her selfe, her conquer'd spoile,
Which she had wonne from all the world afore,
Of all the world was spoyl'd within a while.
    So when the compast course of the vniuerse
In sixe and thirtie thousand yeares is ronne,
305 The bands of th'elements shall backe reuerse
To their first discord, and be quite vndonne:
      The seedes, of which all things at first were bred,
      Shall in great *Chaos* wombe againe be hid.

23

O warie wisedome of the man, that would
That *Carthage* towres from spoile should be forborne,   310
To th'end that his victorious people should
With cancring laisure not be ouerworne;
   He well foresaw, how that the Romane courage,
Impatient of pleasures faint desires,
Through idlenes would turne to ciuill rage,   315
And be her selfe the matter of her fires.
   For in a people giuen all to ease,
Ambition is engendred easily;
As in a vicious bodie, grose disease
Soone growes through humours superfluitie.   320
     That came to passe, when swolne with plenties pride,
     Nor prince, nor peere, nor kin they would abide.

24

If the blinde furie, which warres breedeth oft,
Wonts not t'enrage the hearts of equall beasts,
Whether they fare on foote, or flie aloft,   325
Or armed be with clawes, or scalie creasts;
   What fell *Erynnis* with hot burning tongs,
Did grype your hearts, with noysome rage imbew'd,
That each to other working cruell wrongs,
Your blades in your owne bowels you embrew'd?   330
   Was this (ye *Romanes*) your hard destinie?
Or some old sinne, whose vnappeased guilt
Powr'd vengeance forth on you eternallie?
Or brothers blood, the which at first was spilt
     Vpon your walls, that God might not endure,   335
     Vpon the same to set foundation sure?

25

O that I had the *Thracian* Poets harpe,
For to awake out of th'infernall shade
Those antique *Cæsars*, sleeping long in darke,
340   The which this auncient Citie whilome made:
    Or that I had *Amphions* instrument,
To quicken with his vitall notes accord,
The stonie ioynts of these old walls now rent,
By which th'*Ausonian* light might be restor'd:
345   Or that at least I could with pencill fine,
Fashion the pourtraicts of these Palacis,
By paterne of great *Virgils* spirit diuine;
I would assay with that which in me is,
    To builde with leuell of my loftie style,
350   That which no hands can euermore compyle.

26

Who list the Romane greatnes forth to figure,
Him needeth not to seeke for vsage right
Of line, or lead, or rule, or squaire, to measure
Her length, her breadth, her deepnes, or her hight,
355   But him behooues to vew in compasse round
All that the Ocean graspes in his long armes;
Be it where the yerely starre doth scortch the ground,
Or where colde *Boreas* blowes his bitter stormes.
    Rome was th'whole world, and al the world was *Rome*,
360   And if things nam'd their names doo equalize,
When land and sea ye name, then name ye *Rome*;
And naming *Rome* ye land and sea comprize:
    For th'auncient Plot of *Rome* displayed plaine,
    The map of all the wide world doth containe.

27

Thou that at *Rome* astonisht dost behold   365
The antique pride, which menaced the skie,
These haughtie heapes, these palaces of olde,
These wals, these arcks, these baths, these temples hie;
    Iudge by these ample ruines vew, the rest
The which iniurious time hath quite outworne,   370
Since of all workmen helde in reckning best,
Yet these olde fragments are for paternes borne:
    Then also marke, how Rome from day to day,
Repayring her decayed fashion,
Renewes herselfe with buildings rich and gay;   375
That one would iudge, that the *Romaine Dæmon*
    Doth yet himselfe with fatall hand enforce,
    Againe on foote to reare her pouldred corse.

28

He that hath seene a great Oke drie and dead,
Yet clad with reliques of some Trophees olde,   380
Lifting to heauen her aged hoarie head,
Whose foote in ground hath left but feeble holde;
    But halfe disbowel'd lies aboue the ground,
Shewing her wreathed rootes, and naked armes,
And on her trunke all rotten and vnsound   385
Onely supports herselfe for meate of wormes;
    And though she owe her fall to the first winde,
Yet of the deuout people is ador'd,
And manie yong plants spring out of her rinde;
Who such an Oke hath seene, let him record   390
    That such this Cities honour was of yore,
    And mongst all Cities florished much more.

29
All that which *Aegypt* whilome did deuise,
All that which *Greece* their temples to embraue,
After th'Ionicke, Atticke, Doricke guise,
Or *Corinth* skil'd in curious workes to graue;
  All that *Lysippus* practike arte could forme,
Apelles wit, or *Phidias* his skill,
Was wont this auncient Citie to adorne,
And the heauen it selfe with her wide wonders fill;
  All that which *Athens* euer brought forth wise,
All that which *Afrike* euer brought forth strange,
All that which *Asie* euer had of prise,
Was here to see. O meruelous great change:
  Rome liuing, was the worlds sole ornament,
  And dead, is now the worlds sole moniment.

30
Like as the seeded field greene grasse first showes,
Then from greene grasse into a stalke doth spring,
And from a stalke into an eare forth-growes,
Which eare the frutefull graine doth shortly bring;
  And as in season due the husband mowes
The wauing lockes of those faire yeallow heares,
Which bound in sheaues, and layd in comely rowes,
Vpon the naked fields in stackes he reares:
  So grew the Romane Empire by degree,
Till that Barbarian hands it quite did spill,
And left of it but these olde markes to see,
Of which all passers by doo somewhat pill:
  As they which gleane, the reliques vse to gather,
  Which th'husbandman behind him chanst to scater.

31

That same is now nought but a champian wide,
Where all this worlds pride once was situate.
No blame to thee, whosoeuer dost abide
By *Nyle*, or *Gange*, or *Tygre*, or *Euphrate*,
    Ne *Afrike* thereof guiltie is, nor *Spaine*,   425
Nor the bolde people by the *Thamis* brincks,
Nor the braue warlicke brood of *Alemaine*,
Nor the borne Souldier which *Rhine* running drinks:
    Thou onely cause, O Ciuill furie, art
Which sowing in th'*Aemathian* fields thy spight,   430
Didst arme thy hand against thy proper hart;
To th'end that when thou wast in greatest hight
    To greatnes growne, through long prosperitie,
    Thou then adowne might'st fall more horriblie.

32

Hope ye my verses that posteritie   435
Of age ensuing shall you euer read?
Hope ye that euer immortalitie
So meane Harpes worke may chalenge for her meed?
    If vnder heauen anie endurance were,
These moniments, which not in paper writ,   440
But in Porphyre and Marble doo appeare,
Might well haue hop'd to haue obtained it.
    Nath'les my Lute, whom *Phœbus* deignd to giue,
Cease not to sound these olde antiquities:
For if that time doo let thy glorie liue,   445
Well maist thou boast, how euer base thou bee,
    That thou art first, which of thy Nation song
    Th'olde honour of the people gowned long.

L'Envoy.

Bellay, first garland of free Poësie
450   That France brought forth, though fruitfull of braue wits,
Well worthie thou of immortalitie,
That long hast traueld by thy learned writs,
    Olde Rome out of her ashes to reuiue,
    And giue a second life to dead decayes:
455   Needes must he all eternitie suruiue,
That can to other giue eternall dayes.
    Thy dayes therefore are endles, and thy prayse
Excelling all, that euer went before;
And after thee, gins Bartas hie to rayse
460   His heauenly Muse, th'Almightie to adore.
    Liue happie spirits, th'honour of your name,
    And fill the world with neuer dying fame.

FINIS.

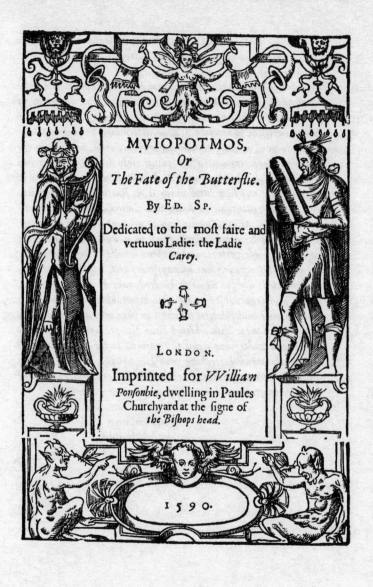

MVIOPOTMOS,
Or
The Fate of the Butterflie.

By Ed. Sp.

Dedicated to the most faire and
vertuous Ladie: the Ladie
Carey.

LONDON.

Imprinted for VVilliam
Ponsonbie, dwelling in Paules
Churchyard at the signe of
the Bishops head.

1590.

To the right worthy and vertuous
Ladie; the La: *Carey*.

*Most braue and bountifull La: for so excellent fauours as I haue
receiued at your sweet handes, to offer these fewe leaues as in
recompence, should be as to offer flowers to the Gods for their
diuine benefites. Therefore I haue determined to giue my selfe*

5   *wholy to you, as quite abandoned from my selfe, and absolutely
vowed to your seruices: which in all right is euer held for full
recompence of debt or damage to haue the person yeelded. My
person I wot wel how little worth it is. But the faithfull minde
and humble zeale which I beare vnto your La: may perhaps be*

10   *more of price, as may please you to account and vse the poore
seruice thereof; which taketh glory to aduance your excellent
partes and noble vertues, and to spend it selfe in honouring you:
not so much for your great bounty to my self, which yet may not
be vnminded; nor for name or kindreds sake by you vouchsafed,*

15   *beeing also regardable; as for that honorable name, which yee
haue by your braue deserts purchast to your self, and spred in the
mouths of al men: with which I haue also presumed to grace my
verses, and vnder your name to commend to the world this smal
Poëme, the which beseeching your La: to take in worth, and of*

20   *all things therein according to your wonted graciousnes to make
a milde construction, I humbly pray for your happines.*

Your La: euer
humbly;
E: S.

Muiopotmos: or
The Fate of the Butterflie.

I sing of deadly dolorous debate,
Stir'd vp through wrathfull *Nemesis* despight,
Betwixt two mightie ones of great estate,
Drawne into armes, and proofe of mortall fight,
Through prowd ambition, and hartswelling hate,   5
Whilest neither could the others greater might
And sdeignfull scorne endure; that from small iarrè
Their wraths at length broke into open warre.

The roote whereof and tragicall effect,
Vouchsafe, O thou the mournfulst Muse of nyne,   10
That wontst the tragick stage for to direct,
In funerall complaints and waylfull tyne,
Reueale to me, and all the meanes detect,
Through which sad *Clarion* did at last declyne
To lowest wretchednes; And is there then   15
Such rancour in the harts of mightie men?

Of all the race of siluer-winged Flies
Which doo possesse the Empire of the aire,
Betwixt the centred earth, and azure skies,
Was none more fauourable, nor more faire,   20
Whilst heauen did fauour his felicities,
Then *Clarion*, the eldest sonne and haire
Of *Muscaroll*, and in his fathers sight
Of all aliue did seeme the fairest wight.

With fruitfull hope his aged breast he fed   25
Of future good, which his yong toward yeares,
Full of braue courage and bold hardyhed,
Aboue th'ensample of his equall peares,
Did largely promise, and to him forered

30

(Whilst oft his heart did melt in tender teares)
That he in time would sure proue such an one,
As should be worthie of his fathers throne.

The fresh yong flie, in whom the kindly fire
Of lustfull yougth began to kindle fast,
35   Did much disdaine to subiect his desire
To loathsome sloth, or houres in ease to wast;
But ioy'd to range abroad in fresh attire,
Through the wide compas of the ayrie coast,
And with vnwearied wings each part t'inquire
40   Of the wide rule of his renowmed sire.

For he so swift and nimble was of flight,
That from this lower tract he dar'd to stie
Vp to the clowdes, and thence with pineons light,
To mount aloft vnto the Christall skie,
45   To vew the workmanship of heauens hight:
Whence downe descending he along would flie
Vpon the streaming riuers, sport to finde;
And oft would dare to tempt the troublous winde.

So on a Summers day, when season milde
50   With gentle calme the world had quieted,
And high in heauen *Hyperions* fierie childe
Ascending, did his beames abroad dispred,
Whiles all the heauens on lower creatures smilde;
Yong *Clarion* with vauntfull lustie head,
55   After his guize did cast abroad to fare;
And theretoo gan his furnitures prepare.

His breastplate first, that was of substance pure,
Before his noble heart he firmely bound,
That mought his life from yron death assure,
60   And ward his gentle corpes from cruell wound:
For it by arte was framed, to endure
The bit of balefull steele and bitter stownd,
No lesse than that, which *Vulcane* made to sheild
Achilles life from fate of *Troyan* field.

And then about his shoulders broad he threw   65
An hairie hide of some wilde beast, whom hee
In saluage forrest by aduenture slew,
And reft the spoyle his ornament to bee:
Which spredding all his backe with dreadfull vew,
Made all that him so horrible did see,   70
Thinke him *Alcides* with the Lyons skin,
When the *Næmean* Conquest he did win.

Vpon his head his glistering Burganet,
The which was wrought by wonderous deuice,
And curiously engrauen, he did set: 75
The mettall was of rare and passing price;
Not *Bilbo* steele, nor brasse from *Corinth* fet,
Nor costly *Oricalche* from strange *Phœnice*;
But such as could both *Phœbus* arrowes ward,
And th'hayling darts of heauen beating hard.   80

Therein two deadly weapons fixt he bore,
Strongly outlaunced towards either side,
Like two sharpe speares, his enemies to gore:
Like as a warlike Brigandine, applyde
To fight, layes forth her threatfull pikes afore,   85
The engines which in them sad death doo hyde:
So did this flie outstretch his fearefull hornes,
Yet so as him their terrour more adornes.

Lastly his shinie wings as siluer bright,
Painted with thousand colours, passing farre   90
All Painters skill, he did about him dight:
Not halfe so manie sundrie colours arre
In *Iris* bowe, ne heauen doth shine so bright,
Distinguished with manie a twinckling starre,
Nor *Iunoes* Bird in her ey-spotted traine   95
So manie goodly colours doth containe.

Ne (may it be withouten perill spoken)
The Archer God, the sonne of *Cytheree*,
That ioyes on wretched louers to be wroken,
100   And heaped spoyles of bleeding harts to see,
Beares in his wings so manie a changefull token.
Ah my liege Lord, forgiue it vnto mee,
If ought against thine honour I haue tolde;
Yet sure those wings were fairer manifolde.

105   Full manie a Ladie faire, in Court full oft
Beholding them, him secretly enuide,
And wisht that two such fannes, so silken soft,
And golden faire, her Loue would her prouide;
Or that when them the gorgeous Flie had doft,
110   Some one that would with grace be gratifide,
From him would steale them priuily away,
And bring to her so precious a pray.

Report is that dame *Venus* on a day,
In spring when flowres doo clothe the fruitful ground,
115   Walking abroad with all her Nymphes to play,
Bad her faire damzels flocking her arownd,
To gather flowres, her forhead to array:
Emongst the rest a gentle Nymph was found,
Hight *Astery*, excelling all the crewe
120   In curteous vsage, and vnstained hewe.

Who being nimbler ioynted than the rest,
And more industrious, gathered more store
Of the fields honour, than the others best;
Which they in secret harts enuying sore,
125   Tolde *Venus*, when her as the worthiest
She praisd', that *Cupide* (as they heard before)
Did lend her secret aide, in gathering
Into her lap the children of the spring.

Whereof the Goddesse gathering iealous feare,
Not yet vnmindfull, how not long agoe   130
Her sonne to *Psyche* secrete loue did beare,
And long it close conceal'd, till mickle woe
Thereof arose, and manie a rufull teare;
Reason with sudden rage did ouergoe,
And giuing hastie credit to th'accuser,   135
Was led away of them that did abuse her.

Eftsoones that Damzel by her heauenly might,
She turn'd into a winged Butterflie,
In the wide aire to make her wandring flight;
And all those flowres, with which so plenteouslie   140
Her lap she filled had, that bred her spight,
She placed in her wings, for memorie
Of her pretended crime, though crime none were:
Since which that flie them in her wings doth beare.

Thus the fresh *Clarion* being readie dight,   145
Vnto his iourney did himselfe addresse,
And with good speed began to take his flight:
Ouer the fields in his franke lustinesse,
And all the champion he soared light,
And all the countrey wide he did possesse,   150
Feeding vpon their pleasures bounteouslie,
That none gainsaid, nor none did him enuie.

The woods, the riuers, and the medowes green,
With his aire-cutting wings he measured wide,
Ne did he leaue the mountaines bare vnseene,   155
Nor the ranke grassie fennes delights vntride.
But none of these, how euer sweete they beene,
Mote please his fancie, nor him cause t'abide:
His choicefull sense with euerie change doth flit.
No common things may please a wauering wit.   160

To the gay gardins his vnstaid desire
Him wholly caried, to refresh his sprights:
There lauish Nature in her best attire,
Powres forth sweete odors, and alluring sights;
165   And Arte with her contending, doth aspire
T'excell the naturall, with made delights:
And all that faire or pleasant may be found,
In riotous excesse doth there abound.

There he arriuing, round about doth flie,
170   From bed to bed, from one to other border,
And takes suruey with curious busie eye,
Of euerie flowre and herbe there set in order;
Now this, now that he tasteth tenderly,
Yet none of them he rudely doth disorder,
175   Ne with his feete their silken leaues deface;
But pastures on the pleasures of each place.

And euermore with most varietie,
And change of sweetnesse (for all change is sweete)
He casts his glutton sense to satisfie,
180   Now sucking of the sap of herbe most meete,
Or of the deaw, which yet on them does lie,
Now in the same bathing his tender feete:
And then he pearcheth on some braunch thereby,
To weather him, and his moyst wings to dry.

185   And then againe he turneth to his play,
To spoyle the pleasures of that Paradise:
The wholsome Saulge, and Lauender still gray,
Ranke smelling Rue, and Cummin good for eyes,
The Roses raigning in the pride of May,
190   Sharpe Isope, good for greene wounds remedies,
Faire Marigoldes, and Bees alluring Thime,
Sweete Marioram, and Daysies decking prime.

Coole Violets, and Orpine growing still,
Embathed Balme, and chearfull Galingale,
Fresh Costmarie, and breathfull Camomill,   195
Dull Poppie, and drink-quickning Setuale,
Veyne-healing Veruen, and hed-purging Dill,
Sound Sauorie, and Bazill hartie-hale,
Fat Colworts, and comforting Perseline,
Colde Lettuce, and refreshing Rosmarine.   200

And whatso else of vertue good or ill
Grewe in this Gardin, fetcht from farre away,
Of euerie one he takes, and tastes at will,
And on their pleasures greedily doth pray.
Then when he hath both plaid, and fed his fill,   205
In the warme Sunne he doth himselfe embay,
And there him rests in riotous suffisaunce
Of all his gladfulnes, and kingly ioyaunce.

What more felicitie can fall to creature,
Than to enioy delight with libertie,   210
And to be Lord of all the workes of Nature,
To raine in th'aire from earth to highest skie,
To feed on flowres, and weeds of glorious feature,
To take what euer thing doth please the eie?
Who rests not pleased with such happines,   215
Well worthie he to taste of wretchednes.

But what on earth can long abide in state?
Or who can him assure of happie day;
Sith morning faire may bring fowle euening late,
And least mishap the most blisse alter may?   220
For thousand perills lie in close awaite
About vs daylie, to worke our decay;
That none, except a God, or God him guide,
May them auoyde, or remedie prouide.

225 And whatso heauens in their secret doome
Ordained haue, how can fraile fleshly wight
Forecast, but it must needs to issue come?
The sea, the aire, the fire, the day, the night,
And th'armies of their creatures all and some
230 Do serue to them, and with importune might
Warre against vs the vassals of their will.
Who then can saue, what they dispose to spill?

Not thou, O *Clarion*, though fairest thou
Of all thy kinde, vnhappie happie Flie,
235 Whose cruell fate is wouen euen now
Of *Ioues* owne hand, to worke thy miserie:
Ne may thee helpe the manie hartie vow,
Which thy olde Sire with sacred pietie
Hath powred forth for thee, and th'altars sprent:
240 Nought may thee saue from heauens auengement.

It fortuned (as heauens had behight)
That in this gardin, where yong *Clarion*
Was wont to solace him, a wicked wight
The foe of faire things, th'author of confusion,
245 The shame of Nature, the bondslaue of spight,
Had lately built his hatefull mansion,
And lurking closely, in awayte now lay,
How he might anie in his trap betray.

But when he spide the ioyous Butterflie
250 In this faire plot dispacing too and fro,
Fearles of foes and hidden ieopardie,
Lord how he gan for to bestirre him tho,
And to his wicked worke each part applie:
His heart did earne against his hated foe,
255 And bowels so withranckling poyson swelde,
That scarce the skin the strong contagion helde.

The cause why he this Flie so maliced,
Was (as in stories it is written found)
For that his mother which him bore and bred,
The most fine-fingred workwoman on ground,   260
Arachne, by his meanes was vanquished
Of *Pallas*, and in her owne skill confound,
When she with her for excellence contended,
That wrought her shame, and sorrow neuer ended.

For the *Tritonian* Goddesse hauing hard   265
Her blazed fame, which all the world had fil'd,
Came downe to proue the truth, and due reward
For her prais-worthie workmanship to yeild
But the presumptuous Damzel rashly dar'd
The Goddesse selfe to chalenge to the field,   270
And to compare with her in curious skill
Of workes with loome, with needle, and with quill.

Minerua did the chalenge not refuse,
But deign'd with her the paragon to make:
So to their worke they sit, and each doth chuse   275
What storie she will for her tapet take.
Arachne figur'd how *Ioue* did abuse
Europa like a Bull, and on his backe
Her through the sea did beare; so liuely seene,
That it true Sea, and true Bull ye would weene.   280

She seem'd still backe vnto the land to looke,
And her play-fellowes aide to call, and feare
The dashing of the waues, that vp she tooke
Her daintie feete, and garments gathered neare:
But (Lord) how she in euerie member shooke,   285
When as the land she saw no more appeare,
But a wilde wildernes of waters deepe:
Then gan she greatly to lament and weepe.

Before the Bull she pictur'd winged Loue,
With his yong brother Sport, light fluttering
Vpon the waues, as each had been a Doue;
The one his bowe and shafts, the other Spring
A burning Teade about his head did moue,
As in their Syres new loue both triumphing:
And manie Nymphes about them flocking round,
And manie *Tritons*, which their hornes did sound.

And round about, her worke she did empale
With a faire border wrought of sundrie flowres,
Enwouen with an Yuie winding trayle:
A goodly worke, full fit for Kingly bowres,
Such as Dame *Pallas*, such as Enuie pale,
That al good things with venemous tooth deuowres,
Could not accuse. Then gan the Goddesse bright
Her selfe likewise vnto her worke to dight.

She made the storie of the olde debate,
Which she with *Neptune* did for *Athens* trie:
Twelue Gods doo sit around in royall state,
And *Ioue* in midst with awfull Maiestie,
To iudge the strife betweene them stirred late:
Each of the Gods by his like visnomie
Eathe to be knowen; but *Ioue* aboue them all,
By his great lookes and power Imperiall.

Before them stands the God of Seas in place,
Clayming that sea-coast Citie as his right,
And strikes the rockes with his three-forked mace;
Whenceforth issues a warlike steed in sight,
The signe by which he chalengeth the place,
That all the Gods, which saw his wondrous might
Did surely deeme the victorie his due:
But seldome seene, foreiudgement proueth true.

290

295

300

305

310

315

320

Then to her selfe she giues her *Aegide* shield,
And steelhed speare, and morion on her hedd,
Such as she oft is seene in warlicke field:
Then sets she forth, how with her weapon dredd
She smote the ground, the which streight foorth did yield   325
A fruitfull Olyue tree, with berries spredd,
That all the Gods admir'd; then all the storie
She compast with a wreathe of Olyues hoarie.

Emongst those leaues she made a Butterflie,
With excellent deuice and wondrous slight,   330
Fluttring among the Oliues wantonly,
That seem'd to liue, so like it was in sight:
The veluet nap which on his wings doth lie,
The silken downe with which his backe is dight,
His broad outstretched hornes, his hayrie thies,   335
His glorious colours, and his glistering eies.

Which when *Arachne* saw, as ouerlaid,
And mastered with workmanship so rare,
She stood astonied long, ne ought gainesaid,
And with fast fixed eyes on her did stare,   340
And by her silence, signe of one dismaid,
The victorie did yeeld her as her share:
Yet did she inly fret, and felly burne,
And all her blood to poysonous rancor turne.

That shortly from the shape of womanhed   345
Such as she was, when *Pallas* she attempted,
She grew to hideous shape of dryrihed,
Pined with griefe of follie late repented:
Eftsoones her white streight legs were altered
To crooked crawling shankes, of marrowe empted,   350
And her faire face to fowle and loathsome hewe,
And her fine corpes to a bag of venim grewe.

This cursed creature, mindfull of that olde
Enfestred grudge, the which his mother felt,
355   So soone as *Clarion* he did beholde,
His heart with vengefull malice inly swelt,
And weauing straight a net with manie a folde
About the caue, in which he lurking dwelt,
With fine small cords about it stretched wide,
360   So finely sponne, that scarce they could be spide.

Not anie damzell, which her vaunteth most
In skilfull knitting of soft silken twyne;
Nor anie weauer, which his worke doth boast
In dieper, in damaske, or in lyne;
365   Nor anie skil'd in workmanship embost;
Nor anie skil'd in loupes of fingring fine,
Might in their diuers cunning euer dare,
With this so curious networke to compare.

Ne doo I thinke, that that same subtil gin,
370   The which the *Lemnian* God framde craftilie,
Mars sleeping with his wife to compasse in,
That all the Gods with common mockerie
Might laugh at them, and scorne their shamefull sin,
Was like to this. This same he did applie,
375   For to entrap the careles *Clarion*,
That rang'd each where without suspition.

Suspition of friend, nor feare of foe,
That hazarded his health, had he at all,
But walkt at will, and wandred too and fro,
380   In the pride of his freedome principall:
Litle wist he his fatall future woe,
But was secure, the liker he to fall.
He likest is to fall into mischaunce,
That is regardles of his gouernaunce.

Yet still *Aragnoll* (so his foe was hight)   385
Lay lurking couertly him to surprise,
And all his gins that him entangle might,
Drest in good order as he could deuise.
At length the foolish Flie without foresight,
As he that did all daunger quite despise,   390
Toward those parts came flying careleslie,
Where hidden was his hatefull enemie.

Who seeing him, with secrete ioy therefore
Did tickle inwardly in euerie vaine,
And his false hart fraught with all treasons store,   395
Was fil'd with hope, his purpose to obtaine:
Himselfe he close vpgathered more and more
Into his den, that his deceiptfull traine
By his there being might not be bewraid,
Ne anie noyse, ne anie motion made.   400

Like as a wily Foxe, that hauing spide,
Where on a sunnie banke the Lambes doo play,
Full closely creeping by the hinder side,
Lyes in ambushment of his hoped pray,
Ne stirreth limbe, till seeing readie tide,   405
He rusheth forth, and snatcheth quite away
One of the litle yonglings vnawares:
So to his worke *Aragnoll* him prepares.

Who now shall giue vnto my heauie eyes
A well of teares, that all may ouerflow?   410
Or where shall I finde lamentable cryes,
And mournfull tunes enough my griefe to show?
Helpe O thou Tragick Muse, me to deuise
Notes sad enough, t'expresse this bitter throw:
For loe, the drerie stownd is now arriued,   415
That of all happines hath vs depriued.

The luckles *Clarion*, whether cruell Fate,
Or wicked Fortune faultles him misled,
Or some vngracious blast out of the gate
420 Of *Aeoles* raine perforce him droue on hed,
Was (O sad hap and howre vnfortunate)
With violent swift flight forth caried
Into the cursed cobweb, which his foe
Had framed for his finall ouerthroe.

425 There the fond Flie entangled, strugled long,
Himselfe to free thereout; but all in vaine.
For striuing more, the more in laces strong
Himselfe he tide, and wrapt his winges twaine
In lymie snares the subtill loupes among;
430 That in the ende he breathelesse did remaine,
And all his yougthly forces idly spent,
Him to the mercie of th'auenger lent.

Which when the greisly tyrant did espie,
Like a grimme Lyon rushing with fierce might
435 Out of his den, he seized greedelie
On the resistles pray, and with fell spight,
Vnder the left wing stroke his weapon slie
Into his heart, that his deepe groning spright
In bloodie streames foorth fled into the aire,
440 His bodie left the spectacle of care.

FINIS.

Visions of the worlds vanitie.

1

One day, whiles that my daylie cares did sleepe,
My spirit, shaking off her earthly prison,
Began to enter into meditation deepe
Of things exceeding reach of common reason;
　Such as this age, in which all good is geason,   5
And all that humble is and meane debaced,
Hath brought forth in her last declining season,
Griefe of good mindes, to see goodnesse disgraced.
　On which when as my thought was throghly placed,
Vnto my eyes strange showes presented were,   10
Picturing that, which I in minde embraced,
That yet those sights empassion me full nere.
　　Such as they were (faire Ladie) take in worth,
　　That when time serues, may bring things better forth.

2

In Summers day, when *Phœbus* fairly shone,   15
I saw a Bull as white as driuen snowe,
With gilden hornes embowed like the Moone,
In a fresh flowring meadow lying lowe:
　Vp to his eares the verdant grasse did growe,
And the gay floures did offer to be eaten;   20
But he with fatnes so did ouerflowe,
That he all wallowed in the weedes downe beaten,
　Ne car'd with them his daintie lips to sweeten:
Till that a Brize, a scorned little creature,
Through his faire hide his angrie sting did threaten,   25
And vext so sore, that all his goodly feature,
　　And all his plenteous pasture nought him pleased:
　　So by the small the great is oft diseased.

3

Beside the fruitfull shore of muddie *Nile*,
30   Vpon a sunnie banke outstretched lay
In monstrous length, a mightie Crocodile,
That cram'd with guiltles blood, and greedie pray
    Of wretched people trauailing that way,
Thought all things lesse than his disdainfull pride.
35   I saw a little Bird, cal'd *Tedula*,
The least of thousands which on earth abide,
    That forst this hideous beast to open wide
The greisly gates of his deuouring hell,
And let him feede, as Nature doth prouide,
40   Vpon his iawes, that with blacke venime swell.
    Why then should greatest things the least disdaine,
    Sith that so small so mightie can constraine?

4

The kingly Bird, that beares *Ioues* thunder-clap,
One day did scorne the simple Scarabee,
45   Proud of his highest seruice, and good hap,
That made all other Foules his thralls to bee:
    The silly Flie, that no redresse did see,
Spide where the Eagle built his towring nest,
And kindling fire within the hollow tree,
50   Burnt vp his yong ones, and himselfe distrest;
    Ne suffred him in anie place to rest,
But droue in *Ioues* owne lap his egs to lay;
Where gathering also filth him to infest,
Forst with the filth his egs to fling away:
55   For which when as the Foule was wroth, said *Ioue*,
    Lo how the least the greatest may reproue.

5

Toward the sea turning my troubled eye,
I saw the fish (if fish I may it cleepe)
That makes the sea before his face to flye,
And with his flaggie finnes doth seeme to sweepe   60
    The fomie waues out of the dreadfull deep,
The huge *Leuiathan*, dame Natures wonder,
Making his sport, that manie makes to weep:
A sword-fish small him from the rest did sunder,
    That in his throat him pricking softly vnder,   65
His wide Abysse him forced forth to spewe,
That all the sea did roare like heauens thunder,
And all the waues were stain'd with filthie hewe.
    Hereby I learned haue, not to despise,
    What euer thing seemes small in common eyes.   70

6

An hideous Dragon, dreadfull to behold,
Whose backe was arm'd against the dint of speare,
With shields of brasse, that shone like burnisht golde,
And forkhed sting, that death in it did beare,
    Stroue with a Spider his vnequall peare: 75
And bad defiance to his enemie.
The subtill vermin creeping closely neare,
Did in his drinke shed poyson priuilie;
    Which through his entrailes spredding diuersly,
Made him to swell, that nigh his bowells brust,   80
And him enforst to yeeld the victorie,
That did so much in his owne greatnesse trust.
    O how great vainnesse is it then to scorne
    The weake, that hath the strong so oft forlorne.

7

85   High on a hill a goodly Cedar grewe,
        Of wondrous length, and streight proportion,
        That farre abroad her daintie odours threwe;
        Mongst all the daughters of proud *Libanon*,
            Her match in beautie was not anie one.
90   Shortly within her inmost pith there bred
        A litle wicked worme, perceiu'd of none,
        That on her sap and vitall moysture fed:
            Thenceforth her garland so much honoured
            Began to die, (O great ruth for the same)
95   And her faire lockes fell from her loftie head,
        That shortly balde, and bared she became.
            I, which this sight beheld, was much dismayed,
            To see so goodly thing so soone decayed.

8

        Soone after this I saw an Elephant,
100   Adorn'd with bells and bosses gorgeouslie,
        That on his backe did beare (as batteilant)
        A gilden towre, which shone exceedinglie;
            That he himselfe through foolish vanitie,
            Both for his rich attire, and goodly forme,
105   Was puffed vp with passing surquedrie,
        And shortly gan all other beasts to scorne.
            Till that a little Ant, a silly worme,
            Into his nosthrils creeping, so him pained,
        That casting downe his towres, he did deforme
110   Both borrowed pride, and natiue beautie stained.
            Let therefore nought that great is, therein glorie,
            Sith so small thing his happines may varie.

9

Looking far foorth into the Ocean wide,
A goodly ship with banners brauely dight,
And flag in her top-gallant I espide,   115
Through the maine sea making her merry flight:
    Faire blew the winde into her bosome right;
And th'heauens looked louely all the while,
That she did seeme to daunce, as in delight,
And at her owne felicitie did smile.   120
    All sodainely there cloue vnto her keele
A little fish, that men call *Remora*,
Which stopt her course, and held her by the heele,
That winde nor tide could moue her thence away.
    Straunge thing me seemeth, that so small a thing   125
    Should able be so great an one to wring.

10

A mighty Lyon, Lord of all the wood,
Hauing his hunger throughly satisfide,
With pray of beasts, and spoyle of liuing blood,
Safe in his dreadles den him thought to hide: 130
    His sternesse was his prayse, his strength his pride,
And all his glory in his cruell clawes.
I saw a wasp, that fiercely him defide,
And bad him battaile euen to his iawes;
    Sore he him stong, that it the blood forth drawes,   135
And his proude heart is fild with fretting ire:
In vaine he threats his teeth, his tayle, his pawes,
And from his bloodie eyes doth sparkle fire;
    That dead himselfe he wisheth for despight.
    So weakest may anoy the most of might.   140

11

What time the Romaine Empire bore the raine
Of all the world, and florisht most in might,
The nations gan their soueraigntie disdaine,
And cast to quitt them from their bondage quight:
145   So when all shrouded were in silent night,
The *Galles* were, by corrupting of a mayde,
Possest nigh of the Capitol through slight,
Had not a Goose the treachery bewrayde.

If then a Goose great *Rome* from ruine stayde,
150   And *Ioue* himselfe, the patron of the place,
Preserud from being to his foes betrayde,
Why do vaine men mean things so much deface,
        And in their might repose their most assurance,
        Sith nought on earth can chalenge long endurance?

12

155   When these sad sights were ouerpast and gone,
My spright was greatly moued in her rest,
With inward ruth and deare affection,
To see so great things by so small distrest:
        Thenceforth I gan in my engrieued brest
160   To scorne all difference of great and small,
Sith that the greatest often are opprest,
And vnawares doe into daunger fall.

        And ye, that read these ruines tragicall
Learne by their losse to loue the low degree,
165   And if that fortune chaunce you vp to call
To honours seat, forget not what you be:
        For he that of himselfe is most secure,
        Shall finde his state most fickle and vnsure.

FINIS.

The Visions of Bellay.

1

It was the time, when rest soft sliding downe
From heauens hight into mens heauy eyes,
In the forgetfulnes of sleepe doth drowne
The carefull thoughts of mortall miseries:
    Then did a Ghost before mine eyes appeare,   5
On that great riuers banck, that runnes by *Rome*,
Which calling me by name, bad me to reare
My lookes to heauen whence all good gifts do come,
    And crying lowd, loe now beholde (quoth hee)
What vnder this great temple placed is: 10
Lo all is nought but flying vanitee.
So I that know this worlds inconstancies,
    Sith onely God surmounts all times decay,
    In God alone my confidence do stay.

2

On high hills top I saw a stately frame,   15
An hundred cubits high by iust assize,
With hundreth pillours fronting faire the same,
All wrought with Diamond after Dorick wize:
    Nor brick, nor marble was the wall in view,
But shining Christall, which from top to base   20
Out of her womb a thousand rayons threw,
On hundred steps of *Afrike* golds enchase:
    Golde was the parget, and the seeling bright
Did shine all scaly with great plates of golde;
The floore of *Iasp* and *Emeraude* was dight.   25
O worlds vainesse. Whiles thus I did behold,
    An earthquake shooke the hill from lowest seat,
    And ouerthrew this frame with ruine great.

3

Then did a sharped spyre of Diamond bright,
30   Ten feete each way in square, appeare to mee,
Iustly proportion'd vp vnto his hight,
So far as Archer might his leuel see:
    The top thereof a pot did seeme to beare,
Made of the mettall, which we most do honour,
35   And in this golden vessell couched weare
The ashes of a mightie Emperour:
    Vpon foure corners of the base were pight,
To beare the frame, foure great Lyons of gold;
A worthy tombe for such a worthy wight.
40   Alas this world doth nought but grieuance hold.
    I saw a tempest from the heauen descend,
    Which this braue monument with flash did rend.

4

I saw raysde vp on yuorie pillours tall,
Whose bases were of richest mettalls warke,
45   The chapters Alablaster, the fryses christall,
The double front of a triumphall Arke:
    On each side purtraid was a Victorie,
Clad like a Nimph, that wings of siluer weares,
And in triumphant chayre was set on hie,
50   The auncient glory of the Romaine Peares.
    No worke it seem'd of earthly craftsmans wit,
But rather wrought by his owne industry,
That thunder-dartes for *Ioue* his syre doth fit.
Let me no more see faire thing vnder sky,
55   Sith that mine eyes haue seene so faire a sight
    With sodain fall to dust consumed quight.

5

Then was the faire *Dodonian* tree far seene,
Vpon seauen hills to spread his gladsome gleame,
And conquerours bedecked with his greene,
Along the bancks of the *Ausonian* streame: 60
    There many an auncient Trophee was addrest,
And many a spoyle, and many a goodly show,
Which that braue races greatnes did attest,
That whilome from the *Troyan* blood did flow.
    Rauisht I was so rare a thing to vew,   65
When lo a barbarous troupe of clownish fone
The honour of these noble boughs down threw,
Vnder the wedge I heard the tronck to grone;
      And since I saw the roote in great disdaine
      A twinne of forked trees send forth againe.   70

6

I saw a Wolfe vnder a rockie caue
Noursing two whelpes; I saw her litle ones
In wanton dalliance the teate to craue,
While she her neck wreath'd from them for the nones:
    I saw her raunge abroad to seeke her food,   75
And roming through the field with greedie rage
T'embrew her teeth and clawes with lukewarm blood
Of the small heards, her thirst for to asswage.
    I saw a thousand huntsmen, which descended
Downe from the mountaines bordring *Lombardie*,   80
That with an hundred speares her flank wide rended.
I saw her on the plaine outstretched lie,
      Throwing out thousand throbs in her owne soyle:
      Soone on a tree vphang'd I saw her spoyle.

7

85   I saw the Bird that can the Sun endure,
With feeble wings assay to mount on hight,
By more and more she gan her wings t'assure,
Following th'ensample of her mothers sight:
    I saw her rise, and with a larger flight
90 To pierce the cloudes, and with wide pinneons
To measure the most haughtie mountaines hight,
Vntill she raught the Gods owne mansions:
    There was she lost, when suddaine I behelde,
Where tumbling through the ayre in firie fold,
95 All flaming downe she on the plaine was felde,
And soone her bodie turn'd to ashes colde.
    I saw the foule that doth the light dispise,
Out of her dust like to a worme arise.

8

    I saw a riuer swift, whose fomy billowes
100 Did wash the ground work of an old great wall;
I saw it couer'd all with griesly shadowes,
That with black horror did the ayre appall:
    Thereout a strange beast with seuen heads arose,
That townes and castles vnder her brest did coure,
105 And seem'd both milder beasts and fiercer foes
Alike with equall rauine to deuoure.
    Much was I mazde, to see this monsters kinde
In hundred formes to change his fearefull hew,
When as at length I saw the wrathfull winde,
110 Which blows cold storms, burst out of *Scithian* mew,
    That sperst these cloudes, and in so short as thought,
    This dreadfull shape was vanished to nought.

9

Then all astonied with this mighty ghoast,
An hideous bodie big and strong I sawe,
With side long beard, and locks down hanging loast,   115
Sterne face, and front full of Saturnlike awe;
    Who leaning on the belly of a pot,
Pourd foorth a water, whose out gushing flood
Ran bathing all the creakie shore aflot,
Whereon the *Troyan* prince spilt *Turnus* blood;   120
    And at his feete a bitch wolfe suck did yeeld
To two young babes: his left the *Palme* tree stout,
His right hand did the peacefull *Oliue* wield,
And head with Lawrell garnisht was about.
    Sudden both *Palme* and *Oliue* fell away,   125
    And faire greene Lawrell branch did quite decay.

10

Hard by a riuers side a virgin faire,
Folding her armes to heauen with thousand throbs,
And outraging her cheekes and golden haire,
To falling riuers sound thus tun'd her sobs.   130
    Where is (quoth she) this whilom honoured face?
Where the great glorie and the auncient praise,
In which all worlds felicitie had place,
When Gods and men my honour vp did raise?
    Suffisd' it not that ciuill warres me made   135
The whole worlds spoile, but that this Hydra new,
Of hundred *Hercules* to be assaide,
With seuen heads, budding monstrous crimes anew,
    So many *Neroes* and *Caligulaes*
    Out of these crooked shores must dayly rayse?   140

11

Vpon an hill a bright flame I did see,
Wauing aloft with triple point to skie,
Which like incense of precious Cedar tree,
With balmie odours fil'd th'ayre farre and nie.
145   A Bird all white, well feathered on each wing,
Hereout vp to the throne of Gods did flie,
And all the way most pleasant notes did sing,
Whilst in the smoake she vnto heauen did stie.
    Of this faire fire the scattered rayes forth threw
150 On euerie side a thousand shining beames:
When sudden dropping of a siluer dew
(O grieuous chance) gan quench those precious flames;
    That it which earst so pleasant sent did yeld,
    Of nothing now but noyous sulphure smeld.

12

155   I saw a spring out of a rocke forth rayle,
As cleare as Christall gainst the Sunnie beames,
The bottome yeallow, like the golden grayle
That bright *Pactolus* washeth with his streames;
    It seem'd that Art and Nature had assembled
160 All pleasure there, for which mans hart could long;
And there a noyse alluring sleepe soft trembled,
Of manie accords more sweete than Mermaids song:
    The seates and benches shone as yuorie,
    And hundred Nymphes sate side by side about;
165 When from nigh hills with hideous outcrie,
A troupe of Satyres in the place did rout,
    Which with their villeine feete the streame did ray,
    Threw down the seats, and droue the Nymphs away.

13

Much richer then that vessell seem'd to bee,
Which did to that sad *Florentine* appeare,   170
Casting mine eyes farre off, I chaunst to see,
Vpon the *Latine* Coast herselfe to reare:
　But suddenly arose a tempest great,
Bearing close enuie to these riches rare,
Which gan assaile this ship with dreadfull threat,   175
This ship, to which none other might compare.
　And finally the storme impetuous
Sunke vp these riches, second vnto none,
Within the gulfe of greedie *Nereus*.
I saw both ship and mariners each one,   180
　And all that treasure drowned in the maine:
　But I the ship saw after raisd' againe.

14

　Long hauing deeply gron'd these visions sad,
I saw a Citie like vnto that same,
Which saw the messenger of tidings glad;   185
But that on sand was built the goodly frame:
　It seem'd her top the firmament did rayse,
And no lesse rich than faire, right worthie sure
(If ought here worthie) of immortall dayes,
Or if ought vnder heauen might firme endure.   190
　Much wondred I to see so faire a wall:
When from the Northerne coast a storme arose,
Which breathing furie from his inward gall
On all, which did against his course oppose,
　Into a clowde of dust sperst in the aire   195
　The weake foundations of this Citie faire.

15

At length, euen at the time, when *Morpheus*
Most trulie doth vnto our eyes appeare,
Wearie to see the heauens still wauering thus,
200   I saw *Typhæus* sister comming neare;
　　Whose head full brauely with a morion hidd,
Did seeme to match the Gods in Maiestie.
She by a riuers bancke that swift downe slidd,
Ouer all the world did raise a Trophee hie;
205　　An hundred vanquisht Kings vnder her lay,
With armes bound at their backs in shamefull wize;
Whilst I thus mazed was with great affray,
I saw the heauens in warre against her rize:
　　Then downe she stricken fell with clap of thonder,
210　　That with great noyse I wakte in sudden wonder.

FINIS.

The Visions of Petrarch.
formerly translated.

1

Being one day at my window all alone,
So manie strange things happened me to see,
As much it grieueth me to thinke thereon.
At my right hand a Hynde appear'd to mee,
   So faire as mote the greatest God delite;   5
Two eager dogs did her pursue in chace,
Of which the one was blacke, the other white:
With deadly force so in their cruell race
   They pincht the haunches of that gentle beast,
That at the last, and in short time I spide,   10
Vnder a Rocke where she alas opprest,
Fell to the ground, and there vntimely dide.
   Cruell death vanquishing so noble beautie,
   Oft makes me wayle so hard a destenie.

2

After at sea a tall ship did appeare,   15
Made all of Heben and white Yuorie,
The sailes of golde, of silke the tackle were,
Milde was the winde, calme seem'd the sea to bee,
   The skie eachwhere did show full bright and faire;
With rich treasures this gay ship fraighted was: 20
But sudden storme did so turmoyle the aire,
And tumbled vp the sea, that she (alas)
   Strake on a rock, that vnder water lay,
And perished past all recouerie.
O how great ruth and sorrowfull assay,   25
Doth vex my spirite with perplexitie,
   Thus in a moment to see lost and drown'd,
   So great riches, as like cannot be found.

3

Then heauenly branches did I see arise
30 Out of the fresh and lustie Lawrell tree,
Amidst the yong greene wood: of Paradise
Some noble plant I thought my selfe to see:
    Such store of birds therein yshrowded were,
Chaunting in shade their sundrie melodie,
35 That with their sweetnes I was rauish't nere.
While on this Lawrell fixed was mine eie,
    The skie gan euerie where to ouercast,
And darkned was the welkin all about,
When sudden flash of heauens fire out brast,
40 And rent this royall tree quite by the roote,
    Which makes me much and euer to complaine:
    For no such shadow shalbe had againe.

4

Within this wood, out of a rocke did rise
A spring of water, mildly rumbling downe,
45 Whereto approched not in anie wise
The homely shepheard, nor the ruder clowne;
    But manie Muses, and the Nymphes withall,
That sweetly in accord did tune their voyce
To the soft sounding of the waters fall,
50 That my glad hart thereat did much reioyce.
    But while herein I tooke my chiefe delight,
I saw (alas) the gaping earth deuoure
The spring, the place, and all cleane out of sight.
Which yet aggreeues my hart euen to this houre,
55   And wounds my soule with rufull memorie,
    To see such pleasures gon so suddenly.

5

I saw a Phœnix in the wood alone,
With purple wings, and crest of golden hewe;
Strange bird he was, whereby I thought anone,
That of some heauenly wight I had the vewe;   60
   Vntill he came vnto the broken tree,
And to the spring, that late deuoured was.
What say I more? each thing at last we see
Doth passe away: the Phœnix there alas
   Spying the tree destroid, the water dride,   65
Himselfe smote with his beake, as in disdaine,
And so foorthwith in great despight he dide:
That yet my heart burnes in exceeding paine,
   For ruth and pitie of so haples plight.
   O let mine eyes no more see such a sight.   70

6

   At last so faire a Ladie did I spie,
That thinking yet on her I burne and quake;
On hearbs and flowres she walked pensiuely,
Milde, but yet loue she proudly did forsake:
   White seem'd her robes, yet wouen so they were,   75
As snow and golde together had been wrought.
Aboue the wast a darke clowde shrouded her,
A stinging Serpent by the heele her caught;
   Wherewith she languisht as the gathered floure,
And well assur'd she mounted vp to ioy.   80
Alas, on earth so nothing doth endure,
But bitter griefe and sorrowfull annoy:
   Which make this life wretched and miserable,
   Tossed with stormes of fortune variable.

[7]

85   When I beheld this tickle trustles state
Of vaine worlds glorie, flitting too and fro,
And mortall men tossed by troublous fate
In restles seas of wretchednes and woe,
    I wish I might this wearie life forgoe,
90   And shortly turne vnto my happie rest,
Where my free spirite might not anie moe
Be vext with sights, that doo her peace molest.
    And ye faire Ladie, in whose bounteous brest
All heauenly grace and vertue shrined is,
95   When ye these rythmes doo read, and vew the rest,
Loath this base world, and thinke of heauens blis:
    And though ye be the fairest of Gods creatures,
    Yet thinke, that death shall spoyle your goodly
        features.

FINIS.

Daphnaïda.

An Elegie vpon the

death of the noble and vertuous
Douglas Howard, *Daughter and*
heire of *Henry* Lord *Howard,* Vis-
count *Byndon, and wife of Ar-*
thure Gorges *Esquier.*

Dedicated to the Right honorable the Lady
Helena, Marquesse of *Northampton.*

By Ed. Sp.

At London
Printed for William Ponsonby, dwelling in
Paules Churchyard at the signe of the
Bishops head 1591.

To the right Hono-
rable and vertuous Lady *Helena*
Marquesse of North-hampton.

I haue the rather presumed humbly to offer vnto your Honor the
dedication of this little Poëme, for that the noble and vertuous
Gentlewoman of whom it is written, was by match neere alied,
and in affection greatly deuoted vnto your Ladiship. The occasion
5   *why I wrote the same, was aswell the great good fame which I*
heard of her deceassed, as the particular goodwill which I beare
vnto her husband Master Arthure Gorges, *a louer of learning and*
vertue, whose house as your Ladiship by mariage hath honoured, so
doo I finde the name of them by many notable records, to be of
10   *great antiquitie in this Realm; and such as haue euer borne*
themselues with honorable reputation to the world, and vnspotted
loyaltie to their Prince and Countrey: besides so linially are they
descended from the Howards, *as that the Lady* Anne Howard,
eldest daughter to Iohn *Duke of* Norfolke, *was wife to Sir*
15   Edmund, *mother to Sir* Edward, *and grandmother to Sir* William
and Sir Thomas Gorges *Knights. And therefore I doo assure*
my selfe that no due honour done to the white Lyon, but will be
most gratefull to your Ladiship, whose husband and children doo
so neerely participate with the bloud of that noble familie. So in
20   *all duetie I recommend this Pamphlet, and the good acceptance*
thereof, to your honorable fauour and protection. London *this*
first of Ianuary.   1591.

Your Honours humbly euer.

E. Sp.

Daphnaïda.

What euer man he be, whose heauie minde
With griefe of mournefull great mishap opprest,
Fit matter for his cares increase would finde:
Let reade the rufull plaint herein exprest
Of one (I weene) the wofulst man aliue;   5
Euen sad *Alcyon*, whose empierced brest
Sharpe sorrowe did in thousand peeces riue.

But who so else in pleasure findeth sense,
Or in this wretched life dooth take delight,
Let him be banisht farre away from hence: 10
Ne let the sacred Sisters here be hight,
Though they of sorrowe heauilie can sing;
For euen their heauie song would breede delight:
But here no tunes, saue sobs and grones shall ring.

In stead of them, and their sweete harmonie,   15
Let those three fatall Sisters, whose sad hands
Doo weaue the direfull threds of destinie,
And in their wrath breake off the vitall bands,
Approach hereto: and let the dreadfull Queene
Of darkenes deepe come from the Stygian strands,   20
And grisly Ghosts to heare this dolefull teene.

In gloomie euening, when the wearie Sun
After his dayes long labour drew to rest,
And sweatie steeds now hauing ouer run
The compast skie, gan water in the west,   25
I walkt abroade to breath the freshing ayre
In open fields, whose flowring pride opprest
With early frosts, had lost their beautie faire.

There came vnto my minde a troublous thought,
Which dayly dooth my weaker wit possesse,
Ne lets it rest, vntill it forth haue brought
Her long borne Infant, fruit of heauinesse,
Which she conceiued hath through meditation
Of this worlds vainnesse and lifes wretchednesse,
That yet my soule it deepely doth empassion.

So as I muzed on the miserie,
In which men liue, and I of many most,
Most miserable man; I did espie
Where towards me a sory wight did cost,
Clad all in black, that mourning did bewray:
And *Iaakob* staffe in hand deuoutlie crost,
Like to some Pilgrim come from farre away.

His carelesse locks, vncombed and vnshorne
Hong long adowne, and beard all ouer growne,
That well he seemd to be sum wight forlorne;
Downe to the earth his heauie eyes were throwne
As loathing light: and euer as he went,
He sighed soft, and inly deepe did grone,
As if his heart in peeces would haue rent.

Approaching nigh, his face I vewed nere,
And by the semblant of his countenance,
Me seemd I had his person seene elsewhere,
Most like *Alcyon* seeming at a glaunce;
Alcyon he, the iollie Shepheard swaine,
That wont full merrilie to pipe and daunce,
And fill with pleasance euery wood and plaine.

Yet halfe in doubt because of his disguize,
I softlie sayd *Alcyon*? There with all
He lookt a side as in disdainefull wise,
Yet stayed not: till I againe did call.
Then turning back he saide with hollow sound,
Who is it, that dooth name me, wofull thrall,
The wretchedst man that treades this day on ground?

One, whome like wofulnesse impressed deepe
Hath made fit mate thy wretched case to heare,   65
And giuen like cause with thee to waile and weepe:
Griefe findes some ease by him that like does beare,
Then stay *Alcyon*, gentle shepheard stay,
(Quoth I) till thou haue to my trustie eare
Committed, what thee dooth so ill apay.   70

Cease foolish man (saide he halfe wrothfully)
To seeke to heare that which cannot be tolde.
For the huge anguish, which dooth multiplie
My dying paines, no tongue can well vnfold:
Ne doo I care, that any should bemone   75
My hard mishap, or any weepe that would,
But seeke alone to weepe, and dye alone.

Then be it so (quoth I) that thou art bent
To die alone, vnpitied, vnplained,
Yet ere thou die, it were conuenient   80
To tell the cause, which thee theretoo constrained:
Least that the world thee dead accuse of guilt,
And say, when thou of none shalt be maintained,
That thou for secret crime thy blood hast spilt.

Who life dooes loath, and longs to bee vnbound   85
From the strong shackles of fraile flesh (quoth he)
Nought cares at all, what they that liue on ground
Deeme the occasion of his death to bee:
Rather desires to be forgotten quight,
Than question made of his calamitie,   90
For harts deep sorrow hates both life and light.

Yet since so much thou seemst to rue my griefe,
And carest for one that for himselfe cares nought,
(Signe of thy loue, though nought for my reliefe:
For my reliefe exceedeth liuing thought)   95
I will to thee this heauie case relate,
Then harken well till it to ende bee brought,
For neuer didst thou heare more haplesse fate.

Whilome I vsde (as thou right well doest know)
My little flocke on westerne downes to keepe,
Not far from whence *Sabrinaes* streame doth flow,
And flowrie bancks with siluer liquor steepe:
Nought carde I then for worldly change or chaunce,
For all my ioy was on my gentle sheepe,
And to my pype to caroll and to daunce.

It there befell as I the fields did range
Fearelesse and free, a faire young Lionesse,
White as the natiue Rose before the chaunge,
Which *Venus* blood did in her leaues impresse,
I spied playing on the grassie playne
Her youthfull sports and kindlie wantonnesse,
That did all other Beasts in beawtie staine.

Much was I moued at so goodly sight;
Whose like before mine eye had seldome seene,
And gan to cast, how I her compasse might,
And bring to hand, that yet had neuer beene:
So well I wrought with mildnes and with paine,
That I her caught disporting on the grene,
And brought away fast bound with siluer chaine.

And afterwards I handled her so fayre,
That though by kind shee stout and saluage were,
For being borne an auncient Lions haire,
And of the race, that all wild beastes do feare;
Yet I her fram'd and wan so to my bent,
That shee became so meeke and milde of cheare,
As the least lamb in all my flock that went.

For shee in field, where euer I did wend,
Would wend with me, and waite by me all day:
And all the night that I in watch did spend,
If cause requir'd, or els in sleepe, if nay,
Shee would all night by mee or watch, or sleepe;
And euermore when I did sleepe or play,
She of my flock would take full warie keepe.

Safe then and safest were my sillie sheepe,
Ne fear'd the Wolfe, ne fear'd the wildest beast: 135
All were I drown'd in carelesse quiet deepe:
My louelie Lionesse without beheast
So carefull was for them and for my good,
That when I waked, neither most nor least
I found miscaried or in plaine or wood.   140

Oft did the Shepeheards, which my hap did heare,
And oft their lasses which my luck enuide,
Daylie resort to me from farre and neare,
To see my Lyonesse, whose praises wide
Were spred abroad; and when her worthinesse   145
Much greater than the rude report they tri'de,
They her did praise, and my good fortune blesse.

Long thus I ioyed in my happinesse,
And well did hope my ioy would haue no end:
But oh fond man, that in worlds ficklenesse   150
Reposedst hope, or weenedst her thy frend,
That glories most in mortall miseries,
And daylie doth her changefull counsels bend
To make new matter fit for Tragedies.

For whilest I was thus without dread or dout,   155
A cruell *Satyre* with his murdrous dart,
Greedie of mischiefe ranging all about,
Gaue her the fatall wound of deadlie smart:
And reft fro me my sweete companion,
And reft fro me my loue, my life, my hart,   160
My Lyonesse (ah woe is mee) is gon.

Out of the world thus was she reft awaie,
Out of the world, vnworthie such a spoyle;
And borne to heauen, for heauen a fitter pray:
Much fitter than the Lyon, which with toyle   165
Alcides slew, and fixt in firmament;
Her now I seek throughout this earthlie soyle,
And seeking misse, and missing doe lament.

Therewith he gan afresh to waile and weepe,
170   That I for pittie of his heauie plight,
Could not abstaine mine eyes with teares to steepe:
But when I saw the anguish of his spright
Some deale alaid, I him bespake againe.
Certes *Alcyon*, painfull is thy plight,
175   That it in me breeds almost equall paine.

Yet doth not my dull wit well vnderstand
The riddle of thy loued Lionesse;
For rare it seemes in reason to be skand
That man, who doth the whole worlds rule possesse
180   Should to a beast his noble hart embase,
And be the vassall of his vassalesse:
Therefore more plaine aread this doubtfull case.

Then sighing sore, *Daphne* thou knewest (quoth he)
She now is dead; ne more endured to say:
185   But fell to ground for great extreamitie,
That I beholding it, with deepe dismay
Was much appald, and lightlie him vprearing,
Reuoked life that would haue fled away,
All were my self through griefe in deadly drearing.

190   Then gan I him to comfort all my best,
And with milde counsaile stroue to mitigate
The stormie passion of his troubled brest,
But he thereby was more empassionate:
As stubborne steed, that is with curb restrained,
195   Becomes more fierce and feruent in his gate;
And breaking foorth at last, thus dearnelie plained.

1   What man henceforth, that breatheth vitall ayre,
Will honour heauen, or heauenlie powers adore?
Which so vniustlie doe their iudgments share;
200   Mongst earthlie wightes, as to afflict so sore
The innocent, as those which do transgresse,
And do not spare the best or fayrest more,
Than worst or fowlest, but doe both oppresse.

If this be right, why did they then create
The world so fayre, sith fairenesse is neglected?   205
Or whie be they themselues immaculate,
If purest things be not by them respected?
She faire, shee pure, most faire, most pure shee was,
Yet was by them as thing impure reiected:
Yet shee in purenesse, heauen it selfe did pas.   210

In purenesse and in all celestiall grace,
That men admire in goodlie womankinde,
Shee did excell and seem'd of Angels race
Liuing on earth like Angell new diuinde,
Adorn'd with wisedome and with chastitie: 215
And all the dowries of a noble mind,
Which did her beautie much more beautifie.

No age hath bred (since fayre *Astræa* left
The sinfull world) more vertue in a wight,
And when she parted hence, with her she reft   220
Great hope; and robd her race of bountie quight:
Well may the shepheard lasses now lament,
For dubble losse by her hath on them light;
To loose both her and bounties ornament.

Ne let *Elisa* royall Shepheardesse   225
The praises of my parted loue enuy,
For she hath praises in all plenteousnesse
Powr'd vpon her like showers of *Castaly*
By her own Shepheard, *Colin* her owne Shepherd,
That her with heauenly hymnes doth deifie,   230
Of rustick muse full hardly to be betterd.

She is the Rose, the glorie of the day,
And mine the Primrose in the lowly shade,
Mine, ah not mine; amisse I mine did say:
Not mine but his, which mine awhile her made: 235
Mine to be his, with him to liue for ay:
O that so faire a flower so soone should fade,
And through vntimely tempest fall away.

She fell away in her first ages spring,
240   Whil'st yet her leafe was greene, and fresh her rinde,
And whil'st her braunch faire blossomes foorth did bring,
She fell away against all course of kinde:
For age to dye is right, but youth is wrong;
She fel away like fruit blowne downe with winde:
245   Weepe Shepheard weepe to make my vndersong.

2 What hart so stony hard, but that would weepe,
And poure foorth fountaines of incessant teares?
What *Timon*, but would let compassion creepe
Into his brest, and pierce his frosen eares?
250   In stead of teares, whose brackish bitter well
I wasted haue, my heart blood dropping weares,
To thinke to ground how that faire blossome fell.

Yet fell she not, as one enforst to dye,
Ne dyde with dread and grudging discontent,
255   But as one toyld with trauaile downe doth lye,
So lay she downe, as if to sleepe she went,
And closde her eyes with carelesse quietnesse;
The whiles soft death away her spirit hent,
And soule assoyld from sinfull fleshlinesse.

260   Yet ere that life her lodging did forsake,
She all resolu'd and ready to remoue,
Calling to me (ay me) this wise bespake;
Alcyon, ah my first and latest loue,
Ah why does my *Alcyon* weepe and mourne,
265   And grieue my ghost, that ill mote him behoue,
As if to me had chanst some euill tourne?

I, since the messenger is come for mee,
That summons soules vnto the bridale feast
Of his great Lord, must needes depart from thee,
270   And straight obay his soueraine beheast:
Why should *Alcyon* then so sore lament,
That I from miserie shall be releast,
And freed from wretched long imprisonment?

Our daies are full of dolor and disease,
Our life afflicted with incessant paine,   275
That nought on earth may lessen or appease.
Why then should I desire here to remaine?
Or why should he that loues me, sorie bee
For my deliuerance, or at all complaine
My good to heare, and toward ioyes to see?   280

I goe, and long desired haue to goe,
I goe with gladnesse to my wished rest,
Whereas no worlds sad care, nor wasting woe
May come their happie quiet to molest,
But Saints and Angels in celestiall thrones   285
Eternally him praise, that hath them blest,
There shall I be amongst those blessed ones.

Yet ere I goe, a pledge I leaue with thee
Of the late loue, the which betwixt vs past,
My yong *Ambrosia*, in lieu of mee   290
Loue her: so shall our loue for euer last.
Thus deare adieu, whom I expect ere long:
So hauing said, away she softly past:
Weep Shepheard weep, to make mine vndersong.

3 So oft as I record those piercing words,   295
Which yet are deepe engrauen in my brest,
And those last deadly accents, which like swords
Did wound my heart and rend my bleeding chest,
With those sweet sugred speaches doo compare,
The which my soule first conquerd and possest,   300
The first beginners of my endles care;

And when those pallid cheekes and ashy hew,
In which sad death his pourtraicture had writ,
And when those hollow eyes and deadly view,
On which the clowde of ghastly night did sit,   305
I match with that sweet smile and chearful brow,
Which all the world subdued vnto it;
How happie was I then, and wretched now?

How happie was I, when I saw her leade
310 The Shepheards daughters dauncing in a rownd?
How trimly would she trace and softly tread
The tender grasse with rosie garland crownd?
And when she list aduance her heauenly voyce,
Both Nimphs and Muses nigh she made astownd,
315 And flocks and shepheards caused to reioyce.

But now ye Shepheard lasses, who shall lead
Your wandring troupes, or sing your virelayes?
Or who shall dight your bowres, sith she is dead
That was the Lady of your holy dayes?
320 Let now your blisse be turned into bale,
And into plaints conuert your ioyous playes,
And with the same fill euery hill and dale.

Let Bagpipe neuer more be heard to shrill,
That may allure the senses to delight;
325 Ne euer Shepheard sound his Oaten quill
Vnto the many, that prouoke them might
To idle pleasance: but let ghastlinesse
And drery horror dim the chearfull light,
To make the image of true heauinesse.

330 Let birds be silent on the naked spray,
And shady woods resound with dreadfull yells:
Let streaming floods their hastie courses stay,
And parching drougth drie vp the christall wells;
Let th'earth be barren and bring foorth no flowres,
335 And th'ayre be fild with noyse of dolefull knells,
And wandring spirits walke vntimely howres.

And Nature nurse of euery liuing thing,
Let rest her selfe from her long wearinesse,
And cease henceforth things kindly forth to bring,
340 But hideous monsters full of vglinesse:
For she it is, that hath me done this wrong,
No nurse, but Stepdame cruell mercilesse,
Weepe Shepheard weepe to make my vnder song.

4 My little flocke, whom earst I lou'd so well,
And wont to feede with finest grasse that grew,   345
Feede ye hencefoorth on bitter *Astrofell*,
And stinking Smallage, and vnsauerie Rew;
And when your mawes are with those weeds corrupted,
Be ye the pray of Wolues: ne will I rew,
That with your carkasses wild beasts be glutted.   350

Ne worse to you my sillie sheepe I pray,
Ne sorer vengeance wish on you to fall
Than to my selfe, for whose confusde decay
To carelesse heauens I doo daylie call:
But heauens refuse to heare a wretches cry,   355
And cruell death doth scorne to come at call,
Or graunt his boone that most desires to dye.

The good and righteous he away doth take,
To plague th'vnrighteous which aliue remaine:
But the vngodly ones he doth forsake,   360
By liuing long to multiplie their paine:
Els surely death should be no punishment,
As the great Iudge at first did it ordaine,
But rather riddance from long languishment.

Therefore my *Daphne* they haue tane away;   365
For worthie of a better place was she:
But me vnworthie willed here to stay,
That with her lacke I might tormented be.
Sith then they so haue ordred, I will pay
Penance to her according their decree,   370
And to her ghost doo seruice day by day.

For I will walke this wandring pilgrimage
Throughout the world from one to other end,
And in affliction wast my better age.
My bread shall be the anguish of my mind,   375
My drink the teares which fro mine eyes do raine,
My bed the ground that hardest I may finde;
So will I wilfully increase my paine.

And she my loue that was, my Saint that is,
380　When she beholds from her celestiall throne,
(In which shee ioyeth in eternall blis)
My bitter penance, will my case bemone,
And pitie me that liuing thus doo die:
For heauenly spirits haue compassion
385　On mortall men, and rue their miserie.

So when I haue with sorowe satisfide
Th'importune fates, which vengeance on me seeke,
And th'heauens with long languor pacifide,
She for pure pitie of my sufferance meeke,
390　Will send for me; for which I daylie long,
And will till then my painfull penance eeke:
Weep Shepheard, weep to make my vnder song.

5 Hencefoorth I hate what euer Nature made,
And in her workmanship no pleasure finde:
395　For they be all but vaine, and quickly fade,
So soone as on them blowes the Northern winde,
They tarrie not, but flit and fall away,
Leauing behind them nought but griefe of minde,
And mocking such as thinke they long will stay.

400　I hate the heauen, because it doth withhold
Me from my loue, and eke my loue from me;
I hate the earth, because it is the mold
Of fleshly slime and fraile mortalitie;
I hate the fire, because to nought it flyes,
405　I hate the Ayre, because sighes of it be,
I hate the Sea, because it teares supplyes.

I hate the day, because it lendeth light
To see all things, and not my loue to see;
I hate the darknesse and the drery night,
410　Because they breed sad balefulnesse in mee:
I hate all times, because all times doo flye
So fast away, and may not stayed bee,
But as a speedie post that passeth by.

I hate to speake, my voyce is spent with crying:
I hate to heare, lowd plaints haue duld mine eares: 415
I hate to tast, for food withholds my dying:
I hate to see, mine eyes are dimd with teares:
I hate to smell, no sweet on earth is left:
I hate to feele, my flesh is numbd with feares:
So all my senses from me are bereft.   420

I hate all men, and shun all womankinde;
The one because as I they wretched are,
The other for because I doo not finde
My loue with them, that wont to be their Starre:
And life I hate, because it will not last,   425
And death I hate, because it life doth marre,
And all I hate, that is to come or past.

So all the world, and all in it I hate,
Because it changeth euer too and fro,
And neuer standeth in one certaine state,   430
But still vnstedfast round about doth goe,
Like a Mill wheele, in midst of miserie,
Driuen with streames of wretchednesse and woe,
That dying liues, and liuing still does dye.

So doo I liue, so doo I daylie die,   435
And pine away in selfe-consuming paine,
Sith she that did my vitall powres supplie,
And feeble spirits in their force maintaine
Is fetcht fro me, why seeke I to prolong
My wearie daies in dolor and disdaine?   440
Weep Shepheard weep to make my vnder song.

6 Why doo I longer liue in lifes despight?
And doo not dye then in despight of death:
Why doo I longer see this loathsome light,
And doo in darknesse not abridge my breath,   445
Sith all my sorrow should haue end thereby,
And cares finde quiet; is it so vneath
To leaue this life, or dolorous to dye?

To liue I finde it deadly dolorous;
450   For life drawes care, and care continuall woe:
Therefore to dye must needes be ioyeous,
And wishfull thing this sad life to forgoe.
But I must stay; I may it not amend,
My *Daphne* hence departing bad me so,
455   She bad me stay, till she for me did send.

Yet whilest I in this wretched vale doo stay,
My wearie feete shall euer wandring be,
That still I may be readie on my way,
When as her messenger doth come for me:
460   Ne will I rest my feete for feeblenesse,
Ne will I rest my limmes for fraïltie,
Ne will I rest mine eyes for heauinesse.

But as the mother of the Gods, that sought
For faire *Eurydice* her daughter deere
465   Throghout the world, with wofull heauie thought;
So will I trauell whilest I tarrie heere,
Ne will I lodge, ne will I euer lin,
Ne when as drouping *Titan* draweth neere
To loose his teeme, will I take vp my Inne.

470   Ne sleepe (the harbenger of wearie wights)
Shall euer lodge vpon mine ey-lids more;
Ne shall with rest refresh my fainting sprights,
Nor failing force to former strength restore,
But I will wake and sorrow all the night
475   With *Philumene*, my fortune to deplore,
With *Philumene*, the partner of my plight.

And euer as I see the starres to fall,
And vnder ground to goe, to giue them light
Which dwell in darknes, I to minde will call,
480   How my faire Starre (that shinde on me so bright)
Fell sodainly, and faded vnder ground;
Since whose departure, day is turnd to night,
And night without a *Venus* starre is found.

But soone as day doth shew his deawie face,
And calls foorth men vnto their toylsome trade,   485
I will withdraw me to some darksome place,
Or some deepe caue, or solitarie shade;
There will I sigh and sorrow all day long,
And the huge burden of my cares vnlade:
Weep Shepheard, weep, to make my vndersong.   490

7 Hence foorth mine eyes shall neuer more behold
Faire thing on earth, ne feed on false delight
Of ought that framed is of mortall moulde,
Sith that my fairest flower is faded quight:
For all I see is vaine and transitorie,   495
Ne will be helde in anie stedfast plight,
But in a moment loose their grace and glorie.

And ye fond men on fortunes wheele that ride,
Or in ought vnder heauen repose assurance,
Be it riches, beautie, or honors pride: 500
Be sure that they shall haue no long endurance,
But ere ye be aware will flit away;
For nought of them is yours, but th'onely vsance
Of a small time, which none ascertaine may.

And ye true Louers, whom desastrous chaunce   505
Hath farre exiled from your Ladies grace,
To mourne in sorrow and sad sufferaunce,
When ye doo heare me in that desert place
Lamenting lowde my *Daphnes* Elegie,
Helpe me to wayle my miserable case,   510
And when life parts, vouchsafe to close mine eye.

And ye more happie Louers, which enioy
The presence of your dearest loues delight,
When ye doo heare my sorrowfull annoy,
Yet pittie me in your empassiond spright,   515
And thinke that such mishap, as chaunst to me,
May happen vnto the most happiest wight;
For all mens states alike vnstedfast be.

And ye my fellow Shepheards, which do feed
520   Your carelesse flocks on hils and open plaines,
With better fortune, than did me succeed,
Remember yet my vndeserued paines,
And when ye heare, that I am dead or slaine,
Lament my lot, and tell your fellow swaines,
525   That sad *Alcyon* dyde in lifes disdaine.

And ye faire Damsels Shepheards dere delights,
That with your loues do their rude hearts possesse,
When as my hearse shall happen to your sightes,
Vouchsafe to deck the same with Cyparesse;
530   And euer sprinckle brackish teares among,
In pitie of my vndeseru'd distresse,
The which I wretch, endured haue thus long.

And ye poore Pilgrimes, that with restlesse toyle
Wearie your selues in wandring desert wayes,
535   Till that you come, where ye your vowes assoyle,
When passing by ye read these wofull layes
On my graue written, rue my *Daphnes* wrong,
And mourne for me that languish out my dayes:
Cease Shepheard, cease, and end thy vndersong.

540   Thus when he ended had his heauie plaint,
The heauiest plaint that euer I heard sound,
His cheekes wext pale, and sprights began to faint,
As if againe he would haue fallen to ground;
Which when I saw, I (stepping to him light)
545   Amooued him out of his stonie swound,
And gan him to recomfort as I might.

But he no waie recomforted would be,
Nor suffer solace to approach him nie,
But casting vp a sdeinfull eie at me,
That in his traunce I would not let him lie,   550
Did rend his haire, and beat his blubbred face
As one disposed wilfullie to die,
That I sore grieu'd to see his wretched case.

Tho when the pang was somewhat ouerpast,
And the outragious passion nigh appeased,   555
I him desirde, sith daie was ouercast,
And darke night fast approched, to be pleased
To turne aside vnto my Cabinet,
And staie with me, till he were better eased
Of that strong stownd, which him so sore beset.   560

But by no meanes I could him win thereto,
Ne longer him intreate with me to staie,
But without taking leaue, he foorth did goe
With staggring pace and dismall lookes dismay,
As if that death he in the face had seene,   565
Or hellish hags had met vpon the way:
But what of him became I cannot weene.

FINIS.

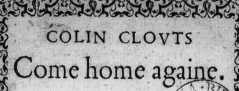

COLIN CLOVTS
Come home againe.

By Ed. Spencer.

LONDON
Printed for VVilliam Ponſonbie.
1595.

TO THE RIGHT
worthy and noble Knight
Sir *Walter Raleigh*, Captaine of her Maiesties
Guard, Lord Wardein of the Stanneries,
and Lieutenant of the Countie of
Cornwall.
(∴)

SIR, that you may see that I am not alwaies ydle as yee thinke,
though not greatly well occupied, nor altogither vndutifull, though
not precisely officious, I make you present of this simple pastorall,
vnworthie of your higher conceipt for the meanesse of the stile,
5 *but agreeing with the truth in circumstance and matter. The which*
I humbly beseech you to accept in part of paiment of the infinite
debt in which I acknowledge my selfe bounden vnto you, for your
singular fauours and sundrie good turnes shewed to me at my
late being in England, and with your good countenance protect
10 *against the malice of euill mouthes, which are alwaies wide open*
to carpe at and misconstrue my simple meaning. I pray continu-
ally for your happinesse. From my house of Kilcolman *the* 27.
of December. 1591.

Yours euer humbly.

Ed. Sp.

COLIN CLOVTS
come home againe.

The shepheards boy (best knowen by that name)
That after *Tityrus* first sung his lay,
Laies of sweet loue, without rebuke or blame,
Sate (as his custome was) vpon a day,
Charming his oaten pipe vnto his peres,   5
The shepheard swaines that did about him play:
Who all the while with greedie listfull eares,
Did stand astonisht at his curious skill,
Like hartlesse deare, dismayd with thunders sound.
At last when as he piped had his fill,   10
He rested him: and sitting then around,
One of those groomes (a iolly groome was he,
As euer piped on an oaten reed,
And lou'd this shepheard dearest in degree,
Hight *Hobbinol*) gan thus to him areed.   15
    Colin my liefe, my life, how great a losse
Had all the shepheards nation by thy lacke?
And I poore swaine of many greatest crosse:
That sith thy *Muse* first since thy turning backe
Was heard to sound as she was wont on hye,   20
Hast made vs all so blessed and so blythe.
Whilest thou wast hence, all dead in dole did lie:
The woods were heard to waile full many a sythe,
And all their birds with silence to complaine:
The fields with faded flowers did seem to mourne,   25
And all their flocks from feeding to refraine:
The running waters wept for thy returne,
And all their fish with languour did lament:
But now both woods and fields, and floods reviue,
Sith thou art come, their cause of meriment,   30
That vs late dead, hast made againe aliue:

But were it not too painfull to repeat
The passed fortunes, which to thee befell
In thy late voyage, we thee would entreat,
Now at thy leisure them to vs to tell.

    To whom the shepheard gently answered thus,
Hobbin thou temptest me to that I couet:
For of good passed newly to discus,
By dubble vsurie doth twise renew it.
And since I saw that Angels blessed eie,
Her worlds bright sun, her heauens fairest light,
My mind full of my thoughts satietie,
Doth feed on sweet contentment of that sight:
Since that same day in nought I take delight,
Ne feeling haue in any earthly pleasure,
But in remembrance of that glorious bright,
My lifes sole blisse, my hearts eternall threasure.
Wake then my pipe, my sleepie *Muse* awake,
Till I haue told her praises lasting long:
Hobbin desires, thou maist it not forsake,
Harke then ye iolly shepheards to my song.

    With that they all gan throng about him neare,
With hungrie eares to heare his harmonie:
The whiles their flocks deuoyd of dangers feare,
Did round about them feed at libertie.

    One day (quoth he) I sat, (as was my trade)
Vnder the foote of *Mole* that mountaine hore,
Keeping my sheepe amongst the cooly shade,
Of the greene alders by the *Mullaes* shore:
There a straunge shepheard chaunst to find me out,
Whether allured with my pipes delight,
Whose pleasing sound yshrilled far about,
Or thither led by chaunce, I know not right:
Whom when I asked from what place he came,
And how he hight, himselfe he did ycleepe,
The shepheard of the Ocean by name,
And said he came far from the main-sea deepe.

35

40

45

50

55

60

65

He sitting me beside in that same shade,
Prouoked me to plaie some pleasant fit,
And when he heard the musicke which I made,   70
He found himselfe full greatly pleasd at it:
Yet æmuling my pipe, he tooke in hond
My pipe before that æmuled of many,
And plaid theron; (for well that skill he cond)
Himselfe as skilfull in that art as any.   75
He pip'd, I sung; and when he sung, I piped,
By chaunge of turnes, each making other mery,
Neither enuying other, nor enuied,
So piped we, vntill we both were weary.

    There interrupting him, a bonie swaine,   80
That *Cuddy* hight, him thus atweene bespake:
And should it not thy readie course restraine,
I would request thee *Colin*, for my sake,
To tell what thou didst sing, when he did plaie.
For well I weene it worth recounting was,   85
Whether it were some hymne, or morall laie,
Or carol made to praise thy loued lasse.

    Nor of my loue, nor of my losse (quoth he)
I then did sing, as then occasion fell:
For loue had me forlorne, forlorne of me,   90
That made me in that desart chose to dwell.
But of my riuer *Bregogs* loue I soong,
Which to the shiny *Mulla* he did beare,
And yet doth beare, and euer will, so long
As water doth within his bancks appeare.   95

    Of fellowship (said then that bony Boy)
Record to vs that louely lay againe:
The staie whereof, shall nought these eares annoy,
Who all that *Colin* makes, do couet faine.

    Heare then (quoth he) the tenor of my tale,   100
In sort as I it to that shepheard told:
No leasing new, nor Grandams fable stale,
But auncient truth confirm'd with credence old.

Old father *Mole*, (*Mole* hight that mountain gray
105 That walls the Northside of *Armulla* dale)
He had a daughter fresh as floure of May,
Which gaue that name vnto that pleasant vale;
Mulla the daughter of old *Mole*, so hight
The Nimph, which of that water course has charge,
110 That springing out of *Mole*, doth run downe right
To *Butteuant*, where spreading forth at large,
It giueth name vnto that auncient Cittie,
Which *Kilnemullah* cleped is of old:
Whose ragged ruines breed great ruth and pittie,
115 To trauailers, which it from far behold.
Full faine she lou'd, and was belou'd full faine,
Of her owne brother riuer, *Bregog* hight,
So hight because of this deceitfull traine,
Which he with *Mulla* wrought to win delight.
120 But her old sire more carefull of her good,
And meaning her much better to preferre,
Did thinke to match her with the neighbour flood,
Which *Allo* hight, Broad water called farre:
And wrought so well with his continuall paine,
125 That he that riuer for his daughter wonne:
The dowre agreed, the day assigned plaine,
The place appointed where it should be doone.
Nath'lesse the Nymph her former liking held;
For loue will not be drawne, but must be ledde,
130 And *Bregog* did so well her fancie weld,
That her good will he got her first to wedde.
But for her father sitting still on hie,
Did warily still watch which way she went,
And eke from far obseru'd with iealous eie,
135 Which way his course the wanton *Bregog* bent,
Him to deceiue for all his watchfull ward,
The wily louer did deuise this slight:
First into many parts his streame he shar'd,
That whilest the one was watcht, the other might

Passe vnespide to meete her by the way;   140
And then besides, those little streames so broken
He vnder ground so closely did conuay,
That of their passage doth appeare no token,
Till they into the *Mullaes* water slide.
So secretly did he his loue enioy: 145
Yet not so secret, but it was descride,
And told her father by a shepheards boy.
Who wondrous wroth for that so foule despight,
In great auenge did roll downe from his hill
Huge mightie stones, the which encomber might   150
His passage, and his water-courses spill.
So of a Riuer, which he was of old,
He none was made, but scattred all to nought,
And lost emong those rocks into him rold,
Did lose his name: so deare his loue he bought.   155
    Which hauing said, him *Thestylis* bespake,
Now by my life this was a mery lay:
Worthie of *Colin* selfe, that did it make.
But read now eke of friendship I thee pray,
What dittie did that other shepheard sing?   160
For I do couet most the same to heare,
As men vse most to couet forreine thing.
That shall I eke (quoth he) to you declare.
His song was all a lamentable lay,
Of great vnkindnesse, and of vsage hard,   165
Of *Cynthia* the Ladie of the sea,
Which from her presence faultlesse him debard.
And euer and anon with singulfs rife,
He cryed out, to make his vndersong
Ah my loues queene, and goddesse of my life,   170
Who shall me pittie, when thou doest me wrong?
    Then gan a gentle bonylasse to speake,
That *Marin* hight, Right well he sure did plaine:
That could great *Cynthiaes* sore displeasure breake,
And moue to take him to her grace againe.   175

But tell on further *Colin*, as befell
Twixt him and thee, that thee did hence dissuade.
   When thus our pipes we both had wearied well,
(Quoth he) and each an end of singing made,
180   He gan to cast great lyking to my lore,
And great dislyking to my lucklesse lot:
That banisht had my selfe, like wight forlore,
Into that waste, where I was quite forgot.
The which to leaue, thenceforth he counseld mee,
185   Vnmeet for man, in whom was ought regardfull
And wend with him, his *Cynthia* to see:
Whose grace was great, and bounty most rewardfull.
Besides her peerlesse skill in making well
And all the ornaments of wondrous wit,
190   Such as all womankynd did far excell:
Such as the world admyr'd and praised it:
So what with hope of good, and hate of ill,
He me perswaded forth with him to fare:
Nought tooke I with me, but mine oaten quill:
195   Small needments else need shepheard to prepare.
So to the sea we came; the sea? that is
A world of waters heaped vp on hie,
Rolling like mountaines in wide wildernesse,
Horrible, hideous, roaring with hoarse crie.
200   And is the sea (quoth *Coridon*) so fearfull?
   Fearful much more (quoth he) then hart can fear:
Thousand wyld beasts with deep mouthes gaping direfull
Therin stil wait poore passengers to teare.
Who life doth loath, and longs death to behold,
205   Before he die, alreadie dead with feare,
And yet would liue with heart halfe stonie cold,
Let him to sea, and he shall see it there.
And yet as ghastly dreadfull, as it seemes,
Bold men presuming life for gaine to sell,
210   Dare tempt that gulf, and in those wandring stremes
Seek waies vnknowne, waies leading down to hell.

For as we stood there waiting on the strond,
Behold an huge great vessell to vs came,
Dauncing vpon the waters back to lond,
As if it scornd the daunger of the same;   215
Yet was it but a wooden frame and fraile,
Glewed togither with some subtile matter,
Yet had it armes and wings, and head and taile,
And life to moue it selfe vpon the water.
Strange thing, how bold and swift the monster was,   220
That neither car'd for wynd, nor haile, nor raine,
Nor swelling waues, but thorough them did passe
So proudly, that she made them roare againe.
The same aboord vs gently did receaue,
And without harme vs farre away did beare,   225
So farre that land our mother vs did leaue,
And nought but sea and heauen to vs appeare.
Then hartlesse quite and full of inward feare,
That shepheard I besought to me to tell,
Vnder what skie, or in what world we were,   230
In which I saw no liuing people dwell.
Who me recomforting all that he might,
Told me that that same was the Regiment
Of a great shepheardesse, that *Cynthia* hight,
His liege his Ladie, and his lifes Regent.   235
If then (quoth I) a shepheardesse she bee,
Where be the flockes and heards, which she doth keep?
And where may I the hills and pastures see,
On which she vseth for to feed her sheepe?
These be the hills (quoth he) the surges hie,   240
On which faire *Cynthia* her heards doth feed:
Her heards be thousand fishes with their frie,
Which in the bosome of the billowes breed.
Of them the shepheard which hath charge in chief,
Is *Triton* blowing loud his wreathed horne: 245
At sound whereof, they all for their relief
Wend too and fro at euening and at morne.

And *Proteus* eke with him does driue his heard
Of stinking Seales and Porcpisces together,
250   With hoary head and deawy dropping beard,
Compelling them which way he list, and whether.
And I among the rest of many least,
Haue in the Ocean charge to me assignd:
Where I will liue or die at her beheast,
255   And serue and honour her with faithfull mind.
Besides an hundred Nymphs all heauenly borne,
And of immortall race, doo still attend
To wash faire *Cynthiaes* sheep, when they be shorne,
And fold them vp, when they haue made an end.
260   Those be the shepheards which my *Cynthia* serue,
At sea, beside a thousand moe at land:
For land and sea my *Cynthia* doth deserue
To haue in her commandement at hand.
Thereat I wondred much, till wondring more
265   And more, at length we land far off descryde:
Which sight much gladed me; for much afore
I feard, least land we neuer should haue eyde:
Thereto our ship her course directly bent,
As if the way she perfectly had knowne.
270   We *Lunday* passe; by that same name is ment
An Island, which the first to west was showne.
From thence another world of land we kend,
Floting amid the sea in ieopardie,
And round about with mightie white rocks hemd,
275   Against the seas encroching crueltie.
Those same the shepheard told me, were the fields
In which dame *Cynthia* her landheards fed,
Faire goodly fields, then which *Armulla* yields
None fairer, nor more fruitfull to be red.
280   The first to which we nigh approched, was
An high headland thrust far into the sea,
Like to an horne, whereof the name it has,
Yet seemed to be a goodly pleasant lea:

There did a loftie mount at first vs greet,
Which did a stately heape of stones vpreare,   285
That seemd amid the surges for to fleet,
Much greater then that frame, which vs did beare:
There did our ship her fruitfull wombe vnlade,
And put vs all ashore on *Cynthias* land.

    What land is that thou meanst (then *Cuddy* sayd)   290
And is there other, then whereon we stand?

    Ah *Cuddy* (then quoth *Colin*) thous a fon,
That hast not seene least part of natures worke:
Much more there is vnkend, then thou doest kon,
And much more that does from mens knowledge lurke.   295
For that same land much larger is then this,
And other men and beasts and birds doth feed:
There fruitfull corne, faire trees, fresh herbage is
And all things else that liuing creatures need.
Besides most goodly riuers there appeare,   300
No whit inferiour to thy *Funchins* praise,
Or vnto *Allo* or to *Mulla* cleare:
Nought hast thou foolish boy seene in thy daies.
But if that land be there (quoth he) as here,
And is theyr heauen likewise there all one?   305
And if like heauen, be heauenly graces there,
Like as in this same world where we do wone?

    Both heauen and heauenly graces do much more
(Quoth he) abound in that same land, then this.
For there all happie peace and plenteous store   310
Conspire in one to make contented blisse:
No wayling there nor wretchednesse is heard,
No bloodie issues nor no leprosies,
No griesly famine, nor no raging sweard,
No nightly bodrags, nor no hue and cries;   315
The shepheards there abroad may safely lie,
On hills and downes, withouten dread or daunger:
No rauenous wolues the good mans hope destroy,
Nor outlawes fell affray the forest raunger.

320   There learned arts do florish in great honor,
      And Poets wits are had in peerlesse price:
      Religion hath lay powre to rest vpon her,
      Aduancing vertue and suppressing vice.
      For end, all good, all grace there freely growes,
325   Had people grace it gratefully to vse:
      For God his gifts there plenteously bestowes,
      But gracelesse men them greatly do abuse.
          But say on further, then said *Corylas*,
      The rest of thine aduentures, that betyded.
330   Foorth on our voyage we by land did passe,
      (Quoth he) as that same shepheard still vs guyded,
      Vntill that we to *Cynthiaes* presence came:
      Whose glorie greater then my simple thought,
      I found much greater then the former fame;
335   Such greatnes I cannot compare to ought:
      But if I her like ought on earth might read,
      I would her lyken to a crowne of lillies,
      Vpon a virgin brydes adorned head,
      With Roses dight and Goolds and Daffadillies;
340   Or like the circlet of a Turtle true,
      In which all colours of the rainbow bee;
      Or like faire *Phebes* garlond shining new,
      In which all pure perfection one may see.
      But vaine it is to thinke by paragone
345   Of earthly things, to iudge of things diuine:
      Her power, her mercy, and her wisedome, none
      Can deeme, but who the Godhead can define.
      Why then do I base shepheard bold and blind,
      Presume the things so sacred to prophane?
350   More fit it is t'adore with humble mind,
      The image of the heauens in shape humane.
          With that *Alexis* broke his tale asunder,
      Saying, By wondring at thy *Cynthiaes* praise,
      Colin, thy selfe thou mak'st vs more to wonder,
355   And her vpraising, doest thy selfe vpraise.

But let vs heare what grace she shewed thee,
And how that shepheard strange, thy cause aduanced?
    The shepheard of the Ocean (quoth he)
Vnto that Goddesse grace me first enhanced,
And to mine oaten pipe enclin'd her eare,   360
That she thenceforth therein gan take delight,
And it desir'd at timely houres to heare,
All were my notes but rude and roughly dight,
For not by measure of her owne great mynd,
And wondrous worth she mott my simple song,   365
But ioyd that country shepheard ought could fynd
Worth harkening to, emongst the learned throng.
    Why? (said *Alexis* then) what needeth shee
That is so great a shepheardesse her selfe,
And hath so many shepheards in her fee,   370
To heare thee sing, a simple silly Elfe?
Or be the shepheards which do serue her laesie,
That they list not their mery pipes applie?
Or be their pipes vntunable and craesie,
That they cannot her honour worthylie?   375
    Ah nay (said *Colin*) neither so, nor so:
For better shepheards be not vnder skie,
Nor better hable, when they list to blow
Their pipes aloud, her name to glorifie.
There is good *Harpalus* now woxen aged,   380
In faithfull seruice of faire *Cynthia:*
And there is *Corydon* though meanly waged,
Yet hablest wit of most I know this day.
And there is sad *Alcyon* bent to mourne,
Though fit to frame an euerlasting dittie,   385
Whose gentle spright for *Daphnes* death doth tourn
Sweet layes of loue to endlesse plaints of pittie.
Ah pensiue boy pursue that braue conceipt,
In thy sweet Eglantine of *Meriflure*,
Lift vp thy notes vnto their wonted height,   390
That may thy *Muse* and mates to mirth allure.

There eke is *Palin* worthie of great praise,
Albe he enuie at my rustick quill:
And there is pleasing *Alcon*, could he raise
His tunes from laies to matter of more skill.
And there is old *Palemon* free from spight,
Whose carefull pipe may make the hearer rew:
Yet he himselfe may rewed be more right,
That sung so long vntill quite hoarse he grew.
And there is *Alabaster* throughly taught,
In all this skill, though knowen yet to few,
Yet were he knowne to *Cynthia* as he ought,
His Eliseïs would be redde anew.
Who liues that can match that heroick song,
Which he hath of that mightie Princesse made?
O dreaded Dread, do not thy selfe that wrong,
To let thy fame lie so in hidden shade:
But call it forth, O call him forth to thee,
To end thy glorie which he hath begun:
That when he finisht hath as it should be,
No brauer Poeme can be vnder Sun.
Nor *Po* nor *Tyburs* swans so much renowned,
Nor all the brood of *Greece* so highly praised,
Can match that *Muse* when it with bayes is crowned,
And to the pitch of her perfection raised.
And there is a new shepheard late vp sprong,
The which doth all afore him far surpasse:
Appearing well in that well tuned song,
Which late he sung vnto a scornfull lasse.
Yet doth his trembling *Muse* but lowly flie,
As daring not too rashly mount on hight,
And doth her tender plumes as yet but trie,
In loues soft laies and looser thoughts delight.
Then rouze thy feathers quickly *Daniell*,
And to what course thou please thy selfe aduance:
But most me seemes, thy accent will excell,
In Tragick plaints and passionate mischance.

395

400

405

410

415

420

425

And there that shepheard of the Ocean is,
That spends his wit in loues consuming smart:
Full sweetly tempred is that *Muse* of his   430
That can empierce a Princes mightie hart.
There also is (ah no, he is not now)
But since I said he is, he quite is gone,
Amyntas quite is gone and lies full low,
Hauing his *Amaryllis* left to mone.   435
Helpe, O ye shepheards helpe ye all in this,
Helpe *Amaryllis* this her losse to mourne:
Her losse is yours, your losse *Amyntas* is,
Amyntas floure of shepheards pride forlorne:
He whilest he liued was the noblest swaine,   440
That euer piped in an oaten quill:
Both did he other, which could pipe, maintaine,
And eke could pipe himselfe with passing skill.
And there though last not least is *Aetion*,
A gentler shepheard may no where be found: 445
Whose *Muse* full of high thoughts inuention,
Doth like himselfe Heroically sound.
All these, and many others mo remaine,
Now after *Astrofell* is dead and gone:
But while as *Astrofell* did liue and raine,   450
Amongst all these was none his Paragone.
All these do florish in their sundry kynd,
And do their *Cynthia* immortall make:
Yet found I lyking in her royall mynd,
Not for my skill, but for that shepheards sake.   455
    Then spake a louely lasse, hight *Lucida*,
Shepheard, enough of shepheards thou hast told,
Which fauour thee, and honour *Cynthia:*
But of so many Nymphs which she doth hold
In her retinew, thou hast nothing sayd;   460
That seems, with none of them thou fauor foundest,
Or art ingratefull to each gentle mayd,
That none of all their due deserts resoundest.

       Ah far be it (quoth *Colin Clout*) fro me,
465   That I of gentle Mayds should ill deserue:
       For that my selfe I do professe to be
       Vassall to one, whom all my dayes I serue;
       The beame of beautie sparkled from aboue,
       The floure of vertue and pure chastitie,
470   The blossome of sweet ioy and perfect loue,
       The pearle of peerlesse grace and modestie:
       To her my thoughts I daily dedicate,
       To her my heart I nightly martyrize:
       To her my loue I lowly do prostrate,
475   To her my life I wholly sacrifice:
       My thought, my heart, my loue, my life is shee,
       And I hers euer onely, euer one:
       One euer I all vowed hers to bee,
       One euer I, and others neuer none.
480   Then thus *Melissa* said; Thrise happie Mayd,
       Whom thou doest so enforce to deifie:
       That woods, and hills, and valleyes thou hast made
       Her name to eccho vnto heauen hie.
       But say, who else vouchsafed thee of grace?
485   They all (quoth he) me graced goodly well,
       That all I praise, but in the highest place,
       Vrania, sister vnto *Astrofell*,
       In whose braue mynd as in a golden cofer,
       All heauenly gifts and riches locked are:
490   More rich then pearles of *Ynde*, or gold of *Opher*,
       And in her sex more wonderfull and rare.
       Ne lesse praise worthie I *Theana* read,
       Whose goodly beames though they be ouer dight
       With mourning stole of carefull wydowhead,
495   Yet through that darksome vale do glister bright;
       She is the well of bountie and braue mynd,
       Excelling most in glorie and great light:
       She is the ornament of womankind,
       And Courts chief garlond with all vertues dight.

Therefore great *Cynthia* her in chiefest grace   500
Doth hold, and next vnto her selfe aduance,
Well worthie of so honourable place,
For her great worth and noble gouernance.
Ne lesse praise worthie is her sister deare,
Faire *Marian*, the *Muses* onely darling: 505
Whose beautie shyneth as the morning cleare,
With siluer deaw vpon the roses pearling.
Ne lesse praise worthie is *Mansilia*,
Best knowne by bearing vp great *Cynthiaes* traine:
That same is she to whom *Daphnaida*   510
Vpon her neeces death I did complaine.
She is the paterne of true womanhead,
And onely mirrhor of feminitie:
Worthie next after *Cynthia* to tread,
As she is next her in nobilitie.   515
Ne lesse praise worthie *Galathea* seemes,
Then best of all that honourable crew,
Faire *Galathea* with bright shining beames,
Inflaming feeble eyes that her do view.
She there then waited vpon *Cynthia*,   520
Yet there is not her won, but here with vs
About the borders of our rich *Coshma*,
Now made of *Maa* the Nymph delitious.
Ne lesse praisworthie faire *Neæra* is,
Neæra ours, not theirs, though there she be,   525
For of the famous Shure, the Nymph she is,
For high desert, aduaunst to that degree.
She is the blosome of grace and curtesie,
Adorned with all honourable parts:
She is the braunch of true nobilitie,   530
Belou'd of high and low with faithfull harts.
Ne lesse praisworthie *Stella* do I read,
Though nought my praises of her needed arre,
Whom verse of noblest shepheard lately dead
Hath prais'd and rais'd aboue each other starre.   535

Ne lesse praisworthie are the sisters three,
The honor of the noble familie:
Of which I meanest boast my selfe to be,
And most that vnto them I am so nie.
540 *Phyllis, Charillis,* and sweet *Amaryllis,*
Phillis the faire, is eldest of the three:
The next to her, is bountifull *Charillis.*
But th'youngest is the highest in degree.
Phyllis the floure of rare perfection,
545 Faire spreading forth her leaues with fresh delight,
That with their beauties amorous reflexion,
Bereaue of sence each rash beholders sight.
But sweet *Charillis* is the Paragone
Of peerlesse price, and ornament of praise,
550 Admyr'd of all, yet enuied of none,
Through the myld temperance of her goodly raies.
Thrise happie do I hold thee noble swaine,
The which art of so rich a spoile possest,
And it embracing deare without disdaine,
555 Hast sole possession in so chaste a brest:
Of all the shepheards daughters which there bee,
And yet there be the fairest vnder skie,
Or that elsewhere I euer yet did see,
A fairer Nymph yet neuer saw mine eie:
560 She is the pride and primrose of the rest,
Made by the maker selfe to be admired:
And like a goodly beacon high addrest,
That is with sparks of heauenle beautie fired.
But *Amaryllis,* whether fortunate,
565 Or else vnfortunate may I aread,
That freed is from *Cupids* yoke by fate,
Since which she doth new bands aduenture dread.
Shepheard what euer thou hast heard to be
In this or that praysd diuersly apart,
570 In her thou maist them all assembled see,
And seald vp in the threasure of her hart.

Ne thee lesse worthie gentle *Flauia*,
For thy chaste life and vertue I esteeme:
Ne thee lesse worthie curteous *Candida*,
For thy true loue and loyaltie I deeme.   575
Besides yet many mo that *Cynthia* serue,
Right noble Nymphs, and high to be commended:
But if I all should praise as they deserue,
This sun would faile me ere I halfe had ended.
Therefore in closure of a thankfull mynd,   580
I deeme it best to hold eternally,
Their bounteous deeds and noble fauours shrynd,
Then by discourse them to indignifie.
     So hauing said, *Aglaura* him bespake:
Colin, well worthie were those goodly fauours   585
Bestowd on thee, that so of them doest make,
And them requitest with thy thankfull labours.
But of great *Cynthiaes* goodnesse and high grace,
Finish the storie which thou hast begunne.
     More eath (quoth he) it is in such a case   590
How to begin, then know how to haue donne.
For euerie gift and euerie goodly meed,
Which she on me bestowd, demaunds a day;
And euerie day, in which she did a deed,
Demaunds a yeare it duly to display.   595
Her words were like a streame of honny fleeting,
The which doth softly trickle from the hiue:
Hable to melt the hearers heart vnweeting,
And eke to make the dead againe aliue.
Her deeds were like great clusters of ripe grapes,   600
Which load the bunches of the fruitfull vine:
Offring to fall into each mouth that gapes,
And fill the same with store of timely wine.
Her lookes were like beames of the morning Sun,
Forth looking through the windowes of the East: 605
When first the fleecie cattell haue begun
Vpon the perled grasse to make their feast.

Her thoughts are like the fume of Franckincence,
Which from a golden Censer forth doth rise:
610 And throwing forth sweet odours mounts fro thence
In rolling globes vp to the vauted skies.
There she beholds with high aspiring thought,
The cradle of her owne creation:
Emongst the seats of Angels heauenly wrought,
615 Much like an Angell in all forme and fashion.
    Colin (said *Cuddy* then) thou hast forgot
Thy selfe, me seemes, too much, to mount so hie:
Such loftie flight, base shepheard seemeth not,
From flocks and fields, to Angels and to skie.
620   True (answered he) but her great excellence,
Lifts me aboue the measure of my might:
That being fild with furious insolence,
I feele my selfe like one yrapt in spright.
For when I thinke of her, as oft I ought,
625 Then want I words to speake it fitly forth:
And when I speake of her what I haue thought,
I cannot thinke according to her worth.
Yet will I thinke of her, yet will I speake,
So long as life my limbs doth hold together,
630 And when as death these vitall bands shall breake,
Her name recorded I will leaue for euer.
Her name in euery tree I will endosse,
That as the trees do grow, her name may grow:
And in the ground each where will it engrosse,
635 And fill with stones, that all men may it know.
The speaking woods and murmuring waters fall,
Her name Ile teach in knowen termes to frame:
And eke my lambs when for their dams they call,
Ile teach to call for *Cynthia* by name.
640 And long while after I am dead and rotten:
Amongst the shepheards daughters dancing rownd,
My layes made of her shall not be forgotten,
But sung by them with flowry gyrlonds crownd.

And ye, who so ye be, that shall surviue:
When as ye heare her memory renewed,   645
Be witnesse of her bountie here aliue,
Which she to *Colin* her poore shepheard shewed.
    Much was the whole assembly of those heards,
Moov'd at his speech, so feelingly he spake:
And stood awhile astonisht at his words,   650
Till *Thestylis* at last their silence brake,
Saying, Why *Colin*, since thou foundst such grace
With *Cynthia* and all her noble crew:
Why didst thou euer leaue that happie place,
In which such wealth might vnto thee accrew?   655
And back returnedst to this barrein soyle,
Where cold and care and penury do dwell:
Here to keep sheepe, with hunger and with toyle,
Most wretched he, that is and cannot tell.
    Happie indeed (said *Colin*) I him hold,   660
That may that blessed presence still enioy,
Of fortune and of enuy vncomptrold,
Which still are wont most happie states t'annoy:
But I by that which little while I prooued:
Some part of those enormities did see,   665
The which in Court continually hooued,
And followd those which happie seemd to bee.
Therefore I silly man, whose former dayes
Had in rude fields bene altogether spent,
Darest not aduenture such vnknowen wayes,   670
Nor trust the guile of fortunes blandishment,
But rather chose back to my sheep to tourne,
Whose vtmost hardnesse I before had tryde,
Then hauing learnd repentance late, to mourne
Emongst those wretches which I there descryde.   675
    Shepheard (said *Thestylis*) it seemes of spight
Thou speakest thus gainst their felicitie,
Which thou enuiest, rather then of right
That ought in them blameworthie thou doest spie.

680   Cause haue I none (quoth he) of cancred will
       To quite them ill, that me demeand so well:
       But selfe-regard of priuate good or ill,
       Moues me of each, so as I found, to tell
       And eke to warne yong shepheards wandring wit,
685   Which through report of that liues painted blisse,
       Abandon quiet home, to seeke for it,
       And leaue their lambes to losse misled amisse.
       For sooth to say, it is no sort of life,
       For shepheard fit to lead in that same place,
690   Where each one seeks with malice and with strife,
       To thrust downe other into foule disgrace,
       Himselfe to raise: and he doth soonest rise
       That best can handle his deceitfull wit,
       In subtil shifts, and finest sleights deuise,
695   Either by slaundring his well deemed name,
       Through leasings lewd, and fained forgerie:
       Or else by breeding him some blot of blame,
       By creeping close into his secrecie;
       To which him needs, a guilefull hollow hart,
700   Masked with faire dissembling curtesie,
       A filed toung furnisht with tearmes of art,
       No art of schoole, but Courtiers schoolery.
       For arts of schoole haue there small countenance,
       Counted but toyes to busie ydle braines,
705   And there professours find small maintenance,
       But to be instruments of others gaines.
       Ne is there place for any gentle wit,
       Vnlesse to please, it selfe it can applie:
       But shouldred is, or out of doore quite shit,
710   As base, or blunt, vnmeet for melodie.
       For each mans worth is measured by his weed,
       As harts by hornes, or asses by their eares:
       Yet asses been not all whose eares exceed,
       Nor yet all harts, that hornes the highest beares.
715   For highest lookes haue not the highest mynd,

Nor haughtie words most full of highest thoughts:
But are like bladders blowen vp with wynd,
That being prickt do vanish into noughts.
Euen such is all their vaunted vanitie,
Nought else but smoke, that fumeth soone away,   720
Such is their glorie that in simple eie
Seeme greatest, when their garments are most gay.
So they themselues for praise of fooles do sell,
And all their wealth for painting on a wall;
With price whereof, they buy a golden bell,   725
And purchace highest rowmes in bowre and hall:
Whiles single Truth and simple honestie
Do wander vp and downe despys'd of all;
Their plaine attire such glorious gallantry
Disdaines so much, that none them in doth call.   730
    Ah *Colin* (then said *Hobbinol*) the blame
Which thou imputest, is too generall,
As if not any gentle wit of name,
Nor honest mynd might there be found at all.
For well I wot, sith I my selfe was there,   735
To wait on *Lobbin* (*Lobbin* well thou knewest)
Full many worthie ones then waiting were,
As euer else in Princes Court thou vewest.
Of which, among you many yet remaine,
Whose names I cannot readily now ghesse: 740
Those that poore Sutors papers do retaine,
And those that skill of medicine professe.
And those that do to *Cynthia* expound
The ledden of straunge languages in charge:
For *Cynthia* doth in sciences abound,   745
And giues to their professors stipends large.
Therefore vniustly thou doest wyte them all,
For that which thou mislikedst in a few.
    Blame is (quoth he) more blamelesse generall,
Then that which priuate errours doth pursew: 750
For well I wot, that there amongst them bee

Full many persons of right worthie parts,
Both for report of spotlesse honestie,
And for profession of all learned arts,
755   Whose praise hereby no whit impaired is,
Though blame do light on those that faultie bee,
For all the rest do most-what fare amis,
And yet their owne misfaring will not see:
For either they be puffed vp with pride,
760   Or fraught with enuie that their galls do swell,
Or they their dayes to ydlenesse diuide,
Or drownded lie in pleasures wastefull well,
In which like Moldwarps nousling still they lurke,
Vnmyndfull of chiefe parts of manlinesse,
765   And do themselues for want of other worke,
Vaine votaries of laesie loue professe,
Whose seruice high so basely they ensew,
That *Cupid* selfe of them ashamed is,
And mustring all his men in *Venus* vew,
770   Denies them quite for seruitors of his.

And is loue then (said *Corylas*) once knowne
In Court, and his sweet lore professed there?
I weened sure he was our God alone:
And only woond in fields and forests here.
775   Not so (quoth he) loue most aboundeth there.
For all the walls and windows there are writ,
All full of loue, and loue, and loue my deare,
And all their talke and studie is of it.
Ne any there doth braue or valiant seeme,
780   Vnlesse that some gay Mistresse badge he beares:
Ne any one himselfe doth ought esteeme,
Vnlesse he swim in loue vp to the eares.
But they of loue and of his sacred lere,
(As it should be) all otherwise deuise,
785   Then we poore shepheards are accustomd here,
And him do sue and serue all otherwise.
For with lewd speeches and licentious deeds,

His mightie mysteries they do prophane,
And vse his ydle name to other needs,
But as a complement for courting vaine.   790
So him they do not serue as they professe,
But make him serue to them for sordid vses,
Ah my dread Lord, that doest liege hearts possesse,
Auenge thy selfe on them for their abuses.
But we poore shepheards whether rightly so,   795
Or through our rudenesse into errour led,
Do make religion how we rashly go,
To serue that God, that is so greatly dred;
For him the greatest of the Gods we deeme,
Borne without Syre or couples of one kynd,   800
For *Venus* selfe doth soly couples seeme,
Both male and female through commixture ioynd.
So pure and spotlesse *Cupid* forth she brought,
And in the gardens of *Adonis* nurst:
Where growing, he his owne perfection wrought,   805
And shortly was of all the Gods the first.
Then got he bow and shafts of gold and lead,
In which so fell and puissant he grew,
That *Ioue* himselfe his powre began to dread,
And taking vp to heauen, him godded new.   810
From thence he shootes his arrowes euery where
Into the world, at randon as he will,
On vs fraile men, his wretched vassals here,
Like as himselfe vs pleaseth, saue or spill.
So we him worship, so we him adore   815
With humble hearts to heauen vplifted hie,
That to true loues he may vs euermore
Preferre, and of their grace vs dignifie:
Ne is there shepheard, ne yet shepheards swaine,
What euer feeds in forest or in field,   820
That dare with euil deed or leasing vaine
Blaspheme his powre, or termes vnworthie yield.
    Shepheard it seemes that some celestiall rage

Of loue (quoth *Cuddy*) is breath'd into thy brest,
825   That powreth forth these oracles so sage,
Of that high powre, wherewith thou art possest.
But neuer wist I till this present day
Albe of loue I alwayes humbly deemed,
That he was such an one, as thou doest say,
830   And so religiously to be esteemed.
Well may it seeme by this thy deep insight,
That of that God the Priest thou shouldest bee:
So well thou wot'st the mysterie of his might,
As if his godhead thou didst present see.

835   Of loues perfection perfectly to speake,
Or of his nature rightly to define,
Indeed (said *Colin*) passeth reasons reach,
And needs his priest t'expresse his powre diuine.
For long before the world he was y'bore
840   And bred aboue in *Venus* bosome deare:
For by his powre the world was made of yore,
And all that therein wondrous doth appeare.
For how should else things so far from attone
And so great enemies as of them bee,
845   Be euer drawne together into one,
And taught in such accordance to agree?
Through him the cold began to couet heat,
And water fire; the light to mount on hie,
And th'heauie downe to peize; the hungry t'eat
850   And voydnesse to seeke full satietie.
So being former foes, they wexed friends,
And gan by litle learne to loue each other:
So being knit, they brought forth other kynds
Out of the fruitfull wombe of their great mother.
855   Then first gan heauen out of darknesse dread
For to appeare, and brought forth chearfull day:
Next gan the earth to shew her naked head,
Out of deep waters which her drownd alway.
And shortly after euerie liuing wight,

Crept forth like wormes out of her slimie nature,   860
Soone as on them the Suns life giuing light,
Had powred kindly heat and formall feature,
Thenceforth they gan each one his like to loue,
And like himselfe desire for to beget,
The Lyon chose his mate, the Turtle Doue   865
Her deare, the Dolphin his owne Dolphinet,
But man that had the sparke of reasons might,
More then the rest to rule his passion,
Chose for his loue the fairest in his sight,
Like as himselfe was fairest by creation.   870
For beautie is the bayt which with delight
Doth man allure, for to enlarge his kynd,
Beautie the burning lamp of heauens light,
Darting her beames into each feeble mynd:
Against whose powre, nor God nor man can fynd   875
Defence, ne ward the daunger of the wound,
But being hurt, seeke to be medicynd
Of her that first did stir that mortall stownd.
Then do they cry and call to loue apace,
With praiers lowd importuning the skie,   880
Whence he them heares, and when he list shew grace,
Does graunt them grace that otherwise would die.
So loue is Lord of all the world by right,
And rules the creatures by his powrfull saw:
All being made the vassalls of his might,   885
Through secret sence which therto doth them draw.
Thus ought all louers of their lord to deeme:
And with chaste heart to honor him alway:
But who so else doth otherwise esteeme,
Are outlawes, and his lore do disobay.   890
For their desire is base, and doth not merit,
The name of loue, but of disloyall lust:
Ne mongst true louers they shall place inherit,
But as Exuls out of his court be thrust.
    So hauing said, *Melissa* spake at will,   895

Colin, thou now full deeply hast divynd:
Of loue and beautie and with wondrous skill,
Hast *Cupid* selfe depainted in his kynd.
To thee are all true louers greatly bound,
900   That doest their cause so mightily defend:
But most, all wemen are thy debtors found,
That doest their bountie still so much commend.

   That ill (said *Hobbinol*) they him requite,
For hauing loued euer one most deare:
905   He is repayd with scorne and foule despite,
That yrkes each gentle heart which it doth heare.

   Indeed (said *Lucid*) I haue often heard
Faire *Rosalind* of diuers fowly blamed:
For being to that swaine too cruell hard,
910   That her bright glorie else hath much defamed.
But who can tell what cause had that faire Mayd
To vse him so that vsed her so well:
Or who with blame can iustly her vpbrayd,
For louing not? for who can loue compell?
915   And sooth to say, it is foolhardie thing,
Rashly to wyten creatures so diuine,
For demigods they be and first did spring
From heauen, though graft in frailnesse feminine.
And well I wote, that oft I heard it spoken,
920   How one that fairest *Helene* did reuile,
Through iudgement of the Gods to been ywroken
Lost both his eyes and so remaynd long while,
Till he recanted had his wicked rimes,
And made amends to her with treble praise:
925   Beware therefore, ye groomes, I read betimes,
How rashly blame of *Rosalind* ye raise.

   Ah shepheards (then said *Colin*) ye ne weet
How great a guilt vpon your heads ye draw:
To make so bold a doome with words vnmeet,
930   Of thing celestiall which ye neuer saw.

For she is not like as the other crew
Of shepheards daughters which emongst you bee,
But of diuine regard and heauenly hew,
Excelling all that euer ye did see.
Not then to her that scorned thing so base,   935
But to my selfe the blame that lookt so hie:
So hie her thoughts as she her selfe haue place,
And loath each lowly thing with loftie eie.
Yet so much grace let her vouchsafe to grant
To simple swaine, sith her I may not loue: 940
Yet that I may her honour paravant,
And praise her worth, though far my wit aboue.
Such grace shall be some guerdon for the griefe,
And long affliction which I haue endured:
Such grace sometimes shall giue me some reliefe,   945
And ease of paine which cannot be recured.
And ye my fellow shepheards which do see
And heare the languours of my too long dying,
Vnto the world for euer witnesse bee,
That hers I die, nought to the world denying,   950
This simple trophe of her great conquest.
    So hauing ended, he from ground did rise,
And after him vprose eke all the rest:
All loth to part, but that the glooming skies
Warnd them to draw their bleating flocks to rest.   955

FINIS.

ASTROPHEL.

A Paſtorall Elegie vpon
the death of the moſt Noble and valorous
Knight, Sir *Philip Sidney.*

Dedicated

*To the moſt beautifull and vertuous Ladie, the Counteſſe
of* Eſſex.

Astrophel.

Shepheards that wont on pipes of oaten reed,
Oft times to plaine your loues concealed smart:
And with your piteous layes haue learnd to breed
Compassion in a countrey lasses hart.
Hearken ye gentle shepheards to my song, 5
And place my dolefull plaint your plaints emong.

To you alone I sing this mournfull verse,
The mournfulst verse that euer man heard tell:
To you whose softened hearts it may empierse,
With dolours dart for death of Astrophel. 10
To you I sing and to none other wight,
For well I wot my rymes bene rudely dight.

Yet as they been, if any nycer wit
Shall hap to heare, or couet them to read:
Thinke he, that such are for such ones most fit, 15
Made not to please the liuing but the dead.
And if in him found pity euer place,
Let him be moov'd to pity such a case.

A gentle Shepheard borne in *Arcady,*
Of gentlest race that euer shepheard bore:
About the grassie bancks of *Hæmony,*
Did keepe his sheep, his litle stock and store.
Full carefully he kept them day and night, 5
In fairest fields, and *Astrophel* he hight.

Young *Astrophel* the pride of shepheards praise,
Young *Astrophel* the rusticke lasses loue:
Far passing all the pastors of his daies,
In all that seemly shepheard might behoue. 10
In one thing onely fayling of the best,
That he was not so happie as the rest.

For from the time that first the Nymph his mother
Him forth did bring, and taught her lambs to feed:
15   A sclender swaine excelling far each other,
In comely shape, like her that did him breed,
He grew vp fast in goodnesse and in grace,
And doubly faire wox both in mynd and face.

Which daily more and more he did augment,
20   With gentle vsage and demeanure myld:
That all mens hearts with secret rauishment
He stole away, and weetingly beguyld.
Ne spight it selfe that all good things doth spill,
Found ought in him, that she could say was ill.

25   His sports were faire, his ioyance innocent,
Sweet without sowre, and honny without gall:
And he himselfe seemd made for meriment,
Merily masking both in bowre and hall.
There was no pleasure nor delightfull play,
30   When *Astrophel* so euer was away.

For he could pipe and daunce, and caroll sweet,
Emongst the shepheards in their shearing feast:
As Somers larke that with her song doth greet
The dawning day forth comming from the East.
35   And layes of loue he also could compose,
Thrise happie she, whom he to praise did chose.

Full many Maydens often did him woo,
Them to vouchsafe emongst his rimes to name,
Or make for them as he was wont to doo,
40   For her that did his heart with loue inflame.
For which they promised to dight for him,
Gay chapelets of flowers and gyrlonds trim.

And many a Nymph both of the wood and brooke,
Soone as his oaten pipe began to shrill:
Both christall wells and shadie groues forsooke,   45
To heare the charmes of his enchanting skill.
And brought him presents, flowers if it were prime,
Or mellow fruit if it were haruest time.

But he for none of them did care a whit,
Yet wood Gods for them often sighed sore: 50
Ne for their gifts vnworthie of his wit,
Yet not vnworthie of the countries store.
For one alone he cared, for one he sight,
His lifes desire, and his deare loues delight.

Stella the faire, the fairest star in skie,   55
As faire as Venus or the fairest faire:
A fairer star saw neuer liuing eie,
Shot her sharp pointed beames through purest aire.
Her he did loue, her he alone did honor,
His thoughts, his rimes, his songs were all vpon her.   60

To her he vowd the seruice of his daies,
On her he spent the riches of his wit:
For her he made hymnes of immortall praise,
Of onely her he sung, he thought, he writ.
Her, and but her of loue he worthie deemed,   65
For all the rest but litle he esteemed.

Ne her with ydle words alone he wowed,
And verses vaine (yet verses are not vaine)
But with braue deeds to her sole seruice vowed,
And bold atchieuements her did entertaine.   70
For both in deeds and words he nourtred was,
Both wise and hardie (too hardie alas).

In wrestling nimble, and in renning swift,
In shooting steddie, and in swimming strong:
75 Well made to strike, to throw, to leape, to lift,
And all the sports that shepheards are emong.
In euery one he vanquisht euery one,
He vanquisht all, and vanquisht was of none.

Besides, in hunting such felicitie,
80 Or rather infelicitie he found:
That euery field and forest far away,
He sought, where saluage beasts do most abound.
No beast so saluage but he could it kill,
No chace so hard, but he therein had skill.

85 Such skill matcht with such courage as he had,
Did prick him foorth with proud desire of praise:
To seek abroad, of daunger nought y'drad,
His mistresse name, and his owne fame to raise.
What needeth perill to be sought abroad,
90 Since round about vs, it doth make aboad?

It fortuned, as he that perilous game
In forreine soyle pursued far away:
Into a forest wide, and waste he came
Where store he heard to be of saluage pray.
95 So wide a forest and so waste as this,
Nor famous *Ardeyn*, nor fowle *Arlo* is.

There his welwouen toyles and subtil traines,
He laid the brutish nation to enwrap:
So well he wrought with practise and with paines,
100 That he of them great troups did soone entrap.
Full happie man (misweening much) was hee,
So rich a spoile within his power to see.

Eftsoones all heedlesse of his dearest hale,
Full greedily into the heard he thrust:
To slaughter them, and worke their finall bale,   105
Least that his toyle should of their troups be brust.
Wide wounds emongst them many one he made,
Now with his sharp borespear, now with his blade.

His care was all how he them all might kill,
That none might scape (so partiall vnto none)   110
Ill mynd so much to mynd anothers ill,
As to become vnmyndfull of his owne.
But pardon that vnto the cruell skies,
That from himselfe to them withdrew his eies.

So as he rag'd emongst that beastly rout,   115
A cruell beast of most accursed brood
Vpon him turnd (despeyre makes cowards stout)
And with fell tooth accustomed to blood,
Launched his thigh with so mischieuous might,
That it both bone and muscles ryued quight.   120

So deadly was the dint and deep the wound,
And so huge streames of blood thereout did flow:
That he endured not the direfull stound,
But on the cold deare earth himselfe did throw.
The whiles the captiue heard his nets did rend,   125
And hauing none to let, to wood did wend.

Ah where were ye this while his shepheard peares,
To whom aliue was nought so deare as hee:
And ye faire Mayds the matches of his yeares,
Which in his grace did boast you most to bee?   130
Ah where were ye, when he of you had need,
To stop his wound that wondrously did bleed?

Ah wretched boy the shape of dreryhead,
And sad ensample of mans suddein end:
135   Full litle faileth but thou shalt be dead,
Vnpitied, vnplaynd, of foe or frend.
Whilest none is nigh, thine eylids vp to close,
And kisse thy lips like faded leaues of rose.

A sort of shepheards sewing of the chace,
140   As they the forest raunged on a day:
By fate or fortune came vnto the place,
Where as the lucklesse boy yet bleeding lay.
Yet bleeding lay, and yet would still haue bled,
Had not good hap those shepheards thether led.

145   They stopt his wound (too late to stop it was)
And in their armes then softly did him reare:
Tho (as he wild) vnto his loued lasse,
His dearest loue him dolefully did beare.
The dolefulst beare that euer man did see,
150   Was *Astrophel*, but dearest vnto mee.

She when she saw her loue in such a plight,
With crudled blood and filthie gore deformed:
That wont to be with flowers and gyrlonds dight,
And her deare fauours dearly well adorned,
155   Her face, the fairest face, that eye mote see,
She likewise did deforme like him to bee.

Her yellow locks that shone so bright and long,
As Sunny beames in fairest somers day:
She fiersly tore, and with outragious wrong
160   From her red cheeks the roses rent away.
And her faire brest the threasury of ioy,
She spoyld thereof, and filled with annoy.

His palled face impictured with death,
She bathed oft with teares and dried oft:
And with sweet kisses suckt the wasting breath,   165
Out of his lips like lillies pale and soft.
And oft she cald to him, who answerd nought,
But onely by his lookes did tell his thought.

The rest of her impatient regret,
And piteous mone the which she for him made: 170
No toong can tell, nor any forth can set,
But he whose heart like sorrow did inuade.
At last when paine his vitall powres had spent,
His wasted life her weary lodge forwent.

Which when she saw, she staied not a whit,   175
But after him did make vntimely haste:
Forth with her ghost out of her corps did flit,
And followed her make like Turtle chaste.
To proue that death their hearts cannot diuide,
Which liuing were in loue so firmly tide.   180

The Gods which all things see, this same beheld,
And pittying this paire of louers trew:
Transformed them there lying on the field,
Into one flowre that is both red and blew.
It first growes red, and then to blew doth fade,   185
Like *Astrophel*, which thereinto was made.

And in the midst thereof a star appeares,
As fairly formd as any star in skyes:
Resembling *Stella* in her freshest yeares,
Forth darting beames of beautie from her eyes,   190
And all the day it standeth full of deow,
Which is the teares, that from her eyes did flow.

That hearbe of some, Starlight is cald by name,
Of others *Penthia*, though not so well:
195   But thou where euer thou doest finde the same,
From this day forth do call it *Astrophel*.
And when so euer thou it vp doest take,
Do pluck it softly for that shepheards sake.

Hereof when tydings far abroad did passe,
200   The shepheards all which loued him full deare:
And sure full deare of all he loued was,
Did thether flock to see what they did heare.
And when that pitteous spectacle they vewed,
The same with bitter teares they all bedewed.

205   And euery one did make exceeding mone,
With inward anguish and great griefe opprest:
And euery one did weep and waile, and mone,
And meanes deviz'd to shew his sorrow best.
That from that houre since first on grassie greene
210   Shepheards kept sheep, was not like mourning seen.

But first his sister that *Clorinda* hight,
The gentlest shepheardesse that liues this day:
And most resembling both in shape and spright
Her brother deare, began this dolefull lay.
215   Which least I marre the sweetnesse of the vearse,
In sort as she it sung, I will rehearse.

[Dolefull Lay of Clorinda]

Ay me, to whom shall I my case complaine,
That may compassion my impatient griefe?
Or where shall I vnfold my inward paine,
That my enriuen heart may find reliefe?
5   Shall I vnto the heauenly powres it show?
Or vnto earthly men that dwell below?

To heauens? ah they alas the authors were,
And workers of my vnremedied wo:
For they foresee what to vs happens here,
And they foresaw, yet suffred this be so.   10
　From them comes good, from them comes also il,
　That which they made, who can them warne to spill.

To men? ah they alas like wretched bee,
And subiect to the heauens ordinance:
Bound to abide what euer they decree,   15
Their best redresse, is their best sufferance.
　How then can they like wretched comfort mee,
　The which no lesse, need comforted to bee?

Then to my selfe will I my sorrow mourne,
Sith none aliue like sorrowfull remaines: 20
And to my selfe my plaints shall back retourne,
To pay their vsury with doubled paines.
　The woods, the hills, the riuers shall resound
　The mournfull accent of my sorrowes ground.

Woods, hills and riuers, now are desolate,   25
Sith he is gone the which them all did grace:
And all the fields do waile their widow state,
Sith death their fairest flowre did late deface.
　The fairest flowre in field that euer grew,
　Was *Astrophel*; that was, we all may rew.   30

What cruell hand of cursed foe vnknowne,
Hath cropt the stalke which bore so faire a flowre?
Vntimely cropt, before it well were growne,
And cleane defaced in vntimely howre.
　Great losse to all that euer him did see,   35
　Great losse to all, but greatest losse to mee.

Breake now your gyrlonds, O ye shepheards lasses,
Sith the faire flowre, which them adornd, is gon:
The flowre, which them adornd, is gone to ashes,
40   Neuer againe let lasse put gyrlond on.
    In stead of gyrlond, weare sad Cypres nowe,
    And bitter Elder, broken from the bowe.

Ne euer sing the loue-layes which he made,
Who euer made such layes of loue as hee?
45   Ne euer read the riddles, which he sayd
Vnto your selues, to make you mery glee.
    Your mery glee is now laid all abed,
    Your mery maker now alasse is dead.

Death the deuourer of all worlds delight,
50   Hath robbed you and reft fro me my ioy:
Both you and me, and all the world he quight
Hath robd of ioyance, and left sad annoy.
    Ioy of the world, and shepheards pride was hee,
    Shepheards hope neuer like againe to see.

55   Oh death that hast vs of such riches reft,
Tell vs at least, what hast thou with it done?
What is become of him whose flowre here left
Is but the shadow of his likenesse gone.
    Scarse like the shadow of that which he was,
60   Nought like, but that he like a shade did pas.

But that immortall spirit, which was deckt
With all the dowries of celestiall grace:
By soueraine choyce from th'heuenly quires select,
And lineally deriv'd from Angels race,
65   O what is now of it become aread.
    Ay me, can so diuine a thing be dead?

Ah no: it is not dead, ne can it die,
But liues for aie, in blisfull Paradise:
Where like a new-borne babe it soft doth lie,
In bed of lillies wrapt in tender wise.   70
   And compast all about with roses sweet,
   And daintie violets from head to feet.

There thousand birds all of celestiall brood,
To him do sweetly caroll day and night:
And with straunge notes, of him well vnderstood,   75
Lull him a sleep in Angelick delight;
   Whilest in sweet dreame to him presented bee
   Immortall beauties, which no eye may see.

But he them sees and takes exceeding pleasure
Of their diuine aspects, appearing plaine,   80
And kindling loue in him aboue all measure,
Sweet loue still ioyous, neuer feeling paine.
   For what so goodly forme he there doth see,
   He may enioy from iealous rancor free.

There liueth he in euerlasting blis,   85
Sweet spirit neuer fearing more to die:
Ne dreading harme from any foes of his,
Ne fearing saluage beasts more crueltie.
   Whilest we here wretches waile his priuate lack,
   And with vaine vowes do often call him back.   90

But liue thou there still happie, happie spirit,
And giue vs leaue thee here thus to lament:
Not thee that doest thy heauens ioy inherit,
But our owne selues that here in dole are drent.
   Thus do we weep and waile, and wear our eies,   95
   Mourning in others, our owne miseries.

Which when she ended had, another swaine
Of gentle wit and daintie sweet deuice:
Whom *Astrophel* full deare did entertaine,
100   Whilest here he liv'd, and held in passing price,
Hight *Thestylis*, began his mournfull tourne,
And made the *Muses* in his song to mourne.

And after him full many other moe,
As euerie one in order lov'd him best,
105   Gan dight themselues t'expresse their inward woe,
With dolefull layes vnto the time addrest.
The which I here in order will rehearse,
As fittest flowres to deck his mournfull hearse.

AMORETTI
AND
Epithalamion.

Written not long since
by Edmunde
Spenser.

Printed for William
Ponsonby. 1595.

To the Right Worship-
full Sir Robart Need-
ham Knight.

Sir, to gratulate your safe return from Ireland, I had nothing
so readie, nor thought any thing so meete, as these sweete
conceited Sonets, the deede of that weldeseruing gentleman,
maister Edmond Spenser: whose name sufficiently warranting
5   the worthinesse of the work: I do more confidently presume
to publish it in his absence, vnder your name to whom (in
my poore opinion) the patronage therof, doth in some re-
spectes properly appertaine. For, besides your iudgement and
delighte in learned poesie: This gentle Muse for her former
10 perfection long wished for in Englande, nowe at the length
crossing the Seas in your happy companye, (though to your
selfe vnknowne) seemeth to make choyse of you, as meetest to
giue her deserued countenaunce, after her retourne: entertaine
her, then, (Right worshipfull) in sorte best beseeming your
15 gentle minde, and her merite, and take in worth my
good will herein, who seeke no more, but to shew my selfe
yours in all dutifull affection.

W. P.

G: W. senior, to the Author

Darke is the day, when *Phœbus* face is shrowded,
  and weaker sights may wander soone astray:
  but when they see his glorious raies vnclowded,
  with steddy steps they keepe the perfect way:
So while this Muse in forraine landes doth stay,   5
  inuention weepes, and pens are cast aside,
  the time like night, depriud of chearefull day,
  and few do write, but (ah) too soone may slide.
Then, hie thee home, that art our perfect guide,
  and with thy wit illustrate Englands fame,   10
  dawnting thereby our neighboures auncient pride,
  that do for poesie, challendge cheefest name.
So we that liue and ages that succeede,
  With great applause thy learned works shall reede.

Ah Colin, whether on the lowly plaine,
  pyping to shepherds thy sweete roundelaies:
  or whether singing in some lofty vaine,
  heroick deedes, of past, or present daies:
Or whether in thy louely mistris praise,   5
  thou list to exercise thy learned quill,
  thy muse hath got such grace, and power to please,
  with rare inuention bewtified by skill,
As who therein can euer ioy their fill.
  O therefore let that happy muse proceede   10
  to clime the height of vertues sacred hill,
  where endles honor shall be made thy meede.
Because no malice of succeeding daies,
  can rase those records of thy lasting praise.

G. W. I.

SONNET. I.

Happy ye leaues when as those lilly hands,
    which hold my life in their dead doing might
    shall handle you and hold in loues soft bands,
    lyke captiues trembling at the victors sight.
5   And happy lines, on which with starry light,
    those lamping eyes will deigne sometimes to look
    and reade the sorrowes of my dying spright,
    written with teares in harts close bleeding book.
And happy rymes bath'd in the sacred brooke,
10   of *Helicon* whence she deriued is,
    when ye behold that Angels blessed looke,
    my soules long lacked foode, my heauens blis.
Leaues, lines, and rymes, seeke her to please alone,
    whom if ye please, I care for other none.

SONNET. II.

Vnquiet thought, whom at the first I bred,
    Of th'inward bale of my loue pined hart:
    and sithens haue with sighes and sorrowes fed,
    till greater then my wombe thou woxen art.
5   Breake forth at length out of the inner part,
    in which thou lurkest lyke to vipers brood:
    and seeke some succour both to ease my smart
    and also to sustayne thy selfe with food.
But if in presence of that fayrest proud
10   thou chance to come, fall lowly at her feet:
    and with meeke humblesse and afflicted mood,
    pardon for thee, and grace for me intreat.
Which if she graunt, then liue and my loue cherish,
    if not, die soone, and I with thee will perish.

SONNET. III.

The souerayne beauty which I doo admyre,
  witnesse the world how worthy to be prayzed:
  the light wherof hath kindled heauenly fyre,
  in my fraile spirit by her from basenesse raysed.
That being now with her huge brightnesse dazed,   5
  base thing I can no more endure to view:
  but looking still on her I stand amazed,
  at wondrous sight of so celestiall hew.
So when my toung would speak her praises dew,
  it stopped is with thoughts astonishment: 10
  and when my pen would write her titles true,
  it rauisht is with fancies wonderment:
Yet in my hart I then both speake and write
  the wonder that my wit cannot endite.

SONNET. IIII.

New yeare forth looking out of Ianus gate,
  Doth seeme to promise hope of new delight:
  and bidding th'old Adieu, his passed date
  bids all old thoughts to die in dumpish spright.
And calling forth out of sad Winters night,   5
  fresh loue, that long hath slept in cheerlesse bower:
  wils him awake, and soone about him dight
  his wanton wings and darts of deadly power.
For lusty spring now in his timely howre,
  is ready to come forth him to receiue: 10
  and warnes the Earth with diuers colord flowre,
  to decke hir selfe, and her faire mantle weaue.
Then you faire flowre, in whom fresh youth doth raine,
  prepare your selfe new loue to entertaine.

SONNET. V.

Rudely thou wrongest my deare harts desire,
  In finding fault with her too portly pride:
  the thing which I doo most in her admire,
  is of the world vnworthy most enuide.
5 For in those lofty lookes is close implide,
  scorn of base things, and sdeigne of foule dishonor:
  thretning rash eies which gaze on her so wide,
  that loosely they ne dare to looke vpon her.
Such pride is praise, such portlinesse is honor,
10 that boldned innocence beares in hir eies:
  and her faire countenance like a goodly banner,
  spreds in defiaunce of all enemies.
Was neuer in this world ought worthy tride,
  without some spark of such self-pleasing pride.

SONNET. VI.

Be nought dismayd that her vnmoued mind
  doth still persist in her rebellious pride:
  such loue not lyke to lusts of baser kynd,
  the harder wonne, the firmer will abide.
5 The durefull Oake, whose sap is not yet dride,
  is long ere it conceiue the kindling fyre:
  but when it once doth burne, it doth diuide
  great heat, and makes his flames to heauen aspire.
So hard it is to kindle new desire,
10 in gentle brest that shall endure for euer:
  deepe is the wound, that dints the parts entire
  with chast affects, that naught but death can seuer.
Then thinke not long in taking litle paine,
  to knit the knot, that euer shall remaine.

SONNET. VII.

Fayre eyes, the myrrour of my mazed hart,
   what wondrous vertue is contaynd in you
   the which both lyfe and death forth from you dart
   into the obiect of your mighty view?
For when ye mildly looke with louely hew,   5
   then is my soule with life and loue inspired:
   but when ye lowre, or looke on me askew,
   then doe I die, as one with lightning fyred.
But since that lyfe is more then death desyred,
   looke euer louely, as becomes you best,   10
   that your bright beams of my weak eies admyred,
   may kindle liuing fire within my brest.
Such life should be the honor of your light,
   such death the sad ensample of your might.

SONNET. VIII.

More then most faire, full of the liuing fire,
   Kindled aboue vnto the maker neere:
   no eies but ioyes, in which al powers conspire,
   that to the world naught else be counted deare.
Thrugh your bright beams doth not the blinded guest   5
   shoot out his darts to base affections wound:
   but Angels come to lead fraile mindes to rest
   in chast desires on heauenly beauty bound.
You frame my thoughts and fashion me within,
   you stop my toung, and teach my hart to speake,   10
   you calme the storme that passion did begin,
   strong thrugh your cause, but by your vertue weak.
Dark is the world, where your light shined neuer;
   well is he borne, that may behold you euer.

SONNET. IX.

Long-while I sought to what I might compare
   those powrefull eies, which lighten my dark spright,
   yet find I nought on earth to which I dare
   resemble th'ymage of their goodly light.
5 Not to the Sun: for they doo shine by night;
   nor to the Moone: for they are changed neuer;
   nor to the Starres: for they haue purer sight;
   nor to the fire: for they consume not euer;
Nor to the lightning: for they still perseuer;
10 nor to the Diamond: for they are more tender;
   nor vnto Christall: for nought may them seuer;
   nor vnto glasse: such basenesse mought offend her;
Then to the Maker selfe they likest be,
   whose light doth lighten all that here we see.

SONNET. X.

Vnrighteous Lord of loue what law is this,
   That me thou makest thus tormented be:
   the whiles she lordeth in licentious blisse
   of her freewill, scorning both thee and me.
5 See how the Tyrannesse doth ioy to see
   the huge massacres which her eyes do make:
   and humbled harts brings captiues vnto thee,
   that thou of them mayst mightie vengeance take.
But her proud hart doe thou a little shake
10 and that high look, with which she doth comptroll
   all this worlds pride bow to a baser make,
   and al her faults in thy black booke enroll.
That I may laugh at her in equall sort,
   as she doth laugh at me and makes my pain her sport.

SONNET. XI.

Dayly when I do seeke and sew for peace,
   And hostages doe offer for my truth:
   she cruell warriour doth her selfe addresse
   to battell, and the weary war renew'th.
Ne wilbe moou'd with reason or with rewth,   5
   to graunt small respit to my restlesse toile:
   but greedily her fell intent poursewth,
   Of my poore life to make vnpittied spoile.
Yet my poore life, all sorrowes to assoyle,
   I would her yield, her wrath to pacify: 10
   but then she seekes with torment and turmoyle,
   to force me liue and will not let me dy.
All paine hath end and euery war hath peace,
   but mine no price nor prayer may surcease.

SONNET. XII.

One day I sought with her hart-thrilling eies
   to make a truce and termes to entertaine:
   all fearelesse then of so false enimies,
   which sought me to entrap in treasons traine.
So as I then disarmed did remaine,   5
   a wicked ambush which lay hidden long
   in the close couert of her guilefull eyen,
   thence breaking forth did thick about me throng.
Too feeble I t'abide the brunt so strong,
   was forst to yeeld my selfe into their hands: 10
   who me captiuing streight with rigorous wrong,
   haue euer since me kept in cruell bands.
So Ladie now to you I doo complaine,
   against your eies that iustice I may gaine.

SONNET. XIII.

In that proud port, which her so goodly graceth,
    whiles her faire face she reares vp to the skie:
    and to the ground her eie lids low embaseth,
    most goodly temperature ye may descry,
5 Myld humblesse mixt with awfull maiesty,
    for looking on the earth whence she was borne,
    her minde remembreth her mortalitie,
    what so is fayrest shall to earth returne.
But that same lofty countenance seemes to scorne
10   base thing, and thinke how she to heauen may clime:
    treading downe earth as lothsome and forlorne,
    that hinders heauenly thoughts with drossy slime.
Yet lowly still vouchsafe to looke on me,
    such lowlinesse shall make you lofty be.

SONNET. XIIII.

Retourne agayne my forces late dismayd,
    Vnto the siege by you abandon'd quite,
    great shame it is to leaue like one afrayd,
    so fayre a peece for one repulse so light.
5 Gaynst such strong castles needeth greater might,
    then those small forts which ye were wont belay;
    such haughty mynds enur'd to hardy fight,
    disdayne to yield vnto the first assay.
Bring therefore all the forces that ye may,
10   and lay incessant battery to her heart,
    playnts, prayers, vowes, ruth, sorrow, and dismay,
    those engins can the proudest loue conuert.
And if those fayle fall downe and dy before her,
    so dying liue, and liuing do adore her.

SONNET. XV.

Ye tradefull Merchants that with weary toyle,
   do seeke most pretious things to make your gain:
   and both the Indias of their treasures spoile,
   what needeth you to seeke so farre in vaine?
For loe my loue doth in her selfe containe   5
   all this worlds riches that may farre be found,
   if Saphyres, loe her eies be Saphyres plaine,
   if Rubies, loe hir lips be Rubies sound:
If Pearles, hir teeth be pearles both pure and round;
   if Yuorie, her forhead yuory weene;   10
   if Gold, her locks are finest gold on ground;
   if siluer, her faire hands are siluer sheene,
But that which fairest is, but few behold,
   her mind adornd with vertues manifold.

SONNET. XVI.

One day as I vnwarily did gaze
   on those fayre eyes my loues immortall light:
   the whiles my stonisht hart stood in amaze,
   through sweet illusion of her lookes delight,
I mote perceiue how in her glauncing sight,   5
   legions of loues with little wings did fly:
   darting their deadly arrowes fyry bright,
   at euery rash beholder passing by.
One of those archers closely I did spy,
   ayming his arrow at my very hart: 10
   when suddenly with twincle of her eye,
   the Damzell broke his misintended dart.
Had she not so doon, sure I had bene slayne,
   yet as it was, I hardly scap't with paine.

SONNET. XVII.

The glorious pourtraict of that Angels face,
　　Made to amaze weake mens confused skil:
　　and this worlds worthlesse glory to embase,
　　what pen, what pencill can expresse her fill?
5　For though he colours could deuize at will,
　　and eke his learned hand at pleasure guide,
　　least trembling it his workmanship should spill,
　　yet many wondrous things there are beside.
The sweet eye-glaunces, that like arrowes glide,
10　　the charming smiles, that rob sence from the hart:
　　the louely pleasance and the lofty pride,
　　cannot expressed be by any art.
A greater craftesmans hand thereto doth neede,
　　that can expresse the life of things indeed.

SONNET. XVIII.

The rolling wheele that runneth often round,
　　The hardest steele in tract of time doth teare:
　　and drizling drops that often doe redound,
　　the firmest flint doth in continuance weare.
5　Yet cannot I with many a dropping teare,
　　and long intreaty soften her hard hart:
　　that she will once vouchsafe my plaint to heare,
　　or looke with pitty on my payneful smart.
But when I pleade, she bids me play my part,
10　　and when I weep, she sayes teares are but water:
　　and when I sigh, she sayes I know the art,
　　and when I waile she turnes hir selfe to laughter.
So doe I weepe, and wayle, and pleade in vaine,
　　whiles she as steele and flint doth still remayne.

SONNET. XIX.

The merry Cuckow, messenger of Spring,
   His trompet shrill hath thrise already sounded:
   that warnes al louers wayt vpon their king,
   who now is comming forth with girland crouned.
With noyse whereof the quyre of Byrds resounded   5
   their anthemes sweet devized of loues prayse,
   that all the woods theyr ecchoes back rebounded,
   as if they knew the meaning of their layes.
But mongst them all, which did Loues honor rayse,
   no word was heard of her that most it ought,   10
   but she his precept proudly disobayes,
   and doth his ydle message set at nought.
Therefore O loue, vnlesse she turne to thee
   ere Cuckow end, let her a rebell be.

SONNET. XX.

In vaine I seeke and sew to her for grace,
   and doe myne humbled hart before her poure:
   the whiles her foot she in my necke doth place,
   and tread my life downe in the lowly floure.
And yet the Lyon that is Lord of power,   5
   and reigneth ouer euery beast in field:
   in his most pride disdeigneth to deuoure
   the silly lambe that to his might doth yield.
But she more cruell and more saluage wylde,
   then either Lyon or the Lyonesse: 10
   shames not to be with guiltlesse bloud defylde,
   but taketh glory in her cruelnesse.
Fayrer then fayrest let none euer say,
   that ye were blooded in a yeelded pray.

SONNET. XXI.

Was it the worke of nature or of Art,
　　which tempred so the feature of her face,
　　that pride and meeknesse mixt by equall part,
　　doe both appeare t'adorne her beauties grace?
5　For with mild pleasance, which doth pride displace,
　　she to her loue doth lookers eyes allure:
　　and with sterne countenance back again doth chace
　　their looser lookes that stir vp lustes impure.
With such strange termes her eyes she doth inure,
10　　that with one looke she doth my life dismay:
　　and with another doth it streight recure,
　　her smile me drawes, her frowne me driues away.
Thus doth she traine and teach me with her lookes,
　　such art of eyes I neuer read in bookes.

SONNET. XXII.

This holy season fit to fast and pray,
　　Men to deuotion ought to be inclynd:
　　therefore, I lykewise on so holy day,
　　for my sweet Saynt some seruice fit will find.
5　Her temple fayre is built within my mind,
　　in which her glorious ymage placed is,
　　on which my thoughts doo day and night attend
　　lyke sacred priests that neuer thinke amisse.
There I to her as th'author of my blisse,
10　　will builde an altar to appease her yre:
　　and on the same my hart will sacrifise,
　　burning in flames of pure and chast desyre:
The which vouchsafe O goddesse to accept,
　　amongst thy deerest relicks to be kept.

SONNET. XXIII.

Penelope for her *Vlisses* sake,
    Deuiz'd a Web her wooers to deceaue:
    in which the worke that she all day did make
    the same at night she did againe vnreaue:
Such subtile craft my Damzell doth conceaue,   5
    th'importune suit of my desire to shonne:
    for all that I in many dayes doo weaue,
    in one short houre I find by her vndonne.
So when I thinke to end that I begonne,
    I must begin and neuer bring to end: 10
    for with one looke she spils that long I sponne,
    and with one word my whole years work doth rend.
Such labour like the Spyders web I fynd,
    whose fruitlesse worke is broken with least wynd.

SONNET. XXIIII.

When I behold that beauties wonderment,
    And rare perfection of each goodly part:
    of natures skill the onely complement,
    I honor and admire the makers art.
But when I feele the bitter balefull smart,   5
    which her fayre eyes vnwares doe worke in mee:
    that death out of theyr shiny beames doe dart,
    I thinke that I a new *Pandora* see;
Whom all the Gods in councell did agree,
    into this sinfull world from heauen to send: 10
    that she to wicked men a scourge should bee,
    for all their faults with which they did offend.
But since ye are my scourge I will intreat,
    that for my faults ye will me gently beat.

SONNET. XXV.

How long shall this lyke dying lyfe endure,
   And know no end of her owne mysery:
   but wast and weare away in termes vnsure,
   twixt feare and hope depending doubtfully.
5 Yet better were attonce to let me die,
   and shew the last ensample of your pride:
   then to torment me thus with cruelty,
   to proue your powre, which I too wel haue tride.
But yet if in your hardned brest ye hide,
10 a close intent at last to shew me grace:
   then all the woes and wrecks which I abide,
   as meanes of blisse I gladly wil embrace.
And wish that more and greater they might be,
   that greater meede at last may turne to mee.

SONNET. XXVI.

Sweet is the Rose, but growes vpon a brere;
   Sweet is the Iunipere, but sharpe his bough;
   sweet is the Eglantine, but pricketh nere;
   sweet is the firbloome, but his braunches rough.
5 Sweet is the Cypresse, but his rynd is tough,
   sweet is the nut, but bitter is his pill;
   sweet is the broome-flowre, but yet sowre enough;
   and sweet is Moly, but his root is ill.
So euery sweet with soure is tempred still,
10 that maketh it be coueted the more:
   for easie things that may be got at will,
   most sorts of men doe set but little store.
Why then should I accoumpt of little paine,
   that endlesse pleasure shall vnto me gaine.

SONNET. XXVII.

Faire proud now tell me why should faire be proud,
  Sith all worlds glorie is but drosse vncleane:
  and in the shade of death it selfe shall shroud,
  how euer now thereof ye little weene.
That goodly Idoll now so gay beseene,   5
  shall doffe her fleshes borowd fayre attyre:
  and be forgot as it had neuer beene,
  that many now much worship and admire.
Ne any then shall after it inquire,
  ne any mention shall thereof remaine: 10
  but what this verse, that neuer shall expyre,
  shall to you purchas with her thankles paine.
Faire be no lenger proud of that shall perish,
  but that which shal you make immortall, cherish.

SONNET. XXVIII.

The laurell leafe, which you this day doe weare,
  giues me great hope of your relenting mynd:
  for since it is the badg which I doe beare,
  ye bearing it doe seeme to me inclind:
The powre thereof, which ofte in me I find,   5
  let it lykewise your gentle brest inspire
  with sweet infusion, and put you in mind
  of that proud mayd, whom now those leaues attyre:
Proud *Daphne* scorning Phæbus louely fyre,
  on the Thessalian shore from him did flie: 10
  for which the gods in theyr reuengefull yre
  did her transforme into a laurell tree.
Then fly no more fayre loue from Phebus chace,
  but in your brest his leafe and loue embrace.

SONNET. XXIX.

See how the stubborne damzell doth depraue
   my simple meaning with disdaynfull scorne:
   and by the bay which I vnto her gaue,
   accoumpts my selfe her captiue quite forlorne.
5 The bay (quoth she) is of the victours borne,
   yielded them by the vanquisht as theyr meeds,
   and they therewith doe poetes heads adorne,
   to sing the glory of their famous deedes.
But sith she will the conquest challeng needs,
10   let her accept me as her faithfull thrall,
   that her great triumph which my skill exceeds,
   I may in trump of fame blaze ouer all.
Then would I decke her head with glorious bayes,
   and fill the world with her victorious prayse.

SONNET. XXX.

My loue is lyke to yse, and I to fyre;
   how comes it then that this her cold so great
   is not dissolu'd through my so hot desyre,
   but harder growes the more I her intreat?
5 Or how comes it that my exceeding heat
   is not delayd by her hart frosen cold:
   but that I burne much more in boyling sweat,
   and feele my flames augmented manifold?
What more miraculous thing may be told
10   that fire which all thing melts, should harden yse:
   and yse which is congeald with sencelesse cold,
   should kindle fyre by wonderfull deuyse?
Such is the powre of loue in gentle mind,
   that it can alter all the course of kynd.

SONNET. XXXI.

Ah why hath nature to so hard a hart,
   giuen so goodly giftes of beauties grace?
   whose pryde depraues each other better part,
   and all those pretious ornaments deface.
Sith to all other beastes of bloody race,   5
   a dreadfull countenaunce she giuen hath:
   that with theyr terrour al the rest may chace,
   and warne to shun the daunger of theyr wrath.
But my proud one doth worke the greater scath,
   through sweet allurement of her louely hew: 10
   that she the better may in bloody bath
   of such poore thralls her cruell hands embrew.
But did she know how ill these two accord,
   such cruelty she would haue soone abhord.

SONNET. XXXII.

The paynefull smith with force of feruent heat,
   the hardest yron soone doth mollify:
   that with his heauy sledge he can it beat,
   and fashion to what he it list apply.
Yet cannot all these flames in which I fry,   5
   her hart more harde then yron soft awhit:
   ne all the playnts and prayers with which I
   doe beat on th'anduyle of her stubberne wit:
But still the more she feruent sees my fit,
   the more she frieseth in her wilfull pryde: 10
   and harder growes the harder she is smit,
   with all the playnts which to her be applyde.
What then remaines but I to ashes burne,
   and she to stones at length all frosen turne?

SONNET. XXXIII.

Great wrong I doe, I can it not deny,
    to that most sacred Empresse my dear dred,
    not finishing her Queene of faëry,
    that mote enlarge her liuing prayses dead:
5 But lodwick, this of grace to me aread:
    doe ye not thinck th'accomplishment of it,
    sufficient worke for one mans simple head,
    all were it as the rest but rudely writ.
How then should I without another wit,
10   thinck euer to endure so tædious toyle,
    sins that this one is tost with troublous fit,
    of a proud loue, that doth my spirite spoyle.
Ceasse then, till she vouchsafe to grawnt me rest,
    or lend you me another liuing brest.

SONNET. XXXIIII.

Lyke as a ship that through the Ocean wyde,
    by conduct of some star doth make her way,
    whenas a storme hath dimd her trusty guyde,
    out of her course doth wander far astray.
5 So I whose star, that wont with her bright ray
    me to direct, with cloudes is ouercast,
    doe wander now in darknesse and dismay,
    through hidden perils round about me plast.
Yet hope I well, that when this storme is past
10   my *Helice* the lodestar of my lyfe
    will shine again, and looke on me at last,
    with louely light to cleare my cloudy grief.
Till then I wander carefull comfortlesse,
    in secret sorow and sad pensiuenesse.

SONNET. XXXV.

My hungry eyes through greedy couetize,
   still to behold the obiect of their paine:
   with no contentment can themselues suffize,
   but hauing pine and hauing not complaine.
For lacking it they cannot lyfe sustayne,   5
   and hauing it they gaze on it the more:
   in their amazement lyke *Narcissus* vaine
   whose eyes him staru'd: so plenty makes me poore.
Yet are mine eyes so filled with the store
   of that faire sight, that nothing else they brooke,   10
   but lothe the things which they did like before,
   and can no more endure on them to looke.
All this worlds glory seemeth vayne to me,
   and all their showes but shadowes sauing she.

SONNET. XXXVI.

Tell me when shall these wearie woes haue end,
   Or shall their ruthlesse torment neuer cease:
   but al my dayes in pining languor spend,
   without hope of aswagement or release?
Is there no meanes for me to purchace peace,   5
   or make agreement with her thrilling eyes:
   but that their cruelty doth still increace,
   and dayly more augment my miseryes?
But when ye haue shewed all extremityes,
   then thinke how litle glory ye haue gayned: 10
   by slaying him, whose lyfe though ye despyse,
   mote haue your life in honour long maintayned.
But by his death which some perhaps will mone,
   ye shall condemned be of many a one.

SONNET. XXXVII.

What guyle is this, that those her golden tresses,
    She doth attyre vnder a net of gold:
    and with sly skill so cunningly them dresses,
    that which is gold or heare, may scarse be told?
5   Is it that mens frayle eyes, which gaze too bold,
    she may entangle in that golden snare:
    and being caught may craftily enfold
    theyr weaker harts, which are not wel aware?
Take heed therefore, myne eyes, how ye doe stare
10   henceforth too rashly on that guilefull net,
    in which if euer ye entrapped are,
    out of her bands ye by no meanes shall get.
Fondnesse it were for any being free,
    to couet fetters, though they golden bee.

SONNET. XXXVIII.

Arion, when through tempests cruel wracke,
    He forth was thrown into the greedy seas:
    through the sweet musick which his harp did make
    allur'd a Dolphin him from death to ease.
5   But my rude musick, which was wont to please
    some dainty eares, cannot with any skill,
    the dreadfull tempest of her wrath appease,
    nor moue the Dolphin from her stubborne will,
But in her pride she dooth perseuer still,
10   all carelesse how my life for her decayse:
    yet with one word she can it saue or spill,
    to spill were pitty, but to saue were prayse.
Chose rather to be praysd for dooing good,
    then to be blam'd for spilling guiltlesse blood.

SONNET. XXXIX.

Sweet smile, the daughter of the Queene of loue,
   Expressing all thy mothers powrefull art:
   with which she wonts to temper angry Ioue,
   when all the gods he threats with thundring dart.
Sweet is thy vertue as thy selfe sweet art,   5
   for when on me thou shinedst late in sadnesse:
   a melting pleasance ran through euery part,
   and me reuiued with hart robbing gladnesse.
Whylest rapt with ioy resembling heauenly madnes,
   my soule was rauisht quite as in a traunce: 10
   and feeling thence no more her sorowes sadnesse,
   fed on the fulnesse of that chearefull glaunce.
More sweet than Nectar or Ambrosiall meat
   seemd euery bit, which thenceforth I did eat.

SONNET. XL.

Mark when she smiles with amiable cheare,
   And tell me whereto can ye lyken it:
   when on each eyelid sweetly doe appeare
   an hundred Graces as in shade to sit.
Lykest it seemeth in my simple wit   5
   vnto the fayre sunshine in somers day:
   that when a dreadfull storme away is flit,
   thrugh the broad world doth spred his goodly ray:
At sight whereof each bird that sits on spray,
   and euery beast that to his den was fled,   10
   comes forth afresh out of their late dismay,
   and to the light lift vp theyr drouping hed.
So my storme beaten hart likewise is cheared,
   with that sunshine when cloudy looks are cleared.

SONNET. XLI.

Is it her nature or is it her will,
   to be so cruell to an humbled foe?
   if nature, then she may it mend with skill,
   if will, then she at will may will forgoe.
5 But if her nature and her wil be so,
   that she will plague the man that loues her most:
   and take delight t'encrease a wretches woe,
   then all her natures goodly guifts are lost.
And that same glorious beauties ydle boast,
10   is but a bayt such wretches to beguile:
   as being long in her loues tempest tost,
   she meanes at last to make her piteous spoyle.
O fayrest fayre let neuer it be named,
   that so fayre beauty was so fowly shamed.

SONNET. XLII.

The loue which me so cruelly tormenteth,
   So pleasing is in my extreamest paine:
   that all the more my sorrow it augmenteth,
   the more I loue and doe embrace my bane.
5 Ne doe I wish (for wishing were but vaine)
   to be acquit fro my continuall smart:
   but ioy her thrall for euer to remayne,
   and yield for pledge my poore captyued hart;
The which that it from her may neuer start,
10   let her, yf please her, bynd with adamant chayne:
   and from all wandring loues which mote peruart,
   his safe assurance strongly it restrayne.
Onely let her abstaine from cruelty,
   and doe me not before my time to dy.

SONNET. XLIII.

Shall I then silent be or shall I speake?
   And if I speake, her wrath renew I shall:
   and if I silent be, my hart will breake,
   or choked be with ouerflowing gall.
What tyranny is this both my hart to thrall,   5
   and eke my toung with proud restraint to tie?
   that nether I may speake nor thinke at all,
   but like a stupid stock in silence die.
Yet I my hart with silence secretly
   will teach to speak, and my iust cause to plead: 10
   and eke mine eies with meeke humility,
   loue learned letters to her eyes to read.
Which her deep wit, that true harts thought can spel,
   will soone conceiue, and learne to construe well.

SONNET. XLIIII.

When those renoumed noble Peres of Greece,
   thrugh stubborn pride amongst themselues did iar
   forgetfull of the famous golden fleece,
   then Orpheus with his harp theyr strife did bar.
But this continuall cruell ciuill warre,   5
   the which my selfe against my selfe doe make:
   whilest my weak powres of passions warreid arre,
   no skill can stint nor reason can aslake.
But when in hand my tunelesse harp I take,
   then doe I more augment my foes despight: 10
   and griefe renew, and passions doe awake,
   to battaile fresh against my selfe to fight.
Mongst whome the more I seeke to settle peace,
   the more I fynd their malice to increace.

SONNET. XLV.

Leaue lady in your glasse of christall clene,
  Your goodly selfe for euermore to vew:
  and in my selfe, my inward selfe I meane,
  most liuely lyke behold your semblant trew.
5 Within my hart, though hardly it can shew
  thing so diuine to vew of earthly eye:
  the fayre Idea of your celestiall hew,
  and euery part remaines immortally:
And were it not that through your cruelty,
10 with sorrow dimmed and deformd it were:
  the goodly ymage of your visnomy,
  clearer then christall would therein appere.
But if your selfe in me ye playne will see,
  remoue the cause by which your fayre beames darkned
    be.

SONNET. XLVI.

When my abodes prefixed time is spent,
  My cruell fayre streight bids me wend my way:
  but then from heauen most hideous stormes are sent
  as willing me against her will to stay.
5 Whom then shall I or heauen or her obay?
  the heauens know best what is the best for me:
  but as she will, whose will my life doth sway,
  my lower heauen, so it perforce must bee.
But ye high heuens, that all this sorowe see,
10 sith all your tempests cannot hold me backe:
  aswage your stormes, or else both you and she,
  will both together me too sorely wrack.
Enough it is for one man to sustaine
  the stormes, which she alone on me doth raine.

SONNET. XLVII.

Trust not the treason of those smyling lookes,
  vntill ye haue theyr guylefull traynes well tryde:
  for they are lyke but vnto golden hookes,
  that from the foolish fish theyr bayts doe hyde:
So she with flattring smyles weake harts doth guyde   5
  vnto her loue and tempte to theyr decay,
  whome being caught she kills with cruell pryde,
  and feeds at pleasure on the wretched pray:
Yet euen whylst her bloody hands them slay,
  her eyes looke louely and vpon them smyle: 10
  that they take pleasure in her cruell play,
  and dying doe them selues of payne beguyle.
O mighty charm which makes men loue theyr bane,
  and thinck they dy with pleasure, liue with payne.

SONNET. XLVIII.

Innocent paper whom too cruell hand
  Did make the matter to auenge her yre:
  and ere she could thy cause wel vnderstand,
  did sacrifize vnto the greedy fyre.
Well worthy thou to haue found better hyre,   5
  then so bad end for hereticks ordayned:
  yet heresy nor treason didst conspire,
  but plead thy maisters cause vniustly payned.
Whom she all carelesse of his griefe constrayned
  to vtter forth th'anguish of his hart: 10
  and would not heare, when he to her complayned,
  the piteous passion of his dying smart.
Yet liue for euer, though against her will,
  and speake her good, though she requite it ill.

SONNET. XLIX.

Fayre cruell, why are ye so fierce and cruell?
   Is it because your eyes haue powre to kill?
   then know, that mercy is the mighties iewell,
   and greater glory thinke to saue, then spill.
5   But if it be your pleasure and proud will,
   to shew the powre of your imperious eyes:
   then not on him that neuer thought you ill,
   but bend your force against your enemyes.
Let them feele th'utmost of your crueltyes,
10   and kill with looks, as Cockatrices doo:
   but him that at your footstoole humbled lies,
   with mercifull regard, giue mercy too.
Such mercy shal you make admyred to be,
   so shall you liue by giuing life to me.

SONNET. L.

Long languishing in double malady,
   of my harts wound and of my bodies griefe:
   there came to me a leach that would apply
   fit medicines for my bodies best reliefe.
5   Vayne man (quod I) that hast but little priefe,
   in deep discouery of the mynds disease,
   is not the hart of all the body chiefe?
   and rules the members as it selfe doth please?
Then with some cordialls seeke first to appease
10   the inward languour of my wounded hart,
   and then my body shall haue shortly ease:
   but such sweet cordialls passe Physitions art.
Then my lyfes Leach doe you your skill reueale,
   and with one salue both hart and body heale.

SONNET. LI.

Doe I not see that fayrest ymages
  Of hardest Marble are of purpose made?
  for that they should endure through many ages,
  ne let theyr famous moniments to fade.
Why then doe I, vntrainde in louers trade,   5
  her hardnes blame which I should more commend?
  sith neuer ought was excellent assayde,
  which was not hard t'atchiue and bring to end.
Ne ought so hard, but he that would attend,
  mote soften it and to his will allure: 10
  so doe I hope her stubborne hart to bend,
  and that it then more stedfast will endure.
Onely my paines wil be the more to get her,
  but hauing her, my ioy wil be the greater.

SONNET. LII.

So oft as homeward I from her depart,
  I goe lyke one that hauing lost the field,
  is prisoner led away with heauy hart,
  despoyld of warlike armes and knowen shield.
So doe I now my selfe a prisoner yeeld,   5
  to sorrow and to solitary paine:
  from presence of my dearest deare exylde,
  longwhile alone in languor to remaine.
There let no thought of ioy or pleasure vaine
  dare to approch, that may my solace breed: 10
  but sudden dumps and drery sad disdayne
  of all worlds gladnesse more my torment feed.
So I her absens will my penaunce make,
  that of her presens I my meed may take.

SONNET. LIII.

The Panther knowing that his spotted hyde
   Doth please all beasts but that his looks them fray:
   within a bush his dreadfull head doth hide,
   to let them gaze whylest he on them may pray.
5 Right so my cruell fayre with me doth play,
   for with the goodly semblant of her hew,
   she doth allure me to mine owne decay,
   and then no mercy will vnto me shew.
Great shame it is, thing so diuine in view,
10   made for to be the worlds most ornament:
   to make the bayte her gazers to embrew,
   good shames to be to ill an instrument.
But mercy doth with beautie best agree,
   as in theyr maker ye them best may see.

SONNET. LIIII.

Of this worlds Theatre in which we stay,
   My loue lyke the Spectator ydly sits
   beholding me that all the pageants play,
   disguysing diuersly my troubled wits.
5 Sometimes I ioy when glad occasion fits,
   and mask in myrth lyke to a Comedy:
   soone after when my ioy to sorrow flits,
   I waile and make my woes a Tragedy.
Yet she beholding me with constant eye,
10   delights not in my merth nor rues my smart:
   but when I laugh she mocks, and when I cry
   she laughes, and hardens euermore her hart.
What then can moue her? if nor merth nor mone,
   she is no woman, but a sencelesse stone.

SONNET. LV.

So oft as I her beauty doe behold,
   And therewith doe her cruelty compare:
   I maruaile of what substance was the mould
   the which her made attonce so cruell faire.
Not earth; for her high thoghts more heauenly are,   5
   not water; for her loue doth burne like fyre:
   not ayre; for she is not so light or rare,
   not fyre; for she doth friese with faint desire.
Then needs another Element inquire
   whereof she mote be made; that is the skye.   10
   for to the heauen her haughty lookes aspire:
   and eke her mind is pure immortall hye.
Then sith to heauen ye lykened are the best,
   be lyke in mercy as in all the rest.

SONNET. LVI.

Fayre ye be sure, but cruell and vnkind,
   As is a Tygre that with greedinesse
   hunts after bloud, when he by chance doth find
   a feeble beast, doth felly him oppresse.
Fayre be ye sure but proud and pittilesse,   5
   as is a storme, that all things doth prostrate:
   finding a tree alone all comfortlesse,
   beats on it strongly it to ruinate.
Fayre be ye sure, but hard and obstinate,
   as is a rocke amidst the raging floods: 10
   gaynst which a ship of succour desolate,
   doth suffer wreck both of her selfe and goods.
That ship, that tree, and that same beast am I,
   whom ye doe wreck, doe ruine, and destroy.

SONNET. LVII.

Sweet warriour when shall I haue peace with you?
   High time it is, this warre now ended were:
   which I no lenger can endure to sue,
   ne your incessant battry more to beare:
5 So weake my powres, so sore my wounds appeare,
   that wonder is how I should liue a iot,
   seeing my hart through launched euery where
   with thousand arrowes, which your eies have shot:
Yet shoot ye sharpely still, and spare me not,
10   but glory thinke to make these cruel stoures.
   ye cruell one, what glory can be got,
   in slaying him that would liue gladly yours?
Make peace therefore, and graunt me timely grace,
   that al my wounds wil heale in little space.

SONNET. LVIII.
By her that is most assured to her selfe.

Weake is th'assurance that weake flesh reposeth
   In her owne powre and scorneth others ayde:
   that soonest fals when as she most supposeth
   her selfe assurd, and is of nought affrayd.
5 All flesh is frayle, and all her strength vnstayd,
   like a vaine bubble blowen vp with ayre:
   deuouring tyme and changeful chance haue prayd
   her glories pride that none may it repayre.
Ne none so rich or wise, so strong or fayre,
10   but fayleth trusting on his owne assurance:
   and he that standeth on the hyghest stayre
   fals lowest: for on earth nought hath enduraunce.
Why then doe ye proud fayre, misdeeme so farre,
   that to your selfe ye most assured arre?

SONNET. LIX.

Thrise happie she, that is so well assured
   Vnto her selfe and setled so in hart:
   that nether will for better be allured,
   ne feard with worse to any chaunce to start,
But like a steddy ship doth strongly part   5
   the raging waues and keepes her course aright:
   ne ought for tempest doth from it depart,
   ne ought for fayrer weathers false delight.
Such selfe assurance need not feare the spight
   of grudging foes, ne fauour seek of friends: 10
   but in the stay of her owne stedfast might,
   nether to one her selfe nor other bends.
Most happy she that most assured doth rest,
   but he most happy who such one loues best.

SONNET. LX.

They that in course of heauenly spheares are skild,
   To euery planet point his sundry yeare:
   in which her circles voyage is fulfild,
   as Mars in three score yeares doth run his spheare.
So since the winged God his planet cleare   5
   began in me to moue, one yeare is spent:
   the which doth longer vnto me appeare,
   then al those fourty which my life outwent.
Then by that count, which louers books inuent,
   the spheare of Cupid fourty yeares containes: 10
   which I haue wasted in long languishment,
   that seemd the longer for my greater paines.
But let my loues fayre Planet short her wayes
   this yeare ensuing, or else short my dayes.

SONNET. LXI.

The glorious image of the makers beautie,
    My souerayne saynt, the Idoll of my thought,
    dare not henceforth aboue the bounds of dewtie,
    t'accuse of pride, or rashly blame for ought.
5 For being as she is diuinely wrought,
    and of the brood of Angels heuenly borne:
    and with the crew of blessed Saynts vpbrought,
    each of which did her with theyr guifts adorne;
The bud of ioy, the blossome of the morne,
10   the beame of light, whom mortal eyes admyre:
    what reason is it then but she should scorne
    base things that to her loue too bold aspire?
Such heauenly formes ought rather worshipt be,
    then dare be lou'd by men of meane degree.

SONNET. LXII.

The weary yeare his race now hauing run,
    The new begins his compast course anew:
    with shew of morning mylde he hath begun,
    betokening peace and plenty to ensew,
5 So let vs, which this chaunge of weather vew,
    chaunge eeke our mynds and former liues amend,
    the old yeares sinnes forepast let vs eschew,
    and fly the faults with which we did offend.
Then shall the new yeares ioy forth freshly send
10   into the glooming world his gladsome ray:
    and all these stormes which now his beauty blend,
    shall turne to caulmes and tymely cleare away.
So likewise loue cheare you your heauy spright,
    and chaunge old yeares annoy to new delight.

SONNET. LXIII.

After long stormes and tempests sad assay,
　Which hardly I endured heretofore:
　in dread of death and daungerous dismay,
　with which my silly barke was tossed sore:
I doe at length descry the happy shore, 5
　in which I hope ere long for to arryue,
　fayre soyle it seemes from far and fraught with store
　of all that deare and daynty is alyue.
Most happy he that can at last atchyue
　the ioyous safety of so sweet a rest: 10
　whose least delight sufficeth to depriue
　remembrance of all paines which him opprest.
All paines are nothing in respect of this,
　all sorrowes short that gaine eternall blisse.

SONNET. LXIIII.

Comming to kisse her lyps, (such grace I found)
　Me seemd I smelt a gardin of sweet flowres:
　that dainty odours from them threw around
　for damzels fit to decke their louers bowres.
Her lips did smell lyke vnto Gillyflowers, 5
　her ruddy cheekes lyke vnto Roses red:
　her snowy browes lyke budded Bellamoures,
　her louely eyes lyke Pincks but newly spred,
Her goodly bosome lyke a Strawberry bed,
　her neck lyke to a bounch of Cullambynes: 10
　her brest lyke lillyes, ere theyr leaues be shed,
　her nipples lyke yong blossomd Iessemynes:
Such fragrant flowres doe giue most odorous smell,
　but her sweet odour did them all excell.

SONNET. LXV.

The doubt which ye misdeeme, fayre loue, is vaine,
    That fondly feare to loose your liberty,
    when loosing one, two liberties ye gayne,
    and make him bond that bondage earst dyd fly.
5 Sweet be the bands, the which true loue doth tye,
    without constraynt or dread of any ill:
    the gentle birde feeles no captiuity
    within her cage, but singes and feeds her fill.
There pride dare not approch, nor discord spill
10   the league twixt them, that loyal loue hath bound:
    but simple truth and mutuall good will,
    seekes with sweet peace to salue each others wound:
There fayth doth fearlesse dwell in brasen towre,
    and spotlesse pleasure builds her sacred bowre.

SONNET. LXVI.

To all those happy blessings which ye haue,
    with plenteous hand by heauen vpon you thrown:
    this one disparagement they to you gaue,
    that ye your loue lent to so meane a one.
5 Yee whose high worths surpassing paragon,
    could not on earth haue found one fit for mate,
    ne but in heauen matchable to none,
    why did ye stoup vnto so lowly state?
But ye thereby much greater glory gate,
10   then had ye sorted with a princes pere:
    for now your light doth more it selfe dilate,
    and in my darknesse greater doth appeare.
Yet since your light hath once enlumind me,
    with my reflex yours shall encreased be.

SONNET. LXVII.

Lyke as a huntsman after weary chace,
    Seeing the game from him escapt away,
    sits downe to rest him in some shady place,
    with panting hounds beguiled of their pray:
So after long pursuit and vaine assay,   5
    when I all weary had the chace forsooke,
    the gentle deare returnd the selfe-same way,
    thinking to quench her thirst at the next brooke.
There she beholding me with mylder looke,
    sought not to fly, but fearelesse still did bide: 10
    till I in hand her yet halfe trembling tooke,
    and with her owne goodwill hir fyrmely tyde.
Strange thing me seemd to see a beast so wyld,
    so goodly wonne with her owne will beguyld.

SONNET. LXVIII.

Most glorious Lord of lyfe that on this day,
    Didst make thy triumph ouer death and sin:
    and hauing harrowd hell didst bring away
    captiuity thence captiue vs to win:
This ioyous day, deare Lord, with ioy begin,   5
    and grant that we for whom thou diddest dye
    being with thy deare blood clene washt from sin,
    may liue for euer in felicity.
And that thy loue we weighing worthily,
    may likewise loue thee for the same agàine: 10
    and for thy sake that all lyke deare didst buy,
    with loue may one another entertayne.
So let vs loue, deare loue, lyke as we ought,
    loue is the lesson which the Lord vs taught.

SONNET. LXIX.

The famous warriors of the anticke world,
   Vsed Trophees to erect in stately wize:
   in which they would the records haue enrold,
   of theyr great deeds and valarous emprize.
5   What trophee then shall I most fit deuize,
   in which I may record the memory
   of my loues conquest, peerelesse beauties prise,
   adorn'd with honour, loue, and chastity?
Euen this verse vowd to eternity,
10   shall be thereof immortall moniment:
   and tell her prayse to all posterity,
   that may admire such worlds rare wonderment.
The happy purchase of my glorious spoile,
   gotten at last with labour and long toyle.

SONNET. LXX.

Fresh spring the herald of loues mighty king,
   In whose cote armour richly are displayd
   all sorts of flowers the which on earth do spring
   in goodly colours gloriously arrayd.
5   Goe to my loue, where she is carelesse layd,
   yet in her winters bowre not well awake:
   tell her the ioyous time wil not be staid
   vnlesse she doe him by the forelock take.
Bid her therefore her selfe soone ready make,
10   to wayt on loue amongst his louely crew:
   where euery one that misseth then her make,
   shall be by him amearst with penance dew.
Make hast therefore sweet loue, whilest it is prime,
   for none can call againe the passed time.

SONNET. LXXI.

I ioy to see how in your drawen work,
    Your selfe vnto the Bee ye doe compare;
    and me vnto the Spyder that doth lurke
    in close awayt to catch her vnaware.
Right so your selfe were caught in cunning snare   5
    of a deare foe, and thralled to his loue:
    in whose streight bands ye now captiued are
    so firmely, that ye neuer may remoue.
But as your worke is wouen all about,
    with woodbynd flowers and fragrant Eglantine: 10
    so sweet your prison you in time shall proue,
    with many deare delights bedecked fyne.
And all thensforth eternall peace shall see,
    betweene the Spyder and the gentle Bee.

SONNET. LXXII.

Oft when my spirit doth spred her bolder winges,
    In mind to mount vp to the purest sky:
    it down is weighd with thoght of earthly things
    and clogd with burden of mortality,
Where when that souerayne beauty it doth spy,   5
    resembling heauens glory in her light:
    drawne with sweet pleasures bayt, it back doth fly,
    and vnto heauen forgets her former flight.
There my fraile fancy fed with full delight,
    doth bath in blisse and mantleth most at ease: 10
    ne thinks of other heauen, but how it might
    her harts desire with most contentment please.
Hart need not wish none other happinesse,
    but here on earth to haue such heuens blisse.

SONNET. LXXIII.

Being my selfe captyued here in care,
   My hart, whom none with seruile bands can tye,
    but the fayre tresses of your golden hayre,
    breaking his prison forth to you doth fly.
5 Lyke as a byrd that in ones hand doth spy
    desired food, to it doth make his flight:
    euen so my hart, that wont on your fayre eye
    to feed his fill, flyes backe vnto your sight.
Doe you him take, and in your bosome bright,
10   gently encage, that he may be your thrall:
    perhaps he there may learne with rare delight,
    to sing your name and prayses ouer all.
That it hereafter may you not repent,
   him lodging in your bosome to haue lent.

SONNET. LXXIIII.

Most happy letters fram'd by skilfull trade,
   with which that happy name was first desynd:
    the which three times thrise happy hath me made,
    with guifts of body, fortune and of mind.
5 The first my being to me gaue by kind,
    from mothers womb deriu'd by dew descent,
    the second is my souereigne Queene most kind,
    that honour and large richesse to me lent.
The third my loue, my liues last ornament,
10   by whom my spirit out of dust was raysed:
    to speake her prayse and glory excellent,
    of all aliue most worthy to be praysed.
Ye three Elizabeths for euer liue,
   that three such graces did vnto me giue.

SONNET. LXXV.

One day I wrote her name vpon the strand,
    but came the waues and washed it away:
    agayne I wrote it with a second hand,
    but came the tyde, and made my paynes his pray.
Vayne man, sayd she, that doest in vaine assay,   5
    a mortall thing so to immortalize,
    for I my selue shall lyke to this decay,
    and eek my name bee wyped out lykewize.
Not so, (quod I) let baser things deuize
    to dy in dust, but you shall liue by fame: 10
    my verse your vertues rare shall eternize,
    and in the heuens wryte your glorious name.
Where whenas death shall all the world subdew,
    our loue shall liue, and later life renew.

SONNET. LXXVI.

Fayre bosome fraught with vertues richest tresure,
    The neast of loue, the lodging of delight:
    the bowre of blisse, the paradice of pleasure,
    the sacred harbour of that heuenly spright.
How was I rauisht with your louely sight,   5
    and my frayle thoughts too rashly led astray?
    whiles diuing deepe through amorous insight,
    on the sweet spoyle of beautie they did pray.
And twixt her paps like early fruit in May,
    whose haruest seemd to hasten now apace: 10
    they loosely did theyr wanton winges display,
    and there to rest themselues did boldly place.
Sweet thoughts I enuy your so happy rest,
    which oft I wisht, yet neuer was so blest.

SONNET. LXXVII.

Was it a dreame, or did I see it playne,
  a goodly table of pure yvory:
  all spred with iuncats, fit to entertayne
  the greatest Prince with pompous roialty?
5 Mongst which there in a siluer dish did ly
  twoo golden apples of vnualewd price:
  far passing those which Hercules came by,
  or those which Atalanta did entice.
Exceeding sweet, yet voyd of sinfull vice,
10 That many sought yet none could euer taste,
  sweet fruit of pleasure brought from paradice
  By loue himselfe and in his garden plaste.
Her brest that table was so richly spredd,
  my thoughts the guests, which would thereon haue
    fedd.

SONNET. LXXVIII.

Lackyng my loue I go from place to place,
  lyke a young fawne that late hath lost the hynd:
  and seeke each where, where last I sawe her face,
  whose ymage yet I carry fresh in mynd.
5 I seeke the fields with her late footing synd,
  I seeke her bowre with her late presence deckt,
  yet nor in field nor bowre I her can fynd:
  yet field and bowre are full of her aspect,
But when myne eyes I thereunto direct,
10 they ydly back returne to me agayne,
  and when I hope to see theyr trew obiect,
  I fynd my selfe but fed with fancies vayne.
Ceasse then myne eyes, to seeke her selfe to see,
  and let my thoughts behold her selfe in mee.

SONNET. LXXIX.

Men call you fayre, and you doe credit it,
   For that your selfe ye dayly such doe see:
   but the trew fayre, that is the gentle wit,
   and vertuous mind is much more praysd of me.
For all the rest, how euer fayre it be,   5
   shall turne to nought and loose that glorious hew:
   but onely that is permanent and free
   from frayle corruption, that doth flesh ensew.
That is true beautie: that doth argue you
   to be diuine and borne of heauenly seed: 10
   deriu'd from that fayre Spirit, from whom al true
   and perfect beauty did at first proceed.
He onely fayre, and what he fayre hath made,
   all other fayre lyke flowres vntymely fade.

SONNET. LXXX.

After so long a race as I haue run
   Through Faery land, which those six books compile,
   giue leaue to rest me being halfe fordonne,
   and gather to my selfe new breath awhile.
Then as a steed refreshed after toyle,   5
   out of my prison I will breake anew:
   and stoutly will that second worke assoyle,
   with strong endeuour and attention dew.
Till then giue leaue to me in pleasant mew,
   to sport my muse and sing my loues sweet praise: 10
   the contemplation of whose heauenly hew,
   my spirit to an higher pitch will rayse.
But let her prayses yet be low and meane,
   fit for the handmayd of the Faery Queene.

SONNET. LXXXI.

Fayre is my loue, when her fayre golden heares,
    with the loose wynd ye wauing chance to marke:
    fayre when the rose in her red cheekes appeares,
    or in her eyes the fyre of loue does sparke.
5   Fayre when her brest lyke a rich laden barke,
    with pretious merchandize she forth doth lay:
    fayre when that cloud of pryde, which oft doth dark
    her goodly light with smiles she driues away.
But fayrest she, when so she doth display
10   the gate with pearles and rubyes richly dight:
    throgh which her words so wise do make their way
    to beare the message of her gentle spright:
The rest be works of natures wonderment,
    but this the worke of harts astonishment.

SONNET. LXXXII.

Ioy of my life, full oft for louing you
    I blesse my lot, that was so lucky placed:
    but then the more your owne mishap I rew,
    that are so much by so meane loue embased.
5   For had the equall heuens so much you graced
    in this as in the rest, ye mote inuent
    som heuenly wit, whose verse could haue enchased
    your glorious name in golden moniment.
But since ye deignd so goodly to relent
10   to me your thrall, in whom is little worth,
    that little that I am, shall all be spent,
    in setting your immortall prayses forth.
Whose lofty argument vplifting me,
    shall lift you vp vnto an high degree.

SONNET. LXXXIII.

My hungry eyes, through greedy couetize,
   Still to behold the obiect of theyr payne:
   with no contentment can themselues suffize,
   but hauing pine, and hauing not complayne.
For lacking it, they cannot lyfe sustayne,   5
   and seeing it, they gaze on it the more:
   in theyr amazement lyke Narcissus vayne
   whose eyes him staru'd: so plenty makes me pore.
Yet are myne eyes so filled with the store
   of that fayre sight, that nothing else they brooke: 10
   but loath the things which they did like before,
   and can no more endure on them to looke.
All this worlds glory seemeth vayne to me,
   and all theyr shewes but shadowes sauing she.

SONNET. LXXXIIII.

Let not one sparke of filthy lustfull fyre
   breake out, that may her sacred peace molest:
   ne one light glance of sensuall desyre
   Attempt to work her gentle mindes vnrest.
But pure affections bred in spotlesse brest,   5
   and modest thoughts breathd from wel tempred sprites,
   goe visit her in her chast bowre of rest,
   accompanyde with angelick delightes.
There fill your selfe with those most ioyous sights,
   the which my selfe could neuer yet attayne: 10
   but speake no word to her of these sad plights,
   which her too constant stiffenesse doth constrayn.
Onely behold her rare perfection,
   and blesse your fortunes fayre election.

SONNET. LXXXV.

The world that cannot deeme of worthy things,
    when I doe praise her, say I doe but flatter:
    so does the Cuckow, when the Mauis sings,
    begin his witlesse note apace to clatter.
But they that skill not of so heauenly matter,
    all that they know not, enuy or admyre,
    rather then enuy let them wonder at her,
    but not to deeme of her desert aspyre.
Deepe in the closet of my parts entyre,
    her worth is written with a golden quill:
    that me with heauenly fury doth inspire,
    and my glad mouth with her sweet prayses fill.
Which when as fame in her shrill trump shal thunder,
    let the world chose to enuy or to wonder.

SONNET. LXXXVI.

Venemous toung tipt with vile adders sting,
    Of that selfe kynd with which the Furies fell
    theyr snaky heads doe combe, from which a spring
    of poysoned words and spitefull speeches well;
Let all the plagues and horrid paines of hell,
    vpon thee fall for thine accursed hyre:
    that with false forged lyes, which thou didst tel,
    in my true loue did stirre vp coles of yre,
The sparkes whereof let kindle thine own fyre,
    and catching hold on thine owne wicked hed
    consume thee quite, that didst with guile conspire
    in my sweet peace such breaches to haue bred.
Shame be thy meed, and mischiefe thy reward,
    dew to thy selfe that it for me prepard.

SONNET. LXXXVII.

Since I did leaue the presence of my loue,
  Many long weary dayes I haue outworne:
  and many nights, that slowly seemd to moue
  theyr sad protract from euening vntill morne.
For when as day the heauen doth adorne,   5
  I wish that night the noyous day would end:
  and when as night hath vs of light forlorne,
  I wish that day would shortly reascend.
Thus I the time with expectation spend,
  and faine my griefe with chaunges to beguile, 10
  that further seemes his terme still to extend,
  and maketh euery minute seeme a myle.
So sorrow still doth seeme too long to last,
  but ioyous houres doo fly away too fast.

SONNET. LXXXVIII.

Since I haue lackt the comfort of that light,
  The which was wont to lead my thoughts astray:
  I wander as in darkenesse of the night,
  affrayd of euery dangers least dismay.
Ne ought I see, though in the clearest day,   5
  when others gaze vpon theyr shadowes vayne:
  but th'onely image of that heauenly ray,
  whereof some glance doth in mine eie remayne.
Of which beholding th'Idæa playne,
  through contemplation of my purest part: 10
  with light thereof I doe my selfe sustayne,
  and thereon feed my loue-affamisht hart.
But with such brightnesse whylest I fill my mind,
  I starue my body and mine eyes doe blynd.

SONNET. LXXXIX.

Lyke as the Culuer on the bared bough,
    Sits mourning for the absence of her mate:
    and in her songs sends many a wishfull vow,
    for his returne that seemes to linger late;
5   So I alone now left disconsolate,
    mourne to my selfe the absence of my loue:
    and wandring here and there all desolate,
    seek with my playnts to match that mournful doue:
Ne ioy of ought that vnder heauen doth houe,
10   can comfort me, but her owne ioyous sight:
    whose sweet aspect both God and man can moue,
    in her vnspotted pleasauns to delight.
Dark is my day, whyles her fayre light I mis,
    and dead my life that wants such liuely blis.

['Anacreontics']

[1]

In youth before I waxed old,
  The blynd boy Venus baby,
For want of cunning made me bold,
  In bitter hyue to grope for honny.
    But when he saw me stung and cry,   5
    He tooke his wings and away did fly.

[2]

As Diane hunted on a day,
  She chaunst to come where Cupid lay,
  his quiuer by his head:
One of his shafts she stole away,   10
And one of hers did close conuay,
  into the others stead:
    With that loue wounded my loues hart,
    but Diane beasts with Cupids dart.

[3]

I saw in secret to my Dame,   15
  How little Cupid humbly came:
  and sayd to her All hayle my mother.
But when he saw me laugh, for shame
His face with bashfull blood did flame,
  not knowing Venus from the other.   20
Then neuer blush Cupid (quoth I)
  for many haue err'd in this beauty.

[4]

Vpon a day as loue lay sweetly slumbring,
    all in his mothers lap:
25 A gentle Bee with his loud trumpet murm'ring,
    about him flew by hap.
Whereof when he was wakened with the noyse,
    and saw the beast so small:
Whats this (quoth he) that giues so great a voyce,
30   that wakens men withall?
In angry wize he flyes about,
    and threatens all with corage stout.

To whom his mother closely smiling sayd,
    twixt earnest and twixt game:
35 See thou thy selfe likewise art lyttle made,
    if thou regard the same.
And yet thou suffrest neyther gods in sky,
    nor men in earth to rest:
But when thou art disposed cruelly,
40   theyr sleepe thou doost molest.
Then eyther change thy cruelty,
    or giue lyke leaue vnto the fly.

Nathlesse the cruell boy not so content,
    would needs the fly pursue:
45 And in his hand with heedlesse hardiment,
    him caught for to subdue.
But when on it he hasty hand did lay,
    the Bee him stung therefore:
Now out alasse (he cryde) and welaway,
50   I wounded am full sore:
The fly that I so much did scorne,
    hath hurt me with his little horne.

Vnto his mother straight he weeping came,
   and of his griefe complayned:
Who could not chose but laugh at his fond game,   55
   though sad to see him pained.
Think now (quod she) my sonne how great the smart
   of those whom thou dost wound:
Full many thou hast pricked to the hart,
   that pitty neuer found: 60
Therefore henceforth some pitty take,
   when thou doest spoyle of louers make.

She tooke him streight full pitiously lamenting,
   and wrapt him in her smock:
She wrapt him softly, all the while repenting,   65
   that he the fly did mock.
She drest his wound and it embaulmed wel
   with salue of soueraigne might:
And then she bath'd him in a dainty well,
   the well of deare delight.   70
Who would not oft be stung as this,
   to be so bath'd in Venus blis?

The wanton boy was shortly wel recured
   of that his malady:
But he soone after fresh againe enured   75
   his former cruelty.
And since that time he wounded hath my selfe
   with his sharpe dart of loue:
And now forgets the cruell carelesse elfe,
   his mothers heast to proue.   80
So now I languish till he please
   my pining anguish to appease.

FINIS.

Epithalamion.

G.B.

[1]

Ye learned sisters which haue oftentimes
Beene to me ayding, others to adorne:
Whom ye thought worthy of your gracefull rymes,
That euen the greatest did not greatly scorne
To heare theyr names sung in your simple layes, 5
But ioyed in theyr prayse;
And when ye list your owne mishaps to mourne,
Which death, or loue, or fortunes wreck did rayse,
Your string could soone to sadder tenor turne,
And teach the woods and waters to lament 10
Your dolefull dreriment:
Now lay those sorrowfull complaints aside,
And hauing all your heads with girland crownd,
Helpe me mine owne loues prayses to resound,
Ne let the same of any be enuide, 15
So Orpheus did for his owne bride,
So I vnto my selfe alone will sing,
The woods shall to me answer and my Eccho ring.

[2]

Early before the worlds light giuing lampe,
His golden beame vpon the hils doth spred, 20
Hauing disperst the nights vnchearefull dampe,
Doe ye awake and with fresh lusty hed,
Go to the bowre of my beloued loue,
My truest turtle doue,
Bid her awake; for Hymen is awake, 25
And long since ready forth his maske to moue,
With his bright Tead that flames with many a flake,
And many a bachelor to waite on him,
In theyr fresh garments trim.
Bid her awake therefore and soone her dight, 30
For lo the wished day is come at last,
That shall for al the paynes and sorrowes past,

Pay to her vsury of long delight,
And whylest she doth her dight,
35   Doe ye to her of ioy and solace sing,
That all the woods may answer and your eccho ring.

[3]
Bring with you all the Nymphes that you can heare
Both of the riuers and the forrests greene:
And of the sea that neighbours to her neare,
40   Al with gay girlands goodly wel beseene.
And let them also with them bring in hand,
Another gay girland
For my fayre loue of lillyes and of roses,
Bound trueloue wize with a blew silke riband.
45   And let them make great store of bridale poses,
And let them eeke bring store of other flowers
To deck the bridale bowers.
And let the ground whereas her foot shall tread,
For feare the stones her tender foot should wrong,
50   Be strewed with fragrant flowers all along,
And diapred lyke the discolored mead.
Which done, doe at her chamber dore awayt,
For she will waken strayt,
The whiles doe ye this song vnto her sing,
55   The woods shall to you answer and your Eccho ring.

[4]
Ye Nymphes of Mulla which with carefull heed,
The siluer scaly trouts doe tend full well,
And greedy pikes which vse therein to feed,
(Those trouts and pikes all others doo excell)
60   And ye likewise which keepe the rushy lake,
Where none doo fishes take,
Bynd vp the locks the which hang scatterd light,
And in his waters which your mirror make,
Behold your faces as the christall bright,
65   That when you come whereas my loue doth lie,
No blemish she may spie.
And eke ye lightfoot mayds which keepe the deere,

That on the hoary mountayne vse to towre,
And the wylde wolues which seeke them to deuoure,
With your steele darts doo chace from comming neer,   70
Be also present heere,
To helpe to decke her and to help to sing,
That all the woods may answer and your eccho ring.

[5]

Wake, now my loue, awake; for it is time,
The Rosy Morne long since left Tithones bed,   75
All ready to her siluer coche to clyme,
And Phœbus gins to shew his glorious hed.
Hark how the cheerefull birds do chaunt theyr laies
And carroll of loues praise.
The merry Larke hir mattins sings aloft,   80
The thrush replyes, the Mauis descant playes,
The Ouzell shrills, the Ruddock warbles soft,
So goodly all agree with sweet consent,
To this dayes merriment.
Ah my deere loue why doe ye sleepe thus long,   85
When meeter were that ye should now awake,
T'awayt the comming of your ioyous make,
And hearken to the birds louelearned song,
The deawy leaues among.
For they of ioy and pleasance to you sing,   90
That all the woods them answer and theyr eccho ring.

[6]

My loue is now awake out of her dreame,
And her fayre eyes like stars that dimmed were
With darksome cloud, now shew theyr goodly beams
More bright then Hesperus his head doth rere.   95
Come now ye damzels, daughters of delight,
Helpe quickly her to dight,
But first come ye fayre houres which were begot
In Ioues sweet paradice, of Day and Night,
Which doe the seasons of the yeare allot,   100
And al that euer in this world is fayre
Doe make and still repayre.

And ye three handmayds of the Cyprian Queene,
The which doe still adorne her beauties pride,
105   Helpe to addorne my beautifullest bride
And as ye her array, still throw betweene
Some graces to be seene,
And as ye vse to Venus, to her sing,
The whiles the woods shal answer and your eccho ring.

[7]

110   Now is my loue all ready forth to come,
Let all the virgins therefore well awayt,
And ye fresh boyes that tend vpon her groome
Prepare your selues; for he is comming strayt.
Set all your things in seemely good aray
115   Fit for so ioyfull day,
The ioyfulst day that euer sunne did see.
Faire Sun, shew forth thy fauourable ray,
And let thy lifull heat not feruent be
For feare of burning her sunshyny face,
120   Her beauty to disgrace.
O fayrest Phœbus, father of the Muse,
If euer I did honour thee aright,
Or sing the thing, that mote thy mind delight,
Doe not thy seruants simple boone refuse,
125   But let this day let this one day be myne,
Let all the rest be thine.
Then I thy souerayne prayses loud wil sing,
That all the woods shal answer and theyr eccho ring.

[8]

Harke how the Minstrels gin to shrill aloud
130   Their merry Musick that resounds from far,
The pipe, the tabor, and the trembling Croud,
That well agree withouten breach or iar.
But most of all the Damzels doe delite,
When they their tymbrels smyte,
135   And thereunto doe daunce and carrol sweet,
That all the sences they doe rauish quite,
The whyles the boyes run vp and downe the street,

Crying aloud with strong confused noyce,
As if it were one voyce.
Hymen io Hymen, Hymen they do shout,   140
That euen to the heauens theyr shouting shrill
Doth reach, and all the firmament doth fill,
To which the people standing all about,
As in approuance doe thereto applaud
And loud aduaunce her laud,   145
And euermore they Hymen Hymen sing,
That al the woods them answer and theyr eccho ring.

[9]

Loe where she comes along with portly pace,
Lyke Phœbe from her chamber of the East,
Arysing forth to run her mighty race,   150
Clad all in white, that seemes a virgin best.
So well it her beseemes that ye would weene
Some angell she had beene.
Her long loose yellow locks lyke golden wyre,
Sprinckled with perle, and perling flowres a tweene,   155
Doe lyke a golden mantle her attyre,
And being crowned with a girland greene,
Seeme lyke some mayden Queene.
Her modest eyes abashed to behold
So many gazers, as on her do stare,   160
Vpon the lowly ground affixed are.
Ne dare lift vp her countenance too bold,
But blush to heare her prayses sung so loud,
So farre from being proud.
Nathlesse doe ye still loud her prayses sing,   165
That all the woods may answer and your eccho ring.

[10]

Tell me ye merchants daughters did ye see
So fayre a creature in your towne before?
So sweet, so louely, and so mild as she,
Adornd with beautyes grace and vertues store,   170
Her goodly eyes lyke Saphyres shining bright,
Her forehead yuory white,

Her cheekes lyke apples which the sun hath rudded,
Her lips lyke cherryes charming men to byte,
175   Her brest like to a bowle of creame vncrudded,
Her paps lyke lyllies budded,
Her snowie necke lyke to a marble towre,
And all her body like a pallace fayre,
Ascending vppe with many a stately stayre,
180   To honors seat and chastities sweet bowre.
Why stand ye still ye virgins in amaze,
Vpon her so to gaze,
Whiles ye forget your former lay to sing,
To which the woods did answer and your eccho ring.

[11]

185   But if ye saw that which no eyes can see,
The inward beauty of her liuely spright,
Garnisht with heauenly guifts of high degree,
Much more then would ye wonder at that sight,
And stand astonisht lyke to those which red
190   Medusaes mazeful hed.
There dwels sweet loue and constant chastity,
Vnspotted fayth and comely womanhood,
Regard of honour and mild modesty,
There vertue raynes as Queene in royal throne,
195   And giueth lawes alone.
The which the base affections doe obay,
And yeeld theyr seruices vnto her will,
Ne thought of thing vncomely euer may
Thereto approch to tempt her mind to ill.
200   Had ye once seene these her celestial threasures,
And vnreuealed pleasures,
Then would ye wonder and her prayses sing,
That al the woods should answer and your echo ring.

[12]

Open the temple gates vnto my loue,
205   Open them wide that she may enter in,
And all the postes adorne as doth behoue,
And all the pillours deck with girlands trim,

For to recyue this Saynt with honour dew,
That commeth in to you.
With trembling steps and humble reuerence,   210
She commeth in, before th'almighties vew,
Of her ye virgins learne obedience,
When so ye come into those holy places,
To humble your proud faces;
Bring her vp to th'high altar that she may   215
The sacred ceremonies there partake,
The which do endlesse matrimony make,
And let the roring Organs loudly play
The praises of the Lord in liuely notes,
The whiles with hollow throates   220
The Choristers the ioyous Antheme sing,
That al the woods may answere and their eccho ring.

[13]

Behold whiles she before the altar stands
Hearing the holy priest that to her speakes
And blesseth her with his two happy hands,   225
How the red roses flush vp in her cheekes,
And the pure snow with goodly vermill stayne,
Like crimsin dyde in grayne,
That euen th'Angels which continually,
About the sacred Altare doe remaine,   230
Forget their seruice and about her fly,
Ofte peeping in her face that seemes more fayre,
The more they on it stare.
But her sad eyes still fastened on the ground,
Are gouerned with goodly modesty,   235
That suffers not one looke to glaunce awry,
Which may let in a little thought vnsownd.
Why blush ye loue to giue to me your hand,
The pledge of all our band?
Sing ye sweet Angels, Alleluya sing,
That all the woods may answere and your eccho ring.   240

[14]

Now al is done; bring home the bride againe,
Bring home the triumph of our victory,
Bring home with you the glory of her gaine,
245 With ioyance bring her and with iollity.
Neuer had man more ioyfull day then this,
Whom heauen would heape with blis.
Make feast therefore now all this liue long day,
This day for euer to me holy is,
250 Poure out the wine without restraint or stay,
Poure not by cups, but by the belly full,
Poure out to all that wull,
And sprinkle all the postes and wals with wine,
That they may sweat, and drunken be withall.
255 Crowne ye God Bacchus with a coronall,
And Hymen also crowne with wreathes of vine,
And let the Graces daunce vnto the rest;
For they can doo it best:
The whiles the maydens doe theyr carroll sing,
260 To which the woods shal answer and theyr eccho ring.

[15]

Ring ye the bels, ye yong men of the towne,
And leaue your wonted labors for this day:
This day is holy; doe ye write it downe,
That ye for euer it remember may.
265 This day the sunne is in his chiefest hight,
With Barnaby the bright,
From whence declining daily by degrees,
He somewhat loseth of his heat and light,
When once the Crab behind his back he sees.
270 But for this time it ill ordained was,
To chose the longest day in all the yeare,
And shortest night, when longest fitter weare:
Yet neuer day so long, but late would passe.
Ring ye the bels, to make it weare away,
275 And bonefiers make all day,
And daunce about them, and about them sing:
that all the woods may answer, and your eccho ring.

[16]

Ah when will this long weary day haue end,
And lende me leaue to come vnto my loue?
How slowly do the houres theyr numbers spend?   280
How slowly does sad Time his feathers moue?
Hast thee O fayrest Planet to thy home
Within the Westerne fome:
Thy tyred steedes long since haue need of rest.
Long though it be, at last I see it gloome,   285
And the bright euening star with golden creast
Appeare out of the East.
Fayre childe of beauty, glorious lampe of loue
That all the host of heauen in rankes doost lead,
And guydest louers through the nights dread,   290
How chearefully thou lookest from aboue,
And seemst to laugh atweene thy twinkling light
As ioying in the sight
Of these glad many which for ioy doe sing,
That all the woods them answer and their echo ring.   295

[17]

Now ceasse ye damsels your delights forepast;
Enough is it, that all the day was youres:
Now day is doen, and night is nighing fast:
Now bring the Bryde into the brydall boures.
Now night is come, now soone her disaray,   300
And in her bed her lay;
Lay her in lillies and in violets,
And silken courteins ouer her display,
And odourd sheetes, and Arras couerlets.
Behold how goodly my faire loue does ly   305
In proud humility;
Like vnto Maia, when as Ioue her tooke,
In Tempe, lying on the flowry gras,
Twixt sleepe and wake, after she weary was,
With bathing in the Acidalian brooke.   310
Now it is night, ye damsels may be gon,
And leaue my loue alone,

And leaue likewise your former lay to sing:
The woods no more shal answere, nor your echo ring.

[18]

315 Now welcome night, thou night so long expected,
That long daies labour doest at last defray,
And all my cares, which cruell loue collected,
Hast sumd in one, and cancelled for aye:
Spread thy broad wing ouer my loue and me,
320 That no man may vs see,
And in thy sable mantle vs enwrap,
From feare of perrill and foule horror free.
Let no false treason seeke vs to entrap,
Nor any dread disquiet once annoy
325 The safety of our ioy:
But let the night be calme and quietsome,
Without tempestuous storms or sad afray:
Lyke as when Ioue with fayre Alcmena lay,
When he begot the great Tirynthian groome:
330 Or lyke as when he with thy selfe did lie,
And begot Maiesty.
And let the mayds and yongmen cease to sing:
Ne let the woods them answer, nor theyr eccho ring.

[19]

Let no lamenting cryes, nor dolefull teares,
335 Be heard all night within nor yet without:
Ne let false whispers breeding hidden feares,
Breake gentle sleepe with misconceiued dout.
Let no deluding dreames, nor dreadful sights
Make sudden sad affrights;
340 Ne let housefyres, nor lightnings helpelesse harmes,
Ne let the Pouke, nor other euill sprights,
Ne let mischiuous witches with theyr charmes,
Ne let hob Goblins, names whose sence we see not,
Fray vs with things that be not.
345 Let not the shriech Oule, nor the Storke be heard:
Nor the night Rauen that still deadly yels,
Nor damned ghosts cald vp with mighty spels,

Nor griesly vultures make vs once affeard:
Ne let th'unpleasant Quyre of Frogs still croking
Make vs to wish theyr choking.   350
Let none of these theyr drery accents sing;
Ne let the woods them answer, nor theyr eccho ring.

[20]

But let stil Silence trew night watches keepe,
That sacred peace may in assurance rayne,
And tymely sleep, when it is tyme to sleepe,   355
May poure his limbs forth on your pleasant playne,
The whiles an hundred little winged loues,
Like diuers fethered doues,
Shall fly and flutter round about your bed,
And in the secret darke, that none reproues,   360
Their prety stealthes shal worke, and snares shal spread
To filch away sweet snatches of delight,
Conceald through couert night.
Ye sonnes of Venus, play your sports at will,
For greedy pleasure, carelesse of your toyes,   365
Thinks more vpon her paradise of ioyes,
Then what ye do, albe it good or ill.
All night therefore attend your merry play,
For it will soone be day:
Now none doth hinder you, that say or sing,   370
Ne will the woods now answer, nor your Eccho ring.

[21]

Who is the same, which at my window peepes?
Or whose is that faire face, that shines so bright?
Is it not Cinthia, she that neuer sleepes,
But walkes about high heauen al the night?   375
O fayrest goddesse, do thou not enuy
My loue with me to spy:
For thou likewise didst loue, though now vnthought,
And for a fleece of woll, which priuily,
The Latmian shephard once vnto thee brought,   380
His pleasures with thee wrought.

Therefore to vs be fauorable now;
And sith of wemens labours thou hast charge,
And generation goodly dost enlarge,
385   Encline thy will t'effect our wishfull vow,
And the chast wombe informe with timely seed,
That may our comfort breed:
Till which we cease our hopefull hap to sing,
Ne let the woods vs answere, nor our Eccho ring.

[22]

390   And thou great Iuno, which with awful might
The lawes of wedlock still dost patronize,
And the religion of the faith first plight
With sacred rites hast taught to solemnize:
And eeke for comfort often called art
395   Of women in their smart,
Eternally bind thou this louely band,
And all thy blessings vnto vs impart.
And thou glad Genius, in whose gentle hand,
The bridale bowre and geniall bed remaine,
400   Without blemish or staine,
And the sweet pleasures of theyr loues delight
With secret ayde doest succour and supply,
Till they bring forth the fruitfull progeny,
Send vs the timely fruit of this same night.
405   And thou fayre Hebe, and thou Hymen free,
Grant that it may so be.
Til which we cease your further prayse to sing,
Ne any woods shal answer, nor your Eccho ring.

[23]

And ye high heauens, the temple of the gods,
410   In which a thousand torches flaming bright
Doe burne, that to vs wretched earthly clods
In dreadful darknesse lend desired light;
And all ye powers which in the same remayne,
More then we men can fayne,
415   Poure out your blessing on vs plentiously,
And happy influence vpon vs raine,
That we may raise a large posterity,

Which from the earth, which they may long possesse,
With lasting happinesse,
Vp to your haughty pallaces may mount,   420
And for the guerdon of theyr glorious merit
May heauenly tabernacles there inherit,
Of blessed Saints for to increase the count.
So let vs rest, sweet loue, in hope of this,
And cease till then our tymely ioyes to sing,   425
The woods no more vs answer, nor our eccho ring.

[24]
Song made in lieu of many ornaments,
With which my loue should duly haue bene dect,
Which cutting off through hasty accidents,
Ye would not stay your dew time to expect,   430
But promist both to recompens,
Be vnto her a goodly ornament,
And for short time an endlesse moniment.

FINIS

Fowre Hymnes,

MADE BY
EDM. SPENSER.

LONDON,
Printed for VVilliam Ponfonby.
1596.

TO THE RIGHT HO-
NORABLE AND MOST VER-
tuous Ladies, the Ladie Margaret Countesse
of Cumberland, and the Ladie Marie
Countesse of Warwicke.

Hauing in the greener times of my youth, composed these former
two Hymnes in the praise of Loue and beautie, and finding that
the same too much pleased those of like age and disposition, which
being too vehemently caried with that kind of affection, do rather
5 *sucke out poyfon to their strong passion, then hony to their honest*
delight, I was moued by the one of you two most excellent Ladies,
to call in the same. But being vnable so to doe, by reason that
many copies thereof were formerly scattered abroad, I resolued at
least to amend, and by way of retractation to reforme them,
10 *making in stead of those two Hymnes of earthly or naturall loue*
and beautie, two others of heauenly and celestiall. The which I
doe dedicate ioyntly vnto you two honorable sisters, as to the most
excellent and rare ornaments of all true loue and beautie, both in
the one and the other kinde, humbly beseeching you to vouchsafe
15 *the patronage of them, and to accept this my humble seruice, in*
lieu of the great graces and honourable fauours which ye dayly
shew vnto me, vntill such time as I may by better meanes yeeld
you some more notable testimonie of my thankfull mind and
dutifull deuotion.
20   *And euen so I pray for your happinesse.*
    Greenwich this first of September.
        1596.

            Your Honors most bounden euer
                in all humble seruice.
25   Ed. Sp.

AN HYMNE IN
HONOVR OF
LOVE.

Loue, that long since hast to thy mighty powre,
Perforce subdude my poore captiued hart,
And raging now therein with restlesse stowre,
Doest tyrannize in euerie weaker part;
Faine would I seeke to ease my bitter smart,   5
By any seruice I might do to thee,
Or ought that else might to thee pleasing bee.

And now t'asswage the force of this new flame,
And make thee more propitious in my need,
I meane to sing the praises of thy name,   10
And thy victorious conquests to areed;
By which thou madest many harts to bleed
Of mighty Victors, with wyde wounds embrewed,
And by thy cruell darts to thee subdewed.

Onely I feare my wits enfeebled late,   15
Through the sharpe sorrowes, which thou hast me bred,
Should faint, and words should faile me, to relate
The wondrous triumphs of thy great godhed.
But if thou wouldst vouchsafe to ouerspred
Me with the shadow of thy gentle wing,   20
I should enabled be thy actes to sing.

Come then, O come, thou mightie God of loue,
Out of thy siluer bowres and secret blisse,
Where thou doest sit in *Venus* lap aboue,
Bathing thy wings in her ambrosiall kisse,   25
That sweeter farre then any Nectar is;
Come softly, and my feeble breast inspire
With gentle furie, kindled of thy fire.

And ye sweet Muses, which haue often proued
30   The piercing points of his auengefull darts;
And ye faire Nimphs, which oftentimes haue loued
The cruell worker of your kindly smarts,
Prepare your selues, and open wide your harts,
For to receiue the triumph of your glorie,
35   That made you merie oft, when ye were sorie.

And ye faire blossomes of youths wanton breed,
Which in the conquests of your beautie bost,
Wherewith your louers feeble eyes you feed,
But sterue their harts, that needeth nourture most,
40   Prepare your selues, to march amongst his host,
And all the way this sacred hymne do sing,
Made in the honor of your Soueraigne king.

Great god of might, that reignest in the mynd,
And all the bodie to thy hest doest frame,
45   Victor of gods, subduer of mankynd,
That doest the Lions and fell Tigers tame,
Making their cruell rage thy scornefull game,
And in their roring taking great delight;
Who can expresse the glorie of thy might?

50   Or who aliue can perfectly declare,
The wondrous cradle of thine infancie?
When thy great mother Venus first thee bare,
Begot of Plentie and of Penurie,
Though elder then thine owne natiuitie;
55   And yet a chyld, renewing still thy yeares;
And yet the eldest of the heauenly Peares.

For ere this worlds still mouing mightie masse,
Out of great Chaos vgly prison crept,
In which his goodly face long hidden was
60   From heauens view, and in deepe darknesse kept,

Loue, that had now long time securely slept
In *Venus* lap, vnarmed then and naked,
Gan reare his head, by *Clotho* being waked.

And taking to him wings of his owne heate,
Kindled at first from heauens life-giuing fyre,   65
He gan to moue out of his idle seate,
Weakely at first, but after with desyre
Lifted aloft, he gan to mount vp hyre,
And like fresh Eagle, make his hardie flight
Through all that great wide wast, yet wanting light.   70

Yet wanting light to guide his wandring way,
His owne faire mother, for all creatures sake,
Did lend him light from her owne goodly ray:
Then through the world his way he gan to take,
The world that was not till he did it make;   75
Whose sundrie parts he from them selues did seuer,
The which before had lyen confused euer.

The earth, the ayre, the water, and the fyre,
Then gan to raunge them selues in huge array,
And with contrary forces to conspyre   80
Each against other, by all meanes they may,
Threatning their owne confusion and decay:
Ayre hated earth, and water hated fyre,
Till Loue relented their rebellious yre.

He then them tooke, and tempering goodly well   85
Their contrary dislikes with loued meanes,
Did place them all in order, and compell
To keepe them selues within their sundrie raines,
Together linkt with Adamantine chaines;
Yet so, as that in euery liuing wight   90
They mixe themselues, and shew their kindly might.

So euer since they firmely haue remained,
And duly well obserued his beheast;
Through which now all these things that are contained
95   Within this goodly cope, both most and least
Their being haue, and dayly are increast,
Through secret sparks of his infused fyre,
Which in the barraine cold he doth inspyre.

Thereby they all do liue, and moued are
100   To multiply the likenesse of their kynd,
Whilest they seeke onely, without further care,
To quench the flame, which they in burning fynd:
But man, that breathes a more immortall mynd,
Not for lusts sake, but for eternitie,
105   Seekes to enlarge his lasting progenie.

For hauing yet in his deducted spright,
Some sparks remaining of that heauenly fyre,
He is enlumind with that goodly light,
Vnto like goodly semblant to aspyre:
110   Therefore in choice of loue, he doth desyre
That seemes on earth most heauenly, to embrace,
That same is Beautie, borne of heauenly race.

For sure of all, that in this mortall frame
Contained is, nought more diuine doth seeme,
115   Or that resembleth more th'immortall flame
Of heauenly light, then Beauties glorious beame.
What wonder then, if with such rage extreme
Fraile men, whose eyes seek heauenly things to see,
At sight thereof so much enrauisht bee?

120   Which well perceiuing, that imperious boy
Doth therwith tip his sharp empoisned darts;
Which glancing through the eyes with countenance coy,
Rest not, till they haue pierst the trembling harts,
And kindled flame in all their inner parts,
125   Which suckes the blood, and drinketh vp the lyfe
Of carefull wretches with consuming griefe.

Thenceforth they playne, and make ful piteous mone
Vnto the author of their balefull bane;
The daies they waste, the nights they grieue and grone,
Their liues they loath, and heauens light disdaine;   130
No light but that, whose lampe doth yet remaine
Fresh burning in the image of their eye,
They deigne to see, and seeing it still dye.

The whylst thou tyrant Loue doest laugh and scorne
At their complaints, making their paine thy play;   135
Whylest they lye languishing like thrals forlorne,
The whyles thou doest triumph in their decay,
And otherwhyles, their dying to delay,
Thou doest emmarble the proud hart of her,
Whose loue before their life they doe prefer.   140

So hast thou often done (ay me the more)
To me thy vassall, whose yet bleeding hart,
With thousand wounds thou mangled hast so sore
That whole remaines scarse any little part,
Yet to augment the anguish of my smart,   145
Thou hast enfrosen her disdainefull brest,
That no one drop of pitie there doth rest.

Why then do I this honor vnto thee,
Thus to ennoble thy victorious name,
Since thou doest shew no fauour vnto mee,   150
Ne once moue ruth in that rebellious Dame,
Somewhat to slacke the rigour of my flame?
Certes small glory doest thou winne hereby,
To let her liue thus free, and me to dy.

But if thou be indeede, as men thee call,   155
The worlds great Parent, the most kind preseruer
Of liuing wights, the soueraine Lord of all,
How falles it then, that with thy furious feruour,
Thou doest afflict as well the not deseruer,
As him that doeth thy louely heasts despize,   160
And on thy subiects most doest tyrannize?

Yet herein eke thy glory seemeth more,
By so hard handling those which best thee serue,
That ere thou doest them vnto grace restore,
165   Thou mayest well trie if they will euer swerue,
And mayest them make it better to deserue,
And hauing got it, may it more esteeme,
For things hard gotten, men more dearely deeme.

So hard those heauenly beauties be enfyred,
170   As things diuine, least passions doe impresse,
The more of stedfast mynds to be admyred,
The more they stayed be on stedfastnesse:
But baseborne mynds such lamps regard the lesse,
Which at first blowing take not hastie fyre,
175   Such fancies feele no loue, but loose desyre.

For loue is Lord of truth and loialtie,
Lifting himselfe out of the lowly dust,
On golden plumes vp to the purest skie,
Aboue the reach of loathly sinfull lust,
180   Whose base affect through cowardly distrust
Of his weake wings, dare not to heauen fly,
But like a moldwarpe in the earth doth ly.

His dunghill thoughts, which do themselues enure
To dirtie drosse, no higher dare aspyre,
185   Ne can his feeble earthly eyes endure
The flaming light of that celestiall fyre,
Which kindleth loue in generous desyre,
And makes him mount aboue the natiue might
Of heauie earth, vp to the heauens hight.

190   Such is the powre of that sweet passion,
That it all sordid basenesse doth expell,
And the refyned mynd doth newly fashion
Vnto a fairer forme, which now doth dwell
In his high thought, that would it selfe excell;
195   Which he beholding still with constant sight,
Admires the mirrour of so heauenly light.

Whose image printing in his deepest wit,
He thereon feeds his hungrie fantasy,
Still full, yet neuer satisfyde with it,
Like *Tantale*, that in store doth sterued ly: 200
So doth he pine in most satiety,
For nought may quench his infinite desyre,
Once kindled through that first conceiued fyre.

Thereon his mynd affixed wholly is,
Ne thinks on ought, but how it to attaine;   205
His care, his ioy, his hope is all on this,
That seemes in it all blisses to containe,
In sight whereof, all other blisse seemes vaine.
Thrise happie man, might he the same possesse;
He faines himselfe, and doth his fortune blesse.   210

And though he do not win his wish to end,
Yet thus farre happie he him selfe doth weene,
That heauens such happie grace did to him lend,
As thing on earth so heauenly, to haue seene,
His harts enshrined saint, his heauens queene,   215
Fairer then fairest, in his fayning eye,
Whose sole aspect he counts felicitye.

Then forth he casts in his vnquiet thought,
What he may do, her fauour to obtaine;
What braue exploit, what perill hardly wrought,   220
What puissant conquest, what aduenturous paine,
May please her best, and grace vnto him gaine:
He dreads no danger, nor misfortune feares,
His faith, his fortune, in his breast he beares.

Thou art his god, thou art his mightie guyde,   225
Thou being blind, letst him not see his feares,
But cariest him to that which he hath eyde,
Through seas, through flames, through thousand
        swords and speares:
Ne ought so strong that may his force withstand,
With which thou armest his resistlesse hand.   230

Witnesse *Leander*, in the Euxine waues,
And stout *Æneas* in the Troiane fyre,
Achilles preassing through the Phrygian glaiues,
And *Orpheus* daring to prouoke the yre
235   Of damned fiends, to get his loue retyre:
For both through heauen and hell thou makest way,
To win them worship which to thee obay.

And if by all these perils and these paynes,
He may but purchase lyking in her eye,
240   What heauens of ioy, then to himselfe he faynes,
Eftsoones he wypes quite out of memory,
What euer ill before he did aby:
Had it bene death, yet would he die againe,
To liue thus happie as her grace to gaine.

245   Yet when he hath found fauour to his will,
He nathemore can so contented rest,
But forceth further on, and striueth still
T'approch more neare, till in her inmost brest,
He may embosomd bee, and loued best;
250   And yet not best, but to be lou'd alone,
For loue can not endure a Paragone.

The feare whereof, O how doth it torment
His troubled mynd with more then hellish paine!
And to his fayning fansie represent
255   Sights neuer seene, and thousand shadowes vaine,
To breake his sleepe, and waste his ydle braine;
Thou that hast neuer lou'd canst not beleeue,
Least part of th'euils which poore louers greeue.

The gnawing enuie, the hart-fretting feare,
260   The vaine surmizes, the distrustfull showes,
The false reports that flying tales doe beare,
The doubts, the daungers, the delayes, the woes,
The fayned friends, the vnassured foes,
With thousands more then any tongue can tell,
265   Doe make a louers life a wretches hell.

Yet is there one more cursed then they all,
That cancker worme, that monster Gelosie,
Which eates the hart, and feedes vpon the gall,
Turning all loues delight to miserie,
Through feare of loosing his felicitie.   270
Ah Gods, that euer ye that monster placed
In gentle loue, that all his ioyes defaced.

By these, O Loue, thou doest thy entrance make,
Vnto thy heauen, and doest the more endeere
Thy pleasures vnto those which them partake,   275
As after stormes when clouds begin to cleare,
The Sunne more bright and glorious doth appeare;
So thou thy folke, through paines of Purgatorie,
Dost beare vnto thy blisse, and heauens glorie.

There thou them placest in a Paradize   280
Of all delight, and ioyous happie rest,
Where they doe feede on Nectar heauenly wize,
With *Hercules* and *Hebe*, and the rest
Of *Venus* dearlings, through her bountie blest,
And lie like Gods in yuorie beds arayd,   285
With rose and lillies ouer them displayd.

There with thy daughter *Pleasure* they doe play
Their hurtlesse sports, without rebuke or blame,
And in her snowy bosome boldly lay
Their quiet heads, deuoyd of guilty shame,   290
After full ioyance of their gentle game,
Then her they crowne their Goddesse and their Queene,
And decke with floures thy altars well beseene.

Ay me, deare Lord, that euer I might hope,
For all the paines and woes that I endure,   295
To come at length vnto the wished scope
Of my desire, or might my selfe assure,
That happie port for euer to recure.
Then would I thinke these paines no paines at all,
And all my woes to be but penance small.   300

Then would I sing of thine immortall praise
An heauenly Hymne, such as the Angels sing,
And thy triumphant name then would I raise
Boue all the gods, thee onely honoring,
305   My guide, my God, my victor, and my king;
Till then, dread Lord, vouchsafe to take of me
This simple song, thus fram'd in praise of thee.

FINIS.

AN HYMNE IN
HONOVR OF
BEAVTIE.

Ah whither, Loue, wilt thou now carrie mee?
What wontlesse fury dost thou now inspire
Into my feeble breast, too full of thee?
Whylest seeking to aslake thy raging fyre,
Thou in me kindlest much more great desyre,   5
And vp aloft aboue my strength doest rayse
The wondrous matter of my fyre to prayse.

That as I earst in praise of thine owne name,
So now in honour of thy Mother deare,
An honourable Hymne I eke should frame,   10
And with the brightnesse of her beautie cleare,
The rauisht harts of gazefull men might reare,
To admiration of that heauenly light,
From whence proceeds such soule enchaunting might.

Therto do thou great Goddesse, queene of Beauty,   15
Mother of loue, and of all worlds delight,
Without whose souerayne grace and kindly dewty,
Nothing on earth seemes fayre to fleshly sight,
Doe thou vouchsafe with thy loue-kindling light,
T'illuminate my dim and dulled eyne,   20
And beautifie this sacred hymne of thyne.

That both to thee, to whom I meane it most,
And eke to her, whose faire immortall beame,
Hath darted fyre into my feeble ghost,
That now it wasted is with woes extreame,   25
It may so please that she at length will streame
Some deaw of grace, into my withered hart,
After long sorrow and consuming smart.

What time this worlds great workmaister did cast
30   To make al things, such as we now behold,
It seemes that he before his eyes had plast
A goodly Paterne to whose perfect mould
He fashiond them as comely as he could,
That now so faire and seemely they appeare,
35   As nought may be amended any wheare.

That wondrous Paterne wheresoere it bee,
Whether in earth layd vp in secret store,
Or else in heauen, that no man may it see
With sinfull eyes, for feare it to deflore,
40   Is perfect Beautie which all men adore,
Whose face and feature doth so much excell
All mortall sence, that none the same may tell.

Thereof as euery earthly thing partakes,
Or more or lesse by influence diuine,
45   So it more faire accordingly it makes,
And the grosse matter of this earthly myne,
Which clotheth it, thereafter doth refyne,
Doing away the drosse which dims the light
Of that faire beame, which therein is empight.

50   For through infusion of celestiall powre,
The duller earth it quickneth with delight,
And life-full spirits priuily doth powre
Through all the parts, that to the lookers sight
They seeme to please. That is thy soueraine might,
55   O *Cyprian* Queene, which flowing from the beame
Of thy bright starre, thou into them doest streame.

That is the thing which giueth pleasant grace
To all things faire, that kindleth liuely fyre,
Light of thy lampe, which shyning in the face,
60   Thence to the soule darts amorous desyre,
And robs the harts of those which it admyre,
Therewith thou pointest thy Sons poysned arrow,
That wounds the life, and wastes the inmost marrow.

How vainely then doe ydle wits inuent,
That beautie is nought else, but mixture made   65
Of colours faire, and goodly temp'rament
Of pure complexions, that shall quickly fade
And passe away, like to a sommers shade,
Or that it is but comely composition
Of parts well measurd, with meet disposition.   70

Hath white and red in it such wondrous powre,
That it can pierce through th'eyes vnto the hart,
And therein stirre such rage and restlesse stowre,
As nought but death can stint his dolours smart?
Or can proportion of the outward part,   75
Moue such affection in the inward mynd,
That it can rob both sense and reason blynd?

Why doe not then the blossomes of the field,
Which are arayd with much more orient hew,
And to the sense most daintie odours yield,   80
Worke like impression in the lookers vew?
Or why doe not faire pictures like powre shew,
In which oftimes, we Nature see of Art
Exceld, in perfect limming euery part.

But ah, beleeue me, there is more then so   85
That workes such wonders in the minds of men.
I that have often prou'd, too well it know;
And who so list the like assayes to ken,
Shall find by tryall, and confesse it then,
That Beautie is not, as fond men misdeeme,   90
An outward shew of things, that onely seeme.

For that same goodly hew of white and red,
With which the cheekes are sprinckled, shal decay,
And those sweete rosy leaues so fairely spred
Vpon the lips, shall fade and fall away   95
To that they were, euen to corrupted clay.
That golden wyre, those sparckling stars so bright
Shall turne to dust, and loose their goodly light.

But that faire lampe, from whose celestiall ray
100   That light proceedes, which kindleth louers fire,
Shall neuer be extinguisht nor decay,
But when the vitall spirits doe expyre,
Vnto her natiue planet shall retyre,
For it is heauenly borne and can not die,
105   Being a parcell of the purest skie.

For when the soule, the which deriued was
At first, out of that great immortall Spright,
By whom all liue to loue, whilome did pas
Downe from the top of purest heauens hight,
110   To be embodied here, it then tooke light
And liuely spirits from that fayrest starre,
Which lights the world forth from his firie carre.

Which powre retayning still or more or lesse,
When she in fleshly seede is eft enraced,
115   Through euery part she doth the same impresse,
According as the heauens haue her graced,
And frames her house, in which she will be placed,
Fit for her selfe, adorning it with spoyle
Of th'heauenly riches, which she robd erewhyle.

120   Therof it comes, that these faire soules, which haue
The most resemblance of that heauenly light,
Frame to themselues most beautifull and braue
Their fleshly bowre, most fit for their delight,
And the grosse matter by a soueraine might
125   Tempers so trim, that it may well be seene,
A pallace fit for such a virgin Queene.

So euery spirit, as it is most pure,
And hath in it the more of heauenly light,
So it the fairer bodie doth procure
130   To habit in, and it more fairely dight
With chearefull grace and amiable sight.
For of the soule the bodie forme doth take:
For soule is forme, and doth the bodie make.

Therefore where euer that thou doest behold
A comely corpse, with beautie faire endewed,   135
Know this for certaine, that the same doth hold
A beauteous soule, with faire conditions thewed,
Fit to receiue the seede of vertue strewed.
For all that faire is, is by nature good;
That is a signe to know the gentle blood.   140

Yet oft it falles, that many a gentle mynd
Dwels in deformed tabernacle drownd,
Either by chaunce, against the course of kynd,
Or through vnaptnesse in the substance fownd,
Which it assumed of some stubborne grownd,   145
That will not yield vnto her formes direction,
But is perform'd with some foule imperfection.

And oft it falles (ay me the more to rew)
That goodly beautie, albe heauenly borne,
Is foule abusd, and that celestiall hew,   150
Which doth the world with her delight adorne,
Made but the bait of sinne, and sinners scorne;
Whilest euery one doth seeke and sew to haue it,
But euery one doth seeke, but to depraue it.

Yet nathemore is that faire beauties blame,   155
But theirs that do abuse it vnto ill:
Nothing so good, but that through guilty shame
May be corrupt, and wrested vnto will.
Nathelesse the soule is faire and beauteous still,
How euer fleshes fault it filthy make: 160
For things immortall no corruption take.

But ye faire Dames, the worlds deare ornaments,
And liuely images of heauens light,
Let not your beames with such disparagements
Be dimd, and your bright glorie darkned quight,   165
But mindfull still of your first countries sight,
Doe still preserue your first informed grace,
Whose shadow yet shynes in your beauteous face.

Loath that foule blot, that hellish fierbrand,
170   Disloiall lust, faire beauties foulest blame,
That base affections, which your eares would bland,
Commend to you by loues abused name;
But is indeede the bondslaue of defame,
Which will the garland of your glorie marre,
175   And quench the light of your bright shyning starre.

But gentle Loue, that loiall is and trew,
Will more illumine your resplendent ray,
And adde more brightnesse to your goodly hew,
From light of his pure fire, which by like way
180   Kindled of yours, your likenesse doth display,
Like as two mirrours by opposd reflexion,
Doe both expresse the faces first impression.

Therefore to make your beautie more appeare,
It you behoues to loue, and forth to lay
185   That heauenly riches, which in you ye beare,
That men the more admyre their fountaine may,
For else what booteth that celestiall ray,
If it in darkenesse be enshrined euer,
That it of louing eyes be vewed neuer?

190   But in your choice of Loues, this well aduize,
That likest to your selues ye them select,
The which your forms first sourse may sympathize,
And with like beauties parts be inly deckt:
For if you loosely loue without respect,
195   It is no loue, but a discordant warre,
Whose vnlike parts amongst themselues do iarre.

For Loue is a celestiall harmonie,
Of likely harts composd of starres concent,
Which ioyne together in sweete sympathie,
200   To worke ech others ioy and true content,
Which they haue harbourd since their first descent
Out of their heauenly bowres, where they did see
And know ech other here belou'd to bee.

Then wrong it were that any other twaine
Should in loues gentle band combyned bee,   205
But those whom heauen did at first ordaine,
And made out of one mould the more t'agree:
For all that like the beautie which they see,
Streight do not loue: for loue is not so light,
As streight to burne at first beholders sight.   210

But they which loue indeede, looke otherwise,
With pure regard and spotlesse true intent,
Drawing out of the obiect of their eyes,
A more refyned forme, which they present
Vnto their mind, voide of all blemishment;   215
Which it reducing to her first perfection,
Beholdeth free from fleshes frayle infection.

And then conforming it vnto the light,
Which in it selfe it hath remaining still
Of that first Sunne, yet sparckling in his sight,   220
Thereof he fashions in his higher skill,
An heauenly beautie to his fancies will,
And it embracing in his mind entyre,
The mirrour of his owne thought doth admyre.

Which seeing now so inly faire to be,   225
As outward it appeareth to the eye,
And with his spirits proportion to agree,
He thereon fixeth all his fantasie,
And fully setteth his felicitie,
Counting it fairer, then it is indeede,   230
And yet indeede her fairenesse doth exceede.

For louers eyes more sharply sighted bee
Then other mens, and in deare loues delight
See more then any other eyes can see,
Through mutuall receipt of beames bright,   235
Which carrie priuie message to the spright,
And to their eyes that inmost faire display,
As plaine as light discouers dawning day.

Therein they see through amorous eye-glaunces,
240 Armies of loues still flying too and fro,
Which dart at them their litle fierie launces,
Whom hauing wounded, backe againe they go,
Carrying compassion to their louely foe;
Who seeing her faire eyes so sharpe effect,
245 Cures all their sorrowes with one sweete aspect.

In which how many wonders doe they reede
To their conceipt, that others neuer see,
Now of her smiles, with which their soules they feede,
Like Gods with Nectar in their bankets free,
250 Now of her lookes, which like to Cordials bee;
But when her words embassade forth she sends,
Lord how sweete musicke that vnto them lends.

Sometimes vpon her forhead they behold
A thousand Graces masking in delight,
255 Sometimes within her eye-lids they vnfold
Ten thousand sweet belgards, which to their sight
Doe seeme like twinckling starres in frostie night:
But on her lips like rosy buds in May,
So many millions of chaste pleasures play.

260 All those, O *Cytherea*, and thousands more
Thy handmaides be, which do on thee attend
To decke thy beautie with their dainties store,
That may it more to mortall eyes commend,
And make it more admyr'd of foe and frend;
265 That in mens harts thou mayst thy throne enstall
And spred thy louely kingdome ouer all.

Then *Iö tryumph*, O great beauties Queene,
Aduance the banner of thy conquest hie,
That all this world, the which thy vassals beene,
270 May draw to thee, and with dew fealtie,
Adore the powre of thy great Maiestie,
Singing this Hymne in honour of thy name,
Compyld by me, which thy poore liegeman am.

In lieu whereof graunt, O great Soueraine,
That she whose conquering beautie doth captiue   275
My trembling hart in her eternall chaine,
One drop of grace at length will to me giue,
That I her bounden thrall by her may liue,
And this same life, which first fro me she reaued,
May owe to her, of whom I it receaued.   280

And you faire *Venus* dearling, my deare dread,
Fresh flowre of grace, great Goddesse of my life,
When your faire eyes these fearefull lines shal read,
Deigne to let fall one drop of dew reliefe,
That may recure my harts long pyning griefe,   285
And shew what wondrous powre your beauty hath,
That can restore a damned wight from death.

FINIS.

AN HYMNE OF
HEAVENLY
LOVE.

Loue, lift me vp vpon thy golden wings,
From this base world vnto thy heauens hight,
Where I may see those admirable things,
Which there thou workest by thy soueraine might,
5   Farre aboue feeble reach of earthly sight,
That I thereof an heauenly Hymne may sing
Vnto the god of Loue, high heauens king.

Many lewd layes (ah woe is me the more)
In praise of that mad fit, which fooles call loue,
10   I haue in th'heat of youth made heretofore,
That in light wits did loose affection moue.
But all those follies now I do reproue,
And turned haue the tenor of my string,
The heauenly prayses of true loue to sing.

15   And ye that wont with greedy vaine desire
To reade my fault, and wondring at my flame,
To warme your selues at my wide sparckling fire,
Sith now that heat is quenched, quench my blame,
And in her ashes shrowd my dying shame:
20   For who my passed follies now pursewes,
Beginnes his owne, and my old fault renewes.

Before this worlds great frame, in which al things
Are now containd, found any being place,
Ere flitting Time could wag his eyas wings
25   About that mightie bound, which doth embrace
The rolling Spheres, and parts their houres by space,
That high eternall powre, which now doth moue
In all these things, mou'd in it selfe by loue.

It lou'd it selfe, because it selfe was faire;
(For faire is lou'd;) and of it selfe begot   30
Like to it selfe his eldest sonne and heire,
Eternall, pure, and voide of sinfull blot,
The firstling of his ioy, in whom no iot
Of loues dislike, or pride was to be found,
Whom he therefore with equall honour crownd.   35

With him he raignd, before all time prescribed,
In endlesse glorie and immortall might,
Together with that third from them deriued,
Most wise, most holy, most almightie Spright,
Whose kingdomes throne no thought of earthly wight   40
Can comprehend, much lesse my trembling verse
With equall words can hope it to reherse.

Yet O most blessed Spirit, pure lampe of light,
Eternall spring of grace and wisedome trew,
Vouchsafe to shed into my barren spright,   45
Some little drop of thy celestiall dew,
That may my rymes with sweet infuse embrew,
And giue me words equall vnto my thought,
To tell the marueiles by thy mercie wrought.

Yet being pregnant still with powrefull grace,   50
And full of fruitfull loue, that loues to get
Things like himselfe, and to enlarge his race,
His second brood though not in powre so great,
Yet full of beautie, next he did beget
An infinite increase of Angels bright,   55
All glistring glorious in their Makers light.

To them the heauens illimitable hight,
Not this round heauen, which we from hence behold,
Adornd with thousand lamps of burning light,
And with ten thousand gemmes of shyning gold,   60
He gaue as their inheritance to hold,
That they might serue him in eternall blis,
And be partakers of those ioyes of his.

There they in their trinall triplicities
About him wait, and on his will depend,
Either with nimble wings to cut the skies,
When he them on his messages doth send,
Or on his owne dread presence to attend,
Where they behold the glorie of his light,
And caroll Hymnes of loue both day and night.

Both day and night is vnto them all one,
For he his beames doth still to them extend,
That darknesse there appeareth neuer none,
Ne hath their day, ne hath their blisse an end,
But there their termelesse time in pleasure spend,
Ne euer should their happinesse decay,
Had not they dar'd their Lord to disobay.

But pride impatient of long resting peace,
Did puffe them vp with greedy bold ambition,
That they gan cast their state how to increase,
Aboue the fortune of their first condition,
And sit in Gods owne seat without commission:
The brightest Angell, euen the Child of light
Drew millions more against their God to fight.

Th'Almighty seeing their so bold assay,
Kindled the flame of his consuming yre,
And with his onely breath them blew away
From heauens hight, to which they did aspyre,
To deepest hell, and lake of damned fyre;
Where they in darknesse and dread horror dwell,
Hating the happie light from which they fell.

So that next off-spring of the Makers loue,
Next to himselfe in glorious degree,
Degendering to hate fell from aboue
Through pride; (for pride and loue may ill agree)
And now of sinne to all ensample bee:
How then can sinfull flesh it selfe assure,
Sith purest Angels fell to be impure?

But that eternall fount of loue and grace,
Still flowing forth his goodnesse vnto all,   100
Now seeing left a waste and emptie place
In his wyde Pallace, through those Angels fall,
Cast to supply the same, and to enstall
A new vnknowen Colony therein,
Whose root from earths base groundworke shold begin.   105

Therefore of clay, base, vile, and next to nought,
Yet form'd by wondrous skill, and by his might:
According to an heauenly patterne wrought,
Which he had fashiond in his wise foresight,
He man did make, and breathd a liuing spright   110
Into his face most beautifull and fayre,
Endewd with wisedomes riches, heauenly, rare.

Such he him made, that he resemble might
Himselfe, as mortall thing immortall could;
Him to be Lord of euery liuing wight,   115
He made by loue out of his owne like mould,
In whom he might his mightie selfe behould:
For loue doth loue the thing belou'd to see,
That like it selfe in louely shape may bee.

But man forgetfull of his makers grace,   120
No lesse then Angels, whom he did ensew,
Fell from the hope of promist heauenly place,
Into the mouth of death to sinners dew,
And all his off-spring into thraldome threw:
Where they for euer should in bonds remaine,   125
Of neuer dead, yet euer dying paine.

Till that great Lord of Loue, which him at first
Made of meere loue, and after liked well,
Seeing him lie like creature long accurst,
In that deepe horror of despeyred hell,   130
Him wretch in doole would let no lenger dwell,
But cast out of that bondage to redeeme,
And pay the price, all were his debt extreeme.

Out of the bosome of eternall blisse,
135   In which he reigned with his glorious syre,
He downe descended, like a most demisse
And abiect thrall, in fleshes fraile attyre,
That he for him might pay sinnes deadly hyre,
And him restore vnto that happie state,
140   In which he stood before his haplesse fate.

In flesh at first the guilt committed was,
Therefore in flesh it must be satisfyde:
Nor spirit, nor Angell, though they man surpas,
Could make amends to God for mans misguyde,
145   But onely man himselfe, who selfe did slyde.
So taking flesh of sacred virgins wombe,
For mans deare sake he did a man become.

And that most blessed bodie, which was borne
Without all blemish or reprochfull blame,
150   He freely gaue to be both rent and torne
Of cruell hands, who with despightfull shame
Reuyling him, that them most vile became,
At length him nayled on a gallow tree,
And slew the iust, by most vniust decree.

155   O huge and most vnspeakeable impression
Of loues deepe wound, that pierst the piteous hart
Of that deare Lord with so entyre affection,
And sharply launching euery inner part,
Dolours of death into his soule did dart;
160   Doing him die, that neuer it deserued,
To free his foes, that from his heast had swerued.

What hart can feele least touch of so sore launch,
Or thought can think the depth of so deare wound?
Whose bleeding sourse their streames yet neuer staunch,
165   But stil do flow, and freshly still redound,
To heale the sores of sinfull soules vnsound,
And clense the guilt of that infected cryme,
Which was enrooted in all fleshly slyme.

O blessed well of loue, O floure of grace,
O glorious Morning starre, O lampe of light,   170
Most liuely image of thy fathers face,
Eternall King of glorie, Lord of might,
Meeke lambe of God before all worlds behight,
How can we thee requite for all this good?
Or what can prize that thy most precious blood?   175

Yet nought thou ask'st in lieu of all this loue,
But loue of vs for guerdon of thy paine.
Ay me; what can vs lesse then that behoue?
Had he required life of vs againe,
Had it beene wrong to aske his owne with gaine?   180
He gaue vs life, he it restored lost;
Then life were least, that vs so litle cost.

But he our life hath left vnto vs free,
Free that was thrall, and blessed that was band;
Ne ought demaunds, but that we louing bee,   185
As he himselfe hath lou'd vs afore hand,
And bound therto with an eternall band,
Him first to loue, that vs so dearely bought,
And next, our brethren to his image wrought.

Him first to loue, great right and reason is,   190
Who first to vs our life and being gaue;
And after when we fared had amisse,
Vs wretches from the second death did saue;
And last the food of life, which now we haue,
Euen himselfe in his deare sacrament,   195
To feede our hungry soules vnto vs lent.

Then next to loue our brethren, that were made
Of that selfe mould, and that selfe makers hand,
That we, and to the same againe shall fade,
Where they shall haue like heritage of land,   200
How euer here on higher steps we stand;
Which also were with selfe same price redeemed
That we, how euer of vs light esteemed.

And were they not, yet since that louing Lord
205   Commaunded vs to loue them for his sake,
Euen for his sake, and for his sacred word,
Which in his last bequest he to vs spake,
We should them loue, and with their needs partake;
Knowing that whatsoere to them we giue,
210   We giue to him, by whom we all doe liue.

Such mercy he by his most holy reede
Vnto vs taught, and to approue it trew,
Ensampled it by his most righteous deede,
Shewing vs mercie miserable crew,
215   That we the like should to the wretches shew,
And loue our brethren; thereby to approue,
How much himselfe that loued vs, we loue.

Then rouze thy selfe, O earth, out of thy soyle,
In which thou wallowest like to filthy swyne
220   And doest thy mynd in durty pleasures moyle,
Vnmindfull of that dearest Lord of thyne;
Lift vp to him thy heauie clouded eyne,
That thou his soueraine bountie mayst behold,
And read through loue his mercies manifold.

225   Beginne from first, where he encradled was
In simple cratch, wrapt in a wad of hay,
Betweene the toylefull Oxe and humble Asse,
And in what rags, and in how base aray,
The glory of our heauenly riches lay,
230   When him the silly Shepheards came to see,
Whom greatest Princes sought on lowest knee.

From thence reade on the storie of his life,
His humble carriage, his vnfaulty wayes,
His cancred foes, his fights, his toyle, his strife,
235   His paines, his pouertie, his sharpe assayes,
Through which he past his miserable dayes,
Offending none, and doing good to all,
Yet being malist both of great and small.

And looke at last how of most wretched wights,
He taken was, betrayd, and false accused,   240
How with most scornefull taunts, and fell despights
He was reuyld, disgrast, and foule abused,
How scourgd, how crownd, how buffeted, how brused;
And lastly how twixt robbers crucifyde,
With bitter wounds through hands, through feet and syde.   245

Then let thy flinty hart that feeles no paine,
Empierced be with pittifull remorse,
And let thy bowels bleede in euery vaine,
At sight of his most sacred heauenly corse,
So torne and mangled with malicious forse,   250
And let thy soule, whose sins his sorrows wrought,
Melt into teares, and grone in grieued thought.

With sence whereof whilest so thy softened spirit
Is inly toucht, and humbled with meeke zeale,
Through meditation of his endlesse merit,   255
Lift vp thy mind to th'author of thy weale,
And to his soueraine mercie doe appeale;
Learne him to loue, that loued thee so deare,
And in thy brest his blessed image beare.

With all thy hart, with all thy soule and mind,   260
Thou must him loue, and his beheasts embrace:
All other loues, with which the world doth blind
Weake fancies, and stirre vp affections base,
Thou must renounce, and vtterly displace,
And giue thy selfe vnto him full and free,   265
That full and freely gaue himselfe to thee.

Then shalt thou feele thy spirit so possest,
And rauisht with deuouring great desire
Of his deare selfe, that shall thy feeble brest
Inflame with loue, and set thee all on fire   270
With burning zeale, through euery part entire,
That in no earthly thing thou shalt delight,
But in his sweet and amiable sight.

Thenceforth all worlds desire will in thee dye,
275   And all earthes glorie on which men do gaze,
Seeme durt and drosse in thy pure sighted eye,
Compar'd to that celestiall beauties blaze,
Whose glorious beames all fleshly sense doth daze
With admiration of their passing light,
280   Blinding the eyes and lumining the spright.

Then shall thy rauisht soule inspired bee
With heauenly thoughts, farre aboue humane skil,
And thy bright radiant eyes shall plainely see
Th'Idee of his pure glorie present still,
285   Before thy face, that all thy spirits shall fill
With sweete enragement of celestiall loue,
Kindled through sight of those faire things aboue.

FINIS.

AN HYMNE OF
HEAVENLY
BEAVTIE.

Rapt with the rage of mine own rauisht thought,
Through contemplation of those goodly sights,
And glorious images in heauen wrought,
Whose wondrous beauty breathing sweet delights,
Do kindle loue in high conceipted sprights: 5
I faine to tell the things that I behold,
But feele my wits to faile, and tongue to fold.

Vouchsafe then, O thou most almightie Spright,
From whom all guifts of wit and knowledge flow,
To shed into my breast some sparkling light   10
Of thine eternall Truth, that I may show
Some litle beames to mortall eyes below,
Of that immortall beautie, there with thee,
Which in my weake distraughted mynd I see.

That with the glorie of so goodly sight,   15
The hearts of men, which fondly here admyre
Faire seeming shewes, and feed on vaine delight,
Transported with celestiall desyre
Of those faire formes, may lift themselues vp hyer,
And learne to loue with zealous humble dewty   20
Th'eternall fountaine of that heauenly beauty.

Beginning then below, with th'easie vew
Of this base world, subiect to fleshly eye,
From thence to mount aloft by order dew,
To contemplation of th'immortall sky,   25
Of the soare faulcon so I learne to fly,
That flags awhile her fluttering wings beneath,
Till she her selfe for stronger flight can breath.

Then looke who list, thy gazefull eyes to feed
30   With sight of that is faire, looke on the frame
Of this wyde *vniuerse*, and therein reed
The endlesse kinds of creatures, which by name
Thou canst not count, much lesse their natures aime:
All which are made with wondrous wise respect,
35   And all with admirable beautie deckt.

First th'Earth, on adamantine pillers founded,
Amid the Sea engirt with brasen bands;
Then th'Aire still flitting, but yet firmely bounded
On euerie side, with pyles of flaming brands,
40   Neuer consum'd nor quencht with mortall hands;
And last, that mightie shining christall wall,
Wherewith he hath encompassed this All.

By view whereof, it plainly may appeare,
That still as euery thing doth vpward tend,
45   And further is from earth, so still more cleare
And faire it growes, till to his perfect end
Of purest beautie, it at last ascend:
Ayre more then water, fire much more then ayre,
And heauen then fire appeares more pure and fayre.

50   Looke thou no further, but affixe thine eye
On that bright shynie round still mouing Masse,
The house of blessed Gods, which men call *Skye*,
All sowd with glistring stars more thicke then grasse,
Whereof each other doth in brightnesse passe;
55   But those two most, which ruling night and day,
As King and Queene, the heauens Empire sway.

And tell me then, what hast thou euer seene,
That to their beautie may compared bee,
Or can the sight that is most sharpe and keene,
60   Endure their Captains flaming head to see?
How much lesse those, much higher in degree,
And so much fairer, and much more then these,
As these are fairer then the land and seas?

For farre aboue these heauens which here we see,
Be others farre exceeding these in light,   65
Not bounded, not corrupt, as these same bee,
But infinite in largenesse and in hight,
Vnmouing, vncorrupt, and spotlesse bright,
That need no Sunne t'illuminate their spheres,
But their owne natiue light farre passing theirs.   70

And as these heauens still by degrees arize,
Vntill they come to their first Mouers bound,
That in his mightie compasse doth comprize,
And carrie all the rest with him around,
So those likewise doe by degrees redound,   75
And rise more faire, till they at last ariue
To the most faire, whereto they all do striue.

Faire is the heauen, where happy soules haue place,
In full enioyment of felicitie,
Whence they doe still behold the glorious face   80
Of the diuine eternall Maiestie;
More faire is that, where those *Idees* on hie
Enraunged be, which *Plato* so admyred,
And pure *Intelligences* from God inspyred.

Yet fairer is that heauen, in which doe raine   85
The soueraine *Powres* and mightie *Potentates*,
Which in their high protections doe containe
All mortall Princes, and imperiall States;
And fayrer yet, whereas the royall Seates
And heauenly *Dominations* are set,   90
From whom all earthly gouernance is fet.

Yet farre more faire be those bright *Cherubins*,
Which all with golden wings are ouerdight,
And those eternall burning *Seraphins*,
Which from their faces dart out fierie light;   95
Yet fairer then they both, and much more bright
Be th'Angels and Archangels, which attend
On Gods owne person, without rest or end.

These thus in faire each other farre excelling,
100   As to the Highest they approch more neare,
Yet is that Highest farre beyond all telling,
Fairer then all the rest which there appeare,
Though all their beauties ioynd together were:
How then can mortall tongue hope to expresse,
105   The image of such endlesse perfectnesse?

Cease then my tongue, and lend vnto my mynd
Leaue to bethinke how great that beautie is,
Whose vtmost parts so beautifull I fynd,
How much more those essentiall parts of his,
110   His truth, his loue, his wisedome, and his blis,
His grace, his doome, his mercy and his might,
By which he lends vs of himselfe a sight.

Those vnto all he daily doth display,
And shew himselfe in th'image of his grace,
115   As in a looking glasse, through which he may
Be seene, of all his creatures vile and base,
That are vnable else to see his face,
His glorious face which glistereth else so bright,
That th'Angels selues can not endure his sight.

120   But we fraile wights, whose sight cannot sustaine
The Suns bright beames, when he on vs doth shyne,
But that their points rebutted backe againe
Are duld, how can we see with feeble eyne,
The glory of that Maiestie diuine,
125   In sight of whom both Sun and Moone are darke,
Compared to his least resplendent sparke?

The meanes therefore which vnto vs is lent,
Him to behold, is on his workes to looke,
Which he hath made in beauty excellent,
130   And in the same, as in a brasen booke,
To reade enregistred in euery nooke
His goodnesse, which his beautie doth declare,
For all thats good, is beautifull and faire.

Thence gathering plumes of perfect speculation,
To impe the wings of thy high flying mynd,   135
Mount vp aloft through heauenly contemplation,
From this darke world, whose damps the soule do blynd,
And like the natiue brood of Eagles kynd,
On that bright Sunne of glorie fixe thine eyes,
Clear'd from grosse mists of fraile infirmities.   140

Humbled with feare and awfull reuerence,
Before the footestoole of his Maiestie,
Throw thy selfe downe with trembling innocence,
Ne dare looke vp with corruptible eye,
On the dred face of that great *Deity*,   145
For feare, lest if he chaunce to looke on thee,
Thou turne to nought, and quite confounded be.

But lowly fall before his mercie seate,
Close couered with the Lambes integrity,
From the iust wrath of his auengefull threate,   150
That sits vpon the righteous throne on hy:
His throne is built vpon Eternity,
More firme and durable then steele or brasse,
Or the hard diamond, which them both doth passe.

His scepter is the rod of Righteousnesse,   155
With which he bruseth all his foes to dust,
And the great Dragon strongly doth represse,
Vnder the rigour of his iudgement iust;
His seate is Truth, to which the faithfull trust;
From whence proceed her beames so pure and bright,   160
That all about him sheddeth glorious light.

Light farre exceeding that bright blazing sparke,
Which darted is from *Titans* flaming head,
That with his beames enlumineth the darke
And dampish aire, wherby al things are red: 165
Whose nature yet so much is maruelled
Of mortall wits, that it doth much amaze
The greatest wisards, which thereon do gaze.

But that immortall light which there doth shine,
170   Is many thousand times more bright, more cleare,
More excellent, more glorious, more diuine,
Through which to God all mortall actions here,
And euen the thoughts of men, do plaine appeare:
For from th'eternall Truth it doth proceed,
175   Through heauenly vertue, which her beames doe breed.

With the great glorie of that wondrous light,
His throne is all encompassed around,
And hid in his owne brightnesse from the sight
Of all that looke thereon with eyes vnsound:
180   And vnderneath his feet are to be found
Thunder, and lightning, and tempestuous fyre,
The instruments of his auenging yre.

There in his bosome *Sapience* doth sit,
The soueraine dearling of the *Deity*,
185   Clad like a Queene in royall robes, most fit
For so great powre and peerelesse maiesty.
And all with gemmes and iewels gorgeously
Adornd, that brighter then the starres appeare,
And make her natiue brightnes seem more cleare.

190   And on her head a crowne of purest gold
Is set, in signe of highest soueraignty,
And in her hand a scepter she doth hold,
With which she rules the house of God on hy,
And menageth the euer-mouing sky,
195   And in the same these lower creatures all,
Subiected to her powre imperiall.

Both heauen and earth obey vnto her will,
And all the creatures which they both containe:
For of her fulnesse which the world doth fill,
200   They all partake, and do in state remaine,
As their great Maker did at first ordaine,
Through obseruation of her high beheast,
By which they first were made, and still increast.

The fairenesse of her face no tongue can tell,
For she the daughters of all wemens race,   205
And Angels eke, in beautie doth excell,
Sparkled on her from Gods owne glorious face,
And more increast by her owne goodly grace,
That it doth farre exceed all humane thought,
Ne can on earth compared be to ought.   210

Ne could that Painter (had he liued yet)
Which pictured *Venus* with so curious quill,
That all posteritie admyred it,
Haue purtrayd this, for all his maistring skill;
Ne she her selfe, had she remained still,   215
And were as faire, as fabling wits do fayne,
Could once come neare this beauty souerayne.

But had those wits the wonders of their dayes,
Or that sweete *Teian* Poet which did spend
His plenteous vaine in setting forth her prayse,   220
Seene but a glims of this, which I pretend,
How wondrously would he her face commend,
Aboue that Idole of his fayning thought,
That all the world shold with his rimes be fraught?

How then dare I, the nouice of his Art,   225
Presume to picture so diuine a wight,
Or hope t'expresse her least perfections part,
Whose beautie filles the heauens with her light,
And darkes the earth with shadow of her sight?
Ah gentle Muse thou art too weake and faint,   230
The pourtraict of so heauenly hew to paint.

Let Angels which her goodly face behold
And see at will, her soueraigne praises sing,
And those most sacred mysteries vnfold,
Of that faire loue of mightie heauens king.   235
Enough is me t'admyre so heauenly thing,
And being thus with her huge loue possest,
In th'only wonder of her selfe to rest.

But who so may, thrise happie man him hold,
240   Of all on earth, whom God so much doth grace,
And lets his owne Beloued to behold:
For in the view of her celestiall face,
All ioy, all blisse, all happinesse haue place,
Ne ought on earth can want vnto the wight,
245   Who of her selfe can win the wishfull sight.

For she out of her secret threasury,
Plentie of riches forth on him will powre,
Euen heauenly riches, which there hidden ly
Within the closet of her chastest bowre,
250   Th'eternall portion of her precious dowre,
Which mighty God hath giuen to her free,
And to all those which thereof worthy bee.

None thereof worthy be, but those whom shee
Vouchsafeth to her presence to receaue,
255   And letteth them her louely face to see,
Wherof such wondrous pleasures they conceaue,
And sweete contentment, that it doth bereaue
Their soule of sense, through infinite delight,
And them transport from flesh into the spright.

260   In which they see such admirable things,
As carries them into an extasy,
And heare such heauenly notes, and carolings,
Of Gods high praise, that filles the brasen sky,
And feele such ioy and pleasure inwardly,
265   That maketh them all worldly cares forget,
And onely thinke on that before them set.

Ne from thenceforth doth any fleshly sense,
Or idle thought of earthly things remaine,
But all that earst seemd sweet, seemes now offense,
270   And all that pleased earst, now seemes to paine.
Their ioy, their comfort, their desire, their gaine,
Is fixed all on that which now they see,
All other sights but fayned shadowes bee.

And that faire lampe, which vseth to enflame
The hearts of men with selfe consuming fyre,   275
Thenceforth seemes fowle, and full of sinfull blame;
And all that pompe, to which proud minds aspyre
By name of honor, and so much desyre,
Seemes to them basenesse, and all riches drosse,
And all mirth sadnesse, and all lucre losse.   280

So full their eyes are of that glorious sight,
And senses fraught with such satietie,
That in nought else on earth they can delight,
But in th'aspect of that felicitie,
Which they haue written in their inward ey;   285
On which they feed, and in their fastened mynd
All happie ioy and full contentment fynd.

Ah then my hungry soule, which long hast fed
On idle fancies of thy foolish thought,
And with false beauties flattring bait misled,   290
Hast after vaine deceiptfull shadowes sought,
Which all are fled, and now haue left thee nought,
But late repentance through thy follies prief;
Ah ceasse to gaze on matter of thy grief.

And looke at last vp to that soueraine light,   295
From whose pure beams al perfect beauty springs,
That kindleth loue in euery godly spright,
Euen the loue of God, which loathing brings
Of this vile world, and these gay seeming things;
With whose sweete pleasures being so possest,   300
Thy straying thoughts henceforth for euer rest.

Prothalamion

Or
A Spousall Verse made by
Edm. Spenser.

IN HONOVR OF THE DOV-
ble mariage of the two Honorable & vertuous
Ladies, the Ladie Elizabeth *and the Ladie* Katherine
Somerset, Daughters to the Right Honourable the
Earle of *Worcester* and espoused to the two worthie
Gentlemen M. *Henry Gilford,* and
M. *William Peter* Esquyers.

AT LONDON.
Printed for *VVilliam Ponsonby.*
1596.

Prothalamion.

I

Calme was the day, and through the trembling ayre,
Sweete breathing *Zephyrus* did softly play
A gentle spirit, that lightly did delay
Hot *Titans* beames, which then did glyster fayre:
When I whom sullein care,
Through discontent of my long fruitlesse stay
In Princes Court, and expectation vayne
Of idle hopes, which still doe fly away,
Like empty shaddowes, did aflict my brayne,
Walkt forth to ease my payne
Along the shoare of siluer streaming *Themmes*,
Whose rutty Bancke, the which his Riuer hemmes,
Was paynted all with variable flowers,
And all the meades adornd with daintie gemmes,
Fit to decke maydens bowres,
And crowne their Paramours,
Against the Brydale day, which is not long:
    Sweete *Themmes* runne softly, till I end my Song.

2

There, in a Meadow, by the Riuers side,
A Flocke of *Nymphes* I chaunced to espy,
All louely Daughters of the Flood thereby,
With goodly greenish locks all loose vntyde,
As each had bene a Bryde,
And each one had a little wicker basket,
Made of fine twigs entrayled curiously,
In which they gathered flowers to fill their flasket:
And with fine Fingers, cropt full feateously
The tender stalkes on hye.
Of euery sort, which in that Meadow grew,
They gathered some; the Violet pallid blew,
The little Dazie, that at euening closes,
The virgin Lillie, and the Primrose trew,

With store of vermeil Roses,
To decke their Bridegromes posies,
Against the Brydale day, which was not long: 35
    Sweete *Themmes* runne softly, till I end my Song.

3

With that I saw two Swannes of goodly hewe,
Come softly swimming downe along the Lee;
Two fairer Birds I yet did neuer see:
The snow which doth the top of *Pindus* strew,   40
Did neuer whiter shew,
Nor *Ioue* himselfe when he a Swan would be
For loue of *Leda*, whiter did appeare:
Yet *Leda* was they say as white as he,
Yet not so white as these, nor nothing neare;   45
So purely white they were,
That euen the gentle streame, the which them bare,
Seem'd foule to them, and bad his billowes spare
To wet their silken feathers, least they might
Soyle their fayre plumes with water not so fayre,   50
And marre their beauties bright,
That shone as heauens light,
Against their Brydale day, which was not long:
    Sweete *Themmes* runne softly, till I end my Song.

4

Eftsoones the *Nymphes*, which now had Flowers their fill,   55
Ran all in haste, to see that siluer brood,
As they came floating on the Christal Flood,
Whom when they sawe, they stood amazed still,
Their wondring eyes to fill,
Them seem'd they neuer saw a sight so fayre,   60
Of Fowles so louely, that they sure did deeme
Them heauenly borne, or to be that same payre
Which through the Skie draw *Venus* siluer Teeme,
For sure they did not seeme
To be begot of any earthly Seede,   65

But rather Angels or of Angels breede:
Yet were they bred of *Somers-heat* they say,
In sweetest Season, when each Flower and weede
The earth did fresh aray,
70 So fresh they seem'd as day,
Euen as their Brydale day, which was not long:
    Sweete *Themmes* runne softly, till I end my Song.

5

Then forth they all out of their baskets drew,
Great store of Flowers, the honour of the field,
75 That to the sense did fragrant odours yield,
All which vpon those goodly Birds they threw,
And all the Waues did strew,
That like old *Peneus* Waters they did seeme,
When downe along by pleasant *Tempes* shore
80 Scattred with Flowres, through *Thessaly* they streeme,
That they appeare through Lillies plenteous store,
Like a Brydes Chamber flore:
Two of those *Nymphes*, meane while, two Garlands
        bound,
Of freshest Flowres which in that Mead they found,
85 The which presenting all in trim Array,
Their snowie Foreheads therewithall they crownd,
Whil'st one did sing this Lay,
Prepar'd against that Day,
Against their Brydale day, which was not long:
90   Sweete *Themmes* runne softly, till I end my Song.

6

Ye gentle Birdes, the worlds faire ornament,
And heauens glorie, whom this happie hower
Doth leade vnto your louers blisfull bower,
Ioy may you haue and gentle hearts content
95 Of your loues couplement:
And let faire *Venus*, that is Queene of loue,
With her heart-quelling Sonne vpon you smile,
Whose smile they say, hath vertue to remoue
All Loues dislike, and friendships faultie guile
100 For euer to assoile.

Let endlesse Peace your steadfast hearts accord,
And blessed Plentie wait vpon your bord,
And let your bed with pleasures chast abound,
That fruitfull issue may to you afford,
Which may your foes confound,   105
And make your ioyes redound,
Vpon your Brydale day, which is not long:
   Sweete *Themmes* run softlie, till I end my Song.

7

So ended she; and all the rest around
To her redoubled that her vndersong,   110
Which said, their bridale daye should not be long.
And gentle Eccho from the neighbour ground,
Their accents did resound.
So forth those ioyous Birdes did passe along,
Adowne the Lee, that to them murmurde low,   115
As he would speake, but that he lackt a tong,
Yeat did by signes his glad affection show,
Making his streame run slow.
And all the foule which in his flood did dwell
Gan flock about these twaine, that did excell   120
The rest, so far, as *Cynthia* doth shend
The lesser starres. So they enranged well,
Did on those two attend,
And their best seruice lend,
Against their wedding day, which was not long: 125
   Sweete *Themmes* run softly, till I end my song.

8

At length they all to mery *London* came,
To mery London, my most kyndly Nurse,
That to me gaue this Lifes first natiue sourse:
Though from another place I take my name,   130
An house of auncient fame.
There when they came, whereas those bricky towres,
The which on *Themmes* brode aged backe doe ryde,
Where now the studious Lawyers haue their bowers,
There whylome wont the Templer Knights to byde,   135

Till they decayd through pride:
Next whereunto there standes a stately place,
Where oft I gayned giftes and goodly grace
Of that great Lord, which therein wont to dwell,
140   Whose want too well, now feeles my freendles case:
But Ah here fits not well
Olde woes but ioyes to tell
Against the bridale daye, which is not long:
    Sweete *Themmes* runne softly, till I end my Song.

9

145   Yet therein now doth lodge a noble Peer,
Great *Englands* glory and the Worlds wide wonder,
Whose dreadfull name, late through all *Spaine* did
        thunder,
And *Hercules* two pillors standing neere,
Did make to quake and feare:
150   Faire branch of Honor, flower of Cheualrie,
That fillest *England* with thy triumphes fame,
Ioy haue thou of thy noble victorie,
And endlesse happinesse of thine owne name
That promiseth the same:
155   That through thy prowesse and victorious armes,
Thy country may be freed from forraine harmes:
And great *Elisaes* glorious name may ring
Through al the world, fil'd with thy wide Alarmes,
Which some braue muse may sing
160   To ages following,
Vpon the Brydale day, which is not long:
    Sweete *Themmes* runne softly, till I end my Song.

10

From those high Towers, this noble Lord issuing,
Like Radiant *Hesper* when his golden hayre
165   In th'*Ocean* billowes he hath Bathed fayre,
Descended to the Riuers open vewing,
With a great traine ensuing.

Aboue the rest were goodly to bee seene
Two gentle Knights of louely face and feature
Beseeming well the bower of anie Queene,   170
With gifts of wit and ornaments of nature,
Fit for so goodly stature:
That like the twins of *Ioue* they seem'd in sight,
Which decke the Bauldricke of the Heauens bright.
They two forth pacing to the Riuers side,   175
Receiued those two faire Brides, their Loues delight,
Which at th'appointed tyde,
Each one did make his Bryde,
Against their Brydale day, which is not long:
    Sweete *Themmes* runne softly, till I end my Song.   180

FINIS.

Commendatory Sonnets.

To the right worshipfull, my singular good frend, M. Gabriell
Haruey, Doctor of the Lawes.

Haruey, the happy aboue happiest men
I read: that sitting like a Looker-on
Of this worldes Stage, doest note with critique pen
The sharpe dislikes of each condition:
5   And as one carelesse of suspition,
Ne fawnest for the fauour of the great:
Ne fearest foolish reprehension
Of faulty men, which daunger to thee threat.
But freely doest, of what thee list, entreat,
10 Like a great Lord of peerelesse liberty:
Lifting the Good vp to high Honours seat,
And the Euill damning euermore to dy.
For Life, and Death is in thy doomefull writing:
So thy renowme liues euer by endighting.

Dublin: this xviij. of Iuly: 1586.

Your deuoted frend, during life,

EDMUND SPENCER.

[Prefixed to *Nennio, or A Treatise of Nobility*]

Who so wil seeke by right deserts t'attaine
    vnto the type of true Nobility,
    And not by painted shewes and titles vaine,
    Deriued farre from famous Auncestrie,
5   Behold them both in their right visnomy
    Here truly pourtray'd, as they ought to be,
    And striuing both for termes of dignitie,
    To be aduanced highest in degree.
    And when thou doost with equall insight see
10   the ods twixt both, of both then deem aright
    And chuse the better of them both to thee,

But thanks to him that it deserues, behight:
To *Nenna* first, that first this worke created,
And next to *Jones*, that truely it translated.

ED. SPENSER.

[Prefixed to *The Historie of George Castriot, surnamed
Scanderbeg*]

Wherefore doth vaine antiquitie so vaunt,
　Her ancient monuments of mightie peeres,
　And old Heroes, which their world did daunt
　With their great deedes, and fild their childrens eares?

Who rapt with wonder of their famous praise,　　　　　5
　Admire their statues, their Colossoes great,
　Their rich triumphall Arcks which they did raise,
　Their huge Pyramids, which do heauen threat.

Lo one, whom later age hath brought to light,
　Matchable to the greatest of those great:　　　　　10
　Great both by name, and great in power and might,
　And meriting a meere triumphant seate.

　The scourge of Turkes, and plague of infidels,
　　Thy acts, ô Scanderbeg, this volume tels.

Ed. Spenser.

[Prefixed to *The Commonwealth and Gouernment of Venice*]

The antique *Babel*, Empresse of the East,
  Vpreard her buildinges to the threatned skie:
And Second *Babell* tyrant of the West,
  Her ayry Towers vpraised much more high.
5 But with the weight of their own surquedry,
  They both are fallen, that all the earth did feare,
And buried now in their own ashes ly,
  Yet shewing by their heapes how great they were.
But in their place doth now a third appeare,
10 Fayre *Venice*, flower of the last worlds delight,
And next to them in beauty draweth neare,
  But farre exceedes in policie of right.
Yet not so fayre her buildinges to behold
  As *Lewkenors* stile that hath her beautie told.

                                        Edm. Spencer.

Attributed Verses

From Sir James Ware's *The Historie of Ireland*, 1633.

Certaine verses of Mr Edm. Spenser's.

A translation made *ex tempore* by Mr *Edm. Spenser* upon this distich,
written on a Booke belonging to the right honorable *Richard Earle*
of *Corke*, &c.

> *Nvlla dies pereat, pereat pars nulla diei,*
> *Ne tu sic pereas, ut periere dies.*

Let no day passe, passe no part of the day,
   Lest thou doe passe, as dayes doe passe away.

Verses upon the said Earles Lute.

Whilst vitall sapp did make me spring,
   And leafe and bough did flourish brave,
I then was dumbe and could not sing,
   Ne had the voice which now I have:
5   But when the axe my life did end,
   The Muses nine this voice did send.
               E. S.

From Thomas Fuller's *The History of the*
Worthies of England, 1662.

> *I was promis'd on a time,*
> *To have reason for my rhyme;*
> *From that time unto this season,*
> *I receiv'd nor rhyme nor reason.*

NOTES

Abbreviations

The Notes cite items listed under Further Reading in the abbreviated form of surname and date of publication. Thus 'cf. Lotspeich (1942), 40' refers to H. G. Lotspeich, *Classical Mythology in the Poetry of Edmund Spenser* (Princeton, 1942), p. 40. The most important primary sources are cited by author and title as follows:

Boccaccio, *Genealogia* (cited by book and chapter)
Camden, *Britain* (cited by page)
Castiglione, *Courtier* (cited by page)
Comes, *Mythologiae* (cited by book and chapter)
ECE (for *Elizabethan Critical Essays*, cited by volume and page)
Ficino, *Commentary* (cited by book and chapter)
Holinshed, *Chronicles* (cited by volume and page)
Servius, *Commentarii* (cited by Virgilian passage)
Wells, *Allusions* (cited by page)

Full details of these works are supplied under Further Reading.

The following abbreviations for Spenser's works are used throughout the Notes:

Amor	*Amoretti*
Ast	*Astrophel*
CCH	*Colin Clovts Come Home Againe*
Comp	*Complaints*
Daph	*Daphnaïda*
DLC	*Dolefull Lay of Clorinda*
Epith	*Epithalamion*
FH	*Fowre Hymnes*
FQ	*The Faerie Queene*
HB	*An Hymne in Honovr of Beavtie*
HHB	*An Hymne of Heavenly Beavtie*
HHL	*An Hymne of Heavenly Love*
HL	*An Hymne in Honovr of Love*
Letters	*Three Proper . . . Letters. Two . . . Commendable Letters*
MHT	*Prosopopoia. Or Mother Hubberds Tale*

Muiop	*Mviopotmos, Or the Fate of the Butterflie*
Prose	*Spenser's Prose Works*, Variorum Edition, vol. 9 (1949)
Proth	*Prothalamion*
RR	*Ruines of Rome: by Bellay*
RT	*The Ruines of Time*
SC	*The Shepheardes Calender*
TM	*The Teares of the Muses*
TW	*A Theatre for Worldlings*
VB	*The Visions of Bellay*
Vewe	*A Vewe of the Present State of Irelande*
VG	*Virgils Gnat*
VP	*The Visions of Petrarch*
VW	*Visions of the Worlds Vanitie*

Other abbreviations used in the Notes and Further Reading are as follows:

CL	*Comparative Literature*
EA	*Études Anglaises*
EIC	*Essays in Criticism*
ELH	*English Literary History*
ELN	*English Language Notes*
ELR	*English Literary Renaissance*
ES	*English Studies*
HLQ	*Huntington Library Quarterly*
JEGP	*Journal of English and Germanic Philology*
JHI	*Journal of the History of Ideas*
JMRS	*Journal of Medieval and Renaissance Studies*
MLN	*Modern Language Notes*
MLQ	*Modern Language Quarterly*
MLR	*Modern Language Review*
MP	*Modern Philology*
N&Q	*Notes and Queries*
OED	*Oxford English Dictionary*
PMLA	*Publications of the Modern Language Association of America*
PQ	*Philological Quarterly*
REL	*Review of English Literature*
RES	*Review of English Studies*
SEL	*Studies in English Literature*
SP	*Studies in Philology*
SpE	*The Spenser Encyclopedia* (ed. Hamilton)
SpN	*Spenser Newsletter*
SR	*Studies in the Renaissance*
SSt	*Spenser Studies*

TLS	*Times Literary Supplement*
TSLL	*Texas Studies in Language and Literature*
UTQ	*University of Toronto Quarterly*
Var	*The Works of Edmund Spenser. A Variorum Edition*
YES	*Yearbook of English Studies*

For the explanation of recurrent words and phrases the reader is referred
to the Glossary of Common Terms. Owing to pressure of space such usages
are not normally glossed in the notes. The majority of archaisms and
dialectical terms used in *The Shepheardes Calender* are adequately explained
by E. K., but the remainder are dealt with either in the notes or the glossary
as appropriate. References to E. K.'s glosses are given in square brackets,
for example *SC, November*, [161].

FROM *A THEATRE FOR WORLDLINGS*

The work which has become known to Spenser's readers as *A Theatre for
Worldlings* was published in 1569 under the full title of *A Theatre wherein
be represented as wel the miseries & calamities that follow the voluptuous
Worldlings, As also the great ioyes and plesures which the faithfull do enioy.
An argument both profitable and delectable, to all that sincerely loue the word
of God.* The author was Jan van der Noot, a Dutch refugee fleeing religious
persecution at the hands of 'that wycked tyrant', the Duke of Alva (fol.
105v) [cf. Forster (1967b)]. How Spenser became involved in the enterprise
remains unknown, although the likeliest explanation is through the influence
of Richard Mulcaster, his schoolmaster at Merchant Taylors', who had
close associations with the émigré Dutch community. It is noteworthy,
however, that the publisher was Henry Bynneman who later produced the
Spenser–Harvey *Letters* (1580). Two previous editions, the first in Dutch
and the second in French, had already appeared from the press of John
Day (1568) [cf. Van Dorsten (1970)]. The English edition is comprised of
a dedicatory epistle to Queen Elizabeth, a series of epigrams and sonnets
accompanied by emblematic illustrations, and a long prose commentary
(heavily indebted to John Bale and Heinrich Bullinger) expounding the
meaning of the preceding 'visions' – a format of text and exegesis designed
to lend the work something akin to scriptural authority [cf. Hyde (1983)].
Despite an overtly eirenic attitude, the work is uncompromising in its
denunciation of the Roman Catholic Church [cf. Prescott (1978)] and in
representing its 'worldliness' as both cause and symptom of the spiritual
malaise of the time [cf. Rasmussen (1980)]. 'Borne of the subversion of the
Empire', the papacy is represented as the successor to imperial tyranny,
and the Church of Rome as the temple of Antichrist (fol. 20v).

From the viewpoint of literary history, *A Theatre* is significant for the development of the sonnet form in three languages, Dutch, French and English. The presence of accompanying illustrations constitutes one of the earliest examples of its kind, establishing a tradition that was to influence *The Shepheardes Calender*. The Dutch and French editions are illustrated by fine copperplate etchings and the English edition by less sophisticated woodcuts. The precise relationship between the two sets of illustrations is problematic, although the traditional attribution of the copperplate engravings to Marcus Gheeraerts the Elder remains possible despite arguments to the contrary [cf. Friedland (1956); Bath (1988)].

The poems are arranged in three groups. The 'Epigrams' are derived from Petrarch's *Rime Sparse* (323) in the French translation of Clément Marot. Sonnets 1–11 derive from the *Songe* (a sequence of fifteen sonnets) appended to Du Bellay's *Antiquitez de Rome* (later translated by Spenser as *Ruines of Rome*). Sonnets 12–15 are original compositions (presumably by Noot) inspired by the Book of Revelation and full of the Apocalyptic excitement of the age. The French edition simply reproduces the poetry of Marot and Du Bellay and it would appear that this was the version from which Spenser worked, but with some knowledge of the Italian in the case of Petrarch. The quality of the English translations, though variable, is generally accurate and there seems little reason to doubt their attribution to the same hand, although Spenser's responsibility for the four 'Apocalyptic' sonnets has been called in question [cf. Satterthwaite (1960)]. The epigrams display a certain insecurity of structure. Marot was faithful to Petrarch's twelve-line format, but Spenser develops epigrams 1 and 3 into English sonnets rhyming *ababcdcdefefgg*. The internal structure, however, remains at odds with the demands of the sonnet form and the problem remained largely unresolved when the epigrams were revised as *The Visions of Petrarch*. Far more successful in this respect were the translations from Du Bellay, the earliest instance of a blank-verse sonnet sequence in English, and doubtless influenced by current theories of neo-classical poetics of the sort discussed in the Spenser–Harvey correspondence. The Roman subject matter would have made the avoidance of rhyme (present in the original) seem theoretically appropriate.

Regarded as a unified sequence, the epigrams and sonnets display a clear thematic progression. The former afford universal, atemporal emblems of the world's vanity while the latter supply historical verification in the specific instance of imperial Rome, the fate of which adumbrates that of its papal successor. The eighth sonnet of Du Bellay's *Songe*, excluded from *A Theatre*, had juxtaposed Revelation's imagery of the beast from the sea with that of the barbarian invasions, thereby fusing the destinies of pagan and papal Rome and, very probably, inspiring the four 'Apocalyptic' sonnets which conclude the sequence.

The influence of *A Theatre* upon Spenser's later work was substantial. By denoting Queen Elizabeth as 'Astreæ' (sig. A6r) and opposing her political influence to that of the Catholic Whore of Babylon, it established the polarized female archetypes which recur throughout *The Faerie Queene*. By presenting a prolonged meditation upon the transience of earthly things and reposing its trust in the 'Lorde of Sabaoth, the Lord of hostes' (fol. 65r), it initiated Spenser's obsessive engagement with the theme of mutability and the ultimate resolution of the long-deferred 'Sabaoths sight' (*FQ*, 7. 8. 2). It was doubtless a contributory factor to the centrality within his work of architectural symbolism, particularly in relation to ancient Rome and to the 'architecture' of the human body. The illustrations helped to foster Spenser's interest in allegorical landscape, and the prophetic *persona* informed the cultivation of his visionary poetics. Equally important was the influence upon the development of the Spenserian sonnet, and the use, fostered by Du Bellay, of archaic diction for specialized effect [cf. Satterthwaite (1960)]. It would be quite unwarranted to identify Spenser's political or religious attitudes with those of Noot, but there can be no doubt as to the importance of *A Theatre* to any study of Spenser's literary development. His preoccupation with the image of the *theatrum mundi*, with pageant, emblem and Apocalyptic symbolism begins here. Cf. Forster (1967a); Van Dorsten (1970).

Epigrams

Epigram 1
TW identifies the 'faire hinde' as Petrarch's Laura and 'the houndes white and black' as 'the daye and night, meaning the time passyng away' (fol. 13v). Cf. Dido as a wounded hind in Virgil, *Aeneid*, 4. 68–73. While preserving its erotic associations, Petrarch endows the hind with spiritual significance (cf. *Rime Sparse*, 190).

Epigram 2
TW identifies the 'faire ship' as Laura, comparing 'her whyte coloured face vnto Ivorie, and hir blackishe browes . . . vnto the wood of Hebene [ebony]'. The cords and ropes represent 'not onely all hir costely rayement or apparell, but also hir . . . excellent vertues' (fols. 13v–14r).

Epigram 3
TW identifies the birdsong as Laura's 'louying and curteous talke' and the 'lyghtenyng and tempest' as 'a burnyng sicknesse' (fol. 14r).

11 *outbrast*: burst out.

Epigrams 4–6

TW characterizes these poems as exercises in *contemptus mundi*. Following Laura's demise, Petrarch reassessed the value of 'worldely love' and 'turned himselfe to Godwarde' (fol. 14v).

Epigram 4

4–8 Cf. *FQ*, 6. 10. 7.

Epigram 5

An ironic reversal of the more usual use of the Phoenix as a symbol of Christ's resurrection.

Epigram 6

The stinging of the lady by the serpent is suggestive of the demise of Eurydice (Ovid, *Metamorphoses*, 10. 8–10) and the fall of Eve (Genesis 3: 1–6), but her assurance of joy recalls the prophecy of ultimate victory over the serpent through the woman's seed, Christ (Genesis 3: 15). The Virgin Mary was commonly regarded as the second Eve, and Petrarch's Laura is complimented by the association.

Epigram 7

Spenser follows Marot in transforming Petrarch's three-line coda into a quatrain comprised of two rhyming couplets.

3 *request*: translating the French 'desir'.

Sonets

Sonnets 1–11

TW asserts that in these sonnets Du Bellay 'goeth about to persuade, that all things here upon earthe, are nothyng but . . . miserable vanitie' (fol. 15v). Because Rome's arrogance was manifest in its architecture its ruins 'beare witnesse' to divine vengeance (fols. 16r–17v).

Sonnet 1

10 *Temple*: the firmament (all that is 'under the sun' in Ecclesiastes 1: 9).
11 Cf. 'Vanity of vanities . . . all is vanity' (Ecclesiastes 1: 2).
14 *confidence*: strengthening the 'hope' expressed by Du Bellay.

Sonnet 2

1 *frame*: underlying structure, base. Here the 'frame' becomes a bier, a word defined by E. K. as 'a frame wheron they vse to lay the dead corse' (*SC*, *November*, [161]).

cubites: ancient standard of measure based on the length of the forearm.

4 *Dorike*: one of the three orders of Greek architecture.

9 *parget*: ornamental plaster-work often indented or in relief.

11 *Iaspis . . . Emeraude*: jasper and emerald, in vain imitation of the New Jerusalem. Cf. Revelation 21: 18–19.

Sonnet 3

14 *flushe*: flash (of lightning).

Sonnet 4

10–11 *his . . . sire*: the god Vulcan was Zeus' armourer.

Sonnet 5

1 *Dodonian tree*: the oak, so called from the oracular oak tree at Dodona in Epirus which was sacred to Zeus.

2 *seuen hilles*: of Rome (*TW*, fols. 14v–15r).

4 *Italian streame*: the Tiber.

10–11 The barbarian invasions of the fourth and fifth centuries AD.

14 *forked trees*: probably alluding to the papacy (which claimed to have secured temporal power under the Donation of Constantine) and to its ally the Holy Roman Empire: 'Daniel and Paule . . . haue foretold that Antechrist should be borne of the subuersion of the Empire' (*TW*, fol. 20v).

Sonnet 6

1 *the birde*: 'the Eagle imperiall' (*TW*, fol. 15r).

13 *foule*: probably the owl, as an emblem of spiritual obscurantism. It was ill-omened (cf. *FQ*, 1. 9. 33). Its wormlike birth from the eagle's ashes parodies the rebirth of the phoenix. *TW* asserts that 'the truth is darkened' in the papacy's rise from the ashes of empire (fol. 19r). Cf. John 3: 19.

Sonnet 7

2 *body*: 'he meaneth the riuer of Tyber' (*TW*, fol. 15r).

3 *side*: long and flowing.

4 *Saturnelike*: sombre, awe-inspiring.

8 *Troyan Duke*: Aeneas, cf. Virgil, *Aeneid*, 12. 697–952. For the Trojan ancestry of the Romans and Britons cf. *FQ*, 3. 9. 38–51.

9–10 The legendary founders of Rome, Romulus and Remus, were suckled by a she-wolf.

11 *tree of peace*: the olive tree. Cf. *SC*, *Aprill*, 123–6, [124].

Palme: an emblem of victory. Cf. *VG*, 113.

12 *Laurel*: an emblem of both political and poetic success and implying an association between the 'renowne of Prince, and Princely Poeta [poet]' (cf. *Prose*, 466). Cf. Petrarch, *Rime Sparse*, 263; *SC*, *Aprill*, [104].

13–14 *Palme . . . Laurel*: the political, cultural and aesthetic decline of Rome, including that of Latin poetry.

Sonnet 8

1 *wailing Nimphe*: representing the City of Rome.

11–12 The Hydra sprouted two heads for every one cut off by Hercules until the wounds were seared with burning brands. It was often identified with the seven-headed beast from the sea of Revelation 13: 1.

14 *Neroes . . . Caligulaes*: standard exemplars of imperial corruption.

15 The coincidence of a fifteen-line sonnet at the centre of a fifteen-sonnet sequence has prompted numerological speculation: fifteen can denote spiritual ascent because there were fifteen steps to the Temple, and as the sum of seven and eight it might suggest the harmony of the Old and New Testaments, or the resolution of time in eternity. Cf. Prescott (1978), 46–7. However, the fifteenth line occurs in neither the Dutch nor the French versions and was deleted in *VB*. One should be wary of interpreting aesthetic inexperience as mystical design.

Sonnet 9

3 *Ceder tree*: cf. the aromatic cedars of Lebanon used in the construction of Solomon's temple (2 Chronicles 2: 3–8).

10 *leames*: rays or beams.

11 *golden shoure*: the golden shower whereby Zeus defloured Danaë was often allegorized as the corrupting power of wealth, and specifically of bribery or simony. Cf. Comes, *Mythologiae*, 7. 18; *FQ*, 3. 11. 31.

Sonnet 10

Cf. *TM*, 265–82.

4 *golden Pactol*: the River Pactolus near Sardis to which Midas transferred his golden touch (Ovid, *Metamorphoses*, 11. 142–5).

Sonnet 11

1–2 *Morpheus . . . eyes*: Morpheus was the god of dreams, the most reliable of which occurred, according to Ronsard, in the early morning. Cf. *Elegies*, 1. 34 ('Discours' 5, lines 1–6).

4 *Typhæus sister*: Typhoeus, the youngest son of Gea (Earth), challenged Zeus for dominion of the lower world and was imprisoned under Mount Etna. His sister is presumably the Titaness Rhea (honoured in Rome as

Cybele) but the exact allusion is obscure. Allegorically she may represent imperial Rome itself. Cf. *FQ* , 7. 6. 2–4.

5 *morian*: a type of helmet without a beaver or visor.

Sonnet 12

The source is Revelation 13.

1 *vgly beast*: 'the congregation of the wicked' (*TW*, fol. 20v).

2 *ten crounes*: 'Signifying their great dominion' (*TW*, fol. 21r).

3 *blaspheming name*: 'What are Popes, Cardinals, patriarks . . . archbishops . . . but names of blasphemie?' (*TW*, fol. 22r).

4–5 *Leopard . . . Lions*: cf. Daniel 7: 3–7. *TW* observes that '*this beast was like the Leopard, spoted and blemished*, tokens of inconstancie . . . and temeritie. *His feete like to a Beares feete*, fearful and horrible . . . signifying crueltie, stubbornesse, stoutnesse and uncleanesse. *And his mouth as the mouth of a Lion*, declaring heereby the . . . wickednesse of those Prelates'. The lion represents the Assyrians and Chaldees, the bear the Medes and Persians, and the leopard the Greeks. The vices of all three are held to inhere in the papacy (*TW*, fols. 23r–v). Cf. *RT*, 64–70.

6 *mightie Dragon*: 'Sathan the Diuell' (*TW*, fol. 24v).

8 *grieuous wounde*: 'through the . . . preaching of the Gospell . . . since the time of John Hus' (*TW*, fol. 26v).

11–14 *sea . . . vp*: this is actually the beast from the earth, not the sea, 'signifying . . . all manner of false Prophets' (*TW*, fol. 33v).

Sonnet 13

The source is Revelation 17–18.

1 *Woman . . . beast*: the Whore of Babylon, understood as Roman Catholicism, upon the Antichrist (*TW*, fols. 43v–45r). Cf. *FQ*, 1. 7. 16–18.

2 *Orenge colour*: for the French 'migrainne', 'scarlet reddish, in token of greate tyrannie, sheddyng of bloud and murthers' (*TW*, fol. 44v).

3 *name of blasphemie*: 'as, your holynesse . . . vicar of God' (*TW*, fol. 44v).

4–5 *seuen . . . hornes*: 'signifying all his subtil practises' (*TW*, fol. 45r).

6–7 *glorie . . . golde*: signifying priestly vestments (*TW*, fol. 45r).

8 *cup*: 'this cup, is hir false and cursed Religion', a parody of the Eucharist (*TW*, fol. 45v). Cf. *FQ*, 1. 8. 14.

10 *Martyrs*: in contemporary terms, victims of the Inquisition.

12 *Angell*: 'Signifying the true ministers and preachers [of the Reformation] sent in these our dayes' (*TW*, fol. 50v).

14 *Babylon*: commonly interpreted by Protestants as Rome.

Sonnet 14

The source is Revelation 19.

1 *white horse*: 'the true and faithfull ministers of the word of God' (*TW*, fol. 63v).
2 *faithfull man*: Christ.
3 *crounes*: 'to signifie that Jesus Christ is the soueraigne king aboue all kings' and that the elect are crowned with grace (*TW*, fols. 64v–65r).
4 *worde*: Christ as the Logos, the 'euerlasting word' (*TW*, fol. 66r).
5 *embrued*: stained (recalling the Passion and Crucifixion).
7 *armie*: 'true and faithfull ministers' (*TW*, fol. 66r).
9 *birdes*: all who 'lead heere in earth an heauenly life' (*TW*, fol. 67v).
10 *eate . . . flesh*: cf. Revelation 19: 17–18. *TW* supplies the more comforting interpretation of 'convert unto the Lord' (fol. 68v).

Sonnet 15

The source is Revelation 21–2. Cf. *FQ*, 1. 10. 53–8.

1 *new . . . Heauen*: traditionally associated with the Second Coming but also representing deliverance of the elect 'here in this worlde from sin' (*TW*, fol. 78r).
2 *the sea*: 'the troublous sea of thys worlde' (*TW*, fol. 78v).
3–4 *Citie . . . spouse*: the New Jerusalem, 'the congregation and churche of god', figured as the bride of Christ (*TW*, fols. 78v–79r).
9 *Square*: 'Whatsoeuer is foure square, abideth firme and vnmoueable' (*TW*, fol. 81r).
   twelue: for twelve as a number of perfection cf. *TW*, fols. 82r–84r.
10 *pearle*: 'for the doctrine of the Gospell is precious and costly without comparison' (*TW*, fol. 82r).
11 *precious stone*: for the allegorical significance cf. *TW*, fols. 84r–87v.
12 *streame*: 'this river signifieth the two testaments of the Lorde, wherby stode that most pleasant tree of lyfe, namely Christ Jesus' (*TW*, fols. 88r–89v). Cf. *FQ*, 1. 11. 29–34, 46–52.

THE SHEPHEARDES CALENDER

The Shepheardes Calender was published towards the close of 1579 at a time of acute political crisis occasioned by the proposed marriage between Queen Elizabeth I and the Catholic Duc d'Alençon, an alliance which seemed to many to threaten the very foundations of English Protestant government [cf. Byrom (1933)]. As I have argued in the Introduction (p. xiii), to praise Elizabeth's virginity at the very moment when she seemed determined to abandon it was intensely dangerous [cf. McLane (1961); McCabe (1995)].

Incongruously, therefore, a work intended to launch the public career of England's 'new Poete' was issued anonymously. The author is 'shadowed' under the complex *persona* of Colin Clout and introduced by the mysterious 'E. K.'. Sensitive issues are discussed through the medium of cautiously ambivalent pastoral dialogue, and amorous complaint cryptically insinuates political discontent. As pastoral verse was traditionally understood to provide a safe medium for covert political allusion and innuendo, Spenser's choice of genre was highly apposite. His archaic diction belies, and simultaneously encodes, the topicality of his material. The publication of the *Calender* marked the beginning of a lifelong engagement with the tortuous politics of the Elizabethan court [cf. Montrose (1980), (1983); Lane (1993)].

For sixteenth-century writers the supreme classical model for pastoral verse was Virgil, but his influence was heavily mediated through that of such Christian pastoralists as Petrarch, Mantuan, Sannazzaro and Clément Marot [cf. Alpers (1996); Cooper (1977); A. Patterson (1986)]. Not surprisingly, therefore, religious, moral and political themes predominate as do the devices of emblem, allegory and fable [cf. MacCaffrey (1969)]. But Spenser is characteristically original in his reception of literary tradition. By locating his eclogues within a calendrical structure he achieves a distinctive unity of design which lends intellectual coherence, in its preoccupation with time, mutability and endurance, to the precocious variety of styles and metres designed to display the new poet's technical versatility [cf. Durr (1957)]. E. K.'s elaborate discourse on the technicalities of the calendar is clearly intended to call equal attention to the cyclicity of temporal duration and to the uncertainty of its human calibration. Within the calendar year the seasonal year begins and ends. Within the seasonal year the opposite occurs, and the two cycles are fated to remain, like nature and society, forever out of phase [cf. McCabe (1989), 22–3].

In terms of the poetic career, to begin with pastoral was to signal a desire to proceed through the Virgilian 'rota' and emerge in the fullness of time as an epic poet. It was not, strictly speaking, a pattern to which Spenser was destined to adhere, but it served at this stage as a convenient vehicle for examining the relationship between aesthetic and political power, poetics and patronage [cf. D. L. Miller (1983); P. Cheney (1993)]. Pervading the moral and political concerns of the *Calender* is an underlying preoccupation with the role of the poet in society and the fear lest he become, like Colin Clout in *Aprill*, too 'alienate and with drawen' to perform his public function. In this respect the *persona* of Colin – and also *October*'s Cuddie – serves to 'shadow' not merely a particular poet, but the poetic profession in general [cf. R. Greene (1987); Helgerson (1978), (1983); Mallette (1979)].

Protracted discussion of the identity of E. K. has tended to distract attention from the far more important issue of his function. While it is certainly possible, as has sometimes been suggested, that E. K. is to be identified with someone such as Edmund Kirke, Spenser's Cambridge contemporary, it is far more likely, particularly in view of the comparably elaborate subterfuge surrounding the publication of the Spenser–Harvey correspondence (1580), that the initials fabricate yet another *persona* under which the new poet 'secretly shadoweth himself', possibly with scholarly assistance from Gabriel Harvey upon whose work E. K. lavishes such unqualified praise. E. K.'s epistle to Harvey constitutes a manifesto both for the new poet and for a new poetics. Like Joachim Du Bellay's *La Défence et Illustration de la Langue Francoyse* (1549), it signals the inauguration of a poetic craft more linguistically refined and generically sophisticated than that of 'the rakehellye route of our ragged rymers' who 'hunt the letter' to the point of extinction. The very fact of protracted annotation serves to elevate the new poet's work to classical status. E. K. is to him what the ancient commentators Donatus and Servius were to Virgil, but he is also something more: not even Virgil enjoyed the services of a commentator for his first edition. The commentary interacts with the text in such a manner as to become an integral part of it. Its gratuitous disclaimers of covert intention, for example, hint at the ambiguous connotations of apparently straightforward vocabulary. At times the 'voice' of E. K. seems to engage in dialogue with the text, qualifying, contradicting and arguing as though participating in the pastoral debates. At other times it serves to distance the reader from the fiction by calling prosaic attention to the conventions and limitations of the genre and, as a result, to the increasingly problematic relationship between image and reality whether it be political, religious or aesthetic [cf. Schleiner (1990); Tribble (1993); Waldman (1988). A checklist of archaisms glossed by E. K. is provided in McElderry (1932), 151–2].

The complexity of the *Calender*'s presentation is greatly increased by the presence of the twelve woodcuts because the interaction of word and picture is seldom straightforward. Indeed, as the headnotes to the relevant eclogues indicate, many of the woodcuts are subtly nuanced to qualify, or even to contradict, the emphases of the verse. Considered as a sequence they lend visual urgency to the passage of time while the allegorical associations of their respective astrological signs frequently correspond to, or ironically contextualize, the themes of the verse. The positioning of particular eclogues under specific signs of the Zodiac was clearly a matter of considerable significance. The structural presentation of the *Calender* forms part of its meaning [cf. Eade (1972); Heninger (1988); Luborsky (1981); Richardson (1989)]. Cf. Berger (1988); Bernard (1989); Cullen (1970); Ettin (1984); Hamilton (1956); Hoffmann (1977); L. S. Johnson (1990); Lerner (1972); Mallette (1981); Norbrook (1984); D. M. Rosenberg (1981); Rosenmeyer (1969); Shepherd (1989); Shore (1985).

Envoy TO HIS BOOKE

1 *Goe . . . booke*: a formal 'envoy' to launch the work. Cf. Chaucer, 'Go, litel bok, go, litel myn tragedye' (*Troilus*, 5. 1786).

3 *president*: combining connotations of president (patron) and precedent (exemplar), to represent Sidney as Castiglione's ideal courtier.

5 *barke*: envy is traditionally figured as canine. Cf. *FQ*, 6. 12. 40.

7 *Vnder . . . wing*: cf. 'under the shadow of thy wings' (Psalms 36: 7).

10 *All as*: while.

13–14 Referring to the work's anonymous publication.

15 *For thy thereof*: on which account.

16 *ieopardee*: alluding to the political danger of publication.

19 *Immeritô*: unworthy or possibly blameless, but deliberately enigmatic either way. Cf. D. Cheney (1989), 144–6.

Epistle *To the most excellent . . .*

1 *VNCOVTHE VNKISTE*: cf. 'Unknowne, unkist', from Pandarus' salacious address to Troilus in Chaucer, *Troilus*, 1. 809.

3 *Lidgate*: cf. John Lydgate, *The Fall of Princes*, 1. 252.

   Loadestarre: guiding star (often the pole star).

5 *Tityrus*: Virgil's *persona* in *Eclogues*, 1. Cf. *October*, 55–60, [55]. For Chaucer as the English Tityrus cf. *June*, 81–96, [81].

8 *Ma. Haruey*: Gabriel Harvey, MA, fellow of Pembroke Hall, Cambridge during Spenser's residence, and his correspondent in *Letters* (1580). Harvey (*c.* 1550–1631) is principally remembered for his marginalia and his controversy with Thomas Nashe. Cf. *September*, [176]; Stern (1979).

9 *brocage*: brokering, in the sexual sense of pimping.

14 *tromp*: trumpet, an emblem of fame, cf. *FQ*, 2. 3. 10.

20 *Decorum*: theory of generic and stylistic propriety. Cf. Puttenham, *Arte of English Poesie*, *ECE*, 2. 173–81.

24 *auncient*: archaic, cf. headnote.

32 *Oratour*: Marcus Tullius Cicero in *De Oratore*, 2. 14. 60.

44 *Valla*: Lorenzo Valla (1407–57), Italian humanist, commented on the Roman historian Livy in *Emendationes in Livium de Bello Punico*.

45 *Saluste*: Caius Sallustius Crispus (86–34 BC), Roman historian, whose style was attacked in Roger Ascham's *The Scholemaster* (1570).

52 *Tullie*: Cicero in *De Oratore*, 3. 38. 153, and *Orator*, 23. 80.

57 *age. yet*: here, as elsewhere, the text reproduces the punctuation of the first quarto. *Var* notes that 'the period varied in force with some printers . . . it seems to have served as a somewhat variable, or even casual, substitute for comma, semicolon, or colon' (*Minor Poems*, 1. 715).

60 *all as in*: just as in.

61 *blaze and portraict*: depict and portray.

70 *dischorde*: for this sentiment cf. *FQ*, 3. 2. 15.

concordaunce: concord, harmony.

71 *Alceus*: ancient Greek poet. Cf. Cicero, *De Natura Deorum*, 1. 28. 79.

75 *hardinesse*: boldness, audacity.

76–7 *marking . . . cast*: misjudging his aim, they complain of the length of the shot. In archery the 'compass' is the curved path described by an arrow.

90 *gallimaufray*: jumble.

hodgepodge: confused medley.

95 *Euanders mother*: Evander led a colony of Arcadians who settled on Mount Palatine (Virgil, *Aeneid*, 8. 51–4). For his mother's archaic diction cf. Aulus Gellius, *Noctes Atticae*, 1. 10. 2, but E. K.'s reference derives from Macrobius, *Saturnalia*, 1. 5. 1.

104 *Nources milk*: 'the Childe that suckethe the milke of the nurse muste of necessitye learne his firste speache of her' (*Prose*, 119).

110 *conne . . . thanke*: thank them (to 'con thanks' is to express gratitude).

120 *spue out*: a biblical formula, cf. Leviticus 18: 28.

rakehellye: debauched. Cf. 'rakehell bands' at *FQ*, 5. 11. 44.

121 *hunt the letter*: affect excessive alliteration.

122 *iangle*: jabber, chatter.

129 *Pythia*: prophetess of Apollo at Delphi, but here alluding to the Cumaean Sybil, who foretells Aeneas' victory in Virgil, *Aeneid*, 6. 77–97.

130 *Os . . . domans*: 'mastering her foaming mouth and fierce heart' (*Aeneid*, 6. 80).

136–7 *Of . . . vnrest*: cf. *June*, 65, 79.

140 *couertly*: it was expected that pastoral should 'under the vaile of homely persons and in rude speeches . . . insinuate and glaunce at greater matters, and such as perchance had not bene safe to have beene disclosed in any other sort'. Cf. Puttenham, *Arte of English Poesie*, *ECE*, 2. 40.

149 *Theocritus*: ancient Greek poet of the third century BC whose *Idylls* were commonly held to have established the pastoral genre.

151 *Mantuane*: Baptista Spagnuoli of Mantua (1448–1516), some of whose Latin eclogues were imitated in English by Alexander Barclay (1515–21).

152 *full somd*: fully 'summed' or grown, fully fledged.

Petrarque: Francesco Petrarch (1304–74), author of the *Rime Sparse*, produced twelve influential Latin eclogues.

Boccace: Giovanni Boccaccio (1313–75), author of *The Decameron*, wrote sixteen Latin eclogues and a pastoral romance, *L'Ameto*, in Italian.

Marot: Clément Marot (1496–1544), French poet celebrated for his translations of the Psalms; two of his eclogues are imitated by Spenser in *November* and *December*.

Sanazarus: Jacobo Sannazzaro (1456–1530), author of *Arcadia* (1504), wrote a series of piscatory eclogues substituting fishermen for shepherds.

156 *principals*: principal or main feathers.

164 *.s.*: here, as elsewhere throughout E. K.'s commentary, an abbreviation for the Latin *scilicet*, 'namely'.

168 *olde name*: *The Kalender of Shepherdes*, an English version of Guy de Marchant's almanac, *Le Compost et Calendrier des Bergers* (1493), frequently updated and reprinted throughout the sixteenth century.

169 *scholion*: learned commentary.

184–5 *Dreames . . . Cupide*: not extant. For 'Dreames' cf. *November*, [195].

212 *Quidams*: certain persons.

221 *Latine Poemes*: cf. *September*, [176].

General argument

7–8 *Æglogaj . . . tales*: reflecting a popular, but false, etymology. Eclogue means 'selection' and derives from the Greek for choice or choosing.

19 ἀνάλυσις: analysis.

20 *sentence*: opinion.

48 *Andalo*: Andalo de Negro, who instructed Boccaccio in astronomy.

48–9 *Macrobius . . . Saturne*: Macrobius' *Convivia Saturnalia* to which E. K.'s discussion of the ancient calendar is heavily indebted.

51 *coumpting*: reckoning.

63 *Iulius Cæsar*: the matter was highly topical. Proposals for reform of the Julian calendar were already circulating. The Gregorian calendar (named after Pope Gregory XIII) was widely adopted in 1582, but not in England until 1752 because of its papal associations. Cf. Parmenter (1936).

66 *Abib*: containing part of March and April. Cf. Exodus 13: 3–4.

72–4 *Bissextilem . . . intercalares*: the Julian calendar introduced in 45 BC established the convention of the leap year in order to regularize the practice of compensating for the discrepancy between the solar year and the calendar year by the irregular introduction of extra or 'intercalary' days or months. The leap year was known as the 'bissextile year' (year of two sixes) owing to the insertion of an intercalary day six days prior to the Calends of March. Cf. Macrobius, *Saturnalia*, 1. 12–14 passim.

79 *Numa Pompilius*: second king of Rome credited with the establishment of much religious ceremonial and observance.

86 *Ianus*: the two-faced Italian god of entrances and beginnings who gives his name to the month of January.

92 *Rabbins*: rabbis.

94 *Tisri*: 'the Babylonian name for the first month of the Jewish civil year, or the seventh month of the ecclesiastical year, corresponding to parts of September and October' (*OED*).

95 *Pauilions*: tabernacles. Cf. Leviticus 23: 34.

102 *seene*: knowledgeable, well versed.

Januarye

The first eclogue serves to introduce the figure of Colin Clout and to establish the mood of dejected alienation that characterizes him throughout the work. Although E. K. maintains that the poet 'secretly shadoweth himself' under this *persona*, the careful introduction at the opening and close of the eclogue of a distinct third-person narrator functions to distance the two. Similarly, although the ostensible theme of the eclogue is that of unrequited love, the choice of vocabulary insinuates the presence of other forms of discontent covertly articulated through the diction of amorous complaint [cf. Marotti (1982)]. Colin's Petrarchan malaise is responsible for the 'ill gouernement' (45) of his flock at a time when Queen Elizabeth's proposed marriage to the Catholic Duc d'Alençon threatened the ruin of Protestant government. As E. K. points out, Colin Clout's name evokes reminiscences of Skelton's anti-court satires and the elegiac complaints of the French Protestant exile, Clément Marot. E. K.'s allusions to Sir Thomas Smith's treatise of good government and to the exiled poet Ovid (in a work avowedly inspired by the politically approved poet Virgil) adumbrate the *Calender*'s political agenda. Comparison with Virgil's first eclogue strongly suggests that Colin's political and emotional kinship is with the disaffected shepherd Meliboeus rather than the secure and contented Tityrus.

A further complication is the effect of Colin's infatuation with Rosalind upon his relationship with Hobbinol (55–60), a subject central to *June*. The lady has supplanted Colin's friend, although the speaker's complaint echoes that of Virgil's homoerotic shepherd, Corydon (*Eclogues*, 2). An ironic tension between form and content is hereby engineered, suggestive of the potentially destructive ambivalence of youthful emotions. Denying the possibility of 'pæderastice', E. K. interprets the relationship between Colin and Hobbinol as Platonic, asserting the superiority of such intellectual associations over those of the body [cf. Goldberg (1992)]. The resulting conflict between friendship (*amicitia*) and love (*eros*) deepens the isolation of the central figure whose obsessive self-absorption is conveyed through pathetic fallacy: although himself in the spring-time of youth he finds in the barren winter landscape a 'myrrhour' of his emotional state (20) [cf. Berger (1983a)]. His journey to the 'neighbour towne' (50) has disabled his capacity both for pastoral life and pastoral song and he therefore breaks his 'pype' (67–72). As the woodcut effectively illustrates, he has fallen out of harmony with seasonal change, but into 'pensife' complicity with seasonal decay [cf. Luborsky (1981)]. His December monologue therefore reprises his opening complaint in the same form and style (six-line stanzas rhyming *ababcc*), but without any notable sense of emotional progress. Appropriately, the temporal movement of the first eclogue is from 'sunneshine day' (3) to 'frosty *Night*' (74) and the weary weight of its concluding alexandrine marks Colin as the *Calender*'s principal casualty of time. Cf. D. Cheney (1989); Moore (1975); A. Patterson (1986); Prescott (1978); B. R. Smith (1991); Vink (1986).

Argument

Pipe: oaten or reed pipes, panpipes. The woodcut, however, illustrates bagpipes.

Januarye

17 *Pan*: amorous Arcadian god of woodlands, song and shepherds, hence the presiding deity of pastoral verse. Often identified allegorically with Nature, the universe or Christ. Cf. *Aprill*, [50]; *Maye*, [54].

27 *stoures*: distresses, turmoils, emotional crises. Cf. *FQ*, 4. 9. 39.

44 *knees . . . fare*: cf. Psalms 109: 24.

55 *Hobbinol*: Gabriel Harvey. Cf. *September*, [176].

58 *cracknelles*: light, crisp biscuits. Cf. *November*, 96.

67–72 Colin's abandonment of music recalls that of Virgil's disaffected Meliboeus who vows to 'sing no more' (*Eclogues*, 1. 77).

71 *shall . . . abye*: shall meanwhile pay the penalty.

73 *Phœbus*: Apollo, the sun god.

74 *waine*: waggon, an appropriately pastoral term for Apollo's chariot.

76 *pensife*: sad, brooding.

78 *Whose . . . weepe*: an alexandrine (i.e. a line of six metrical feet).

80 *Anchôra speme*: Italian for 'still [there is] hope', with a pun on the Latin *anchora spei*, the 'anchor of hope', a common Christian emblem which appears on the title-page of *FQ* (1596).

Gloss

[1] *COLIN Cloute*: in imitation of the satiric *persona* employed by John Skelton in *Colyn Cloute* (1529), an attack upon ecclesiastical abuse and, in particular, Cardinal Wolsey. Spenser's plaintive note, however, owes more to the *persona* of Colin from Clément Marot's *Eglogue sur le Trépas de ma Dame Loyse de Savoye* (1531) imitated in *November*.

vnlikelyhoode: dissimilarity, discrepancy.

[10] Cf. Sir Thomas Smith, *De Republica Anglorum* (1. 9). As the work was not published until 1583 Harvey must have had access to a manuscript copy. Smith (1513–77) was the first Regius Professor of Civil Law at Cambridge and Queen Elizabeth's ambassador to France.

[57] *Rusticus . . . Alexis*: 'You are a bumkin, Corydon, and Alexis does not care for your gifts' (Virgil, *Eclogues*, 2. 56).

[59] *pæderastice*: love of boys, pederasty.

  Alcybiades: cf. the pseudo-Platonic *Alcibiades*, 1. 131c.

  Xenophon: cf. *Symposium*, 8.

  Maximus Tyrius: cf. *Dissertationes*, 21. 8.

  gynerastice: love of women.

  Lucian: ribald Greek satirist (*c.* AD 115–200), author of *Dialogues of the Gods* and *Dialogues of the Dead*.

  Vnico Aretino: Pietro Aretino (1492–1556), notorious, and highly popular, for his pornographic verses.

  Perionius: Joachim Perion, author of *In Petrum Aretinum Oratio* (1551).

[60] *Ouide . . . Corynna*: cf. Ovid, *Tristia*, 4. 10. 60.

  Iulia: Ovid's association with Julia was commonly supposed to have contributed to his exile from Rome.

  Aruntius Stella . . . Statius: cf. Statius' *Epithalamion in Stellam et Violentillam* in *Silvae*, 1. 2. 197–8 where Stella's wife is called Asteris. Martial calls her Ianthis at *Epigrams*, 6. 21; 7. 14.

  Madonna Cælia: cf. *Lettre Amorose di Madonna Coeli Gentildonna Romana. Scritte al suo Amante* (1562).

  Petrona: unidentified.

[61] *Epanorthosis*: rhetorical figure involving correction and often entailing the repetition of a key word.

Februarie

The second eclogue introduces the element of pastoral dialogue that is crucial to the complex, dialectical ethos of the *Calender*. The dispute between Thenot and Cuddie reflects the traditional antagonism between youth and age, and is often held to illustrate the contrast between 'hard' and 'soft' versions of pastoral in that the young man resents the suffering inherent in seasonal change (1–8) whereas the old man accepts it as a necessary part of the natural order (9–24). So far as the participants are concerned such attitudes remain polarized and the debate breaks off, as the emblems indicate, in rancorous disagreement, yet the speeches are designed to betray the multiple ironies underlying both viewpoints [cf. Alpers (1972)]. The voice of experience is also that of sexual envy (57–68, 80–84), the voice of complaint is 'greene' in judgement as well as in 'yeares' (85–90) [cf. L. S. Johnson (1990), 63–71]. The setting of the dispute in February, commonly regarded as the last month of the year [cf. *FQ*, 7. 7. 43], serves to remind us that youth and age are not polar opposites but form part of a continuum: Thenot has once been young, as Cuddie will one day be old.

Age is in dispute with its own past, youth with its own future [cf. Berger (1988), 416–41].

Not surprisingly, therefore, the application of Thenot's fable of the oak and the briar is more problematical than the teller himself realizes. Hence the attribution of the story to Tityrus, or Chaucer (92), the master of narrative irony, and hence too the repetition within the fable of so much of the vocabulary of the preceding debate. Lacking Tityrus' subtlety, Thenot draws a simplistic, self-comforting moral from the demise of the 'ambitious brere', but ignores the clear implication (emphasized by E. K.'s gloss) that the oak is at least partially responsible for its own downfall in rendering itself vulnerable to the briar's complaints (207–12). The re-teller is inadequate to the tale. Its political and religious imagery is largely irrelevant to the personal circumstances of Thenot and Cuddie but serve to widen its application to the public domain. Spenser's audience is not Thenot's audience. Despite the assertion in the 'Argument' that the eclogue is 'rather morall and generall, then bent to any secrete or particular purpose' the choice of vocabulary suggests otherwise. The briar's flowers are 'meete to clothe a mayden Queene' (132), the oak is one of the husbandman's 'trees of state' (146), the husbandman himself is addressed as 'my soueraigne' (163), and the decay of the 'auncient tree' is associated with the 'foolerie' of 'popishe' superstition (209–11). In this manner the fable is made to reflect obliquely on the politics of court faction, the perils of 'root and branch' reformation, the relentless dynamics of social change, and the rising xenophobia engendered by Elizabeth's proposed marriage to d'Alençon. Such reflections are seasonally appropriate because wood-cutting was traditionally associated with February [cf. Luborsky (1981)].

As William Webbe observed in 1586, the style and metre are characteristic of Spenser's 'satyricall reprehensions' (cf. *ECE*, 1. 270). The coarse, archaic and dialectical diction and the rough tetrameter couplets (with line lengths varying from eight to ten syllables and frequent substitution of anapaestic for iambic feet) preserve the decorum of 'clownish' discourse while anticipating the concerns of the ecclesiastical eclogues and evoking reminiscences of Langland's *Piers Plowman*. Various attempts have been made to identify specific allusions in the fable, but the style would suggest a preference for studied ambiguity over consistent reference, for issues over personalities. Thenot speaks bluntly *ad hominem*, but his creator is considerably more discreet. Cf. Bond (1981); Friedland (1954); Greco (1982); King (1990); McCabe (1995); McLane (1961); Marx (1985); Watson (1993).

Argument

vnlustinesse: lack of strength or vigour, but sexual innuendo informs all such usages throughout the eclogue.

some Picture: for the association of poetry and painting cf. Horace, *Ars Poetica*, 361–5.

Februarie

7 *wrigle*: wriggling.

8 *Perke*: brisk, pert, self-satisfied.

auales: droops, falls.

11–13 'World' and 'worse' were held to be etymologically connected: 'when the world woxe old, it woxe warre old, / (Whereof it hight)' (*FQ*, 4. 8. 31).

14 *former fall*: first fall of Adam and Eve.

17 *threttie*: thirty.

27 *accord full nie*: precisely correspond.

28 *wrye*: bent, twisted.

35 *loytring*: idling.

35–50 Cf. Mantuan, *Eclogues*, 6. 19–25.

36 *broomes*: yellow shrub common on heath and pasture.

40 *pypes . . . corne*: cf. Chaucer, *The House of Fame*, 1224.

41 *Lords . . . yeare*: like lords of misrule.

42 *eft*: afterwards (an archaic usage).

47 *corage*: boldness, mettle, desire. Cf. line 80 below.

52 *youngth*: youth (an archaic form).

57 *lopp*: small branches and twigs, faggot wood. 'Lop and top' was a common phrase.

65 *gyrdle of gelt*: gilded belt or waistband (often used as an emblem of chastity, cf. *FQ*, 4. 5. 3–6).

66 *buegle*: tube-shaped glass beads usually coloured black.

71 *brag*: briskly, haughtily.

72 *smirke*: neat, trim.

74 *dewelap*: fold of loose skin about the throat.

77 *can*: have 'conned' or learned.

78 *lustlesse*: listless. Cf. *FQ*, 1. 4. 20.

81 *blowen bags*: swollen udders.

85 *wote . . . kenst*: I know you know.

86 *headlesse hood*: empty hood, hence empty-headedness.

88 *wage is death*: 'For the wages of sin is death' (Romans 6: 23).

90 *stoopegallaunt*: that humbles gallants. *OED* notes that the term was originally used of the sweating sickness.

95 *nouells*: short tales.

101 *hearken . . . end*: listen to the outcome.

102–14 For the image of the oak cf. Lucan, *Pharsalia*, 1. 136–43; *RR*, 379–92.

109 *mochell mast*: much forest fruit, here many acorns.

111 *rine*: rind, bark.

115 *brere*: briar, here a wild rose bush.

116 *Thelement*: the air.

119 *wonned*: used, was accustomed (wont). E. K.'s gloss is incorrect.

128 *stocke*: trunk.

130 *white . . . redde*: colours associated with the queen, cf. *Aprill*, [68].

134 *dirks*: darkens.

141 *adawed*: subdued, daunted. Cf. *FQ*, 3. 7. 13.

149 *stirring . . . strife*: cf. Proverbs 10: 12; 15: 18.

160 *painted*: feigned, plausible.

162 *crime*: charge, accusation.

179 *cancker wormes*: caterpillars and other insect larvae.

182 *defast*: defaced.

187 *sufferance*: indulgence.

192 *noulde . . . leasure*: would not wait or delay.

207–12 Deftly fusing pagan and Roman Catholic rituals to the detriment of the latter. Cf. Luke 3: 9 for the necessary destruction of decayed trees.

217 *In fine*: in the end.

236 *brouzed*: bruised or cropped (from browsed).

242 *graffed*: grafted.

   breche: breeches or buttocks.

243 *frorne*: frozen (an archaism).

248–9 *Iddio . . . essempio*: 'Because he is old, God makes his own to his own pattern', or 'Because God is old, take him for an example'.

251–2 *Niuno . . . Iddio*: 'No old man fears God'.

Gloss

[4] *Gride*: *OED* cites a variant of Lydgate's *Troy Book*, 2. 4209, taking *gryde* as a form of the verb gird. The *Middle English Dictionary* lists the forms 'girds' and 'grides' as interchangeable.

[25] *Thenot*: cf. Marot, *Eglogue sur le Trépas de ma Dame Loyse de Savoye* (1531), imitated in *November*.

[33] *Mimus Publianus*: Publilius Syrus, Latin mime writer of the first century BC, best known through the popular anthology, *Publilii Syri Mimi Sententiae*, of which Erasmus published an edition in 1514.

   Improbè . . . facit: 'It is an outrage for a man who is twice shipwrecked to blame Neptune' (Publilius Syrus, *Sententiae*, 331).

[35] *Chaucers verse*: cf. *The House of Fame*, 1225–6.

[63] *Phyllis*: the name does not occur in Theocritus, but is found in Virgil (*Eclogues*, 3. 78) and Mantuan (*Eclogues*, 4. 176).

526 NOTES TO *MARCH*

[83] *Rather*: early, born early in the year.

[92] *Tityrus*: for Chaucer as Tityrus cf. *June*, 81–96, [81].

[96] *Well thewed*: replete with good morals. Cf. *FQ*, 2. 6. 26; *HB*, 137.

[102] *Æsopes*: cf. the reed and the olive tree, *Fables*, no. 143.

Hypotyposis: sketch, pattern, type.

[149] *Sterne strife*: cf. the pseudo-Chaucerian *Plowman's Tale*, 55.

[176] κατ᾿ εἰκασμόν: as a comparison.

[215] *Saxa . . . grauido*: 'The rocks groaned under the heavy blow'. Not found in Virgil.

[244] *startuppe*: a rustic boot.

Emblem

counterbuff: rebuff.

tydes: times.

Ape . . . fables: Aesop has a fox rather than an ape. Cf. *Fables*, no. 42.

Erasmus: Desiderius Erasmus (1466–1536), Dutch humanist, friend of Sir Thomas More, author of *The Praise of Folly* (1509), translator and textual editor of the New Testament (1516). His *Adages* (1500), an edited compilation of Latin and Greek proverbs, were highly popular.

Nemo . . . Iouem: 'No old man fears Jove.' Not found in Erasmus.

March

This is the first of four 'recreatiue' eclogues 'which conceiue matter of loue, or commendation of special personages'. The choice is appropriate because 'the yeare beginneth in March', according to the old calendar, 'for then the sonne reneweth his finished course, and the seasonable spring refresheth the earth'. As the woodcut illustrates, the two speakers are also in the springtime of life, and the ram of Aries, under which they stand, traditionally signified lust or desire [cf. *FQ*, 7. 7. 32]. Their tentative accommodation to the imperatives, and dangers, of sexual awakening is mediated through their excited reports of encounters with Cupid (either direct or indirect) and the natural imagery is replete with erotic innuendo (14–17) [cf. Spitzer (1950)]. In Bion's fourth idyll, upon which the central episode is based (61–102), a 'fowler-lad' discovers Cupid's identity from an elder 'fowler', but here the boys are left to their own uncertain devices with only Willye's report of his father's experiences to serve by way of a guide (104–14). In *Februarie* Cuddie's enthusiasm for spring and love is countered by Thenot's cautious experience, but now it falls to E. K. to decode the iconography of Cupid [79], explain the sexual significance of Thomalin's wound [97], and warn of the psychological changes wrought by age when 'we fynde our bodyes and wits aunswere not to such vayne iollitie and lustful pleasaunce' [cf. Berger (1983b)]. In this respect *March* constitutes a sort of 'gloss' on the preceding eclogue, just as *Februarie* does on *Januarye*.

Despite the evident lightness of tone and metre (a variety of 'tail-rhyme', jauntily alternating pairs of tetrameter lines with single trimeters in a rhyme scheme of *aabccb*), the attitude towards love is somewhat sour. Even the goddess Flora is lent an unflattering gloss [16]. The abrupt allusion to a lady called 'Lettice' (20), glossed merely as 'the name of some country lasse', may glance at the Earl of Leicester's clandestine and potentially ruinous marriage to Lettice Knollys, while the bitter pun in Thomalin's emblem (assisted by an orthography which substitutes 'Gaule' for 'gall') contrives to offer an oblique insult to Elizabeth's much reviled French suitor. In the spring of 1579 love was indeed the Achilles' heel of Elizabethan policy (95–102). To be politically 'wise and eke to loue' would appear to be an impossibility [cf. McCabe (1995)]. Cf. Allen (1968); Hoffman (1977); Luborsky (1981); Mounts (1952); Nelson (1963).

Argument
make purpose: broach the subject of, discourse of.

March
13–15 Note the reminiscences of the briar of *Februarie*, 115–26.
13 *studde*: stem.
14 *bragly*: ostentatiously, boastfully.
15 *vtter*: put or thrust forth.
25 *assott*: muddled, confused.
28 *How kenst thou*: how do you know.
35 *preuie*: peculiar, particular.
38–9 A common pastoral motif, cf. Virgil, *Eclogues*, 5. 12.
39 *Ylike*: alike (an archaic form).
41 *whott*: hot, choleric. But cf. note to 106–14 below.
43 *seeing*: supervision, overseeing.
46 *sithens . . . morowe*: it is but three days since.
50 *clouted*: wrapped in clouts, bandaged in rags.
52 *unioynted*: dislocated, disjointed.
53 *ioynted*: disjointed, broken. Cf. *FQ*, 5. 11. 29.
55 *Thelf*: The elf.
56 *But . . . good*: but now I hope she knows better.
58–60 These three lines, delicately poised between past and future, serve as the structural centre of the eclogue, dividing 57 lines of dialogue from 57 lines of mythological anecdote.
59 *forecast*: anticipated, considered in advance.
62 *groomes*: lackeys, servants.
65 *bolts*: arrows.

528 NOTES TO MARCH

66 *tooting*: searching.

67 *Yuie*: with erotic associations. In Bion, *Idylls*, 4 it is a box-tree.

73 *thicke*: thicket.

74 *quicke*: living creature.

81 *lope*: leapt.

85 *leuelde*: aimed.

89 *pumie*: pumice stones.

91 *wimble*: nimble.

wight: agile, brisk.

95 *earst*: at first (an archaism).

105 *token*: sign, mark.

106–14 Possibly intended to recall Vulcan's entrapment of the adulterous Venus and Mars (March is the month of Mars) – and raising some questions about Willye's family. Cf. D. Cheney (1989).

111 *Peeretree*: possibly recalling the adulterous liaison of Chaucer's *Merchant's Tale*, 2207–11.

115 *thicks*: darkens. Cf. 'light thickens', *Macbeth*, 3. 2. 50.

116 *steepes*: bathes.

118 *Willyes Embleme*: cf. Publilius Syrus, *Sententiae*, 22.

121 *Thomalins Embleme*: from Plautus, *Cistellaria*, 1. 69–70.

Both emblems are found in Georg Major, *Sententiae Veterum Poetarum* (1551), 82, 85.

Gloss

Theocritus: actually Bion, *Idylls*, 4, possibly through Ronsard's version, *L'Amour Oyseau* (1560), or Politian's Latin translation (1512). Cf. note to [79] below.

[16] *Tacitus*: not in Tacitus. Cf. Lactantius, *Institutiones Divinae*, 1. 20. 6 cited in Boccaccio, *Genealogia*, 4. 61.

Andronica: not identified.

[17] *Macrobius*: cf. *Saturnalia*, 1. 12. 19. For Maia cf. *Epith*, 307–10 and notes.

[20] *Lettice*: possibly an oblique allusion to Lettice Knollys (mother by her first husband of the second Earl of Essex) who married the Earl of Leicester in 1578 to the Queen's great displeasure. D'Alençon disclosed the marriage to Elizabeth in 1579. Cf. headnote.

[23] *Lethe*: the gloss is confused. Lethe was the river of oblivion from which the souls were required to drink. Cf. Virgil, *Aeneid*, 6. 703–51.

[33] *Poetes*: cf. 'purpureas pueri . . . alas' at Ovid, *Remedia Amoris*, 701.

[40] *Virgils verse*: 'I have a father at home, and a harsh stepmother' (*Eclogues*, 3. 33).

[54] *Chaucer*: misquoted from *Sir Thopas*, 893.

[79] *Propertius*: cf. *Elegies*, 2. 12.

Moschus ... Politianus: Moschus, *Idylls*, 1 as translated in the *Epigrammata* (1512) of Angelo Poliziano (1454–94), known in England as Politian, and renowned as a scholar, poet and textual critic.

thys Poets: Spenser's translation is not extant but the material may be reworked at *FQ*, 3. 6. 11–26.

[91] *deliuer*: nimble, agile.

[97] *Homer*: not in Homer. Cf. Fulgentius, *Mythologia*, 3. 7 cited in Boccaccio, *Genealogia*, 12. 52.

Eustathius: Eustathius of Constantinople, a twelfth-century commentator upon the Homeric Hymns. But E. K.'s source is again Boccaccio, *Genealogia*, 12. 52.

Hipocrates: famous Greek physician of the fifth century BC. Cf. Hippocrates, *Of Airs, Waters, Places*, 22.

[116] *Periphrasis*: circumlocution.

Aprill

Although *Aprill* is a 'recreatiue' eclogue written 'to the honor and prayse of our most gracious souereigne, Queene Elizabeth', Colin Clout is too 'alienate and with drawen' to take part in the seasonal celebrations. His intricately wrought 'laye / Of fayre *Elisa*' (33–4) is therefore sung in his absence by his disconsolate friend Hobbinol, and the joy of times past is considerably qualified by the despondency of the present. Colin has abandoned poetry and the pastoral world is accordingly diminished. The stark contrast between the rough quatrains of the opening dialogue (1–36) and the complex patterning of the 'laye' (37–153), with its subtle interplay of long and short lines (rhyming *ababccddc*) and delicate variations of mood and tone, serves to illustrate the magnitude of the loss. Far from inspiring poetry, love now impedes it. Viewed in this context, Elisa seems fortunate in her virginal independence. As the daughter of Pan and Syrinx she is the living embodiment of pastoral poetry, being herself a poet and the inspiration of poets (50–51, 91–4). The messianic interpretation of Virgil's fourth eclogue, Spenser's closest classical model, reinforces such impressions: 'so sprong her grace / Of heauenly race, / No mortall blemishe may her blotte' (52–4). Yet at the time of publication Elizabeth was thought to favour the abandonment of her virginal status for marriage to d'Alençon. In the popular imagination she, no less than Colin Clout, was thought to have 'so little skill to brydle loue' (20) – as the sly pun on 'brydle' may well be intended to suggest. The imagery of the lay resembles that of an epithalamion or wedding hymn – 'The pretie Pawnce, / And the Cheuisaunce, / Shall match with the fayre flowre Delice' (142–4) – yet marriage with the French 'fleur-de-lis' was precisely what Protestant England feared [cf. McLane (1961), 13–26].

Read in historical context the lay may be seen to express as much anxiety as admiration. It reminds the Queen of the importance of her public image at a time when her proposed marriage to an 'alien' was threatening to alienate the people from the crown [cf. McCabe (1995)]. The timeless icon of the virgin queen is located squarely within the cyclical mutability of the year under the sign of Taurus, often identified by Spenser with the 'bull from the sea' which carried off the virgin Europa [cf. *FQ*, 7. 7. 33; Richardson (1989), 269–70]. Recounting that myth in the *Metamorphoses*, Ovid remarks that 'majesty and love do not go well together, nor tarry long in the same dwelling place' (2. 846–7). Spenser's message would appear to be similar: by insisting for so long upon her virginity the Queen has rendered it integral to her sovereignty. Her 'modest eye' guarantees 'Her Maiestie' (70–71) and the public icon must now be maintained by personal sacrifice. One detects similar tensions throughout the lay: Elisa seems strangely oblivious to Colin's, and possibly to the country's, sufferings (99), and although he terms her his 'goddesse' (97) he warns of the dangers inherent in attributing divinity to any mortal (86–90). The 'Redde rose medled with the White yfere' (68) in Elisa's countenance recalls the turbulent history that the mythology of Pan and Syrinx elides.

As the Introduction to the present edition notes, the witty choice of emblems functions in a similar fashion. When dressed like a nymph of Diana, Venus cuts an intensely ambivalent figure, fusing, and even confounding, the *personae* of virgin and mistress, mother and whore [cf. Di Matteo (1989)]. By means such as these, the enigmatic quality of the verse is rendered politically resonant. The 'pastoral of power' interrogates its own mythology. Cf. Cain (1978); Cullen (1970); Luborsky (1981); McCoy (1997); Micros (1993); Montrose (1980), (1983); Watkins (1995).

Argument

abruptely: in abbreviated fashion.

Aprill

8 *thristye*: thirsty.

14–15 *Pipe . . . broke*: cf. *Januarye*, 71–2.

16 *outwent*: excelled, surpassed.

18 *pinching*: in the sense of painful or distressing.

21 *Southerne . . . boye*: Spenser was secretary to John Young (1534?–1605), Bishop of Rochester. Cf. *September*, 171 and note.

24 *Forcing*: endeavouring, urging (i.e. by pressing gifts upon him).

25 *is starte*: has bolted, has rushed away.

27 *bredde*: occasioned.

29 *trimly dight*: deftly composed or constructed. Here as elsewhere 'dight' lends a consciously archaic quality to the verse.

36 Cf. Theocritus, *Idylls*, 1. 7–8.

37–153 For classical models for Colin's 'laye' cf. Theocritus, *Idylls*, 17 and Virgil, *Eclogues*, 4.

50 *without spotte*: stainless, immaculate (like the Virgin Mary). Cf. Song of Songs 4: 7.

52 *grace*: in both the social and spiritual senses.

54 *blotte*: stain, tarnish.

57 *Scarlot*: a colour emblematic of royalty.

58 *Ermines*: signifying purity, as in the celebrated 'Ermine Portrait'. Cf. Strong (1987), 113–15.

59 *Cremosin coronet*: presumably a garland of red roses (often associated with Venus).

60 *Damaske roses*: red or pink roses traditionally believed to have originated in Damascus.

 Daffadillies: daffodils.

61 *Bayleaues*: emblematic of conquest and virginity. Cf. E. K.'s gloss at [104].

62 *Primroses*: cf. *Februarie*, [166].

63 *Violet*: emblematic of modesty and love.

69 *depeincten*: depict.

77–8 *blusht . . . showe*: a Petrarchan conceit. Cf. *Rime Sparse*, 115.

81 *haue . . . ouerthrowe*: to be defeated.

82 *Cynthia*: Diana, as goddess of the moon.

86–7 *Latonaes . . . Niobe*: cf. E. K.'s gloss, fourth from the end. It is displaced from its proper position in the first quarto.

99 *Albee*: although, but with a possible play on Albion (England).

109 *foote*: dance.

113 *fourth grace*: normally Venus, but here the goddess is supplanted by the queen. Cf. *FQ*, 6. 10. 12–16 where the queen herself is displaced by Colin's lady.

114 *yeuen*: given (an archaism).

123 *Coronall*: wreath or garland.

126 *principall*: befitting a prince (a typical Spenserian pun). Cf. *Muiop*, 380.

128 *hye . . . apace*: hurry there speedily.

131 *whereas*: where.

133 *fillets*: ribbons for binding the hair.

135 *finesse*: elegance.

 tawdrie lace: silk waistband (more usually a neckband). St Audrey was said to have died of a throat tumour visited upon her in retribution for the youthful vanity of her necklaces. Hence the contraction 'tawdrie'.

136 *Cullambine*: columbine.

137 *Gelliflowres*: gillyflowers or clove pinks.

138 *Coronations*: carnations (with a political pun).

   Sops in wine: clove pinks or gillyflowers.

141 *Kingcups*: buttercups (with a political pun).

142 *Pawnce*: pansy.

143 *Cheuisaunce*: not identified as a flower but used by Spenser for chivalric enterprise. Cf. *Maye*, [92]; *FQ*, 2. 9. 8.

144 *flowre Delice*: fleur-de-lis, the royal emblem of France and, as opponents of the d'Alençon match argued, already part of Elizabeth's blazon owing to the monarchy's ancestral claim on France [McCabe (1995), 27–8].

148 *echeone*: each one.

152 *Damsines*: damsons (a variety of small plum).

153 *part*: share.

156 *taking*: condition, plight.

157 *lewdly bent*: basely or foolishly inclined.

163 *O . . . virgo?*: 'How shall I address you, maiden?' (Virgil, *Aeneid*, 1. 327).

165 *O . . . certe*: 'Surely a goddess' (Virgil, *Aeneid*, 1. 328).

Gloss

[5] *delaye*: temper with moisture, assuage. Cf. *FQ*, 3. 12. 42.

[19] *make . . . Poetes*: cf. Sidney, *Apology for Poetry*, *ECE*, 1. 155.

[21] *lasse of Kent*: cf. *Februarie*, 74.

[26] *glenne*: glen or wild valley. E. K.'s gloss is in error.

   Hamlet: cf. *Januarye*, 49–50.

   Theocritus: cf. *Idylls*, 7. 97.

   Petrarches Goddesse: cf. *Rime Sparse*, 5 where Petrarch expounds the significance of the form 'Lauretta'.

   Stesichorus: Greek lyric poet (*c.* 632–553 BC). Himera was his home town not his mistress. For his blinding cf. Plato, *Phaedrus*, 243a–b.

[33] *Roundelayes*: short simple lyrics with a refrain, cf. *August*, 53–124.

   Virelayes: short lyric poems using only two rhymes.

[37] *Exordium . . . animos*: 'a formal introduction to prepare the readers' minds'.

[41] For the Muses' genealogy cf. Comes, *Mythologiae*, 4. 10; 7. 15.

[42] *Helicon*: properly a mountain in Boeotia containing the sanctuary of the Muses with the spring of Hippocrene just below the summit, but itself regarded as a spring by Chaucer. Cf. *House of Fame*, 521–2.

   Castalius: cf. *VG*, 21–4; Virgil, *Culex*, 15–17; *November*, [30].

   Pegasus: cf. Ovid, *Metamorphoses*, 5. 254–63.

[46] *siluer song*: the Greek phrase quoted ('silver song') is not in Hesiod.

[50] *Syrinx*: cf. Ovid, *Metamorphoses*, 1. 689–712.

   Homeres saying: 'Proud is the heart of kings, fostered of heaven; for their honour is from Zeus, and Zeus, god of counsel, loveth them' (cf. *Iliad*, 2. 196–7).

Christ himselfe: as the 'good shepherd' Christ is Pan (John 10: 14). The primary influence is Marot who alludes to Francis I as Pan in *Eglogue au Roy soubz les noms de Pan et Robin* and to Christ as Pan in *La Complaincte d'un Pastoureau Chrestien* in which the speaker addresses his complaint to God 'under the *persona* of Pan, the god of shepherds'.

[100] *Signat . . . gestu*: 'Polyhymnia signifies everything with her hand and speaks through gesture'. Cf. Ausonius, *De Musarum Inventis*, 9. This poem is ascribed to Virgil by Dumaeus in the edition of 1542 (which Spenser used for *VG*) and by Comes, *Mythologiae*, 7. 15. For Polyhymnia cf. *TM*, 541–94.

[104] *Arbor . . . Poëti*: 'Victorious triumphal tree / The honour of Emperors and of Poets', Petrarch, *Rime Sparse*, 263.

[109] *Graces*: cf. Seneca, *De Beneficiis*, 1. 3; Servius, *Commentarii (Aeneid*, 1. 720); Comes, *Mythologiae*, 4. 15; *FQ*, 6. 10. 21–4.

Pasithea: cf. Homer, *Iliad*, 14. 276.

Boccace saith: cf. Boccaccio, *Genealogia*, 5. 35.

[120] *King Arthure*: Roger Ascham had attacked Arthurian romances in *The Scholemaster* (1570) and Arthur's historical existence was a matter of contemporary controversy. The issue was topical in view of the Tudor family's claim to Arthurian descent.

Ladyes . . . Lake: the Lady of the Lake featured in Leicester's famous entertainment for Elizabeth at Kenilworth in 1575.

[122] *Cloris*: the goddess Flora. Cf. *March*, [16]; *Proth*, 2 and notes; Ovid, *Fasti*, 5. 195–220. Chaucer associates Zephyrus with the month of April, cf. 'General Prologue', 5–7.

[124] *Neptune and Minerua*: cf. Servius, *Commentarii (Georgics*, 1. 12).

[136] *Flos delitiarum*: 'Flower of delights'.

[99] *Forswonk and forswatt*: from *The Plowman's Tale* ('Prologue', 14), commonly attributed to Chaucer at this period.

[86–7] *Niobe*: cf. Ovid, *Metamorphoses*, 6. 146–311.

Emblem

Æneas . . . Venus: cf. Virgil, *Aeneid*, 1. 314–414.

Maye

This is the first of Spenser's ecclesiastical eclogues designed to explore the religious divisions of contemporary England. The literary conventions upon which it draws were long established and universally familiar. The spiritual dimension of pastoral imagery, greatly developed in the eclogues of Petrarch,

Mantuan and Marot, originates in Psalm 23, 'The Lord is my shepherd', and in the Gospel of John where Christ declares himself to be 'the good shepherd' (10: 14). As a result of the Reformation, however, there were now, as the 'Argument' informs us, two distinct 'formes of pastoures or Ministers . . . the protestant and the Catholique'. The former are represented by Piers, spiritual kinsman of Langland's Piers Plowman, and the latter by the more worldly Palinode.

The structure is similar to that of *Februarie* with the opening dialogue (1–173) serving as a prelude to an elaborate moral parable after the manner of Aesop's fables and the medieval cycle of Reynard the Fox (174–305). The conclusion is strikingly problematic in that Palinode appears to appreciate Piers's story but to miss – or to dismiss – its polemic point (306–17). This is inevitable because the preceding debate confronts us not merely with conflicting doctrines but with conflicting temperaments. Devoted to things spiritual, Piers reads the pastoral landscape allegorically: his Pan is Christ and he has followed St Paul's injunction to 'put away childish things' (17–18). Palinode, by contrast, responds to the sheer 'iouysaunce' of the pastoral world (25): his Pan is the god of 'the greene Wood' and he retains the spirit of youth in elder years. While Piers's rugged tetrameters evoke the moral ethos of *The Plowman's Tale*, those of Palinode are attuned to the infectious music of May Day – his heart dances to the playing of the pastoral pipe (26). As in the case of *Februarie*, therefore, the stark, intellectual dichotomies of the debate are considerably obscured by the personalities of the participants, and it remains unclear how the music of the green wood may be reconciled to the morality of the good shepherd. Piers's sentiments frequently sound harsh and E. K. is at pains to dissociate them from the 'malitious' opinions of radical Puritans [121]. The opening exchanges are so finely balanced as to afford little clear evidence of the author's outlook – in marked distinction to the typical Puritan dialogue.

The fable, however, is somewhat less opaque in responding to the perceived threat of crypto-Catholic infiltration. This was an anxiety by no means exclusive to Puritans but common to all shades of Protestant opinion. The Queen's excommunication (1570), the ongoing Jesuit mission to England, and the perilous influence of the Catholic Duc d'Aubigny on the youthful James VI of Scotland combined to lend urgency to the matter [cf. McLane (1961), 77–91]. It was widely feared that in the event of any change in religious policy – such as might be occasioned by the Queen's proposed marriage – the crypto-Catholic fox would transform itself once again into the Roman wolf [cf. King (1990), 37–9]. Hence E. K.'s allusion to the St Bartholomew's Day massacre [304]. The marriage of Flora, attended by a 'fayre flocke of Faeries', to the Lord of the May (27–33) may pose a danger to 'the faerie queene' because female lust is alleged to be unquenchable (134–5).

The outlook of the eclogue is considerably more complex than its 'Argument' suggests. The woodcut assigns central position to the triumph of Palinode's May Lord and Queen but surrounds their joyous procession – in a wagon drawn by winged horses resembling Pegasus – with cautionary vignettes from Piers's moral fable [cf. Luborsky (1981)]. Palinode's name implies 'recantation' or 'retraction', but it is left to the reader to decide which, if either, of the two speakers, or the two Pans, should make such a gesture, and what sort of moral or aesthetic accommodation it might involve [cf. Herman (1992)]. Cf. Brennan (1986); Hume (1969), (1984); L. S. Johnson (1990); King (1982), (1985); Waters (1974).

Argument

credit: credence, belief.

counterpoynt: counterstroke, complete deception.

Maye

4 *gawdy greene*: bright or yellowish green (an archaic usage).

12 *eare*: ere.

13 *Eglantine*: wild rose.

14 *Sopps in wine*: cf. *Aprill*, 138 and note.

17–18 Echoing St Paul's sentiments at 1 Corinthians 13: 11.

17 *Palinode*: the name means 'retraction' or 'recantation' (a palinode was a poem or song made in retraction of some former piece). No retraction is made in *Maye* but cf. note to *Julye*, 181.

18 *tway*: two (a dialectical form to suggest rusticity).

19 *lenger*: longer (an archaic form).

22 *Tabrere*: drummer (a tabor is a small drum).

28 *May*: May-lord, a young man chosen to preside over the festivities.
  musicall: musical accompaniment.

30 *attone*: at one with him, in harmony with him. Cf. *FQ*, 2. 1. 29.

31 *Flora*: cf. *March*, [16]; *Aprill*, [122]; *Proth*, 2 and notes.

34 *Maybush*: a branch of hawthorn.

35 *Piers*: the name recalls that of Piers Plowman. An allusion to Bishop John Piers of Salisbury (1523–94) has also been suggested, but the evidence is slight. Cf. McLane (1961), 175–87.

41 *sparely*: frugally, cautiously.

45–50 An attack on the prevalent abuse of pluralism whereby unqualified deputies were hired at a pittance to serve as ministers while the absentee holders of the benefice (laymen as well as clerics) enjoyed the bulk of its income without performing any pastoral duties. The imagery is informed by Christ's attack upon hirelings at John 10: 12–15.

49 *fallen*: befalls, happens to.

50 *peece*: portion.

51–4 Cf. Christ's concern for the lost sheep, Matthew 18: 11–14.

51 *muse*: wonder.

55 *of spight*: from spite.

58 *All . . . foe*: although it were by my foe.

68 *other moe*: many others.

74 *touches . . . defilde*: cf. Ecclesiasticus 13: 1.

75 *Algrind*: an anagram of Grindal. Edmund Grindal (1519–83) became Archbishop of Canterbury in 1576 but was sequestered from his office the following year owing to his support for Puritan 'prophesyings', religious gatherings at which scripture was expounded. He was Master of Pembroke Hall, Cambridge from 1559 to 1562. Cf. headnote to *Julye*.

77 *With . . . heire*: 'it is fitting for them to take care of their heirs'. The issue of clerical marriage was still controversial. The Queen was known to disapprove of it although it was allowed in the Anglican Church and widely championed as preferable to Roman Catholic celibacy.

80 *wont countenaunce*: customary status or public repute.

82 *foresay*: renounce (a rare usage giving an archaic effect).

84 *spard*: spared, saved.

88 *trust*: property entrusted to him (by bequest).

90 *misgouernaunce*: ill-management.

95–100 For this ape lore cf. Pliny, *Natural History*, 8. 80. 216.

105 *shepeheards . . . inheritaunce*: cf. Deuteronomy 18: 1.

106 *fee in sufferaunce*: allowance of revenues. Technically speaking sufferance is 'the condition of the holder of an estate who, having come in by lawful right, continues to hold it after the title has ceased without the express leave of the owner' (*OED*).

109 *ywis*: indeed, truly.

110 *forgoe*: give up, renounce.

111 *Pan . . . inheritaunce*: cf. Deuteronomy 10: 9.

112 *little . . . serued*: little sufficed.

117 *tract*: passage.

120 *obeysaunce*: obedience.

121 *gouernaunce*: temporal authority or power.

123 *Lordship*: Puritans regarded the Anglican retention of episcopacy as a betrayal of the Reformation. They objected to the temporal power of the episcopate as reflected in such titles as 'Lord Bishop'. As E. K. suggests at [121], they regarded the temporal ambitions of the papacy as responsible for the corruption of the Church's spiritual mission.

126 *somewhile*: at some time.

127 *Wolues*: cf. Christ's condemnation of false prophets (Matthew 7: 15).

131 *nill . . . borrowe*: will not be delivered by surety or pledge. The metaphor is that of spiritual imprisonment. At line 150 Christ is identified as the 'borrowe' or 'common pledge' of redemption. The etymology of 'borrowe' is discussed in *Letters* (cf. *Prose*, 213). Cf. *September*, 96.

132 *Three thinges*: the formula is common in Proverbs.

133 *outragious*: excessive, beyond all bounds.

135 *Hardly forbearen*: scarcely refrain.

137 *Wanting*: lacking.

138 *thristie*: thirsty.

157 *beare of*: shake off, withstand.

164 *list . . . make*: I desire to make no agreement.

167 *leuer*: rather.

168 Cf. 'And what communion hath light with darkness' (2 Corinthians 6: 14).

169 *peace . . . Lambe*: a biblical topos, cf. Isaiah 11: 6; 65: 25.

172 *felowship*: companionship, comradery. But fellowship in the theological sense is what Piers wishes to avoid: 'what fellowship hath righteousness with unrighteousness?' (2 Corinthians 6: 14).

173 *Ladde . . . straying*: a common topos, cf. Virgil, *Eclogues*, 5. 12.

177 *Gate*: given the theological context of the fable the use of goat and kid may be intended to recall Christ's reference to the segregation of the sheep (the saved) from the goats (the damned) at Matthew 25: 32–3.

   dame: mother, but possibly with the political connotations of great lady in oblique allusion to the Queen who is 'dame *Eliza*' at *Aprill*, 150.

180 *But for*: because.

181 *wit to beware*: sense to be cautious.

184 *fauour*: attractiveness, good looks.

185 *Vellet*: velvet.

188 *ranckly*: luxuriantly, abundantly (possibly also a sign of 'rank' lust).

192 *iollitee*: (jollity) exuberance, cheerfulness.

206 *hauty . . . weld*: wield his lofty horns.

210 *made . . . breache*: broke upon her anew.

212 *lineaments*: characteristics, features.

219 *Foxe*: the traditional enemy is the wolf, but the fox had particular contemporary associations with crypto-Catholicism. Cf. such polemic tracts as William Turner's *The Huntyng of the Romishe Foxe* (1543); *September*, 155 and note; King (1990), 37–9.

227 *schooled*: instructed.

232 *dispraised*: spoken ill of, deplored.

234 *sperred . . . fast*: bolted securely.

239 *trusse*: bundle, pack.

241 *Biggen*: cap or hood (possibly a night-cap).

245 *me*: colloquially employing the ethical dative.

250 *lengd*: longed (a dialectical form implying rusticity).

251 *Wickets*: little door's.

254 *double eyed*: because deceit is two faced.

258 *carrion*: putrefying, rotting.

264 *lack of*: short of.

266 *donne*: dun, dark.

267 *traueile*: combining the senses of travel and travail.

277 *nought . . . iewell*: he thought nothing too dear to pay for the jewel.

281 *descried . . . trayne*: recognized by what trailed behind him.

284 *after . . . chere*: either in accordance with his (now cheerful) mood or following his kindly reception.

can: did.

286 *knack*: knick-knack, trinket.

288 *saue*: except.

294 *doubtfull*: apprehensive (entertaining doubts about the kid's safety).

hyde: hied, hurried.

298 *merchandise*: a stock term of denigration for what Protestants regarded as the worthless ceremonial trappings of Roman Catholicism.

304 *does . . . remayne*: does await them all.

306 *beside . . . wit*: mistaken.

309 *sir Iohn*: a common term of opprobrium for an unlearned priest. Puritans complained of the ignorance of the non-preaching clergy, 'dumb-mouth' hirelings such as those deplored by Piers. If 'our sir Iohn' implies that the priest is Roman Catholic, or inclined towards that cause, Palinode's remark lends an ironic twist to the conclusion of the dialogue.

312 *But . . . if*: but if.

319 *Palinodes Embleme*: 'everyone without faith is suspicious'.

321 *Piers . . . Embleme*: 'What faith then is in the faithless?'

Gloss

[6] *redoundeth*: is superfluous. Cf. *Aprill*, [155].

[9] *straunge*: because of the use of 'where' as a noun.

[39] *Faytours*: more properly understood as impostors or cheats.

[54] *good shepherd*: cf. 'I am the good shepherd' (John 10: 11, 14).

Eusebius: cf. *Praeparatio Evangelica*, 5. 17.

Plutarch: cf. *De Defectu Oraculorum*, 17.

Lauetere: cf. Ludwig Lavater, *De Spectris*, translated by Robert Harrison as *Of Ghostes and Spirites Walking by Nyght* (1572), 1. 19. E. K.'s allusions to Eusebius and Plutarch derive from Lavater.

[57] *Malim . . . miserescere*: 'I would prefer everyone to envy me rather than to pity me'. The source remains untraced but cf. Pindar, *Pythian Odes*, 1. 85; Herodotus, *History*, 3. 52.

[61] *syncope*: deletion of letters or syllables from a word.

[69] *Sardanapalus*: Assyrian monarch notorious for sensuality.

Tullie: Cicero. Cf. *Tusculan Disputations*, 5. 35. 101.

All . . . others: these lines recur with minor variations in *Letters* where Spenser claims to have translated them extempore (cf. *Prose*, 16). This is sometimes regarded as providing evidence for his identification with E. K. Cf. notes to *Letters*, 'That which I eate'.

Erle of Deuonshire: Edward de Courtenay, Earl of Devon (*c.* 1357–1419). The verses are thought to derive from his monument at Tiverton. Cf. *Complete Peerage*, 4. 325–6.

smacke: trace, touch.

[92] *Chaucer*: cf. *The Shipman's Tale*, 1519, 1581.

[111] *Deuteronomie*: cf. Deuteronomy 10: 9.

[121] *fatherly . . . gouernaunce*: the gloss tactfully diverts Piers's criticism from Anglicanism to Rome, but Puritan polemicists emphasized the similarity between the English and Roman episcopates. Despite E. K.'s disclaimer, Piers's complaints are dangerously reminiscent of those which caused 'vnrest and hinderaunce' to the Church.

[142] *Atlas . . . shoulders*: for the Euhemeristic interpretation of this myth cf. Boccaccio, *Genealogia*, 4. 31; Comes, *Mythologiae*, 4. 7.

[160] *Chaucer*: cf. *The Complaint of Mars*, 52.

[174] *Æsops fables*: cf. the fable of the wolf and the goat, *Fables*, no. 220.

Catastrophe: denouement.

[189] πάθος: pathetic expression.

[193] *Hyperbaton*: a rhetorical figure involving the separation of words normally belonging together. The parenthesis interrupts the goat's speech and emphasizes the pathos of her reminiscence.

[205] *Sic . . . ferebat*: 'Such were his eyes, his very hand, and face' (Virgil, *Aeneid*, 3. 490).

[232] *Lorde Hastingues*: cf. Holinshed, *Chronicles*, 3. 381–2.

[240] *Paxes*: small golden or silver tablets bearing sacred images kissed by the celebrant at mass and circulated to the congregation.

[251] *Chaucer*: cf. *The Merchant's Tale*, 2046, 2117.

[304] *Epiphonema*: sententious summary.

Charles . . . nynth: alluding to the massacre of Huguenots on St Bartholomew's Day, 24 August 1572, ordered by Charles IX, allegedly at the instigation of his mother, Catherine de Medici.

Emblem

Theognis: not in Theognis and otherwise unidentified.

June

The relationship between Colin and Hobbinol, touched upon briefly in *Januarye* and *Aprill*, now moves centre stage in a dialogue which explores the tension between the 'recreatiue' and 'plaintiue' modes of Spenserian pastoral [cf. Bernard (1989), 54–61]. Ideally, as E. K.'s 'Generall argument' informs us, 'matter of loue' should fall into the 'recreatiue' category, but Colin's disaffection is such that the traditional lover's complaint threatens to develop into a solipsistic love of complaint. He has grown increasingly isolated from pastoral society: 'I play to please my selfe' (72), he asserts, yet he ironically admits that 'I am not, as I wish I were' (105). He is, therefore, the one person wholly excluded from the recreative effects of his verse. Whereas in *Januarye* his mood might be said to reflect the season, he is now out of harmony with the annual cycle, although in bygone years his music is said to have surpassed the 'larke in Sommer dayes' (51). His January emblem held out the possibility of hope but his current emblem denies it. He speaks morbidly of his advancing years (33–40) in marked contrast to Palinode, the elderly but young-at-heart protagonist of the preceding eclogue. His outlook precludes entrance to the recreative space (or state) of Hobbinol's 'paradise', a 'locus amoenus' of personal contentment in which the 'wandring mynde' finds repose (2) – at least for the moment, for the *Calender* as a whole denies the possibility of recreating Eden on earth [cf. Hoffman (1977), 61–9]. It is clear, however, that Colin can no longer find even temporary satisfaction in Hobbinol's friendship, or in his love.

Like the unfortunate Meliboeus of Virgil's first eclogue, Colin can 'nowhere fynd, to shroude my lucklesse pate' (16). But Meliboeus was a victim of political circumstance and it is likely that Colin's disaffection with the 'faithlesse' Rosalind (115) may reflect, albeit obliquely, the country's growing dissatisfaction with its Tudor 'rose' [cf. McLane (1961), 27–46]. It is noteworthy, for example, that Colin's emotional frustration impedes his artistic development. Although revered by Hobbinol as an Orphic poet whose 'oaten pype' is sufficiently potent to charm even the Muse of heroic verse (53–64), he disclaims all lofty poetic ambitions (65–72) and channels his remaining energies into a lament for the deceased Tityrus (81–96). The immediate allusion is to Chaucer, but lurking in the background is the figure of Virgil who was commonly believed to have 'shadowed' himself under the *persona* of Tityrus, the fortunate shepherd of the first eclogue who secured the patronage of Augustus and retained possession of the pastoral paradise from which Colin is exiled. Echoes of the *Aeneid* in Colin's lamentations (14–16) serve to confirm this pattern of ironic associations. Far from ascending from pastoral to epic, the bucolic poet is suffering epic torments and 'Rosalind' seems oblivious to his plight.

Yet even the poetics of desolation retains a certain 'recreatiue' effect: the versatile eight-line stanza organized upon a mere two rhymes (*ababbaba*) is something of a technical tour-de-force and the eloquence of Colin's lament for Tityrus anticipates that of his superb elegy for Dido in *November*.

Although E. K. tells us that Colin's journey southwards 'is no poetical
fiction' [18], many other details clearly fall into this category, and the
relationship between author and *persona* remains as elusive as ever. Colin's
pipe is broken but Spenser's continues to play. Despite the loss of Rosalind,
June ends, as it begins (9), on a note of benediction: the flocks are 'blessed'
(118) and the concluding lines evoke something of the muted satisfaction
of Virgil's final eclogue. Sorrow and mutability are acknowledged, but so
too are the joys of summer. Cf. Berger (1969); Cullen (1970); Goldberg
(1992); L. S. Johnson (1990).

Argument
vowed: devoted.

June
3 *what . . . delyte?*: what do I lack to occasion delight?
8 *attemper*: bring into harmony. Cf. *Aprill*, 36.
9–16 Adapting Virgil, *Eclogues*, 1. 1–5.
14–16 Echoing Virgil, *Aeneid*, 1. 1–4.
16 *shroude*: shelter. Cf. *June*, 54; *Julye*, 3. The first edition has 'shouder',
a reading defended in Brooks-Davies (1992).
17 *list . . . be*: wish to be advised.
19 *me*: for me (the ethical dative. Cf. *Maye*, 245).
　harbrough: harbour, in the sense of refuge or resting place.
20 *witche*: wych elm.
24 *gastly*: ghastly, frightful.
　owles: generally regarded as ill-omened. Cf. *TW*, sonnet 6. 13; *RT*, 130;
Epith, 345 and notes.
25–7 Possibly influenced by Horace, *Odes*, 1. 4. 5–7.
25 *Graces*: cf. *Aprill*, [109] and note.
27 *trimly . . . traces*: featly footed measures or dance steps.
28 *systers nyne*: the nine Muses. Cf. *Aprill*, [41].
　Parnasse: Mount Parnassus. Cf. *Aprill*, [42].
30 *Pan*: cf. *Januarye*, 17 and note.
34 *lincks*: chains.
39 *wexen . . . aboue*: grown worn or frayed on the surface of the fabric.
43 *Queene apples*: an early variety of apple, or possibly quinces.
45 *gaudy*: fine, gay.
　comen: common, in the sense of habitual, usual.
46 *rype*: mature.
46–8 Cf. 'when I became a man, I put away childish things' (1 Corinthians
13: 11).
49 *roundelayes*: cf. *Aprill*, [33] and note.
52 *Echo*: cf. Virgil, *Eclogues*, 1. 4–5. There may be an ironic allusion to the

myth of Narcissus for whose love the nymph Echo pined away. Cf. Ovid, *Metamorphoses*, 3. 359–401; *August*, 160. E. K. associates 'the author' with Narcissus in his gloss to Diggon's emblem in *September*.

53–64 Hobbinol credits Colin with Orphic powers. Cf. note to line 96 below.

57 *Calliope*: Muse of heroic poetry. Cf. *Aprill*, [100].

59 *Luyts . . . Tamburins*: lutes and tabors (small drums), denoting lyric and heroic poetry respectively.

62–4 A Virgilian topos, cf. *Eclogues*, 4. 55–7.

64 *outgoe*: excel, surpass.

65 *conne no skill*: have no knowledge. This line and line 79 are quoted in the 'Dedicatory Epistle' to illustrate the author's humility.

66 *daughters . . . Ioue*: for the Muses as daughters of Jove and Memory (Mnemosyne) cf. Cicero, *De Natura Deorum*, 3. 21. 54. For Apollo and Memory as their parents cf. *Aprill*, [41] and note.

67 *quill*: pen or pipe.

70 *Parnasse*: symbolizing epic poetry, as opposed to pastoral's 'lowly groue'.

76 *where . . . best*: wherever is best for them (where the best befalls them).

79 *paint out*: graphically describe (exploiting the common analogy between poetry and painting. Cf. Horace, *Ars Poetica*, 361–5).

80 *poore*: pour.

82 *make*: compose poetry. For the poet as 'maker' see George Puttenham, *Arte of English Poesie*, *ECE*, 2. 3.

84 *loue ytake*: taken or captivated by love. Alluding not only to the lovers' complaints in *Troilus and Cressida*, *The Knight's Tale* and *Romaunt of the Rose*, but also to such pseudo-Chaucerian pieces as *The Complaint of the Black Knight* and *La Belle Dame Sans Merci*.

85 *Well . . . wayle*: he well knew how to bewail.

87 *mery tales*: *The Canterbury Tales*.

91 *passing*: fusing the senses of surpassing and transient.

94 *spring*: cf. 'Dan *Chaucer*, well of English vndefyled' (*FQ*, 4. 2. 32).

95 *learne*: teach.

96 *trees . . . shedde*: in imitation of the bereaved Orpheus whose poetry had the power to move trees. Cf. Ovid, *Metamorphoses*, 10. 86–144.

110 *fere*: companion, mate (often used of a spouse).

117–20 Cf. Virgil, *Eclogues*, 10. 75–7.

119 *forsloe*: delay or hinder.

122 *Gia . . . spenta*: 'Hope utterly extinguished'.

Gloss

[10] *Eden*: cf. Genesis 2: 8.

Mesopotamia: literally 'land between the rivers'.

Diodorus Syculus: cf. *The Library of History*, 17. 53. 3.

Tygris . . . Euphrates: cf. Genesis 2: 14 (where the Tigris is called Hiddekel).

denominate: named.

[18] For the implications of this gloss for Spenser's biography see *Var, Minor Poems*, 1. 312–14. Debate has centred upon the interpretation of 'the Northpartes', and 'the North countrye' [19]. Inconclusive attempts have been made to link the poet to the Spensers of Hurstwood in east Lancashire. Other critics have regarded 'north' as a relative term and believe that E. K. alludes to Spenser's move from Cambridge to Kent – although Cambridgeshire is conspicuously devoid of lofty 'hylles'.

[21] *Kantsh . . . woodie*: for this etymology cf. William Lambard, *A Perambulation of Kent* (1576), 7, where the name is clearly identified as Briton and not Saxon as E. K. maintains.

[25] *opinion of Faeries*: belief in the existence of fairies.

religiously: tenaciously.

shauelings: monks with shaven or tonsured crowns.

nousell: nurture.

distraicte: divided.

Guelfes . . . Gibelins: the Guelfs supported the papal cause and the Ghibellines that of the empire during the conflict between Frederick II and the papacy (1227–50). The association with elfs and goblins is fanciful.

Lord Thalbot: John Talbot (1388?–1453), first Earl of Shrewsbury, whose exploits in France are celebrated in Shakespeare's *1 Henry VI*.

[25] *Graces*: cf. *Aprill*, [109].

Musæus: cf. *Hero and Leander*, 63–5.

Pageaunts: these works are not extant.

[43] *Ipse . . . mala*: 'My own hands will gather quinces, pale with tender down' (Virgil, *Eclogues*, 2. 51). For Spenser's use of this eclogue cf. headnote to *Januarye*.

[57] *Calliope*: cf. *Aprill*, [100].

staffe: stanza.

[59] *Tamburines*: tabors or drums. A clarion is a trumpet.

[68] *Pan . . . Phœbus*: cf. Ovid, *Metamorphoses*, 11. 146–93.

[81] *Tullie . . . lyfe*: cf. Cicero, *Post Reditum in Senatu*, 4. 8.

[102] *Menalcas*: a speaker in Virgil's third and fifth eclogues.

[103] *vnderfonge*: in this context the term effectively means 'seduce'.

Julye

Spenser is indebted to the eighth eclogue of Mantuan for the central conceit of *Julye*, the opposition between hill and dale, but he explores it in the light of Isaiah 40: 4, 'Every valley shall be exalted, and every mountain and hill shall be made low'. The metre is the old 'fourteener' (here generally divided into alternating lines of eight and six syllables) familiar to Spenser's readers from George Turberville's translation of Mantuan (1567) and Sternhold and Hopkins's translation of the Psalms (1562).

The debate between Thomalin (possibly based upon Thomas Cooper, Bishop of Lincoln) and Morrell (possibly based upon John Aylmer, Bishop of London) rehearses many of the issues raised, and left unresolved, in *Maye* [cf. McLane (1961), 188–215]. For Thomalin, as for Piers, the pastoral landscape is the site of moral choice. He will not 'clime' (9) to the sort of ecclesiastical lordship despised by his counterpart [cf. *Maye*, 121–5], nor will he acknowledge any Pan but Christ (179). His condemnation of Rome, like that of Piers, reflects obliquely upon the 'popish' abuses alleged to survive in the reformed church (179–204) and has a direct bearing upon contemporary controversies concerning episcopacy, pluralism, the use of clerical vestments and the intellectual calibre of the Elizabethan clergy. He rejects the remarkable, poetic eloquence of Morrell's defence of high station (49–52, 57–92), and proffers a rugged proverbial wisdom designed to undermine its exotic ethos (93–108). In particular he objects to the indiscriminate conflation of biblical and classical imagery which informs Morrell's argument. For him, Mount Olivet and Mount Ida are distinct: the former was the precinct of Christ, the latter was home to the bad shepherd Paris who deserted his flock and brought destruction in his wake (141–52). As in *Maye*, the two speakers inhabit conflicting imaginative, as well as moral, worlds. Accordingly, they read the pastoral landscape differently. From Thomalin's viewpoint, Morrell appropriates the spiritual significance of mountains in support of social climbing. From Morrell's viewpoint, Thomalin distorts the traditional symbolism of valleys in order to denigrate legitimate social eminence.

The matter is complicated, however, by the introduction of Algrind (Archbishop Edmund Grindal), a figure admired by Thomalin despite his attainment of high ecclesiastical office. Grindal had sought to promote reform from within the Anglican Church but had fallen into the Queen's disfavour owing to his support for Puritan 'prophesyings', unlicensed religious gatherings at which scripture was expounded and discussed [cf. Collinson (1979), 233–52]. By refusing to suppress these activities (in a letter tactlessly modelled upon St Ambrose's excommunication of Theodosius) he precipitated a conflict between spiritual and secular authority and was sequestered from his office [cf. McCabe (1995)]. At the time of the *Calender*'s publication, therefore, the 'queene of shepheardes all' (*Aprill*, 34) – the supreme governor of the Anglican Church – was in conflict with the best of shepherds (associated as he is with Abel, Moses and Aaron). The material was dangerous but Spenser handles it discreetly. The female eagle that occasions Algrind's downfall is responsible in deed alone, not in intention

(221–6). She attempts to smash a 'shell fishe' – presumably the disputed practices – and not the innocent shepherd sitting 'vpon a hyll' (217). As here presented, Algrind is the victim of circumstance, not vice [cf. King (1990), 41–4]. His fate confirms Thomalin in his personal preference for the mean estate, but does not point to any necessary association between ecclesiastical eminence and pride. On the contrary, by Thomalin's own testimony, Algrind remained a good shepherd however 'great in gree' (215). As in *Maye*, the polarity of the debate is drawn to a studied inconclusiveness encapsulated in the conflicting emblems: as E. K.'s gloss observes, it is the paradoxical nature of Christ to be both humble and exalted. It remains unclear, however, how such a condition is be realized (or imitated) within the sphere of ecclesiastical government. Cf. J. H. Anderson (1970); Hoffman (1977); Shore (1985).

Julye

3 *shrowde*: shelter. Cf. *June*, 16 and note.

5 *swayne*: servant or labourer. Cf. Chaucer, *The Reeve's Tale*, 4027.

6 *hyll*: cf. Isaiah 40: 4; King (1990), 41–2.

10 *looke alofte*: cf. *Maye*, 124.

11 *reede is ryfe*: proverb is common.

14 *trode . . . tickle*: path is not so treacherous.

16 *misse . . . mickle*: loss is not much.

19 *Cuppe*: the constellation Crater.

20 *Diademe*: Corona Borealis.

33–40 Cf. Mantuan, *Eclogues*, 8. 8–14.

33 *thous*: you are (thou art).

36 *blere . . . eyes*: blur my eyes, hoodwink or deceive me.

43 *S. Brigets bowre*: unidentified.

45 *con . . . skill*: have knowledge of the Muses.

46 *sayne . . . what*: mostly say.

50 *Oliuet*: cf. Matthew 21: 1; 24: 3; 26: 30.

51 *Feeding . . . Dan*: cf. Ezekiel 34: 14–15. Dan was one of the twelve tribes of Israel.

52 *which . . . beget*: which He (as God) begot, or which begot Him (in the sense that Christ was born into the nation of Israel).

55 *bloudy sweat*: during the agony in Gethsemane 'his sweat was as it were great drops of blood falling down to the ground' (Luke 22: 44).

56 *Wolues*: in his role of 'good shepherd', cf. John 10: 11–14.

57–68 Cf. Mantuan, *Eclogues*, 8. 45–9.

69 *foresayd*: forbidden, prohibited (a rare usage).

70 *places of delight*: for Paradise cf. *June*, [10].

71 *For . . . weene*: for this reason I believe.

75 *strow my store*: spread out or display my stock of examples. Cf. Mantuan, *Eclogues*, 8. 56–7.

77 *resourse*: used loosely in the sense of resort (or recourse), but informed by the underlying sense of 'renewal'.

78 *haunten rathe*: soon, or speedily, resort.

79–84 In *Letters* Spenser mentions his '*Epithalamion Thamesis* . . . setting forth the marriage of the Thames . . . and . . . all the Riuers throughout Englande, whyche came to this Wedding' (*Prose*, 17). Cf. *FQ*, 4. 11. 8–53.

85 *Melampode*: black hellebore.

86 *Teribinth*: the turpentine tree.

98 *old . . . sawe*: ancient proverb.

101 *Alsoone*: as soon (archaic).

105–12 For the final segregation of sheep and goats cf. Matthew 25: 32–3.

116 *han . . . yore*: have died of old.

118 *goe*: gone.

119 *sample*: example.

120 *als . . . soe*: that we also might do so.

124 *why . . . disease*: why do we disturb or trouble them.

125–36 For Abel, the 'first shepheard', cf. Mantuan, *Eclogues*, 7. 14–22.

126 *Algrind*: cf. *Maye*, 75 and note.

131 *in . . . degree*: in every respect.

145–52 Cf. *August*, 137–8; S. Stewart (1988).

148 *to deare*: too dear.

151 *ouerlayd*: overwhelmed, overpowered.

157–64 Cf. Mantuan, *Eclogues*, 7. 29–31.

158 *sawe . . . face*: cf. Exodus 33: 11.

159 *His face*: either God's face or that of Moses: 'the skin of Moses' face shone' (Exodus 34: 35).

160 *in place*: in his presence, cf. *FQ*, 1. 5. 36.

162 *cote*: coat, signifying his clerical profession. As the founder of the priesthood Aaron was the first 'man of the cloth'.

164 *that . . . hote*: that I mentioned (or named) formerly.

165 *lowe . . . lief*: humble and amenable or willing.

170 *amend*: amended.

171 *nighly wore*: niggardly or sparingly worn.

173 *pall*: a woollen vestment worn by popes and archbishops.

174 *blist*: blessed.

176 *lord it*: cf. lines 185–6 and note to *Maye*, [123].

181 *Palinode*: if this is the Palinode of *Maye* he would seem to have discovered the justice of Piers's complaints and made a sort of 'recantation'. It is suggestive that the first edition actually assigns Thomalin's emblem to 'Palinode'. Cf. note to *SC, Maye*, 17.

184 *misusage*: abuse or corruption.

185 *leade*: lead their lives or behave themselves.

186 *Lordes*: cf. similar complaints in *The Plowman's Tale*, 701–8.

187–200 Cf. Marot, *Le Complaincte d'un Pastoreau Chrestien*, 179–209.

188 *chippes*: parings of bread crust.

    chere: fare, proper food.

191 *corne is theyrs*: cf. *The Plowman's Tale*, 'Prologue', 43.

193 *thriftye stockes*: thriving livestock.

199 *leany*: lean (a rare usage).

201 *misgone*: gone astray.

202 *heapen . . . wrath*: cf. Romans 2: 5.

206 *lacke of telling*: inadequacy or defect in the relating.

211 *rancke*: abundant (but with connotations of corruption).

234 *In . . . virtus*: 'Virtue resides in the middle', alluding to the golden mean of Aristotelian philosophy. Cf. *FQ*, 2. 2. 35–9.

236 *In . . . fœlicitas*: 'Felicity lies at the summit', a Platonic adage adapted to worldly ends by Morrell.

Gloss

[1] *scrypture*: cf. Matthew 25: 32–3.

[9] *Clymbe*: for the implications of the imagery cf. John 10: 1.

[12] *Seneca*: not in Seneca, but cf. Horace, *Odes*, 2. 10. 10, a passage quoted by E. K. at [91].

    Decidunt . . . lapsu: 'Lofty things suffer a heavier fall.'

[17] *sonne*: possibly to be understood allegorically as the Son of God in view of the eschatological overtones of the segregation of the sheep from the goats at [1]. At Mark 13: 6–26 Christ predicts wars, earthquakes, unprecedented affliction and the rise of false prophets until 'they see the Son of man coming in the clouds with great power and glory'.

[33] *Lurdane*: worthless rascal or dullard, from Old French 'lourdain', but for E. K.'s etymology cf. Holinshed, *Chronicles*, 1. 709; 5. 256.

    Feuer Lurdane: disease of laziness.

[51] *Synecdochen*: a rhetorical figure whereby the part represents the whole.

[59] *Diodorus Syc.*: Diodorus Siculus, *The Library of History*, 17. 7. 6–7, but the primary source is Mantuan, *Eclogues*, 8. 45–9.

    Ida: Endymion slept on Mount Latmus not Mount Ida. Cf. *Epith*, 380.

[64] *Endymion*: cf. Boccaccio, *Genealogia*, 4: 16; Comes, *Mythologiae*, 4: 8.

[63] *follye . . . thence*: cf. Genesis 3: 23–4.

[73] *Synah*: (Sinai) where Moses received the commandments, cf. Exodus 19–20.

[74] *Ladyes bowre*: angels were said to have transported the house of the Virgin Mary to Loreto in Italy (Mantuan, *Eclogues*, 8. 52). It was a popular

place of Roman Catholic pilgrimage and a common target of Protestant satire.

[79] *Rochester*: the topography would be familiar to Spenser in his capacity of secretary to Thomas Young, Bishop of Rochester.

[85–6] *Mantuane*: cf. *Eclogues*, 8. 15–18.

Theocritus: misquoted from *Epigrams*, 1. 6: 'the white he-goat crops the terebinth tree's outer twigs'.

[91] *Feriuntque ... montes*: 'lightning strikes the mountain summits' (Horace, *Odes*, 2. 10. 11–12 substituting 'fulmina' for 'fulgura').

[127] *Abell ... Cain*: cf. Genesis 4: 2.

[143] *twelue ... Iacob*: Jacob's twelve sons are named at Exodus 1: 1–4.

[146] *Hecubas dreame*: cf. Hyginus, *Fables*, 91; Apollodorus, *The Library*, 3. 12. 5; Boccaccio, *Genealogia*, 6. 22.

[147] *Venus ... Paris*: Paris' choice of Aphrodite (Venus) over Hera and Athene was often allegorized as a preference for love (or lust) over wisdom and virtue. Cf. Comes, *Mythologiae*, 6. 23; *FQ*, 3. 9. 33–5.

[154] *Argus ... Io*: cf. Ovid, *Metamorphoses*, 1. 588–750. The detail of the hoof print was probably suggested by lines 649–50 ('instead of words she told the sad tale ... with letters traced in the dust with her hoof') from which commentators extrapolated E. K.'s explanation. Cf. *October*, [32].

[161] *Decorum*: sense of generic and stylistic propriety.

meanenesse: lowliness.

[163] *Not so true*: because Aaron fashioned the idolatrous golden calf (Exodus 32: 1–6).

[173] *In purple*: applied to Rome by E. K. but politically sensitive owing to the continuing controversy concerning the use of clerical vestments within the Anglican Church.

[177] *Chaucer*: cf. the pseudo-Chaucerian *Plowman's Tale*, 134, 162.

I. Goore: John Gower (1330?–1408), author of *Confessio Amantis* (1390).

[213] *Æschylus*: cf. Pliny, *Natural History*, 10. 3. 7. Grindal had used the story in a sermon of 1564. Cf. *Remains of Archbishop Grindal* (1843), 8.

Embleme

sequestred: obliquely glancing at Grindal's sequestration.

hys cote: his clerical coat or cloth, as at line 162.

doctour: unidentified.

Suorum ... humillimus: 'Christ the humblest of his own.'

Suorum ... altissimus: 'God the most exalted of his own.'

August

This eclogue, like that assigned to June, illustrates the disquietingly sym-
biotic relationship between the 'recreatiue' and 'plaintiue' modes of pastoral,
between the social powers of art and the isolating forces of distress. Although
the theme of unrequited love, common to Perigot and Colin, is handled in
radically dissimilar ways, the juxtaposing of apparently discordant forms
suggests an unsettling relationship between them. Just as Willye provides
an ironic 'vndersong' (128) to Perigot's complaint, so the roundelay consti-
tutes a sort of comic counterpoint to Colin's lamentation and is, in turn,
qualified by it. From the artistic viewpoint with 'mery thing its good to
medle sadde' (144) and the eclogue provides a dazzling showcase for
Spenser's versatility as he turns from one complex form to another [cf.
D. L. Miller (1979)]. As the 'Argument' indicates, the singing contest was
a staple of the pastoral genre but the addition of Colin's 'proper song' is
an original touch. The energies of emotional distress are channelled through
a sequence of elaborately patterned and self-reflexive verse forms with the
result that grief becomes something of a performing art.

The opening dialogue reprises the six-line stanza of Colin's *Januarye*
monologue (rhyming *ababcc*), but significantly divides it between two
speakers. Unlike Colin, Perigot still feels himself to be part of a rustic
community. Although confined to couplets for the first twenty-four lines,
he grows in confidence with the prospect of the wager and, having acted
as mere respondent in the initial verses, takes the initiative in the roundelay.
For the first forty-two lines the weight of the exchange is two to one against
him, but thereafter the proportions equalize. The roundelay itself is an
interactive form which, like a pastoral duet, accommodates both complaint
and commentary. Almost imperceptibly its vibrant rhythms modulate the
initial tone of grief into a lighter key so that Perigot ends by seeming quite
dissimilar to Colin whose complex lament has no 'undersong' but the
'hollow Echo of my carefull cryes' (160). Dwelling 'apart / In gastfull
groue' (169–70) he seems to have become increasingly remote from the
very community in which his 'song' is performed and appreciated [cf.
Montrose (1979)]. Yet, in obvious anticipation of *November*, his poetics of
desolation looks certain to win him the pastoral crown (145–6). Even a
despondent Colin is 'the shepheards ioye' (190). His is a severely formal
complaint, a variant of the Provençal sestina, in which the end words of
each line are redeployed throughout the poem in a complex pattern (123456,
612345, 561234 etc.) until all six are repeated in a three-line coda in the
exact order in which they appear in the opening verse. Though uttered in
the 'wild woddes' the poem retains the formal sophistication of intensely
civilized expression and, through the imagery of the nightingale, reaches

for the sympathy of the very community from which it asserts its isolation (187–9). Because Virgil associates the nightingale with Orpheus' lament for the loss of Eurydice, it may be seen to function here as a metaphor for the transformative powers of art, the distillation of grief into song [cf. *Georgics*, 4. 511–15]. If it also points, as has been argued, towards an eventual transcendence of sorrow, Colin himself would appear to remain unaware of this possibility [cf. Cheney (1993), 98–100; Tylus (1988)].

The discussion of love is conducted, ironically, under the sign of Virgo and its ill-effects are more evident than its benefits. The woodcut casts its pastoral figures against an active georgic background, yet Colin tells us in *December* that 'my haruest hastened all to rathe: / The eare that budded faire, is burnt and blasted' (98–9). His sense of alienation is bad for his flock. 'Neuer knewe I louers sheepe in good plight' (20), remarks Willye, recalling the 'ill gouernement' (45) of Colin's sheep in *Januarye*. Cuddie's judgement of the singing contest is compared to the ill-fated judgement of Paris, and Venus appears in the woodcut holding the golden ball awarded to her by the shepherd that 'left hys flocke, to fetch a lasse, / whose loue he bought to deare' [cf. *Julye*, 147–8; S. Stewart (1988)]. Through this complex network of associations Spenser again activates contemporary anxieties concerning the d'Alençon match and its religious implications. Willye's 'mazer' (26), an object fit for 'any harvest Queene' (36), displays a shepherd rushing to save an 'innocent' lamb from 'the Wolues iawes' (31–3) thereby recalling the concerns of *Maye* and *Julye* and anticipating those of *September*. But the true harvest queen, as the woodcut implies, is Virgo, and Virgo is the birth sign of England's (still) virgin Queen. Cf. Berger (1988); Hoffman (1977); Mallette (1979).

Argument

delectable: delightful.
Theocritus: cf. *Idylls*, 5, 6.
vmpere: umpire, arbiter.
neatheards: cowherd's.
cause: contention, contest.
proper: excellent (i.e. worthy the name of a song).

August

1 *game*: sport or diversion in the specific sense of a contest.
2 *Wherefore*: with which.
3 *renne . . . frame*: run out of order or out of tune.
5 *assayde*: afflicted. Cf. *FQ*, 1. 2. 24.
6 *apayd*: contented, at ease.
16 *younglings*: young lambs (as Willye's reply makes clear).
21 *But . . . if*: but if.

24 *dared*: daunted, scared (taking up the challenge or 'dare' of line 2).

26–36 Cf. Theocritus, *Idylls*, 1. 27–56; Virgil, *Eclogues*, 3. 36–48.

26 *mazer*: wooden drinking bowl, such as the 'Valence Mary Cup' kept at Pembroke Hall, Cambridge.

  warre: knot, burr.

30 *Yuie*: ivy was sacred to Bacchus. Cf. *Muiop*, 299 and note.

31 *Thereby*: adjacent, nearby.

38 *nis . . . another*: there is not such another.

39 *Dambe*: dam, mother.

40 *rafte*: deprived.

41 *purchast . . . field*: acquired from me openly or fairly (i.e. in a fair contest).

43 *make . . . brother*: i.e. you may expect the same to befall his brother.

47 *But for*: because.

53 *holly*: holy.

55 *shrieue*: shrive, hear confessions and absolve sins.

56 *roundelay*: cf. *Aprill*, [33] and note.

60 *selfe . . . spill*: wasted or ruined himself (by falling in love).

61 *Bellibone*: fair maid, bonny lass. Cf. *Aprill*, [92].

67 *Kirtle*: skirt.

  saye: fine quality woollen cloth.

79 *roude*: roved, shot (arrows) at random.

87 *lightsome . . . shroudes*: radiant lightning hides itself.

92 *pitteous plight*: pathetic effect or state of affairs.

97 *raunch*: pluck, pull.

99 *hart roote*: inmost heart.

100 *desperate*: to be despaired of, incurable.

104 *curelesse*: incurable. Echoing the complaint of Oenone to Paris at Ovid, *Heroides*, 5. 149. For Paris cf. lines 137–8; *Julye*, [146], [147].

105 *bale*: bail, delivery or release, but punning on 'bale' or destruction.

107 *Yet . . . thought*: yet this girl would not leave my mind.

108 *to*: too.

110 *pinching*: cf. *Aprill*, 18 and note.

113 *gracelesse greefe*: grief occasioned by the lack of 'grace' or favour.

120 *mocke*: sign of derision, but playing on the dual senses of ridicule and (empathic) imitation.

125 *roundle*: roundel or roundelay. Cf. *Aprill*, [33] and note.

128 *vndersongs*: burdens, refrains.

  addrest: applied, directed.

131 *gayned*: won, gained the victory.

133 *for*: because.

  payned: taken such pains, made such an effort.

134 *wroughten*: ornamented, designed.

139 *yshend*: put to shame (an archaic usage).

145 *ycrouned*: crowned (an archaic usage).

148 *matter . . . deede*: material of his making.

151–89 As E. K. provides no gloss to Colin's sestina it may have been added to the poem at a relatively late stage of composition. Its repetitive structure made the sestina an appropriate form for complaint.

154 *make a part*: form part of the melody or counterpoint.

160 *Echo*: cf. note to *June* 52; L. S. Johnson (1990), 122.

161 *part*: depart.

164 *voyd*: leave, withdraw.

170 *gastfull*: dreadful, terrible.

173–4 *byrds . . . death*: shriek owls, regarded as harbingers of death.

174 *deadly*: deathlike, dismal.

178 *yrksome*: distressing, painful.

183 *Nightingale*: Philomela, raped by Tereus, was transformed into a nightingale (Ovid, *Metamorphoses*, 6. 424–674). Her song was regarded as the archetypal lover's complaint. Cf. *November*, [141]; Petrarch, *Rime Sparse*, 311.

188 *apart*: at a remove or distance from the singer.

189 *sounder*: deep or profound, playing on 'sound' at line 187. The 'sound' of Colin's lament 'sounds' the depth of their tranquil sleep.

191 *turning*: fashioning, with particular reference to the sestina's intricate rhyme scheme.

197 *Vincenti . . . victi*: 'The glory of the vanquished goes to the victor'. Cf. Gabriel Harvey, *Marginalia* (1913), 192.

199 *Vinto . . . vitto*: 'Vanquished not subdued'.

201 *Felice . . . può*: either 'Let him be happy who can' or, as E. K. prefers, 'He is happy who can'.

Gloss

[19] *Infelix . . . pecus*: 'O ever luckless flock of sheep' (*Eclogues*, 3. 3).

[26] *Theocritus . . . Virgile*: cf. *Idylls*, 1. 23–56; 5. 20–30; *Eclogues*, 3. 28–51.

[46] *Pousse*: pulse, field of peas.

[131] *Et . . . hic*: 'You deserve the heifer and he also' (*Eclogues*, 3. 109).
    enterchaunge: exchange.

[138] *Paris*: cf. *Julye*, [146], [147] and note.

[138] *pryce*: award, trophy.

Emblem

dew: due.

moderate: control, restrain.

leaue of with: quit or end with.

September

September, the third and last of Spenser's ecclesiastical eclogues, is directed, according to the 'Argument', against the 'loose liuing of Popish prelates'. Its model is Mantuan's ninth eclogue which attacks the depravity of the Roman curia and extols, by way of contrast, the virtues of the good shepherd. Yet the 'farre countrye' deplored by Diggon Davie is never expressly identified, and the term 'popish' is richly ambiguous. Frequently, as the following notes indicate, overt satire of Rome insinuates oblique satire of the Anglican establishment, a circumstance that accounts for Hobbinol's fear that his friend may speak 'to plaine' (136). The setting of topical satire in a 'forraine' location is a standard device of the form: the corruption of the 'other' is found within a divided self.

Diggon Davie has been convincingly identified with Richard Davies, bishop of the Welsh diocese of St David's, a figure well placed to speak from experience. His own diocese had suffered at the hands of greedy courtiers (122–35) and he had served on Archbishop Grindal's commission of inquiry into ecclesiastical abuses [cf. McLane (1961), 216–34]. From his viewpoint, a mercenary market in religious commodities has supplanted Christ's spiritual generosity (34–7; 96–9). Not surprisingly, therefore, the moral complaints of *Maye* and *Julye* are aggravated here in the same 'flatt' diction (105) and rugged tetrameters. The structure is also similar with dialogue giving way to moralized fable (180–225).

While the precise details of Roffy's 'particular Action' (as E. K. terms it, [180–225]) have eluded interpretation, his discovery of a wolf in sheep's clothing – in a country in which 'wolves' are supposed to have been exterminated (150–55) – is suggestive of a successful act of opposition to the Jesuit mission. His call for 'watchfulnesse' (230–35) would probably evoke a more optimistic response from Protestant readers than it elicits from Hobbinol (236–41) who sympathizes with the endeavour but despairs of success [cf. Hume (1984), 37–9]. This is all the more significant in that the pastoral topos underlying the satire traditionally pits a corrupt town against an innocent country. But Hobbinol's pastoral paradise seems far less idyllic than it did in *June* (1–13). Now 'the Westerne wind bloweth sore' (49) and he feels 'stiffe' and 'stanck' (47). Evils abound in Arcadia too, and innocence, in itself, is no guarantee of immunity [cf. Gless (1994), 19–22]. Echoes of Virgil's first and ninth eclogues – poems of war, wolves and dispossession – exacerbate the sombre mood with the result that the contrast between home and abroad is considerably blurred.

Since Roffy is certainly to be identified with Bishop John Young, Spenser has followed Mantuan in denoting his own patron as the archetypal good shepherd, a potent counter-example to the prevailing corruption. By insisting upon the association between Roffy and Colin (176–9) he forges a link between *September* and *August* where the vigilance of the good shepherd is depicted on Willye's mazer (*August*, 31–4). But Mantuan's good shepherd is himself a poet whose art is said to surpass that of Orpheus [cf. *Eclogues*, 9. 215], while Roffy's 'boye' seems increasingly inclined to agree with Virgil's Moeris that song alone cannot save, or create, the good place [cf. *Eclogues*, 9. 7–16]. As E. K. observes, Diggon's emblem is equally applicable to Colin who is again said to represent 'the Authour selfe' [176]. In the fullness of time both will be driven 'for neede to come home agayne' (67), but to an imperfect country. Cf. Berger (1988); L. S. Johnson (1990); King (1990); Lane (1993); Lindheim (1990).

September

1 *Diggon Dauie*: Diggon is the Welsh form of Diccon, a nickname for Richard. The name suggests that of the candid Davy Diker of Thomas Churchyard's *Davy Dycars Dreame* (*c*. 1552). Cf. King (1990), 25.

   her: him, a Welsh usage probably designed, like others, to prompt the identification of Davie as Richard Davies, bishop of St David's, who translated the New Testament and prayer book into Welsh.

2 *missaye*: speak incorrectly, mistake. Cf. line 106.

7 *dight*: maltreated, abused.

10 *at mischiefe*: in (or by) misfortune.

12 *gall*: chafe.

13 *ripeth vp*: (painfully) opens up.

24 *astate*: state, condition.

26 *of yore*: of old.

30 *dempt*: deemed, thought.

33 *being*: living, livelihood.

   truely mene: are honestly intentioned or disposed.

34–5 *But . . . remaine*: 'But there is no better country to be in for those who profit from deceit.'

36 *setten . . . shame*: shamefully sell their wares (referring to simony).

37 *Mart*: a common topos of anti-Catholic satire, cf. *Maye*, 298 and note.

39 *baytes*: baits, traps.

40–41 *Or . . . throte*: possibly glancing at the prevalent traffic in ecclesiastical fines and the displacement of worthy ministers from wealthy benefices. If so, apparent satire of Rome encodes oblique satire of Anglicanism.

44 *Bulls*: a biblical image. Cf. note to line 124 below.

   bate: fed.

46 *cranck*: boldly, vigorously.

50 *souereigntee*: supremacy.

52 *vnder . . . hill*: in the shelter of the hill.

61 *Dogge . . . mouth*: Aesop relates how a dog lost the meat it was carrying when it attempted to snatch the reflection. Cf. *Fables*, no. 185.

65 *pyne*: pain, pangs of hunger. Cf. *FQ*, 1. 9. 35.

74 *wote ne*: know not.

81 *ledde of*: lead by.

83 *casten to compasse*: contrive or plot to accomplish.

89 *holy water*: a standard topic of Protestant satire, cf. *Februarie*, [209].

　doen . . . drench: drown them all.

90 *high way*: an ironic claim since the broad highway leads to hell, the strait and narrow way to heaven (cf. Matthew 7: 13–14).

91 *vndersaye*: say by way of reply or riposte.

93 *balk*: either miss by error or avoid by intention.

94–7 Roman Catholic rites of exorcism were commonly associated with black magic by Protestant polemicists.

95 *paund*: pawned, staked.

96 *Marrie*: by Mary (a common oath).

　great Pan: Christ, cf. *Aprill*, [50] and note.

　borrow: pledge, security. Cf. *Maye*, 131 and note.

99 *For . . . drawe*: for which reason (they) would draw.

100 *a . . . name*: in God's name.

101 *brewed*: brought about, caused.

102 *dirke*: darkly, in the sense of obscurely or enigmatically.

103–21 Diggon rehearses the complaints of *Maye*, 73–94 but qualifies their impact by ascribing them to those who 'missay' the clergy. Once again, satire of Rome encodes oblique criticism of Anglicanism: Roman Catholic priests might have mistresses and illegitimate offspring but only Anglican priests had the worldly 'care' of wives and families.

103 *to*: too.

104 *speake . . . what*: what most concerns shepherds.

105 *flatt*: plain, unadorned.

106 *Their . . . missay*: their bad behaviour causes men to speak ill of them.

107 *faye*: faith (archaic).

108 *world . . . war*: cf. *Februarie*, 11–13 and note.

109 *All for*: because.

　beastly . . . blont: sensual and stupid.

110 *note*: know not (i.e. a contraction of ne wot).

111 *cote*: either sheep-cote or clerical garb. Cf. *Julye*, 162 and note.

112 *sticke . . . say*: do not hesitate or scruple to say.

　whote . . . tongue: possibly derived from Isaiah 6: 6–7.

113 *graseth*: 'moves on devouring' (*OED*).

114 *casten . . . care*: make too much account of worldly concerns.

115 *deck . . . Dame*: dress their wife (or mistress).

116–19 The perceived decline in hospitality was often attributed to absenteeism, enclosure of common land and materialism.

116 *encheason*: reason. Cf. *Maye*, 147.

117 *reeking*: smoking.

120 *steads*: farms, farmsteads.

121 *Monster*: the many-headed Hydra slain by Hercules was often allegorized as the multitude.

122–35 Diggon lends support to the criticism of rapacious patrons who levied extortionate rents upon the incumbents of the livings to which they presented. Prominent courtiers such as Burghley and Leicester were alleged to be complicit in the abuse. Cf. *MHT*, 515–40.

122 *shooten . . . pricke*: hit nearest the mark or the bull's-eye.

123 *other . . . lick*: proverbial expression for appropriating the profits of someone else's labours. Cf. *MHT*, 78.

124 *Bulles of Basan*: cf. Psalms 22: 12–13. Cf. line 44.

130 *wagmoires*: quagmires.

132 *wind*: draw or pull in twisting movements.

134 *of*: off.

135 *leese . . . grosse*: lose the whole.

136 *to*: too.

138 *cleanly couer*: gloss over, conceal.

139 *forced*: enforced, imposed upon us.

140 *creepe*: apparently in the sense of 'get by' or 'make do'.

143 *But . . . choyce*: unless he calls them when they want to be called.

146 *But . . . cal*: but it would be better for them to come at their call.

148 *yrent*: rent, torn apart.

149 *All . . . nould*: because they would not.

154 *soth*: truth.

155 *Foxes*: the fox signifies both crypto-Catholics within the Anglican Church, and Catholics who, denied the power to be persecutors (wolves), scheme to regain control. Cf. *Maye*, 219 and note.

156–61 Cf. 'Beware of false prophets, which come to you in sheep's clothing, but inwardly they are ravening wolves' (Matthew 7: 15). Probably a topical allusion to the Jesuit missions of 1578–80.

156 *wise*: manner.

158 *widely*: at large, freely over a wide range.

159 *raungers*: forest rangers, gamekeepers. The 'ranging' of the keepers curtails the 'wide ranging' of the wolf, cf. line 195.

160 *prolling*: prowling.

162 *priue . . . pert*: clandestinely or openly.

164 *ball*: an odd usage if employed as a common noun. Osgood (1915) and Herford (1932) take it to be the dog's name. Cf. note to line 190 below.

169 *mayntenaunce*: demeanour, behaviour (a Chaucerian usage).

171 *Roffynn*: John Young (1534?–1605), Bishop of Rochester ('Roffensis' in Latin) and, prior to that, Master of Pembroke Hall, Cambridge during Spenser's residence. Cf. *Aprill*, 21 and note.

172 *hight*: entails or purports, a pseudo-archaic usage found only in Spenser (*OED*).

173 *betight*: betide, befall.

174 *merciable*: merciful.

175 *conuenable*: consistent.

176 *selfe boye*: his own boy. Spenser was Bishop Young's secretary.

180 *Thilk . . . marke*: this same shepherd I may well note.

183 *and if but*: but if.

185 *gulfe*: voracious appetite (the abyss or 'gulf' of his stomach).

186 *repayre*: make his way, betake himself.

190 *ball*: (bawl) howl.

202 *practise*: ploy, stratagem.

203 *Argus*: cf. Ovid, *Metamorphoses*, 1. 624–7; *Julye*, [154].

206 *counterfect*: counterfeit.

210 *widder*: wider.

211 *hidder . . . shidder*: young male and female sheep (specifically those between eight or nine months old and their first shearing, *OED*).

217 *Lowder*: a common dog's name.

227 *All for*: because.

  deuoyr: duty.

230 *watchfulnesse*: cf. Matthew 24: 42–3; 25: 1–13.

238 *fleshe*: cf. 'the spirit indeed is willing, but the flesh is weak' (Matthew 26: 41).

240 *chaungeable rest*: rest by way of change from labour, periodic rest.

255–7 Echoing Virgil, *Eclogues*, 1. 79–83 but in a gloomier key.

259 *lite*: light upon, encounter.

261 *Inopem . . . fecit*: 'Plenty makes me poor.'

Gloss

[10] *vsurped of*: used by.

  Lidgate . . . Chaucer: cf. Lydgate, *Falls of Princes*, 8, epigraph; Chaucer, *The Romaunt of the Rose*, 4552.

[47] *Stanck*: a neologism coined from Italian *stanco*, 'weary'.

[54] *Debes . . . ventis*: 'Beware lest you become the winds' laughing stock' (Horace, *Odes*, 1. 14. 15–16).

[57] *Soote*: not used in *September*.

[76] *Mantuane*: cf. *Eclogues*, 6. 8–9.

[83] *Per Syncopen*: 'By deletion of letters or syllables.' E. K.'s explanation is incorrect; 'emprise' and 'enterprise' are wholly distinct.

[119] *Crumenall*: a neologism, coined from the Latin *crumena*, 'purse'.

[151] *yeare . . . Lorde*: Edgar reigned from AD 959 to 975. The dates appear to have been accidentally omitted in E. K.'s gloss.

proper policie: Edgar demanded an annual tribute of three hundred wolves from the king of Wales thereby eradicating the species. Cf. Holinshed, *Chronicles*, 1. 695.

[153] *Ethelbert*: Ethelbert, king of Kent, received St Augustine in 597, converted to Christianity and established the new religion at Canterbury although he did not impose it on his subjects. Ethelbert, king of Wessex, was also for a time king of Kent (855–60). His reign was marred by Danish invasions. E. K.'s explanation is spurious.

[162] *Chaucer*: cf. the pseudo-Chaucerian *La Belle Dame Sans Mercy*, 174.

[171] *Roffy*: Raffy Lyonnois is mentioned not in Marot's *Eglogue au Roy soubz les noms de Pan et Robin* but in *Eglogue sur le Trépas de ma Dame Loyse de Savoye* (42). Spenser has merely adapted the name, the persons are quite distinct.

[176] *Musarum Lachrymæ*: *Smithus, vel Lachrymae Musarum* (1578) commemorates the death of Sir Thomas Smith (1577), assigning one lament to each of the nine Muses, a format adapted in *TM*. For Smith, cf. *Januarye*, [10] and note.

Gratulationum Valdinensium: *Gratulationes Valdinenses* (1578) consists of four books of Latin verse addressed to the Queen and various prominent courtiers including Lord Burghley, the Earl of Leicester and Sir Philip Sidney. The manuscript was presented to the Queen during the progress of 1578 at Audley End in Essex, and the printed version at Hadham Hall in Hertfordshire, the home of Harvey's friend Arthur Capel.

Tyrannomastix: not extant.

Ode Natalitia: published in 1575 to commemorate the death of the rhetorician Peter Ramus in the Massacre of St Bartholomew's Day (1572). Harvey was a leading exponent of Ramist rhetoric at Cambridge.

Rameidos: not extant, but the title suggests a further celebration of the life and thought of Peter Ramus.

Philomusus: not extant, and it is unclear whether this is a separate title or a constituent element of the preceding or succeeding titles.

Anticosmopolita: not extant, an epic poem (subtitled 'Britanniae Apologia') in celebration of Queen Elizabeth mentioned in *Letters* (cf. *Prose*, 460).

[240] *Quod . . . est*: 'Whatever lacks periodic rest does not endure' (Ovid, *Heroides*, 4. 89).

Emblem

Narcissus in Ouid: cf. *Metamorphoses*, 3. 466; *June*, 52 and note; *Amor*, 35; *FQ*, 1. 4. 29.

October

The October eclogue explores the stark contrast between the sublime aspirations of poetry and the material needs of the poet. Mediating between them is the elusive figure of the patron. No less is at stake here than the role of literature in Elizabethan society, and the hopes and fears of the *Calender*'s 'new Poete' are accordingly canvassed through the medium of pastoral debate [cf. Helgerson (1978)]. The eclogue is quoted in the Spenser–Harvey *Letters* (1580) where Harvey notes the financial concerns of '*Cuddie, alias* you know who' by way of emphasizing the pressing need to secure commercial success (cf. *Prose*, 470–71). Ideally, as the 'Argument' asserts, poetry is properly considered to be a 'diuine gift', rather than a mere 'arte', and the 'glory' is 'much greater then the gayne' (20), but in the real world poets must 'feede' (34) and Platonic values entail a financial cost [cf. Schleiner (1985)]. Cultivation of the poet's divine gift demands a reciprocal generosity on the part of man. The sour tones of Mantuan's fifth eclogue, with its miserly patron and embittered poet, echo in the background [cf. Hoffman (1977), 13–21], as do those of Theocritus' attack upon the crass philistinism of his own mercenary age [cf. *Idylls*, 16]. By contrast, Virgil, 'the Romish *Tityrus*' patronized by Maecenas and inspired by Augustus, proceeded from pastoral, through georgic, to epic poetry thereby establishing a paradigm for the careers of both poet and patron (55–60). As Mantuan observes, 'good fortune gave him eloquence' [cf. *Eclogues*, 5. 89]. The woodcut suggests the possibility of a similar progression in that Cuddie looks beyond the central emblem of the panpipes, proffered by Piers, towards the classical temples in the background [cf. Luborsky (1981)]. The positions are reversed in the dialogue, however, where Piers espouses artistic aspirations while Cuddie laments the moral and social decline which stifles poetic endeavour (67–78).

It is surprising to find Cuddie, rather than Colin, described as 'the perfecte paterne of a Poete' but, as E. K. observes, 'some doubt, that the persons be different' [1]. Through this complex presentational device Cuddie is made to stand in relation to Colin as Colin stands to 'the authour selfe'. Notably absent from all of the 'Satyricall' eclogues, Colin, as it were, dons the *persona* of Cuddie to criticize 'the contempte of Poetrie' evident in 'Princes pallace' (81). The verse form is an adaptation of the six-line stanza of Colin's *Januarye* monologue (now rhyming *abbaba*). It falls to Piers, the moral spokesman of *Maye*, to advance the cause of '*Elisa*' and 'the worthy whome shee loueth best' (45–7) as suitable themes for heroic verse while insisting upon the centrality of poetry to the spiritual well-being of the nation. In this manner the eclogue attempts to pre-empt its own reception by inspiring the heroic milieu of which it appears to despair. For the poet to perceive the celestial in the material – by regarding Queen Elizabeth, for example, as an 'immortall mirrhor' of the divine (93) – it is essential that those he considers 'worthy' of his 'payne' be 'also fauourers of hys skil and faculty' [43].

The strength of that faculty is evident in the structure of the eclogue itself with its complex pattern of thematic and symbolic correspondences between strategically placed verses. The central stanzas (10–11), for example, concentrate upon Virgil, the supreme exemplar of the well-patronized poet, while the fifth and sixteenth focus upon the poet's Orphic potential. Both the power and the limitations of poetry are hereby acknowledged in what constitutes a remarkably perceptive accommodation of the spirit to an incipient aesthetics of cultural materialism. It is noteworthy, however, that, in anticipation of *November*, the Virgilian *rota* has undergone a Christian recension with religious verse apparently displacing epic as the supreme goal of Orphic flight [cf. P. Cheney (1993), 30–31]. The implication would appear to be that the poet may be forced to look beyond earthly love and power – which commonly entail disappointment (61–72) and tyranny (98–9) – to higher forces. Thus the dialogue pulls in opposite directions simultaneously while creating poetry from the conflict. The ultimate 'defence' of poetry is poetry itself. Cf. Berger (1988); Goldberg (1986), 63–7; Richardson (1989); Watkins (1995).

Argument

heauenly instinct: aptitude instilled by heaven.

ἐνθουσιασμὸς: 'enthusiasmos' or divinely inspired poetic frenzy (cf. Plato, *Phaedrus*, 245a). Sir Philip Sidney defines it as 'a very inspiring of a divine force, farre above mans wit'. At issue is the distinction between the poet as craftsman or 'maker', and the poet as *vates* or 'prophet' (*Apology for Poetry*, *ECE*, 1. 154–5, 158–9, 192). Cf. *Aprill*, [19]; *October*, [21]; *CCH*, 823; *HB*, 1–3 and notes.

English Poete: not extant.

October

1–5 Cf. Mantuan, *Eclogues*, 5. 1–5.

2 *chace*: hurry on, hasten (often used of driving cattle or sheep).

3 *weary . . . race*: wear away the languorous hours of daytime.

5 *bydding base*: to 'bid the base' was to challenge a player to run from home base in a running contest (cf. *FQ*, 5. 8. 5), but the expression was also used of offering challenges in a singing contest.

9 *spared store*: reserve stock, what she had saved.

11–12 Cf. Aesop's fable of the ant and the grasshopper, *Fables*, no. 336.

12 *straine*: press hard upon, distress.

15 *bett . . . thy*: better for that.

16 *sclender prise*: meagre reward.

17 *I . . . flye*: he flushes out the birds but others catch them.

19–24 For the moral influence of poetry cf. *TM*, 451–4.

23 *pleasaunce . . . vaine*: pleasure of your poetic vein or style.

24 *trayned*: drawn, trailed along.

25 *in frame*: in harmony, in order.

26 *routes*: throngs.

   cleaue: cling.

27 *Seemeth*: it seems that.

28 *All as*: just as.

29 *balefull bowre*: menacing or deadly abode, the underworld.

30 *hound*: Cerberus, guardian of the underworld. Cf. *VG*, 345–52.

31 *traine*: tail.

33 *ere . . . thy*: ever the more for that.

35 *sheddeth*: dissipate, evaporate.

37–42 Cf. Mantuan, *Eclogues*, 5. 126–8.

37 *base . . . clowne*: low and uncouth rustic.

39 *giusts*: jousts.

40 *weld . . . crowne*: possess or bear the awesome crown, reign.

41 *doubted*: redoubted, dreaded.

42 *vnbruzed*: undented.

45 *rest*: stop, repose (having found a suitable theme).

46 *bigger . . . sing*: i.e. sing in loftier style. Cf. *FQ*, 7. 7. 1.

48 *white . . . stake*: the Dudley crest displayed a white bear shackled to a ragged staff or stump. Cf. notes to *RT*, 184, 561.

50 *tenor*: tension, tautness.

53 *All*: although.

55–60 Virgil's progress from pastoral (*Eclogues*) through bucolic (*Georgics*) to epic poetry (*Aeneid*) was described in four lines commonly printed as a preface to the *Aeneid*: 'I am he who formerly tuned my song on a slender reed, then, leaving the woodland, compelled the neighbouring fields to obey the husbandman, however grasping, a work pleasing to farmers: but now I turn to Mars [war]'. They established a paradigm for the poetic career, cf. Mantuan, *Eclogues*, 5. 86–8; *FQ*, 1 Proem 1. The matter is appropriately recalled here as October was Virgil's birth month.

56 *Mecænas*: Caius Cilnius Maecenas (73–08 BC), close ally of the Emperor Augustus and renowned as the patron of Horace and Virgil.

58 *laboured*: tilled, ploughed. An allusion to Virgil's *Georgics*.

   timely eare: seasonable harvest.

65–6 Cf. Mantuan, *Eclogues*, 5. 153–6.

67–72 Cf. Mantuan, *Eclogues*, 5. 157–9.

67 *vertue*: manliness, manly daring (Italian *virtu*).

68 *a bedde of*: to bed by (i.e. manhood is enervated by ease).

69 *pease*: pea.

70 *preace*: press, in the sense of crowd or throng, but playing on printing press. *OED* tentatively explains 'to put in preace' as 'to put in practice' but this is the only example cited.

73–6 Cf. Mantuan, *Eclogues*, 5. 148–52.

74 *stocke*: source or trunk (continuing the metaphor implicit in 'buddes' and 'shoote').

75 *Or . . . fayne*: either it must conceal men's follies.

76 *rybaudrye*: ribaldry.

79 *pierlesse*: without peer or equal, but with a play on 'Piers'. Poetry has no such advocate as Piers in 'Princes pallace'.

85 *to*: too.

87 *peeced pyneons*: patched wings.

88 *Colin fittes*: it is fitting or proper for Colin.
    scanne: climb. Cf. *FQ*, 7. 6. 8.

89 *bedight*: abused, afflicted. Cf. *September*, 7 and note.

92 *lyftes . . . myre*: alluding to the Platonic doctrine of progressive ascent from earthly to spiritual love. Cf. *HL*, 176–82 and notes.

93 *immortall mirrhor*: according to Platonic theory mortal beauty reflects that of immortality. Cf. *HL*, 196. Ficino asserts that 'the single face of God shines successively in three mirrors . . . the Angelic Mind, the World Soul and the [material] Body of the World' (*Commentary*, 5. 4). The phrase may be intended to suggest that Colin will find his true inspiration not in Rosalind but in the queen. Cf. *FQ*, 1 Proem 4.

94 *aboue . . . skie*: above the firmament, the sphere of fixed stars.

101 *crabbed*: harsh, perverse.

103 *casts . . . prise*: determines to attain an important goal or prize.

105 *thriftie bitts*: either frugal cuts or prime cuts.

106 *Bacchus . . . wise*: Bacchus, the god of wine, is friendly to Apollo, the god of poetry: i.e. drink aids poetic invention. Cf. Clements (1955), 802–3. However, Cuddie's confidence is perhaps misplaced: it was during the celebrations of Bacchus that Orpheus, noted as the archetypal pattern of the vatic poet at lines 28–30, was torn to pieces.

108 *nombers*: metres, rhythms.

110 *distaind*: stained.

111 *Yuie*: ivy is used to crown poets at Virgil, *Eclogues*, 7. 25; 8. 12–13.

112 *Muse*: Melpomene, the Muse of tragedy.

114 *Bellona*: goddess of war.

117 *assayde*: assailed us.

119 *Gates . . . layd*: goats have given birth.

122 *Agitante . . . illo*: cf. Ovid, *Fasti*, 6. 5, 'est deus in nobis; agitante calescimus illo [there is a god within us; we grow inflamed as he afflicts us]'. Ovid is claiming the role of divinely inspired *vates*, or 'prophet'.

Gloss

Theocritus: cf. *Idylls*, 16. The indebtedness is slight.

Hiero . . . Syracuse: Hieron II of Syracuse (*c*. 360–215 BC), claimed descent from Hieron I, the 'tyrant'.

Mantuane: cf. *Eclogues*, 5, a principal source for *October*.

[1] *Cantion*: song (cf. the Italian *canzona*).

[8] *Auena*: Latin for 'reed pipe'. Cf. Virgil, *Eclogues*, 1. 2.

[12] *vnlustye*: dull, listless.

[21] *conspyre*: agree.

Plato . . . Legibus: not in Plato's *Laws*, and unidentified elsewhere.

vatem: seer or prophet.

[27] *Plato . . . Pythagoras*: Plato cites Pythagoras at *Phaedo*, 86b–d.

compassion: sympathy.

Alexander . . . Timotheus: the story is recounted in this form in the popular encyclopaedia known as *Suidas*, under 'Timotheus'.

Plato . . . brests: the gloss is garbled. Plato discusses the moral and emotional effects of certain melodies, and draws an analogy between musical and political standards (*Laws*, 2. 655a–660a; 3. 700a–701b). Certain types of music and poetry are barred from his ideal state (*Republic*, 10. 605c–607d). Spenser discusses the power of music to alter national character in *Vewe* (cf. *Prose*, 121). E. K.'s reference to Aristotle may be a vague reminiscence of *Politics*, 8. 7.

[28] *Orpheus*: a type of the vatic poet. Cf. *June*, 96 and note. For his recovery and subsequent loss of Eurydice cf. Virgil, *Georgics*, 4. 453–527.

[32] *Argus*: cf. *Julye*, [154] and note.

[43] *faculty*: poetic faculty or ability.

[47] *Erle of Leycester*: By the time of publication Robert Dudley, Earl of Leicester, was out of favour with Elizabeth owing to his clandestine marriage to Lettice Knollys and his opposition to the Queen's proposed marriage to d'Alençon.

cognisance: crest.

other: others of his family, for example.

[55] *Romish Tityrus*: cf. note to 'Epistle', 5.

Mecænas: cf. *October*, 56 and note.

[57] *Georgiques*: the first and second quartos read 'Bucoliques'.

[65] *Oration of Tullies*: cf. Cicero, *Pro Archia Poeta*, 10. 24.

Giunto . . . Trouasti: 'When Alexander came to the famous tomb of the fierce Achilles he said sighingly, "O fortunate man who found so clear a trumpet"' (Petrarch, *Rime Sparse*, 187. 1–4).

Scipio . . . Ennius: for Scipio Africanus' patronage of the poet Ennius cf. Horace, *Odes*, 4. 8. 13–20; Cicero, *Pro Archia Poeta*, 9. 22.

Alexander . . . Pindarus: cf. Pliny, *Natural History*, 7. 29. 109; Plutarch, *Alexander*, 11.

Darius . . . pillowe: for variants of this story cf. Plutarch, *Alexander*, 8, 26; Pliny, *Natural History*, 7. 29. 108.

[78] *Tom Piper*: nickname for local village piper, often associated with those who accompany Morris dancers.

[90] *one . . . sonetts*: not extant. For the swan as an emblem of the poet cf. Clements (1955), 784–9. Cf. *RT*, 589–600 and note. Ovid compares his *Tristia* to the song of a dying swan (5. 1. 14).

[93] *Fiorir . . . affanni*: '[the noble tree, i.e. the laurel signifying his lady Laura] . . . made my weak wit blossom in its shade and grow in my troubles' (Petrarch, *Rime Sparse*, 60. 3–4).

[96] *Cacozelon*: stylistic affectation.

[100] *Mantuanes . . . Poscit*: 'Divine [poetry] demands a mind empty of cares.' The line is not in Mantuan but cf. *Eclogues*, 5. 69–70; Cicero, *Epistulae Ad Quintum Fratrem*, 3. 4. 4.

[105] *Fœcundi . . . disertum*: 'Whom have brimming goblets not made eloquent?' (Horace, *Epistles*, 1. 5. 19).

[110] *Poetical furie*: illustrating the 'enthusiasm' or divine frenzy commended in the 'Argument' to *October*. Sir Philip Sidney cites Plato's *Ion* (534a–e) as a source for the notion, cf. *Apology for Poetry*, *ECE*, 1. 192.

numbers: metres.

[113] *buskin*: boot worn by Greek tragic actors.

stockes: socks or stockings worn by Greek comic actors.

Sola . . . cothurno: 'Your songs alone are worthy of the buskin of Sophocles' (Virgil, *Eclogues*, 8. 10).

Magnum . . . cothurno: '[Aeschylus taught] magniloquence and buskined gait' (Horace, *Ars Poetica*, 280).

[114] *Queint*: E. K.'s gloss is probably correct but the term also has the connotations of 'skilled' or 'haughty'.

Bellona . . . Pallas: in classical mythology Bellona and Pallas are distinct but Renaissance commentators sometimes conflate them. Cf. Boccaccio, *Genealogia*, 5. 48.

Lucian: cf. *Dialogues of the Gods*, 'Hephaestus and Zeus', 225–6.

saucinesse: forwardness.

[114] *Æquipage*: more properly to be understood as martial accoutrement rather than, as E. K. maintains, 'order', but retinue is also possible.

[118] *Charmes*: magic spells.

Aut si carminibus: 'Or if in songs' (not in Ovid).

Emblem

Piers answereth: Piers's reply is missing in all editions.

Epiphonematicos: by way of pithy summary, sententiously.

Nouember

In *November* death comes to Arcadia. Invited by Thenot to resume the poetic career cut short by 'loues misgouernaunce' (4), Colin responds with a pastoral elegy suitable to the 'sollein season' of the year (17) and to his own dejected mood. The primary model is Clément Marot's *Eglogue sur le Trépas de ma Dame Loyse de Savoye* (1531) – in which the speakers are Thenot and Colin – but the tradition stretches back through Virgil's fifth eclogue (generally regarded as a lament for Julius Caesar) to Moschus, Bion and Theocritus. According to E. K. the identity of Dido 'is unknowen and closely buried in the Authors conceipt' [38], but the obvious structural and linguistic correspondences with the *Aprill* eclogue, combined with the argument's description of Dido as a 'mayden of great bloud', lend an implicitly political dimension to 'loues misgouernaunce' [cf. McLane (1961), 47–60]. Both Virgil and Marot were perceived to have written elegies of state, and the choice of the name Dido, recalling the unfortunate Virgilian queen who destroyed herself for love of a foreign prince, suggests an allusion to the proposed match with d'Alençon, an event which, according to Sir Philip Sidney, would accomplish 'the manifest death' of the Queen's 'estate' [cf. McCabe (1995), 34]. The olive branches which served in *Aprill* as symbols of Elizabethan 'Peace and quietnesse' [124] now serve as garlands for Dido's bier (144). Thus Eliza is indeed 'buried', figuratively speaking, 'in the Authors conceipt' and contemporary readers might well remember that Virgil's alternative name for Dido was 'Elissa'. They would certainly know that November is the month of Elizabeth's accession day with all of its attendant celebrations.

And yet, despite the elegiac theme, it is not true that 'All Musick sleepes, where death doth leade the daunce' (105). Like the nightingale to which he is compared, Colin transforms grief into 'song' (25) thereby creating a paradoxical effect of 'doolful pleasaunce' (204), the very essence of the poetic elegy. Consigning Marot's relatively unsophisticated interlocking quatrains to the opening dialogue (rhyming *abab bcbc* etc.), Spenser conspicuously outdoes his model by creating for the elegy itself an elaborate ten-line stanza (rhyming *ababbccdbd*) opening with an alexandrine (a line of six iambic feet) and skilfully deploying a repeated pattern of pentameters, tetrameters and dimeters to achieve increasingly subtle effects of rhythmic and tonal variation. Through Colin's 'vatic' artistry the earthly calamity of Dido's death is transformed into a vision of Christian transcendence: 'I see thee blessed soule, I see, / Walke in *Elisian* fieldes so free' (178–9) [cf. P. Cheney (1991)]. In marked contrast to Virgil's Dido, who is fated to inhabit the 'Mourning Fields' ('lugentes campi'), Spenser's Dido–Elissa is ushered into the pastoral care of the good shepherd and the refrain alters accordingly from 'O heauie herse . . . O carefull verse' (160–62) to 'O happye herse . . . O ioyfull verse' (170–72). A spiritual springtime of 'fresh' fields and 'greene' grass is hereby recovered at the very onset of winter (189).

But who is 'the good shepherd'? According to E. K. the Elysian fields 'be deuised of Poetes to be a place of pleasure like Paradise' [179], and the vision of Dido's apotheosis – a traditional component of the elegiac genre – is a 'liuely Icon, or representation as if he saw her in heauen present' [178]. The 'herse' referred to in the refrain signifies not merely the bier or decorative catafalque but, as E. K. notes, the funeral obsequies themselves [60], including the elegy rehearsed, or recited, by Colin [cf. Berger (1988), 400–401]. If Eliza is fated to die, she desperately needs her poet to place her in the 'Elisian fieldes'. In the woodcut Dido's funeral cortège is consigned to the background while pride of place is assigned to the coronation of Colin Clout as the undisputed 'souereigne of song' [cf. Luborsky (1981)]. Ideally art and faith fuse, but only ideally. The deepest political theme of the *Calender* – underlying all particular examples – is the role of images in Elizabethan society, the relationship between the art of politics and the politics of art. Virgil's transformation of Dido from faithful widow to desperate lover was itself politically informed [cf. D. Cheney (1989), 154–61; Watkins (1995), 79–82], as was Marot's presentation of Louise de Savoy, whose religious policies he bitterly opposed, as 'the shepherdess of Peace' [cf. A. Patterson (1986)]. By recalling both the chaste and the passionate Dido, *November* registers in a darker key the radical ambivalence towards Queen Elizabeth evident even in *Aprill*, and, like Thenot, the reader is left uncertain whether to 'reioyce or weepe for great constrainte' (205). Cf. Davies (1981); Hoffman (1977); Kay (1990); Mallette (1981); Martin (1987); Montrose (1979); Parmenter (1936); Pigman (1985); Reamer (1969); Sacks (1985); Sagaser (1989); Whipp (1990).

Argument

bloud: family, descent.

required: inquired.

Marot . . . Queene: cf. Clément Marot, *Eglogue sur le Trépas de ma Dame Loyse de Savoye* (1531). Queen Louise of Savoy was the mother of King Francis I.

November

3 *to*: too.

5 *somewhat*: something.

7–8 Both Spenser and Marot imitate Virgil, *Eclogues*, 5. 10–11.

8 *Pan*: cf. *Januarye*, 17 and note.

12 *cocked*: arranged in conical heaps or cocks (hay-cocks).

15 *laye*: lair or couch.

17 *Thilke . . . aske*: this sullen season requires a sadder mood or state of mind.

21 *algate*: in any case (an archaic usage).

22 *vnderfong*: undertake.

24 *Relieue*: lift up or restore to use.

25–8 Cf. Marot, *Eglogue sur le Trépas*, 29–32.

25 *Nightingale*: cf. *August*, 183 and note.

26 *Titmose*: tomtit.

30 *han be*: have been.

35 *quill*: pipe.

37 *drent*: drowned. Virgil's Dido mounted her own funeral pyre and slew herself with Aeneas' sword (*Aeneid*, 4. 642–705).

41–6 Cf. Marot, *Eglogue sur le Trépas*, 37–44; Theocritus, *Idylls*, 1. 23–8.

42 *Cosset*: cf. E. K.'s gloss at [46].

43 *rownd . . . rufull*: full and doleful.

46 *Then*: than.

48 *contempt*: contemptuously disregarded, spurned.

50 *vaine*: poetic vein or style. Cf. *October*, 23.

51 *rugged*: harsh, lacking polish.

52 *strayne*: exert or stretch to the limit (with a play on the common phrase of 'straining' the voice by singing vigorously).

53–202 The fifteen stanzas of Colin's elegy have been related to the fifteen rungs of Jacob's ladder ascending from earth to heaven. Cf. Davies (1981).

60 *herse*: not merely the bier, but as E. K. notes, the obsequies themselves including the song 'rehearsed' or recited by Colin. Cf. *August*, 193; *RT*, 255.

71 *Breake . . . pypes*: a symbolic gesture. Cf. *Januarye*, 72.

76 *ygoe*: gone (an archaic form).

83–92 A common biblical and classical topos: cf. Job 14: 7–10; Moschus, *Idylls*, 3. 99–104; Marot, *Eglogue sur le Trépas*, 178–81.

87 *of . . . availe*: of most benefit or advantage.

91 *quaile*: fade, wither.

96 *cracknells*: light, crisp biscuits. Cf. *Januarye*, 58.
　chere: food.

99 *clouted*: clotted.

104 *dolors dint*: sorrow's stroke or blow.

105 *death . . . daunce*: alluding to the topos of the Dance of Death as illustrated, for example, by Holbein.

107 *blew . . . gray*: colours emblematic of life and hope are replaced by colours emblematic of death and bereavement. For gray cf. *August*, [66].

109 *embraue*: embellish, splendidly adorn.

115 *chiefe*: head of a flower.

116 *gilte Rosemaree*: either a special variety of 'golden' rosemary or ordinary rosemary adorned with gilt.

129 *tourne*: change.

131 *without remorse*: without remittance or intermission.

133–4 Cf. Marot, *Eglogue sur le Trépas*, 107–9.

135–7 Ibid., 118–21.

138–41 Ibid., 126–9.

138 *Turtle*: turtle dove, an emblem of love. Cf. *FQ*, 4. 8. 3–5.

141 *steepe*: bathe, soak. Cf. *March*, 116.

144–7 Cf. Marot, *Eglogue sur le Trépas*, 240–51; Virgil, *Eclogues*, 5. 20–21.

144 *Oliue*: an emblem of peace, cf. *Aprill*, 123–6, [124].

146 *bayes*: an emblem of poetry. Cf. *TW*, sonnet 7. 12 and note.

147 *Eldre*: black-berried elder. Elder was the tree upon which Judas was said to have hanged himself. The berries are bitter. Cf. *DLC*, 42.

153 *slipper*: slippery, unreliable.

155 *marked scope*: target.

158 *mould*: form or frame (cf. *FQ*, 2. 7. 42), playing on the alternative sense of earth or dust (from which the body is made and to which it must return).

163–72 For this technique of transition cf. Virgil, *Eclogues*, 5. 56–80.

167 *remorse*: remittance.

170–72 For the device of altering the pastoral refrain cf. Theocritus, *Idylls*, 1. 127; Moschus, *Idylls*, 3. 119–20.

175 *saintes*: those received into heavenly bliss.

184 *doome of*: judgement for.

185 *vntil*: unto.

186 *Dye . . . dayly*: cf. 1 Corinthians 15: 31.

   expert: experience (a rare usage).

187–9 Cf. Virgil, *Eclogues*, 5. 60–61; Marot, *Eglogue sur le Trépas*, 194–6, 202–3.

203–8 Cf. Marot, *Eglogue sur le Trépas*, 262–5, 270–78. Thenot's six-line coda adopts the rhyme pattern of *Januarye* (*ababcc*) and thus forms a link to *December*.

203 *francke*: generous or sincere. Cf. Marot's 'O franc Pasteur' (*Eglogue sur le Trépas*, 262).

204 *doolful pleasaunce*: mournful pleasure.

206 *gotte*: earned.

208 *mizzle*: drizzle.

210 *La . . . mord*: translated by E. K. as 'Death biteth not', this is Clément Marot's personal emblem as supplied in the 1539 edition of the *Œuvres*.

Gloss

[13] *Welked*: the term can also mean cause to fade or darken, cf. *Januarye*, 73 and note; *FQ*, 1. 1. 23.

[16] *Pisces*: a notorious crux. As the woodcuts make clear, the sun is in Sagittarius in November and Pisces in February. McLane (1961) suggests that the error is deliberate and intended to alert the reader to an allusion to the Catholic (fish-eating) Duc d'Alençon (pp. 53–4), in his capacity as Dauphin or 'dolphin'. Richardson (1989) reviews the astrological background and conjectures that the error reflects Colin's unbalanced state of mind although this hardly explains E. K.'s acquiescence (pp. 503–10). Brooks-Davies (1995) suggests that the allusion is not to the sign of Pisces but to the twelfth astrological house traditionally correlated with the sign of Pisces and the planet Venus (pp. 403–8). Confusion may have arisen from the equally problematic statement in Virgil's *Georgics* that the Pleiades set in November 'fleeing before the star of the watery fish' (4. 234–5) which Servius took as an allusion to the star known as the Southern Fish, sometimes alternatively identified with the Dolphin. Modern commentators regard it as an allusion to the sign of Pisces used loosely to designate the winter season. Cf. D. Cheney (1989); L. S. Johnson (1987).

pad: pannier, basket.

[21] *Virelaies*: cf. *Aprill*, [33] and note.

[30] *Castalias*: a fountain on Mount Parnassus sacred to Apollo and the Muses. Cf. Virgil, *Georgics*, 3. 291–3; *Aprill*, [42]; *VG*, 21–4 and notes.

[38] *Pan*: identified with Henry VIII at *Aprill*, [50]. The overt disclaimer may be intended both to suggest political allusion and render it safe. For Pan cf. *Januarye*, 17 and note.

[53] *Melpomene . . . boatu*: 'Melpomene proclaims dismal events in a resounding tragic voice'. Not in Virgil but Ausonius, *De Musarum Inventis*, 4. Cf. *Aprill*, [100] and note.

[55] *Hecuba . . . Seneca*: the gloss is confusing. The ghost of Polydorus appears in Euripides' *Hecuba* and that of Tantalus in Seneca's *Thyestes*.

[60] *obsequie*: ritual, rite.

[73] *Epanorthosis*: cf. *Januarye*, [61] and note.

[83] *A . . . maius*: 'From lesser to greater.'

[108] *as is vsed*: as is customary in.

[113] *Lobbin*: a possible allusion to the Earl of Leicester, represented as lamenting the symbolic 'death' of his queen. Cf. *CCH*, 735–6 and note.

[141] *Philomele*: cf. *August*, 183 and note.

sisters husbande: Tereus.

George Gaskin: George Gascoigne (?1525–77) to whose *Complaynt of Phylomene* E. K. refers. Spenser's allusion to the 'Titmose' at line 26 may be a direct borrowing (cf. *Phylomene*, 25–6).

[148] *fatall sisters*: cf. *FQ*, 4. 2. 47–8.

Herebus . . . Nighte: cf. Cicero, *De Natura Deorum*, 3. 17. 44; Comes, *Mythologiae*, 3. 12.

Clotho . . . occat: 'Clotho bears the distaff, Lachesis draws out the thread, Atropos cuts it' (*Anthologia Latina*, 729R).

[164] *Persephone*: an error for Tisiphone repeated at *TM*, 164. Cf. *VG*, 422–3 where the mistake apparently originated in Spenser's misreading of Virgil, *Culex*, 261–2. Persephone is properly Proserpina, spouse of Hades and queen of the underworld.

[179] *Elysian fieldes*: abode of the blessed in Virgil's underworld (cf. *Aeneid*, 6. 637–59, 743–7). By contrast, Virgil's unfortunate (*infelix*) Dido inhabits the Mourning Fields (6. 440–66). Spenser is punning on 'Elissa', the alternative name of Virgil's Dido, thereby consolidating a pattern of allusions to the 'Eliza' of *Aprill*. Cf. Marot, *Eglogue sur le Trépas*, 192.

[186] *Phædone*: cf. *Phaedo*, 61b–c where willingness to die characterizes the philosophical temperament.

[195] *Manna in scripture*: cf. Exodus 16: 4–35.

proper: appropriate, relevant.

Hebe: cupbearer to the gods. The source is unidentified.

dreames: not extant. According to *Letters*, Spenser intended to publish the work with both gloss and illustrations: 'I take best my *Dreames* shoulde come forth alone, being growen by meanes of the Glosse . . . full as great as my *Calendar*. Therin be some things excellently, and many things wittily discoursed of *E. K.* and the Pictures so singularly set forth, and purtrayed, as if *Michael Angelo* were there, he could (I think) nor amende the best, nor reprehende the worst' (cf. *Prose*, 18).

Emblem

trespasse . . . one: cf. 1 Corinthians 15: 21–2.

Chaucer: cf. the opening sentences of *The Parson's Tale* quoting Jeremiah 6: 16.

Death . . . all: cf. 1 Corinthians 15: 55.

December

Having composed an elegy for Dido in *November*, Colin now composes what is, in effect, an elegy for himself, evoking the collective resonances of the Narcissus myth associated with his *persona* throughout the *Calender* [cf. L. S. Johnson (1990), 109–14]. Because the final eclogue concludes 'euen as the first beganne' with 'a complaynte of Colin to God Pan', he has become his own 'echo', a figure locked in solipsistic dialogue with himself. The stanza form is that of *Januarye* and the season is again winter, but from Colin's viewpoint this structural circularity entails emotional entrapment. He therefore 'proportioneth his life to the foure seasons of the yeare' even though, as the calendrical form inevitably dictates, he is scarcely a year older than when he began. His premature apprehension of senescence functions as a potent metaphor for his emotional state: what he attributes to time is, paradoxically, the product of despondent immaturity.

As in *Januarye* the 'new Poete' is careful to distinguish his voice from that of Colin. The first stanza is spoken by an omniscient narrator, and E. K.'s comment upon Colin's missing 'embleme' transforms what might have been a despairing epitaph into a celebration of artistic achievement on a par with that of Horace and Ovid. Similarly the 'Epilogue' reverts to the first person singular of the opening 'envoy' to assert the triumph of art over time: 'Loe I haue made a Calender for euery yeare, / That steele in strength, and time in durance shall outweare'. From the viewpoint of the author structural circularity indicates completion. By composing twelve eclogues he looks beyond Virgil's pastoral achievement to the twelve books of the *Aeneid* anticipating his own progress from bucolic to heroic verse. His epilogue takes the form of a 'square poem' comprised of twelve lines of twelve syllables each because twelve is the Virgilian number of poetic perfection. In terms of quality his work has won a 'free passeporte' to posterity, but the issue of political 'ieopardee', raised in the 'envoy', remains unresolved. By invoking both Horace and Ovid, E. K. reminds us of the contrasting fortunes of these two Augustan poets, the one officially patronized, the other driven into exile. The author's assertion of achievement subtly fuses echoes of both, just as Colin's *Januarye* and *December* monologues evoke ironic reminiscences of both of the speakers of Virgil's first eclogue, the politically secure Tityrus and the victimized Meliboeus.

The mood of political anxiety is underscored by Spenser's use of his principal model, Clément Marot's *Eglogue au Roy soubz les noms de Pan et Robin*. In that poem, despite his experience of religious exile, and the dangers still attendant upon his position, Marot (Robin) imagines that Francis I (Pan) has heard his prayer for assistance (259–60). Colin, by contrast, is far less assured of the support of the 'shepheards God' – 'perdie God was he none' (50). Nowhere indeed is the distinction between the royal and the divine Pan so acute. In his companion piece, *La Complaincte d'un Pastoureau Chrestien*, in which Christ, and not the king, is addressed as Pan, Marot voices the distress of the dispossessed more overtly, but Spenser has combined both complaints in the one poem. Both Robin (205) and Colin (141–2) hang their pipes upon trees, but only Robin undertakes to retrieve the instrument and sing anew under royal protection (243–6) [cf. A. Patterson (1986)]. The *December* woodcut, contradicting the text, shows Colin's pipe lying broken at his feet [cf. Luborsky (1981)]. As so often in the *Calender*, Colin's personal discontent appears to serve as an index of national disquiet, but both are subject to structural qualification.

From Colin's perspective 'after Winter dreerie death does hast' (144), but the work's calendrical form implies otherwise. Not death but spring follows winter and, despite political opposition, Ovid has survived no less than Horace or Virgil. And Colin too is destined to survive both as a literary artefact and an enduring instrument of Spenser's complex self-reflection. Cf. Kennedy (1980); D. L. Miller (1979), (1983); Reamer (1969).

December

2 *brere*: briar.

7–12 Cf. Marot, *Eglogue au Roy soubz les noms de Pan et Robin*, 6–14 and *La Complaincte d'un Pastoureau Chrestien*, 28–40. For Pan cf. note to *Aprill*, [50].

8 *keepe*: care.

12 *Then*: than.

14 *Oaten reede*: cf. *October*, 8, [8] and note.

15 *sonet*: short lyric poem. Cf. Marot's 'chansonnettes', *Eglogue au Roy*, 12.

17 *greene cabinet*: Marot's 'verd cabinet' which anticipates the 'verte maison' of the court (*Eglogue au Roy*, 13, 259).

19–36 Cf. Marot, *Eglogue au Roy*, 15–32.

22 *doubted*: dreaded. Cf. *October*, 41.

25 *raunge*: wander at will.

27 *Pricket*: buck in its second year with straight, unbranched horns.

29 *wreaked*: recked, cared.

31 *craggie*: steep and rugged.

32 *All to*: just to.
   of: off.

37–40 Cf. Marot, *Eglogue au Roy*, 40–48; Virgil, *Eclogues*, 9. 32–4.

37 *for*: because.

39 *tomuch*: too much.

40 *Somedele ybent*: somewhat disposed.

41 *Wrenock*: possibly Richard Mulcaster (?1530–1611), headmaster of the Merchant Taylors' School and author of two influential treatises on education, *The Positions* (1581) and *The Elementarie* (1582). Marot, *Eglogue au Roy*, 49 pays similar tribute to his father, also a poet. The play on 'wren' continues the avian imagery associated with poetic endeavour.

45 *Hobbinol*: Gabriel Harvey. Cf. 'Epistle', 8; *September*, [176] and note.

51 *hurtlesse pleasaunce*: harmless pleasure.

53 *gaue me checkmate*: a popular love metaphor from chess.

60 *reigned . . . seate*: was ascendant in the astrological house of Venus.

63 *whether*: whither.

63–4 *vnbridled . . . bitte*: evoking the celebrated image of the passions as horses in Plato, *Phaedrus*, 246a–b, 253c–254e. Cf. *FQ*, 1. 1. 1.

68 *formall rowmes*: symmetrical combs.

70 *Paddocks*: toads, perhaps glancing at d'Alençon, cf. Adler (1981), 257.

72 *Owle*: for owls cf. Isaiah 34: 15; *June*, 24; *Epith*, 345 and note.
grieuous . . . keepe: makes her doleful dwelling.

73–8 Cf. Marot, *Eglogue au Roy*, 109–11.

81 *winding*: interwoven, wound.

83–90 Cf. Marot, *Eglogue au Roy*, 124–33.

85 *tryed time*: experience, greater maturity.

93 *ene*: one (an archaic form).

95–6 Cf. *Amor*, 25.

97–8 Cf. Marot, *Eglogue au Roy*, 199–202.

98 *to rathe*: too quickly.

102 *brakes*: bracken or briars.

105 *now at erst*: already.

106 *flattring*: delusively enticing or promising.

107 *mellow*: sweet and juicy.

118 *vnsoote*: unsweet.

119 *loser*: wanton.

120 *One*: Rosalind.

121–2 Cf. Virgil, *Eclogues*, 5. 35–7.

123 *sheaue*: sheaf.

124 *Cockel*: a weed prevalent in wheat crops. Cf. 'Let thistles grow instead of wheat, and cockel instead of barley' (Job 31: 40).

125 *fynd*: refined, winnowed.

127 *terme*: terminus, limit.

136 *myne . . . wright*: crowfeet (wrinkles) are drawn about my eyes. Colin himself has become a text, his lines 'written' by time.

141 Cf. Marot, *Eglogue au Roy*, 205, 243–6.

151–4 Cf. Theocritus, *Idylls*, 1. 115–18.

157 *Colins Embleme*: omitted in all editions. Hughes (1715) suggested 'Vivitur ingenio, caetera mortis erunt' ('His intellect endures, the rest is mortal') from *Elegiae in Maecenatem* (1. 38), falsely attributed to Virgil in the Dumaeus edition of 1542 which Spenser used for *VG*.

Gloss

[4] *Tityrus*: cf. 'Epistle', 5; *June*, 81–96 and notes.

[11] *Pan . . . magistros*: 'Pan cares for sheep and the keepers of sheep' (Virgil, *Eclogues*, 2. 33). Cf. Marot, *Eglogue au Roy*, 6–8.

[17–18] *Cabinet . . . diminutiues*: imitating Marot, *Eglogue au Roy*, 13–14.

[40] *Qui . . . musicam*: '[competition for the palm] is open to all who practise poetry' (Terence, *Phormio*, 'Prologue', 18).

[81] *leapes*: baskets.

[84] *Cauda . . . Draconis*: 'tail or head of the dragon'.

[84] *Theocritus*: cf. *Idylls*, 7. 52–3; 13. 25–6.

[87] *Liuie*: cf. Livy, *History of Rome*, 9. 36, but E. K.'s source is Cicero, *De Divinatione*, 1. 41. 92.

[88] *Dea . . . herbis*: 'The cruel goddess with potent herbs' (Virgil, *Aeneid*, 7. 19).

Emblem

Exegi . . . vorax: 'I have completed a monument more lasting than bronze . . . which neither rain nor the voracious North wind [can destroy]', misquoted from Horace, *Odes*, 3. 30. 1–3.

Grande . . . vetustas: 'I have completed a great work which neither the wrath of Jove, nor fire, nor sword, nor gnawing time can erode', misquoted from Ovid, *Metamorphoses*, 15. 871–2.

Epilogue *Loe I haue . . .*

The epilogue is symbolically cast as a 'square' poem comprised of twelve lines of twelve syllables each. Puttenham identified this 'quadrangle equilater' as 'the figure of most solliditie and stedfastnesse' and associated it with Aristotle's 'constant minded man euen egal [equal] and direct on all sides, and not easily ouerthrowne by euery litle aduersitie, *hominem quadratum*, a square man' (*Arte of English Poesie*, *ECE*, 2. 104). Together with the references to Horace and Ovid the device enforces the claims of artistic independence. For the significance of the number twelve cf. *TW*, sonnet 15. 9 and note.

4 *worlds dissolution*: end of the world.

5–6 *teach . . . keepe*: referring specifically to the 'moral' eclogues.

7–12 Cf. Chaucer, *Troilus and Criseyde*, 5. 1786–92.

7 *passeporte*: licence to travel, safe-conduct.

9 *Tityrus*: Virgil (and possibly Chaucer). Cf. 'Epistle', 5; *June*, 81–96 and notes.

10 *Pilgrim . . . Ploughman*: *The Plowman's Tale* was generally attributed to Chaucer ('the Pilgrim'), but E. K. may refer to Langland's *Piers Ploughman*.

11–12 Cf. Statius, *Thebaid*, 12. 816–19. It is notable that Statius' references to 'magnanimous Caesar' (814) are omitted.

13 *Merce . . . mercede*: the meaning is ambiguous, possibly 'For reward not hire' alluding to the conflict between political patronage and artistic independence. 'Grace not wages' is also possible implying that love, poetry and religion constitute their own reward [cf. Kennedy (1980)].

FROM *LETTERS (1580)*

The Spenser–Harvey correspondence was published in 1580 under two separate title-pages (only the first of which is reproduced in the present edition): *Three Proper, and wittie, familiar Letters: lately passed betwene two Vniuersitie men: touching the Earthquake in Aprill last, and our English refourmed Versifying. With the Preface of a wellwiller to them both* (containing the verses beginning 'See yee the blindefoulded pretie God' and 'That which I eate'), followed by *Two Other, very commendable Letters, of the same mens writing: both touching the foresaid Artificiall Versifying, and certain other Particulars: More lately deliuered vnto the Printe*r (containing 'Iambicum Trimetrum' and 'Ad Ornatissimum virum'). As the first three letters are ascribed to 1580 and the last two to 1579, the volume defies the normal expectations of epistolary chronology thereby appearing to corroborate the claim of unauthorized publication and intensifying the fiction of disclosed intimacy. The correspondence provides important information concerning Spenser's intellectual ethos, his attitude towards poetic language and metrics, and the nature of his relationships with Leicester, Sidney and Harvey. Despite disclaimers to the contrary, the letters were clearly intended, or at least edited, for publication and are best regarded as carefully crafted exercises in self-promotion. Cf. Goldberg (1992), 63–101; Quitslund (1996); Stern (1979).

Iambicum Trimetrum

In this poem Spenser attempts to demonstrate the application of classical quantitative metres to English versification following the rules 'that *M. Philip Sidney* gaue me, being the very same which *M. Drant* [i.e. Thomas Drant] deuised, but enlarged with *M. Sidneys* own iudgement, and augmented with my Obseruations' (cf. *Prose*, 16). The problem, as he recognized, was that the results often conflicted with the natural speech rhythms of the language. By way of solution he proposed a separate system of verse pronunciation, a proposal cogently dismissed by Harvey. Although the methods Spenser employed were ill-judged and quickly abandoned, the enterprise itself is characteristic of his determination to rival the ancients and possess 'the kingdome of our owne Language' (cf. *Prose*, 16, 473–5). For Harvey's specific criticisms of the metrics of 'Iambicum Trimetrum' cf. *Prose*, 442. For full discussions of the movement to reform English versification after the classical manner cf. Attridge (1974); Helgerson (1992), 25–40; S. Weiner (1982).

5 *boorde*: table.
6 *Virginals*: a form of spinet set in a case.

11 *appall*: sicken, enfeeble.
21 *Immerito*: Spenser's pseudonym from *SC*, 'Envoy', 'To His Booke'.

Ad Ornatissimum virum

Although the accompanying letter of 5 October 1579 was allegedly dis-
patched from Leicester House, and Spenser undertakes to travel abroad in
'his Honours service', there is no evidence that he left England at this time
and Harvey casts considerable doubt upon the enterprise: 'as for your
speedy and hasty trauell . . . you shall not, I saye, bee gone ouer Sea, for
al your saying, neither the next, nor the nexte week' (*Prose*, 444). The
poem, which adopts the form and style of a Horatian epistle, is best regarded
as an elaborate literary exercise adumbrating some of the major themes and
aspirations of Spenser's epic verse and exploring the conflict between virtue
and expediency. Cf. Rambus (1993), 17–19. The Latin is often obscure
and sometimes inaccurate but I suggest the following translation:

> To the most eminent Mr G. H., already distinguished by many honour-
> able titles, his friend Immerito, soon about to journey into Gaul, sends
> his best wishes.

[1–17] Thus a minor poet salutes a major poet, a not unfriendly poet salutes
a friendly bard, a new poet salutes an established master, and wishes him
fair weather on his return after many years abroad, fairer weather, indeed,
than he himself enjoys. Look how the god of the Sea – if he may truly be
deemed to be a god who incites the unwilling to crime and dissolves sworn
affections – gives me clear signs [of departure] and smoothes the oceans
through which my sail-bearing ship is soon to plough. And see, also, how
father Aeolus quells the mighty wrath of the North Wind. Everything is
ready for my journey: I alone am unprepared. For my affections, wounded
I know not how, have lately tossed about on perilous tides, as Love, that
potent pilot, drives the impotent prow this way and that. Reason with its
wiser counsels is distracted from the pursuit of immortal renown by Cupid's
swift bow. Tortured in this dilemma, I founder in the very port.

2 *nouus . . . Poëtam*: alluding to the 'newe Poete' of *SC*.
4 *reducem*: there is no evidence for Harvey's being abroad but he speaks of
a prospective trip to Italy. Cf. *Prose*, 444; Stern (1979), 176.
7 *Deus . . . Marinus*: Neptune, god of the sea.
9 *Æolus*: god of the winds (cf. Homer, *Odyssey*, 10. 1–27).
10 *Aquilonis*: the north wind.
12 *mens . . . vulnere*: the marriage of one 'Edmounde Spenser', probably
the poet, to Maccabaeus Chylde is recorded at St Margaret's Church,
Westminster on 27 October 1579.
16 *Cupidinis Arcu*: for Cupid's iconography cf. *SC*, *March*, [79]; *CCH*,
799–822 and notes.

[17–33] Loose these knots and I shall regard you – you who despise quiver-backed Cupid (and I beseech the gods not to allow you to enjoy such a reputation with impunity!) – as my great Apollo. Your noble spirit, I know full well, drives you to seek the highest honours and to handle weightier themes than those of trifling love – yet not all love is to be deemed inconsequential. Thus it is that you account nothing comparable to everlasting fame or to the hallowed image of such glory. All that the madding crowd adores – whether it be land, connections, real estate or money, or whatever pleases the eyes, such as beauties, pageants or amours, you trample underfoot like dirt, dismissing them as sensual delusions. Your philosophy is certainly worthy of the Harvey I admire, of the eloquent orator and the noble soul. It is a philosophy that the ancient Stoics would not fear to prescribe as eternally binding; yet all men's tastes are not alike.
20 *Apollo*: in his capacity as healer, to cure the malady of love. Cf. Virgil, *Eclogues*, 3. 104.

[34–46] It is said that the smooth-tongued son of decrepit Laertes, despite long exile on tempestuous seas, continually buffeted beneath strange skies, spurned immortality and the boudoirs of the gods for the embrace of his tearful wife. So great was the power of Love, and of a Woman mightier still than Love. But such is your loftiness of mind that you mock Ulysses also, and in comparison with the overshadowing image of such great glory and the renown born of true merit, you condemn all that the madding crowd admires whether it be land, connections, livestock, property, wealth or whatever pleases the eyes, such as beauties, pageants or amours, or whatever delights the taste or hearing.
34–8 *Dicitur . . . beatos*: Odysseus preferred his mortal wife Penelope to the nymph Calypso who offered him immortality. In Homer she addresses him as 'son of Laertes' (*Odyssey*, 5. 148–281).

[47–65] You are indeed sublimely wise, but wisdom is not common sense. The man who stoops to trivial follies often wins the palm from the supercilious sage. The sour tribe of Sophists derided Aristippus for speaking mild words to a purple-clad Tyrant, but he in turn ridiculed the empty doctrines of the Sophists who were tormented by the flitting shade of a gnat. Whoever has striven to please high-ranking men has studied folly, for thus does fortune favour fools. In summary, whoever desires to adorn his temples with garlands of laurel and to ingratiate himself in public favour, learns to play the fool, and solicits the base applause of inglorious folly. Although reputed to be the one wise man amongst a million fools, even father Ennius was praised for wildly pouring forth drunken ditties while deep in his cups. Nor, by your leave, may you, the Great Cato of our age, win the sacred name of honoured poet, however nobly you sing or however lofty be your song, unless you yield yourself to folly – the world is so full of fools!

47 *Sapor at sapientia*: distinguishing between the worldly wisdom needed to survive and the more abstract, uncompromising variety.

50–51 *Aristippum . . . Tyranno*: the precise anecdote is unidentified. Aristippus was often credited with founding the Cyrenaic school of philosophy noted for its hedonistic tendencies. Horace, however, credits him with a quick-witted sense of practicality (*Epistles*, 1. 17. 13–14), and Diogenes Laertius with the ability to adapt himself 'to place, time and person' (*Lives of the Eminent Philosophers*, 2. 8. 65, 68). The 'purple Tyrant' was Dionysius I of Syracuse.

53 *Culicis umbra*: possibly alluding to Socrates who described himself as a 'gadfly' sent by the gods to sting Athens out of its moral lethargy (cf. *Apology*, 30e–31a). His 'shade' continues to torment the Sophists.

59–61 *Ennius . . . vino*: cf. Horace, *Epistles*, 1. 19. 7–8. For wine as a source of poetic inspiration cf. *SC*, *October*, 103–14 and notes.

62 *Cato*: probably the famous censor, Marcus Porcius Cato (234–149 BC), renowned for the severity of his moral and social views.

65 *Stultorum . . . plena*: adapting Cicero's famous adage, 'stultorum plena sunt omnia', the world is full of fools (*Familiar Letters*, 9. 22. 4).

[66–77] The safest plan is to chart a mid-course through the abyss, for he alone may be accounted a sage who desires to seem neither too foolish nor too wise. On the one side you drown, on the other side you burn. Nor, if you are prudent, should you over zealously condemn luxuriant pleasures, nor a mistress finally won in marriage, nor the offer of gold – leave such pitiable sophistries to such poor chaps as the Curii and the Fabrii, the honour of their own age, but the scorn of ours – nor, on the other hand, should you seek such delights excessively. Both extremes are highly culpable. The man who understands this much (if any man understands so much) you may record, even though Socrates disagree, as the one wise man.

71 *Dominam*: Harvey refers to 'Domina Immerito, mea bellissima Collina Clouta' (Mistress Immerito, the charming Mrs Colin Clout). Cf. *Prose*, 476.

venientem in vota: probably intended as a double-entendre meaning either 'won in marriage' or 'brought to bed'.

72 *Curijs . . . Fabricijsque*: Manius Curius Dentatus and Gaius Fabricius Luscinus, jointly celebrated by Horace for their incorruptibility, were heroes of Rome's war with Pyrrhus (cf. *Odes*, 1. 12. 40–41).

[78–94] One virtue makes men religious, another makes them just, another gives them stout and steadfast hearts: but he wins every vote who blends utility with delight. Long ago the gods gave me the gift of delight but they have never given me the gift of being useful. Would that, even now, they had granted me the gift of being useful as well as the gift of pleasing! Oh would that the gods, to whom the greatest miracles are no more difficult than the least, might give me – unless they begrudge such happiness to mortals – the twin gifts of delight and utility at a stroke! But such is your good fortune that you enjoy the gifts of delight and utility in equal measure and whenever you please. But I, born under an inauspicious star, must seek my fortune from afar, across the desolate Caucasus, the mountainous Pyrenees, the foul terrain of Babylon, and if I do not find it there I must seek it still further off, wandering endlessly like the companions of Ulysses across the immense Ocean through the midst of the waves, following in the weary footsteps of the grieving goddess from whose search the earth concealed its glorious spoil.

80 *Omne . . . dulci*: quoted from Horace, *Art of Poetry*, 343.

83 *aequiualia*: Grosart suggests the emendation 'aequalia'.

88–9 *Caucasa . . . turpem*: doubtless humorous in view of the proposed trip 'in Gallias' (into France). 'Babilonaque turpem' probably refers to Rome, the 'new Babylon' of Protestant polemic. Cf. *TW*, sonnet 13. 14. For 'inhospita Caucasa' cf. Horace, *Odes*, 1. 22. 6–7.

90 *quaesitum*: Grosart suggests the emendation 'quaesitam'.

92 *Vlyssis*: using Ulysses as the archetypal wanderer.

93–4 *Deam . . . orbis*: alluding to Ceres' worldwide search for her daughter Proserpina, abducted by Pluto (cf. Ovid, *Metamorphoses*, 5. 438–571; *Daph*, 463–5 and note).

[95–117] For it is shameful for a young man, whose talents are not too ignoble, to lurk at home in the inglorious shadows, wasting his prime years in menial tasks, watching his promised harvest fail. Therefore I shall leave at once (who wishes me farewell?), and trek wearily across the precipitous Alps. But who, in my absence, will send you little letters seasoned with British dew, or wanton love songs? Beneath the peak of the Oebalian mountain my forsaken Muse shall endlessly lament the long periods of silence and weep because sacred Helicon has fallen dumb. And my dear Harvey (equally dear to one and all, and justly so, since he virtually surpasses all of them put together), my Angel and my Gabriel, though accompanied by innumerable friends and surrounded by a charmingly talented circle, will none the less inquire after Immerito, his one absent friend, and express the wish, 'Would that my Edmund had been here! He would have sent me news, and have confided his amours, and often with the kindest, heartfelt words have wished me well. May God guide him safely back at last etc.'

The Graces bid me say more, but the Muses are unwilling. Farewell, a fond farewell, my beloved Harvey, far dearer to my heart than any other.

103 *Oebalij . . . montis*: presumably Mount Vesuvius. Oebaldus was the grandson of Sebethus, the god of a river which flowed by Naples. Cf. Virgil, *Aeneid*, 7. 733–6.

108 *Angelus et Gabriel*: Gabriel was particularly auspicious because he announced the conception of Christ to the Virgin Mary (cf. Luke 1: 26–38).

111 *Edmundus*: a deliberate clue to the identity of 'Immerito'.
115 *Charites*: the Graces. Cf. *SC*, *Aprill*, [109] and note.
Musas: for the Muses cf. *SC*, *Aprill*, [41] and note.

From *Letter to Harvey* . . .

[1]
1 *God*: Cupid. Cf. note to 'Ad Ornatissimum virum', 16.

[2]
A couplet alleged to have been carved upon the tomb of King Sardanapalus of Syria, a notorious epicure (cf. Cicero, *Tusculan Disputations*, 5. 35. 101) and previously published in *SC*, *Maye*, [69]. For William Webbe's analysis of the metre cf. *A Discourse of English Poetrie* (1586), *ECE*, 1. 283–4.

COMPLAINTS

Complaint, like satire, is more properly regarded as a mode than a genre, but the nine separate works gathered together in Spenser's *Complaints* constitute an anthology of its major kinds, ranging from the conventionally disconsolate, rhetorically charged female complaints of *The Ruines of Time* and *The Teares of the Muses*, through the colloquial estates' satire of *Mother Hubberds Tale* and the playful mock-heroic lamentations of *Virgils Gnat* and *Muiopotmos*, to the ponderous despondency of Du Bellay's *Ruines of Rome* and the sombre reflections of the various visionary sequences with which the volume concludes. Inclusiveness, contrast and variety are the principles most evident in the selection of materials. Classical mythology is juxtaposed with medieval beast fable, massive ruins with butterflies, translations with original works. The diversity of verse forms is also remarkable: rhyme royal, ottava rima, heroic couplets, sextains, English, Petrarchan and Spenserian sonnets. Equally evident, however, is an underlying unity of concern. In his prefatory address to 'the *Gentle Reader*' the printer William Ponsonby notes that all of the pieces chosen for inclusion 'containe like matter of argument . . . being all complaints and meditations of the worlds vanitie'. He also indicates that publication was encouraged by the 'fauourable passage', or popular reception, of *The Faerie Queene* a year previously.

It would be ill-advised, however, to take Ponsonby's letter at face value given the disingenuous tactics employed in the publication of *The Shepheardes Calender* and the Spenser–Harvey *Letters*. Although it has recently been argued that Spenser played little or no part in the preparation of *Complaints* the evidence of the dedications to *The Ruines of Time*, *The Teares of the Muses*, *Mother Hubberds Tale* and *Muiopotmos* (all dignified by separate title-pages) argues otherwise [cf. Brink (1991)]. It is clear from the language employed that these dedications were written with a view to publication rather than private presentation. Thus Spenser speaks of 'eternizing' the fame of the Dudley family in *The Ruines of Time* and of making his affection for Lady Strange 'uniuersallie known to the world' in *The Teares of the Muses*. More pertinent still is the assertion that he has been 'mooued to set . . . foorth' *Mother Hubberds Tale* (a poem written 'long sithens') by his devotion to Lady Compton and Mountegle, 'setting forth' being the term Ponsonby uses for the publication of *The Faerie Queene*. Similarly, the dedication to *Muiopotmos* speaks of Spenser's intention 'to commend to the world this smal Poëme'.

Complaints was entered in the Stationers' Register on 29 December 1590 and published before 19 March 1591, and the most recent documentary evidence suggests that Spenser was in England during this period but that he left soon after as a result of the ensuing controversy [cf. Peterson (1997)]. Internal allusion indicates that *The Teares of the Muses* was revised as late as April 1590. The obvious inference is that Spenser fully co-operated with Ponsonby in capitalizing upon the interest aroused by the publication of his epic and wrote a series of new dedications for old materials with a view to imminent publication. There is no evidence that any of the works involved were prepared for publication on any other occasion, and corrections made to some copies at the proof stage may indicate authorial intervention although they cannot be taken as conclusive in themselves.

If Ponsonby's letter was intended as a safeguard against official reaction it failed conspicuously. Contemporary allusions by Harvey, Nashe and Robert Parsons indicate that passages in both *The Ruines of Time* and *Mother Hubberds Tale* were interpreted (correctly) as attacks upon Lord Burghley and his son Robert Cecil, and that attempts were made to have the volume called in, although the number of extant copies suggests that public curiosity largely frustrated such efforts [cf. Wells, *Allusions*, 24, 27]. It is noteworthy, however, that the volume was not republished until its incorporation in the first folio edition of Spenser's works in 1611 when (as the following notes indicate) significant alterations were made to *The Ruines of Time* and *Mother Hubberds Tale* was entirely omitted.

As the headnotes to the individual works point out, dates of composition are notoriously hard to determine. *Complaints* contains material dating from as early as 1569 to as late as 1590 and the problem is greatly complicated by the likelihood that works such as *Mother Hubberds Tale* (the concluding section of which may date from 1579–80) have undergone considerable revision prior to publication. What is clear, however, is Spenser's enduring concern with the course of public affairs, with the importance of patronage, and the association between the state of literature and the state of the nation. His complaints range from the minutely specific to the universal, from personal lampoon to spiritual anguish, but with little sense of disjunction or dislocation. Rather, personal emotions are articulated through skilful translations, ancient and modern anxieties coalesce and particular places serve, through their very specificity, as backdrops for limitless speculation. Nowhere is Spenser's imaginative enthusiasm for decay more evident than in his protests against it. Situated among the ruins of time, fallen heroes and dead butterflies, the various speakers find a vicarious consolation in the powerful energies of convention, an aesthetic pleasure in the artistry of complaint. Cf. P. Cheney (1993); Maclean (1978); Manley (1982); Nelson (1963); Peter (1956); H. Smith (1961); Stein (1934).

The Printer to the Gentle Reader

1 *late . . . foorth*: about a year previously. William Ponsonby published *FQ*, 1–3 early in 1590 and *Complaints* in the first quarter of 1591.
4 *accomplishment*: completion, fulfilment.
8 *departure*: probably referring to 1580 when he first went to Ireland, but possibly intended to create the impression that he had returned there in 1591 before the publication of *Comp*. Cf. the headnote.
10 *parcels*: pieces, items.
15–20 *Ecclesiastes . . . Psalmes*: not extant. The influence of Ecclesiastes is felt throughout Spenser's poetry in relation to the vanity of worldly aspiration, and the Song of Songs (Canticles) informs much of his mystical imagery. *A senights [seven nights] slumber* may be related to *My Slumber* alluded to, together with *The dying Pellican*, in *Letters* (cf. *Prose*, 6, 17). *The seuen Psalmes* was probably a translation of the seven penitential psalms (6, 32, 38, 51, 102, 130, 143), popular with English writers from Wyatt to Mary Sidney. For the 'lost poems' cf. *SpE*, 737–8.
24 *new Poet*: recalling E. K.'s dedicatory epistle to Harvey in *SC*.

The Ruines of Time

Central to the ethos of visionary complaint which informs *The Ruines of Time* is the complex relationship between its various speakers [cf. Rasmussen (1981)]. Verlame's 'doubtfull speach' (485) gives voice to an intensely enigmatic, and occasionally nightmarish, mentality preoccupied with the issue of mutability. She laments the destruction of Verulamium (1–175) and the deaths of Leicester and Sidney (176–343) as instances of the vanity of human wishes, yet hers is a 'sinfull' fallen world (44) and she is beset by 'greislie shades, such as doo haunt in hell' (125). Particularly insidious is her solipsistic obsession with the past: as an admirer of William Camden – and specifically of her own image in William Camden – she condemns herself to the temporal and spatial confinement from which she affects to desire release. Her future is a constant rehearsal of her past; her fame is inextricable from her fall.

In seeking to answer the crucial question of 'how can mortall immortalitie giue?' (413) Verlame places her faith in the endurance of poetry (344–469), as though speaking for the poet himself, or his *alter ego* Colin Clout (253–9), and reaffirming the commonplaces of contemporary humanism. Yet despite Spenser's undoubted interest in promoting the posthumous fame of his erstwhile patrons, the effect is to afford the reader a critical perspective on Verlame. Hers is not the city of God. Her days are merely 'earthlie daies' (312) and within the overall structure of the poem her perspective is shown to be limited and self-contradictory. The biblical resonance of her language ironically undermines her humanist idealism by mediating her highest sentiments through the admonitory diction of Ecclesiastes. In this respect her voice both echoes and parodies the lyricism of Psalm 137 by contriving to lament both the power and the fall of 'Babylon'. Not surprisingly, her utterance leaves the narrator in a state of 'anguish' and 'horror' (482–3), but affords little consolation. The six 'pageants' which appear spontaneously to his grieving mind, and are presumably to be regarded as symptoms of depression, illustrate the destruction of various wonders of the ancient world or their equivalents (491–574), and thereby seem to corroborate Verlame's world view, until an appropriately disembodied, Apocalyptic 'voyce' (580) points the way towards 'hope of heauen' (585) by conjuring up another series of pageants specifically intended as moral *exempla* (582). While they too insist upon the transience of worldly things in their emblematic representation of the death of Sir Philip Sidney, they also afford visions of transcendence through images of stellification or apotheosis (589–672). The poet is recognized to be as mortal as other men, but death opens the pathway to 'a second life' (669) and Pegasus flies to heaven (657–8). The value of human endeavour is hereby located not in its earthly endurance but in its spiritual worth. It is the 'spirite' that proves to be 'immortall' (673) and proper aspiration is directed towards God (685). As recorded by his friend Fulke Greville, Sidney's last words invited bystanders to observe in his death 'the end of this world with all her vanities' [cf. Greville (1986), 83].

As the number seven could be understood *both* as a symbol of permanence *and* of mutability [cf. Nelson (1961), 99; Fowler (1964), 58], the structure of the poem would seem to embody the ambivalence of its message in that seventy stanzas of rhyme royal (stanzas of seven lines rhyming *ababbcc*) are followed by two visionary sequences of seven sections apiece in the same format. While lamentable in themselves, the deaths of Sidney and Leicester had also robbed Spenser of his most influential patrons and the thinly veiled attacks on Lord Burghley, judiciously attributed to Verlame, reflect the frustration of very worldly ambition and lend the work a keenly topical edge (216–17, 447–53). Although the poem may contain sections of early material, particularly in the first of the emblematic sequences, the allusion to the death of Walsingham indicates that the text was revised as late as 6 April 1590 (435–41). As so often in the Spenserian canon, the most sublime of speculations are rooted in the anxieties, and the needs, of the moment. Cf. Cartmell (1985); DeNeef (1979); Herendeen (1981); Kerrigan (1991); MacLure (1973); Manley (1982); Nelson (1961), (1963); Orwen (1941); Satterthwaite (1960).

Dedication *To the right Noble . . .*

Marie . . . Pembrooke: Mary Sidney (1561–1621), sister to Sir Philip Sidney, married Henry Herbert, second Earl of Pembroke in 1577. Renowned as a patron of letters, she completed her brother's translation of the Psalms, oversaw the posthumous publication of his literary works and translated Mornay's *Discourse of Life and Death*, Garnier's *Antonius* and Petrarch's *Triumph of Death*. She is celebrated as Urania at *CCH*, 486–91.

3 *brother deceased*: Sir Philip Sidney died at Zutphen in 1586.
7 *spired*: put forth, produced.
8 *disdeigned . . . world*: deemed the world unworthy.
13 *late cumming*: probably in 1589.

The Ruines of Time

1 *on*: one.
2 *siluer streaming*: cf. *Proth*, 11. For the significance of the setting in relation to Psalm 137 cf. Cartmell (1985).
2–3 *Thamesis . . . yore*: the popular belief that the Thames once flowed by Verulamium was denied by Holinshed and Camden (*Chronicles*, 1. 323; *Britain*, 411). Cf. note to lines 148–54 below.
3 *Verlame*: the Roman city of Verulamium, close to St Albans.
5 *little moniment*: 'of the old compasse of the walles of Verolamium there is now small knowledge to be had by the ruines' (Holinshed, *Chronicles*, 1. 322). Cf. Camden, *Britain*, 408.
9 *Woman . . . wailing*: 'How doth the city sit solitary, that was full of people . . . She weepeth sore in the night' (Lamentations 1: 1–2). Cf. the city of Rome at *VB*, 127–40; *TW*, sonnet 8.
12 *railing*: gushing. Cf. Lamentations 1: 16.
13 *broken rod*: symbolic of lost authority.
17 *doubt*: am uncertain, unsure.
  fatall Impes: the Fates. Cf. *SC, November*, [148].

19 *Genius*: the 'genius loci' or spirit of the place. Cf. Virgil, *Aeneid*, 5. 95; 7. 136. For Genius in general cf. Comes, *Mythologiae*, 4. 3.

20–21 *perplexed . . . vexed*: with biblical connotations. Cf. *VP*, 26 and note.

36–42 Verulamium was 'a citie infranchised and indued with Roman priuileges' rather than a mere colony, cf. Holinshed, *Chronicles*, 1. 322.

36 *garland wore*: as a sign of pre-eminence.

41 *that I was*: what I was.

45 *first . . . date*: from birth to death, beginning to end.

47 *ingate*: entrance. For the 'gates' of birth and death cf. *FQ*. 3. 6. 31–2.

48–9 *woomb . . . toomb*: a common conceit, cf. Genesis 3: 19.

56 *vapour . . . decaie*: cf. James 4: 14.

59–63 The traditional 'ubi sunt' ('where are they now?') topos.

63 *raine*: reign, dominion (the Roman *imperium*).

64–70 Cf. Daniel 7: 3–7. The Geneva Bible identifies the lion with Assyria, the bear with Persia and the leopard with Alexander the Great. Cf. *TW*, sonnet 12. 4–5 and note. Cf. Rasmussen (1981), 161.

65 *footing*: footprints, trace.

70 *whelps*: the officers who partitioned Alexander's empire, collectively known as the Diadochi ('Successors').

71 *seuen . . . beast*: conflating the beast of Daniel 7: 7 with the seven-headed beast of Revelation 13: 1–2 commonly interpreted as Rome. Cf. *TW*, sonnet 13; *VB*, 103–6 and notes.

74 *in . . . necke*: i.e. as though harnessing them.

80 *equall*: in the sense of well disposed, equalling Rome's success.

85–98 'If I were disposed . . . to reckon up what great store of Romane peeces of coine, how many cast images of gold and silver, how many vessels, what a sort of modules or Chapters of pillars . . . have beene digged up, my words would not carry credit: The thing is so incredible' (Camden, *Britain*, 411). Cf. Holinshed, *Chronicles*, 1. 322–3.

96 *imageries*: carved figures, statuary. Cf. *VG*, 103.

98 *rust*: corrosion.

102 *Troynouant*: for London as the new Troy founded by the Trojan Brutus cf. *FQ*, 3. 9. 33–51.

103 *my . . . bee*: Verulamium was 'not onlie nothing inferior to London it selfe, but rather preferred before it' (Holinshed, *Chronicles*, 1. 321).

104 *Pendragon*: Uther Pendragon, father of King Arthur. Camden records his 'seven yeeres siege' (*Britain*, 412).

106 *Bunduca*: Boudica, queen of the Iceni whose revolt against Rome was crushed in AD 61. Her career is celebrated at *FQ*, 2. 10. 54–6.

112 *foyld . . . assailed*: history has been altered for rhetorical effect. Tacitus, Holinshed and Camden all record the fall of Verulamium to the Britons (*Annals*, 14. 33; *Britain*, 409; *Chronicles*, 1. 499).

114 *Saxons*: as recorded in Camden, *Britain*, 410.

116 *prizde . . . Generall*: taken as a prize at the cost of the general's life.

123 *turnd to smoake*: cf. Isaiah 51: 6.

130 *Shriche-owle*: screech owls, regarded as harbingers of death. Cf. Isaiah 34: 15; *FQ*, I. 9. 33. Cf. *SC*, *June*, 24; *Epith*, 345 and notes.

131 *Nightingale*: cf. *SC*, *August*, 183; *November*, [141] and notes.

133 *Mewes*: gulls.

Plouers: wading birds such as lapwings.

135 *channell*: i.e. course.

140 *moorish*: marshy.

148–54 Holinshed records how workmen digging in the ruins 'happened oftentimes upon Lempet shels, peeces of rustie anchors, and keeles of great vessels, whereupon some by and by gathered that either the Thames or some arme of the sea did beat upon that towne' (*Chronicles*, I. 323).

151 *lake*: in the uncommon sense of river or stream of water (*OED*).

157 *no . . . mone*: no one else does mourn.

158 *dolefull dreriment*: gloomy sadness or melancholy.

168 *true-seeming sort*: in truthful and fitting fashion.

169 *Cambden*: William Camden (1551–1623), headmaster of Westminster School, Clarenceux King-of-Arms, and celebrated antiquary. *Britannia*, the chorographical study to which Verlame alludes, appeared in 1586 and the *Annales*, a history of Queen Elizabeth's reign, in 1615.

176 *wight*: person, but often applied, as here, to spectres or ghosts.

184 *mightie Prince*: Robert Dudley, Earl of Leicester, died in 1588.

renowmed race: *Letters* refers to an unpublished poem entitled *Stemmata Dudleiana*, a celebration of Leicester's family (cf. *Prose*, 18), some of which may be incorporated here.

188 *Sate . . . bosome*: enjoyed the confidence of, or was on terms of intimacy with.

189 *Right . . . loyall*: a translation of Leicester's motto, 'Droict et Loyal'.

190 *I . . . die*: rhetorical exaggeration. Leicester died at Cornbury Lodge in Oxfordshire, not in St Albans.

191 *meane . . . beare*: Leicester's funeral was both costly and magnificent.

196 *Requiem*: originally a Roman Catholic mass for the repose of the soul, but here presumably referring to the Anglican funeral rites.

199 *halfe happie*: an ironic belittlement.

202 *courting masker*: i.e. fawning actor.

louteth: bows.

204 *oaker*: ochre, mineral of clay and ferric oxide used as a pigment.

212 Cf. Matthew 6: 19–20 on laying up treasures in heaven.

213 *come . . . dread*: what he dreaded has come to pass.

214 *now dead*: now that he (Leicester) is dead.

vpbraid: decry, criticize.

215 *baid*: bayed, barked.

216–17 *Foxe . . . Badger*: 'The foxe doth fight with the Brocke [badger] for dens, and defileth the Brockes den with his urine and with his dirte' (Stephen Bateman, *Batman upon Bartholome* (1582), 385). Leicester's death benefited his arch-rival William Cecil, Lord Burghley (1520–98), figured here as the fox. The insult is considerable.

219 *vapoured*: evaporated, dissipated into vapour.

223 *reuiue*: restore to life (by celebrating his memory).

226 *vp to raise*: i.e. to play.

230 *quite*: acquit, clear. Verlame accuses Spenser of the dereliction of duty to which he admits in the dedication.

233 *bounteous . . . trie*: experienced his liberal disposition.

236 *applie*: contribute.

239 *his brother*: Ambrose Dudley, first Earl of Warwick, died in 1590.

244 *dearest Dame*: Anne Russell, daughter of Francis Russell, second Earl of Bedford. She is one of the two dedicatees of *FH*. Cf. *CCH*, 492–503 and note.

260 *his sister*: Mary Dudley, sister of the Earl of Leicester, wife of Sir Henry Sidney and mother of Sir Philip Sidney, died in 1586.

thy father: Francis Russell, second Earl of Bedford, died in 1585.

266 *his sonne*: actually his grandson, Edward Russell, third Earl of Bedford, as the following line makes clear.

268 *Vnder . . . countenaunce*: sheltered under your protection.

272 *Impe*: offspring, child.

273 *count . . . Countie*: i.e. value wisdom more than your lands.

274 *husbands sister*: Mary Dudley (as at line 260).

279 *sacred brood*: Sir Philip Sidney.

281 *gentle spirite*: Sidney.

breathed . . . aboue: cf. *TM*, 361.

282 *bosome . . . blis*: applied to Christ at *HHL*, 134 and here implying a comparison with Christ elaborated at lines 297–301.

284 *natiue propertis*: natural (pure) conditions.

289 *influence*: flowing in, like the influence of the stars.

291 *too soone*: Sidney died from battle wounds at the age of thirty-two.

natiue place: heaven, completing the Neoplatonic notion of descent into matter and return to the world of spirit implicit at lines 281–2.

296 *goale*: jail.

298 *bodie . . . sacrifise*: cf. Romans 12: 1.

301 *life exchanging*: giving his life in exchange.

305 *cumbrous*: troublesome, oppressive.

317 *thine . . . sister*: Mary Sidney, Countess of Pembroke.

318–22 *sings . . . anoy*: *DLC* published with *Ast* in 1595 purports to be by Mary Sidney.

324 *valiance*: courage, heroism.

325–9 Celebrating Sidney's *Arcadia* first published in 1590.

330–36 Socrates was reputed to regard the company of poets as among the principal delights of the afterlife. Cf. Plato, *Apology*, 41a.

332 *Elisian fields*: cf. *SC*, *November*, [179] and note.

333 *Orpheus*: the archetypal vatic poet, cf. *SC*, *October*, [28] and note.

   Linus: credited with teaching Orpheus. Cf. Virgil, *Eclogues*, 6. 67–73.

349 *rustie*: in the sense of corroding or spoiling.

354 *mortall hous*: the body. Cf. *FQ*, 2. 9. 17–58.

356 *breath . . . nostrels*: cf. Isaiah 2: 22.

358–71 A classical topos, cf. Theocritus, *Idylls*, 16; Horace, *Odes*, 4. 8, 9.

361 *sponge*: pieces of moist sponge were used to erase writing.

368–9 *daughters . . . Ioue*: cf. *SC*, *June*, 66 and note; Boccaccio, *Genealogia*, 11. 2.

369 *father of eternitie*: as the dispenser of fame and immortality. Cf. Boccaccio, *Genealogia*, 11. 1.

373 *Proserpina*: consort of Hades, and queen of the underworld.

374–6 *power . . . day*: as in the case of Orpheus and Eurydice at lines 391–2, but perhaps also recalling Christ's (more successful) harrowing of hell.

379–82 *brood . . . spirite*: in Seneca's *Hercules Oetaeus* the hero, in agony from the poisoned shirt of Nessus, burns himself to death on Mount Oeta but reappears to his mother Alcmena as an immortal (1758–1996). Cf. Ovid, *Metamorphoses*, 9. 229–72.

380 *golden girt*: said of Hippolyta in Seneca, *Hercules Furens*, 543.

384–5 *Hebes . . . Paramoure*: Hebe, daughter of Hera and Zeus, was given as a bride to Hercules after his apotheosis (Hesiod, *Theogony*, 950–95; Homer, *Odyssey*, 11. 601–4). She was often allegorized as the perpetual life, or fame, accruing to heroism (Boccaccio, *Genealogia*, 9. 2.) Cf. *HL*, 283; *Epith*, 405 and notes.

386–9 *Ledaes . . . orient*: Castor and Pollux, the Dioscuri, were twin sons of Leda but only Pollux was born immortal. On Castor's death Pollux was granted permission to share immortality with his brother by the expedient of their spending alternate days in Hades and on Olympus. Cf. Virgil, *Aeneid*, 6. 121–2; Ovid, *Fasti*, 5. 693–720; *Proth*, 42–4, 173 and notes.

389 *orient*: ascending or rising.

391 *Orpheus . . . Eurydice*: cf. *SC*, *October*, [28] and note.

394 *Pierian . . . sisters*: the Muses, alluding to their haunt of Pieria in Thessaly. Cf. Virgil, *Eclogues*, 8. 63.

395 *impacable*: that cannot be pacified, implacable.

399 *Nectar . . . Ambrosia*: divine food and drink. Cf. *SC*, *November*, [195].

402 *numbers*: metre.

407–13 Poetry's superiority to architecture is noted by Du Bellay, *La Défence et Illustration de la Langue Francoyse*, 2. 5.

408 *aspired*: lifted up, elevated.

408–14 *Pyramides . . . wonder*: the Pyramids, the Colossus of Rhodes and the Tomb of Mausolus at Halicarnassus were among the seven wonders of the ancient world. 'Brasen Pillours' and 'Shrines' may allude to two others, the temple of Artemis at Ephesus and the Statue of Zeus at Olympia. Cf. lines 491–546 below; *RR*, 15–28 and notes.

410 *fired*: destroyed by fire.

411 *metall . . . desired*: gold. Cf. *VB*, 34.

413 *mortal . . . giue*: for a provocative reply cf. *Amor*, 75. 5–8.

416 *Marcellus*: several temples were struck by lightning when the Roman consul Marcellus (271–208 BC) attempted to dedicate a temple inappropriately to two gods (cf. Plutarch, *Life of Marcellus*, 28).

417 *Lisippus*: Lysippus, ancient Greek sculptor, famed for a colossal statue of Hercules at Sicyon, and numerous depictions of Alexander the Great.

418 *Edmond . . . gaine*: Camden deplores Henry VIII's suppression of the monastery at Bury St Edmunds for material gain (*Britain*, 461).

421–4 *fame . . . away*: adapting Virgil's description of rumour at *Aeneid*, 4. 173–7.

426 *Pegasus*: the winged horse commonly employed as a symbol of poetic inspiration. Its hoof struck Mount Helicon thereby producing the spring Hippocrene frequented by the Muses. Cf. Ovid, *Metamorphoses*, 5. 250–68.

428–9 *Lethe . . . Thetis*: Thetis bathed her son Achilles in the River Styx, but the mistake is ironically appropriate since Lethe is the river of oblivion. Cf. *SC*, *March*, [97].

430 *blinde bard*: Homer.

431 *Castalie*: a fountain on Mount Parnassus. Cf. Boccaccio, *Genealogia*, 10. 27; *SC*, *November*, [30] and note.

432 *Easterne Conquerour*: Alexander the Great. Cf. Du Bellay, *La Défence et Illustration de la Langue Francoyse*, 2. 5; *SC*, *October*, [65] and note.

436 *Melibæ . . . Poet*: Sir Francis Walsingham, the Secretary of State, died in April 1590 and Thomas Watson published his commemorative *Meliboeus* in Latin together with an English version, *An Eglogue upon the death of the Right Honourable Sir Francis Walsingham*. Spenser included a dedicatory sonnet to Walsingham in *FQ* (1590) comparing him to Maecenas. He complimented Watson on his *Amyntas* at *FQ*, 3. 6. 45. Watson urged Spenser to console the Queen for Walsingham's death (*An Eglogue*, 371–410).

442–4 *two . . . Salomon*: 'There be two things that grieve mine heart . . . a man of war that suffereth poverty; and men of understanding that are not set by' (Ecclesiasticus 26: 28). The book was commonly attributed to Solomon.

447 *he . . . will*: probably Lord Burghley, cf. headnote. The Textual

Apparatus lists a series of revisions made to lines 447–55 in the folio edition of 1611 in order to eliminate personal allusions to Burghley.

452–5 Reversing the fable of the oak and the briar at *SC*, *Februarie*, 102–238.

457 *ouerkest*: overcast (in the sense of obscuring perception).

458 *see . . . confusion*: realize that they are on the road to destruction.

460 *infest*: molest, harass.

477–90 Cf. *VW*, 1–14.

485 *muzing at*: pondering or reflecting upon.

doubtfull: ambiguous, cryptic.

488 *demonstration*: illustration, manifestation.

490 *Pageants*: the following visions may preserve material from Spenser's lost 'Dreames'. Cf. *SC*, *November*, [195] and note. E. K. refers to Spenser's 'Pageaunts' (possibly a separate work) at *June*, [25].

491 *Image*: combining allusions to the Statue of Zeus at Olympia, one of four wonders of the ancient world alluded to in pageants 1–4, with reminiscences of the colossal idol set up in Daniel 3: 1–11.

496 *Assyrian tyrant*: Nebuchadnezzar II who captured Jerusalem in 586 BC.

497 *holie brethren*: Shadrach, Meshach and Abednego defied the king and were miraculously preserved in the fiery furnace (cf. Daniel 3: 12–30).

498 *staid*: stood.

499 *brickle*: brittle, weak. For the idol's feet of clay cf. Daniel 2: 33–5.

504 *dearelie*: deeply, grievously.

505 *Towre*: possibly resembling the Pharos lighthouse at Alexandria.

508 *sandie ground*: cf. Matthew 7: 26–7; *FQ*, 1. 4. 5 (the House of Pride).

509 *great Towre*: the Tower of Babel (cf. Genesis 11: 4–9).

511 *Ninus*: Nimus, founder of Nineveh, was frequently confused with Nimrod who built Babel. Cf. *FQ*, 2. 9. 21.

514 *flit*: in the sense of vanish away or perish.

517 *dust*: 'dust thou art, and unto dust shalt thou return' (Genesis 3: 19).

519 *Paradize*: combining allusions to the hanging gardens of Babylon, and accounts of the 'fools' paradise'. Cf. *VB*, 155–68.

523–5 *Merlin . . . Belphœbe*: no such incident occurs in extant versions of *FQ*, but cf. the 'earthly Paradize' to which Belphoebe takes Timias, Prince Arthur's squire (3. 5. 39–40).

525 *staine*: obscure its lustre, eclipse.

533–9 *Giaunt . . . boast*: combining allusions to the Colossus of Rhodes, popularly believed to have straddled the harbour entrance (as at lines 540–41), with the biblical Goliath (cf. 1 Samuel 17: 4–51).

547 *Bridge*: recalling Xerxes' bridge over the Hellespont which collapsed in a storm (cf. Herodotus, 7. 33–5; Lucan, *Pharsalia*, 672–7).

551 *Traian*: the Emperor Trajan's bridge over the Danube (cf. Dio Cassius, *History*, 68. 13).

553 *equall vewing*: i.e. to the impartial observer.

561 *two Beares*: the Earls of Leicester and Warwick, from the white bear on the Dudley family crest. Cf. *SC, October*, 48, [47] and note to line 616 below.

575–88 Cf. *VB*, 1–14 and notes.

577 *bereaued quight*: utterly bereft of power.

580–81 *voyce . . . appalled*: with Apocalyptic overtones (cf. Revelation 8: 13).

583 *vanitie . . . minde*: cf. Ecclesiastes 1: 14.

590 *Swan*: Sir Philip Sidney. Cf. *SC, October*, [90] and note.

593 *Strimonian*: the swans of River Strymon in Thrace lament the death of the poet Bion at Moschus, *Idylls*, 3. 14–18.

598 *fit*: playing on the dual senses of musical 'fit' (or strain) and of paroxysm. The swan's song heralds its death throes.

601 *signe*: the constellation Cygnus.

604–8 *Harpe . . . lead*: Orpheus' harp continues to sound after his death as it floats midstream at Ovid, *Metamorphoses*, 11. 50–53.

603 *Lee*: a tributary of the Thames (cf. *Proth*, 38). If no specific reference is intended 'lee' may simply mean meadow (lea).

607 *Dan*: a title of honour employed by Chaucer.

609 *Philisides*: star-lover, Sidney's pastoral *persona* in *Arcadia*.

611 *diuin'd*: made divine.

612 *heauenly noyse*: suggesting apotheosis, cf. Revelation 19: 6–7; *FQ*, 1. 12. 39.

613 *strings . . . wind*: like an Aeolian harp, blending nature and art.

615 *signe*: the constellation Lyra (for the stellification of Orpheus' harp cf. Comes, *Mythologiae*, 7. 14).

616 *Harpe . . . Beare*: suggesting the celestial reunion of Sidney and Leicester (figured here as the constellation of the Great Bear). Cf. note to line 561 above.

618 *Coffer*: possibly Sidney's coffin, or his ship, *The Black Pinnace*, in which his remains were brought home for burial. At lines 621–8 it recalls Noah's ark (and the ark of the covenant), an emblem of salvation.

629 *starre*: possibly the constellation Argo, the stellified ship which contained the Golden Fleece ('heauenly treasures'). Philisides or Astrophil, the star-lover, has himself become a star.

631–44 These lines employ the imagery of the mystical union of the soul (the virgin) with Christ (the bridegroom). Cf. Song of Songs, passim; Revelation 19: 7–9.

633 *be red*: be taken.

646–51 *Knight . . . gras*: the death of the knight-poet Sidney at Zutphen.

646 *winged steed*: Pegasus. Cf. note to line 426 above.

647 *Medusaes blood*: cf. Ovid, *Metamorphoses*, 4. 765–86.

648 *Perseus . . . seed*: Perseus was the son of Zeus by Danaë.

649 *Andromeda*: cf. Ovid, *Metamorphoses*, 4. 670–764.

657 *heauen . . . bore*: alluding to the constellations of Pegasus and Perseus.

659–72 Cf. *TW*, sonnet 3; *VB*, 29–42.

659 *Arke . . . golde*: vessel or urn, recalling the ark of the covenant which held the 'testimony' of God (Exodus 25: 10–16).

661 *ashes . . . hold*: Sidney's remains.

663 *glorifie*: praise.

665 *Whether . . . those*: which of those.

666 *wing footed*: Ovid's 'alipes' (cf. *Metamorphoses*, 4. 756; 11. 312).

Mercurie: appropriate both as the god who leads souls to the underworld and the patron of eloquence and learning.

680 *faire Ladie*: Mary Sidney, Countess of Pembroke.

684–6 Cf. *HB*, 43–9.

The Teares of the Muses

The poem borrows its title and format from *Smithus, vel Lachrymae Musarum* (1578), Gabriel Harvey's elegy on the death of Sir Thomas Smith which is praised in the gloss to the September eclogue of *The Shepheardes Calender* [176]. The six-line stanza, rhyming *ababcc*, is identical to that of the *Januarye* and *December* eclogues, and is therefore associated with Spenserian moods of dejection and complaint. The Muses are represented in traditional fashion not merely as patrons of the arts but as the supreme repositories and conduits of 'Sapience' (135), anticipating the importance of that theme in *An Hymne of Heavenly Beautie* [cf. Bennett (1932)]. Their lament encompasses not just the decline in aristocratic patronage and the denial of poets' honourable 'meed' (453) or financial 'fee' (471) but, as in Du Bellay's *La Musagnoeomachie*, the apparent triumph of 'vgly Barbarisme' (187) and 'ignorance, the enemie of grace' (497). Viewed from this perspective the lamentable state of the arts functions as an index of the degeneration of the race (436) for which a 'discipline of vice' (336) has supplanted 'heauenlie discipline' (518). Both society and the arts are perceived to lack 'due Decorum' (214), and heroic verse is deemed impossible in a land unfit for heroes (439–50). The decline of poetry is both cause and symptom of the prevalent malaise. Images of alienation and exile, akin to those regularly associated with Colin Clout, are frequent, and the Muses' vocabulary is infused with echoes of biblical lament.

The starkness of the presentation, which some critics deem inapplicable to the cultural landscape of the 1590s, has given rise to the suggestion that the poem must date from an earlier decade. The internal evidence is inconclusive, however, and the conventions of the form demand stylistic hyperbole and artistic hauteur: the 'true' devotees of the Muses were traditionally regarded as few and exclusive [cf. Snare (1969)]. The conspicuous praise of Queen Elizabeth, from whom Spenser had recently received an annual pension of fifty pounds, as both poet and patron (571–82) is doubtless intended to arouse a desire for emulation among her courtiers while obliquely castigating the current lack of courtly patronage also deplored in *Colin Clouts Come Home Againe* [cf. Fox (1995)].

Like Colin Clout, the Muses end by breaking their 'learned instruments' in frustration (599), but the poem itself is carefully structured as a counter example to the culture of decay. With the exception of Euterpe, each of the Muses utters nine stanzas of complaint and the narrator begins with nine stanzas of introduction, the number nine being commonly regarded as symbolic of the soul and intellect [cf. Fowler (1964), 274]. Euterpe's additional stanza allows for a clear break at line 300, the exact centre of the poem, with five speakers accommodated in each half. As 'Eulogies turne into Elegies' (372) the structural coherence of the form lends ironic authority to the vision of decline. Cf. Roche (1989b); Stein (1934).

Dedication *To the right honorable . . .*

Ladie Strange: Alice Spencer, daughter of Sir John Spencer of Althorp and wife to Ferdinando Stanley, Lord Strange, fifth Earl of Derby. She is celebrated in *CCH* as 'sweet Amaryllis' (540, 564–71). Milton's *Arcades* was written for her and *A Maske presented at Ludlow Castle* for her stepson (and son-in-law), the Earl of Bridgewater.

8 *bands of affinitie*: for Spenser's claims of kinship to the Spencers of Althorp cf. the dedications to *MHT* and *Muiop*; *CCH*, 536–9; *Proth*, 130–31.

The Teares of the Muses

1 *Sisters nine*: the portrayal of the Muses is indebted to Ausonius, *De Musarum Inventis*, attributed to Virgil in the Dumaeus edition of 1542 which Spenser used for *VG*. Cf. *SC*, *Aprill*, [100]; *November*, [53] and notes. The Muses' order of appearance follows that of Ausonius.

2 *Apolloes*: for Apollo as father of the Muses cf. *SC*, *Aprill*, [41]; *June*, 66 and note; Snare (1969), 49.

5 *Helicone*: for Helicon as a spring rather than a mountain cf. *SC*, *Aprill*, [42] and note.

7 *Phœbus . . . sonne*: Phaeton, son of Apollo, attempted to drive the chariot of the sun and was destroyed by Zeus in order to save the world from incineration. Cf. Ovid, *Metamorphoses*, 2. 1–328; *VG*, 197–200. The myth is used as an *exemplum* of pride at *FQ*, 1. 4. 9.

8 *Ythundered*: (was) killed by a thunderbolt.

10 *compasse . . . path*: beyond the appointed pathway traced by the Zodiac.

13–15 *Calliope . . . Palici*: the mythology is confused. Calliope mourned for her poet son Orpheus. The nymph Thalia (distinct from the Muse of the same name) was the mother of the Palici, two minor rural deities. Cf. Macrobius, *Saturnalia*, 5. 19. 15–31 (commenting on Virgil, *Aeneid*, 9. 585).

16 *fatall Sisters*: the three Fates. Cf. *SC, November*, [148].

28 *consorts*: harmony of several voices (here of the elements).

54a *Clio*: properly the Muse of history, but as the recorder of heroic deeds her province overlaps with that of Calliope, the Muse of epic poetry.

57–8 *Castalie . . . Parnasse*: cf. *SC, Aprill*, [42]; *November*, [30] and notes.

70 *type*: acme or summit.

72 *Despise . . . Sapience*: 'whoso despiseth wisdom . . . is miserable . . . and their works unprofitable' (Wisdom 3: 11). For sapience cf. *HHB*, 183–287.

73 *sectaries*: adherents, followers.

75–8 Cf. *RT*, 452–3 and note.

75 *Impes*: shoots or saplings.

77 *vnderkeep*: suppress.

89 *God . . . praised*: cf. Proverbs 8: 22–31.

94 *Armes*: heraldic coats of arms.

112 *humour*: moisture.

114a *Melpomene*: the Muse of tragedy. Cf. Horace, *Odes*, 1. 24. 2–4.

115–16 *powre . . . dryde*: cf. Jeremiah 9: 1.

117–19 *brasen . . . sides*: cf. Virgil, *Aeneid*, 6. 625–7; Ovid, *Tristia*, 1. 5. 53–4.

126 *vassals . . . sin*: cf. John 8: 34; Ephesians 2: 3; 2 Peter 2: 19.

127–30 A classical topos, cf. Virgil, *Georgics*, 2. 490–92.

128 *vnderstanding*: 'Wisdom is the principal thing; therefore get wisdom: and with all thy getting get understanding' (Proverbs 4: 7).

130 *freakes*: capricious changes.

133 *patience*: ability to endure suffering (Latin *patientia*).

134 *throwes*: thrustings. Cf. *FQ*, 2. 5. 9.

142 *helme . . . sway*: a common Spenserian image, cf. *FQ*, 2. 7. 1.

143 *euent*: fate.

144 *intendiment*: understanding.

145–6 *foolish . . . riches*: cf. Proverbs 3: 13–15; Wisdom 8: 5.

152 *buskin*: cf. *SC, October*, [113] and note.

160 *Trophees*: triumphal memorials often decked, as the following line suggests, with the spoils of victory.

164 *Megera*: Megaera, one of the three Furies.

Persephone: queen of the underworld. Cf. *SC, November*, [164] and note.

173 *next in rew*: next in line, but playing on 'rue', grief.

174a *Thalia*: the Muse of comedy. In *Letters* Harvey reminds Spenser of his '*Nine Comoedies* . . . to which you giue the names of the *Nine Muses*' and compares them favourably with those of Ariosto (cf. *Prose*, 471).

176 *sock*: cf. *SC, October*, [113] and note.

180 *Graces*: cf. *SC, Aprill*, [109] and note.

184 *roome*: place.

187–8 Influenced by Erasmus's colloquy, *Conflictus Thaliae et Barbariae.*

188–90 *Ignorance . . . bredd*: 'The Ignorance of mortals, which is the Night of the mind, is the parent and nurse of nearly all the calamities that afflict human beings' (Comes, *Mythologiae*, 3. 12). Cf. Lotspeich (1942), 72.

192 *Scene*: stage (Latin *scaena*).

   disguize: disfigure.

194 *vulgare entertaine*: cf. 'odi profanum vulgus et arceo [I hate the profane mob and keep aloof from them]', Horace, *Odes*, 3. 1. 1.

197 *Counterfesaunce*: counterfeiting (i.e. dramatic personation).

198 *Delight . . . Laughter*: Sidney advises that 'the end of the comicall part bee not upon such scornefull matters as stirreth laughter onely, but mixt with it, that delightful teaching which is the end of Poesie' (*Apology for Poetry, ECE*, 1. 200).

202 *limned*: portrayed, depicted.

205–6 *Nature . . . imitate*: the popular notion of drama as an imitation of life (or mimesis) found in Aristotle's *Poetics* and Donatus' commentary on Terence.

206 *mock*: in the combined senses of ridicule and imitate.

207 *kindly . . . shade*: good natured, or lifelike, counterfeiting or imitation by way of mimicry or play-acting.

208 *Willy*: unidentified, but possibly Sidney who died in 1586. His 'Lady of May' might qualify him for honourable mention by Thalia.

211–16 Cf. *SC, October*, 73–8.

214 *Decorum*: rhetorical theory of generic and stylistic propriety.

217 *gentle Spirit*: unidentified.

222 *sell*: deliver up.

226 *losels*: worthless people, good-for-nothings.

232 *breaches . . . supply*: filled the pauses between her sobs.

234a *Euterpe*: properly Muse of flute music, but endowed with the reed pipe in Ausonius' *De Musarum Inventis*, and consequently taken here for the Muse of pastoral poetry. Cf. note to line 1 above.

236 *Philomele*: the nightingale. Cf. *SC, August*, 183 and note.

238 *diuers*: various.

244 *charmes*: songs (Latin *carmina*). Cf. *Ast*, 46 and note.

253–64 Cf. Du Bellay, *La Musagnoeomachie*, 37–44.

256 *Cymerians*: in Homer the Cimmerians live in total darkness at the margins of the earth (*Odyssey*, 11. 14–16). Cf. *VG*, 370.

259–63 *Ignorance . . . Night*: cf. note to lines 188–90 above.

264 *Syre . . . brother*: incestuous distortion of familial relationships is frequently employed as a metaphor for intellectual or spiritual confusion.

265–82 *He . . . hard*: cf. *TW*, sonnet 10; *VB*, 155–66.

268 *Faunes . . . Satyres*: cf. *VB*, 166 and note.

raced: razed, demolished.

271 *horsefoot Helicon*: mistaking Helicon for Hippocrene. Cf. note to *RT*, 426.

273 *Castalion*: cf. *SC*, *Aprill*, [42] and note.

283 *Shriekowles*: screech owls were regarded as ill-omened. Cf. *TW*, sonnet 6. 13; *SC*, *June*, 24; *RT*, 130 and notes.

285 *Eccho*: for the myth of Echo cf. *SC*, *June*, 52 and note.

300a *Terpsichore*: properly the Muse of dance, but here championing the moral value of true art against its abusers. Cf. Boccaccio, *Genealogia*, 11. 2; *MHT*, 809–38; *CCH*, 775–94.

303 *Feareles*: not fearing.

308 *bosome . . . sit*: cf. John 1: 18.

309 *virgin Queenes*: an oblique compliment to Queen Elizabeth.

315–18 Cf. the note to line 264 above.

322 *ranke*: combining the senses of fecund and gross.

327 *schooles*: seats of learning, universities.

336 *discipline of vice*: thereby subverting the moral purpose of art. Cf. Sidney, *Apology for Poetry*, *ECE*, 1. 178–80.

340 *discountenaunce*: show disapproval or disfavour towards.

346 *compassion*: pity, sympathize with.

353 *pittilesse*: unpitied.

360a *Erato*: Muse of the lyre, here taken as the patron of love poetry (cf. Plato, *Phaedrus*, 259d). Her name was etymologically associated with Eros. The lofty conception of love suggests Platonic influence, but the emphasis on possession of the loved one (365) effects an accommodation of the physical to the spiritual akin to the notion of married chastity in *FQ*, 3.

361 *gentle Spirits*: cf. *RT*, 281 where Sidney is among them.

breathing: expressing, uttering. They breathe forth what has been breathed into them (or 'inspired') from above.

362 *Venus . . . bred*: cf. the 'pleasant arbour' of Venus and Adonis where Cupid is reconciled to Psyche, *FQ*, 3. 6. 43–52.

365–6 Cf. *HL*, 273–9.

370 *compasse*: circumference, circle.

389 *bosome . . . nests*: cf. *RT*, 282 and note.

392 *cannot gesse*: cannot even form a conjecture of.

395 *at riot*: without restraint or artistic control.

396 *what . . . behoue*: what is fitting or proper for it.

397 *Cytheree*: Venus, reputedly born on the island of Cythera.

398 *maist go pack*: depart with her belongings, a colloquial phrase designed to create a mock-heroic tone.

401 *gay Sonne*: Cupid.

402 *ruffed*: ruffled.

403 *three Twins*: the three Graces, cf. *SC*, *Aprill*, [109] and note. 'Twins' was not infrequently used for triplets at this period.

406 *Aggrate*: please, gratify.

410 *Court or Schoole*: the two natural centres of poetic learning.

412 *lent to*: granted to, bestowed upon.

420a *Calliope*: Muse of epic poetry, but in Spenser her function overlaps with that of Clio. Cf. *SC*, *Aprill*, [100].

429–30 *off-spring . . . fill*: the heroes of Greek mythology were usually descendants of the gods.

433–44 Cf. *RT*, 449–55.

433 *rust*: in the sense of corrosion.

447 *Irus*: a beggarly messenger in Homer's *Odyssey* (18. 1–116), here used as a type of lowly insignificance.

Inachus: an Argive king, often cited as a type of high birth and prestige. Cf. Horace, *Odes*, 2. 3. 21–4; *FQ*, 4. 11. 15.

461 *Bacchus . . . Hercules*: Bacchus was renowned for his conquest of the East and Hercules for his twelve labours. They were both deified for their devotion to justice. Cf. Horace, *Odes*, 3. 3. 9–15; *FQ*, 5. 1. 2.

462 *Charlemaine*: Charlemagne, king of the Franks, and emperor of the West (742–814), together with his twelve Paladins, was the subject of countless *chansons de geste*. The constellation of Charles's Wain (the Plough) is so called from a corruption of his name.

Starris seauen: the seven bodies of the solar system then known.

463 *Clarion*: trumpet.

466 *prize of value*: an ambiguous phrase, possibly 'proof of valour'.

480a *Vrania*: the Muse of astronomy, here Christianized, as was customary in Renaissance classical dictionaries, as the Muse of heavenly knowledge. In Plato she is patroness of philosophers (cf. *Phaedrus*, 259d), but by emphasizing her contemplative nature Spenser makes her akin, if not quite identical, to Sapience (*HHB*, 183–301). He may have been influenced by Du Bartas's *Uranie* (1574) to which he alludes at *RR*, 459–60.

481 *influence*: the astrological term for the operation of stellar force (literally a 'flowing in' of stellar fluid).

489 *ornaments of wisdome*: 'For there is a golden ornament upon her [learning], and her bands are purple lace' (Ecclesiasticus 6: 30). As the 'ornaments' of learning the poets too are 'bereft'.

495 *loadstarre*: guiding star (often the pole-star).

499–510 Cf. *HHB*, 22–105.

503 *knowledge . . . knowe*: the adage 'know thyself' was central to Renaissance philosophy. Cf. Sir John Davies, *Nosce Teipsum* (1599).

506 *Christall firmament*: the crystalline sphere or ninth heaven, located between the primum mobile and the sphere of fixed stars. Cf. *HHB*, 41.

507 *great Hierarchie*: the ascending order of the eight spheres leading ultimately to God.

509 *Spirites . . . Intelligences*: the spheres were imagined to possess conscious souls or 'intelligences' which were sometimes identified with the Muses. Cf. Macrobius, *Somnium Scipionis*, 2. 3; Heninger (1977), 136–8.

520 *schoole*: schooling, discipline.

530 *would . . . breed*: would generate for them.

531 *loathsome den*: reminiscent of the Platonic 'cave' in which the unenlightened dwell in ignorance (cf. *Republic*, 7. 514a–516a).

532 *ghostly*: spiritual.

540a *Polyhymnia*: the Muse of rhetoric, who laments the lack of artistic discipline in contemporary writing. Cf. *Aprill*, [100] and note.

542 *curious complements*: ingenious (stylistic) formalities.

549 *Diapase*: diapason or octave, often used figuratively for concord or harmony. Cf. Heninger (1977), 132–40.

553–8 Sidney complains of 'a confused masse of words, with a tingling sound of ryme, barely accompanied with reason' (*Apology for Poetry*, *ECE*, 1. 196).

553 *vphoorded*: hoarded or heaped up.

556 *intelligence*: understanding.

558 *fantasie*: the intellectual faculty which creates and associates images. Without the government of reason it borders on lunacy. Cf. *FQ*, 2. 9. 49–52.

559–64 The sacred origin of poetry was a Renaissance commonplace. Cf. Puttenham, *Arte of English Poesie*, *ECE*, 2. 6–10.

566–7 *prophaned . . . vulgar*: cf. note to line 194 above.

571 *One onelie*: Queen Elizabeth I.

572 *myrrour . . . maiestie*: as the earthly reflection of divine monarchy. Cf. *SC*, *October*, 93 and note.

576 For Elizabeth's contemporary reputation as a poet cf. Puttenham, *Arte of English Poesie*, *ECE*, 2. 66; *CCH*, 188–91.

578 *Pandora*: the name means 'all gifts', but the sinister associations of Pandora, created by Jove to plague mankind, are hard to eradicate. Cf. Comes, *Mythologiae*, 2. 6; 4. 6; *RR*, 260; *Amor*, 24. 8 and notes.

579 *Diuine Elisa*: cf. *SC*, *Aprill*, 34.

586 *influence*: comparing the queen's effect to that of the stars. Cf. the note to line 481 above.

590 *Acorns*: the traditional food of primitive man. Cf. *VG*, 206–8.

599 *breake*: a symbolic gesture, cf. *SC*, *Januarye*, 72.
600 *louing*: amended to 'living' in the first folio (1611).

Virgils Gnat

Preoccupation with deciphering the hidden meaning signalled in the prefatory sonnet has long obscured the wider thematic concerns and artistic claims of *Virgils Gnat*. Most influential has been the suggestion that Spenser, in the *persona* of the gnat, laments his relegation – for real or imagined offences – to the 'waste wildernesse' of Ireland (369). This would place the date of composition around 1580 but there is no corroboratory evidence and an appointment as private secretary to the Lord Deputy of Ireland might well have been regarded as an act of patronage rather than punishment. By the time of publication Leicester was dead (1588), but the issue of patronage was still very pressing. Because the *Culex*, of which Spenser's poem is largely an amplified translation, was attributed to Virgil, its opening address to the future emperor Augustus could be taken to exemplify the ideal relationship between prince and poet, a relationship founded on reciprocal support and respect. By contrast, the dedicatory sonnet to *Virgils Gnat* functions to cast the translator as an Ovidian 'outcast' (330), a victim of official neglect rather than a Virgilian laureate. The translation may thus be seen to develop the themes of cultural alienation and aesthetic decline explored in *The Ruines of Time* and *The Teares of the Muses* by insinuating that the patron's obligation to promote the poet's fame is no less compelling than the poet's duty to celebrate his sponsor (57–64, 687–8). The concluding couplet is replete with proleptic irony: Spenser's own grave was fated to lack a fitting monument for many years.

While Spenser generally sticks close to the original text (as printed in Dumaeus's edition of 1542), the transformation of Virgil's unrhymed hexameters into stanzas of *ottava rima* (rhyming *abababcc*) has the effect of increasing the total length from 414 to 688 lines. Descriptive adjectives are frequently expanded into whole phrases, the mock-heroic ethos of the narrative is reinforced, and the voice of the gnat is rendered characteristically Spenserian in its concern for 'vanitie' and 'mutabilitie' (559–60), predominant themes of *Complaints*. Indeed throughout the translation generally the Virgilian world view is deftly appropriated to the Spenserian. Thus, for example, 'naiads' become 'fairies' (179), Orpheus becomes 'Dan *Orpheus*' (180) and Spenser's favourite adjectives abound. The beauty of the pastoral setting is severely compromised by dark mythological allusions (e.g. 171–6) and the 'huge great Serpent' takes on a Satanic demeanour (250–64), an effect powerfully enhanced by the sombre vocabulary chosen to render the gnat's descent to the classical underworld, here significantly translated as 'hell' (e.g. 462, 475). Even the mistranslations identified in the notes (e.g. 169–74, 200–206) seem to be informed by Spenser's pervasive interests since moral interpretation invariably compensates for defective comprehension. Whatever private meaning Leicester may have found in the poem, its aesthetic significance does not depend upon our ability to 'glose vpon' such covert allusions. Rather, the act of publication lends public resonance to private complaint, and serves to illustrate the complex social and political uses of classical translation. Cf. Adler (1981); Brink (1996); Greenlaw (1932); Heninger (1987); Lotspeich (1935); D. L. Miller (1983); Mounts (1952); Rosenberg (1955); Van Dorsten (1981).

Dedication *Long since dedicated . . .*

Leicester: Robert Dudley, Earl of Leicester, died in 1588. Cf. *SC*, *March*, [20]; *October* [47]; *RT*, 184 and notes.

1–14 *Wrong'd . . . knowen*: A Spenserian sonnet (rhyming *ababbcbccdcdee*) which suggests the presence of a cryptic meaning in *VG*.

3 *clowdie teares*: tears that cloud the eyes.

5 *Oedipus*: mentioned for having solved the riddle of the sphinx.

6 *diuining*: prophetic, with second sight.

10 *glose vpon*: comment upon, interpret.

Virgils Gnat

1–64 Translating the *recusatio* of *Culex* (1–41) which makes a formal denial of epic intentions, and thereby establishing an appropriately ironic context for the mock-heroic ethos of the poem proper.

1 *Augustus*: first emperor of Rome (63 BC–AD 14), but addressed as Octavius in *Culex*, being still a boy ('puer') at the alleged time of dedication, hence Spenser's 'sacred childe' at lines 37 and 54.

2 *tender Muse*: identified in *Culex* as Thalia, the Muse of comedy, and appropriate, despite the tone of complaint, to the mock-heroic ethos.

3 *cobweb*: a mistranslation. *Culex* refers to the weaving of little spiders ('araneoli', *Culex*, 2). Cf. note to *Muiop*, 385.

5 *history*: narrative, tale.

11 *bigger notes*: loftier, epic strains ('graviore sono', *Culex*, 8). Cf. *SC*, *October*, 46 and note.

allure: poetry's power to move the emotions was regarded as crucial to its nature. Cf. Sidney, *Apology for Poetry*, *ECE*, 1. 171.

13 *Latona*: mother by Jove of Apollo and Diana. Cf. *FQ*, 2. 12. 13.

14 *ornament*: most illustrious.

15 *Phœbus*: Apollo, god of poetry and father of the Muses.

16 *harp*: Apollo's seven-stringed lyre was taken to symbolize the harmony of the spheres. Cf. Heninger (1977), 136–8.

18 *Poets Prince*: in *Culex* the 'princeps' is Apollo himself, but the ambiguity may be intended as an oblique compliment to Elizabeth I, celebrated as a poet at *TM*, 571–6; *CCH*, 188–91.

19 *Xanthus . . . blood*: Bellerophon slew Chimera, a hybrid monster, part lion, part dragon and part goat, on the banks of the River Xanthus.

20 *Astery*: the island of Delos, birthplace of Apollo. Asteria, daughter of the Titan Coeus, hurled herself into the sea off its shores.

21–3 *Parnasse . . . Castaly*: cf. *SC, Aprill*, [42].

21 *brood*: nesting place, home.

22 *forhead . . . hornes*: the two peaks of Parnassus, rising above Delphi, between which flows the stream of Castalia.

26 *Pierian streames*: streams of Pieria in Thessaly sacred to the Muses.

Naiades: properly water nymphs but here identified with the Muses (cf. Virgil, *Eclogues*, 10. 10–12).

28 *Adorne*: honour with their presence ('celebrate', *Culex*, 19).

Pales: Roman goddess of agriculture and fertility. Cf. Ovid, *Fasti*, 4. 722–4.

30 *successe*: succession.

33 *Professing*: declaring belief in, acknowledging allegiance to.

40 *Giants . . . Phlegræan*: Jove fought the Giants on the plain of Phlegra in Macedonia. Cf. *FQ*, 5. 7. 10.

41–2 *Centaures . . . Lapithaes*: conflict broke out between the Centaurs and Lapiths at the marriage of Pirithous and Hippodamia when the Centaur Eurytus attempted to rape the bride. Cf. Ovid, *Metamorphoses*, 12. 210–535; *FQ*, 4. 1. 23. For the bestial nature of Centaurs cf. Comes, *Mythologiae*, 7. 4.

42 *at bord*: at the (wedding) table.

43–50 Herodotus recounts how Xerxes burned the Acropolis (8. 53), dug a canal across the isthmus between Athos and the Greek mainland (7. 22–5), and madly attempted to fetter the sea (7. 35). Cf. *RT*, 547 and note.

46 *abord*: across, an unusual usage with a play on 'aboard'.

48 *renowne*: make famous, celebrate.

49 *Hellespont*: the Dardanelles.

65 *hight*: high.

66 *each where*: everywhere.

67 *Charet*: chariot.

68 *Aurora*: goddess of the dawn.

heare: hair.

75 *ment*: mixed or mingled.

82 *brouze*: browse upon.

84 *stud*: stem. Cf. *SC, March*, 13.

86 *chaw*: chew.

89–152 The traditional topos of the happy pastoral life. Cf. Virgil, *Georgics*, 2. 458–540; *FQ*, 6. 9. 19–33.

94 *macerate*: vex, fret or waste.

99 *vnderlayes*: underlies.

100 *summer beames*: supporting beams, rafters.

104 *Bætus . . . Alcons*: ancient Greek engravers. For Boethus cf. Pliny, *Natural History*, 33. 55. 55.

105 *whelky*: formed in shells ('conchea baca', *Culex*, 68).

108 *display*: stretch out ('prosternit', *Culex*, 69).

111 *from*: away from, free from.

119 *neate*: sparkling bright, pure.

123 *greedy riches*: the transferred epithet from *Culex*, 81, 'avidas . . . opes'.

124 *warlick*: warlike.

133 *Panchæa*: Panchaia, an Arabian district famed for frankincense.

139 *flow*: abound.

141 *resolu'd*: relaxed.

145 *Faunes*: translating 'Panes' (Pans), *Culex*, 94. The woodland god Faunus was often identified with Pan. For Faunus cf. *FQ*, 7. 6. 42–50.

146 *Tempe*: a celebrated valley in Thessaly.

  countrey Nymphs: dryads or wood nymphs.

149 *Ascræan bard*: the Greek poet Hesiod, author of *Works and Days* and the *Theogony*, born in Ascra in Boeotia.

152 *turmoyle*: vex, trouble.

154 *batt*: staff.

156 *Hyperion*: Apollo, the sun god.

158 *world*: the heavens ('aetherio . . . mundo', *Culex*, 102).

162 *draue*: drove.

163 *cærule*: sky-blue.

164 *goord*: gourd. The comparison is Spenser's own.

169–70 The awkward syntax mirrors that of *Culex*, 111–14. The sense is 'soon he saw them placed in the sacred wood to which . . .'

170 *Delian Goddesse*: Diana, goddess of woodlands, born on Delos.

171–2 *bad . . . Agaue*: Agave, daughter of Cadmus, tore her son Pentheus to pieces during frenzied Bacchic rites. Cf. Ovid, *Metamorphoses*, 3. 710–33.

173 *king Nictileus*: Spenser's translation is mistaken. Nyctelius is properly a name for Bacchus.

178 *Dryades*: dryads or wood nymphs.

179 *Fairies*: for 'Naiadum coetu' (band of water nymphs), *Culex*, 117.

180 *Dan Orpheus*: for 'Dan' as a title of honour cf. *RT*, 607. For Orpheus cf. *SC*, October, [28] and note.

181 *Hebrus*: a river in Thrace stopped by the music of Orpheus.

183 *Peneus*: a river of Thessaly flowing through Tempe, not mentioned in *Culex*. Cf. *Proth*, 78.

190–224 Cf. the catalogue of trees at *FQ*, 1. 1. 8–9.

190 *Palme trees*: for 'platinus' (plane trees), *Culex*, 124.

193 *Lotos*: the lotus flower induced an intoxicating lethargy in Ulysses' companions (Homer, *Odyssey*, 9. 92–104).

196 *stay*: detained.

198 *Sunnes . . . daughters*: the Heliades, daughters of Apollo and sisters of Phaeton, lamented their brother's death so grievously that they were transformed into poplars. Cf. Ovid, *Metamorphoses*, 2. 340–66.

199 *Phaeton*: cf. *TM*, 7 and note.

201–3 Thinking herself deserted by Theseus' son, Demophoon, his lover Phyllis died of grief and was transformed into an almond tree. Spenser mistranslates 'cui' (to whom) as 'in which' (*Culex*, 131), thereby excluding Phyllis and suggesting that Demophoon was transformed.

204–5 *Oke . . . charmes*: supposing this to be another case of metamorphosis, Spenser misinterprets an allusion to the oracular Dodonian oaks. Cf. *TW*, sonnet 5. 1 and note.

206 *Acornes . . . foode*: cf. *TM*, 590 and note.

207–8 Upon the restoration of her daughter Proserpina, Ceres, goddess of agriculture, supplied Triptolemus with grain and instructed him to spread the gift among his fellow men. Cf. Ovid, *Metamorphoses*, 5. 642–61.

210–11 *Argoan . . . signe*: the Argo, in which Jason sought the Golden Fleece, was transformed into the constellation Argo. Cf. *RT*, 629 and note.

215 *Holme*: the holm-oak ('ilicis . . . nigrae', *Culex*, 140).

219–20 *Poplar . . . strokes*: in *Culex* the ivy binds the arms of the poplars to prevent the Heliades' grief from turning to self-mutilation (141–2). The translation is confused and appears to blend the 'strokes' suffered by Phaeton in his fall with those of his sisters.

221 *lythe*: pliant, supple.

223–4 *Myrtle . . . reproach*: Myrsine, a priestess of Venus, was transformed into a myrtle to keep her from a lover. Cf. Servius, *Commentarii* (*Aeneid*, 3. 23). *Culex* mentions her fate not her 'reproach' (145), and Spenser may have confused her with the incestuous Myrrha who was transformed into a myrrh tree. Cf. Ovid, *Metamorphoses*, 10. 488–502.

225 *embowring*: nesting, lodging.

229 *frogs*: cf. *Epith*, 349 and note.

   scowring: scum, dirt.

232 *Echo*: cf. *SC*, *June*, 52 and note.

237 *stocke*: livestock.

242 *dispredd*: spread out.

250 *pide*: blotched, mottled.

251 *trace*: move (leaving his trace or track in his wake).

254 *brandisht*: vibrating (and on display).

   gride: pierce. Cf. *SC*, *Februarie*, [4] and note.

255 *boughts*: coils, folds.

259 *proud vaunt*: arrogant bearing or demeanour.

265 *dispace*: move (a Spenserian coinage). Cf. *Muiop*, 250.

268 *grand*: huge. It is the snake that is huge ('ingens') in *Culex*, 174.

280 *outstrained*: outstretched.

281 *at point*: fittingly, suitably.

309 *slowth*: sloth (playing on the previous 'slowe').

310 *ghastly*: in the sense of aghast.

311 *blent . . . sense*: cheated or deceived his senses.

313–14 *night . . . Herebus*: Night was sister and wife of Erebus, god of darkness.

315 *Vesper*: Hesperus, the evening star.

316 *Oeta*: a mountain range in Thessaly. Cf. Virgil, *Eclogues*, 8. 30.

324 *Image*: spectre ('effigies', *Culex*, 208).

333 *in lieu*: in reward or recompense.

338 *Lethes*: the river of oblivion in the underworld, but Charon is more usually associated with the Styx. Cf. *RT*, 428 and note.

339 *spoyld of*: seized by, carried off by.

   Charon: son of Night and Erebus, ferryman of the River Styx.

342 *Tisiphone*: one of the three Furies.

345 *Cerberus*: three-headed dog that guarded the entrance to Hades.

348 *cralling*: crawling.

357 *piteous*: compassionate.

359–60 For the departure of Astraea, goddess of justice, from the earth cf. *MHT*, 1–4; *Daph*, 218 and note.

364 *render*: given in return.

368 *relent*: mitigate, soften.

369 *waste wildernesse*: possibly alluding to Spenser's departure to Ireland in 1580. Cf. *FQ*, dedicatory sonnets to Grey and Ormond.

370 *Cymerian shades*: infernal darkness. Cf. *TM*, 256 and note.

373–5 *Othos . . . Ephialtes*: the twin sons of the giant Aloeus who tried to tear down the heavens and overthrow Jove. Cf. Virgil, *Aeneid*, 6. 582–4.

374 *inuades*: enters into, penetrates.

377–8 *Tityus . . . Latona*: Tityos, a giant son of Jove, was slain by Apollo for offering violence to Latona, Apollo's mother. Cf. Virgil, *Aeneid*, 6. 595–600.

385–8 Tantalus revealed ('did . . . bewray') the banquets of the gods by stealing divine food and giving it to mortals. Cf. *HL*, 200 and note; *FQ*, 2. 7. 57–60.

389–92 Sisyphus was condemned to the perpetually frustrated task of rolling a stone up a hill. The suggestion that he was punished for refusing to pray is Spenser's own. Cf. Ovid, *Metamorphoses*, 4. 460; *FQ*, 1. 5. 35.

393 *damosells*: when forced to wed their cousins all but one of the fifty Danaides slew them on the wedding night and were condemned to fill a bottomless cistern with water from sieves. Cf. Ovid, *Metamorphoses*, 4. 462–3; 10. 44.

394 *Erynnis*: a Fury. Cf. *RR*, 327. (Erinyes is the collective name for the Furies.)

    tynde: lit, kindled.

395 *Hymen*: the god of marriage.

397 *Colchid mother*: Medea, a native of Colchis, slew her children to revenge herself on her husband Jason. Cf. Seneca, *Medea*.

401–5 *Pandionian . . . Lapwing*: Philomela and Procne, daughters of King Pandion of Athens, killed Itys, the son of King Tereus of Thrace, to gain revenge for Tereus' brutal rape of Philomela. She was transformed into a nightingale, Procne into a swallow and Tereus into a hoopoe (*epos*). Cf. Ovid, *Metamorphoses*, 6. 424–674. Arthur Golding translated *epos* (674) as 'lapwing' in his version of 1565–7. Cf. *SC*, *November*, [141].

409 *Cadmus blood*: Eteocles and Polynices, sons of Oedipus and descendants of Cadmus, contested the sovereignty of Thebes.

421 *Elisian plaine*: abode of the blest in the underworld. Cf. *SC*, *November*, 179 and note.

422 *Persephone*: Proserpina, queen of Hades, mistaken by Spenser for one of the Furies. Cf. *TM*, 164 and note.

423 *fellow Furies*: 'comites heroidas' (heroine throng), *Culex*, 261.

425 *Alceste*: Alcestis chose to die in place of her husband Admetus who had offended the goddess Artemis.

430 Penelope remained true to the absent Odysseus despite pressure to remarry from a throng of unwanted suitors. Cf. *Amor*, 23. 1–4 and notes.

431 *rulesse*: either pitiless (rueless) or unruly (ruleless).

433–80 For Orpheus and Eurydice cf. *SC*, *October*, [28] and note.

435 *looking back*: her husband's act of looking back, not hers.

440 *Stygian*: infernal (from the River Styx).

441 *Phlegeton*: a river of fire in Hades. Cf. *FQ*, 2. 4. 41.

442 *compassed*: surrounded, encircled.

443 *rustie*: rust-red (i.e. the colour of Phlegeton's molten flow).

    fowle fashion: hideous sights (i.e. things of foul appearance).

444 *Tartar*: Tartarus, abode of the wicked in the underworld.

446 The judges of the underworld were Minos, Rhadamanthus and Aeacus. Cf. Plato, *Gorgias*, 523e–524a; Ovid, *Metamorphoses*, 9. 434–41.

455 *shrill*: for 'sonorae' (echoing, sonorous), *Culex*, 281.

459 *monthly*: alluding to Diana's lunar cycle.

462 *Queene of hell*: Proserpina.

463 *fere*: spouse, mate.

465 *approoued*: found or proved by experience.

468 *arere*: backwards (arrear).

473–80 Greatly expanded from *Culex*, 294–6.

481 *Aeacus*: son of Jupiter, was made a judge in the underworld as a reward for his justice on earth. Cf. Ovid, *Metamorphoses*, 13. 25–8.

489 *th'one*: Telamon wedded his captive Hesione, the sister of King Priam of Troy, and fathered Teucer.

rauisht of: captivated by.

491 *th'other . . . Thetis*: Peleus fathered Achilles by Thetis, a goddess of the sea. Cf. Ovid, *Metamorphoses*, 11. 217–28.

492 *Nereus*: a god of the sea.

493–6 *youngman . . . fyre*: Ajax, son of Telamon, who prevented Hector from burning the Greek ships.

495 *Argolick*: Grecian (from the city of Argos).

496 *Bett*: beat.

497 *diuorces*: divisions or contentions (Latin *divortium*).

500 *Teucrian*: Trojan (from Teucer, first king of Troy).

501 *Sigæan*: Trojan (from Sigeum, a promontory of the Troad).

502 *Simois . . . Xanthus*: rivers near Troy.

503 *Hector*: son of King Priam and principal defender of Troy.

505 *Ida*: a mountain of Phrygia near Troy. Cf. *SC*, *Julye*, [59], [146] and notes.

511 *Rhetæan*: Trojan (from Rhoeteum, a promontory of the Troad).

513 *sonne of Telamon*: Ajax.

514 *thwarting*: holding crosswise.

523 *Argos*: Greece (from Argos, capital city of Argolis in the Peloponnesus).

defend: fend off, ward off.

524 *Vulcane*: the god of fire.

525 *th'one Aeacide*: one grandson of Aeacus, Ajax.

526 *th'other*: Achilles.

Phrygian: Trojan. Troy lay in Phrygia in Asia Minor.

528 *thrice*: according to Virgil, *Aeneid*, 1. 483.

530 *vnfaithfull Paris*: Paris, son of Priam, stole Helen from her husband Menelaus and slew Achilles by piercing him in the heel.

531–2 *him . . . ambushment*: distorting *Culex*, 325–6. Ajax went mad and killed himself when Ulysses outwitted him in the contest for Achilles' arms. There was no ambush (cf. Ovid, *Metamorphoses*, 13. 1–398).

533 *Laërtes sonne*: Ulysses.

535 *Strymonian Rhæsus*: Rhesus, son of the Thracian river god Strymon, was murdered by Ulysses and Diomede to frustrate the prophecy that Troy would not fall once his horses drank from the River Xanthus.

536 *Dolons . . . surprysall*: Dolon was a Trojan spy cunningly ambushed and killed by Ulysses (cf. Homer, *Iliad*, 10. 314–464).

537 *Cycones*: Thracian allies of Troy (cf. Homer, *Odyssey*, 9. 39–61).

538 *Læstrigones*: enormous cannibals who destroyed all of the Greek ships except for Ulysses' own (cf. Homer, *Odyssey*, 10. 80–132).

539 *Scilla*: the daughter of Phorcus who was transformed by Circe into a hybrid sea monster, having a female form girdled with savage dogs.

541 *Aetnean Cyclops*: The Cyclopses acted as assistants to the god Vulcan whose forge was situated under Mount Etna.

542 *Charybdis*: a whirlpool in the straits of Messina.

543 *Tartarie*: Tartarus (alluding to Ulysses' descent to the lower world).

545 *Agamemnon*: king of Mycenae, leader of the Greeks at Troy.

546 *Tantalus*: great-grandfather of Agamemnon.

549 *Dorick*: Greek (the Dorians were a Hellenic tribe).

Iliack: Trojan (from Ilion, Homer's name for Troy).

552 *Hellespont*: used loosely here for the Aegean. The Greeks suffered shipwreck off the coast of Euboea.

557 *type*: summit.

glaunce: blow, impact.

562 *Ericthonian*: Trojan (Erichthonius was the son of Dardanus, king of Troy).

564 *scowre*: pass rapidly over, traverse rapidly.

567 *Nereïs*: a Nereid, i.e. a daughter of the sea-god Nereus.

568 *claue*: cleaved, cut.

573 *loadstarre*: guiding star by which to navigate.

576 *impeach*: hinder, prevent.

586 *Caphareus*: a promontory of Euboea.

587 *Euboick*: of the island of Euboea, east of the Greek mainland.

588 *Hercæan*: unidentified, as Spenser indicates (possibly a corruption of Aegean).

599–600 *Fabij ... Horatij*: famous Roman families. Quintus Fabius Maximus frustrated Hannibal; P. Decius Mus sacrificed his life in the Latin War; Horatius Cocles defended the Sublician bridge in the war with Lars Porsenna.

601 *Camill*: Marcus Furius Camillus captured the Etruscan city of Veii and saved Rome from the Gauls.

602 *Curtius*: Manius Curtius plunged into a mysterious chasm in the Forum (later known as the Lacus Curtius) thereby causing it to close.

606 *Mutius*: Mucius Scaevola demonstrated Roman defiance of Lars Porsenna by thrusting his hand into a flame.

609 *Curius*: Manius Curius Dentatus conquered the Sabines and defeated King Pyrrhus.

611 *Flaminius*: unidentified, but the pun on 'flamma' (flame) at *Culex*, 368 may suggest Caecilius Metellus who lost his sight rescuing the Palladium (a sacred image of Pallas) from the burning temple of Vesta.

613–16 The unclear syntax reflects textual ambiguity at *Culex*, 370–71.

613 *either Scipion*: Scipio Africanus (236–183 BC) defeated Hannibal at the battle of Zama thereby assuring victory in the second Punic War; Scipio

Aemilianus (185–129 BC) destroyed Carthage itself thereby concluding the third Punic War.

615 *vow'd*: for 'devota' (doomed to destruction), *Culex*, 370.

623 *Minos*: king of Crete, and son of Zeus, one of the three judges of the lower world. Cf. note to line 446 above.

632 *intollerable*: unbearable, insupportable.

638 *seuer*: scatter, disperse.

641 *fit*: bout, spell.

651 *squaring . . . compasse*: fashioning all around, playing on the notion of squaring the circle ('orbem') of the gnat's tomb, *Culex*, 396.

well beseene: of pleasant aspect.

657 *hoorded*: stacked, piled.

664 *scape*: escape.

670 *Costmarie*: a form of chrysanthemum grown as a flavouring herb. Cf. *Muiop*, 195.

671 *Saffron . . . Cilician*: Cilicia in Asia Minor was famed for saffron (*Crocus sativus*). Cf. Ovid, *Fasti*, 1. 76.

672 *Lawrell*: associated with Phoebus Apollo as the god of poetry. Cf. *TW*, sonnet 7. 12 and note.

673 *Rhododaphne*: oleander.

Sabine flowre: savin (*Juniperus sabina*), a small evergreen shrub. Cf. *FQ*, 3. 2. 49.

676 *Box . . . offence*: for 'bocchus' at *Culex*, 406, named after King Bocchus of Mauretania who betrayed his son-in-law Jugurtha to the Romans (Sallust, *Jugurtha*, 113–14).

677 *Amaranthus*: in Thomas Watson's *Amynta* (1585), adapted from Tasso's pastoral play, Amintas dies for love and is transformed into an amaranthus. Abraham Fraunce translated the work into English in 1587.

679 *Narcisse*: dying through self-love, Narcissus was transformed into the flower of the same name. Cf. Ovid, *Metamorphoses*, 3. 339–510.

687 *in lieu*: see note to line 333 above.

Prosopopoia. Or Mother Hubberds Tale

George Puttenham defines 'prosopopoia' as 'the Counterfait in Personation' (cf. *ECE*, 2. 170), and Spenser's use of the term seems to apply both to his own literary skill in 'counterfeiting' the poem's *personae* and to the malign social impersonations of the fox and the ape. The work takes the form of four beast fables, loosely inspired by the cycle of Renard the Fox – available to Spenser in the translations of Caxton (1481) and Gaultier (1550) – and narrated by the traditional story-teller Mother Hubberd at a time of plague, like the stories narrated in Boccaccio's *Decameron*. The astrological detail of the opening lines obliquely signals the work's satiric emphasis in recalling the departure of Virgo (Astraea or Justice) from a corrupt world (1–8): the golden age, we learn, has been succeeded by an age of iron (141–53, 254). Thereafter the work is carefully structured to present, in ascending order of seriousness, a wide range of political and ecclesiastical abuses stretching from the impostures of masterless vagabonds at one end of the social scale to the systematic, but disconcertingly similar, abuse of courtly office at the other. Implicit in the account is the responsibility of the 'sleeping' or 'sluggish' lion (952–4, 1327), representing the permissive or careless monarch, for the worst of the nation's troubles. No less than divine intervention is necessary to awaken royal vengeance (1225–332) – a political achievement to which the poem itself would seem to aspire.

The pervasive pastoral imagery links the poem's concerns with those of *The Shepheardes Calender*. The fox and the ape first abuse their position as shepherds (303–40), then as pastors or spiritual 'shepherds' (431–574), and finally as courtiers or political 'shepherds' (1205–22). In the mode of medieval estates' satire their trail of corruption encompasses the citizenry, the church, the court and ultimately the monarchy itself. Yet the maintenance of the traditional social hierarchy is perceived to be vital to social stability: the radicalism of the fox's philosophy with its emphasis upon 'libertie' and community of goods taps the deepest anxieties of a conservative society (129–53).

Spenser's assertion in his dedication that the poem was 'long sithens composed in the raw conceipt of my youth' has occasioned much debate concerning the date of composition. If, as is generally suspected, the fourth episode reflects worries concerning the Queen's proposed marriage to the Duc d'Alençon (whose ambassador Simier is thought to be figured in the ape) and the possible alienation of the crown to the House of Valois, some version of the text must date from 1579 or 1580. As Lord Burghley was commonly believed to favour the French match, he is a good candidate for the fox (cf. *The Ruines of Time*, 216–17). At the time of publication, however, the Queen's marriage was no longer an issue yet contemporary evidence suggests that attempts were made to have the poem 'called in' thereby increasing both its popularity and its price [cf. Peterson (1997)]. Writing in 1592 Gabriel Harvey observes that 'Mother-Hubbard in the heat of choler, forgetting the pure sanguine of her sweete Feary Queene, wilfully over-shot her malcontented selfe' (*Works*, 1. 164), and the account is largely substantiated by Thomas Nashe (*Works*, 1. 281–2). As the following notes demonstrate, thinly veiled criticism of Lord Burghley and his son Robert Cecil is likely to have prompted official action. In view of Burghley's position as Lord Treasurer, the fox's obsession with the accumulation of 'treasure' (1171–2, 1306), the illegal enrichment of his 'cubs' (1151–8) and the formulation of devious 'pollicie' (1036) seem to underscore Spenser's satiric intention. Whereas passages obliquely critical of Burghley in *The Ruines of Time* were tacitly altered in the folio edition of 1611, *Mother Hubberds Tale* was not republished until after the death of Robert Cecil.

It would therefore appear that a poem originally composed during the crisis of the French match was cleverly revised for publication in 1591. That it retained its power to occasion such a vigorous reaction bears testimony to Spenser's skill in analysing not merely the personalities but the very power structures of the Elizabethan regime. His rhyming couplets serve as a potent vehicle for the distillation of rich social detail and, in places, anticipate the rhythmic poise and balance of the Augustans. The work is noteworthy for its variety of styles, ranging from the plain (305–24) to the grand (1257–70), and for its complex interplay of voices as the unnamed narrator retells the tale of Mother Hubberd and linguistically 'personates' all of the other characters through the rehearsal of her 'bad' and blunt language (1388). The celebrated portrait of the perfect courtier eloquently delineates the ideal from which the court is seen to have derogated and supplies the value-system against which the 'beasts' are judged (717–93). Cf. Atchity (1973); T. M. Greene (1963); Greenlaw (1932); B. Harris (1941); Judson (1948); Oakeshott (1971); Stein (1934); Van der Berg (1978).

Dedication *To the right Honourable* . . .

Ladie . . . Mountegle: Anne Spencer, daughter of Sir John Spencer of Althorp, celebrated as Charillis at *CCH*, 536–63. She married first William Stanley, Lord Mountegle (died 1581), second Henry, Lord Compton (died 1589) and third Robert Sackville (died 1609), second Earl of Dorset and eldest son of Lord Buckhurst, one of the dedicatees of *FQ*.

4 *that House*: the Spencers of Althorp with whom Spenser claims kinship in the dedications to *TM*, *Muiop*, and at *CCH*, 536–9 and *Proth*, 130–31.

11 *personated*: represented allegorically or by fictitious *personae*.

Prosopopoia

1–8 *month . . . death*: in August the sun, and the dog-star Syrius, leave the sign of Leo and enter that of Virgo. The influence of Syrius was held to occasion the sickness of the 'dog-days'. Cf. *SC*, *Julye*, 21–4, [21].

1 *righteous Maide*: Astraea, goddess of justice, identified with the constellation Virgo. Cf. Comes, *Mythologiae*, 2. 2; *VG*, 359–60; *Daph*, 218 and notes.

2 *vpbraide*: condemnation, censure.

6 *chafed*: vexed.

10 *did to die*: caused to die.

15 *griefe*: pain, affliction.

19 *wise*: manner.

21–32 The motif of storytelling as a distraction from sickness or plague recalls the opening of Boccaccio's *Decameron*.

22 *forgoe*: forsake.

23 *deceaue*: beguile.

24 *reaue*: take away, remove.

26 *idle stound*: indolent period.

27 *cast in course*: determined, undertook.

   waste: wile away, occupy.

35 *seem'd*: beseemed, befitted.

40 *diseased*: disquieted, troubled.

41 *Ile . . . say*: I'll write in such terms as she used in telling the same story, i.e. the style will be appropriately colloquial.

45 *ciuill*: civilized.

47 *hard estate*: straitened circumstances, lowly condition.

48 *lyeke*: like.

49 *vnhappie*: mischievously (prone to occasion mischief).

50 *fellowes*: companions, comrades.

   fitted: well-matched, suited.

53 *Gossip*: friend, crony.

54 *tide*: tied.

55 *trustely complaine*: lament in confidence.

72 *awhape*: confound, amaze.

78 *beard . . . swept*: cf. *SC, September*, 123 and note.

80 *about to throwe*: turn about at once, go directly on the other tack.

84 *vncouth wize*: unfamiliar or unaccustomed manner.

85 *Lymiter*: mendicant friar licensed to beg within certain limits.

86 *Gipsen*: gypsy.

94 *like*: please.

96 *expell*: reject, refuse.

100 *disaduentrous*: unfortunate, disastrous.

   fortuneless: unprofitable, unrewarding.

109 *heauens windowes*: a biblical formula, cf. Genesis 7: 11.

110 *habiliments*: clothing, apparel.

112 *wey*: weigh (in the sense of consider).

113 *aduise*: deliberate.

114 *Sir Reynold*: in imitation of Renard the Fox.

119 *occasion*: opportunity.

121 *anie*: any one.

124 *anon*: straightaway, forthwith.

125 *motioned*: broached, brought forward.

128 *miswend*: go astray, come to grief.

135–50 The fox's appeal to the communal life of the Golden Age was a staple of political radicalism from John Ball in the reign of Richard II to the Levellers. Cf. the arguments of the 'egalitarian' giant at *FQ*, 5. 2. 32–8. Biblical authority was found in Acts 4: 34–7; 5: 1–10. Supporters of the established order argued that the right to private property was consistent with the principles of natural law and it was endorsed in the thirty-eighth article of the Anglican Church.

137 *chalenge to*: claim for, demand for.

139 *in . . . mugger*: privately, secretly.

142 *ylike . . . bought*: redeemed at the same high price (by Christ).

143 *partition*: division.

147 *liuelode*: livelihood.

151 *golden . . . Saturne*: cf. Ovid, *Metamorphoses*, 1. 89–112.

154 *plot*: plan, project.

157 *droyle*: toil, drudge.

163 *swinke . . . sweate*: cf. *SC, Aprill*, 99.

171 *state*: condition, circumstances.

173 *ordinaunce*: device, contrivance.

176 *aduizement*: reflection, consideration.

178 *complot*: conspiracy, covert plan.

186–8 *pasport . . . eare*: under the terms of the 1572 'Act for the Punishment of Vagabonds' (14 Elizabeth c. 5) vagrants needed a licence or warrant from the appropriate local authorities to secure safe passage. Among the penalties for default was burning with a hot iron through 'the grystle of the ryght eare'.

192 *defie*: disdain.

197 *Souldiers*: a common abuse of the day.

198 *ciuile*: civil in the sense of publicly acceptable.

201 *occasion*: necessity or opportunity.

203 *ended*: concluded upon, determined.

209–12 *Scotch . . . Portugese*: cf. note to line 677 below.

213 *heeling*: heel-piece of a stocking.

217 *bat*: staff or stick.

221 *mysterie*: occupation, profession.

230 *yeoman*: a freeholder, cultivating his own land.

231 *gay*: bright and ostentatious, showy. Cf. James 2: 3.

241 *straine*: exert, force.

244 *loosly*: at random, at will.

245 *enquire of custome*: make the customary polite inquiry.

248 *good*: goods, possessions.

256 *abate*: bring down, depress.

264 *thetch*: thatch.

268 *balke*: lay out of the way.

269 *slipt . . . handsomly*: dexterously declined the task.

275 *painfull*: laborious.

280 *ghostly father*: father confessor.

287 *paine*: exertion, troublesome toil.

288 *sustaine*: bear, support.

290 *keep*: keeping.

294 *coste*: side (coast).

296 *Belwether*: leading sheep of the flock with a bell about its neck.

298 *endeuourment*: endeavour, industry.

301 *accompt*: account.

315 *treason*: treachery (with political implications for the allegory).

323 *acquite themselues*: give satisfactory account of themselves.

324 *flatly . . . abord*: completely at sea, wholly confounded. Cf. *RR*, 185.

328 *doubting*: suspecting.

329 *bad*: bade, commanded.

330 *meaning*: purpose, intention.

332 *afterclaps*: unexpected strokes or consequences.

  preuent: anticipate, forestall.

338 *complement*: fulfilment, completion.

340 *Carried*: transported, borne.

342 *fortunes . . . tosse*: 'to toss about in the changing currents of fortune'.

344 *Abusing*: deceiving.

354 *cassocke*: close-fitting ecclesiastical tunic.

  sidelong: long, hanging far down. Cf. *VB*, 115.

356 *state*: condition.

357 *pas*: passport, warrant.

358 *Clerkes booke-redd*: the 1572 'Act for the Punishment of Vagabonds' (14 Elizabeth c. 5) embraced 'all Scollers of the Universities of Oxeforde or Cambridge' who begged without authority.

361 *formall*: precise, prim (with the implication of being a priest only in outward form or demeanour). The ensuing portrait summarizes contemporary complaints about unworthy, illiterate clergy.

371 *squib*: man, fellow.

372 *snib*: reprove, rebuke.

382 *euidence*: document.

  will: last testament.

385–91 Parodying the views of those who regarded an ignorant clergy as politically advantageous.

390 *Sir*: cf. *SC, Maye*, 309 and note.

393 *read Homelies*: the Elizabethan *Book of Homilies* was issued in its final form in 1571. Puritans complained that it degraded the office of preaching into an office of reading.

394–5 *done . . . please*: cf. *SC, Maye*, 39–44.

400 *bootles boad*: unprofitably dwell or abide.

406 *haue ... troad*: have not yet (chosen) the course of any (particular) pathway, i.e. have not yet chosen their way of life.

412 *bondmen*: bondsmen (in the sense of debtors).

419–24 Cf. *SC, Maye*, 120–25.

420 *grow ... prize*: 'advance by degrees to a significant office'.

421 *Commissaries*: ecclesiastical officers exercising jurisdiction as representatives of a bishop or deputizing for him in his absence.

422 *Principalls*: heads of religious houses.

Prebendaries: stipendiary canons of a cathedral.

424 *spite ... neare*: 'whatever spiteful men may say' [Renwick (1928), 237].

431–6 Distorting Christ's injunction to 'feed his sheep' (John 21: 15–17).

432 *hath ... threat*: i.e. a grievous penalty is threatened for failure.

438 *bread ... place*: the manna of the Old Testament and the Eucharistic bread of the New Testament were associated by Christ (cf. John 6: 31–5).

439 *he ... rod*: Aaron's rod 'brought forth buds, and bloomed blossoms' (Numbers 17: 8), but the priest displays his ignorance in misattributing the following quotation to Aaron.

440 *All ... God*: cf. Isaiah 54: 13.

441 *That same*: the bread of life.

raught: stretched out, given.

443 *Shepheard*: 'I am the good shepherd' (John 10: 11, 14). The priest abuses Christ's declaration in order to abnegate responsibility for his flock.

447–58 The priest exploits the Reformers' abolition of Roman Catholic rituals and hostility to the doctrine of salvation through 'works' (rather than faith) as a pretext for spiritual indolence. Cf. *SC, Maye*, 149–57.

451 *Anthemes*: antiphonal chant or song.

452 *penie Masses*: masses said for a penny's fee.

Complynes: the last service of the day completing the canonical hours.

453 *Dirges*: offices of the dead (so called from the anthem beginning 'Dirige, Domine Deus meus', from Psalms 5: 8).

Trentals: set of thirty requiem masses.

shrifts: confessions (or possibly penances).

454 *memories*: services of commemoration, especially for the dead.

458 *motion*: impulse.

459–74 The priest exploits genuine Anglican arguments for the use of clerical vestments as a pretext for ostentation. The passage need not indicate Spenser's sympathy with the Puritans in the vestiarian controversy. Cf. *SC, Julye*, [173] and note.

460 *twist*: thread.

463 *Aarons*: cf. Exodus 28: 1–43.

469 *Lord of hoasts*: the Lord of Sabaoth (cf. Romans 9: 28–9; James 5: 4–8; *FQ*, 7. 8. 2).

474 *heare*: hair.

477 *wilfull*: in the sense of perverse or obstinate.

478 *free libertie*: cf. 'Stand fast therefore in the liberty wherewith Christ hath made us free' (Galatians 5: 1). The Reformers asserted the clergy's right to marry but the priest exploits this liberty as a pretext for sensual indulgence.

479 *ghostly*: dealing with religious matters, spiritual (an ironic usage).

482 *Benefice*: a church living.

484 *thereout*: upon that matter, concerning that.

486 *Beneficiall*: a benefice or a letter of presentation to one.

491 *zealous*: a term frequently associated with Puritans.

497 *Radegund*: St Radigund's devotion to virginity was such that she refused to consummate her marriage. She was noted for miraculous cures.

499 *curtesie*: curtsy, obeisance.

501 *or*: ere.

506 *companie*: play the obsequious companion.

507 *beetle stock*: hammer handle, a common figure for dullness and lack of personal initiative or independence.

509 *mock . . . Benefice*: gain a benefice by buffoonery.

510 *coniure by deuice*: conjure up by magic.

511 *cast a figure*: calculate (a horoscope) astrologically.

512 *schoole-trick*: a mere academic exercise.

516–20 For these abuses cf. *SC, September*, 122–35 and note.

517 *Beneuolence*: an enforced contribution, ironically named.
   gage: pledge.

518 *Primitias*: first year's income.

519 *forpas . . . by*: escape them, slip past them.

520 *gelt*: mulcted, curtailed.

523 *compound . . . penie*: come to a better financial arrangement.

527 *cope . . . thee*: make a bargain with you.

540 *peeces riuen*: by the patron's exploitation of the revenues.

542 *Common place*: common theme or topos.

543 *shriuing*: confession.

545 *by my hallidome*: by my holiness (a familiar oath).

547 *discipline*: teaching, instruction.

561 *constraind*: enforced, drawn upon themselves.

562 *Ordinarie*: bishop of the diocese or his deputy.

565 *Pursiuants*: warrant officers.

569 *Visitation*: official visit of inspection by the bishop or archdeacon.
   cyted: summoned.

571 *composition*: financial arrangement or deal.

572 *light condition*: easy terms.

579 *for . . . tourne*: to suit their purposes.

587 *requite*: salute in return. Cf. *FQ*, 1. 9. 49.

611 *portracture*: image, representation.

622 *Lyon*: alluding to Queen Elizabeth I ('she' of line 629). The lion figured prominently on the royal arms.

624 *Enchaste*: bound or enclosed, i.e. the queen employs her favour as a strategy of control.

626 *buxome*: compliant, submissive.

628 *late chayne*: may refer either to the Earl of Leicester's marriage to Lettice Knollys (1578) or to the Earl of Essex's clandestine marriage to Frances Walsingham, widow of Sir Philip Sidney (1590).

629 *she*: the lion is female here and at line 901 but male at line 953 in the more politically sensitive context of the final episode.

636 *cost*: expense, outlay.

639 *gainfull*: profitable.

656 *aguize*: attire, dress.

658 *successe*: fortune, outcome.

665 *Magnifico*: cf. 'like Magnificoes, not a beck but glorious in shew' (Gabriel Harvey, *Letters*, in *Prose*, 467).

667 *counterfesaunce*: dissimulation, counterfeiting.

668 *credite*: (false) repute, cf. line 689.

   countenaunce: semblance.

670 *basen wide*: as wide as a basin, a common phrase.

671 *what . . . wight*: what sort of person.

672 *accoustrements*: apparel, outfits.

673 *queint deuises*: strange or bizarre designs.

677 *Alla Turchesca*: after the Turkish fashion. Adoption of foreign fashions was a prevalent courtly abuse. Castiglione complains that 'there are also those who dress in the manner of Turks' (*Courtier*, 134).

680 *strangenesse*: distance, aloofness.

681 *secrete*: covert, underhand.

   state: rank, status.

682 *hire*: bribe.

683 *couerture*: deceitful strategy.

698 *read*: foretell, predict.

700 *iuggle*: cheat, beguile.

701 *legier demaine*: sleight-of-hand, trickery.

709 *other . . . wits*: other vain wits like himself.

714 *gybe . . . fleare*: jeer and sneer.

716 *ill . . . spill*: spoil with an ill interpretation (or intention).

717–93 For the ideal courtier cf. Castiglione, *Courtier*, 61–4 (martial and physical exercise), 88–92 (learning and literature), 94–5 (music), 125 (service of the prince), 126–7 (conversation and demeanour).

742 *ring . . . beare*: to ride at the ring, i.e. to carry off on the point of a lance a metal ring suspended on a post.

745 *enlarge . . . breath*: develop his breathing.

747 *Eughen*: made of yew.

749 *gowned beast*: caparisoned horse.

750–51 *Persian . . . foe*: a garbled allusion. Cyrus the Great defeated the king of Babylon who controlled Assyria (Herodotus, *History*, 1. 188–91). Athenaeus records that 'the Persian king was never seen on foot outside the palace' (*Deipnosophistae*, xii. 514c).

754 *recoyle*: retire.

756 *toyled*: exhausted by toil, weary.

759 *pause*: rest.

770 *vpshot*: mark (a metaphor from archery).

775 *his grace*: his prince's favour.

778 *In . . . personage*: in whatever service he is pleased to employ his person.

781 *amenaunce*: conduct, bearing.

784 *Courting*: his presence in court, or his role as a courtier.
    applie: devote, employ.

785 *enterdeale*: negotiation, intercourse.

796 *descrie*: discover or disclose.

802 *mumming*: disguising (as in a mummers' play).

803 *balliards*: billiards.

804 *misseeming*: misbecoming, inappropriate to.

807 *Ne . . . scorne*: nor, in order to please them, would he think it beneath him sometimes.

808 *Pandares*: possibly glancing at Simier's role in promoting the d'Alençon match. The Queen called Simier her 'monkey'.

809–20 For the courtly abuse of poetry cf. *CCH*, 775–94.

822 *relieu'd*: relieved his penury with money.

826 *charmes*: songs, poems.

827 *strong conceipts*: forceful fancies or images.

833 *Sectaries*: adherents, devotees.

835 *mewd*: confined, cooped up.

842 *progression*: step by step, stage by stage.

843 *professe*: acknowledge their faith in, preach.

849 *He . . . choyce*: he did not care.

851 *brocage*: procuring, pimping.
    shifts: contrivances, tricks.

854 *purchase*: booty, pillage.

856 *close conueyance*: underhand dealing.

857 *coosinage*: (cozenage) fraud, deception.
    cleanly: deft, adroit, dexterous.

867 *fee-simples*: landed estates belonging absolutely to the owner and his heirs.

869 *Broker*: agent, middleman.

876 *countenaunce*: patron, supporter (i.e. countenancing his actions).

881 *preuent*: forestall, anticipate.

882 *ment*: had intended, or had in mind.

887 *In case*: provided that, on condition that. Cf. line 962.

recompenst . . . reason: reasonably rewarded or requited.

889 *friuolous*: inconsequential, worthless.

893 *had ywist*: had I but known. Cf. the proverbial expression 'beware of had I wist'.

908 *tendance*: waiting in expectation, attendant anticipation.

909 *meane*: lowly (or possibly moderate, the comfortable 'mean' betwixt the high and low estates).

913 *himselfe . . . trie*: prove himself to be a jackdaw or fool.

922 *fowlie . . . entreate*: treated harshly.

925 *huckster*: mercenary, money-making.

928 *countenaunce*: public demeanour or bearing.

930 *vncased*: stripped in the sense of threadbare.

939 *copesmate*: accomplice, confederate.

945 *That . . . repented*: that they regretted.

948 *hipps*: fruit of the wild rose.

950–1380 Cf. Aesop's fable of the ass in lion's skin (*Fables*, no. 279).

950 *rechlesse*: heedlessly, aimlessly (i.e. with no object in view).

960 *scope*: mark, goal.

978 *gest*: action, deed.

980 *soueraign see*: royal seat, throne.

982 *name . . . place*: reckon his lowly position.

986 *cowardree*: cowardice.

996 *Tickled*: excited, stirred.

rash: impulsive.

997 *whether*: which of them.

999 *theretoo*: to the matter.

1005 *aduenter*: venture.

1010 *For . . . noyse*: for fear of making noise.

1021 *stryfull*: contentious.

1023 *rayne*: sovereignty (or possibly the realm).

1026 A common adage. Cf. Seneca, *Thyestes*, 444.

1057–8 For this political sentiment cf. Cicero, *De Officiis*, 3. 21. 82.

1060 *inly quooke*: inwardly quaked.

1062 *did*: donned.

1085 *entertayne*: entertainment, reception.

1088 *raged*: spoke furiously, stormed.

1090 *inuasion*: attack, assault.

1098 *warne*: summon.

1099 *it to defend*: present a legal defence of it.

1103 *stomack*: pride. Cf. *FQ*, 2. 7. 41.

1108 *Conge*: ceremonious leave.

1115 *pointed*: appointed.

1116 *issue*: passage.

1118 *equipage*: retinue.

1119 *forreine beasts*: allegorically alluding to foreign troops. It was feared that d'Alençon would bring French troops to England.

1121 *strange ayde*: foreign military support.

1123–4 *Bred . . . Centaures*: griffins had the head and wings of an eagle and the body of a lion; the Minotaur had a bull's head and a man's body; Centaurs had a human torso attached to a horse's body; dragons were commonly pictured as winged reptiles; crocodiles and beavers were accounted part fish and part beast because of their amphibious nature.

1128 *Like as*: even as, just as.

1132 *season*: appropriate time.

1137–224 Possibly intended as an attack on Lord Burghley who, as Lord Treasurer, was especially vulnerable to charges of financial corruption.

1139 *put in proofe*: put in practice.

1140 *counterpoint*: combination of contrary actions (analogous to the counterpoint of contrasting melodies producing one harmony).

1141 *reach*: device, scheme.

breach: breach of the laws.

1144 *Fiaunt*: warrant.

1145 *lept*: passed rapidly.

1148 *purchase for*: provide for, make provision for.

1150 *little . . . pas*: little did he care.

1151 *his cubs*: Robert Parsons, writing in 1592, detected an allusion to Lord Burghley's children. Cf. Wells, *Allusions*, 24.

1154 *malefices*: mischiefs, evil deeds.

1155 *colours . . . white*: because white is the colour of innocence.

1158 *weight . . . broken*: Robert Cecil, Burghley's son, was a hunchback.

1159 *chaffred*: trafficked in, sold.

Chayres . . . set: the sees or seats of bishops, bishoprics.

1160 *priuie ferme*: private farming. The collection of public taxes was sometimes farmed out to a private individual for a fixed fee. The 'farmer' could then make a hefty profit by over-charging the tax-payers.

1167 *ought*: anything (aught).

1168 *platforme*: basis or foundation.

1173 *loftie towres*: the extravagant building projects of the newly rich or ennobled were the subject of constant satirical attack. Burghley was engaged in building the palace of Theobalds from 1564 to 1585.

1183 *no . . . Nobilitie*: made no account of the nobility, in the sense that he did not value them. Burghley was not of an ancient family.

1190 *streigned*: restrained.

1193 *rascall*: rabble.

1202 *by . . . addresse*: by his own introduction (or possibly by application to him).

1204 *auaile*: profit, advantage.

1212 *order . . . thing*: the state of affairs or sequence of events.

1214 *rash*: rashly, recklessly.

1218 *thwart*: oppose, speak against.

1224 *boxe*: the coffer or money box.

1228 *blacklidded*: cf. the Homeric 'black-browed' (*Iliad*, 1. 528); *FQ*, 7. 6. 22.

1233 *guile suborn'd*: equipped or endowed with guile.

1234 *subuerst*: overturned, ruined.

1237 *dewest*: fittest or rightful.

1240 *Him to auenge*: take vengeance upon him.

1246 *Mercurie*: messenger of the gods. Cf. Virgil, *Aeneid*, 1. 297–304.

1248 *breed*: dwell (an archaic usage).

1250 *stearne*: stern (in the ironic sense of resolute and commanding).

1254 *remitted*: put back, restored.

1255 *treachours*: traitors.

1257 *Sonne of Maia*: Mercury was the son of Zeus by Maia, daughter of Atlas and one of the Pleiades. Cf. *Epith*, 307 and note; *FQ*, 4. 3. 42.

1258 *cleau'd*: penetrated, passed through (literally 'divided').

1261 *prescript*: instruction or direction.

1262 *stouping*: bending or curving downwards.

1264 *easie paine*: light effort or exertion.

1267 *Ambrosiall*: celestial.

1274 *blandishment*: cajolery, flattering lures.

1276 *realme and raine*: kingdom and sovereignty.

1279–91 Conflating Mercury's cap with Pluto's magic hat of darkness which Mercury lent to Perseus. Cf. Ovid, *Metamorphoses*, 1. 672; Comes, *Mythologiae*, 7. 11.

1281 *mocketh*: deludes, deceives.

1283 *runnes . . . swerds*: passes unscathed through enemy swords.

1287 *cunning theeueries*: a notable feature of Mercury's childhood.

1292 *Caduceus*: a miraculous wand entwined by snakes, often employed as an emblem of concord. Cf. Virgil, *Aeneid*, 4. 242–6; Comes, *Mythologiae*, 5. 5; *FQ*, 2. 12. 41; 4. 3. 42; 7. 6. 18.

1293 *damned ghosts*: Mercury conducted the spirits of the deceased to Hades, hence his common epithet 'psychopompus' (conductor of souls).

1294 *Tartare*: abode of the wicked in Hades.

1299 *Syre . . . Alcumena*: while Hermes (Mercury) stood guard, Zeus slept with Alcmene in the form of her husband, Amphitryon, and commanded the sun not to rise for three days. Cf. Plautus, *Amphitryo*; *Epith*, 328–9; *FQ*, 3. 11. 33.

1306 *fild*: filled.

1310 *raigning*: holding sway, flourishing.

1313 *tolde*: numbered, counted.

1314 *lothfull*: reluctant (loath to see).

1317 *auengement for*: retribution for.

1321 *wicked weed*: the detail of a soporific herb placed underneath the lion's head has not been previously mentioned.

1324 *him auize*: bethink himself, reflect.

1330 *blent*: polluted, stained.

1334 *grating*: smiting, striking.

1356 *as . . . reft*: as one bereft of their wits.

1364 *turning . . . confusion*: either attributing everything to the ape's disorderly conduct or explaining everything in such a way as to undo the ape (and save himself).

1366 *stay at ease*: remain unconstrained or untroubled.

1371 *strange*: cf. note to line 1121 above.

1388 *bad*: rude, coarse.

    bluntly: coarsely, without delicacy or refinement.

Ruines of Rome: by Bellay

Ruines of Rome is translated from Joachim Du Bellay's *Les Antiquitez de Rome contenant une generale description de sa grandeur, et comme une deploration de sa ruine*, a work first published in 1558 together with *Une Songe ou Vision sur le mesme subject*, an appendage which Spenser translated for Jan Van der Noot's *A Theatre for Voluptuous Worldling*s (1569) and substantially revised for publication in *Complaints* under the new title of *The Visions of Bellay*. Some version of *The Ruines of Time* may therefore date from the late 1560s, but the reference to Du Bartas's *Uranie* (459–60) indicates that the 'Envoy' was composed after 1574 and whatever early materials Spenser may have had to hand are likely to have undergone extensive revision for publication in 1591. As the following notes indicate, the translation is generally accurate but contains some elementary errors which seriously distort the meaning of the original. Spenser's style is generally less assured than Du Bellay's whose Petrarchan sonnets (observing the traditional break between octave and sestet) are here refashioned into English sonnets of three quatrains and a couplet (rhyming *ababcdcdefefgg*).

    The alteration in form reflects a significant difference in outlook.

Spenser's first translations from the Catholic Du Bellay appeared in the staunchly Protestant context of *A Theatre for Worldlings*, and *The Ruines of Time* displays a similar shift of emphasis. Although Du Bellay was by no means an uncritical admirer of the Renaissance papacy, the speaker's attitude towards Rome is rendered even more problematic in Spenser. Du Bellay's meditation upon the ruins of empire involves a reappraisal of the whole humanist enterprise, casting doubt upon the wisdom of emulating a culture in many respects so alien to the Christian ethos [cf. Greene (1982)]. Not infrequently his stance resembles that of the disappointed Petrarchan lover [cf. Rebhorn (1980)]. For Spenser, however, the image of Rome is refracted through the lens of Protestant polemic (365–78). Whereas the cause of the city's decline is variously attributed to civil discord (127–40), divine intervention (43–56), invasion (141–54), time (36), social decadence (309–22), or the cyclical process of history (211–24), there is an implicit suggestion that even the highest worldly aspirations necessarily breed corruption, that earthly greatness somehow entails a concomitant depravity. Regarded as the epitome of the world (359), Rome is awesome in its very devastation and inspires 'sacred horror' (13) in the beholder – and in all those who might harbour hopes of a *translatio imperii*. The scale of its fall challenges the value of all worldly ambition, including the literary aspirations of modern poets intent on emulating Virgil and refashioning, through a sort of poetic necromancy (1–14), the Roman heritage in vernacular literature (337–50). By association with Babylon (15) Rome emerges as the antithesis of the New Jerusalem envisaged in Revelation, and the concluding reference to Du Bartas may be intended to imply that the 'heauenly Muse' directs one's attention away from images of decay 'th'Almightie to adore' (460) [cf. Fichter (1981)]. But this is to oversimplify the matter: it is noteworthy that neither in Du Bellay nor Spenser does the speaker's protracted meditation upon the 'tragick sights' (85) of Rome's 'ruin'd pride' (208) serve to resolve the fundamental ambivalence of his outlook. Rome's 'heauenly spirites' reside, incongruously, in 'darkest hell' (1–6), and a reluctant 'wonder' (182) for the city and its 'braue writings' persists (68). Paradoxically, aspiration and degradation converge, the 'lowest earth, ioin'd to the heauen hie' (106). The dark tension thus generated may well have influenced Shakespeare's sonnets [cf. Hieatt (1983)]. Cf. Allen (1968); Ferguson (1982); Janowitz (1990); Manley (1982); Prescott (1978); Stapleton (1990); Tucker (1990).

Ruines of Rome

2 *opprest*: pressed down, overwhelmed.

4 *faire verses*: Latin poetry.

5 *shrilling*: piercing.

8 *shreiking yell*: simply 'mon cry' in Du Bellay (1. 7).

9–11 *Thrice . . . Thrice*: creating an effect of ritual incantation owing to the magical properties ascribed to the number three. Cf. Virgil, *Eclogues*, 8. 73–8.

9 *veale*: veil.

10 *Your . . . all*: 'the solemn extent of your tombs'. A badly garbled version of Du Bellay's 'trois fois cernant sous le voile des cieux / De voz tumbeaus le tour devocieux' (1. 9–10).

12 *antique furie*: Du Bellay's 'antique fureur' (1. 12), presumably in the sense of the Latin *manes* or 'ghost' rather than an avenging fury.

13 *sacred horror*: reverend awe (but preserving the sense of dread).

15–24 *Babylon . . . Colosse*: for the seven wonders of the ancient world cf. *RT*, 408–14 and note.

15 *Babylon*: cf. *TW*, sonnet 13. 14 and note.

16 *sharped steeples*: Du Bellay's 'vergers en l'air' (2. 2) or the Hanging Gardens, but Spenser is presumably alluding to the Tower of Babel often confusedly associated with Babylon.

17 *Ephesian buildings*: the temple of Diana at Ephesus.

20 *Ioues . . . Olympus*: the temple of Zeus at Olympia (not Mount Olympus).

21 *Mausolus . . . Carians*: the tomb of Mausolus, satrap of Caria, at Halicarnassus.

22 *Labyrinth*: the labyrinth at Knossus built for King Minos was not generally accounted among the seven wonders.

23–4 *Rhodian . . . Memorie*: the Colossus of Rhodes was erected to commemorate the raising of the siege of Rhodes (305–304 BC).

26 *magnifie*: extol.

29–42 Du Bellay's source was a Latin epigram attributed to Janus Vitalis for which cf. Du Bellay (1966), 275; Kelly (1994).

31 *arches*: triumphal arches.

44 *One . . . Morning*: one foot in the west, the other in the east. Thetis, a sea-goddess, represents the ocean into which the sun sets. Cf. note to line 270 below.

45 *One . . . More*: one hand on the east, the other on the west, complementing line 44. Scythia lay north of the Black and Caspian Seas, and the 'More' are the ancient inhabitants of Mauretania.

48–9 *Giants . . . hills*: cf. note to lines 155–8 below. For Rome's association with the Giants cf. *TW*, sonnet 11. 4 and note. For Giants and Titans (whom Spenser often conflates) as types of arrogance cf. Comes, *Mythologiae*, 6. 20–21.

51–6 *Vpon . . . meete*: the pinning down of Rome is modelled upon that of the giant Typhoeus under Sicily. Cf. Ovid, *Metamorphoses*, 5. 346–58.

54 *noysome Esquiline*: because of its sewers. Cf. *FQ*, 2. 9. 32.

57–8 A Petrarchan topos. Cf. *Rime Sparse*, 248. 1–2.

59 *In case*: if so be that.

   gesse in harte: form some conjecture or mental image of.

60 *picture*: image, representation.

61 *shade*: spirit or ghost (Latin *umbra*).

66–7 *spirite . . . masse*: garbling Du Bellay's allusion to the 'spiritus mundi', or world spirit (5. 11). Cf. Virgil, *Aeneid*, 6. 724–7.

69 *of . . . dust*: a biblical topos, cf. Genesis 2: 7.

70 *Idole*: image, likeness.

71–3 *Berecynthian . . . light*: Cybele or Magna Mater, to whom Mount Berecyntus in Phrygia was sacred, was usually depicted wearing a turreted crown because she invented the art of fortification. Cf. Virgil, *Aeneid*, 6. 784–7; *FQ*, 4. 11. 28.

74 *fownd*: found or discovered to be.

75 *Phrygian mother*: Cybele.

76 *famous progenie*: Cybele was mother of the gods.

85–98 Du Bellay's source was Castiglione's sonnet 'Superbi colli, e voi sacre ruine'. Cf. Castiglione, *Opere* (Padua, 1733), 326.

91 *flie*: hasten.

92 *fable*: common talk.

   spoyle: the Roman ruins were used as stone quarries.

93 *frames*: structures.

94 *ruinate*: destroy, bring crashing down.

99–112 Du Bellay adapts George Buchanan's epigram 'Roma armis terras, ratibusque subegerat undas'. Cf. Buchanan, *Franciscus et Fratres et Opera Alia* (Geneva, 1584), 46.

99 *vassals*: mistranslating Du Bellay's 'vaisseaux' (vessels, 8. 1).

101 *in roundnes*: in total compass, thoroughly.

103 *fruitfull*: prolific, fecund.

104 *nephewes*: descendants.

108 *quight*: freed, liberated from.

111 *head . . . deep*: alluding to the legend that the Capitol takes its name from the human head (*caput*) discovered by workmen digging the foundations of the temple of Jupiter. Cf. Varro, *De Lingua Latina*, 5. 41.

114 *stepdame Nature*: for this topos cf. Quintilian, *Institutes*, 12. 1. 2.

115 *course of kinde*: normal or customary course of nature.

119 *palaces*: the rhyme scheme is defective here whether deliberately or by accident.

122 *beneath . . . Moone*: only sublunary things were supposed to be subject to change, but *FQ* often suggests otherwise. Cf. *FQ*, 5 Proem 5–8; 7. 6. 8–14. For the contemporary controversy cf. McCabe (1989), 149–53.

123 *temporall*: subject to time, transitory.

126 *this whole*: the whole universe.

127–8 *sonne . . . land*: Jason, son of Aeson and leader of the Argonauts, took the Golden Fleece from Colchis on the Black Sea with the aid of Medea's magic spells or 'charmes'.

129–30 *earth . . . sand*: fully armed men sprang from the serpent's teeth sown by the king of Colchis but turned upon one another when Jason cast a rock among them. Cf. Ovid, *Metamorphoses*, 7. 121–42.

132 *Hydra*: the many-headed monster slain by Hercules as his second labour. Cf. *TW*, sonnet 8. 11–12 and note.

134 *one . . . hous*: obscure in Du Bellay (10. 8), possibly earth and sky.

140 *earthborn brethren*: Ovid's 'terrigenae . . . fratres' (*Metamorphoses*, 7. 141).

141 *head*: ascendancy, power.

142 *off-spring*: Romulus and Remus, legendary founders of Rome.

148 *Gothicke colde*: because the Goths were a northern tribe.

149 *Nation . . . brood*: the Goths, regarded as a new race of Giants.

152 *mothers bosome*: Gea or earth (hence the spelling 'geaunts' in *FQ*).

153 *all . . . it*: although it were.

Ioue . . . sire: ambiguous in Du Bellay (11. 13). Here presumably alluding to the Titan Cronus, Jove's father.

155–8 The Giants piled Mount Ossa upon Mount Pelion in an attempt to storm heaven. Cf. Virgil, *Georgics*, 1. 278–83; Ovid, *Metamorphoses*, 1. 151–5.

167 *scorned*: contemptible (in comparison with lost glory).

168 *secure*: free from apprehension or anxiety.

169 *aspiring*: rising or mounting up.

174 *rust*: in the sense of erosion.

175 *vnstable*: fickle, changeable.

176 *opposd' . . . puissance*: in the civil wars.

178 *that God*: the Tiber. Cf. Ovid, *Fasti*, 5. 637–62.

snakie-paced: moving in a sinuous, serpentine course, Du Bellay's 'tortueux' (13. 10).

180 *abaced*: cast down, humbled.

185 *aboord*: adrift (apparently a unique usage).

189 *vaine foolhardise*: empty or feigned bravado.

191–2 *Troy . . . colde*: cf. Homer, *Iliad*, 22. 369–75.

191 *dastards*: despicable cowards.

192 *braue*: swagger.

202–3 *Styx . . . three*: the River Styx encircled Hades nine times. Cf. Virgil, *Aeneid*, 6. 439.

203 *wards*: defensive circuits.

207 *accrewe*: increase.

211–14 *Like . . . poyse*: cf. Virgil, *Georgics*, 3. 237–40.

213 *shouldred narre*: shoved or thrust nearer.

214 *poyse*: impact.

215 *Boreas*: the north wind, a Titan in Greek mythology. Cf. line 358.

218 *cariere*: career, course.

220 *spyre*: spiral upwards.

225–6 *Bird . . . fire*: the eagle, emblem of imperial Rome, traditionally bore Jove's thunderbolts. Cf. Ovid, *Metamorphoses*, 12. 560–61.

233 *Germane . . . disguise*: Spenser has misunderstood Du Bellay where the raven disguises itself as the eagle, i.e. the new Gothic kingdoms assume the imperial mantle and, ultimately, the Holy Roman Empire arises from Rome's fall.

234 *cleaue asunder*: Spenser mistakes Du Bellay's 'feindre' (feign) for 'fendre' (cleave) (17. 10).

239–52 For this motif cf. Propertius, *Elegies*, 4. 1; Ovid, *Fasti*, 5. 93–4.

241 *maystred*: overcome, subdued.

244 *hynde*: farmer, shepherd.

245–8 *yearely . . . tooke*: Roman consuls held office for a year, dictators for six months but with much wider powers. Julius Caesar became perpetual dictator thereby paving the way to empire.

250 *Peters successor*: the Pope, alluding to the 'Donation of Constantine' whereby imperial power was allegedly transferred to the papacy.

   betooke: delivered, handed over.

252 *all . . . being*: cf. *FQ*, 7. 7. 58.

253–4 Cf. note to line 122 above.

260 *Pandora . . . store*: Pandora's chest, a wedding gift from Zeus, was variously reported to contain all worldly blessings or evils. Cf. *TM*, 578; *Amor*, 24. 8–12 and note.

261 *huge Chaos*: Rome itself, as a chaotic blend of good and evil.

   turmoyling: agitating, throwing into a state of turmoil.

269 *compas arch't*: arched in a circle (as a rainbow).

270 *Tethys bosome*: the ocean. Tethys, a Titan, and wife to Oceanus, personified the fecundity of the sea. Du Bellay confuses her with Thetis, a lesser sea-goddess and mother of Achilles (20. 4). Cf. note to line 44 above. The two figures were often conflated. Cf. Comes, *Mythologiae*, 8. 2.

271–4 *mounting . . . horld*: cf. Lucretius, *De Rerum Natura*, 6. 451–534.

272 *spreds*: overspreads, extends over.

274 *horld*: hurled.

279 *vade*: fade, perish.

281–94 For the topos of Rome's self-destruction cf. Horace, *Epodes*, 16. 1–10; Lucan, *Pharsalia*, 1. 1–32.

281 *Pyrrhus*: king of Epirus and antagonist of Rome during the Pyrrhic Wars (282–272 BC).

281–2 *puissance of Afrike*: the city of Carthage, Rome's opponent in the three Punic Wars. Du Bellay refers more specifically to 'le Mars de Libye' or Hannibal (21. 1).

282 *braue Citie*: Rome.

285 *freakes*: vagaries, unpredictable upsets.

289 *obiect*: external enemies, the external object of her valour.

292 *for*: because of.

294 *port . . . riue*: proverbial for the destruction of arrogant success.

296 *Byze*: Byzantium.

300 *Harten*: take heart or courage.

304 *sixe . . . ronne*: the duration of the 'great year' which marked the return of all of the heavenly bodies to their point of origin (their 'compass course') was variously estimated. Cf. Boccaccio, *Genealogia*, 8. 2.

307–8 *seedes . . . Chaos*: cf. Lucan, *Pharsalia*, 1. 72–82; for the seeds of creation cf. Ovid, *Metamorphoses*, 1. 5–20; the Gardens of Adonis, *FQ*, 3. 6. 30–38.

309 *the man*: Scipio Nasica opposed Cato's call for the destruction of Carthage. Cf. Plutarch, *Cato Major*, 27.

    would: willed or wished.

310 *spoile . . . forborne*: should be preserved from destruction.

312 *cancring laisure*: corrupting leisure.

316 *matter*: material, substance.

320 *humours superfluitie*: an excess of one of the four bodily humours of blood, phlegm, black bile and yellow bile.

322 *prince . . . kin*: a garbled version of Du Bellay's 'du beaupere et du gendre' (of the father-in-law and son-in-law), referring to Pompey's marriage to Caesar's daughter Julia (23. 14).

323 *blinde furie*: the spirit of civil war, cf. Horace, *Epodes*, 7. 13–20; Lucan, *Pharsalia*, 1. 8.

324 *equall*: of the same species, uniform.

327 *Erynnis*: a Fury. Cf. 'civilis Erinys', the frenzy of civil war at Lucan, *Pharsalia*, 4. 187; *VG*, 394 and note.

328 *grype*: grasp, clutch.

    imbew'd: inspired.

332 *old sinne*: Rome was often considered to be cursed for the destruction of Carthage.

334 *brothers blood*: the murder of Remus by Romulus was held to have entailed the curse of civil war. Cf. Horace, *Epodes*, 7. 17–20.

334–5 *spilt . . . walls*: for this detail cf. Lucan, *Pharsalia*, 1. 95.

336 *foundation sure*: cf. Luke 6: 48–9.

337 *Thracian . . . harpe*: Orpheus' harp. Cf. Comes, *Mythologiae*, 7. 14; *SC*, *October*, [28] and note.

341 *Amphions*: Amphion's music built the walls of Thebes. Cf. Horace, *Ars Poetica*, 394–6; Boccaccio, *Genealogia*, 5. 30.

344 *Ausonian*: Italian, from Ausonia an antique name for southern Italy common in Virgil.

347 *paterne*: example, model (i.e. by imitating Virgil).

349 *leuell*: punning on a builder's spirit-level. Cf. '*Virgils* spirit diuine' at line 347.

350 *compyle*: put (back) together, reconstruct.

351 *forth to figure*: imagine, form a conception of.

352 *vsage right*: correct use or employment.

353 *line*: plumb-line.

    lead: bob or lump of lead at the end of a plumb-line.

    rule: ruler.

    squaire: set square for measuring right angles.

355 *in . . . round*: right around, the whole circumference.

357 *where . . . ground*: tropical Africa.

    yerely starre: Du Bellay's 'l'Astre annuel', the sun (26. 7).

358 *where . . . Boreas*: the Arctic regions. Cf. note to line 215 above.

360 *equalize*: match, coincide with. The notion that names encode the true nature of things is both biblical and Platonic. Cf. Genesis, 2. 19–20; Plato, *Cratylus*.

362 *comprize*: include, comprehend.

363 *Plot*: ground-plan, map.

367 *heapes*: with biblical nuances, cf. Isaiah 25: 2.

371 *helde . . . best*: held in highest esteem.

372 *Yet*: still, Du Bellay's 'encor' (27. 8).

    paternes borne: taken for models or exemplars. Du Bellay's 'servent d'exemples' (27. 8).

375 *buildings . . . gay*: substituted for Du Bellay's 'd'œuvres divines' (27. 11) to suggest the 'Whore of Babylon'. Cf. *MHT*, 231 and note.

376 *Romaine Dæmon*: the Genius or guardian spirit of Rome. Cf. *RT*, 19 and note.

377 *himselfe . . . enforce*: strive or exert himself.

378 *pouldred*: reduced to dust, pulverized (powdered).

379–92 Du Bellay applies to Rome a comparison Lucan applied to Pompey (*Pharsalia*, 1. 136–43). Cf. *SC, Februarie*, 102–14, 207–12 and notes.

382 *foote*: root.

384 *wreathed*: twisted, contorted.

387 *owe . . . winde*: is bound to fall with the first gust of wind.

388 *deuout*: in the sense of superstitious.

394 *embraue*: embellish, adorn.

395–6 *Ionicke . . . Corinth*: the standard architectural orders as listed by Du Bellay (29. 2–3). The general term 'Atticke' (Athenian) embraces them all.

396 *graue*: carve, engrave.

397 *Lysippus*: cf. note to *RT*, 417 above.

practike: skilful, experienced.

398 *Apelles*: ancient Greek painter of the courts of Philip of Macedon and Alexander the Great. Cf. Pliny, *Natural History*, 35. 36. 79–97.

Phidias: ancient Greek sculptor famed for the statue of Zeus at Olympia. Cf. *RT*, 491 and note.

402 *strange*: unfamiliar, marvellous (from the proverb 'ex Africa semper aliquid novi', Africa always produces something strange).

403 *of prise*: of great value (that was highly prized).

407–10 An ironic application of a simile used in the Gospels to describe the imperishable Kingdom of God. Cf. Mark 4: 26–9.

412 *heares*: ears.

414 *reares*: sets up, raises.

418 *pill*: pillage, plunder (as though it were a stone quarry).

419 *gleane*: gather stray ears of corn left by the reapers.

421–34 For Rome's self-destruction cf. note to lines 281–94 above.

421 *champian*: level open country or plain.

424 *Nyle . . . Euphrate*: the four rivers which fostered ancient civilization.

426 *Thamis brincks*: banks of the Thames.

427 *Alemaine*: Germany.

428 *Rhine . . . drinks*: drinks the running waters of the Rhine. Possibly alluding to Gideon's preference for warriors who lapped up river water over those who knelt to drink it. Cf. Judges 7: 4–8.

430 *Aemathian fields*: Lucan's phrase for the battlefield of Pharsalia where Caesar defeated Pompey (*Pharsalia*, 1. 1); Emathia was in Macedonia.

431 As at line 322 Spenser has missed, or deleted, Du Bellay's specific reference to the conflict between Caesar and Pompey (31. 11).

proper: own.

435–48 For artistic immortality cf. E. K.'s gloss to *SC, December*, 'Embleme' and the concluding epilogue; *RT*, 400–406.

437–8 *that . . . meed*: that such poor harp's work (poetry) may ever claim the reward of immortality.

441 *Porphyre*: porphyry, a form of reddish marble.

443 *Phœbus*: Apollo, as patron of music and poetry.

446–8 *how . . . long*: adapting Horace, *Odes*, 3. 30. 12–14.

448 *gowned long*: wearing the toga. Cf. Virgil's description of the Romans as 'gentemque togatam', people of the toga (*Aeneid*, 1. 282).

449–62 Spenser's addition to the sequence, and in form partly an English sonnet and partly Spenserian (rhyming *ababcdcddedeff*).

449 *garland*: in the figurative sense of 'glory' or adornment.

452 *writs*: writings.

454 *dead decayes*: lifeless ruins.

459–60 *Bartas . . . Muse*: alluding to Du Bartas's *Uranie* (1574). Cf. *TM*, 480a and note. A translation from a Roman Catholic poet ends with praise of a staunchly Protestant poet. Spenser was much impressed by Du Bartas's most famous work, *La Semaine* (1578).

Mviopotmos, or The Fate of the Butterflie

The playful beast fable of *Muiopotmos* affords a striking contrast to the ponderous solemnity of the preceding poem yet continues its exploration of mutability and decay in a different key. Underlying the whole narrative lies a learned pun: the Greek word *psyche* means both 'soul' and 'butterfly' and the mock-heroic style of Spenser's epyllion (or little epic) is brilliantly designed to exploit this ambiguity. Depending upon the reader's viewpoint the tale means everything or nothing – or both. The myth of Cupid and Psyche, to which the narrative alludes (129–36), was traditionally allegorized as the soul's journey towards God and Spenser had recently developed its deeper applications in *The Faerie Queene* (3. 6. 50–52). Not surprisingly, therefore, *Muiopotmos* has often been interpreted as a 'tragick' (413) variant on the same theme with the butterfly (as the soul) falling prey to the devilish Aragnoll (433–6) through the 'riotous excesse' (168) of sensual indulgence (179) or vainglorious presumption (41–5, 209–14). Such a reading is possible but reductive. Clarion's youthful beauty and innocence are just as evident as his folly (169–84). He is a 'foolish Flie without foresight' (389) who mistakes the world for 'Paradise' (186) and roams about, unaware of the existence of spiders, in 'the pride of his freedome principall' (380) and 'regardles of his gouernaunce' (384). Yet while such false security certainly contributes to his downfall, he is also the innocent victim of ancestral malice (241–56), envy (337–52) and 'fell spight' (436), and his 'fate' has sometimes been regarded as a warning to unwary courtiers and princes of the need for prudence and circumspection. Spenser's appeal to Lady Carey to place 'a milde construction' on his work, combined with his allusion to the 'rancour' of 'mightie men' (16), has fuelled the search for topical allusions but none of those suggested is particularly compelling. Uncertainty as to the date of composition greatly complicates the matter. The title-page gives a date of 1590, a year earlier than the other title-pages of *Complaints*, but this may simply refer to the date of printing and may conceivably be old style (referring to the first three months of 1591).

The mock-heroic description of the butterfly owes much to Virgil's *Culex* (which Spenser translated – also in *ottava rima* – as *Virgils Gnat*) and to his description of the kingdom of the bees in the *Georgics*. As the latter work reminds us that the spider 'is hateful to Minerva' (4. 246–7) it forms a bridge between the main storyline and the mythological insets, borrowed from Ovid's *Metamorphoses*, describing the weaving contest of Pallas (Minerva) and Arachne and the latter's transformation into a spider (257–352). The transformation of Astery into a butterfly (113–44) is original to Spenser but Ovidian in manner. The insertion of such passages lends considerable complexity to an otherwise simple narrative and the interpretation of the work largely depends upon the perceived thematic relationship between the various episodes. Spenser's use of Ovidian materials has been interpreted, for example, as commenting obliquely upon the fraught relationship between artistic liberty and political control, the poet finding safe haven – figured here in the branches of the peaceful olive tree (326–36) – only within the aesthetic constraints of political patronage, flourishing or perishing within the politician's web [cf. Bernard (1989), 118–22].

On a more general level the conflict between Pallas and Arachne gives prominence to the imagery of weaving and thereby to the relationship between art and life (280, 329–36) [cf. Dundas (1975)]. Clarion's fate is 'wouen' (235) by Jove as surely as the butterfly which occasions Arachne's transformation is woven into Pallas' tapestry. Yet Arachne's skill survives her fall: art becomes nature in the person of the spider who weaves the net that entraps Clarion (357). Pallas' artificial butterfly seems alive, but the real butterfly dies in the 'curious networke' of Aragnoll's web (368), and all of these fictitious creatures are themselves spun into the verbal tapestry of Spenser's text. In the pleasure gardens frequented by Clarion 'Arte' aspires to 'excell the naturall' (165–6), yet the text reminds us that nothing earthly 'can long abide in state' (217). Cf. Allen (1956); J. H. Anderson (1971); Bender (1972); Bond (1976); Brinkley (1981); Grant (1979); B. Harris (1944); Hulse (1981); Macfie (1990); Morey (1988), (1995); A. D. Weiner (1985); W. Wells (1945).

Dedication *To the right worthy* . . .

Ladie . . . *Carey*: Elizabeth Spenser (1557–1618), daughter of Sir John Spencer of Althorp, married Sir George Carey, Lord Hunsdon (later patron of the Lord Chamberlain's Men) in 1574. She is celebrated as 'Phyllis' at *CCH*, 541–7 and is one of the dedicatees of *FQ*.

7 *person yeelded*: the body itself delivered up.

13 *vnminded*: disregarded.

13–14 *name* . . . *vouchsafed*: Spenser also claims kinship to the Spencers of Althorp in the dedications to *TM*, *MHT* and at *CCH*, 536–9; *Proth*, 130–31.

19 *take in worth*: take in good part.

20 *milde construction*: innocent interpretation. Spenser disavows and simultaneously encourages political interpretation.

Muiopotmos

1 *sing . . . debate*: a mock-heroic opening in imitation of Homer's *Iliad*.

2 *Nemesis*: goddess of divine retribution, often dealing destruction to the arrogant, vainglorious or those guilty of hubris.

3 *mightie ones*: possibly Minerva and Arachne [cf. W. Wells (1945)]. Ovid's Arachne is lowly born but gains renown through her skill (*Metamorphoses*, 6. 7–16). The application of the first two stanzas to the rest of the poem is problematic and does not accord well with the story of Clarion and Aragnoll. Topical allusion is possible.

10 *Muse*: Melpomene. Cf. *SC*, *November*, 53; *TM*, 115–74.

14 *Clarion*: trumpet, an emblem of fame. Cf. *RT*, 434; *TM*, 457–63. The sense of the Latin *clarus*, 'brilliant' or 'bright', may also be present.

14–15 *declyne . . . wretchednes*: regarding tragedy as the 'fall of great men' after the fashion of Chaucer's *Monk's Tale*. Cf. *RT*, 43–56; *TM*, 151–62.

15–16 *And . . . men*: adapting Virgil's question about the gods (*Aeneid*, 1. 11).

17 *Flies*: insects.

18 *Empire . . . aire*: cf. note to line 212 below.

23 *Muscaroll*: from the Latin *musca*, 'a fly'.

26 *toward*: promising.

28 *equall peares*: his contemporaries, his fellows.

29 *forered*: betoken, predict.

39 *inquire*: investigate, explore.

44–5 *mount . . . hight*: a mock-heroic version of Platonic ascent from the earthly to the celestial. Cf. *HL*, 57–70.

48 *tempt . . . winde*: assay the tempestuous wind.

51 *Hyperions . . . childe*: Ovid's periphrasis for Apollo (*Metamorphoses*, 4. 192, 241). The Titan Hyperion was the father of the sun god.

55 *guize*: characteristic manner or customary fashion.

56 *furnitures*: armour, military equipment.

57–96 Imitating the epic topos of the arming of the hero. Cf. *Iliad*, 11. 15–46.

62 *bit*: bite (played upon in 'bitter').

63 *Vulcane . . . sheild*: Achilles' mother Thetis presented him with armour specially made by Vulcan. Cf. Homer, *Iliad*, 18. 369–617; 19. 1–20.

69 *spredding*: spreading over, covering.

71 *Alcides*: Hercules, a descendant of Alceus.

72 *Næmean Conquest*: the first of Hercules' twelve labours involved slaying the Nemean lion. Cf. Hesiod, *Theogony*, 326–32; *FQ*, 7. 7. 36.

73 *Burganet*: light helmet with visor.

77 *Bilbo*: the steel of Bilbao in Spain was renowned.

brasse . . . Corinth: for the fame of Corinthian brass cf. Pliny, *Natural History*, 34. 1. 1.

78 *Oricalche . . . Phœnice*: orichalcum was a precious alloy of copper. The detail derives from the arming of Turnus at Virgil, *Aeneid*, 12. 87; Phoenicia was on the Syrian coast. The association may derive from the manufacturing of orichalcum from 'Phoenician earth'. Cf. Knowlton (1980).

79 *Phœbus arrowes*: sunbeams (i.e. arrows of Apollo).

82 *outlaunced*: launched or projected outwards.

84 *Brigandine*: a small galley with rams. Cf. *FQ*, 4. 2. 16.
    applyde: fitted, readied.

85 *threatfull*: threatening.

86 *engines*: machines, instruments.

93 *Iris* : goddess of the rainbow. Cf. Virgil, *Aeneid*, 4. 700–701.

95 *Iunoes . . . traine*: Juno placed the hundred eyes of the giant Argus in the peacock's tail. Cf. Ovid, *Metamorphoses*, 1. 720–23.

98 *Archer . . . Cytheree*: Cupid, son of Venus. Cf. *SC, March*, [79].

99 *wroken*: avenged. For Cupid's cruelty cf. *FQ*, 3. 11. 29–52.

101 *changefull*: diverse, varied.

104 *manifolde*: many times.

110 *grace*: favour.

113–44 Spenser has here created a new myth designed to contrast with the Ovidian transformation of Arachne into a spider (345–52).

119 *Astery*: the name derives from that of Asteria who transformed herself into a quail to escape the advances of Zeus. She is a subject of Arachne's tapestry at *Metamorphoses*, 6. 108. Cf. *VG*, 20 and note.

120 *usage*: behaviour, manner.

123 *fields honour*: a Latin expression, cf. Virgil, *Georgics*, 2. 404.

129 *iealous*: suspicious.

131–3 *sonne . . . teare*: Cupid visited Psyche by night enjoining her not to look on him. When she disobeyed and discovered his identity she was condemned to countless trials before their eternal reunion. Cf. Apuleius, *The Golden Ass*, 7–9; *FQ*, 3. 6. 50. Psyche means both 'soul' and 'butterfly'.

136 *led away*: misled.

148 *franke lustinesse*: free or unrestrained vigour.

149 *champion*: the open plain.

152 *gainsaid*: refused.

154 *measured*: traversed, travelled.

159 *choicefull*: fickle, capricious.

163–5 *Nature . . . Arte*: for the contention of nature and art cf. *FQ*, 2. 12. 59. The implication is one of hidden danger.

171 *curious*: inquisitive.

178 *all . . . sweete*: only to the unwary, cf. lines 217–20.

184 *weather him*: take the air.

187–200 Cf. the flower passages at *SC, Aprill*, 59–63; 136–44; *VG*, 665–80. Poets were expected to know 'the power of herbs' (*SC, December*, 88).

Cf. Gerard's *Herball* (1597) and Culpeper's *Complete Herbal* (1653) to which the following notes are indebted.

187 *wholsome Saulge*: sage was known as 'the holie herb' for its curative properties.

Lauender . . . gray: spike lavender has 'long hoarie leaves' and its distilled waters were considered good for headaches and epilepsy.

188 *Ranke . . . Rue*: Gerard records its 'ranke smell' and lists a wide range of medicinal properties.

Cummin . . . eyes: aromatic herb believed to clear bloodshot eyes.

190 *Sharpe Isope*: hyssop was used as a gargle for mouth ulcers, a purgative and to heal wounds.

191 *Marigoldes*: the 'flower of the Sunne' considered good for the heart.

Bees . . . Thime: Virgil recommends planting thyme to attract bees (cf. *Georgics*, 4. 31–2, 112).

192 *Sweete Marioram*: an aromatic culinary herb noted for its 'marvellous sweete smell' and used medicinally.

Daysies: used for wounds and ulcers and to clear the eyes.

decking prime: adorning springtime.

193 *Coole Violets*: oil of violets is 'colde and moist' and was used to cool inflammations or distempers of the blood.

Orpine . . . still: also known as livelong ('growing still') and regarded as curative and cleansing for wounds.

194 *Embathed Balme*: the garden herb balm gentle or balm-mint, used as an unguent for wounds and also in tonics.

chearfull Galingale: English galingale or sedge, noted for 'refreshing the spirits and exhilarating the mind'.

195 *Fresh Costmarie*: alecost (a form of chrysanthemum), used to flavour ale and as a purgative. Cf. *VG*, 670.

breathfull Camomill: camomile, an aromatic creeping herb, noted for expelling phlegm, opening pores and clearing head-colds.

196 *Dull Poppie*: the poppy was valued for its soporific qualities.

Setuale: setwall or valerian, used as a stimulant and also in antidotes (hence 'drink-quickning').

197 *Veyne-healing Veruen*: vervain, used for cleansing wounds.

hed-purging Dill: used for curing hiccups and stimulating the brain.

198 *Sound Sauorie*: savory was used as a tonic and to ease melancholy.

Bazill hartie-hale: basil was 'good for the hart and for the head'.

199 *Fat Colworts*: coleworts or cabbages, 'good for sinews and joints'.

comforting Perseline: parsley, 'agreeable' to the stomach and believed to clear internal obstructions.

200 *Colde Lettuce*: lettuce 'cooleth a hot stomacke' or heartburn.

refreshing Rosmarine: rosemary, used in perfumery and held to quicken the senses and freshen the breath.

206 *embay*: bathe.

207 *suffisaunce*: abundance (but the alternative sense of 'sufficiency' underlines the 'riotous' character of the butterfly's attitude).

212 *raine . . . aire*: with potentially sinister connotations. The devil was prince of the air (cf. Ephesians 2: 2).

217 *abide in state*: remain in the same (flourishing) condition.

227 *Forecast*: predict (with a view to forestalling).

229 *all . . . some*: one and all.

230 *importune*: ceaselessly pressing, grievous.

234 *vnhappie happie*: playing on the sense of 'hap' or chance.

257–352 Based on Ovid, *Metamorphoses*, 6. 1–145 but with significant alterations. In Ovid the tapestries are described in the reverse order and the goddess, incensed to find her work equalled by Arachne, destroys her rival's tapestry and transforms her into a spider when she attempts to hang herself. In Spenser the transformation is the self-induced effect of envy (cf. *FQ*, 3. 10. 58–60) and the detail of the butterfly (329–36) is original.

262 *Pallas*: the goddess Athena, also known as Minerva.

265 *Tritonian Goddesse*: Minerva, so called from her birthplace of Lake Tritonis in Libya. Cf. Ovid, *Metamorphoses*, 6. 1.

    hard: heard.

272 *quill*: bobbin.

274 *paragon to make*: to compete with her.

276 *tapet*: tapestry.

277 *figur'd*: portrayed, depicted.

281–96 In Ovid Arachne depicts twenty-one amorous scenes but Spenser elaborates upon the first, drawing also upon *Metamorphoses*, 2. 843–75; Moschus, *Idylls*, 2.

289 *winged Loue*: Cupid.

290 *Sport*: Iocus (Joy) accompanies Cupid at Horace, *Odes*, 1. 2. 34.

292 *Spring*: young man, youth.

296 *Tritons*: sea-gods, traditionally depicted blowing horns.

297 *empale*: surround, encircle.

299 *Yuie*: ivy, sacred to Bacchus (who is one of Arachne's subjects in Ovid) and fitting for scenes of sensual indulgence. Cf. *SC*, *August*, 30.

301 *Enuie pale*: as at Ovid, *Metamorphoses*, 2. 775.

302 *venemous . . . deuowres*: cf. Ovid, *Tristia*, 4. 10. 123–4.

305–6 *debate . . . Athens*: for the dispute between Athena and Neptune over Athens cf. *SC*, *Aprill*, [124] and note.

306 *trie*: strive, venture.

315 *three-forked mace*: the trident. Cf. Comes, *Mythologiae*, 2. 8.

316 *steed*: Neptune's gift was a salt-water spring, but Spenser reads 'ferum' (horse) for 'fretum' (*Metamorphoses*, 6. 77).

320 *foreiudgement*: in the sense of rash or premature judgement. The sentiment is Spenser's addition.

321 *Aegide shield*: following Comes, Spenser conflates Minerva's aegis (a sort of goat-skin breast plate) and shield (*Mythologiae*, 7. 11).

326 *Olyue*: Ovid associates the olive with peace (*Metamorphoses*, 6. 101). Cf. *SC*, *Aprill*, [124].

333 *nap*: down (cleverly combining the physical attributes of the insect with the 'nap' of the cloth upon which it is woven).

337 *ouerlaid*: overcome, overwhelmed.

341 *dismaid*: with a play on her ensuing loss of maiden's shape.

347 *dryrihed*: dreariness or sorrow.

362 *twyne*: thread.

364 *dieper*: diaper, a kind of fine linen.
   damaske: silk.
   lyne: linen.

365 *embost*: ornamented with bosses or studs.

366 *loupes*: loops.

369–73 Vulcan trapped his wife Venus in the act of adultery with Mars. Cf. Ovid, *Metamorphoses*, 4. 176–89.

370 *Lemnian God*: Vulcan, whose seat was on the island of Lemnos.

371 *compasse in*: enclose, entrap.

376 *rang'd*: roved, roamed.

380 *principall*: princely, royal.

385 *Aragnoll*: possibly from the Latin *aranea*, 'spider' or 'cobweb'. The diminutive *araneoli* ('little spiders') is translated as 'cobweb' at *VG*, 3.

394 *tickle*: tingle.

403 *by . . . side*: from behind.

405 *readie tide*: opportune moment, ready opportunity.

412 *runes*: utterances, discourses (a poetic usage).

413 *Tragick Muse*: cf. note to line 10 above.

414 *bitter throw*: grievous death-throe as at *FQ*, 1. 10. 41.

415 *drerie stownd*: dismal moment.

420 *Aeoles raine*: the realm of Aeolus, god of the winds. Cf. Virgil, *Aeneid*, 1. 52–63; *FQ*, 4. 9. 23.
   on hed: headlong.

427 *laces*: fine threads.

429 *lymie*: sticky (as if coated in bird-lime).

434 *Lyon*: the devil is so described at 1 Peter 5: 8.

435–40 Recalling the closing lines of Virgil's *Aeneid* (12. 945–52) in which Aeneas exacts vengeance upon Turnus for the death of Pallas (whose spoils Turnus is wearing).

Visions of the worlds vanitie

This sequence of emblematic sonnets is original to Spenser but heavily influenced by, and designed to complement, *The Visions of Bellay* and *The Visions of Petrarch*, first translated for *A Theatre for Worldlings* and subsequently revised for publication in *Complaints*. Their ethos is visionary: the 'strange showes' here 'presented' to the speaker's 'eyes' (10) proceed from 'meditation deepe' (3) and afford perspectives on contemporary life 'exceeding [the] reach of common reason' (4). Yet the subject matter is highly conventional. Sonnets 4 and 9 rehearse material familiar from Alciati's *Emblems*, with which the work shares a strong generic connection, and the rest may be regarded as variations upon well-worn commonplaces. Their application, however, is somewhat unusual. The format is that of a series of miniature beast fables emblematically illustrating the insecurity of power but designed to lead, in the climactically positioned sonnet 11, to a perception of the value of 'mean things' or lowly persons (152). Noteworthy also is the speaker's potentially radical decision 'to scorne all difference of great and small' (160) and his admonition to those who attain to 'honours seat' – the self-made Lord Burghleys of the world, perhaps – to 'forget not what you be' (166). At times one senses a grim satisfaction battling with 'inward ruth and deare affection' (157) in the representation of the various 'ruines tragicall' (163). As in *Virgils Gnat* 'small' things have their day and, like the prefatory sonnet to *Virgils Gnat*, these sonnets are all Spenserian in form (rhyming *ababbcbccdcdee*), anticipating in their structural experimenta-tion the more mature specimens of *Amoretti*. This is significant in that one detects here a personal and artistic assertiveness absent from the other sequences of vision poems. Both the voice and the form are now distinctly Spenserian. Cf. Clements (1955); Hyde (1983); Satterthwaite (1957).

1–14 Cf. *RT*, 477–90; *VB*, 1–14; *VP*, 1–14.
2 *earthly prison*: the body.
6 *debaced*: looked down upon, despised.
7 *declining season*: it was commonly supposed that the world had reached its final age. Cf. McCabe (1989), 28–9.
10 *showes*: visions.
11 *embraced*: held, in the sense of contemplated.
12 *empassion . . . nere*: moved me deeply or intimately.
13 *Ladie . . . worth*: possibly Elizabeth Carey who is asked to 'take in worth' (take in good part, or be content with) the preceding *Muiopotmos*, or the Countess of Pembroke to whom the whole volume is dedicated.
15–28 Modelled on Aesop's fable of the gnat and the lion (cf. *Fables*, no. 188).

15 *Phœbus*: Apollo, the sun god.

17 *embowed*: bow-shaped, convex.

24 *Brize*: a breeze or gadfly.

28 *diseased*: annoyed, discomfited.

31 *Crocodile*: for its evil associations cf. *FQ*, 1. 5. 18; 5. 7. 6–7.

35 *Tedula*: presumably the trochilus credited with this practice by Pliny, *Natural History*, 8. 37. 90.

43–56 Cf. Aesop's fable of the eagle and the beetle (cf. *Fables*, no. 4), illustrated in Alciati's *Emblems* (no. 168) under the motto 'a minimis quoque timendum' (the least are also to be feared).

43 *kingly Bird*: the eagle.

44 *Scarabee*: scarab or dung beetle.

49 *kindling fire*: an alteration to the usual version in which the scarab breaks the eagle's eggs.

58 *cleepe*: call (an archaism).

60 *flaggie*: pendulous, or possibly flaccid.

62–3 *Leuiathan . . . sport*: cf. Psalms 104: 26. For Leviathan as Egypt (sometimes identified by the Reformers with Rome) cf. Psalms 74: 14; Ezekiel 29: 3–5. Cf. note to lines 71–4 below.

64 *sword-fish*: for its belligerence cf. Pliny, *Natural History*, 32. 6. 15.

66–8 *spewe . . . hewe*: cf. the monster Error at *FQ*, 1. 1. 20. The correspondence may indicate an application to Rome.

71–4 *Dragon . . . beare*: cf. the Leviathan of Job 41: 15–34; and the dragon of *FQ*, 1. 11. 11–12.

75 *vnequall peare*: a deliberate oxymoron: the spider seems inferior to the dragon but proves to be its equal.

77 *vermin*: noxious creature.

83 *vainnesse*: stupidity, foolishness.

84 *forlorne*: destroyed, ruined (from the verb 'forlese').

85–112 At Job 40: 17 the monster Behemoth, sometimes identified with the elephant, 'moveth his tail like a cedar' and the associations may inform Spenser's choice of subjects for these two sonnets.

85–9 *Cedar . . . one*: for the cedar of Lebanon as a type of towering pride brought low by God cf. Ezekiel 31: 3–14. Cf. also *VB*, 57–70; *VP*, 29–42.

86 *proportion*: shape or figure.

90 *pith*: the medulla or inner tissue.

91 *worme*: the cedar was popularly believed to be invulnerable to the tree worm. Cf. Bartholomaeus Anglicus, *De Proprietatibus Rerum*, 17. 23.

100 *bosses*: ornamental knobs.

101 *batteilant*: combatant, prepared for combat.

110 *stained*: blemished, defiled.

112 *varie*: alter, overturn.

113–26 Cf. *VP*, 15–28.

115 *top-gallant*: platform at the head of the main mast.

122 *Remora*: the sucking fish. Pliny laments the human insignificance ('vanitas') exposed by its power (*Natural History*, 32. 1. 1–6). Alciati applies it to those who are easily drawn from virtue (cf. *Emblems*, no. 82).

123 *heele*: bottom or keel.

126 *wring*: afflict, distress.

127–40 Cf. Aesop's fable of the gnat and the lion (cf. *Fables*, 188).

130 *dreadles*: secure.

141–54 The events described form part of the early, legendary history of Rome and pre-date the empire by many centuries.

141 *raine*: sovereignty, dominion.

146–8 *Galles . . . Goose*: conflating two distinct episodes. In the time of Romulus the Sabines gained access to the citadel by bribing Tarpeia, daughter of the custodian, while a Gaulish attack on the Capitol in 390 BC was foiled by the cackling of the sacred geese. Cf. Livy, 1. 11; 5. 47.

148 *bewrayde*: betrayed, disclosed.

163 *ruines*: connecting the visions with *RT*.

164 *loue . . . degree*: cf. *SC, Julye*, 219–20.

168 *fickle*: uncertain, unreliable.

The Visions of Bellay

Appended to Du Bellay's *Antiquitez de Rome* (translated in *Complaints* as *Ruines of Rome*) is *Une Songe ou Vision sur le Mesme Subject* of which the present work is a close translation. The *Songe* is comprised of a sequence of fifteen Petrarchan sonnets collectively presented as a dream vision and designed to reflect emblematically upon the universal implications of the preceding poem. Spenser had contributed an earlier version in blank verse to *A Theatre for Worldlings* (1569), omitting sonnets 6, 8, 13 and 14. These are now restored to their proper positions and all fifteen are recast as English sonnets (rhyming *ababcdcdefefgg*). The process of transition occasions localized distortions and inversions of syntax with some loss of accuracy but, as a comparison between the two versions of sonnet 1 will demonstrate, such faults are generally offset by an increased musicality of language and assurance of metrical control. The revised sequence is remarkably coherent, with no evidence of major stylistic variation in the four newly-added sonnets. The restoration of the eighth sonnet with its pseudo-Apocalyptic imagery serves to underscore the relationship between pagan and papal Rome, between worldly and spiritual 'vanitee' (11). The rise of the papacy and the Holy Roman Empire are presented as particularly ill consequences of

Rome's decline (cf. sonnets 5, 7 and 11). Sonnet 14 explicitly contrasts the city of God with the city of man and allows the speaker's voice to merge momentarily with that of St John. The episode recalls St George's mystical experience in *The Faerie Queene* (1. 4. 4–5; 10. 55–9) and suggests something of the centrality of Du Bellay's influence to the wider Spenserian canon. Cf. T. M. Greene (1982); Prescott (1978); Tucker (1990).

See also the notes to *TW*, sonnets 1–11.

16 *assize*: standard measurement.

21 *rayons*: rays, beams.

22 *golds enchase*: golden inlay, relief or engraving. Cf. *SC*, *August*, 27.

32 *leuel*: aim, mark. Cf. *MHT*, 770–72.

45 *chapters*: capitals.

fryses: friezes.

49 *chayre*: chariot.

58 *gleame*: radiance, brightness. *TW* has 'shade', translating the French 'umbrage' (sonnet 5. 2).

60 *Ausonian streame*: the Tiber. Cf. Virgil, *Aeneid*, 3. 477–9; *RR*, 344 and note.

68 *wedge*: instrument used for splitting wood and, by extension, the blade of an axe.

72 *two whelpes*: Romulus and Remus were suckled by a wolf 'oute of whose breastes they . . . sucked all manner of crueltie' (*TW*, fol. 15v).

74 *wreath'd*: turned or twisted away from.

for . . . nones: for the moment.

79 *thousand huntsmen*: Barbarian invaders.

83 *soyle*: filthy pool of blood.

84 *spoyle*: hide, skin.

91 *haughtie*: lofty.

92 *raught*: reached.

94 *in . . . folde*: lapped or engulfed in flames.

103–6 *beast . . . deuoure*: cf. the beast from the sea, Revelation 13: 1.

104 *coure*: cower, crouch in fear.

107 *kinde*: shape, form.

109–10 *winde . . . burst*: alluding to the Barbarian invasions.

110 *Scithian mew*: confinement in Scythia. Cf. *RR*, 45 and note.

115 *loast*: loose, unbound.

117 *belly*: bulging side.

119 *creakie*: full of creeks (*OED*).

aflot: in a state of overflow or submersion ('afloat', *OED*).

129 *outraging*: rending, tearing.

151 *siluer dew*: probably simony. 'Ambition begot Simonie. Simonie begot the Pope and the Cardinals' (*TW*, fol. 91v).

155 *rayle*: flow, gush.

157 *grayle*: obsolete form of 'grail', gravel. Cf. *FQ*, 1. 7. 6.

166 *Satyres*: representing the bestial in man. Cf. *FQ*, 3. 10. 43–52. For their association with ruin and desolation cf. Isaiah 34: 14.

167 *ray*: pollute, defile.

170 *sad Florentine*: Petrarch. Cf. *VP*, 15–28.

179 *Nereus*: a god of the sea and here virtually synonymous with it. Not mentioned in Du Bellay.

183 *gron'd*: lamented.

184–5 *Citie . . . glad*: alluding to St John's vision of the New Jerusalem, Revelation 21–2. Cf. *TW*, sonnet 15.

186 *sand . . . built*: cf. Matthew 7: 26–7; and Lucifera's palace, *FQ*, 1. 4. 5.

187 *rayse*: graze, scrape.

192 *Northerne . . . storme*: the Barbarian invasions.

The Visions of Petrarch

This brief work is a translation from Petrarch's *Rime Sparse* (323), a sequence of six twelve-line meditations on the death of Laura which culminate in a three-line conclusion expressing the speaker's 'sweet desire for death' ('un dolce di morir desio'). The first five emblems lament the loss of various aspects of Laura's physical and spiritual beauty, the sixth introduces an image of the lady herself allegorically represented as stung by a snake while walking among flowers. The circumstances of her fall recall those of Eve and Eurydice [cf. Genesis 3: 1–7; Ovid, *Metamorphoses*, 10. 8–10], but her departure for the next world 'not merely confident but happy' ('lieta si dipartio, non che secura') evokes the prophecy that the Virgin Mary, as the second Eve, will defeat the serpent: 'I will put enmity between thee and the woman, and between thy seed and her seed; it shall bruise thy head, and thou shalt bruise his heel' (Genesis 3: 15). Spenser had contributed an earlier version to *A Theatre for Worldlings* (1569), working from the French translation of Clément Marot, but possibly with some knowledge of the original. However, whereas Marot had reproduced Petrarch's twelve-line format, Spenser developed the first and third sections into English sonnets (rhyming *ababcdcdefefgg*). He now completes that process by casting all six sections in the same form but without achieving consistency in the positioning of the 'volta', or turn of thought, which occurs in Petrarch precisely at the midpoint [cf. Bath (1988)]. The insecurity of the new form – which may well be deliberate – is therefore at odds with the clear, dichotomous dynamics of the original structure.

Marot had expanded Petrarch's conclusion into a four-line coda, or

643 NOTES TO DAPHNAÏDA

'envoy', which Spenser reproduced in the earlier version, but it is now developed into a full Spenserian sonnet (rhyming *ababbcbccdcdee*) which more successfully appropriates the Petrarchan vision to a characteristically Spenserian preoccupation with mutability and *contemptus mundi*. In particular, as the notes point out, the new echoes of Ecclesiastes serve to underscore the biblical influence informing Spenser's reading of Petrarch. It is hardly coincidental that in his prefatory address to the reader of *Complaints* William Ponsonby lists a translation of Ecclesiastes among Spenser's unpublished works.

If the 'faire Ladie' addressed in the concluding sonnet (and at line 13 of *Visions of the worlds vanitie*) is Lady Carey, the dedicatee of *Muiopotmos*, the last four contributions to *Complaints* may be intended as an extended contemplation, in divergent moods, upon the ultimate 'vanitie' of even the most innocent of human aspirations. Cf. J. C. Bondanella (1978); Forster (1969); Roche (1989).

See also the notes to *TW*, epigrams 1–6.

26 'All is vanity and vexation of spirit' (Ecclesiastes 1: 14). Cf. 'vext with sights' at line 92.
85 *tickle*: mutable, uncertain.
93 *faire Ladie*: Lady Carey is the person most recently addressed (in the dedication to *Muiop*) but the Countess of Pembroke is also possible as the dedicatee of the entire volume.

DAPHNAÏDA

Though closely related to Chaucer's *Book of the Duchess*, *Daphnaïda*, written in memory of 'the noble and vertuous Douglas Howard', is as strikingly dissimilar in tone and outlook as it is in metre and form. Indeed, by choosing for his stanza a variant of rhyme royal subtly altered to avoid the resolution of the concluding couplet (rhyming *ababcbc* rather than the traditional *ababbcc*), Spenser virtually ensured the divergence of the two poems. Chaucer's swift octosyllabic couplets express life even as they explore death, but Spenser's slowly measured iambic pentameters evoke a very different mood. Chaucer begins in spring, Spenser in autumn; Chaucer lingers over reminiscences of past happiness, Spenser broods on the sorrows of the moment [cf. Harris and Steffen (1978)]. As a result, *Daphnaïda* has often been regarded as a particularly morbid exercise in excess, but this is to mistake the nature of its literary conventions.

As a 'rufull plaint' (4) and a 'meditation / Of this worlds vainnesse and lifes wretchednesse' (33–4) *Daphnaïda* announces its kinship to the volume of *Complaints* published the same year, but its form is that of the pastoral

NOTES TO *DAPHNAÏDA* 643

elegy and its fictive strategies function to locate private distress within a wider, and potentially qualifying, context [cf. Martin (1987)]. Alcyon and the narrator are afflicted by a similar malaise – we may even be intended to conclude that they are both widowers (64–6) – but the former is obsessed and inconsolable whereas the latter seeks companionship and desires consolation (554–60). The choice of names is also significant: in Chaucer, in an inset Ovidian episode, the lady Alcyone dies from bereavement (62–214), and Spenser's transference of a female name to his male protagonist may be intended to suggest the emasculating effects of excessive grief – a common Renaissance topos. In this manner the poem contrives to respond to the depth of Alcyon's grief while resisting his surrender to it [cf. Pigman (1985), 75–81]. The extreme formality of the complaint assigned to him, moving in seven well-ordered sections of seven stanzas apiece, suggests a sense of disciplined control, and potential consolation, of which the speaker remains unaware [cf. Røstvig (1963); Kay (1990)]. He seems incapable of sharing Daphne's 'gladnesse' in her own death (282), or of responding to her request that he live for their daughter and 'in lieu of mee / Loue her' (290–91). The sense of emotional dislocation wrought by his grief is embodied in the work's structure. The poem's central stanza records Daphne's assertion, quoted by her grieving husband, that she will dwell eternally amid 'Saints and Angels in celestiall thrones' (281–7), but the central stanza of his own lament records his tormented exclusion from that 'better place' (366) [cf. Fukuda (1987)]. He regards her death as 'against all course of kinde: / For age to dye is right, but youth is wrong' (242–3), but the autumnal setting reminds us that 'early frosts' are in the nature of things (28).

It would therefore appear that *Daphnaïda* demands a guarded response from its readers. We are provided with a perspective upon Alcyon which he, in his distressed condition, is incapable of sharing. Although he is not consoled within the poem, the starkness of the conclusion illustrates the choice facing his real life counterpart, Sir Arthur Gorges, Douglas Howard's husband: resignation or death. In this respect the poem may be intended as an oblique caution [cf. Oram (1981)]. In Ovid, Alcyone is transformed into a bird, despair into elevation, and it is noteworthy that in *Colin Clouts Come Home Againe* Gorges is advised to channel his emotional energies away from sorrow into joyful poetry that 'may thy *Muse* and mates to mirth allure' (391). Within *Daphnaïda* itself the elaborate artistry of formal complaint makes it possible to articulate 'that which cannot be tolde' (72). The relationship between art and grief is thus shown to be potentially transformative: the Fates, it would appear, may serve as Muses after all (11–19). Cf. D. Cheney (1983); DeNeef (1982); Lambert (1976); Sandison (1928).

The title (meaning 'Of Daphne') is both personally and generically appropriate in that Sir Arthur Gorges addressed several poems to his wife under the name of 'Daphne' and both Theocritus (*Idylls*, 1) and Virgil (*Eclogues*, 5) lament the death of characters called 'Daphnis'.

Dedication *To the right . . .*

Marquesse of North-hampton: Helena von Suavenberg or Snachenbergh (1549–1635), a Swede, came to England in 1565 and married William Parr, Marquis of Northampton and brother of Queen Catherine Parr. Following his death in 1571 she married Sir Thomas Gorges, Arthur Gorges's uncle. Her favoured position at court is celebrated at *CCH*, 508–15. She was the chief mourner at Queen Elizabeth's funeral. Cf. Sjøgren (1978).

3 *Gentlewoman*: Douglas Howard (1572–90), wife of Sir Arthur Gorges and daughter of Henry Howard, second Viscount Byndon.

7 *Arthure Gorges*: Sir Arthur Gorges (1557–1625) was a cousin and close ally of Sir Walter Ralegh whose exploits at the Azores (1597) he chronicled in his *Relation of the . . . Iland Voyage*. He translated Lucan's *Pharsalia* (1614) and Bacon's *Wisdom of the Ancients* (1619) into English and Bacon's *Essays* into French. In *The Olympian Catastrophe* (1612), an elegy on the death of Prince Henry, he repeats some of the speeches Spenser here assigns to Alcyon. His bereavement is also commemorated at *CCH*, 384–91.

13 *Howards*: like his wife, Sir Arthur Gorges was descended from John Howard, the first Duke of Norfolk (1430–85) whose daughter Anne married Sir Edmund Gorges. Spenser's genealogy is accurate.

17 *white Lyon*: one of the heraldic supporters of the Norfolk arms.

22 *1591*: as Douglas Howard died in August 1590 the date is probably new style, taking January not March as the beginning of the year (i.e. the poem was published in 1591 not 1592). Cf. Sandison (1928), 650.

Daphnaïda

6 *Alcyon*: on the death of her husband Ceyx, Alcyone attempted suicide but was transformed into a halcyon (cf. Ovid, *Metamorphoses*, 11. 384–748). In Chaucer she dies 'for sorwe' (cf. *Book of the Duchess*, 62–214). The alteration from the feminine to the masculine form of the name evokes the common topos of the emasculating effects of excessive grief. Alcyon later compares himself to Ceres (463) and Philomela (475).

8 *who . . . sense*: whoever can experience pleasure.

16 *fatall Sisters*: the three Fates, cf. *SC*, *November*, [148]. Chaucer invokes Tisiphone at *Troilus and Criseyde*, 1. 6–14.

17 *direfull*: terrible.

18 *bands*: threads.

19 *Queene*: Proserpina, wife of Hades, or possibly Hecate.

20 *Stygian strands*: shores of the infernal River Styx.

27 *opprest*: overwhelmed, crushed.

35 *yet*: still.

38–40 Cf. *Book of the Duchess*, 444–57.

39 *cost*: approach.

41 *Iaakob staffe*: a pilgrim's staff, particularly associated, like the scallop shell, with St James (Latin *Jacobus*).

crost: held as though making the sign of the cross.

46–7 Cf. *Book of the Duchess*, 460–61.

57–60 Cf. ibid., 502–18.

57 *disguize*: strange, unaccustomed dress.

59 *wise*: manner.

67–70 Cf. *Book of the Duchess*, 548–57.

67 *Griefe . . . beare*: translating the Latin proverb 'solamen miseris socios habuisse doloris'.

70 *apay*: requite, repay.

78–84 Cf. *Book of the Duchess*, 721–41.

78 *bent*: inclined, resolved.

80 *conuenient*: befitting, appropriate.

88 *occasion*: cause.

90 *question . . . of*: doubts or questions raised about.

99–168 Cf. *Book of the Duchess*, 617–86 where the man in black employs the imagery of chess to signify his loss.

99 *Whilome I vsed*: in the past I was accustomed to.

101 *Sabrinaes streame*: the River Severn. Sabrina, the illegitimate daughter of King Locrine, was drowned in the Severn by the jealous Queen Guendolen, cf. *FQ*, 2. 10. 17–19. The allusion is perplexing since the Gorges family held lands in Somerset and Dorset.

103–5 Cf. *Book of the Duchess*, 797–802.

107 *Lionesse*: the white lion supported the Norfolk (Howard) arms.

108–9 *White . . . impresse*: according to one version of the myth Venus pricked her feet on thorns as she rushed to succour the dying Adonis and her blood dyed the flowers red. More commonly roses were said to spring from Adonis' own blood. Cf. Bion, 'Lament for Adonis', 64–7; Ovid, *Metamorphoses*, 10. 728–39; Comes, *Mythologiae*, 5. 16.

111 *kindlie wantonnesse*: natural exuberance.

112 *staine*: obscure, eclipse.

116 *bring to hand*: make tame.

120 *handled*: treated.

121 *stout*: proud, resolute.

122 *auncient . . . haire*: she was sole heir to Henry Howard, Viscount Byndon. The lion is, therefore, heraldically appropriate.

124 *fram'd*: disposed, made receptive.

bent: purpose, design.

130 *if nay*: if not required.

133 *warie*: carefull, circumspect.

138 *good*: both property and well-being.

140 *miscaried*: lost or perished.

  or: either.

146 *rude*: common, ill-informed.

  tri'de: found by experience, ascertained.

147 *blesse*: congratulate, praise (but possibly with the ironic implication of piously warding off harm).

151 *her*: the goddess Fortuna (Fortune).

154 *Tragedies*: for this concept of tragedy cf. *TM*, 151–62.

155 *dout*: apprehension.

156 *Satyre*: representing the negative forces of nature, satyrs are commonly destructive in Spenser. Cf. *TM*, 268; *VB*, 166 and notes.

163–4 *spoyle . . . pray*: the terms suggest a contest between earth and heaven for possession of the lady.

165–6 *Lyon . . . firmament*: Hercules slew the Nemean lion which Zeus then placed among the constellations as Leo. Cf. *FQ*, 7. 7. 36.

171 *abstaine*: refrain.

173 *Some . . . alaid*: somewhat abated.

176–82 Cf. *Book of the Duchess*, 721–48.

177 *riddle*: enigmatic account.

178 *in . . . skand*: when rationally assessed or considered.

183–4 Cf. *Book of the Duchess*, 1300–1310.

185 *extreamitie*: extreme or utmost suffering.

188 *Reuoked*: revived (literally 'called back').

189 *drearing*: grief (a Spenserian coinage).

196 *dearnelie plained*: dismally complained.

197–539 A formal 'complaint' symmetrically organized into seven sections of seven stanzas apiece. For the thematic implications of the numerological patterns of seven and nine cf. Kay (1990), 49–51.

199 *share*: allot, apportion.

200–201 *afflict . . . transgresse*: a biblical topos, cf. Genesis 18: 23.

200 *so sore*: as sorely.

203 *oppresse*: afflict, crush.

206 *immaculate*: spotless, pure.

208–12 Cf. *Book of the Duchess*, 484–6.

214 *diuinde*: made divine or heavenly.

218 *Astræa*: goddess of justice, whose departure from the earth signalled the onset of corruption. Cf. Ovid, *Metamorphoses*, 1. 149–50; *MHT*, 1–4; *VG*, 359–60 and notes; *FQ*, 5. 1. 11.

225 *Elisa*: Queen Elizabeth I. Cf. *SC*, *Aprill*, 34.

228 *Castaly*: a fountain on Mount Parnassus sacred to Apollo and the Muses. Cf. *RT*, 431; *TM*, 273 and notes.

229 *Colin*: Colin Clout, Spenser's poetic *persona*. Cf. *SC*, *Aprill*, 33–161.

230 *deifie*: honoured as a goddess.

239 *first . . . spring*: she was just nineteen years old.

240 *rinde*: bark.

248 *Timon*: the famous misanthrope Timon of Athens, cf. Plutarch, *Life of Antony*, 70; Lucian, *Timon, or the Misanthrope*.

251 *dropping weares*: wastes or drains away drop by drop.

265 *ill . . . behoue*: that might ill become him.

266 *tourne*: event, accident.

268 *bridale feast*: cf. 'the marriage supper of the lamb', Revelation 19: 9. Cf. also Matthew 22: 1–14.

280 *toward*: coming, future.

285–6 *Saints . . . blest*: cf. Revelation 7: 9–11.

288 *pledge*: token.

290 *Ambrosia*: their daughter Ambrosia Gorges, probably named after her godfather Ambrose Dudley, Earl of Warwick.

297–8 *swords . . . chest*: cf. Luke 2: 35.

299 *sugred*: dulcet.

309–15 Cf. *Book of the Duchess*, 848–54.

311 *trimly*: featly, finely.

314 *nigh . . . astownd*: she nearly astounded or astonished.

317 *virelayes*: spring poems, short lyrics using only two rhymes.

323 *Bagpipe*: a pastoral instrument, cf. *SC*, *Aprill*, 3.

327 *idle pleasance*: leisured enjoyment.

330–43 *birds . . . song*: a pastoral topos, cf. Virgil, *Eclogues*, 8. 52–60.

330 *spray*: branch.

336 *vntimely howres*: i.e. beyond the nocturnal hours to which they were traditionally believed to be confined.

338 *Let . . . wearinesse*: take a rest from her long wearisome labours.

342 *Stepdame*: cf. *RR*, 114 and note.

346 *Astrofell*: unidentified, as at *Ast*, 181–96. The bog asphodel, common on English moorlands, may be intended here.

347 *Smallage*: wild parsley, noted for its pungent quality.

    Rew: rue, noted for its bitter, strongly scented leaves.

348 *mawes*: stomachs.

    corrupted: infected, sickened.

353 *confusde decay*: dissolution into disordered elements.

354–7 Cf. Chaucer, *The Pardoner's Tale*, 720–38.

364 *riddance*: deliverance.

375–6 *bread . . . teares*: cf. Psalms 80: 5.

379 *Saint*: in the sense that she is now among the blessed.

387 *importune*: grievous, severe.

413 *post*: post-rider, courier.

424 *Starre*: like Sir Philip Sidney's Stella.

432 *Mill wheele*: implying, by association with the mill stone, the idea of being ground down by misery.

434–6 Cf. *Book of the Duchess*, 587–8.

435 *I . . . die*: cf. 1 Corinthians 15: 31.

442–55 *Why . . . send*: for this motif cf. Petrarch, *Rime Sparse*, 268.

447 *vneath*: distressing, troublesome.

450 *drawes*: draws on, entails.

452 *forgoe*: relinquish, give up.

453 *it . . . amend*: alter it for the better, improve it.

463–5 *mother . . . world*: Eurydice is an error for Proserpina. After her abduction by Hades, her mother Ceres, often identified with Cybele or Magna Mater, sought her throughout the world. Cf. Ovid, *Metamorphoses*, 5. 385–571. For Eurydice cf. *VG*, 433–72.

468 *Titan*: the sun god, Phoebus Apollo.

469 *loose*: release from harness.

470 *harbenger*: inn-keeper or host. 'Lodge' (471) develops the metaphor.

475 *Philumene*: for Philomela's transformation into a nightingale cf. *SC*, *August*, 183 and note; *November*, [141].

479 *dwell in darknes*: the Antipodeans, but for religious associations cf. Isaiah 9: 2; Luke 1: 79.

483 *Venus*: Vesper or the evening star. Cf. *Epith*, 286–94.

489 *vnlade*: put off, lay down.

494 *fairest . . . faded*: cf. Psalms 103: 15–16.

503 *vsance*: usage.

504 *none . . . may*: none may be assured or certain of.

505 *desastrous chaunce*: ill-starred or ill-fated fortune.

507 *sufferaunce*: suffering (with connotations of endurance).

525 *in . . . disdaine*: deliberately ambiguous: either disdained by life or disdaining life, having adopted an attitude of 'contemptus mundi'.

529 *Cyparesse*: cypress was symbolic of mourning. Cf. *FQ*, 2. 1. 60.

540–45 Cf. *Book of the Duchess*, 461–503.

545 *Amooued*: aroused.

stonie swound: insensible swoon.

546 *recomfort*: console, encourage.

556–67 The invitation enacts a Virgilian pastoral topos (cf. *Eclogues*, 1. 79–83), but the non-Virgilian refusal signifies the depth of Alcyon's grief.

558 *Cabinet*: little cabin.

562 *intreate*: beseech, implore.

COLIN CLOVTS COME HOME AGAINE

If Edmund Spenser were Colin Clout the title of this poem might indicate a public resolution of private conflicts, a final attainment of security. But Colin Clout is simply the name by which the author is 'best knowen' (1), his voyage abroad is Spenser's homecoming, his homecoming is Spenser's exile [cf. McCabe (1993)]. The title is therefore richly ambiguous and the complex pastoral dialogue, set in place by an unidentified third-person narrator, is carefully designed to exploit that ambiguity through a persistent shifting of emotional and spatial perspectives. Through the *persona* of Colin Clout we learn of the present state of Ireland, of the colonist's sense of dislocation in a 'waste' landscape 'where I [according to a view attributed to Ralegh] was quite forgot' (183). But through Colin's eyes also, the critical eyes of a supposed stranger, we see the corruption of the Elizabethan court where, despite appearances to the contrary, poets go unpatronized and 'each one seeks with malice and with strife, / To thrust downe other into foule disgrace' (690–91). Colin's return 'home' is thus grimly ironic: the harsh and violent environment of Ireland is preferable to the 'guilefull' (699), 'ydle' (704), 'lewd' and 'licentious' (787) atmosphere of the court. Yet Colin distils into the description of Cynthia herself all of the passionate idealism from which her court conspicuously derogates (330–51, 596–647), and his appeal on behalf of William Alabaster, a poet engaged, like Spenser, in the writing of an Elizabethan epic, insinuates an oblique request for a very different sort of homecoming: 'O call him forth to thee, / To end thy glorie which he hath begun' (408–9).

The difficulty is that the association between Cynthia and Elizabeth is every bit as problematic as that between Colin and Spenser. As employed by Sir Walter Ralegh, Spenser's 'shepheard of the Ocean' (66), the figure of Cynthia is used to explore the complex, contradictory and ultimately unfulfilled relationship between the Queen and her admirers. The possibility therefore arises that poetic vision eclipses reality, that Colin's perception of Elizabeth transcends its source of inspiration. The vision of Cynthia, no less than that of Cupid (799–894), is a testimony to the mythopoetic powers of the Orphic or vatic poet enlightened by 'some celestiall rage' [cf. Mallette (1979)], and the work is structured in such a way as to exacerbate the underlying dichotomy by a series of abrupt transitions from vision to experience – as when Thestylis suddenly asks Colin why he decided to leave Cynthia despite his avowed admiration for her (651–9). The bitter satire of a shallow court 'full of loue, and loue, and loue my deare' (777) is greatly intensified by Colin's personal apprehension of a more transcendent, creative force from whose sublime influence most of Elizabeth's attendants deserve to be exiled (893–4).

Such attitudes serve to remind us that, as previously in *The Shepheardes Calender*, the matter of love is highly politicized through the skilful employment of the imagery of courtship in its various senses. Colin's unsuccessful pursuit of Rosalind seems intended to reflect upon the poem's political disappointments. The work revolves about idealized images of circularity and reciprocation, its various sections, as the following notes indicate, are elaborately and meticulously balanced [cf. Burchmore (1977)], yet the effect is one of disjunction and disharmony. Violations of stylistic decorum suggest violations of social and moral decorum as the poem ascends to eulogy only to plunge to satire. Its publication with the elegiac *Astrophel* serves to strengthen the impression that the glory days of the Elizabethan court are over. It would thus appear that the poem occupies a pivotal position in the Spenserian canon. Its dedication is dated 27 December 1591, but internal allusions indicate revision as late as April 1594 (434–5), and the poem was published in the same year as *Amoretti and Epithalamion* (1595), works in which the completion of *The Faerie Queene* is said to have been deferred and Spenser treats of the courtship of his second wife without recourse to the *personae* of Colin or Rosalind. Cf. Bernard (1989); D. Cheney (1983); Comito (1972); Edwards (1971); Ellrodt (1960); Hoffman (1977); Meyer (1969); Oram (1990); Sandison (1934); Shore (1985).

Dedication *To the right . . .*

Raleigh: Sir Walter Ralegh (1554–1618) served in Lord Grey's Irish wars (1580–82) and was instrumental in the notorious massacre of foreign mercenaries at Smerwick, an incident that Spenser vigorously defended in *Vewe* (cf. *Prose*, 161–2). Ralegh was the poet's fellow undertaker in the ill-fated plantation of Munster and is one of the dedicatees of *FQ*. He fell from royal favour owing to his relationship with Elizabeth Throckmorton, a maid of honour whom he married clandestinely in 1592. The matter is represented allegorically in *FQ* in the story of Timias and Belphoebe (4. 7. 23–47; 4. 8. 1–18).

Stanneries: the districts of Cornwall and Devon containing the tin mines and smelting works. The warden guarded crown interests, and conducted the business of the stannery courts.

3 *precisely officious*: punctiliously dutiful.

4 *meanesse*: lowness or rudeness. The poem is written in the 'mean' or middle style appropriate to the pastoral genre, although Colin's praise of Elizabeth consciously violates generic decorum (590–619).

9 *late . . . in*: recent sojourn in.

   protect: protected.

12 *Kilcolman*: Spenser's new residence at the site of an old Desmond castle two miles north-west of the town of Doneraile in County Cork.

13 *1591*: for the dating of the poem see the headnote.

Colin Clouts Come Home Again

1–7 Apart from the opening seven lines (rhyming *ababcbc*) and the concluding five (rhyming *ababa*) the poem is written in continuous quatrains rhyming *abab*. Cf. Burchmore (1977), 398.

1 *best . . . name*: testifying to the popularity of *SC* which had gone through four editions.

2 *Tityrus*: Virgil. Cf. *SC*, 'Epistle', 5 and note.

5 *Charming*: playing or tuning, but with connotations of magical control or skill. Cf. *SC*, *October*, [118].

  oaten pipe: the traditional pastoral instrument.

6 *play*: relax, disport themselves.

7 *listfull*: attentive. Cf. *FQ*, 5. 1. 25.

8 *astonisht*: amazed or stunned.

12 *groomes*: shepherds.

14 *dearest in degree*: in the highest degree, dearest of all.

15 *Hobbinol*: identified as Gabriel Harvey at *SC*, *September*, [176], but there is no evidence that Harvey ever visited Ireland.

  areed: addressed himself, spoke.

18 *I . . . crosse*: i.e. I suffer the greatest affliction of any.

21 *blythe*: joyous.

22–31 *Whilest . . . aliue*: the traditional topos of pathetic fallacy. Cf. Virgil, *Eclogues*, 1. 38–9; 7. 55–60; *SC*, *November*, 123–36.

23 *sythe*: sigh.

39 *dubble vsurie*: double interest.

40 *that Angels*: i.e. Queen Elizabeth's.

46 *bright*: fair lady, beauty.

50 *forsake*: refuse, decline.

53 *harmonie*: melody, concord of word and music.

56 *trade*: custom (and also pastoral occupation).

57 *Mole*: the range of Ballyhoura and Galtee Mountains to the north of Kilcolman. Cf. *FQ*, 7. 6. 36.

59 *Mullaes*: the River Awbeg (meaning 'little river'), a tributary of the River Blackwater, skirting Spenser's property. Cf. *FQ*, 4. 11. 41.

60 *straunge shepheard*: Ralegh.

62 *yshrilled*: sounded out.

65 *ycleepe*: call or name (an archaism).

66 *shepheard . . . Ocean*: recalling Ralegh's unfinished poem to Elizabeth, the *Booke of the Ocean to Scinthia*. He was Vice-Admiral of Devon and Cornwall, and his interest in New World exploration was well known.

69 *Prouoked*: urged.

  fit: a song or some verses of a song.

72 *æmuling*: emulating, desiring to rival (a unique usage).

73 *before . . . many*: that many had previously tried to rival or emulate.

77 *By . . . turnes*: alternating by turn.

81 *atweene*: i.e. in between Colin's speeches.

82 *readie . . . restraine*: interrupt the ready flow or order of discourse.

86–7 *hymne . . . carol*: poetic forms associated with the pastoral mode and specifically with *SC*.

88 *loue . . . losse*: of the lady Rosalind, lamented in *SC*.

90 *For . . . me*: for love had forsaken me and been forsaken by me.

92 *Bregogs*: the River Bregoge (meaning 'deceitful') flows underground for two miles before emerging to join the River Awbeg (Mulla) above Doneraile. Colin's song is in the nature of an aetiological fable. Cf. Henley (1928), 85–7; R. M. Smith (1935).

100 *tenor*: substance or matter.

105 *Armulla dale*: presumably the valley of the River Blackwater.

113 *cleped*: called, named (an archaism).

114 *ragged*: dilapidated, broken-down. Possibly alluding to the ruins of the Franciscan friary at Buttevant.

120 *good*: well-being (but also, as the next line indicates, worldly good).

121 *preferre*: advance (socially or materially).

123 *Allo . . . Broad water*: Allo was properly a tributary of the River Blackwater (commonly called Broadwater at the time). Cf. *FQ*, 4. 11. 41.

131 *good will*: in the formal sense of agreement or consent.

134 *ieolous*: vigilant, suspicious.

141 *besides*: side by side.

151 *water-courses spill*: destroy his channels.

156 *Thestylis*: the poetic *persona* of Lodowick Bryskett, Spenser's friend and colleague in Ireland. Bryskett's *The Mourning Muse of Thestylis* was published with *Ast* following *DLC*. He is addressed at *Amor*, 33. Spenser features as a speaker in Bryskett's *Discourse of Civill Life* (1606).

164–71 Depending upon the dating of this section of the poem the allusion may be to Ralegh's relegation from court in 1589, or to his imprisonment in July 1592 following the disclosure of his marriage to Elizabeth Throckmorton. The 'song' alluded to may be some version of the *Booke of the Ocean to Scinthia*, but the refrain or 'undersong' given at lines 170–71 is not found in any extant poem of Ralegh's. Cf. *FQ*, 3 Proem 4–5.

168 *singulfs rife*: abundant sobs (from Latin *singultus*, 'sobbing').

177 *did . . . dissuade*: did divert you away from here.

180 *lore*: artistic skill.

188 *peerlesse skill*: for Elizabeth as a poet cf. *TM*, 576 and note.

   making: composing. Sidney explains that the term poet 'commeth of this word *Poiein*, which is to make' (*Apology for Poetry*, *ECE*, 1. 155).

195 *needments*: necessaries, luggage.

197–8 *waters . . . mountaines*: cf. Ovid's passage into exile, *Tristia*, 1. 2. 19.

209 *presuming*: presumptuously daring or venturing.

210 *stremes*: currents.

217 *Glewed*: fastened.

subtile matter: fine substance.

223 *againe*: in return or in reply.

226–7 *farre . . . appeare*: cf. Virgil, *Aeneid*, 3. 192–3.

228–63 Adapting the mode of piscatory pastoral developed by Sannazzaro in his *Piscatorial Eclogues* (1526). Cf. *SC*, 'Epistle', 152 and note.

232 *recomforting*: encouraging, reassuring. Cf. *Daph*, 546–7.

233 *Regiment*: domain.

235 *liege*: sovereign.

Regent: ruler, governor.

237 *keep*: tend, care for.

239 *vseth*: was accustomed, made it her practice.

242 *frie*: offspring.

244 *charge in chief*: the Lord High Admiral in 1595 was Lord Howard of Effingham.

245 *Triton*: a sea-god. Cf. Ovid, *Metamorphoses*, 1. 332–42; *FQ*, 4. 11. 12.

wreathed: twisted.

248 *Proteus*: a sea-god with prophetic powers and the ability to change shape. Cf. Virgil, *Georgics*, 4. 387–414; *FQ*, 3. 8. 30.

249 *Porcpisces*: porpoises, regarded as sea-swine as the orthography indicates.

251 *Compelling*: driving, herding.

whether: whithersoever, to whatever place (he chooses).

252–3 *I . . . assignd*: Ralegh was Vice-Admiral of Devon and Cornwall.

270 *Lunday*: the Isle of Lundy off the Devon coast.

271 *first . . . showne*: first to be spotted off the west coast of England.

273 *ieopardie*: danger, obliquely alluding to the danger of invasion.

279 *red*: seen or found.

281 *high headland*: Land's End at the southerly tip of Cornwall.

282 *horne . . . has*: because of Cornwall's tapering shape its name was commonly held to derive from the Briton word *corn* ('horn').

283 *lea*: meadow-land.

284 *loftie mount*: presumably St Michael's Mount at Penzance.

286 *fleet*: float.

288 *vnlade*: unload.

290–99 The exchange recalls the sense of wonder inspired by the 'New World' discoveries in which Ralegh was an active agent.

292 *thous a fon*: you are a fool, recalling the colloquial tone of the pastoral dialogues in *SC* (cf. *Februarie*, 69; *Julye*, 33).

301 *Funchins*: the River Funcheon flows parallel to the River Awbeg and joins the River Blackwater further downstream. Cf. *FQ*, 7. 6. 44.

praise: worth or value.

305 *all one*: just the same (as here).

313 *issues*: discharges. A malady cured by Christ, cf. Matthew 9: 20.

314 *griesly famine*: cf. Spenser's graphic account of the Munster famine in *Vewe* (*Prose*, 158).

 sweard: sword.

315 *bodrags*: raids or incursions. Presumably a corruption of the Celtic *buaidhreamh* ('molestation') or *buadre* ('tumult'). Cf. *FQ*, 2. 10. 63.

318 *wolues*: for Irish wolves cf. *FQ*, 7. 6. 55.

319 *raunger*: game-keeper.

321 *price*: estimation or regard.

322 *Religion . . . her*: religion has the support of the lay or civil authority.

324 *For end*: in conclusion.

324–7 *grace . . . abuse*: note the play upon the various senses of the term 'grace', natural, civil and divine. Cf. *FQ*, 6. 10. 22–4.

332–51 This is more in the nature of an icon of sacral monarchy than a description of the Queen. The recurrent symbol of the circle denotes perfection. Cf. *FQ*, 1 Proem 4; 5 Proem 10–11; 6 Proem 7.

336 *her . . . read*: i.e. if I might account anything earthly to be like her.

340 *circlet . . . Turtle*: the coloured band about the neck of a turtle dove.

342 *Phebes garlond*: the lunar aura. Phoebe is Diana or Cynthia, goddess of the moon.

355 *vpraising*: extolling, praising.

357 *cause*: business.

359 *grace*: favour (but with spiritual connotations).

364 *measure*: standard or capacity.

365 *mott*: appraised (past participle of the verb mete).

366 *fynd*: devise, invent.

370 *in . . . fee*: in her service.

371 *Elfe*: creature.

373 *applie*: employ, put to use.

374 *craesie*: cracked.

380–455 Of the poets accorded fictional names only three, Alcyon (Gorges), Amyntas (Stanley) and Astrofell (Sidney) can be identified with certainty (see notes below).

380 *Harpalus*: possibly George Turberville.

382 *Corydon*: variously identified as Abraham Fraunce or Edward Dyer.

384 *Alcyon*: Sir Arthur Gorges, the death of whose wife Spenser had lamented in *Daphnaïda*. Cf. *Daph*, 'Dedication' and notes.

386 *Daphnes*: Douglas Gorges, poetically addressed by her husband as Daphne.

389 *Eglantine of Merifleure*: an unfinished pastoral poem by Gorges.

392 *Palin*: tentatively identified as George Peele.

394 *Alcon*: variously identified as Thomas Lodge or Thomas Watson.

396 *Palemon*: possibly Thomas Churchyard.

400 *Alabaster*: William Alabaster (1568–1640), author of the Latin tragedy *Roxana* and the unfinished Latin epic *Elisaeis*, in celebration of Queen Elizabeth, to which Spenser alludes at line 403.

406–11 The tone suggests a measure of identification between Spenser and Alabaster in respect of their need for royal patronage.

409 *glorie*: praise (i.e. the work that confers praise).

412 *Po . . . Tyburs*: Tasso (or possibly Ariosto) and Virgil respectively.

415 *pitch*: height, summit.

416 *new shepheard*: identified at line 424 as Samuel Daniel (1563–1619). In 1592 he published the sonnet sequence *Delia* referred to at line 419 and the *Complaint of Rosamond* possibly alluded to at line 427. His tragedy *Cleopatra* appeared in 1594 and the *Civil Wars* between 1595 and 1609.

422 *tender*: fledgling.

424 *rouze*: ruffle or raise (cf. *FQ*, 1. 11. 9).

428 *shepheard . . . Ocean*: Ralegh, as at line 66.

430 *sweetly tempred*: delicately natured, finely constituted.

434 *Amyntas*: Ferdinando Stanley, Lord Strange, fifth Earl of Derby died on 16 April 1594.

435 *Amaryllis*: Alice Spencer, daughter of Sir John Spencer of Althorp and widow of Lord Strange, fifth Earl of Derby. Cf. *TM*, 'Dedication' and notes.

442 *maintaine*: support (by patronage).

444 *Aetion*: possibly Michael Drayton (1563–1631). He had adopted the heroically sounding *persona* of Rowland in *Idea. The Shepheards Garland* (1593) to which Spenser may allude at line 447. Less probable is an allusion to Shakespeare.

446 *inuention*: inventiveness, ingenuity.

449 *Astrofell*: Sir Philip Sidney whose death (1586) is lamented in *Ast*.

452 *sundry kynd*: various types (alluding to their different genres).

455 *that shepheardes*: i.e. the shepherd of the ocean, Ralegh.

466 *For that*: because.

467 *one*: Rosalind of *SC*.

468 *beame . . . aboue*: the ray of beauty shot out (like a spark) from heaven.

473 *martyrize*: sacrifice (by suffering love pangs).

477 *onely*: playing on 'one-ly'.

euer one: 'For truth is one, and right is euer one' (*FQ*, 5. 2. 48). Queen Elizabeth's motto was 'semper eadem', 'always the same'.

478 *all*: wholly, entirely.

481 *enforce*: endeavour, strive.

485–583 Identification of many of the ladies celebrated is necessarily conjectural owing to the conventional quality of Spenser's descriptions.

Contemporary annotations to the poem supply some clues. Cf. Koller (1935). The twelve ladies-in-waiting complement the twelve poets.

487 *Vrania . . . Astrofell*: Mary Herbert, Countess of Pembroke (1561–1621), sister and literary executor of Sir Philip Sidney. The choice of the heavenly Muse Urania (cf. *TM*, 481–540) may allude to her translations of the Psalms. She is the supposed speaker of *DLC*.

490 *gold of Opher*: a biblical formulation, cf. Psalms 45: 9.

492 *Theana*: Anne Russell, daughter of the Earl of Bedford, and widow of Ambrose Dudley, first Earl of Warwick, who died in 1590. She is celebrated at *RT*, 244–52 and is one of the two dedicatees of *FH*.

493 *ouer dight*: cloaked, covered over.

495 *glister*: sparkle, glitter.

505 *Marian*: presumably Margaret Russell, daughter of the Earl of Bedford, and wife of George Clifford, Earl of Cumberland. She is one of the two dedicatees of *FH*.

507 *pearling*: forming pearl-like drops or beads.

508 *Mansilia*: Helena, Countess of Northampton. Cf. *Daph*, 'Dedication' and notes.

511 *her neeces*: Douglas Howard, wife of Sir Arthur Gorges. Cf. *Daph*, 'Dedication' and notes.

512 *paterne*: model.

514 *tread*: walk (in court processions).

516 *Galathea*: presumably Frances Howard, daughter of the Earl of Nottingham and wife to Henry Fitzgerald, twelfth Earl of Kildare.

522–3 *Coshma . . . Maa*: Frances Howard's jointure included Croom and Adare on the River Maigue, from which the barony of Coshma derived its name. Spenser doubled the vowel in Maa in imitation of the long Irish 'a' [á]. Cf. Henley (1933), 464.

524 *Neæra*: Elizabeth Sheffield, daughter of John Lord Sheffield and wife of Thomas Butler, tenth Earl of Ormond, one of the dedicatees of *FQ*.

526 *famous Shure*: the River Suir which rises in the Slieve Bloom mountains and flows through Waterford. Cf. *FQ*, 4. 11. 42–3.

532 *Stella*: here, and at *Ast* 55, Frances Walsingham, widow of Sir Philip Sidney. The Stella of Sidney's *Astrophil and Stella*, however, was Penelope Devereux, Lady Rich.

538 *I . . . be*: Spenser also claims kinship to the Spencers of Althorp in the dedications to *TM*, *MHT*, *Muiop*, and at *Proth*, 130–31.

540 *Phyllis*: Elizabeth Spencer, daughter of Sir John Spencer of Althorp, wife of Sir George Carey, Lord Hunsdon. Cf. *Muiop*, 'Dedication' and notes.

Charillis: Anne Spencer, daughter of Sir John Spencer of Althorp. Cf. *MHT*, 'Dedication' and notes. Her third husband, Robert Sackville, second Earl of Dorset, is the 'noble swaine' of line 552.

Amaryllis: cf. note to line 435 above.

546 *reflexion*: a throwing back of light or iridescence.

547 *rash*: lacking caution, unprepared.

551 *temperance*: self-control, humility.

552–3 *swaine . . . possest*: Anne Spenser wed Robert Sackville in 1592.

560 *primrose*: in the sense of prime rose. Cf. *SC*, *Februarie*, 166.

562 *high addrest*: mounted or kindled on high.

567 *doth . . . dread*: fears to risk entering the bands of another marriage.

572–4 *Flauia . . . Candida*: unidentified and possibly added by way of consolation to those ladies excluded from particular mention. The names mean blonde (literally 'yellow') and white.

582 *shrynd*: enshrined or enclosed (in his thoughts).

583 *indignifie*: dishonour, demean.

586 *make*: eulogize, by 'making' or composing poetry.

596–7 *words . . . hiue*: a biblical simile, cf. Proverbs 16: 24; Song of Songs 4: 11.

600–601 *deeds . . . vine*: adapting Song of Songs 7: 7–8 where the lady's breasts are compared to 'clusters of grapes' and 'clusters of the vine'. The childless Elizabeth is 'fruitfull' in virtuous deeds.

603 *wine*: cf. Song of Songs 1: 2; 4: 10; 7: 9.

605 *windowes . . . East*: cf. Genesis 7: 11.

606 *fleecie cattell*: sheep.

607 *perled*: pearled (with dew drops). Cf. note to line 507 above.

608 *Franckincence*: cf. Exodus 30: 34; Song of Songs 3: 6; Revelation 8: 3–4.

612–15 The queen's contemplation ascends in Neoplatonic fashion to the realm of pure angelic intellect and to her own heavenly 'idea'.

615 *fashion*: demeanour.

616–17 *forgot . . . selfe*: he has forgotten pastoral decorum after the manner of the rustic speakers in the Wakefield Shepherds' Plays when they contemplate divinity. The breach of convention is itself a convention.

618 *seemeth*: befits, suits.

621 *measure*: boundary or limit.

622 *furious insolence*: frenzied exultation. For poetic frenzy cf. notes to *SC*, *October*, 'Argument' and line 823 below.

623 *yrapt in spright*: in rapturous ecstasy.

626–7 *when . . . worth*: i.e. the inadequacy of his language betrays the inadequacy of his thought.

630 *vitall bands*: the bonds of life.

632–3 *name . . . grow*: cf. Virgil, *Eclogues*, 10. 53–4; *FQ*, 4. 7. 46.

632 *endosse*: inscribe, write.

634 *each where*: everywhere.

engrosse: write in large letters.

635 *fill*: i.e. fill the letters carved in the earth.

637 *knowen*: well-known, familiar.

645 *renewed*: recalled, revived.

646 *bountie*: possibly Spenser's pension and his land at Kilcolman.

648 *heards*: shepherds.

655 *vnto . . . accrew*: fall to you, come your way.

659 *Most . . . tell*: he is most wretched who cannot explain the cause of his wretchedness.

660–730 For court satire cf. *TM*, 67–108; *MHT*, 581–942.

662 *vncomptrold*: unhindered, unrestrained.

664 *that . . . prooued*: by what I experienced during my short stay.

666 *hooued*: arose or swelled up.

667 *followd*: dogged.

670 *aduenture*: undertake, venture upon.

671 *blandishment*: allurement, attraction.

673 *hardnesse*: hardship, severity.

678 *of right*: rightfully, reasonably.

680 *cancred*: malignant, spiteful. This disclaimer is common to most satirists of the period.

681 *demeand*: treated.

682 *selfe-regard . . . ill*: consciousness of, or concern for, his personal fortunes, whether good or ill.

687 *losse*: destruction, ruin.

694–5 The absence of a rhyme for 'wit' at line 693 may indicate the loss of a line of text.

695 *his*: some other man's.

696 *fained forgerie*: fraudulent deceit.

697 *breeding*: occasioning, causing.

   blot of blame: mark of defamation or disgrace.

698 *secrecie*: confidence.

700 *dissembling curtesie*: the antithesis of the ideal expounded in *FQ*, 6.

701 *filed*: smooth. Cf. *FQ*, 1. 1. 35.

   tearmes of art: artful language.

702 *schoole*: academic learning or discipline.

   schoolery: instruction, teaching.

703 *countenance*: support, patronage.

705 *professours*: those who profess learning or the arts.

707–8 *Ne . . . applie*: a complaint repeated at *FQ*, 6. 12. 41.

709 *shouldred*: thrust or shoved aside. Cf. *FQ*, 5 Proem 5.

   shit: shot.

711 *weed*: clothing.

713 *exceed*: are of excessive size.

714 *harts . . . beares*: alluding to the cuckold's horns.

719–20 *Euen . . . away*: cf. Psalms 68: 2.

724 *painting . . . wall*: cf. Shakespeare, *Sonnets*, 146. 1–4.

727 *single*: threadbare, meanly attired (continuing the clothing motif).

729 *gallantry*: finery, splendour.

732 *too generall*: too all-embracing or undiscriminating.

733 *of name*: of repute, or of noble name.

736 *Lobbin*: possibly Robert (or Robbin) Dudley, Earl of Leicester (died 1588). At *SC, November*, 113–22 Lobbin laments the death of Dido.

738 *else*: elsewhere.

740 *ghesse*: think of, call to mind.

741 *Those . . . retaine*: presumably those who seek to further the requests of impoverished suitors, retaining rather than discarding their petitions.

744 *ledden*: meaning (literally 'tongue' or 'diction'). Cf. *FQ*, 4. 11. 19.
 in charge: by way of duty.

745 *sciences*: knowledge, various branches of learning.

746 *professors*: proficients, practitioners.

749 *Blame . . . generall*: a common disclaimer of contemporary satire.

750 *priuate*: personal, particular to a specific individual.

754 *profession*: practice.

757 *most-what*: mostly, for the most part.

761 *diuide*: assign, give over.

763 *Moldwarps nousling*: moles nuzzling or burrowing.
 lurke: idle.

766 *professe*: avow.

771 *once*: at all.

772 *lore professed*: doctrine avowed or acknowledged.

776 *writ*: inscribed in the sense of engraved or carved.

778 *studie*: thought, intellectual concern.

780 *badge*: token of favour or esteem.

781 *ought*: aught, of any value.

786 *sue . . . serue*: attend and cater to. Cf. *FQ*, 2. 7. 9.

789 *vse . . . name*: use his name idly or take it in vain.

790 *complement*: ceremonious courtesy (with a play on compliment).
 courting: playing upon the senses of wooing and courtly behaviour.

793 *liege*: loyal.

794 *abuses*: perversions or violations.

797 *Do . . . go*: are punctiliously scrupulous lest we act rashly.

799–822 The Cupid presented here is largely the imperious god of medieval love poetry (cf. *FQ*, 3. 11. 47–9; 12. 22–3), but his birth from a bisexual Venus and his nursing in the gardens of Adonis suggest the more sublime conception of love as a cosmic, creative force developed at lines 835–94 (cf. *HL*, 43–119; *FQ*, 3. 6. 49–50).

800 *couples*: copulation.

801–2 *Venus*: the bisexual Venus is virtually identical to the goddess Nature. Cf. Lucretius, *De Rerum Natura*, 1. 1–23; *FQ*, 4. 10. 39–47; 7. 7. 5–7. For her allegorical significance cf. Comes, *Mythologiae*, 4. 13.

801 *soly . . . seeme*: appears to be both sexes in one.

805 *perfection*: maturity, fulfilment.

807 *shafts . . . lead*: according to Ovid the gold occasions love, the lead hate (*Metamorphoses*, 1. 468–71).

810 *godded*: deified.

812 *randon*: random.

814 *Like . . . spill*: just as he pleases to preserve or destroy us.

818 *Preferre*: advance.

    grace vs dignifie: either make us worthy of their favour or ennoble us through the influence of their favour.

822 *termes*: words, expressions.

    yield: speak, utter.

823 *celestiall rage*: divine madness or 'furor' of which Ficino identified four species: poetic, mystic, prophetic and amatory, associated respectively with the Muses, Dionysus, Apollo and Venus. Amatory madness is declared to be the noblest of the four. Cf. *Commentary*, 7. 13–15; Plato, *Phaedrus*, 244a–245a.

826 *possest*: in the technical sense of possession by a god.

833 *mysterie*: secret doctrine or rite. Colin is initiated into the sacred 'mysteries' of Cupid.

835–94 For love as a cosmic creative force cf. *HL*, 64–119; Ficino, *Commentary*, 3. 2; *FQ*, 4. 10. 31–6. For Cupid cf. Comes, *Mythologiae*, 4. 14.

839 *long . . . y'bore*: cf. *HHL*, 22–35.

843 *so . . . attone*: so far from being at one or in harmony.

844 *so . . . bee*: and such great enemies of one another. The four elements were regarded as mutually antipathetic. Cf. Ovid, *Metamorphoses*, 1. 15–31; *HL*, 83 and note.

849 *peize*: sink (under their own weight).

850 *voydnesse*: emptiness, vacuity.

853 *kynds*: sorts of creatures.

854 *wombe . . . mother*: i.e. the womb of Chaos which supplied 'substance' for creation. Cf. *HL*, 58 and note; *FQ*, 3. 6. 36.

855–70 Skilfully blending classical and biblical accounts of creation. Cf. Ovid, *Metamorphoses*, 1. 416–37; Genesis 1: 1–25.

859–61 *wight . . . light*: for spontaneous generation cf. Ovid, *Metamorphoses*, 1. 416–37; *FQ*, 1. 1. 21; 3. 6. 8.

862 *kindly*: natural (in the sense of enlivening).

    formall feature: distinct form.

871 *bayt*: lure.

872 *enlarge . . . kynd*: propagate his species, but also 'enlarge' or develop his nature. Cf. 2 Corinthians 6: 11.

878 *stir*: stir up, excite, provoke.

880 *importuning*: imploring.

884 *saw*: command, decree.

886 *secret sense*: inner feeling, instinct or intuition.

893 *inherit*: obtain, gain.

894 *Exuls*: exiles.

896 *divynd*: interpreted, explained (in his role as Cupid's priest).

898 *depainted*: depicted, described.

906 *yrkes*: annoys, vexes.

910 *That . . . defamed*: who ('that') had far otherwise ('else') proclaimed ('defamed') her bright glory (i.e. by hiding her cruelty). It is through Colin's laments, however, that the lady is 'defamed' in the other sense.

914 *who . . . compell*: almost proverbial, cf. *FQ*, 3. 1. 25; 4. 1. 46.

918 *graft . . . feminine*: implanted into matter, which was regarded as feminine and therefore 'frail' (cf. *FQ*, 3. 6. 36–7). Cf. Shakespeare's 'frailty, thy name is woman' (*Hamlet*, 1. 2. 146).

920 *one . . . reuile*: the poet Stesichorus was struck blind for defaming Helen of Troy. Cf. *SC*, *Aprill*, [26] and note.

921 *ywroken*: punished.

925 *I . . . betimes*: I advise before it is too late.

927–40 Cf. *Amor*, 61.

937 *hie . . . thoughts*: referring either to thoughts concerning her or to her own elevation of mind.

938 *loath*: loathsome, hateful.

   loftie: directed to high objects, aspiring.

939 *grace*: favour, indulgence.

941 *paravant*: pre-eminently, before all others.

950–51 *die . . . conquest*: for this imagery cf. *Amor*, 69.

950 *nought*: in no way, not at all.

954–5 *glooming . . . rest*: cf. Virgil, *Eclogues*, 1. 83; 10. 75–7.

Astrophel

Responding to the evident artificiality of pastoral elegy, Dr Johnson lamented what he regarded as the lack of sincerity in Milton's *Lycidas*, and the modern reader, even less familiar with the conventions of the genre, is likely to dismiss *Astrophel* for similar reasons. Yet the poem itself is much concerned with the problematical efficacy of artifice in the face of bereavement, and with the degree of consolation, if any, that may be drawn from tapping the energies of poetic tradition. Regarded from this viewpoint its stylistic formality may be seen to facilitate the expression of emotion rather than to impede it [cf. Dundas (1989)].

Pastoral elegy afforded an appropriate form in which to lament the death of the author of *Arcadia*, the supreme pastoral 'maker', but also to question the broader issues arising from his loss. By skilfully adapting Ronsard's *L'Adonis* (1563) to the circumstances of Sidney's death in battle, Spenser examines the personal and public catastrophe through the medium of a highly ambivalent myth [cf. P. E. and J. C. Bondanella (1971)]. Starkly figured as the 'hunting' of a 'brutish nation', the Protestant campaign in which Sidney gave his life (generally regarded in the 1590s as a failure) seems scarcely adequate to the sacrifices it occasioned. There is a sense in which Adonis has recklessly courted his own destruction (79–90), and is fated to survive only through the literature he had abandoned in adopting the martial life (181–96) [cf. Steinberg (1990)]. But this is very much the perspective of a 'shepheard' poet addressing his fellows and, perhaps, staking his claim to the poetic succession [cf. Falco (1993); Sacks (1985), 51–63].

Written in the *persona* of Sidney's sister, the *Dolefull Lay of Clorinda* which immediately follows offers a more personal perspective and recognizes the tormented psychology of a literary form which habitually sees us 'mourning in others, our owne miseries' (96). The true victims of Sidney's death are now identified as the survivors, while he is envisaged in Paradise, lying amid flowers 'like a new-borne babe' (69) rather than transformed into a flower like the classical Adonis. In this respect he resembles the dynamic, living figure of *The Faerie Queene*'s Gardens of Adonis (3. 6. 47) rather than the cunningly woven but deceptive artefact of the House of Malecasta (3. 1. 38). As in *The Ruines of Time* (589–686), spirituality is seen to transcend art. Authorship of the *Dolefull Lay* has sometimes been attributed to Mary Sidney, but the poem is clearly designed, both in theme and structure, as a counterpart to *Astrophel* which it follows without separate heading or title-page. It employs the same stanza form (rhyming *ababcc*) and is exactly half the length of the preceding work (108 lines in 18 stanzas to 216 lines in 36 stanzas) – a structural proportion of 2:1 commonly found in epideictic poems and implying a resolution of complaint in the perception of Sidney's apotheosis [cf. O'Connell (1971)]. In the absence of evidence documenting collaboration between Spenser and Mary Sidney it would seem prudent to ascribe both pieces to the same author.

As the concluding lines indicate, the *Dolefull Lay* enhances the impression of communal grief by serving to introduce further elegies by Lodowick Bryskett, Matthew Roydon, Sir Walter Ralegh and Sir Edward Dyer (or possibly Fulke Greville). The first of Bryskett's two contributions was entered in the Stationers' Register as early as 22 August 1587, but the second may have been written to complement *Astrophel* [cf. Tromly (1986)]. The other pieces had already appeared in *The Phoenix Nest* (1593). The republication of such material in 1595, appended to Spenser's poems, represented a crucial stage in the evolution of Sidney's personal mythology [cf. Falco (1992)] and exercised a considerable influence upon the format of the elegiac anthology to the time of Milton [cf. Kay (1990), 53–66]. Whereas the present edition supplies only Spenser's contributions to the volume the complete text is reprinted in de Sélincourt's edition of *Spenser's Minor Poems* (1910). Cf. Falco (1994); Friedrich (1936); Martin (1987); Pigman (1985); Strickland (1992).

The title alludes to the protagonist of Sidney's *Astrophil and Stella*, two editions of which appeared in 1591. The altered orthography may be intended to suggest the lover's demise, cf. 'Astrofell' at *CCH*, 449. For Spenser's intention to write such an elegy cf. *RT*, 'Dedication'.

Dedication *To the most beautifull . . .*
Countesse of Essex: Frances Walsingham, daughter of Sir Francis Walsingham and widow of Sir Philip Sidney, married Robert Devereux, second Earl of Essex, in 1590. The matter was delicate in that she was not the 'Stella' of Sidney's sonnets nor did she die through grief as the poem suggests. Cf. notes to lines 55, 175–80 and 183–96 below.

Proem
1 *oaten reed*: the traditional pastoral instrument. Cf. *SC*, *October*, 8, [8] and note.
3 *breed*: generate, occasion.
10 *dolours dart*: pang of sorrow.
12 *wot . . . dight*: know that my verses are coarsely composed.
13 *nycer wit*: finer intellect or sensibility.

Astrophel
1 *Arcady*: Arcadia, a traditional setting for pastorals, but with specific allusion to Sidney's *Arcadia* first published in 1590 and republished in 1593. Sidney represents himself as the shepherd Philisides. Cf. *RT*, 673.
2 *gentlest race*: Sidney was the grandson of John Dudley, Duke of Northumberland.
3 *Hæmony*: Haemonia, an ancient name for Thessaly.
7–24 Cf. the description of Calidore at *FQ*, 6. 1. 2–3.
9 *pastors*: shepherds.
10 *In . . . behoue*: in everything befitting a decent (or handsome) shepherd.
13 *Nymph . . . mother*: Mary Dudley, daughter of the Duke of Northumberland and sister of Robert Dudley, Earl of Leicester.

20 *vsage . . . demeanure*: conduct and behaviour.

30 *When . . . away*: whenever Astrophel was absent.

42 *chapelets*: wreaths for the head, coronets.

46 *charmes*: songs (from Latin *carmina*), but with connotations of magical enchantment. Cf. *TM*, 244.

53 *sight*: sighed.

55 *Stella*: here, as at *CCH*, 532, Sidney's widow, but Penelope Devereux, Lady Rich in *Astrophil and Stella* which contains two sonnets strongly indicative of this identification (24, 35). Spenser may imply that Sidney's wife supplanted his former lover as his guiding 'star'.

66 *esteemed*: valued.

67–78 Cf. the more sensual description in Ronsard, *L'Adonis*, 15–28.

67 *wowed*: wooed, courted.

70 *atchieuements*: accomplishments, feats.

72 *too . . . alas*: because his courage led to his death in battle.

80 *infelicitie*: in the dual senses of unhappiness and misfortune.

87 *To . . . y'drad*: to seek adventure abroad, afraid of nothing.

89–90 Cf. Bion, 'Lament for Adonis', 60–61.

92 *forreine . . . away*: Sidney was fatally wounded at Zutphen in September 1586 during Leicester's campaign in the Netherlands.

96 *Ardeyn*: the Forest of Ardennes.

fowle Arlo: the woods of Aherlow north of the Galtee Mountains and close to Spenser's home at Kilcolman were infested with wolves and outlaws. Cf. *FQ*, 7. 6. 36, 55.

97 *toyles . . . traines*: nets and cunning snares (or lures).

98 *enwrap*: entangle, embroil.

103 *all*: wholly, completely.

hale: health, well-being.

104 *greedily*: eagerly.

111–12 *Ill . . . owne*: so intent upon causing ill to others that he was heedless of his own peril.

113–14 *But . . . eies*: but excuse his distraction because the cruelty of heaven diverted his attention towards his enemies and away from his own safety.

116 *brood*: kind, species.

118–24 Cf. Bion, 'Lament for Adonis', 7–10.

119 *Launched*: pierced. Sidney was shot in the left thigh at Zutphen.

mischieuous might: devastating or lethal force.

120 *ryued quight*: completely severed or torn asunder.

123 *endured*: withstood.

126 *let*: hinder, prevent.

129–32 Cf. Theocritus, *Idylls*, 1. 66–8; Virgil, *Eclogues*, 10. 9–10.

133 *shape of dreryhead*: image of sorrow.

136 *vnplaynd*: unlamented.

137–8 Cf. Bion, 'Lament for Adonis', 10–12.

139 *sewing . . . chace*: pursuing the hunt.

140 *raunged*: traversed.

147–74 Sidney was carried to Arnhem, and his wife hastened from Flushing to be with him.

147 *wild*: willed.

149 *beare*: bier.

151–74 Cf. Bion, 'Lament for Adonis', 29–31, 40–61.

154 *fauours*: love tokens.

163 *impictured . . . death*: marked with the signs of death.

172 *like*: equivalent, similar.

  inuade: intrude upon, penetrate.

175–80 Neither 'Stella' suffered such a fate. Lady Sidney survived and married Robert Dudley, Earl of Essex. Lady Rich was divorced by her husband for adultery and married Charles Blount, Lord Mountjoy.

177 *Forth with*: immediately.

178 *make*: mate.

  Turtle: turtle dove.

183–96 *Transformed . . . Astrophel*: Adonis is traditionally transformed into roses and anemones. 'Astrophel' is unknown as a flower (although the sound suggests asphodel) but signifies Sidney's literary endurance through Spenser's elegy and his own *Astrophil and Stella* (which aesthetically joins lover and lady even as it records their separation). Cf. Bion, 'Lament for Adonis', 64–6; Ovid, *Metamorphoses*, 10. 728–39; Ronsard, *Adonis*, 299–302; *Daph*, 346 and note.

191 *deow*: dew.

194 *Penthia*: from the Greek for sorrow.

211 *his sister*: the Countess of Pembroke. Cf. *CCH*, 487 and note.

213 *shape . . . spright*: appearance and spirit.

Dolefull Lay of Clorinda

The 108 lines of the lay may allude to the 108 sonnets of *Astrophil and Stella*, presuming Spenser had access to a complete manuscript. Only 107 sonnets had been published. Cf. Kay (1990), 59.

1 *complaine*: lament, bemoan.

4 *enriuen*: split apart, broken.

12 *warne*: prevent or forbid.

17 *like*: similarly, equally.

22 *vsury*: interest.

41–2 *Cypres . . . Elder*: emblems of bereavement. Cf. *SC*, November, 145–7, [145].

45 *riddles*: witty conundrums, puzzles.

47 *laid . . . abed*: playing on the erotic sense.

57–8 Referring to his transformation into a flower, cf. *Ast*, 181–92.

62 *dowries*: endowments, gifts.

67–88 Continuing the comparison with Adonis. Cf. *FQ*, 3. 6. 46–9.

73–84 Astrophel attains Neoplatonic ascent to the pure form or essence of beauty denied to the protagonist of *Astrophil and Stella*. Cf. *RT*, 589–686.

78 *eye . . . see*: cf. 1 Corinthians 2: 9.

83 *forme*: shape or, in the philosophical sense, essence.

89 *waile . . . lack*: lament the privation of his absence or loss.

90 *vowes*: supplications, prayers.

95 *wear*: wear out, waste.

97–108 These lines serve as an introduction to the anthology of laments by different hands which immediately follow in the first edition.

99 *entertaine*: hold in affection, cherish.

101 *Thestylis*: Lodowick Bryskett. Cf. *CCH*, 156 and note.

106 *vnto . . . addrest*: fashioned for the occasion.

107 *rehearse*: recite, but, in anticipation of line 108, playing on the sense of decking a hearse with flowers or elegies. Cf. Kay (1990), 61–2.

AMORETTI AND EPITHALAMION

This volume was entered in the Stationers' Register on 19 November 1594 and published the following year. The title-page announces that the contents were written 'not long since', but sonnet 8 has been shown to date from the early 1580s and it is possible that other early material may have been reworked for publication [cf. L. Cummings (1964)]. It is generally agreed, however, that the published volume commemorates Spenser's marriage to his second wife, Elizabeth Boyle, and that it is designed to be read as a unity, proceeding through the stages of courtship and betrothal in the *Amoretti* to matrimony in the *Epithalamion* [cf. Kaske (1978)].

In the eighty-nine sonnets of the *Amoretti* Petrarchan and Neoplatonic influences, though clearly evident, are qualified by Protestant matrimonial idealism [cf. Dubrow (1990); J. L. Klein (1989)], and this independence of attitude is formally signalled by the adoption of an original sonnet form whose complex, interlocking structure (rhyming *ababbcbccdcdee*) distinguishes it both from the dialectical (and occasionally dichotomous) Petrarchan form and the potentially segmented 'English' or Shakespearean variety [cf. Spiller (1992), 142–9]. The influence of Petrarch is itself mediated through that of Ronsard, Desportes and Tasso [cf. Kastner (1908–9); Kostic (1959)]. Whereas the Petrarchan lover is invariably locked into an intensely introspective, not to say solipsistic, meditation upon the pangs of unrequited love from which he gains release only by the abandonment or sublimation of his desire, the Spenserian lover seeks the fulfilment, and even sanctification, of carnal desire within matrimony and moves from the language of personal complaint to that of public celebration [cf. Dasenbrook (1985); Roche (1989), 1–69]. His distinctive progress is appropriately charted against *both* the seasonal and the ecclesiastical calendars (natural and spiritual time) moving from 'sad Winters night' (sonnet 4) through spring (sonnet 19) and Lent (sonnet 22) to Easter (sonnet 68), and onwards in the *Epithalamion* to St Barnabas's Day (11 June) which marks the date of the summer solstice [cf. W. C. Johnson (1990)]. Unlike his Neoplatonic counterpart he does not endeavour to climb the 'ladder of ascent' from particular to universal beauty and, as a result, remains as disturbed by the 'absence' of his lady as any purely sensual lover [cf. Casady (1941); Gibbs (1990), 139–74; Bieman (1988), 162–75]. Not infrequently his more Petrarchan and Neoplatonic poses are undercut by his sense of self-conscious irony [cf. sonnets 54 and 88]. The conclusion of the sequence in three sonnets of absence (87–9) fittingly emphasizes his urgent need for the physical consummation celebrated in the *Epithalamion*.

Whereas one detects a movement in the sonnets from a Narcissistic, self-centred desire (sonnet 35) towards a more generous sense of mutuality (sonnets 65, 68), the repetition of sonnet 35 as sonnet 83 reinforces the persistence of appetite and the inadequacy of mere betrothal. Its relevance to both the earlier and later stages of the sequence suggests the ineradicable selfishness of all desire and, perhaps, of consciousness itself. Elsewhere the imagery of flight is juxtaposed with that of feeding (sonnet 72), and even in the *Epithalamion* a subtextual resonance of the myth of Narcissus and Echo may be detected in the refrain [cf. Loewenstein (1986)]. Considered as an extended dramatic monologue the poems disclose more about the speaker than he realizes. His struggle for mastery, inimical to the mutuality of wedded love, is never wholly renounced despite the movement from 'I' to 'we' in the concluding stanzas [cf. Copeland (1988); W. C. Johnson (1993)]. In this regard, as the notes indicate, the short sequence of 'Anac-reontics' positioned between the sonnets and the wedding song serves to explore the multiple ironies of desire through the distancing medium of mythology.

The autobiographical components of the sequence are curiously overt yet highly elusive. The speaker twice reminds us that he is the author of *The Faerie Queene* (sonnets 33 and 80), addresses personal friends (sonnet 33), declares himself to be forty years old (sonnet 60) and compares his relationships with the three Elizabeths in his life, his queen, his mother and his wife (sonnet 74). Yet even such specific allusions serve to promote consideration of larger thematic issues such as the relationship between amorous and epic poetry, the vulnerability of love to time, and the potentially conflicting claims of private and public loyalties. For instance, whereas sonnet 33 expresses weariness with the epic task, sonnet 80 envisages its eventual continuance while also slyly announcing the completion of three, as yet unpublished, books [cf. Dunlop (1980)]. As love poetry moves from impeding epic to inspiring it, the amorous courting of Elizabeth Boyle is precariously poised against the political courting of Elizabeth Tudor [cf. Bates (1992), 138–51; Marotti (1982)].

The structure of the *Amoretti* is highly symmetrical: 21 sonnets precede and 21 follow a central group of 47 designed to move from Ash Wednesday (sonnet 22) to Easter Sunday (sonnet 68). The central sonnet (45) concentrates upon the lady's immortal 'Idea' but in a context which deftly captures the actual ambivalence of the speaker's apparently Platonic stance. Covert allusion to the ecclesiastical calendar for 1594 has been detected in the central section in that the number of sonnets exactly corresponds to the forty-seven days between Ash Wednesday (13 February) and Easter (31 March). By the same calculation sonnet 62 falls, quite accurately, on 25 March or Lady Day [cf. Dunlop (1969), (1970)]. Spenser would therefore appear to have encrypted within the sequence a series of very precise, and highly personal, temporal references designed to locate the eternal in the mundane and produce a sequence for every year from the experiences of one. The lovers' destinies are played out against an elaborate astrological backdrop [cf. Eade (1972)].

The numerological design of the *Epithalamion* reinforces this aspect of the poem's presentation. It is now generally agreed that its twenty-four sections (although unnumbered in the original edition) represent the diurnal and sidereal hours and that the 365 long lines (the sum total of pentameters and alexandrines) represent the annual cycle in which the wedding day is necessarily contained. Night falls at line 300 thereby precisely denoting the sixteen and one quarter hours of daylight specified for 11 June 1594 in contemporary almanacs. It has also been argued that the seven-line envoy or 'tornata' compensates for the 'shortcomings' of the sun which accomplishes a mere 359 days (the number of long lines in the 23 full stanzas) while the sphere of fixed stars completes a full revolution of 360 degrees [cf. Fowler (1970a), 161–73; Hieatt (1960); Wickert (1968)]. By means such as these the patterns of transience are subsumed into the patterns of art. It has been argued more recently that similar numerological schemes inform the structure of the entire volume, thereby uniting its various components, but the calculations involved seem forbiddingly complex and problematic [cf. Fukuda (1988); Thompson (1985)]. More evident in Spenser's text is the sheer vibrancy of excited energy which resists formal predictability: the 'hours' of the *Epithalamion* are of uneven length, the stanza structure (based on the Italian canzone) and rhyme patterns vary continually, and the refrain is constantly altering [cf. Warkentin (1990)].

Although the epithalamium was a recognized classical genre, Spenser responded to his models (the most significant being Catullus, Statius and Claudian) in a highly original fashion [T. M. Greene (1957); Tufte (1970); Welsford (1967)]. As the bridegroom is also a poet he sings his own wedding song – contrary to tradition – and in so doing contemplates the relationship between literature, love and mutability. The immediacy of his experience is expressed and simultaneously contained through the formality of the rhetoric. The poem is structured to move through the twenty-four hours of the wedding day, with their appropriate preparations, emotions and ceremonial activities, from the eager anticipation of morning to the rapturous consummation of night. With the fall of darkness the refrain alters from positive to negative (314) and the poetry seeks to ward off, as by a charm, the imagined terrors of the night (323–52). Although the prevailing tone is joyous, and even triumphal, the imagery insinuates more sombre and solemn elements. Allusions to Orpheus (16), Tithonus (75) and Medea (189–90) reflect the various anxieties incident to love and art, while echoes of the marriage service and Song of Songs articulate their spiritual aspirations [cf. D. Anderson (1984)]. According to the Book of Common Prayer, marriage was held to signify 'the misticall union that is betwixte Christe and his Churche' and the bridegroom is anxious that his wedding day be recorded as a 'holy' day, yet its sanctity accommodates the rowdy 'fescennine' jesting characteristic of classical epithalamia and lends validation to the sensuality of the *Amoretti* (137–9). The 'endlesse matrimony' anticipated in the poem's central line (217) sanctifies the body and sexualizes the soul. The offspring of the couple's carnal love will populate heaven (417–23).

The bride's submission to her husband in 'proud humility' (306) resolves the tension between love and virtue explored in the *Amoretti* and finally distinguishes her from Petrarch's Laura who dies 'humble in herself, but proud against love' (*Rime Sparse*, 323. 64). In keeping with the conventions of the genre the poem locates the couple's union within a communal context and gestures beyond private acts to social consequences. Public ambitions, it would seem, are vicariously fulfilled through personal relationships. The bride is 'lyke some mayden Queene' (158), virtue 'raynes' within her 'as Queene in royal throne' (194) and the wedding night resembles that upon which Jove 'begot Maiesty' (331). Yet even now 'Cinthia' peeps disconcertingly through the window and the speaker begs her blessing while fearing her envy (372–87).

As the concluding 'tornata' indicates, the poem is optimistic but not escapist [cf. Neuse (1966)]. The pressures of time and contingency are fully recognized. Presented 'in lieu of many ornaments' (427) the 'song' compensates for the inadequacies of the wedding day while also (such is the studied ambiguity of the syntax) apologizing for its own. Though self-presented as a figure of considerable poetic authority the speaker remains fully aware of the fate of Orpheus.

For *Amoretti* cf. D. Cheney (1983); P. Cheney (1993); Gibbs (1990); Hardison (1972); Loewenstein (1987); MacArthur (1989); Prescott (1985); Turner (1988). For *Epithalamion* cf. Chinitz (1991); Cirillo (1968); Gleason (1994); Graves (1986); Hieatt (1961); Miller (1970); Steen (1961).

Dedication *To the Right Worshipfull . . .*

Needham: Sir Robert Needham, later Vice-President of the Council of the Marches of Wales, was knighted on 1 September 1594 by Lord Deputy Russell and the dedication must have been written subsequently. He left Ireland on 25 September 1594 and returned on 7 April 1596.

2–3 *sweete conceited*: delightfully ingenious or devised.

12–13 *meetest . . . countenaunce*: fittest to lend her well-deserved support.

18 *W. P.*: William Ponsonby, who also published *Comp* and *FQ*.

Dedicatory sonnets

G: W. senior and G. W. I. are probably Geoffrey Witney Sr and his son Geoffrey Witney Jr. The latter was author of *A Choice of Emblemes* (1586) and a friend of Sir Robert Needham's wife.

'Darke is the day'

1 *Phœbus*: Apollo, the sun.

6 *inuention*: literary creativity in general. In particular the selection or fabrication of material, the basis of the art of rhetoric.

8 *slide*: slip.

10 *illustrate*: shed lustre upon, make renowned.

11 *dawnting*: breaking, quelling.

'Ah Colin'

2–4 *pyping . . . daies*: alluding to *SC* and *FQ*.

2 *roundelaies*: short, simple lyrics. Cf. *SC*, *Aprill*, [33] and note.

9 *who . . . fill*: who can ever be satiated with your poetry.

14 *rase*: erase, obliterate.

Amoretti

Sonnet 1

1 *when as*: when.

2 *dead doing*: murderous. Cf. *FQ*, 2. 3. 8.

3 *bands*: bonds (the fingers).

4 *captiues . . . sight*: adopting the *persona* of the enslaved courtly lover.

6 *lamping*: beaming, resplendent.

   deigne: condescend.

7 *spright*: vital spirit, 'a most subtle vapour' begotten in the heart from the blood and enabling the soul to operate in the body. Cf. Robert Burton, *Anatomy of Melancholy*, Part 1, Sect. 1, Memb. 2, Subs. 2.

8 *harts . . . book*: for the imagery cf. 2 Corinthians 3: 2–3.

close bleeding: secretly or inwardly bleeding.

10 *Helicon*: cf. *SC, Aprill*, [42] and note.

11 *Angels*: applied to Queen Elizabeth at *SC, Aprill*, 64; *CCH*, 40.

Sonnet II

1 *Vnquiet thought*: for the lover's psychology cf. *HL*, 217–24.

2 *hart*: the heart was regarded as the seat of the intellectual faculties.

4 *wombe*: Spenser often describes the heart or breast as pregnant with desire. Cf. *FQ*, 4. 9. 17; Ficino, *Commentary*, 6. 14.

6 *vipers brood*: cf. Matthew 3: 7. Vipers were held to eat their way out of the womb. Cf. Bartholomaeus Anglicus, *De Proprietatibus Rerum*, 18. 117.

11 *humblesse*: humility.

12 *grace*: favour (the amorous equivalent of divine grace).

13 *cherish*: foster, hold dear.

Sonnet III

1–8 In Neoplatonic philosophy earthly beauty was held to reflect its celestial counterpart. Depending upon the nature of the beholder, it might inspire sensual or spiritual love. Cf. Plato, *Phaedrus*, 250d–251a; Ficino, *Commentary*, 6. 18; note to *HHB*, 115.

1 *souerayne*: because she is queen of his affections. For the privileges and duties of such 'sovereignty' cf. *FQ*, 6. 8. 1–2.

admyre: wonder at. This establishes the key note of the sonnet.

3–8 *heauenly . . . hew*: for the ennobling effect of love cf. *HHB*, 15–28.

3 *heauenly fire*: i.e. the fire of love. Cf. *FQ*, 3. 3. 1.

5 *That*: so that.

dazed: dazzled.

9–14 A traditional topos. Cf. Petrarch, *Rime Sparse*, 20, 49.

10 *thoughts astonishment*: stupefaction or paralysis of mind.

11 *titles*: continuing the image of sovereignty.

12 *fancies*: imagination's.

14 *endite*: commit to writing.

Sonnet IIII

1 *New Yeare*: presumably January 1, although the rest of the sonnet suggests the old style of 25 March. The matter was controversial. Cf. *SC*, 'Generall Argument' and notes.

Ianus gate: a gate was the symbol of Janus, the Roman god of beginnings, often depicted with a double-faced head looking backwards and forwards.

Before his deification his reign at Rome was regarded as analogous to the
Golden Age. He gives his name to the month of January.

4 *dumpish spright*: dull or melancholic spirit.

8 *wings . . . darts*: cf. *SC*, *March*, [79]; *CCH*, 799–822 and notes.

9 *lusty*: lively, vigorous (but also with sexual connotations).

10 *him*: love or Cupid.

11 *warnes*: gives timely notice or advice.

   colord. . .flowre: variously coloured flowers. Possibly with oblique allusion
to the seasonal coming of Flora. Cf. *SC*, *March*, [16].

Sonnet v

2 *portly*: imposing, dignified.

4 *vnworthy*: commenting either upon the world or the envy.

   enuide: disliked, grudged at.

5 *close implide*: i.e. her public demeanour reflects her private moral standards.

7 *rash*: presumptuous, impetuous.

   so wide: so immodestly or so far reaching, depending upon whether the
phrase modifies 'thretning' or 'gaze'.

8 *that . . . her*: that they do not dare to look upon her wantonly.

10 *boldned*: emboldened, courageous.

11 *banner*: in Petrarch's *Rime Sparse*, 140 love sets its banner (*insegna*) in
the lover's face.

Sonnet vi

1 *nought*: not at all, beginning a pattern of puns which culminate in the
marriage 'knot' of the final line.

2 *rebellious*: refractory, intractable.

3 *baser kynd*: lower nature.

5 *durefull Oake*: durable oak. The tree was symbolic of durability.

6 *kindling*: punning on the dual sense of igniting and giving birth.

7 *diuide*: give forth in various directions, distribute.

8 *aspire*: mount, rise.

10 *gentle brest*: traditionally held to be the most responsive to love.

11 *parts entire*: inward parts. Cf. *Amor*, 85. 9 and note.

14 *knot*: bond of wedlock. Cf. *Epith*, 44; *FQ*, 1. 12. 37.

Sonnet vii

1 *eyes*: beauty 'attracts . . . the gaze of others, and entering through their
eyes impresses itself upon the human soul' (Castiglione, *Courtier*, 326).

   myrror: 'in the same way in which a mirror, struck . . . by the light of
the sun . . . sets on fire a piece of wool placed next to it . . . that part of the
soul which they call the dark fancy and the memory, like a mirror, is struck

by an image of Beauty itself . . . the force of desire is kindled and the soul loves' (Ficino, *Commentary*, 7. 1).

2 *vertue*: cf. 'true Beautie Vertue is indeed / Whereof this Beautie can be but a shade' (Sidney, *Astrophil and Stella*, 5).

4 *obiect*: himself.

5 *louely hew*: loving aspect.

6 *inspired*: animated, infused.

7 *askew*: askance.

10 *louely*: lovingly.

Sonnet VIII

Note the Shakespearean form (rhyming *ababcdcdefefgg*). For the theme cf. Petrarch, *Rime Sparse*, 151, 154.

2 *Kindled . . . neere*: cf. *HL*, 65; Ficino, *Commentary*, 2. 5.

3 *conspire*: combine, co-operate.

5 *blinded guest*: Cupid, usually represented blindfolded. Cf. note to *HL*, 226.

6 *wound*: some editors add a question mark to clarify the sense.

8 *heauenly beauty*: cf. *HHB*, 267–80.

9–12 *frame . . . weak*: cf. *HL*, 190–96.

13 *Dark . . . light*: the lady's beauty reflects God's creative light (cf. Genesis 1: 2–3; 1 John 1: 5).

Sonnet IX

For the rhetorical device of *comparatio* or comparison, cf. Shakespeare, *Sonnets*, 18, 130.

4 *resemble*: liken, compare.

   th'ymage: the aspect, appearance.

5–12 Employing the rhetorical figure of *expeditio* whereby a number of possibilities are rejected in favour of one solution.

7 *purer sight*: in being closer to the celestial heaven.

12 *glasse*: for its lowly status in comparison with crystal cf. *FQ*, 1. 10. 58.

13–14 *Maker . . . see*: cf. 'God is light' (1 John 1: 5) the proposition on which the central conceit depends. Cf. also John 1: 4.

Sonnet X

For the central conceit cf. Petrarch, *Rime Sparse*, 121.

3 *licentious*: lawless, but playing on the sense of wanton. Her purity defies the 'law' of love.

4 *freewill*: 'free' of the influence of love. The term insinuates a subtle compliment since, according to Calvin, free will was the prerogative of unfallen man. Cf. *Institutes of the Christian Religion*, 1. 15. 8; 2. 2–5.

10 *comptroll*: control, govern.

11 *bow . . . make*: i.e. bend her lofty glance unto a 'base' or lowly lover, in this case the speaker himself.

14 *as . . . sport*: metrically an alexandrine as at *Amor*, 45. 14.

Sonnet XI

1 *sew*: beg, petition.

2 *truth*: troth, fidelity.

3 *cruell warriour*: for love as warfare cf. Ovid, *Amores*, 1. 9; Petrarch, *Rime Sparse*, 21. Venus is frequently depicted vanquishing Mars.

4 *weary*: wearisome, exhausting.

Sonnet XII

For the central conceit cf. Petrarch, *Rime Sparse*, 2, 3.

1 *thrilling*: in the dual sense of piercing and exciting.

5 *disarmed*: i.e. defenceless.

7 *close couert*: secret shelter or hiding place.

9 *brunt*: assault, onslaught.

11 *captiuing*: taking captive.

Sonnet XIII

1–8 The lady's elevated face and downward look symbolize her spiritual aspiration and apprehension of worldly corruption. Cf. the goddess Nature at *FQ*, 7. 7. 57. According to Ovid, man was endowed with an erect posture in order to contemplate heaven (*Metamorphoses*, 1. 84–6).

1 *port*: deportment, bearing.

2 *reares*: raises, lifts.

3 *low embaseth*: lowers.

4 *temperature*: temperament. Her 'humours' are well balanced.

6–8 *earth . . . returne*: cf. Genesis 2: 7; 3: 19.

9 *lofty*: haughty, proud.

10 *heauen . . . clime*: alluding to the Neoplatonic ladder of ascent from earthly to celestial things, cf. *HHB*, 267–87.

12 *drossy*: impure, feculent.

13 *Yet . . . me*: still deign to regard me, even though I am lowly.

14 *lowlinesse . . . be*: such condescension will elevate you. Cf. 'he that shall humble himself shall be exalted' (Matthew 23: 12).

Sonnet XIIII

Employing the traditional conceit of storming the castle of love.

4 *peece*: stronghold, fortress (but also person).
6 *were . . . belay*: were accustomed to besiege (but also waylay).
12 *engins*: engines of war, devices.
    conuert: convert to love, win over.

Sonnet XV

Cf. Philippe Desportes, *Diane*, 1. 32; *Epith*, 167–203; Whidden (1993).

1 *tradefull*: engaged or engrossed in trade.
2 *gain*: profit.
3 *both . . . Indias*: the East and West Indies.
7–14 Using the device of blazon whereby a lover's physical attributes are itemized and celebrated. Cf. Song of Songs 5: 11–16; *Epith*, 171–80. For the body as a microcosm of the world's mineral wealth cf. Ezekiel 28: 13.
11 *locks . . . gold*: cf. Song of Songs 5: 11.

Sonnet XVI

3 *stonisht*: astonished, stunned.
4 *sweet illusion*: enjoyable deception.
5 *glauncing sight*: flashing glances.
6 *loues*: Cupids ('amoretti'). Cf. *Epith*, 357–9; *HB*, 240.
8 *rash*: reckless (being bold enough to look on her).
11 *twincle*: blink.
12 *misintended*: evilly intended, maliciously aimed.

Sonnet XVII

A variation on Petrarch, *Rime Sparse*, 77, 78 where, by contrast, a portrait has actually been made.

2 *confused skil*: disordered reason.
4 *pencill*: paint-brush designed for delicate work.
    expresse . . . fill: represent her satisfactorily, do her complete justice.

Sonnet XVIII

Developing an Ovidian topos cf. *Ars Amatoria*, 1. 473–6; Petrarch, *Rime Sparse*, 265; Desportes, *Les Amours d'Hippolyte*, 51.

2 *teare*: break, split apart.
3 *redound*: overflow, drip over.
4 *weare*: wear down, or wear away.
9–12 For the enactment of love cf. *Amor*, 54; for the lady's incredulity cf. Petrarch, *Rime Sparse*, 203.

Sonnet XIX

1 *Cuckow* ... *Spring*: a traditional association, but the cuckoo is also associated with illicit sex, and particularly cuckoldry. Cf. Shakespeare, *Love's Labour's Lost*, 5. 2. 890–903.

3 *king*: Cupid. Cf. *Amor*, 70. 1.

6 *anthemes*: songs, but with a suggestion of antiphonal response.

7 *rebounded*: reverberated, re-echoed.

12 *ydle*: frivolous, insignificant.

14 *let* ... *be*: let her be regarded as a rebel (or possibly prevent her from being a rebel, taking 'let' in the sense of hinder or disallow).

Sonnet XX

3–8 *whiles* ... *yield*: the lion lore is traditional (cf. Ovid, *Tristia*, 3. 5. 33–4), but the lady regards the speaker as unworthy of leonine clemency.

14 *blooded*: stained with blood (with oblique sexual connotations).

Sonnet XXI

Cf. Petrarch, *Rime Sparse*, 154.

1 *Art*: cosmetic art was widely denigrated. Petrarch refers to the creative 'arts' of heaven and nature (*Rime Sparse*, 154. 1–2).

2 *tempred*: set or blended in balanced harmony.

6 *loue*: the first edition reads 'loues', possibly alluding to the Cupids or 'amoretti' in her eyes. Cf. *Amor*, 16. 5–8.

9 *With* ... *inure*: accustomed her eyes to move within such strangely ill-sorted bounds (i.e. of enticement and discouragement).

13 *traine*: combining the senses of entice and discipline, thereby fusing the dual operations of the lady's beauty.

Sonnet XXII

Cf. Desportes, *Diane*, 1. 43.

1 *holy season*: Lent.

4 *Saynt*: recalling Dante's Beatrice. Cf. *HL*, 211–17.

5 *temple* ... *mind*: playing on the familiar notion of contemplation as building a 'temple' in one's thoughts.

6 *glorious ymage*: 'in the course of time lovers do not see the loved one in their true image received through the senses, but ... in an image already remade by the soul according to the likeness of its own Idea, an image which is more beautiful than the body itself' (Ficino, *Commentary*, 6. 6). Cf. *HL*, 197–9; *HB*, 211–17; Casady (1941).

9 *author*: creator, but playing on the literary sense: she 'writes' his bliss as he writes his woe.

10–11 Cf. Psalms 51: 16–17 which formed part of the service for the

Lenten ritual of Ash Wednesday, the specific day to which the sonnet may refer.

12 *burning . . . desyre*: 'just as material fire refines gold, so this most sacred fire consumes and destroys everything that is mortal in our souls and quickens . . . the celestial part' (Castiglione, *Courtier*, 341).

Sonnet XXIII

1 *Penelope*: chaste wife of Odysseus who refused to entertain suitors until she had completed Laertes' shroud, but unravelled by night what she wove by day. Cf. Homer, *Odyssey*, 2. 93–105; *VG*, 428–32 and note.

4 *vnreaue*: unravel, undo.

5 *subtile*: ingenious, devious.

9 *that*: that which.

12 *years*: possibly intended to indicate the length of the speaker's suit.

13–14 Petrarch asserts that all worldly weaving is mere cobwebs (*Rime Sparse*, 173. 6–7).

Sonnet XXIIII

1 *beauties wonderment*: wonderful pattern of beauty.

3 *complement*: fulfilment, accomplishment.

4 *makers art*: alluding to the familiar notion of nature as God's art.

8 *Pandora*: Pandora (meaning 'all gifts') was sent to earth as a punishment for Prometheus' theft of fire. Her curiosity led her to release from their casket all of life's ills – but also hope. Cf. Hesiod, *Works and Days*, 60–105; *Theogony*, 571–612; *TM*, 578 and note.

Sonnet XXV

Cf. Petrarch, *Rime Sparse*, 134; *HL*, 162–8.

2 *her owne*: life's own.

3 *termes*: conditions or periods of time.

4 *depending doubtfully*: hanging uncertainly.

14 *turne*: return.

Sonnet XXVI

A floral sonnet placed fourth after Ash Wednesday (22) while its counterpart, sonnet 64, is placed fourth before Easter (68). It deals with the 'lower' senses of taste, touch and smell (cf. Castiglione, *Courtier*, 334).

1 *brere*: briar, cf. *SC, Februarie*, 115.

2 *Iunipere*: juniper, an evergreen shrub.

3 *Eglantine*: wild rose, cf. *SC, Maye*, 13.

  nere: deeply, near to the bone.

4 *firbloome*: fur-bloom or furze.

5 *Cypresse*: cf. *SC*, *November*, [145].
   rynd: bark.
6 *pill*: shell.
7 *broome-flowre*: a shrub whose twigs are used for sweeping.
8 *Moly*: magic herb with white flower and black root given to Odysseus to counter the spells of Circe. Cf. Homer, *Odyssey*, 10. 320–26; Ovid, *Metamorphoses*, 14. 291–2.
13 *accoumpt of*: consider significant, make much of.

Sonnet XXVII

A classical topos, cf. Horace, *Odes*, 4. 10.

3 *shroud*: anticipating the clothing imagery at lines 5–6.
4 *how . . . weene*: however little consideration you give the matter now.
5 *Idoll*: implying the 'idolatry' of Narcissism. Cf. *Amor*, 35. 7 and note.
   gay beseene: ostentatiously apparelled.
6 *doffe*: put off.
   fleshes . . . attyre: for flesh as clothing, cf. Job 10: 11.
10–14 *ne . . . paine*: cf. *RT*, 253–9, 400–406.
12 *thankles*: because she displays ingratitude.
13 *that*: that which.

Sonnet XXVIII

1 *laurell*: emblem of poetry and conquest, recalling Petrarch's Laura. Cf. *Rime Sparse*, 5; Ronsard, *Astrée*, 11; *SC*, *Aprill*, [104] and note.
7 *infusion*: pouring in.
9–12 Adapting the standard account whereby Daphne was transformed to save her from being ravished. Cf. Ovid, *Metamorphoses*, 1. 452–567.
10 *Thessalian*: of Thessaly, in north-eastern Greece.
14 *leafe*: both laurel leaves and the leaves of his poetry.

Sonnet XXIX

1 *depraue*: pervert in the sense of misinterpret or misconstrue.
2 *simple*: innocent.
3 *bay*: bay or laurel leaves, as in the preceding sonnet.
4 *accoumpts*: accounts, considers.
9 *sith . . . needs*: since she feels compelled to contest my victory.
12 *trump of fame*: the trumpet was a traditional emblem of fame.
   blaze: blow (and by blowing proclaim).

Sonnet XXX

For the topos of ice and fire cf. Petrarch, *Rime Sparse*, 134, 202.

6 *delayd*: quenched (as at *FQ*, 3. 12. 42).

7 *boyling*: perhaps playing upon the surname of Spenser's second wife Elizabeth Boyle. She was a cousin of Sir Richard Boyle, first Earl of Cork, and distantly related to the Spencers of Althorp.

10 *that*: than that.

11 *sencelesse*: lifeless, numb.

12 *wonderfull deuyse*: astonishing contrivance or sleight.

Sonnet XXXI

Cf. Petrarch, *Rime Sparse*, 265; Desportes, *Cléonice*, 74.

3 *depraues*: perverts, spoils.

5 *beastes . . . race*: creatures of prey.

9 *scath*: harm, injury.

Sonnet XXXII

1–4 For the blacksmith imagery cf. *FQ*, 5. 5. 7–8.

1 *paynefull*: painstaking.
   feruent: glowing, searing.

2 *mollify*: soften, make malleable.

3 *sledge*: sledge hammer.

4 *to . . . apply*: to whatever shape or purpose he chooses.

5 *fry*: burn.

6 *soft awhit*: soften at all.

11 Proverbial: 'the more you beat iron the harder it grows'.

12 *applyde*: directed, addressed.

14 *stones*: possibly hailstones, but cf. *Amor*, 54. 14 and note.

Sonnet XXXIII

The new Elizabeth in the poet's life has displaced his queen, as at *FQ*, 6. 10. 25–8. Cf. *Amor*, 80.

2 *Empresse*: Elizabeth I, as Queen of England, Ireland, France and Virginia, and so described on the title-page of *FQ* (1590, 1596).
   dear dred: as both beloved and awe-inspiring. Cf. *FQ*, 1 Proem 4.

4 *enlarge . . . dead*: magnify her posthumous fame.

5 *lodwick*: Lodowick Bryskett. Cf. *CCH*, 156 and note.
   of . . . aread: be gracious or kind enough to explain to me.

8 *all*: even.

11 *sins*: since.

Sonnet XXXIIII

For the ship imagery cf. Petrarch, *Rime Sparse*, 189, 235; *TM*, 139–44.

2 *conduct*: guidance.

8 *hidden perils*: allegorically the perils of sensual desire.

10 *Helice*: the constellation of the Great Bear by which Greek mariners navigated. Cf. Ovid, *Fasti*, 3. 107–8. The name also recalls Helicon, the source of poetic inspiration.

   lodestar: the pole-star was actually in the Lesser Bear or Cynosure.

Sonnet XXXV

Repeated with minor alterations as sonnet 83 but in a new context. Here, incipient notions of Platonic ascent from body to soul (9–14) are submerged in 'the lust of the flesh, and the lust of the eyes' (1 John 2: 15–16). Thus 'hungry eyes' replace Petrarch's 'weary eyes' (*Rime Sparse*, 14. 1).

1 *couetize*: avarice, cf. note to line 8.

3 *suffize*: satisfy.

7 *Narcissus*: cf. *SC*, *June*, 52 and note. Ficino interprets the myth as signifying how the soul is 'seduced by bodily beauty', which is a mere shadow of the divine, and therefore cannot attain true satisfaction (*Commentary*, 6. 17).

8 *staru'd*: because he could not 'feed' on what he saw.

   plenty . . . poore: translating Ovid's phrase 'inopem me copia fecit' and used as the emblem to *SC*, *September* (cf. *Metamorphoses*, 3. 466). The phrase is applied to avarice at *FQ*, 1. 4. 29.

10 *brooke*: endure, find agreeable.

13–14 Ironically overlooking the lady's own mortality. Cf. 'the world passeth away and the lust thereof' (1 John 2: 17).

Sonnet XXXVI

6 *thrilling*: piercing, exciting.

9 *extremityes*: utmost acts of rigour or severity.

Sonnet XXXVII

1 *golden tresses*: resembling Petrarch's Laura, *Rime Sparse*, 90. 1.

2 *attyre*: dress, do up.

6 *golden snare*: loose hair usually symbolizes wantonness, bound hair chastity. The very emblem of the lady's virtue excites the speaker's desire. Cf. *Amor*, 81. 1–2; *Epith*, 62.

8 *harts*: blond locks bind hearts at Petrarch, *Rime Sparse*, 253. 3–4.

NOTES TO *AMORETTI*   681

Sonnet XXXVIII

1–4 *Arion . . . ease*: Arion was thrown overboard by thieves but saved by a dolphin through the influence of the poet's god, Apollo (cf. Ovid, *Fasti*, 2. 79–118). For the imagery of passion as a tempest cf. *Amor*, 40, 41. In the wedding masque at *FQ*, 4. 11. 23 Arion precedes the bridegroom.

1 *wracke*: violence, ruin.

4 *ease*: save, relieve.

9 *perseuer*: persevere.

Sonnet XXXIX

1 *Queene of loue*: Venus. Cf. *Proth*, 96–100.

3 *Ioue*: Zeus or Jupiter, father of the gods.

5 *art*: with a play on Venus' 'powrefull art'.

8 *reuiued . . . robbing*: a deliberate paradox to signify the enigmatic operations of love.

9–10 *heauenly . . . traunce*: this ecstatic experience confounds the mystical in the sensual, subverting the spiritual vision of Platonic love.

12–14 *fed . . . eat*: the lover was commonly held to derive nourishment from the sight and sound of his lady. Cf. Castiglione, *Courtier*, 334–5; *HB*, 248–50.

13 *Nectar . . . meat*: cf. *SC*, *November*, [195].

Sonnet XL

Cf. Petrarch, *Rime Sparse*, 192.

4 *Graces*: cf. SC, *Aprill*, [109]; *June*, [25] and notes. The Graces are fittingly recalled in view of the etymology of their names: Aglaia ('bright'), Euphrosyne ('cheerful'), Thalia ('festive'). Cf. Hesiod, *Theogony*, 907–11.

7 *flit*: passed, gone.

9 *spray*: twig, small branch.

Sonnet XLI

1 *nature*: natural condition or temperament.

will: personal volition, cf. the 'freewill' of *Amor*, 10. 4 and note.

3–8 Employing the trope of *divisio* or *dialysis*, a mode of arguing towards a conclusion through disjunctive propositions.

9 *beauties . . . boast*: beauty's empty ostentation or show.

Sonnet XLII

6 *acquit*: released, delivered.

8 *pledge*: pawn.

9 *which*: referring to his heart.

start: deviate or swerve away.

10 *adamant*: unbreakable. Cf. *HL*, 89.
11 *peruart*: lead astray, corrupt.
12 *safe assurance*: fidelity. Cf. *Amor*, 58 and 59.
14 *doe*: make, cause.

Sonnet XLIII

For this topos cf. Tasso, *Rime*, 2. 246 (no. 164); 2. 248 (no. 166).

8 *stupid stock*: senseless block (of wood).
9–14 Silence, a virtue most commonly associated with 'womanhood' (*FQ*, 4. 10. 51), is here assigned to the male and endowed with semi-mystical significance. The lady's 'wit' will enable her to decipher the language of silence and the emotional alphabet of glances. The emblem of silence was a musical notation composed solely of rests or pauses. Cf. *Epith*, 353 and note.
13 *spel*: decipher, comprehend.
14 *construe*: translate or interpret (the language of love).

Sonnet XLIIII

Orpheus acted as the coxswain for the Argonauts on their voyage to attain the golden fleece and quelled their disputes with song. Cf. Apollonius Rhodius, *Argonautica*, 1. 492–515; Comes, *Mythologiae*, 7. 14; *FQ*, 4. 1. 23. For Orpheus cf. *SC*, *October*, [28]; *VG*, 433–80 and notes.

7 *warreid*: ravaged.

Sonnet XLV

1–4 Plato asserts that the loved one is 'as it were a mirror in which the lover beholds himself' (*Phaedrus*, 255d). The sonnet employs Platonic notions to witty effect throughout. Cf. *Amor*, 7 and note.
1 *glasse*: looking-glass, mirror.
  clene: clear.
2 *euermore*: for all future time (but the possible sense of 'continually' would imply that the lady was vain).
4 *liuely lyke*: lifelike.
6 *vew*: sight, perusal.
7 *Idea*: in Platonic philosophy ideas are the abstract 'forms' of things perceptible to the intellect (not the sight) and hence more 'real' than material objects. The lady will apprehend her true image in the 'mirror' of the speaker's heart. Cf. Michael Drayton, *Ideas Mirrour* (1594).
10 *dimmed . . . deformd*: the 'mirror' is distorted by the speaker's grief at unrequited love, but Plato would identify the cause as sensual passion.
11 *ymage*: mental picture.
14 *remoue . . . be*: an alexandrine, as at *Amor*, 10. 14.

Sonnet XLVI

1 *abodes*: stay's or visit's.
8 *lower heauen*: alluding to the common cosmological distinction between the material and celestial (or perhaps the crystalline) heavens. The former should function as a reflection of the latter.
12 *sorely wrack*: severely injure or punish.

Sonnet XLVII

Cf. Tasso, *Rime*, 2. 128 (no. 88).

3–4 *golden . . . hyde*: i.e. the enticing glitter of the gold disguises the danger of the hook.
6 *decay*: decline, ruin.
10 *louely*: lovingly, affectionately.
12 *of . . . beguyle*: elude the sensation of pain (by self-delusion).

Sonnet XLVIII

There is a loose resemblance to Desportes, *Diane*, 2. 75.

2 *matter*: as both the cause and victim (or object) of her wrath.
5 *hyre*: recompense, reward.
6 *hereticks*: the burning of alleged heretics was a feature of the reign of Queen Mary, widely regarded by Protestants as a tyrant.
8 *plead*: pleaded.
 payned: caused to suffer pain.
9 *constrayned*: compelled.
12 *passion*: suffering.
14 *speake . . . good*: speak well of her.

Sonnet XLIX

Cf. Tasso, *Rime*, 2. 107 (no. 74).

3 *mighties iewell*: adornment of the powerful.
10 *Cockatrices*: hybrid monsters with the head, wings and feet of a cock and the tail of a serpent, able to kill with a glance and often identified with the basilisk.
12 *regard*: look (but also consideration).

Sonnet L

Cf. Desportes, *Les Amours d'Hippolyte*, 53.

1 *languishing*: suffering, pining.
3 *leach*: physician.
7 *hart . . . chiefe*: Thomas Vicary asserts that the heart is 'King of al

members' but that the brain is 'the gouernour or the treasurie of the fyue wittes' (*The Anatomie of the Bodie of Man*, chapters 4, 7).

9 *cordialls*: medicines designed to invigorate the heart (playing on the Latin *cor*, 'heart').

13 *lyfes Leach*: the lady (a role assigned to Christ in religious poetry).

Sonnet LI

1 *ymages*: likenesses.

2 *of purpose*: deliberately.

4 *ne*: nor.

6 *hardnes*: hardness of heart is identified by Christ as an impediment to salvation (Mark 16: 14), but is here intrinsic to the lady's chastity. Cf. *Amor*, 54. 12–14 and notes.

7–8 *sith . . . end*: since no excellent feat was ever attempted which was accomplished, and concluded, without great difficulty.

9–14 Cf. *Amor*, 25, 26.

9 *attend*: attend to it (or possibly wait for it, or bide his time).

10 *allure*: entice, draw.

11 *bend*: incline, dispose (towards myself).

13 *paines*: painful endeavours.

Sonnet LII

Cf. Petrarch, *Rime Sparse*, 242.

4 *knowen*: familiar, marked with his family arms or device.

11 *dumps*: fits of melancholy or dejection.

13 *absens*: 'the lover who is intent only on physical beauty loses all his good and happiness as soon as the woman he loves, by her absence, leaves his eyes deprived of their splendour' (Castiglione, *Courtier*, 337).

Sonnet LIII

1–4 This habit is ascribed to both panthers and tigers in Bartholomaeus Anglicus, *De Proprietatibus Rerum*, 18. 82.

6 *semblant . . . hew*: appearance of her form or figure.

9 *view*: appearance.

10 *most ornament*: greatest adornment.

11 *make*: turn or transform into.

12 *good . . . instrument*: it is shameful for good to become the instrument of evil.

Sonnet LIIII

Cf. Tasso, *Rime*, 3. 265 (no. 213).

1 *worlds Theatre*: a familiar topos. Ortelius' famous atlas was entitled *Theatrum Orbis Terrarum* (1570), effectively the 'theatre' of the world.
3 *pageants*: scenes or performances (with connotations of self-dramatization and deception).
7 *flits*: alters, changes.
9 *constant*: steady, fixed (in the sense of emotionally unmoved).
12 *hardens . . . hart*: cf. *Amor*, 51. 6 and note.
14 *woman . . . stone*: Anaxarete was turned to stone for spurning her lover Iphis. Ovid tells the story as a warning to ladies against hardness of heart (cf. *Metamorphoses*, 14. 693–764).

Sonnet LV

2 *compare*: for the rhetorical device of *comparatio* cf. *Amor*, 9.
3 *mould*: clay, earth. According to Coverdale's Bible, God made Adam 'of the moulde of the earth' (Tobit 8: 6).
5–8 *earth . . . fyre*: the four mutable elements of which the sublunary world is composed. Cf. *FQ*, 7. 7. 17–25.
6 *loue . . . fyre*: a familiar Petrarchan topos.
7 *light*: playing on the sense of fickle, changeable.
9 *another Element*: everything above the sphere of the moon was held to be composed of the fifth element, the quintessence or ether. It was believed to be latent in all things and alchemists laboured to distil it.
11 *haughty*: lofty, exalted (but with connotations of pride).
14 *mercy*: an attribute of God.

Sonnet LVI

Cf. Tasso, *Rime*, 4. 69 (no. 523).

2 *Tygre*: an emblem of cruelty. Cf. *FQ*, 1. 6. 26; 5. 8. 49.
8 *ruinate*: destroy.
9 *obstinate*: playing upon the Latin *obstare*, 'to stand in the way'.
11 *succour desolate*: destitute of help.

Sonnet LVII

Cf. Petrarch, *Rime Sparse*, 21; Du Bellay, *L'Olive*, 70.

3 *sue*: pursue, but playing upon the sense of 'woo' or 'court'.
4 *incessant battry*: cf. *Amor*, 14. 10. The speaker's plans have recoiled upon himself.
7–9 *seeing . . . still*: cf. *HL*, 122–6; *HB*, 239–45 and notes.
13 *graunt . . . grace*: grant me grace in good time.

Sonnet LVIII

If we take 'by her' in its usual sense, this sonnet is attributed to the lady who complains of worldly security ('assurance') after the fashion of *VW* (153), and concludes with an address to women. Deuteronomy warns that 'thou . . . shalt have none assurance of thy life' (28: 66). Cf. also 2 Corinthians 1: 9. However, the intermingling of possessive pronouns ('her . . . her . . . his . . . your') affords ironic applications to both parties. The lady may be too assured of her power to reject a lover, the speaker may be too assured of the power of the flesh in promoting his suit. If we interpret 'by her' as 'concerning her', then the speaker, mindful of the 'safe assurance' pledged in sonnet 42, warns the 'proud fayre' against false security. Assurance also connoted betrothal, a mutual agreement transcending the isolated self. It has been pointed out that the two contrasting sonnets on assurance, 58 and 59, face or 'mirror' one another in the first edition. Cf. Fukuda (1988).

2 *her*: its (the flesh is gendered female, cf. note to *CCH*, 918).
5 *All . . . frayle*: a biblical topos. Cf. Isaiah 40: 6–8; 1 Peter 1: 24.
6 *vaine bubble*: cf. *SC, Februarie*, 87.
7 *deuouring tyme*: cf. Ovid, 'tempus edax rerum', time devours all (*Metamorphoses* 15. 234).
11–12 Cf. 1 Corinthians 10: 12.

Sonnet LIX

1 *Thrise happie*: a common formula of benediction.
3–4 *better . . . worse*: neither will she be enticed into deviation by hopes of better fortune nor frightened into it by the prospect of worse. Overt praise of the lady's emotional independence insinuates a reminiscence of the marriage vows 'for better or for worse'.
5–8 Cf. *Amor*, 34 and 56. 9–12.
11 *stay*: support, but continuing the nautical metaphor by playing upon the sense of 'stay' as a rope supporting the mast.

Sonnet LX

Cf. Desportes, *Cléonice*, 4.

1–4 Each planet has its own 'year' or period of revolution about the sun. Ptolemy established that of Mars as seventy-nine earth years. Spenser's 'three score' is inaccurate; four score may have been intended or the mistake may have arisen from a desire to co-ordinate the astronomical period with the number of the sonnet.
2 *point*: determine, fix.
   his sundry: its distinct or specific (i.e. peculiar to itself).
3 *her*: their.

4 *Mars*: chosen for its association with the god of war and appropriate to the amatory 'battle' fought out in the sequence.

spheare: planetary orbit.

5 *winged God*: Cupid (love).

planet cleare: shining planet, Venus as the bright 'evening star'.

6 *one yeare*: the actual revolution of Venus is somewhat shorter.

8 *fourty*: perhaps autobiographical – or just a conveniently round figure. Cf. Cheney (1983).

outwent: passed through, went through.

9 *louers books*: reckoning the time expended in love is a Petrarchan topos (cf. *Rime Sparse*, 79, 212).

11 *languishment*: affliction, suffering.

13 *short*: shorten.

wayes: pathways through the heavens.

Sonnet LXI

1–2 *image* . . . *Idoll*: as the 'image' of its creator, the lady's beauty should direct the lover's thoughts towards God, but sensual lovers make an 'idol' of the flesh. The suggestion of idolatry evokes the ambivalence of the speaker's feelings, as developed at line 13. The validity of the worship of saints and images was a matter of fierce religious controversy.

3 *dare not*: an imperative apparently directed to the self.

6 *brood*: parentage.

Angels: cf. *Amor*, 1. 11 and note. Ficino asserts that sensual and spiritual love 'struggle with each other in man: the former banishes him down to the animal and voluptuous life; the latter raises him on high to the angelic and contemplative life' (*Commentary*, 7. 1).

7 *vpbrought*: reared, brought up.

8 *each* . . . *guifts*: a clever variation of the Pandora ('all gifts') image. Cf. note to *Amor*, 24. 8.

12 *bold*: boldly, rashly.

13 *formes* . . . *worshipt*: intentionally ambivalent and alluding either to physically beautiful shapes or to the glorious spiritual essences which such shapes were held to embody. Cf. Ficino, *Commentary*, 7. 1.

Sonnet LXII

1–14 A crucial sonnet of change and renewal as the fusion of seasonal and religious vocabularies suggests. It is positioned at the very centre of the volume, counting all of the stanzas of the 'Anacreontics' and *Epithalamion* continuously with the sonnets.

2 *new begins*: on 25 March or Lady Day, the feast of the Annunciation. It marked the conception of Christ and was often regarded as the day of

creation. The competing claims of the two new year's days (1 January and 25 March) are discussed by E. K. in the 'Generall argument' to *SC*.

5 *which . . . vew*: who perceive this change of weather.

10 *glooming*: dark, gloomy.

   gladsome: cheering, uplifting.

11 *blend*: conceal, obscure.

12 *caulmes*: calms.

Sonnet LXIII

1 *tempests . . . assay*: storms' distressing onslaughts or trials.

3 *in . . . dismay*: in fear of death and dismayed by dangers.

4 *sore*: severely, grievously.

6 *in which*: on or at which.

7 *far*: afar, far off.

8 *of . . . alyue*: of all that is precious and valuable in life.

10 *sweet a rest*: according to Camden, the name Elizabeth signified 'Peace of the Lord, or quiet rest of the Lord', from the Hebrew 'eli-sabbath' (*Remains Concerning Britain* (1674), 102). The etymology was used as a compliment to Queen Elizabeth, and Elizabeth Boyle is here offered a private share in her public glory.

11 *depriue*: remove, take away.

13–14 *All . . . blisse*: cf. *Amor*, 25. 9–14.

Sonnet LXIIII

The kiss represents the most intimate contact with the lady that the speaker has enjoyed. In Castiglione it is argued that a kiss should be permitted only in Platonic relationships 'for as a kiss is a union of body and soul, there is a risk that the sensual lover may incline more to the body than the soul'. Its spiritual significance is expounded with reference to Song of Songs 1: 2 (*Courtier*, 336–7). Cf. Sidney, *Astrophil and Stella*, 79–82.

2 *gardin . . . flowres*: for the lady as a fragrant garden cf. Song of Songs 4: 12–16. Each of the flowers and fruits mentioned by Spenser is emblematic of both sensual and spiritual love, thereby capturing the fusion of eroticism and spirituality apparent in the Hebrew. Cf. *Amor*, 26 and note.

5 *Gillyflowers*: cf. *SC*, *Aprill*, 137 and note.

7 *Bellamoures*: meaning 'fair loves' but the flower is unidentified.

8 *Pincks*: sweet-smelling plants with white, pink or crimson flowers.

10 *Cullambynes*: with a pun on the Latin *collum* ('neck') and *columba* ('dove'), an emblem of love. Cf. *SC*, *Aprill*, 136 and note.

12 *Iessemynes*: jasmines.

Sonnet LXV

From this point onwards the sequence echoes the Anglican marriage service, as the constricting 'bonds' of earlier sonnets are converted into the self-imposed 'bands' (5) of mutual love. Cf. *Amor*, 68; Prescott (1985).

4 *bond*: bound.
10 *league*: union, alliance.
11 *mutuall . . . will*: according to the prayer book marriage was ordained 'for the mutuall societie, helpe, and comforte, that the one ought to have of the other'. Ficino observes that 'whenever two people are brought together in mutual affection . . . they mutually exchange identities . . . in such a way that each receives the other in return' (*Commentary*, 2. 8).
13 *brasen*: strong. Brass was emblematic of strength.
14 *pleasure*: cf. *Amor*, 76; *HL*, 273–86 and notes.

Sonnet LXVI

3 *disparagement*: disgrace of an unworthy marriage.
5 *paragon*: playing on the dual senses of 'exemplar' and 'consort'.
9 *gate*: get.
10 *sorted*: consorted, allied yourself.
11 *dilate*: diffuse, spread wide.
13 *light*: cf. *Amor*, 8. 13; 9. 13–14 and notes.
  enlumind: thrown light upon, illuminated.
14 *reflex*: reflection.

Sonnet LXVII

A provocative variation on Petrarch, *Rime Sparse*, 190 where the hind rejects her pursuer in favour of God who has set her 'free'. In Spenser, marriage reconciles physical and spiritual love to such an extent that freedom may be sacrificed (12–14): the hounds are 'beguiled' of their prey, but the lady is 'beguyld' by love and surrenders voluntarily. Cf. Prescott (1985). In Virgil's parodic anti-epithalamium Damon comments satirically that 'the timid deer shall come with hounds to drink' (*Eclogues*, 8. 28). In Spenser the impossible has occurred. Cf. Tasso, *Rime*, 2. 429 (no. 1).

4 *beguiled*: cheated, disappointed.
7–8 *deare . . . brooke*: cf. Psalms 42: 1.
9–10 *beholding . . . bide*: cf. Proverbs 5: 19.
12 *goodwill*: freewill, an essential prerequisite for marriage.
  fyrmely tyde: St Paul advised wives to 'submit' to their husbands (Ephesians 5: 22).
13 *wyld*: cf. *Daph*, 121 and note.
14 *beguyld*: entrapped, won over.

Sonnet LXVIII

For this sonnet cf. John 13: 31–5 where the 'glorified' Christ commands his followers to 'love one another'.

1 *Lord . . . lyfe*: cf. Acts 3: 13–15; *FQ*, 2. 7. 62.

this day: Easter Sunday. The feast is significant to the progress towards mutuality in love. Ficino observes that 'there is only one death in mutual love, but there are two resurrections, for a lover dies within himself the moment he forgets about himself, but he returns to life immediately in his loved one as soon as the loved one embraces him in loving contemplation' (*Commentary*, 2. 8).

2 *triumph . . . sin*: cf. 1 Corinthians 15: 55–7; Romans 6: 9; Prescott (1990).

3 *harrowd hell*: the apocryphal Gospel of Nicodemus records Christ's descent to hell between Good Friday and Easter Sunday to liberate the souls of the just.

4 *captiuity . . . captiue*: cf. Ephesians 4: 8; Prescott (1990).

7 *blood . . . sin*: cf. Revelation 1: 5; 7: 14.

9 *weighing worthily*: valuing properly.

11 *all . . . buy*: cf. 1 Corinthians 6: 20.

14 *lesson . . . taught*: cf. John 15: 12; Kaske (1977).

Sonnet LXIX

Written in the manner of a triumph of love. Cf. Du Bellay, *L'Olive*, 34; Desportes, *Cléonice*, 11.

2 *wize*: manner.

3 *enrold*: inscribed, registered.

4 *valarous emprize*: courageous enterprise.

8 *honour . . . chastity*: i.e. their love does not derogate from her virtue.

9–12 For this topos cf. *Amor*, 27. 10–14.

12 *wonderment*: object of wonder.

13–14 Recalling *Amor*, 25. 11–14.

13 *purchase*: attainment, acquisition. Cf. Acts 20: 28.

Sonnet LXX

The second spring poem, cf. *Amor*, 19. Cf. Song of Songs 2: 11–13.

1 *king*: Cupid. Cf. *Amor*, 19. 3.

2 *cote armour*: vest of richly embroidered material worn by knights over their armour and also worn by heralds.

8 *forelock*: opportunity was iconographically depicted with a long forelock which had to be grasped while occasion offered. Cf. *FQ*, 2. 4. 4.

11 *misseth . . . make*: has failed to acquire a mate or partner.

12 *amearst*: punished.

13–14 Summarizing the 'carpe diem' theme implicit in the whole sonnet.
13 *prime*: spring, period of maximum sexual vigour and energy.

Sonnet LXXI

1 *drawen work*: embroidery (drawn-thread work).
2 *Bee*: symbolizing the sweet and bitter aspects of love, the honey and the sting. The spider and bee were traditional opponents.
3 *Spyder*: at *Amor*, 23. 7 the speaker 'weaves' his suit to the lady but now she weaves the spider-speaker into her own web.
4 *close awayt*: hidden ambush.
8 *remoue*: depart, escape.
9 *about*: often emended to 'above' to preserve the rhyme scheme.
10 *woodbynd . . . Eglantine*: honeysuckle and wild rose respectively, both emblematic of love. Cf. *SC, Maye*, 13.

Sonnet LXXII

Castiglione notes that 'those who reach this stage of love are like fledgelings which on their feeble wings can lift themselves a little in flight but dare not stray far from the nest or trust themselves to the winds of the open sky' (*Courtier*, 339). St Paul notes that marriage acts as a spiritual distraction (1 Corinthians 7: 32–4). Cf. Tasso, *Rime*, 2. 98 (no. 67).

4 *clogd*: burdened or impeded, as by fetters or clogs (wooden blocks).
10 *mantleth*: spreads its wings. Since only perched hawks were said to mantle their wings the image complements that of the opening lines.

Sonnet LXXIII

Cf. Tasso, *Rime*, 2. 319 (no. 222).

1 *care*: sorrow, distress.
6–8 *desired . . . feed*: the imagery of taste indicates the persistence of sensual appetite. Cf. 'Desire still cries, "give me some food"' (Sidney, *Astrophil and Stella*, 71).
9 *bright*: radiant, beautiful.
10 *encage*: confine, enfold. Cf. *Amor*, 65. 7–8.

Sonnet LXXIIII

1 *skilfull trade*: artful practice (of letters or writing).
2 *desynd*: signified.
3 *three . . . thrise*: corresponding to the number of letters in her name. Cf. note to *Amor*, 63. 10.
4 *body . . . mind*: Plato discriminates between the claims of body, soul and wealth, placing those of wealth last (cf. *Letters*, 8. 355b).
5 *kind*: birth.

7 *kind*: gracious (but also rightful).

8 *honour . . . richesse*: referring to Spenser's reception by the Queen, his annual pension, and the granting of an estate at Kilcolman in Munster.

  lent: bestowed, granted.

9 *liues*: life's.

10 *spirit . . . raysed*: cf. *HL*, 176–9.

13 *three Elizabeths*: this is the sole occasion upon which Spenser refers to the names of his mother and his second wife.

14 *graces*: playing on 'Graces', the three classical deities. Cf. *SC*, *Aprill*, [109]; *Amor*, 40. 4 and notes.

Sonnet LXXV

1 *strand*: sandy beach, shore.

3 *wrote . . . hand*: wrote it out a second time.

9 For poetic immortality cf. *RT*, 344–455; *Amor*, 27. 11–14.

14 *later . . . renew*: i.e. give them poetic immortality.

Sonnet LXXVI

The sensual imagery of this and the following sonnet captures the ambivalence of a love both spiritual and sensual, such as is described at Song of Songs 4: 10–15; 7: 3–6. As the goal is marriage, and not a Platonic relationship, the claims of sensuality cannot be denied. The reference to the 'bowre of blisse' (3) recalls the dangers of sexual desire (cf. *FQ*, 2. 12. 42–87), but that to 'pleasure' (3) recalls the lawful enjoyment of the Gardens of Adonis, devoted to fertility and procreation (cf. *FQ*, 3. 6. 50–51). Cf. note to *Amor*, 65. 14; Tasso, *Rime*, 3. 133 (no. 94).

3 *paradice*: 'a Garden of pleasure' (*SC*, *June*, [10]). Cf. *HL*, 273–86.

4 *harbour*: dwelling, bower.

5 *How . . . rauisht*: cf. Song of Songs 4: 9.

6 *rashly*: imprudently, impulsively.

7 *insight*: vision. As at *Amor*, 72 contemplation may actually frustrate Neoplatonic ascent contrary to more pious expectations.

9 *paps*: breasts, nipples.

  May: traditionally associated with love. Cf. *SC*, *Maye*, 1–2, [1].

11 *loosely*: lasciviously, without restraint.

Sonnet LXXVII

Employing the 'banquet of sense' motif and suggesting, through the ambivalent imagery of apples, the dual nature of the speaker's love. His very 'thoughts' (14) are bodily.

2 *yvory*: cf. Song of Songs 5: 14. But in Virgil false dreams proceed from the underworld through ivory gates (*Aeneid*, 6. 895–6).

3 *iuncats*: delicacies, confectionery.

4 *pompous*: magnificent, splendid.

6 *vnualewd*: inestimable.

7–8 *Hercules ... Atalanta*: as one of his twelve labours Hercules stole the golden apples of the Hesperides by defeating the attendant dragon. Atalanta vowed to marry any man who could defeat her in a race, but Hippomenes gained victory by casting three golden apples (sometimes identified with the apples of the Hesperides) in her path. The apples were often related to the apple of Genesis and taken to signify sinful baits. Cf. *FQ*, 2. 7. 54; Comes, *Mythologiae*, 7. 7. Cf. Tasso, *Rime*, 3. 133 (no. 94).

11 *paradice*: Petrarch's Laura 'was surely born in Paradise' (*Rime Sparse*, 126. 55). Both the evil Bowre of Blisse and the creative Gardens of Adonis are described as paradisal (cf. *FQ*, 2. 12. 58; 3. 6. 29).

14 *thoughts ... fedd*: in Castiglione it is the sensual lover whose thoughts demand the 'delicious food' of the body (*Courtier*, 338).

Sonnet LXXVIII

This is directly related to the preceding sonnet in that, according to Castiglione, the sensual lover cannot bear the lady's absence and craves physical sustenance because he is unable to contemplate the image of pure beauty in his soul (*Courtier*, 338). Cf. Petrarch, *Rime Sparse*, 126, 127.

2 *fawne ... hynd*: cf. Horace, *Odes*, 1. 23 where the lady is the fawn. The reversal of imagery bears an ironic relationship to that of *Amor*, 67.

5 *synd*: marked (with her footprints).

6 *bowre*: abode or bedchamber.

8 *aspect*: appearance (i.e. the remembrance of her presence).

12 *fed ... vayne*: cf. *Amor*, 77. 14; *HHB*, 288–94 and notes.

14 *thoughts ... mee*: the Platonic lover should 'turn his desire completely away from the body to beauty alone' and contemplate it without fear of loss. Cf. Castiglione, *Courtier*, 338.

Sonnet LXXIX

Cf. Tasso, *Rime*, 3. 142 (no. 102).

1 *credit*: either believe or lend validity to.

4–9 *vertuous ... beautie*: cf. *Amor*, 7. 2 and note.

9–10 *argue ... seed*: cf. *Amor*, 61. 6 and note.

11–12 *deriu'd ... proceed*: the Neoplatonic doctrine succinctly expounded. Cf. *HHB*, 8–14.

14 *vntymely fade*: unseasonably wither.

Sonnet LXXX

1–2 *After . . . compile*: since *Amor* was entered in the Stationers' Register on 19 November 1594 this would imply that *FQ*, 4–6 were already completed by this time although not published until 1596.

2 *compile*: fabricate, constitute.

3 *fordonne*: exhausted, worn out.

4 *new breath*: both physical breath and poetic inspiration.

5–8 The mood strongly contrasts with *Amor*, 33. As the consummation of his private love approaches, he appears to gain enthusiasm for his public duty. For the imagery of the steed cf. Virgil, *Aeneid*, 11. 492–9.

6 *prison*: stall or stable.

7 *stoutly*: vigorously, energetically.

assoyle: assail (in the sense of endeavour).

8 *strong endeuour*: strenuous effort.

attention: concentration.

9 *mew*: cage, but wittily playing on 'mews' (stables). His 'steed' is the winged horse Pegasus.

10 *sport*: entertain, indulge.

12 *pitch*: highest point a bird may reach.

14 *handmayd . . . Queene*: cf. *FQ*, 6. 10. 25–8.

Sonnet LXXXI

Adopting the form of a blazon or formal itemizing of attributes. Cf. Tasso, *Rime*, 2. 25 (no. 17).

2 *loose*: free, untrammelled (but with suggestions of sensuality either in the lady or the observer). Cf. *Amor*, 37. 6 and note.

marke: notice, observe.

4 *fyre of loue*: in Castiglione 'vivacious spirits shining from the lady's eyes constantly add fresh fuel to the fire' (*Courtier*, 334). Cf. *HL*, 122–4 and note.

7 *cloud of pryde*: for the theme of pride cf. *Amor*, 5, 31, 32, 38, 58, 59; *Epith*, 164, 306 and notes.

10 *pearles . . . rubyes*: her teeth and lips. Cf. *Amor*, 15. 8–9.

11–12 *words . . . spright*: 'although the mouth is part of the body . . . it provides a channel for words, which are the interpreters of the soul, and for the human breath or spirit' (Castiglione, *Courtier*, 336).

13 *natures wonderment*: i.e. the wonders of physical nature.

14 *harts*: cf. *Amor*, 2. 2 and note.

Sonnet LXXXII

5 *equall*: equitable, impartial.

6 *mote inuent*: might find.

7 *enchased*: engraved, or set in relief.
13 *argument*: theme, subject.
14 *high degree*: by ascending from the merely physical to the spiritual.

Sonnet LXXXIII

Repeating *Amor*, 35 with the minor variants of 'seeing' for 'hauing' (6) and 'shewes' for 'showes' (14). The new context lends the sonnet a different application. The lover's 'plenty' is now that of betrothal, but the lady's virtue still deprives him of consummation. Cf. Introduction.

Sonnet LXXXIIII

Cf. Tasso, *Rime*, 2. 194 (no. 120).

1 *Let not*: the formula has the force of a prayer or prophylactic charm designed to ward off evil. Cf. *Epith*, 334–52.
7 *bowre of rest*: bedchamber – the 'pure affections' (5) and 'modest thoughts' (6) still gravitate to this location.
8 *angelick delightes*: associated in Neoplatonism with spiritual love when the soul 'flies to unite itself with the angelic nature' and partakes of 'the feast of the angels' (Castiglione, *Courtier*, 340, 342).
12 *stiffenesse*: firmness, moral resolution.
14 *election*: alluding either to his choice of the lady or to her choice of him. Either way 'election' has theological connotations of undeserved grace. Like the elect, the speaker is 'saved' despite his unworthiness.

Sonnet LXXXV

Cf. Ronsard, *Hélène*, 1. 10.

3 *Cuckow*: cf. *Amor*, 19. 1 and note.
  Mauis: song-thrush. Cf. *Epith*, 81.
4 *clatter*: babble, chatter.
8 *deeme . . . aspyre*: ambiguously phrased but probably meaning 'aspire to comprehend or celebrate her worth'.
9 *closet*: private chamber or recess.
  parts entyre: inward parts, i.e. deep in the intimacy of his heart. Cf. *Amor*, 6. 11 and note.
11 *heauenly fury*: divinely inspired poetic frenzy. Cf. *SC*, *October*, 'Argument' and notes.

Sonnet LXXXVI

For the theme of envy and misrepresentation cf. *Rime Sparse*, 206.

1 *Venemous toung*: the traditional iconography, cf. *FQ*, 5. 12. 33–6.

2–3 *Furies . . . combe*: infernal goddesses who sit at the gates of hell, as described by Ovid at *Metamorphoses*, 4. 451–4.

3–4 *spring . . . well*: cf. the description of Sclaunder at *FQ*, 4. 8. 26. For the imagery of 'spring' and 'well' cf. *FQ*, 4. 2. 32.

6 *hyre*: payment.

8 *coles of yre*: in Song of Songs the 'coals' of jealousy are 'coals of fire' (8: 6).

9–10 *thine . . . hed*: cf. 'thou shalt heap coals of fire upon his head' (Proverbs 25: 22) but the application is radically dissimilar.

13 *Shame . . . meed*: cf. 'Shame be his meede [reward] . . . that meaneth shame' (*FQ*, 4. 6. 6), the motto of the Knights of the Garter.

14 *dew*: due.

Sonnet LXXXVII

2 *outworne*: passed wearily. The days have worn him out.

4 *sad protract*: tedious duration or extent.

10 *faine*: combining the senses of contrive and pretend.

11 *terme . . . extend*: prolong its duration, extend its limit.

12 *myle*: i.e. the time it would take to walk a mile.

Sonnet LXXXVIII

2–3 *lead . . . wander*: because of the ambivalent nature of his love, he may go astray either with her or without her.

7 *th'onely . . . ray*: in Castiglione the lady's beauty is 'a ray of the supernatural' (*Courtier*, 334).

8 *glance*: gleam, flash.

9 *Idæa*: cf. *Amor*, 45. 7 and note.

10 *contemplation . . . part*: in Castiglione the lover is advised to combat physical absence by contemplating abstract beauty (*Courtier*, 338).

13–14 Neoplatonic strategies fail to satisfy a love desiring bodily consummation. The 'image' produces blindness not insight.

Sonnet LXXXIX

Cf. Petrarch, *Rime Sparse*, 353. The difference is that Laura is dead.

1 *Culuer*: dove, emblem of faithful love. Cf. *TM*, 246.

6 *mourne*: lament.

8 *match*: equal, emulate.

9 *houe*: remains, or hovers (continuing the bird imagery).

12 *vnspotted pleasauns*: unsullied or innocent pleasantness or charm.

14 *liuely*: invigorating, life-giving. Petrarch 'lived' solely in Laura's love (*Rime Sparse*, 206. 2).

Anacreontics

In the first edition these poems follow sonnet 89 without any title. The first two stanzas are printed together on one page but all of the rest are assigned a page each. Their manner is that of the Greek poet Anacreon, much in vogue among the poets of the Pléiade (cf. *HHB*, 219–24), and they reprise the erotic joys and frustrations of the sonnet sequence while anticipating the resolution of spiritual and physical love in *Epith*. Cf. D. Anderson (1984); Hester (1993); Kaske (1978); Miola (1980); Neely (1978).

2 *blynd . . . baby*: Cupid, cf. *SC*, *March*, [79] and note.

3 *cunning*: wisdom (especially that born of experience).

4–5 *honny . . . stung*: cf. *Amor*, 71. 2 and note. For the erotic associations of honey cf. Song of Songs 4: 11.

7–14 A version of Clément Marot, *Epigrams*, 3. 5.

7 *Diane*: Diana, goddess of the hunt and chastity, is often figured as hostile to Cupid (cf. *FQ*, 3. 6. 20–25).

13 *With that*: with the arrow that inspires chastity rather than desire.

　hart: heart, but playing on the sense of 'hart' (deer).

14 *Diane . . . dart*: the arrows of chastity (i.e. the force of the lady's virtue) incite rather than suppress bestial or physical desire, a paradox that encapsulates the dilemma of the preceding sonnet sequence.

15–22 A version of Clément Marot, *Epigrams*, 3. 24.

19 *flame*: blush.

20 *the other*: the speaker's love.

22 *err'd*: i.e. confused the lady with Venus, much as Elizabeth I is taken for Venus at *SC*, *Aprill*, 'emblems'.

23–62 Adapted from Theocritus, *Idylls*, 19 and *Anacreontea*, 35 (also adapted by Ronsard at *L'Inspiration Anacréontique*, 6). The last two stanzas (63–82) are substantially original to Spenser. Cf. Hutton (1941).

25 *gentle Bee*: cf. *Amor*, 71. 2 for the lady as a 'gentle bee'.

32 *corage stout*: doubtless with sexual connotations.

33 *closely*: privately (i.e. she smiled to herself).

42 *fly*: flying insect.

45 *hardiment*: audacity, boldness.

48 *therefore*: i.e. for what he had done.

52 *horne*: sting (with sexual innuendo).

62 *spoyle . . . make*: made his prey, or his booty.

64 *smock*: chemise, with obvious sexual overtones.

67–70 Cf. the imagery of wounding and healing in *Amor*, 50, 65.

67 *embaulmed*: anointed.

68 *salue . . . might*: remedy (or balm) of supreme efficacy. For the erotic associations cf. *FQ*, 3. 5. 50.

70 *well . . . delight*: anticipating the consummation of *Epith*.

73 *recured*: cured, recovered from. Cf. *HB*, 285.

75 *enured*: put into practice, renewed.

79 *elfe*: mischievous imp.

80 *heast to proue*: carry out his mother's behest or bidding.

Epithalamion

The Latin word *epithalamium* (from the Greek *epithalamos*) means '[song] before the bridal door' but was used for wedding songs generally.

1 *learned sisters*: the Muses, Ovid's 'doctae . . . sorores' (*Fasti*, 6. 811). Cf. *SC, Aprill*, [41].

3 *gracefull*: in the dual sense of elegant and conferring grace.

4 *greatest*: Queen Elizabeth (who had received Spenser personally).

7 *owne . . . mourne*: as in *TM*.

8 *rayse*: occasion, cause.

9 *tenor*: combining the senses of pitch and mood. Cf. *SC, October*, [50]; *HHL*, 13–14.

11 *dolefull dreriment*: cf. *SC, November*, [36]; *RT*, 158 and notes.

14 *resound*: proclaim, but often associated with making echoes.

16 *Orpheus*: cf. *SC, October*, [28] and note. Orpheus' attempts at epithalamium were ill-omened (cf. Ovid, *Metamorphoses*, 10. 1–10).

17 *selfe . . . sing*: cf. *SC, June*, 72. Perhaps recalling the Narcissus imagery of *Amor*, 35. 7, particularly in view of the allusion to 'Eccho' at line 18.

18 *woods . . . ring*: the refrain may be intended to recall, and to ward off, the tragic 'echo' of Orpheus' final lament (cf. Virgil, *Georgics*, 4. 526–7; *TM*, 285–6). The nymph Echo pined away through unrequited love for Narcissus (cf. Ovid, *Metamorphoses*, 3. 359–401). In Spenser loss is transformed into consummation. For propitious echoes cf. Claudian, *Epithalamium of Palladius and Celerina*, 23–5.

22 *lusty hed*: vigour, but clearly with sexual connotations.

24 *turtle doue*: cf. *Amor*, 89. 1 and note. In Song of Songs the lady is often addressed as a 'dove' (2: 14; 5: 2; 6: 9).

25 *Hymen*: the god of marriage and often regarded as the son of Apollo and the Muse Clio (or sometimes Calliope or Urania). His emblems were the torch, the flute and a crown of flowers. He is traditionally invoked in epithalamia. Cf. Catullus, 61. 1–4, 39–40, 49–50 etc.

27 *Tead*: torch, as at Catullus, 61. 15 ('pineam . . . taedam').
   flake: stray flame or spark.

28 *bachelor*: young knight or unmarried man.

29 *trim*: elegant.

33 *vsury*: interest.

37 *Nymphes*: minor goddesses of woods, rivers and countryside. They are also summoned to attend the queen at *SC, Aprill*, 120, [120].

that . . . heare: that can hear you.

40 *goodly . . . beseene*: exceptionally beautiful or well favoured.

41–3 Cf. Catullus 61. 6–7.

43 *lillyes . . . roses*: emblematic of chastity and love.

44 *trueloue wize*: into a love knot. Cf. *Amor*, 6. 14 and note.

riband: perhaps also alluding to the marriage girdle, destined to be unloosed by the bridegroom.

45 *poses*: posies, flowers.

47 *deck . . . bowers*: a traditional practice.

49 *feare . . . wrong*: cf. Psalms 91: 12.

51 *diapred . . . mead*: as diversified as a multi-coloured meadow. A diaper was a textile of threads crossed diamond-wise, so reflecting light diversely.

56 *Mulla*: the River Awbeg. Cf. *CCH*, 59 and note.

58 *vse*: are accustomed.

60 *rushy lake*: possibly the lake at Kilcolman.

62 *Bynd . . . locks*: cf. *Amor*, 37. 6 and note.

64 *christall bright*: cf. *SC, Julye*, 159.

65 *whereas*: where.

67 *lightfoot mayds*: cf. *TM*, 31; Horace, *Odes*, 1. 1. 31.

68 *towre*: i.e. by brandishing their antlers aloft.

69 *wolues*: endemic to Ireland. Cf. *CCH*, 318 and note.

74 *Wake . . . awake*: cf. Song of Songs 2: 10–13.

75 *Rosy . . . Tithones*: Aurora (Eos) the goddess of dawn fell in love with Tithonus, son of Laomedon, and gained for him eternal life but without eternal youth. Cf. Homer, *Iliad*, 11. 1–2. 'Rosy' is the traditional epithet.

76 *coche*: couch.

77 *Phœbus*: Apollo, the sun god.

80 *Larke*: the traditional herald of morning.

mattins: morning songs, but with a play on mourning prayers.

81 *Mauis*: song-thrush. Cf. *Amor*, 85. 3.

82 *Ouzell . . . Ruddock*: blackbird and robin redbreast.

86 *meeter*: more fit or appropriate.

87 *make*: mate.

92 *dreame*: often emended to 'dreames' to preserve the rhyme scheme.

95 *Hesperus*: Venus as the morning star, propitious for marriage. Cf. *Proth*, 164–5 and note.

96 *damzels*: bridesmaids.

daughters of delight: used of the Graces at *FQ*, 6. 10. 15 and tending to elevate the bridesmaids to similar status.

98 *houres*: the Horae or Hours were commonly regarded as the daughters of Zeus and Themis, and presided over growth in nature and order in

society. They therefore evoke the dual nature of wedlock. At *FQ*, 7. 7. 45 they are daughters of Jove and Night. Cf. Comes, *Mythologiae*, 4. 16.

99 *Ioues . . . paradice*: cf. Plato, *Symposium*, 203b–c where love is born in the garden of Zeus. Cf. also *FQ*, 3. 6. 29–42.

103 *handmayds*: the three Graces. Cf. *SC*, *Aprill*, [109] and note.

Cyprian Queene: Venus, born off the coast of Cyprus. Cf. Hesiod, *Theogony*, 176–206; *FQ*, 2. 12. 65; *HB*, 55.

104 *pride*: magnificence, splendour.

110 *loue . . . come*: cf. Catullus 61. 76–7, 117–18.

111 *virgins*: bridesmaids.

112 *boyes*: groom's attendants.

113 *he . . . strayt*: cf. Catullus 61. 187.

115 *ioyfull day*: cf. Catullus' 'hilari die' (61. 11).

117 *Sun*: for the sun as the author of life cf. Comes, *Mythologiae*, 4. 10.

118 *lifull*: full of life, life-giving.

119 *sunshyny*: Apocalyptic imagery (cf. Revelation 12: 1; *FQ*, 1. 12. 23).

120 *disgrace*: mar, blemish.

121 *Phœbus . . . Muse*: cf. *SC*, *Aprill*, [41] and note.

124 *boone*: entreaty, request.

127 *souerayne*: supreme, paramount.

129 *shrill*: sound shrilly.

131 *tabor*: small drum.

Croud: six-stringed fiddle.

134 *tymbrels*: tambourines.

136 *sences . . . rauish*: cf. *SC*, *October*, [27] and note.

137–9 *boyes . . . voyce*: cf. the Fescennine jesting at Catullus 61. 122–31.

140–46 A traditional topos. Cf. Claudian, *Fescennine Verses*, 4. 35–7.

144 *approuance*: approval.

145 *her*: their. Cf. *SC*, *Maye*, [160].

laud: praise, but in view of the play on mattins at line 80, possibly alluding to lauds, the traditional morning prayer incorporating Psalms 148–50 which frequently employ the Latin word *laudate* ('praise ye').

148 *portly*: stately.

149 *Phœbe*: (Diana) goddess of the moon. Cf. *SC*, *Aprill*, [65]. For the imagery cf. Psalms 19: 5.

151 *white*: the first of many echoes of the mystical union of the lamb and his bride at Revelation 19: 1–9. Cf. *FQ*, 1. 12. 37–40.

seemes: beseems, becomes.

153 *angell*: cf. *Amor*, 1. 11; 61. 6 and notes.

154 *wyre*: thread. Cf. *FQ*, 2. 3. 30.

155 *perling*: studding, sprinkling.

157 *greene*: 'greene is for maydens meete' (*SC*, *August*, 68).

158 *mayden Queene*: recalling Una at *FQ*, 1. 12. 8 and again associating the lady with Queen Elizabeth. Cf. note to *Amor*, 63. 10.

159 *modest eyes*: 'modestie' is one of the principal virtues of 'womanhood' (192). Cf. *FQ*, 4. 10. 51; Catullus 61. 79.

164 *proud*: for the theme of pride cf. *Amor*, 81. 7 and note.

167 *merchants daughters*: stressing the social context of the wedding.

171–7 For the topos of the blazon cf. *Amor*, 15, 81 and notes.

171 *Saphyres*: reputedly good for the eyes. Cf. Song of Songs 5: 14.

172 *yuory*: cf. Song of Songs 5: 14; 7: 4.

173 *apples*: cf. *Amor*, 77. 7–8 and note.

   rudded: reddened, made ruddy. Cf. *Amor*, 64. 6.

174 *cherryes*: suggesting the 'banquet of sense' motif.

175 *vncrudded*: uncurdled.

176 *paps*: breasts, nipples. Cf. *Amor*, 76. 9.

   lyllies: symbolic of purity. Cf. Song of Songs 4: 5.

177 *marble towre*: a variation of Song of Songs 4: 4.

180 *honors seat*: in her mind.

   bowre: (bed)chamber. Cf. line 299. She combines sensuality with chastity.

186 *inward . . . spright*: cf. *Amor*, 79 and notes. For Neoplatonists physical beauty reflects spiritual beauty. Cf. Plato, *Symposium*, 210a–e.

187 *Garnisht*: adorned or furnished.

189 *red*: beheld.

190 *Medusaes*: one of the three Gorgons, whose hair was a writhing mass of snakes and whose look turned beholders to stone. Petrarch used images of petrification to express the peril of beauty (cf. *Rime Sparse*, 125. 30–32; 129. 51–2). Cf. Comes, *Mythologiae*, 7. 11; Mazzola (1992).

192 *Vnspotted fayth*: cf. Song of Songs 4: 7.

   womanhood: as opposed to 'maydenhed'. Cf. *FQ*, 3. 6. 28 where the two are discriminated. Chastity, however, is common to both.

194 *vertue . . . throne*: cf. Seneca, *Moral Epistles*, 114. 23. 24.

201 *vnreuealed pleasures*: cf. 1 Corinthians 2: 9.

204–5 *Open . . . in*: cf. Isaiah 26. 2; Catullus 61. 76–7.

206–7 *postes . . . trim*: a traditional practice, cf. Catullus 64. 292–3; *SC*, *Maye*, 11–14.

208 *Saynt*: cf. *Amor*, 22. 4 and note. The marriage takes place on St Barnabas's Day (cf. lines 265–72) but the bride herself is a 'saint'.

215 *altar*: altars had been replaced by communion tables in Protestant churches, but the word is doubtless retained for its ceremonial grandeur.

217 *endlesse matrimony*: suggesting the mystical union of the lamb and his bride at Revelation 19: 1–9. Death shall not part them. This line appropriately marks the midpoint of the poem.

218 *roring*: in the sense of booming or resounding.

220 *hollow*: fully open.

221 *Antheme*: hymn or antiphonal song.

226–7 *red . . . snow*: a traditional association. Cf. Tibullus 3. 4. 30–32.

227 *vermill*: vermilion.

228 *dyde in grayne*: i.e. fast dyed.

229 *Angels*: cf. Revelation 7: 11; *FQ*, 1. 12. 39.

230 *remaine*: linger, abide.

236 *looke . . . awry*: discipline of the glance is essential to chastity. Cf. *FQ*, 3. 1. 65; 3. 3. 24.

237 *vnsownd*: wanton, wicked.

239 *pledge . . . band*: token of our union (playing on 'band' as ring).

240 *Alleluya*: cf. Revelation 19: 1.

243–4 *triumph . . . gaine*: cf. *Amor*, 69; *HL*, 33–5.

248 *liue long*: an intensive form of long.

250 *stay*: restraint.

252 *wull*: will.

253 *postes*: door posts. This was a Roman marriage custom.

255 *Bacchus*: god of wine and revelry.

257 *Graces daunce*: cf. *SC, Aprill*, 109–12, [109]. The Graces dance around Colin Clout's lady at *FQ*, 6. 10. 14–15.

265–72 *sunne . . . night*: in the Elizabethan calendar St Barnabas's Day, 11 June, usually marked the summer solstice. Hence the proverb 'Barnaby bright, Barnaby bright, / The longest day and the shortest night'.

267 *by degrees*: gradually, and by astrological degrees.

269 *Crab*: the sign of Cancer. The sun enters Leo in mid-June leaving Cancer 'behind his back'. Cf. *FQ*, 7. 7. 35–6; Campbell (1987).

273 *late*: at last, finally.

278–9 *Ah . . . loue*: cf. Claudian, *Epithalamium of Honorius*, 14–15.

280 *numbers*: i.e. numbers of minutes and numbers on the clock face.

281 *feathers*: Time is traditionally depicted with wings.

282 *fayrest Planet*: the sun, as one of the traditional seven 'planets'.

283 *fome*: sea.

284 *tyred steedes*: as at Virgil, *Aeneid*, 11. 913–14.

285 *gloome*: grow dark or dusky.

286 *euening star*: Hesperus, the planet Venus.

287 *East*: presumably a printer's error for west.

288–9 *Fayre . . . lead*: cf. Catullus 62. 20–31; 64. 328–32; Bion, *Idylls*, 9.

289 *host of heauen*: biblical phrasing. Cf. Isaiah 34: 4; Jeremiah 8: 2.

290 *nights*: often emended to 'nightes' (i.e. with two syllables) to aid the metre.

292 *atweene*: between.

294 *these . . . many*: this joyous multitude.

296–7 *Now . . . youres*: cf. Catullus 61. 227–8.

296 *forepast*: previous.

299 *bring . . . boures*: cf. Catullus 61. 179.

301 *bed . . . lay*: cf. Catullus 61. 182–4.

304 *Arras*: the French town of Arras was famous for richly embroidered tapestries. For the lady's bedding cf. Catullus 64. 46–51.

306 *proud humility*: the oxymoron encapsulates the essence of the lady's moral character. Cf. *Amoretti*, 56.

307 *Maia*: mother of Hermes and one of the Pleiades, renowned for her modesty. Cf. *The Homeric Hymns*, 4. 1–6; *MHT*, 1257 and note.

308 *Tempe*: Maia was a nymph of Mount Cyllene not of Tempe, site of the myth of Apollo and Daphne.

310 *Acidalian brooke*: associated not with Maia but Venus. The Graces bathed in the fountain of Acadalia in Boeotia. Cf. Servius, *Commentarii* (*Aeneid*, 1. 720); *FQ*, 4. 5. 5; 6. 10. 8.

313 *leaue*: cease.

315 *Now . . . expected*: Catullus 62. 1–2. Cf. also Pearcy (1981).

316 *defray*: discharge by payment.

317–18 *cares . . . aye*: recalling the imagery of lines 32–3 above.

318 *cancelled*: i.e. paid or recompensed in full.

319 *broad wing*: for this iconography cf. Virgil, *Aeneid*, 8. 369.

321 *sable mantle*: a traditional detail. Cf. *FQ*, 1. 1. 39.

323 *treason*: recalling the perilous political state of Ireland.

326 *quietsome*: quiet, peaceful.

328 *Ioue . . . Alcmena*: cf. *MHT*, 1299 and note.

329 *Tirynthian groome*: Hercules of Tiryns. The phrase translates Ovid's 'iuvenis Tirynthius' (cf. *Fasti*, 2. 305).

330–31 *selfe . . . Maiesty*: the mythology is apparently original to Spenser. In Ovid Majesty is the child of Honour and Reverence (cf. *Fasti*, 5. 23–6).

334–51 The warding off of evils is a convention of the genre. Cf. Claudian, *Epithalamium of Honorius*, 191–3.

339 *sad affrights*: disturbing terrors.

340 *helpelesse harmes*: ills for which there is no protection or remedy.

341 *Pouke*: Puck, the hobgoblin Robin Goodfellow, sometimes identified with the devil.

343 *names . . . not*: names of spirits undetectable by our senses.

345–8 *shriech . . . vultures*: the owl, the stork, the raven and the vulture are declared to be abominations in Leviticus 11: 13–19. Cf. *SC*, *June*, [23]; *FQ*, 2. 7. 23. For the owl cf. Pliny, *Natural History*, 10. 16. 34–5.

349 *Frogs*: they serve as one of the plagues of Egypt at Exodus 8: 1–14 and as hosts for 'unclean spirits' at Revelation 16: 13. Cf. *VG*, 229–30.

351 *drery*: gloomy.

353 *Silence*: the initial invocation of the Muses appropriately gives way to that of Silence. Cf. *Amor*, 43. 9–14 and note.

354 *assurance*: confidence, security. Cf, *Amor*, 58 and notes.

356 *poure*: an ingenious usage, as though the 'limbs' of sleep were liquid. Possibly inspired by Virgil, *Aeneid*, 5. 836–7, but cf. *FQ*, 1. 7. 7.

playne: the sense is unclear, either the 'plain', or countryside, in which the lovers rest or the 'pleasant complaint' of the lady on her wedding night as she enjoys both the pain and pleasure of love.

357 *winged loues*: Cupids. Cf. *Amor* 16. 6; *HB*, 240.

358 *doues*: sacred to Venus and emblems of love.

363 *couert*: secretive.

364 *sonnes of Venus*: Cupids or putti.

play . . . will: translating 'ludite ut lubet', Catullus 61. 207.

365 *pleasure*: pleasure is the offspring of love at *FQ*, 3. 6. 50–52. Cf. *Amor*, 65. 14; 76 and notes.

374 *Cinthia*: (Diana) born on Mount Cynthus on the isle of Delos. Often applied to Queen Elizabeth whose blessing is thus obliquely evoked. Cf. *SC*, *Aprill*, 82; *CCH*, 66 and notes.

378 *vnthought*: no longer regarded, forgotten.

379–81 *fleece . . . wrought*: Endymion of Latmos seduced the moon goddess Phoebe (Cynthia) with the gift of a fleece and was doomed to perpetual sleep. Cf. *SC*, *Julye*, [64]; Theocritus, *Idylls*, 20. 37–9.

383–7 *wemens . . . breed*: a conventional topos. Cf. Catullus, 61. 207–26.

383 *labours . . . charge*: Diana (Artemis) controlled the pain of childbirth.

384 *enlarge*: increase, multiply.

386 *informe*: infuse, animate.

387 *comfort*: delight (and the eventual 'support' of children).

388 *hopefull hap*: i.e. the good fortune for which we are hoping.

390 *Iuno*: for Juno as guardian of wedlock cf. Virgil, *Aeneid*, 4. 59.

awful: awe-inspiring.

391 *patronize*: promote, uphold.

392 *religion*: fidelity.

faith . . . plight: at the betrothal.

394–5 *comfort . . . women*: when in labour Roman women cried out 'Juno Lucina fer opem' ('Juno Lucina lend assistance'). Cf. Ovid, *Fasti*, 2. 449–52.

398 *Genius*: the god of generation and guardian spirit. Cf. *FQ*, 2. 12. 46–8; 3. 6. 31–2; Comes, *Mythologiae*, 4. 3.

399 *geniall bed*: translating the Latin *lectus genialis*, the 'marriage-bed' as a bed of generation. Cf. Servius, *Commentarii* (*Aeneid*, 6. 603).

403–4 *fruitfull . . . fruit*: with biblical connotations. Cf. 'blessed is the fruit of thy womb' (Luke 1: 42).

405 *Hebe*: daughter of Hera and goddess of youth, often associated with the Muses and the Horae. Cf. Comes, *Mythologiae*, 2. 5; *RT*, 384–5; *HL*, 283 and notes.

411 *clods*: lumps of clay.

412 *dreadful . . . light*: cf. Luke 1. 78–9 where the light is Christ.

413 *powers*: one of the nine ranks of angels and often identified with the intelligences which governed the spheres. Cf. *HHB*, 86 and note.

416 *influence*: in the astrological sense of an 'in-flowing' of power.

420 *haughty*: lofty.

422 *heauenly . . . inherit*: inherit celestial dwellings, conflating the sense of Matthew 25: 34 and Revelation 21: 3.

423 *Saints*: the elect. Cf. *FQ*, 1. 10. 61; 2. 1. 32.

424 *this*: the lack of a rhyme for this word may indicate the loss of a following short line.

425 *tymely*: in the dual sense of opportune and temporal.

429 *cutting . . . accidents*: the circumstances are unknown.

430 *Ye*: presumably applying to the poem itself.

    stay: tarry, wait.

    dew: due, appropriate (the time needed for completion).

    expect: await.

431 *both to recompens*: the sense is unclear; 'both' may refer to the 'many ornaments' and the song itself, or to the bride and time or to some other combination of these elements.

433 *short . . . moniment*: a studied oxymoron recalling the 'Epilogue' to *SC*. In *FQ* 'short time' is associated with mutability (7. 8. 1–2) and the coming of the Lord of Sabaoth who 'will finish the work, and cut it short in righteousness' (Romans 9: 28). The short stanza may indicate that the poem itself has been cut short by 'hasty accidents'. The poem is both an eternal 'monument' and a fragmentary casualty of time.

FOWRE HYMNES

Published in 1596 together with the second edition of *Daphnaïda*, the *Fowre Hymnes* represent a new literary departure for Spenser. The genre of the classical hymn had been revived in the Renaissance but in two distinct, if related, modes. Whereas some writers employed it exclusively for mythological subjects after the classical manner, others retained the form while insisting that the subject matter be Christianized [cf. Rollinson (1968), (1971)]. The issue was highly controversial and Spenser would appear to have exploited the divergence of opinion in order to display his prowess in both modes: his first and second hymns are dedicated to Cupid and Venus, his third and fourth to Christ and Lady Sapience. In the dedication Spenser asserts that the first two hymns were written 'in the greener times of my youth' and have since exercised a corrupting influence upon the young. He now claims to have resolved 'at least to amend, and by way of retractation to reforme them, making in stead of those two Hymnes of earthly or naturall loue and beautie, two others of heauenly and celestiall'. Whatever the literal truth of this, readers would recognize the employment of a standard literary device: a mature poet's apology for the follies of his youth. As so often in Spenser, allegedly biographical detail serves aesthetic design. It is note-worthy in this regard that the dedication speaks not of 'retraction' but of 'retractation' (a process of rehandling or revision) and proceeds to publish the offending hymns together with those supposedly written 'in stead' of them [cf. Oates (1983)]. They are not rejected so much as recontextualized, not displaced so much as relocated.

As even the most cursory examination reveals, the resulting volume is conceived as a unity and if the first two hymns are indeed of earlier composition they have undoubtedly undergone revision. All four hymns are written in stanzas of rhyme royal (seven-line stanzas rhyming *ababbcc*), and all four display the same tripartite format of invocation, celebration and exhortation or prayer [cf. Welsford (1967)]. The style is appropriately elevated because the hymn was regarded as equivalent in status, or even superior, to the epic [cf. P. Cheney (1993), 201–5]. The relationship between the two pairs of hymns cannot, therefore, be understood merely, or even principally, in terms of contrast. The vocabulary of renunciation – which is certainly present – is invariably offset by the imagery of sublimation. Eros is not discarded but sanctified [cf. Bieman (1988), 153–62]. Thus the Christ of *An Hymne of Heavenly Love* emerges as the fulfilment rather than merely the antithesis of the Cupid of *An Hymne in Honour of Love* [cf. Mulryan (1971); Hyde (1986)]. Although represented as an essential creative force for the species, Cupid is a blind guide for the individual (*HL*, 225–6) and his followers often fail (*HL*, 231–7), but Christ embraces Cupid's creativity while 'blinding the eyes and lumining the spright' (*HHL*, 280). In Baconian terms the former is an 'idol' of the mind, a narrow human conception of the deity, but the latter is God, the divine Cupid. What is adumbrated in the first hymn is realized in the third where mere opinion is represented as giving way to universal truth.

Throughout the first hymn Neoplatonic and Petrarchan imagery are intertwined so inextricably as to suggest the frustrating mixture of creative and destructive energies in 'earthly or naturall loue', but in the third hymn Christ emerges as the true Petrarchan lover suffering selflessly for man. It is not so much an ascent from Eros to Agape as a discovery that, properly considered, Eros is Agape. Similarly the figure of Venus, celebrated in *An Hymne in Honour of Beautie*, is made to prefigure that of Sapience in *An Hymne of Heavenly Beautie*. Whereas the beauty of Venus is ultimately solipsistic, inspiring the spirit to seek the flesh, that of Sapience, the heavenly Venus, is transcendent, inspiring the flesh to seek the spirit [cf. Quitslund (1969)]. In her realm the 'hungry soule' finally secures food because the fusion of wisdom and beauty in the one person is seen to guarantee the significance of love, and even of existence (*HHB*, 281–94). The paradisal visions which conclude the first two hymns are therefore designed to stand in relation to those that conclude the final two as mere 'shadowes' do to substance (*HHB*, 291). In this manner, through a series of complex structural and thematic correspondences, the genre of the pagan hymn is, ideally at least, subsumed into that of the Christian, and Christianity is seen to fulfil the highest aspirations of pagan society – a notion central to Renaissance humanism. Yet, as I argue in the Introduction, formal resolution is somewhat undercut by the persistence of irresolute imagery: the spiritual appetite is remarkably sensual.

If the hymns do not afford a simple dichotomy between the earthly and the celestial neither do they afford the progressive, systematic rise from one to the other envisaged in the Neoplatonic 'ladder of ascent'. The first two hymns supply the language of ascent without the experience, the final two celebrate the achievement of ascent through the descent of grace and the inspiration of the Holy Spirit. For Spenser, this is to acknowledge that Christianity is a revealed religion whose God is 'found' only when he discloses himself. Not surprisingly, therefore, meditation on the life of Christ is crucial to *An Hymne of Heavenly Love* (225–59). Similarly 'those *Idees* . . . which *Plato* so admyred' are afforded due recognition in the Christian cosmology of *An Hymne of Heavenly Beautie* (82–3), but only by way of 'retractation': Plato did not glimpse Sapience residing in the 'bosome' of God far above the admired ideas (183) because she is an aspect of the Christian deity revealed through 'grace' alone (240). Furthermore, although the higher reaches of mysticism breed disaffection with the material world, 'heauenly loue', in a passage reminiscent of *Amoretti* 68, inspires us to 'loue our brethren' (197–210) rather than to forsake them [cf. W. C. Johnson (1992)]. The dedicatees of *Fowre Hymnes* are complimented as 'ornaments of all true loue and beautie, *both in the one and the other kinde*' (my emphasis), and the pervasive influence of Christian Neoplatonists such as Ficino, Benivieni and Castiglione through the first pair of hymns establishes a complex dialectical continuity with the second [cf. Ellrodt (1960), 141–70]. As in the fourth book of *The Faerie Queene*, the number four serves as the sign of cosmic harmony, ideally reconciling opposites to produce unity and concord [cf. Fletcher (1911); Fowler (1964), 24–33]. Cf. Bjorvand (1975); Comito (1977); DeNeef (1982); Jayne (1952); P. Johnson (1972); Lewis (1954); Nelson (1963); Rice (1958); Rogers (1983); Røstvig (1971); Sowton (1962); J. Stewart (1957).

Dedication *To the Right* . . .

Cumberland . . . Warwicke: the first lady is Margaret Russell, third daughter of the Earl of Bedford, and wife of George Clifford, Earl of Cumberland. Her daughter erected Spenser's monument in Westminster Abbey in 1620. Cf. *CCH*, 504–7 and note. 'Marie Countesse of Warwicke' is an error for Anne Russell, eldest daughter of the Earl of Bedford, and widow of Ambrose Dudley, first Earl of Warwick who died in 1590. Cf. Quitslund (1985); *RT*, 240–52; *CCH*, 492–503 and notes.

1 *greener*: immature, callow.

2 *praise of Loue*: by contrast cf. Spenser's vigorous defence of love as an epic theme likely to inspire the young at *FQ*, 4 Proem 1–3.

5 *poyson . . . hony*: recalling the traditional opposition between the spider and the bee. Cf. *Amor*, 71 and notes.

9 *retractation*: more in the sense of rehandling (as the words 'amend' and 'reforme' suggest) than recantation. St Augustine published a book of 'Retractations' shortly before his death. Cf. P. Cheney (1993), 196–7.

10–11 *earthly . . . celestiall*: cf. the two Aphrodites of Plato's *Symposium*, the heavenly Aphrodite–Urania and the earthly Aphrodite–Pandemus: 'for love is not of himself either admirable or noble, but only when he moves us to love nobly' (180d–181d). Cf. Ficino, *Commentary*, 2. 7.

21 *Greenwich*: where the court was on 1 September 1596.

An Hymne in Honovr of Love

1–21 Cf. Ovid, *Amores*, 1. 2; Girolamo Benivieni, *Canzona della Amore*, 1–18 for the text of which cf. Fletcher (1911).

13 *Victors*: i.e. those more accustomed to inflicting wounds on others.

14 *darts*: cf. line 121. Cupid had arrows tipped with gold and arrows tipped with lead. The former caused attraction, the latter aversion. Cf. Ovid, *Metamorphoses*, 1. 468–71.

16 *bred*: caused.

17 *faint*: grow weak.

18 *triumphs*: recalling Petrarch's *Triumph of Love*. Cf. *Amor*, 69 and notes; *FQ*, 3. 12. 5–26.

20 *shadow . . . wing*: cf. Psalms 36: 7. Wings are traditional attributes of Cupid. In Plato they serve to elevate earthly desires to the heavens (*Phaedrus*, 246c–e). Cf. lines 176–89.

24 *Venus lap*: combining the sensuous and spiritual aspects of love. Venus and Cupid recall the Virgin and child. Cf. the common phrase 'in the lap of the gods' and note to line 62 below.

25–6 *ambrosiall . . . Nectar*: cf. *SC*, November, [195].

28 *furie*: divinely inspired poetic frenzy. Cf. *SC*, *October*, 'Argument'; *CCH*, 823 and notes. Here poetic and amorous 'furie' fuse.

29 *Muses*: more commonly regarded as virgins, but Calliope was the mother of Orpheus. Cf. *SC*, *Aprill*, [41].

38–9 *eyes . . . harts*: for this lover's malady cf. *Amor*, 35 and notes.

41–2 *hymne . . . king*: cf. 'raising our voices in harmony with the heavenly song of Love' (Plato, *Symposium*, 197e).

43 *Great . . . god*: cf. Plato, *Symposium*, 178a.

45 *Victor of gods*: as illustrated at *FQ*, 3. 11. 29–45.

46 *Lions . . . Tigers*: a traditional topos, cf. *FQ*, 4. 10. 46.

52–3 *Venus . . . Penurie*: Spenser conflates two separate myths. Cupid is traditionally the son of Venus but, according to Plato, Love is born of Porus (Resource) and Penia (Penury). Cf. *Symposium*, 203b–c. Ficino translated Porus as Plenty (*Commentary*, 6. 7). Effectively, therefore, the desire for beauty breeds love. Cf. Comes, *Mythologiae*, 4. 14.

54–6 *elder . . . eldest*: a Neoplatonic paradox. Divine love led to creation and gave rise to creation's love for God. Ficino asserts that 'love is the beginning and the end, the first and last of the gods' (*Commentary*, 5. 10).

57–98 For this conception of creation by love cf. Plato, *Symposium*, 178a–b; Ficino, *Commentary*, 3. 2. For Spenser's cosmology cf. *CCH*, 835–94; *HB*, 29–56, *HHL*, 22–42; *HHB*, 29–105.

58 *Chaos*: Ficino asserts that 'by "Chaos" the Platonists mean the world in its formless state; but by "world" they mean Chaos endowed with form' (*Commentary*, 1. 3).

62 *Venus lap*: see note to line 24 above. Cf. Benivieni, *Canzona della Amore*, 55–8.

63 *Clotho*: one of the three Fates with particular influence over birth. Ficino discusses the relationship between love and necessity at some length (*Commentary*, 5. 11). Cf. *SC*, *November*, [148].

64–8 *wings . . . hyre*: the Angelic Mind, the first created being, 'was illumined by the glory of God Himself . . . when its whole passion was kindled, it drew close to God, and in cleaving to Him, assumed form' (Ficino, *Commentary*, 1. 3).

69 *Eagle*: a symbol of resurrection because it was supposed to regain its youth periodically. Cf. Psalms 103: 5; Isaiah 40: 31; *FQ*, 1. 11. 34.

70 *wast . . . light*: cf. Genesis 1: 2.

71–3 *light . . . ray*: Venus is here identified as beauty and Ficino asserts that beauty is light (Ficino, *Commentary*, 2. 5; 6. 17).

78–91 For creation through the reconciling of opposites cf. Plato, *Symposium*, 188a; Ficino, *Commentary*, 3.2; *FQ*, 4. 10. 32–5.

79 *raunge . . . array*: station themselves in vast ranks.

83 *Ayre . . . fyre*: the four elements which constitute the material universe. Cf. *Clout*, 844 and note; *FQ*, 7. 7. 17–25.

84 *relented*: cooled, abated.

86 *meanes*: intermediaries. 'God placed water and air in the mean between fire and earth . . . and thus he bound and put together a visible and tangible heaven' (Plato, *Timaeus*, 32b–c).

88 *raines*: realms, domains.

89 *Adamantine chaines*: the 'unbreakable bonds' of the chain of being. Cf. Ficino, *Commentary*, 3. 3.

91 *mixe themselues*: i.e. intermingle creatively, and contrary to the views of the Giant at *FQ*, 5. 2. 32–40.

95 *cope*: canopy or vault (of the heavens).

98 *inspyre*: breathe into.

99–105 Animals were credited with no higher purpose than lust, but man was held to be inspired by a desire to perpetuate himself. Cf. Plato, *Symposium*, 207a–209a.

100 *multiply*: cf. 'Be fruitful, and multiply' (Genesis 1: 22, 28).

104–12 *eternitie . . . Beautie*: Ficino defines human love as 'the desire of generation in the beautiful so that everlasting life may be preserved in mortal things' (*Commentary*, 6. 11).

106 *deducted*: drawn down, i.e. emanating from heaven.

107 *sparks . . . fyre*: i.e. the embodied soul retains something of the desire for heavenly beauty and is therefore driven towards its earthly reflection. Cf. Plato, *Phaedrus*, 249d–250d.

108 *enlumind*: illuminated, enlightened.

111 *That*: that which.

112 *Beautie . . . race*: in Castiglione earthly beauty is regarded as a 'ray of the supernatural' (*Courtier*, 334).

117 *rage*: passion.

119 *enrauisht*: enraptured.

120 *imperious boy*: Cupid as the god of carnal desire.

122–4 *glancing . . . parts*: Castiglione explains how the lover's 'vital spirits' enter the loved one's eyes, penetrate the heart and 'infect the blood' so as to make it receptive (*Courtier*, 268). Cf. *Amor*, 81. 4 and note.

127–33 *playne . . . dye*: a conventional account of lovers' malady reprising much of *Amor*. Cf. Castiglione, *Courtier*, 326–7.

131–2 *light . . . eye*: i.e. their mental image of the lady. Cf. *Amor*, 88. 7–14 and notes.

134–7 *tyrant . . . triumph*: cf. the sadistic Cupid of *FQ*, 3. 12. 22–3.

137 *decay*: decline.

138 *dying to delay*: i.e. in order to prolong their pain.

139 *emmarble*: make as hard as marble. Cf. *Amor*, 51. 2.

141–68 The lover's sufferings are made, in accordance with literary precedent, to resemble those of Christ at the same point in *HHL*, 141–68. The structural coincidence ironically enforces the spiritual dissimilarity.

152 *slacke*: abate.

154 *liue . . . dy*: cf. *Amor*, 10.

156 *Parent . . . preseruer*: 'Love is called the author and Preserver of everything' (Ficino, *Commentary*, 3. 2).

159 *afflict*: cf. 'whom the Lord loveth he chasteneth' (Hebrews: 12: 6).

 not deseruer: the innocent.

162–8 Cf. the similar sentiments of *Amor*, 6. 51.

169–72 The syntax is convoluted but the sense is as follows: 'Just as divine things are least affected by passion, these heavenly beauties are equally difficult to inflame with love, and should be admired all the more by constant minds as they themselves are devoted to constancy.'

169 *enfyred*: enkindled or inflamed (with passion).

173–5 Castiglione distinguishes between lovers who pursue worthy, resolute ladies and those who opt for the easily seduced (*Courtier*, 263–4).

177 *Lifting . . . dust*: cf. Psalms 113: 7.

178 *golden plumes*: cf. note to line 20 above and *Amor*, 72.

182 *moldwarpe*: mole.

183 *dunghill thoughts*: with biblical resonance (cf. 1 Samuel 2: 8).

187 *generous*: noble-minded.

193–4 *fairer . . . thought*: 'even as if the beloved were a god, the lover fashions for himself as it were an image, and adorns it to be the object of his veneration and worship' (Plato, *Phaedrus*, 252d). Ideally this forms the second stage on the ladder of spiritual enlightenment (Plato, *Symposium*, 210a–211e). Here, however, as in *Amor*, the 'image' itself excites physical desire. Cf. *Amor*, 22. 6; 61. 1–2; *HB*, 90–91, 214–17; *HHL*, 259 and notes.

196 *mirrour*: because it reflects divine beauty. Cf. 2 Corinthians 3: 18; *Amor*, 45; *HHB*, 115 and notes.

197 *image*: cf. *Amor*, 22. 6; 61. 1–2; *HB*, 211–17 and notes.

198 *feeds . . . fantasy*: fantasy is the imaginative faculty, but the phrase suggests the possibility of delusion. Plato observes that sensual lovers 'feed upon the food of semblance' (*Phaedrus*, 248b). Cf. *HHL*, 196; *HHB*, 286.

200 *Tantale*: Tantalus was condemned to stand in water he could never drink overhung by fruit he could never pluck. Cf. *VG*, 385–8 and note.

204 *affixed wholly*: entirely concentrated.

210 *faines*: imagines (but with the potential for self-delusion).

211 *And . . . end*: i.e. although he does not accomplish his desire.

216 *then*: than.

 fayning: image forming, imagining (and potentially deceptive).

217 *sole aspect*: unique appearance.

218–24 For the heroic effects of love cf. Plato, *Symposium*, 179a–b.

218 *vnquiet thought*: cf. *Amor*, 2. 1.

220 *hardly wrought*: achieved with great difficulty.

225–30 Although the sense is complete this stanza is one line short. In the first edition, as in the present text, the words 'swords and speares' run over into a new line of slightly indented text, although metrically they form an integral part of line 4. Some commentators have regarded the omission as thematically appropriate, as though the incomplete form comments, positively or adversely, upon 'blind' Cupid. Perhaps he cannot see where he leads, or perhaps the stanza cannot 'withstand' his 'force'.

226 *blind*: Cupid's blindness was often interpreted as the blindness of sensual desire, but Neoplatonists sometimes regarded it as the blindness of joy or self-abnegation. Cf. *SC*, *March*, [79]; Wind (1967), 62.

230 *resistlesse*: irresistible.

231–7 *Leander . . . Orpheus*: the passage is indebted to Plato's *Symposium* (179b–e), with Leander and Aeneas substituted for Alcestis who died for her husband. Leander swam the Hellespont (not the Euxine Sea) to reach his lover Hero but finally drowned (cf. Ovid, *Heroides*, 18, 19). Aeneas rescued his father and son from the fires of Troy and is primarily an example of familial love, but, more pertinently, he rushed back into the flames in a vain attempt to save his wife (cf. Virgil, *Aeneid*, 2. 736–95). Although warned that he would die in battle, Achilles entered the fray at Troy in order to avenge his lover Patroclus (cf. Homer, *Iliad*, 18–22). Orpheus failed to redeem Eurydice from Hades and is condemned by Plato for lacking the courage to join her in death. Cf. *SC*, *October*, [28] and note.

233 *Phrygian glaiues*: Trojan swords (or spears).

235 *get . . . retyre*: i.e. to get his loved one to return, to bring her back.

237 *worship*: honour, renown. Cf. *FQ*, 1. 1. 3.

239 *purchase*: procure.

244 *grace*: favour.

254 *fayning fansie*: recalling lines 198, 210, 216.

259 *gnawing enuie*: the traditional iconography. Cf. *FQ*, 1. 4. 30.

260 *distrustfull showes*: untrustworthy appearances or pretences.

263 *vnassured*: uncertain, or causing insecurity.

265 *wretches hell*: the printer's preface to *Comp* lists 'The hell of louers, his Purgatorie' as one of Spenser's allegedly missing works. Cf. *FQ*, 4. 6. 32.

267 *cancker-worme*: caterpillar.

268 *gall*: bile. For the contemporary psychology of jealousy cf. Robert Burton, *The Anatomy of Melancholy*, Pt. 3, Sec. 3, Membs. 1–4.

278 *Purgatorie*: the imagery implies a sort of 'divine comedy' of love but without discarding the sensual elements.

280–87 *Paradize . . . Pleasure*: cf. *FQ*, 3. 6. 49–51 where Psyche (the soul) is reunited with Cupid after many trials in the 'Paradise' of the Gardens of Adonis and gives birth to Pleasure. The myth derives from Apuleius' *Golden Ass* and was allegorized to represent either the earthly fulfilment of desire or the transcendence of carnal passion. Here the former would appear to be indicated. Cf. *Amor*, 76 and notes; McCabe (1989), 146–9.

282 *Nectar*: drink of the gods. Cf. *SC, November*, [195].

283 *Hercules . . . Hebe*: cf. *RT*, 379–85; *Epith*, 405 and notes.

290 *quiet*: resolving the 'vnquiet thought' of line 218.

293 *well beseene*: well-appointed or provided.

296 *scope*: object.

300 *penance*: often applied to the sufferings of Purgatory.

305 *My . . . king*: cf. the first stanza of *HHL* where Christ supplants or sublimates Cupid.

An Hymne in Honovr of Beavtie

1–3 *Ah . . . thee*: the 'fury' of divine possession was attributed both to poets (by the Muses) and lovers (by Venus). Cf. Ficino, *Commentary*, 7. 14; *CCH*, 823 and note.

2 *wontlesse*: unwonted, unaccustomed.
  inspire: breathe.

3 *full of thee*: cf. Horace's 'tui plenum' (*Odes*, 3. 25. 1–2).

7 *matter*: subject matter.

9 *Mother*: Venus, mother of Cupid.

12 *gazefull*: staring, gazing intently.

14 *enchaunting*: enrapturing.

15–18 *Goddesse . . . sight*: for Venus cf. *CCH*, 801–2 and note.

17 *kindly dewty*: natural office or function.

23 *faire . . . beame*: cf. *HL*, 112, 122–6 and notes.

26 *streame*: pour, cause to flow.

27 *deaw*: dew, moisture.

29–42 For creation cf. *CCH*, 835–94; *HL*, 57–98; *HHL*, 22–42; *HHB*, 29–105.

29 *workmaister*: resembling Plato's Demiurge (*Timaeus*, 28–9).

32 *Paterne*: the 'Idea' or plan which informs all creation. Cf. *HHB*, 78–84. According to Ficino 'the pattern of the whole world' resides in the Angelic Mind and World Soul (successive emanations from God) 'much more exactly than . . . in the material world' (*Commentary*, 5. 4).

36–9 *Paterne . . . deflore*: the question of whether the Platonic forms transcended creation or were immanent in it remained unresolved.

39 *deflore*: deflower, in the sense of defile.

40 *Beautie . . . adore*: Neoplatonists often identified Venus–Urania with beauty and regarded beauty as the sum of the Platonic Ideas (cf. *HL*, 71–3 and note). Plato contends that the love of physical beauty springs from a residual memory of divine beauty (*Phaedrus*, 249e–250a). Spenser appears to regard it as instinctive.

41–2 *face . . . tell*: i.e. the idea of beauty transcends all of its embodiments and is essentially ineffable.

43–9 *Thereof . . . empight*: according to Ficino beauty 'sows Nature with Seeds; and provides Matter with Forms'. The beauty of the soul was held to impress itself upon matter and so refine it (*Commentary*, 2. 5; 5. 6).

46 *myne*: i.e. a quarry or source for shapeless matter.

49 *empight*: implanted.

50–54 *infusion . . . please*: Ficino defines beauty as 'activity, vivacity, and a certain grace shining in the body because of the infusion of its own idea' (*Commentary*, 5. 6).

51 *quickneth*: animates, enlivens.

52 *life-full spirits*: equivalent to the vital spirits in the body. Cf. note to line 102 below.

55 *Cyprian Queene*: cf. *Epith*, 103 and note.

flowing: referring to astrological 'influence', an inflowing of stellar power.

56 *bright starre*: Hesperus, the evening star.

57–63 *That . . . marrow*: 'This beauty is an influx of the divine goodness which, like the light of the sun, is shed over all created things but especially displays itself in all its beauty when it discovers and informs a countenance which is well proportioned . . . thus it attracts to itself the gaze of others, and entering through their eyes it impresses itself upon the human soul . . . inflaming it with passion' (Castiglione, *Courtier*, 325–6).

61 *which it admyre*: who admire it.

62–3 *arrow . . . marrow*: because beauty is regarded as essentially incorporeal, the 'fire' of desire cannot be quenched in 'the river of matter' (Ficino, *Commentary*, 5. 3). Cf. note to lines 92–8 below.

62 *pointest*: i.e. furnish with a point or tip.

64–77 'The proximate cause of physical beauty is . . . the beauty of the soul which since it shares in true supernatural beauty makes whatever it touches resplendent and lovely' (Castiglione, *Courtier*, 332).

66–7 *temp'rament . . . complexions*: balancing of pure humours or elements, Ficino's 'temperate combination of the four elements' which help to constitute physical beauty (*Commentary*, 5. 6).

69–70 *comely . . . disposition*: Ficino lists the requirements for physical beauty as 'arrangement, proportion, and adornment' (*Commentary*, 5. 6).

70 *meet disposition*: suitable order or arrangement.

74 *stint . . . smart*: stop his painful suffering.

78–9 *blossomes . . . hew*: cf. Matthew 6: 28–9.

79 *orient hew*: resplendent colour or lustre.

81 *like*: similar.

83–4 *Nature . . . Exceld*: i.e. we see nature outdone by art.

84 *limming*: painting, representing (limning).

85 *more . . . so*: more than physical beauty.

88 *list . . . ken*: wishes to know or experience similar tests or trials.

89 *by tryall*: by experience, by making the attempt.

90–91 *Beautie . . . seeme*: according to Ficino 'the beauty of some person pleases the soul not insofar as it exists in exterior matter, but insofar as its image is comprehended . . . by the soul through sight' (*Commentary*, 5. 3).

92–8 Ficino argues that the corruptibility of matter indicates that true beauty is spiritual (*Commentary*, 5. 3).

94 *rosy leaues*: i.e. comparable to thin layers of 'gold leaf' and therefore prone to flake and decay. For roses and mutability cf. *FQ*, 2. 12. 74–5.

97 *golden wyre*: the lady's hair. Cf. *Epith*, 154 and note.

   sparckling stars: the lady's eyes.

99 *faire lampe*: the beauty of the lady's soul. Ficino argued that beauty was light. Cf. *HL*, 71–3 and note.

102 *vitall spirits*: 'baser than the soul but purer and finer than the body' they functioned to bind soul to matter (Ficino, *Commentary*, 6. 4; 6. 6). Cf. *Amor*, 1. 7 and note.

   expyre: not 'die' but pass out of the body with the last breath.

103 *natiue planet*: each soul was held to have a guiding planet from which it derived particular formative qualities and to which it would ultimately return. Cf. Benivieni, *Canzona della Amore*, 91–100.

105 *parcell*: part, portion.

107 *immortal Spright*: God. Plato, by contrast, believed in the pre-existence of souls (*Phaedrus*, 248–9).

111 *starre*: the sun. Benivieni asserts that the soul descends from 'the highest parts [of the sky] that lodge the sun' (*Canzona della Amore*, 92–4).

112 *carre*: chariot.

113–33 Beauty 'with her heavenly power . . . rules over material nature and with her light dispels the darkness of the body' (Castiglione, *Courtier*, 332). For Neoplatonists generally, the better the soul the more beautiful the body. Cf. note to line 139 below.

114 *seede*: generative seed, progeny (effectively 'matter', cf. *FQ*, 2. 10. 50).

   enraced: implanted (i.e. made part of the mortal human race).

117 *frames . . . placed*: i.e. fashions the body in which it will dwell. For the architectural imagery cf. Benivieni, *Canzona della Amore*, 100–108; Ficino, *Commentary*, 5. 5.

119 *robd erewhyle*: acquired formerly ('robbed' in the sense of being snatched from heaven to earth).

125 *Tempers so trim*: conditions so finely or deftly.

126 *virgin Queene*: cf. the body as the house of the 'virgin' Alma at *FQ*, 2. 9. 18–58; *Epith*, 194 and note.

130 *habit*: reside, dwell.

132–3 *soule . . . make*: cf. note to lines 43–9 above; Ficino, *Commentary*, 5. 5; *FQ*, 3. 6. 37.

135 *endewed*: endowed.

137 *faire . . . thewed*: trained in good manners or morals.

138 *seede . . . strewed*: cf. the parable of the sower, Matthew 13: 3–8, 18–23.

139 *faire . . . good*: 'in some manner the good and the beautiful are identical, especially in the human body' (Castiglione, *Courtier*, 332). Cf. Plato, *Symposium*, 201c; *HHB*, 133.

140 *gentle*: love was particularly associated with the 'gentle heart'.

141–7 Ficino noted that 'seed' or matter might be 'not well adapted' to the influence of the soul and so frustrate the production of physical beauty (*Commentary*, 6. 6). Cf. Castiglione, *Courtier*, 332.

141 *falles*: occurs, happens.

144 *vnaptnesse*: inaptitude.

  substance: matter.

147 *perform'd*: made up, constituted.

152 *bait . . . scorne*: in Castiglione 'suggestive immodesty' is considered to be unworthy of the 'sacred name' of beauty (*Courtier*, 333).

153 *sew*: plead (by wooing or courtship).

155–8 'I shall not deny that we can find . . . beautiful women who are unchaste. But it is . . . not their beauty that makes them so' (Castiglione, *Courtier*, 332).

157–8 *Nothing . . . will*: cf. *CCH*, 324–7.

158 *corrupt*: corrupted.

  will: evil will (effectively evil desire).

161 *things . . . take*: cf. 1 Corinthians 15: 42, 53–4. It was generally agreed, however, that the soul could be corrupted by sin.

164 *disparagements*: dishonours, disgraces.

166 *first countries*: heaven's. Life was traditionally regarded as a pilgrimage home. Cf. Hebrews 11: 13–16.

167 *informed*: imparted or instilled.

168 *shadow*: in the sense of reflected image.

170 *blame*: fault.

171 *bland*: flatter, blandish.

173 *defame*: slander or disgrace.

179–82 *light . . . impression*: 'a lover imprints a likeness of the loved one upon his soul, and so the soul of the lover becomes a mirror in which is reflected the image of the loved one' (Ficino, *Commentary*, 2. 8). Cf. Plato, *Phaedrus*, 255d. Spenser's notion is that the double reflection of two mirrors corrects the distortion that a single mirror produces and thereby reveals the lady's true image, i.e. the image of the lady in the lover's soul is reflected back on to the mirror of her own soul. The two 'fires' of love provide the light necessary for reflection. The idea owes more to witty conceit than to logical argument.

186 *fountaine*: source (i.e. divine beauty).

190–203 Ficino asserts that 'likeness generates love'. Those who are born under the same star, and are therefore endowed with similar virtues, have souls which are naturally sympathetic (*Commentary*, 2. 8; 6. 6).

190 *aduize*: consider, reflect upon.

194 *loosely*: wantonly, promiscuously.

respect: discrimination.

198 *likely*: similar.

composd of: made up of, constituted by.

concent: concord, alluding to the harmonious music of the spheres and the compatibility of the lovers' guiding planets or stars.

202–3 *bowres . . . bee*: Ficino explains that for lovers born under the same star (and therefore of similar nature) 'the image of the more beautiful corresponds to and agrees completely with a like image formed from its very generation . . . in the inner part of the soul' (*Commentary*, 6. 6).

204–6 *twaine . . . ordaine*: cf. Matthew 19: 5–6.

207–9 *mould . . . loue*: 'It happens that a man loves, not always those who are most beautiful, but his own, that is, those who have a like birth [i.e. being 'made out of one mould' or pattern], even though they may be less beautiful than many others' (Ficino, *Commentary*, 6. 6).

214–17 *forme . . . infection*: the lover 'should contemplate beauty . . . in its own simplicity and purity, create it in his imagination as an abstraction distinct from any material form . . . and by the power of his imagination he will make [the lady's] beauty far more lovely than it is in reality' (Castiglione, *Courtier*, 338). Here, however, the 'image' never becomes free of the body. Cf. *HL*, 193–4 and note.

218 *conforming*: bring into accord with, or fashioning in accordance with. Cf. note to lines 202–3 above.

220 *first Sunne*: cf. note to line 111 above.

223 *entyre*: completely or sincerely.

224 *mirrour*: i.e. the image or reflection.

228 *fantasie*: imaginative faculty, but with suggestions of potential self-delusion. The lover has not transcended carnal desire.

229 *setteth*: locates, establishes.

232–59 For the function of 'eyes' generally cf. *HL*, 122–6 and note.

237 *faire*: beauty.

240 *Armies of loues*: amoretti or Cupids. Cf. *Amor*, 16. 6; *Epith*, 357–9.

247 *conceipt*: conception, but with potential connotations of 'fancy' and hence of self-delusion.

249 *Nectar*: cf. *SC, November*, [195].

bankets free: lavish or plentiful banquets.

250–51 *lookes . . . words*: sight and hearing were regarded as the two higher faculties 'which have little to do with corporeal things' (Castiglione, *Courtier*, 334). Cf. *Amor*, 39. 12–14 and note.

250 *Cordials*: restorative medicines, good for the heart (Latin *cor*).

251 *embassade*: on an embassy, as ambassadors.

254 *Graces*: cf. *SC, Aprill*, [109]; *Amor*, 40. 4; *FQ*, 2. 3. 25.
    masking: dancing in a masque.

256 *belgards*: loving looks.

257 *twinckling . . . night*: cf. Chaucer, *General Prologue*, 267–8.

260 *Cytherea*: Venus, born off the Aegean island of Cythera. Cf. *TM*, 397
and note.

267 *Iö tryumph*: chanted at the triumph of Cupid in Ovid, *Amores*, 1. 2. 34
and serving to link the conclusion of *HB* to that of *HL*.

270 *fealtie*: fidelity, loyalty (specifically of vassal to lord).

272 *Hymne*: cf. *HL*, 41, 302.

273 *liegeman*: vassal, follower.

274 *In . . . whereof*: in return for which.

277 *grace*: favour, but with pseudo-theological connotations in anticipation
of line 287.

279 *reaued*: robbed.

281 *deare dread*: cf. *Amor*, 33. 2 and note.

282 *flowre of grace*: but cf. *HHL*, 169

An Hymne of Heavenly Love

1 *golden wings*: cf. *HL*, 20, 178; *HHB*, 92–3 and notes. Plato asserts that
'as soon as [the true lover] beholds the beauty of this world, he is reminded
of true beauty, and his wings begin to grow, then is he fain to lift his wings
and fly upward; yet he has not the power' (*Phaedrus*, 249e). Remembering
that 'God is love' (1 John 4: 8), Spenser seeks the requisite power by
invoking God not Cupid, replacing the promised hymn to Venus (*HB*,
272) with a Christian hymn (*HHL*, 6).

3 *admirable things*: as promised by St Paul at 1 Corinthians 2: 9.

7 *god . . . king*: the Christian God, not the Cupid of *HL*, 305.

8–21 This is in the Petrarchan tradition of recantation, or 'retractation' as
the dedication to *FH* terms it (cf. *Rime Sparse*, 364). Cf. *HHB*, 288–94.

8 *lewd*: combining the senses of ignorant and lascivious.

12 *reproue*: reject.

13 *turned . . . string*: i.e. have changed the pitch or key by turning the pegs
that tune the strings of his instrument.

24 *flitting*: fleeting. Time is traditionally depicted with wings. Plato regarded
it as 'the moving image of eternity' created simultaneously with the heavens
(*Timaeus*, 37d–38b).
    eyas: fledgeling, youthful (like those of an eyas, or young hawk).

25–6 *mightie . . . space*: the primum mobile, the outermost sphere which set the others in motion, was spatially divided into twenty-four 'hours' which were used to calculate sidereal time as the sky was perceived to rotate around the earth.

29–30 *lou'd . . . begot*: the idea originates in Plato (cf. *Symposium*, 206c–e; *Timaeus*, 28–9) but had become part of orthodox Christian theology.

31 *eldest . . . heire*: Christ was 'the only begotten Son' of God (John 1: 18).

34 *dislike*: antipathy or aversion.

36 *prescribed*: preordained.

38–9 *third . . . Spright*: the Holy Spirit was usually held to proceed from the reciprocal love of Father and Son by 'spiration' (breathing out) not generation. According to St Augustine, he 'inflames man to the love of God and of his neighbour, and is Himself love' (*De Trinitate*, 15. 17).

42 *equall*: adequate.

44 *wisedome*: the particular gift of the Holy Spirit (Ecclesiasticus 39: 6; Wisdom 7: 7; 9: 17). The passage anticipates the role of wisdom in *HHB*.

47 *sweet . . . embrew*: saturate with sweet infusion.

50 *pregnant*: prolific, abounding.

51 *get*: beget.

53 *second brood*: not strictly orthodox since they were created not begotten (cf. Hebrews 1: 4–8). The metaphor of pregnancy has distorted the theology.

55 *increase*: proliferation, multiplying.

57 *heauens . . . hight*: the empyrean heaven beyond the primum mobile.

64 *trinall triplicities*: Pseudo-Dionysius (long believed to be the Dionysius of Acts 17: 34) divided the angels into three hierarchies, each of which contained three orders (or choirs): (1) Seraphim, Cherubim, Thrones; (2) Dominations, Virtues, Powers; (3) Principalities, Archangels, Angels. Cf. *FQ*, 1. 12. 39.

66–7 *nimble . . . send*: only archangels and angels officiated in this way. Cf. *FQ*, 2. 8. 1–2.

71–3 *day . . . none*: cf. Revelation 21: 23–5; 22: 5; *HHB*, 69–70.

75 *termelesse*: limitless. They enjoyed perpetuity rather than eternity. Cf. McCabe (1989), 133–4.

78–91 *pride . . . fell*: cf. 2 Peter 2: 4; Jude 6; Revelation 12: 7–9; 20: 2–3.

82 *commission*: authority.

83 *Child of light*: Lucifer. Cf. Isaiah 14: 12.

89 *lake . . . fyre*: cf. Revelation 21: 8.

94 *Degendering*: degenerating.

97 *it . . . assure*: make or think itself secure.

100 *flowing*: pouring.

106–19 These stanzas deftly combine biblical (cf. Genesis 1: 26–7) and Platonic material (cf. *Timaeus*, 28b–30a) by conflating the notion of creation in accordance with a perfect idea or 'pattern' with that of creation in the image of a benign God.

109 *wise foresight*: i.e. divine providence.

112 *Endewd*: endowed.

118–19 *loue . . . bee*: cf. *HB*, 202–3 and note.

123 *dew*: due.

128 *meere*: pure, sheer.

130 *despeyred*: desperate, hopeless.

133 *all . . . extreeme*: although his debt was extremely great. Cf. 1 Corinthians 6: 20; 7: 23.

134–5 *bosome . . . syre*: by contrast with *HL*, 61–3.

136–7 *descended . . . attyre*: cf. John 1: 14; Philippians 2: 7–8.

136 *demisse*: humble, base.

138 *pay . . . hyre*: cf. 'the wages of sin is death' (Romans 6: 23).

141–5 *flesh . . . himselfe*: cf. Romans 8: 3; 1 Corinthians 15: 21.

144 *misguyde*: misguided behaviour, sin.

145 *slyde*: slip (in the moral sense).

149 *reprochfull*: shameful, disgraceful.

151 *despightfull shame*: spiteful opprobrium.

152 *Reuyling*: reviling, cf. Matthew 27: 39.

  that . . . became: that ill or vilely became them or suited them.

153 *gallow*: gallows.

154 *the iust*: Christ. Cf. Acts 5: 30–31; 7: 52.

157 *entyre*: complete, sincere.

164–8 *bleeding . . . slyme*: cf. 'the blood of Jesus Christ . . . cleanseth us from all sin' (1 John 1: 7). For the imagery cf. John 19: 34; Revelation 7: 14.

165 *redound*: spill over, overflow.

167 *infected*: corrupting, contaminating.

169–73 A series of invocations modelled upon the liturgical litany.

169 *well of loue*: cf. John 4: 14.

  floure of grace: supplanting or sublimating the Venus of *HB*, 282.

170 *Morning starre*: cf. Revelation 22: 16.

  lampe of light: contrast with *HB*, 59. Cf. 2 Samuel 22: 29.

171 *image . . . face*: cf. Hebrews 1: 3.

172 *King of glorie*: cf. Psalms 24: 7–10.

  Lord of might: cf. Ephesians 6: 10.

173 *lambe of God*: cf. John 1: 29, 36.

  behight: promised or ordained.

175 *prize*: equal in value, recompense.

176 *lieu*: return.

177 *loue . . . guerdon*: i.e. our love by way of reward.

180 *gaine*: profit, interest.

183–9 *life . . . wrought*: cf. Galatians 5: 13–14.

184 *band*: cursed (banned).

187 *band*: bond (playing on the notion of freedom and bondage).

188–99 *loue . . . we*: cf. Matthew 22: 37–9.

189 *to . . . image*: i.e. in his image.

190–91 *first . . . gaue*: cf. 1 John 4: 19.

193 *second death*: damnation. Cf. Revelation 21: 8.

194–5 *food . . . sacrament*: the Eucharist. Cf. John 6: 35.

196 *feede*: by contrast with the feeding of *HL*, 198, 268.

   lent: gave.

197 *loue . . . brethren*: cf. John 13: 34.

199 *That we*: that we were made of (and by).

   to . . . fade: as dust to dust. Cf. Genesis 3: 19.

200 *heritage of land*: the meagre space of earth needed for burial.

201 *how . . . stand*: however much higher we are now in social terms.

203 *That we*: that we were redeemed.

205–7 *Commaunded . . . spake*: cf. John 15: 17.

207 *last bequest*: his final will or command (before the ascension).

208 *needs partake*: i.e. relieve their needs by sharing our possessions.

209–10 *Knowing . . . liue*: cf. Matthew 25: 35–40.

211–17 For this doctrine of mercy cf. Luke 6: 36.

212 *approue*: prove.

218–24 Compare the effects of love at *HL*, 176–89.

218 *earth*: i.e. man considered as a purely physical creature. Cf. Genesis 2: 7; 1 Corinthians 15: 47.

   soyle: mire or muddy bog in which boars wallow.

219 *filthy swyne*: cf. 2 Peter 2: 22; and 'Grille' at *FQ*, 2. 12. 86–7.

220 *moyle*: defile.

226 *cratch*: manger ('cratch' is used in the Geneva version of Luke 2: 7).

   wad: bundle.

233 *carriage*: demeanour, bearing.

234 *cancred*: malignant, spiteful.

235 *sharpe assayes*: keen afflictions.

238 *malist*: regarded or treated with malice.

239–45 Cf. Matthew 26–7; Mark 14–15; Luke 22–3; John 18–19.

241 *fell despights*: cruel insults.

242 *reuyld . . . abused*: reviled. Cf. Matthew 27: 26–44; John 19: 1–35.

246 *flinty hart*: hardness of heart was condemned by Christ (Mark 16: 14). Cf. *Amor*, 51. 6; 54. 12–14 and notes.

255 *meditation*: in the technical sense of a contemplative exercise designed to move from the literal facts of the Gospels to their spiritual significance.

256 *weale*: well-being.

259 *image*: cf. *HL*, 193–4; *HB*, 214–17 and notes. The 'image' of Christ, the mind's apprehension of his spiritual being, has eclipsed the image of physical beauty. Cf. *Amor*, 22. 6 and note.

267–87 Expressing the transcendental rapture of Neoplatonic ascent. Cf. Plato, *Symposium*, 211a–e; Castiglione, *Courtier*, 342.

263 *fancies*: imaginations. Cf. *HL*, 198 and note.

271 *part entire*: inner part. Cf. *Amor*, 6. 11; 85. 9 and notes.

273 *amiable*: lovable.

276 *pure sighted*: clear-sighted.

277 *blaze*: radiance, brilliance.

280 *Blinding . . . spright*: articulating the spiritual paradox that the flesh becomes blind so that the spirit may see. Cf. *HL*, 226 and note.

  lumining: illuminating, enlightening.

281–7 Alluding to the highest reaches of mystical ascent wherein the mind enjoys angelic vision. Cf. Ficino, *Commentary*, 6. 18–19; 7. 1.

284 *Idee*: employing the Platonic notion of ideas to signify the relationship between the incarnate Christ and his 'idea', the glorified Christ. Cf. *Amor*, 45. 7 and note.

286 *enragement*: rapture, ecstasy.

An Hymne of Heavenly Beavtie

1–14 *Rapt . . . distraughted*: Plato regards this as 'the best of all forms of divine possession' in which the lover 'gazes upward like a bird, and cares nothing for the world beneath' and is commonly considered to be 'demented' (*Phaedrus*, 249d). The ineffability of mystical vision is a traditional topos. Cf. Benivieni, *Canzona della Amore*, 1–18.

3 *images*: Christian versions of the Platonic 'ideas'.

5 *high conceipted*: high-minded, intellectual.

7 *fold*: falter.

8 *almightie Spright*: the Holy Spirit.

9 *all guifts*: among the seven gifts of the Holy Spirit were understanding, here termed 'wit', and wisdom. Cf. Proverbs 2: 6; John 14: 26; Tuve (1966), 101–2.

10–12 *light . . . beames*: cf. Matthew 5: 14–16.

11 *Truth*: the Holy Spirit is 'the Spirit of truth' at John 14: 17.

13 *immortall beautie*: Psalms 90: 17.

14 *distraughted*: distracted (by love of divine beauty).

17 *feed . . . delight*: cf. *HL*, 198 and note.

19 *faire formes*: supplanting or sublimating the 'fairer forme' of *HL*, 193.

20 *zealous*: fervent.

22–105 This follows the 'ladder of ascent' from the created to the creator which formed an essential part of contemplative devotion. Cf. *TM*, 499–528; Wallerstein (1950), 204–24. For the Platonic equivalent cf. *Symposium*,

211c–d. Spenser employs the model of the Ptolemaic universe, ascending from earth through the celestial spheres to the empyrean heaven.

23 *fleshly eye*: Plato regarded sight as 'the keenest mode of perception' (*Phaedrus*, 250d).

25 *contemplation*: 'through just this kind of contemplation we advance to beholding Him who shines forth from within His handiwork' (Ficino, *Commentary*, 5. 4).

26 *Of*: from.

soare faulcon: a red hawk, i.e. a hawk in its first year before it has moulted its red plumage.

27 *flags*: flaps feebly.

wings: cf. note to *HHL*, 1.

28 *breath*: take breath.

29 *gazefull*: cf. *HB*, 12 and note.

31 *reed*: perceive or discern (by 'reading' the 'book' of creation).

33 *aime*: conjecture.

34 *respect*: consideration, care.

36 *Earth . . . pillers*: cf. 1 Samuel 2: 8.

adamantine: cf. note to *HL*, 89.

37 *Sea . . . bands*: cf. Job 26: 10–11.

engirt: encircled.

brasen bands: unbreakable (i.e. strong as brass) bounds or defences.

38 *flitting*: restless, ever-moving.

39 *pyles . . . brands*: the invisible 'element of fire' which was supposed to surround the earth just below the sphere of the moon.

41 *christall wall*: for the crystalline sphere cf. *TM*, 506 and note.

46 *his*: its.

49 *heauen . . . pure*: composed of 'ether', the 'quintessence' or fifth element. Cf. *Amor*, 55. 9 and note.

50–56 Cf. Wisdom 13: 1–5.

52 *Gods*: the planetary deities were commonly identified with the 'intelligences' supposed to guide the spheres. Cf. *TM*, 509 and note.

53 *sowd . . . stars*: alluding to the sphere of fixed stars positioned above the planetary spheres.

55–6 *two . . . sway*: the sun and moon, cf. Genesis 1: 16.

60 *Captains*: the sun's.

65–70 The traditional tripartite division into the sublunary, celestial (stretching from the sphere of the moon to the primum mobile) and empyrean heavens (regarded as infinite). Cf. Lewis (1964), 92–121.

69–70 *Sunne . . . theirs*: cf. *HHL*, 71–3 and note.

71 *these heauens*: the visible celestial heavens.

72 *first . . . bound*: i.e. to the boundary of the primum mobile.

73 *comprize*: contain, enclose.

75–7 *those . . . striue*: Benivieni asserts that the loving soul moves upwards 'grade by grade to the uncreated sphere' (*Canzona della Amore*, 113–15).

75 *redound*: climb or proceed upwards.

78–81 *heauen . . . Maiestie*: the empyrean heaven where the souls of the blessed see God 'face to face' (1 Corinthians 13: 12).

82–3 *Idees . . . Plato*: cf. *Phaedrus* 247d–e. Neoplatonists located the ideas (the universal forms or patterns) in the Angelic Mind (Ficino, *Commentary*, 5. 4). Cf. *HHB*, 32 and note.

84 *Intelligences*: originally the minds or souls which guided the planetary spheres but later identified as angels. Cf. Lewis (1964), 115–16.

86–97 *Powres . . . Archangels*: for the nine orders of angels cf. *HHL*, 64 and note. The series should ascend from common angels to the Seraphim, but Spenser's sequence elevates the lowest ranks to the highest position. Cf. *Epith*, 413 and note.

89 *Seates*: usually called Thrones.

91 *fet*: fetched, drawn.

92–3 *Cherubins . . . wings*: cf. the golden wings of the cherubim on God's 'mercy seat', mentioned at line 148 below (cf. Exodus 25: 18–20).

93 *ouerdight*: covered all over.

94 *burning Seraphins*: seraphim were usually depicted as flame-coloured to express the fervency of their love. Cf. Isaiah 6: 2.

99–105 Ficino asserts that the glory of God's countenance is 'universal Beauty' and that the desire for it is 'universal Love' (*Commentary*, 5. 4).

99 *faire*: fairness, beauty.

108 *vtmost*: outermost.

109 *parts*: attributes.

115 *looking glasse*: cf. 'beholding as in a glass the glory of the Lord' (2 Corinthians 3: 18). Ficino comments that 'the single face of God shines successively in these three mirrors . . . the Angelic Mind, the World Soul and the Body of the World' (*Commentary*, 5. 4). Cf. *HB*, 179–82 and note.

117–26 *vnable . . . sparke*: cf. note to lines 145–7 below.

122 *But*: except.

rebutted: thrown back, reflected.

127–33 *meanes . . . faire*: cf. Romans 1: 20.

130 *brasen*: i.e. as long-lasting as brass.

132 *goodnesse . . . declare*: according to Ficino 'goodness is said to be the outstanding characteristic of God' and the ultimate source of divine beauty. Whoever sees and loves beauty in the creatures 'seeing the glow of God in these . . . sees and loves God Himself' (*Commentary*, 2. 5).

133 *good . . . faire*: cf. *HB*, 139 and note.

134 *speculation*: combining the senses of vision and contemplation (mental vision). Cf. Rogers (1983).

135 *impe*: engraft with feathers (an image from falconry).

wings ... mynd: cf. Petrarch, *Rime Sparse*, 362; *HL*, 20; *HHL*, 1 and notes.

137 *damps*: mists, fogs.

138–9 *Eagles ... eyes*: cf. 'Eagles eye, that can behold the Sunne' (*FQ*, 1. 10. 47). The eagle was the emblem of St John, commonly believed to be the author of Revelation.

142 *footestoole*: cf. Psalms 99: 5.

145–7 *face ... confounded*: 'Thou canst not see my face: for there shall no man see me, and live' (cf. Exodus 33: 20).

148 *mercie seate*: it was placed above the ark of the covenant (cf. Exodus 25: 17–21).

149 *Couered ... integrity*: covered with the imputed righteousness of Christ, the sacrificial 'lamb of God'. Cf. Revelation 5: 7–8.

152 *throne ... Eternity*: cf. Psalms 45: 6; Hebrews 1: 8.

153 *steele or brass*: emblems of permanence. Cf. Horace, *Odes*, 3. 30. 1.

155 *scepter ... Righteousnesse*: cf. Psalms 45: 6–7.

156 *bruseth*: crushes.

157 *great Dragon*: Satan. Cf. Revelation 12: 9; *FQ*, 1. 11. 8–14.

159 *Truth*: cf. John 14: 6.

160 *her*: truth's (traditionally gendered female).

162–75 'The light possessed by the eyes and the colours possessed by bodies are not enough to make vision complete unless they are aroused and strengthened by ... the one light itself above the many ... The perpetual and invisible light of the divine sun is always present to everything: it sustains, stimulates, arouses, completes and strengthens' (Ficino, *Commentary*, 2. 2).

163 *Titans*: Apollo's (as the sun god).

165 *red*: seen, perceived.

166 *maruelled*: wondered at.

168 *wisards*: wise men, sages.

172–3 *God ... appeare*: cf. 1 Chronicles 28: 9.

177 *throne*: cf. Psalms 47. 8; Revelation 4. 2.

178–9 *hid ... vnsound*: cf. 1 Timothy 6: 16.

181–2 *thunder ... yre*: cf. Revelation 4: 5.

183 *in ... bosome*: the location of Christ at *HHL*, 134–5. Cf. John 1: 18. For wisdom by the throne of God cf. Wisdom 9: 4.

Sapience: Spenser's Sapience has been variously identified with the Holy Spirit, Christ (as the Logos), the Virgin Mary and the Schekhina (Wisdom) of the Cabala [cf. Quitslund (1969)]. None is lacking in theological precedent but all sit uneasily with the details of the verse. In Neoplatonic terms Sapience is closest to the Angelic Mind (itself often identified with Venus–Urania) which held the ideas that informed creation (cf. Ficino, *Commentary*, 2. 7; 5. 4). Ficino asserts that 'the single light of the single truth is the beauty of the Angelic Mind' (*Commentary*, 6. 18). Plato notes the beauty of wisdom at *Phaedrus*, 250d. However, Spenser's treatment seems more heavily influenced by the Hebraic tradition of Proverbs 5–9 and Wisdom 7–9 which personifies wisdom as an attribute of God directly involved in the creation and maintenance of the universe. Sapience (the knowledge of God through beatific vision) was regarded as the supreme gift of the Holy Spirit who is invoked at the outset of the hymn.

184 *dearling*: darling. Cf. Proverbs 8: 30.

185 *Queene . . . robes*: cf. *HB*, 126.

186 *powre . . . maiesty*: cf. Wisdom 7: 23.

187 *gemmes . . . gorgeously*: cf. Proverbs 3: 15; 8: 11.

188–9 *brighter . . . cleare*: cf. 'For she is more beautiful than the sun, and above all the order of stars' (Wisdom 7: 29).

193 *rules . . . hy*: cf. Ecclesiasticus 24: 4.

194 *menageth*: directs, regulates.

195 *in . . . same*: by virtue of that.

196 *powre imperiall*: cf. Proverbs 8: 15.

197–8 *heauen . . . containe*: cf. Wisdom 8: 1; Proverbs 8: 13–41.

199 *fulnesse . . . fill*: cf. Wisdom 1: 7.

200–203 *state . . . increast*: cf. Proverbs 8: 27–30.

204–10 'Love pursues what is beautiful, and most beautiful of all is wisdom' (Ficino, *Commentary*, 6. 10).

204 *fairenesse . . . tell*: cf. Wisdom 6: 12; Psalms 45: 2.

205–6 *daughters . . . excell*: cf. Psalms 45: 2.

207 *Sparkled . . . face*: cf. Wisdom 7: 25–6.

211 *Painter*: Apelles (4th century BC), famed for his depiction of Aphrodite rising from the sea. Cf. Pliny, *Natural History*, 35. 36. 91–2; *FQ*, 4. 5. 12.

212 *curious quill*: ingenious pen (or brush).

214 *maistring*: masterly.

215 *she*: Venus.

219 *Teian Poet*: Anacreon of Teos in Ionia. Cf. *Anacreontea*, 57.

220 *vaine*: talent, genius.

221 *pretend*: set forth, proffer for consideration.

223 *Idole*: cf. *Amor*, 61. 1–2; *HL*, 193–4; *HB*, 90–91, 214–17; *HHL*, 259 and notes.

234 *mysteries vnfold*: 'we speak the wisdom of God in a mystery, even the hidden wisdom, which God ordained before the world unto our glory' (1 Corinthians 2: 7).

238 *In th'only*: only in the wonder.

239 *thrise happie*: surpassing the happiness at *HL*, 209.

241 *Beloued to behold*: cf. Wisdom 8: 2, 21.

245 *wishfull*: longed for, desired.

246–50 For the imagery of opulence cf. 'wisedome is most riches' (*FQ*, 6. 9. 30); Proverbs 8: 21; Wisdom 7: 14; 8: 5.

246 *threasury*: cf. Baruch 3: 15.

247 *Plentie of riches*: cf. Ephesians 2: 7; 3: 8.

249 *closet*: cabinet, repository.

251–5 *giuen . . . see*: the operation of grace is left mysterious: the 'worthy' are the chosen. Cf. McCabe (1989), 169–84.

255 *letteth . . . see*: cf. Wisdom 6: 12–16.

260 *admirable things*: cf. *HHL*, 3 and note.

261 *extasy*: ecstasy involves a state of mystical rapture in which the body is insensible to sensation while the mind contemplates celestial visions. Cf. 2 Corinthians 12: 2–4.

263 *brasen*: i.e. resounding to the blare of brass trumpets.

269 *offense*: offensive.

271–2 *ioy . . . see*: cf. Wisdom 8: 16–18.

273 *shadowes*: because the spiritual is the real, recalling Plato's image of the shadowy cave (cf. *Republic*, 7. 514a–515e).

274 *faire lampe*: cf. note to *HB*, 99 above.

276 *blame*: faultiness.

278–9 *honor . . . drosse*: cf. Job 28: 15–19; Wisdom 7: 8–9.

280 *mirth . . . losse*: cf. Philippians 3: 8.

284 *aspect*: beholding or apprehension.

285 *inward ey*: cf. 'the mind's eye begins to see clearly when the outer eyes grow dim' (Plato, *Symposium*, 219a).

286 *feed*: i.e. take spiritual sustenance. Cf. *HL*, 198 and note.

fastened: settled, steadfast.

289 *fancies*: cf. *HL*, 198; *HHL*, 263 and notes.

295–7 *looke . . . spright*: 'the light and beauty of God . . . is called . . . infinite beauty. But infinite beauty demands a vast love also . . . you must worship God truly with infinite love' (Ficino, *Commentary*, 6. 18). Cf. John 1: 9.

298–9 *loathing . . . world*: cf. *FQ*, 1. 10. 62–4.

300 *pleasures*: cf. note to *HL*, 280–87 above.

301 *straying . . . rest*: attaining the spiritual sabbath. Cf. *FQ*, 7. 8. 2.

PROTHALAMION

As its title-page indicates, *Prothalamion* was published in 1596 to mark the double wedding of the two daughters of the Earl of Worcester, Elizabeth and Katherine Somerset. What the poem celebrates, however, is not their marriages but their betrothals and it must therefore have been composed sometime between mid-August, when the Earl of Essex returned from the Cadiz expedition, and 8 November when the wedding took place at Essex

House. As its title indicates the poem marks the creation of a new literary genre, that of the 'pre-wedding' song, based upon the wedding hymns of Catullus, Claudian and Statius, and incorporating a brief epithalamic 'lay' (91–108) reminiscent of Spenser's own *Epithalamion* [cf. J. N. Smith (1959)]. If the journey of the two 'swans' to London is intended to represent an actual procession, a possibility entirely consistent with Elizabethan ceremonial practice, the party would appear to have sailed down the River Lea which joins the Thames opposite Greenwich (where the court was then in residence) and to have continued past the Temple to Essex House.

Among Spenser's contemporary sources for the swan and river imagery were John Leland's *Cygnea Cantio* (1545), William Camden's *De Connubio Tamis et Isis*, fragments of which had appeared in his *Britannia* (1586) and William Vallans's *A Tale of Two Swannes* (1590). Spenser may also have drawn upon his own 'Epithalamion Thamesis' (cf. *Prose*, 17), parts of which may also be incorporated into the fourth book of *The Faerie Queene* (4. 11. 10–53). But *Prothalamion* is distinguished from such precursors, and also from the classical epithalamium, by the intrusive role of its unhappy narrator whose mood of complaint serves as an incongruously elegiac 'vndersong' (110) to the celebration of marriage [cf. Hollander (1987)]. The swan was a traditional emblem of the poet and its employment signals a direct relationship between the narrator's personal circumstances and the substance of his vision. The journey of the swan-brides towards love and matrimony is also the narrator's journey towards hope and renewal. At Essex House, formerly home to the Earl of Leicester, Spenser's erstwhile patron, the sisters find their partners and the 'freendles' (140) poet finds a potential protector [cf. Ericksen (1993)]. The poem may thus be regarded as a celebration of the transformative effects of poetry itself [cf. P. Cheney (1987)].

Discontented by his 'fruitlesse stay' in 'Princes court' (6–7) the poet seeks consolation in nature, but nature manifests an artificial design: the banks that 'hem' the river's waters are 'paynted all with variable flowers' and the surrounding meadows are 'adornd with daintie gemmes' (12–14). Located within this elaborately embroidered landscape the speaker, like the protagonist of a medieval dream vision, 'chaunced to espy' (20) a pageant of 'Fowles so louely' as to seem 'heauenly borne' (61–2), an oxymoronic transfiguration of foul nature into immaculate icon so complete that even the 'siluer streaming *Themmes*' (11) 'seem'd foule' (48) in comparison. The pattern of puns is thus made to serve a crucial thematic purpose since the symbolic 'birds' of stanzas 3–7 are destined, like the children of Lir, to re-metamorphize into the courtly 'brides' of stanza 10 when the signifier is dramatically translated into the signified. And yet, this very *tour de force* which marks the height of the poet's powers also demonstrates their limitation. The vision that lifts him out of temporal despondency returns him to historical circumstance [cf. Berger (1965)]. Like all such aristocratic alliances, the Somerset marriages served a political purpose and Essex House was a hotbed of factional intrigue [cf. Strong (1977), 27–8]. Such is the immediate power of the speaker's vision, however, that Essex appears 'like Radiant *Hesper*' (164) and the bridegrooms 'like' the constellation of Gemini (173–4), but such comparisons also serve to remind us of the potential gap between vision and reality. 'Radiant *Hesper*' was also known as Lucifer and, as the opening of the poem acknowledges, river banks are traditional sites for personal and political 'complaint'.

The river 'Themmes', with all of its potent political associations, is also the river of time (Latin *tempus*), its flow denoting both permanence and transience [cf. Wine (1962)], and our journey downstream takes us from sunlight to starlight. The poet 'sings' in the present tense of transformative visions experienced in the past but destined to be fulfilled at the 'Brydale day' which, according to the careful varying of the refrain, 'is' or 'was' not far off. Such variation is significant in that it complicates the temporal perspectives of a poem greatly preoccupied with the notion of endurance through change – just as the eighteen-line canzone stanza constantly varies the flow of its rhyme-scheme within established parameters. We are left uncertain as to whether the speaker's poetic consummation will or will not coincide with that of the lovers, whether his is the 'braue muse' which, under Essex's patronage and at the 'appointed tyde' (177), will celebrate 'great *Elisaes* glorious name' (157–9). As the poem ends his 'song' has not yet concluded and he is still imploring the Thames to 'runne softly'. Cf. Cain (1971); Fowler (1975); Manley (1982); Norton (1944); S. R. Patterson (1979–80); Rogers (1977); Shire (1978); Woodward (1962).

Title-page

The word 'prothalamion' was coined by Spenser on the model of 'epithalamion' (wedding song) to signify a pre-nuptial poem. Cf. note to the title of *Epith*.

Elizabeth . . . Katherine Somerset: the daughters of Edward Somerset, the fourth Earl of Worcester, who married, respectively, Henry (later Sir Henry) Guilford of Hemstead and William Petre (later second Baron Petre of Writtle) on 8 November 1596 at Essex House.

Prothalamion

1 *trembling*: in the haze of the heat, but also denoting anxiety.
2 *Zephyrus*: god of the west wind, associated with the coming of spring and more generally, as here, with rebirth and renewal (cf. Virgil, *Georgics*, 1. 43–4). The first two stanzas are subtly informed by the erotic subtexts of

Zephyr's rape of Chloris who was transformed into the vernal goddess Flora (cf. Ovid, *Fasti*, 5. 195–224; *SC*, *Aprill*, [122] and note), and Pluto's abduction of Proserpina (cf. Ovid, *Fasti*, 4. 417–54; *Metamorphoses*, 5. 385–408).

3 *spirit*: breeze.

   lightly: gently (with a possible play on wantonly).

   delay: allay, assuage.

4 *Titans*: the sun's. Cf. *SC*, *Julye*, [59] and note.

   glyster: shine brilliantly, glitter.

5 *sullein care*: melancholy anxiety.

11 *Themmes*: for the Thames cf. *FQ*, 4. 11. 24–7.

12 *rutty*: rooty. Roots were believed to make the bank secure.

   hemmes: encloses, restrains (but with a play on the 'hem' of an embroidered garment).

13 *paynted . . . flowers*: cf. Ovid, *Fasti*, 4. 430; *Epith*, 51.

16 *Paramours*: lovers.

17 *Against*: in anticipation of, or in preparation for.

   which . . . long: which is not far off (cf. *FQ*, 4. 4. 12), but also recalling the diminishing hours of daylight at this time of year.

18 *runne softly*: Orpheus was credited with the power of halting rivers, but the speaker is less ambitious. Cf. *VG*, 180–81 and note.

21 *Flood*: river.

22 *goodly*: comely.

   greenish: for fertility. Cf. the sea nymphs 'with long greene haire' at *FQ*, 4. 11. 48.

   loose vntyde: with erotic undertones. Cf. *Amor*, 37. 6 and note.

24–6 *wicker . . . flowers*: cf. Ovid, *Fasti*, 4. 435.

25 *fine*: delicate.

   entrayled curiously: ingeniously entwined. Cf. *SC*, *August*, 30.

26 *flasket*: a long shallow basket.

27 *feateously*: nimbly, dexterously.

28 *on hye*: presumably a variant of 'in hie' meaning 'hastily'.

29–34 For equivalent flower passages cf. *SC*, *Aprill*, 136–44; *Muiop*, 187–200; *Epith*, 41–51 and notes.

30. *Violet . . . blew*: cf. Virgil's 'pallentis violas', 'pale violets' (*Eclogues*, 2. 47). Cf. Ovid, *Fasti*, 4. 437.

32 *virgin Lillie*: the flower that the virgin Proserpina was plucking when she was abducted by Hades (cf. Ovid, *Fasti*, 4. 442).

   Primrose: cf. *SC*, *Februarie*, [166].

33 *vermeil*: crimson, scarlet.

34 *posies*: bouquets, garlands.

37 *Swannes*: here representing the two ladies, but more commonly an emblem of the poet. Cf. *SC*, *October*, [90] and note. The swan features in the insignia of the brides' mother's family.

38 *Lee*: the River Lea, a tributary of the Thames. Cf. *FQ*, 4. 11. 29.

39 *fairer Birds*: because 'birds' may also mean 'ladies' this anticipates the transformation to 'faire brides' at line 176.

40 *Pindus*: a mountain range in Thessaly often associated with Apollo or the Muses. Cf. *FQ*, 3. 4. 41.

42-3 *Joue . . . Leda*: Jove, assuming the form of a swan, ravished Leda and she laid the egg from which hatched the Dioscuri, Castor and Pollux, with whom the bridegrooms are compared at line 173. Like their ladies, the bridegrooms too are swanlike. Cf. Ovid, *Metamorphoses*, 6. 109; *FQ*, 3. 11. 32; *RT*, 386–9 and note.

48-9 *spare / To wet*: refrain from wetting.

49 *least*: lest.

50 *Soyle . . . fayre*: possibly denoting the ladies' reluctance to sully their virginity through love. Cf. Berger (1965).

56 *brood*: offspring (particularly of birds).

57 *Christal Flood*: cf. the description of the Thames at *FQ*, 4. 11. 27.

63 *Venus*: for Venus' swans cf. Horace, *Odes*, 4. 1. 10; Ovid, *Metamorphoses*, 10. 717–18; Vallans, *A Tale of Two Swannes*.

  Teeme: strictly the chain or pole by which a harness was attached to a wagon but used poetically for the vehicle itself (as was the Latin *temo*).

65 *Seede*: origin, generation.

66 *Angels . . . breede*: alluding to the 'donna angelica' of the Petrarchan tradition. Cf. *Amor*, 1. 11; 61. 6 and notes.

67 *Somers-heat*: punning on the ladies' surname of Somerset and supplying a clue, in traditional fashion, to the meaning of the vision.

74 *honour . . . field*: anticipating the description of Essex at line 150.

78-80 *Peneus . . . Thessaly*: the River Peneus rose on Mount Pindus (line 40) and ran through the vale of Tempe in Thessaly in north-eastern Greece. Cf. Catullus 64. 278–93. Peneus was the father of the nymph Daphne who fled from Apollo's love and was transformed into a laurel tree (cf. Ovid, *Metamorphoses*, 1. 452–67). Cf. *Epith*, 308 and note.

82 *Brydes . . . flore*: cf. *Epith*, 45–7.

85 *presenting*: displaying, exhibiting.

  trim Array: elegant order or arrangement.

92 *glorie*: adornment (something in which heaven itself glories).

93 *blisfull bower*: the bridal bower (cf. *Epith*, 47), with the erotic associations of a 'bowre of blisse'. Cf. *FQ*, 2. 12. 42.

95 *couplement*: union, coupling.

96-106 *let . . . redound*: the traditional blessing. Cf. Catullus, 61. 228–31; Claudian, *Epithalamium of Honorius*, 190–281; *Epith*, 353–423.

97 *quelling*: vanquishing.

  Sonne: Cupid.

  smile: for its significance in love cf. *Amor*, 39, 40.

98 *vertue*: strength, power.

99 *Loues dislike*: dislike of love. Cf. *HHL*, 34.

faultie guile: blameworthy deceit (i.e. the sort of deceit that undermines friendship).

101–2 *Peace . . . Plentie*: cf. *Amor*, 62. 4. For Plenty as the parent of love cf. *HL*, 52–3 and note.

104 *afford*: provide, yield.

106 *redound*: overflow (but also resound or re-echo).

109 *So . . . she*: for this formula cf. *TM*, 113, 359 etc.

110 *vndersong*: refrain, burden. Cf. *SC*, *August*, 128. For its elegiac implications cf. *Daph*, 245.

112 *Eccho*: cf. *Epith*, 18 and note.

neighbour ground: cf. *SC*, *Januarye*, [50]; *June*, [52].

113 *accents:* voices.

115 *Lee*: cf. note to line 38 above.

118 *making . . . slow*: as the River Tiber did for Aeneas (cf. Virgil, *Aeneid*, 8. 86–9).

121–2 *Cynthia . . . starres*: Cynthia, goddess of the moon, is a common name for Queen Elizabeth (*SC*, *Aprill*, 82; *Epith*, 374). The imagery is classical (cf. Horace, *Odes*, 1. 12. 46–8) but also occurs in Vallans, *A Tale of Two Swannes*.

122 *enranged*: ranked, arranged in order.

127 *mery*: delightful, pleasant.

128 *kyndly Nurse*: benevolent or native hometown, Spenser's sole reference to his birthplace.

129 *sourse*: origin (maintaining the river imagery).

130–31 *place . . . fame*: Spenser claimed kinship to the Spencers of Althorp who claimed descent from the ancient family of Despencers. Cf. the dedications to *TM*, *MHT*, *Muiop*, and *CCH*, 537–9.

135 *There . . . byde*: the Inner Temple, one of the Inns of Court, had originally been in the possession of the Knights Templars until their suppression by Edward II. The Earl of Worcester and the two bridegrooms were affiliated to the Inns of Court. Cf. Wilkin (1990).

137 *stately place*: Essex House, formerly known as Leicester House.

138 *goodly grace*: kind favour.

139 *great Lord*: the Earl of Leicester who died in 1588. Cf. *SC*, *October*, [47]; *RT*, 184; *VG*, 'Dedication' and notes.

140 *Whose . . . case*: my friendless state feels his loss all too well.

141 *fits . . . well*: is not fitting or appropriate.

145 *lodge*: live.

noble Peer: Robert Devereux, second Earl of Essex (1567–1601), Leicester's stepson. Cf. *SC*, *March*, [20] and note.

148 *Hercules . . . pillors*: the two promontories of the Straits of Gibraltar, said to have been erected by Hercules to mark the boundary of his travels.

150 *flower of Cheualrie*: probably with specific allusion to the Knights of the Garter. Worcester, the brides' father, was also a member of the order.

152 *noble victorie*: alluding to his famous raid on Cadiz in June 1596 which impaired Spanish preparations for a second Armada.

153 *happinesse . . . name*: punning on the name of Devereux as *devenir heureux*, 'to become happy'.

157 *Elisaes*: Queen Elizabeth's. Cf. *SC, Aprill*, [33].

158 *Alarmes*: calls to arms (or warlike warnings to her enemies).

159 *braue muse*: possibly Spenser's own, cf. *SC, October*, 43-8.

161 *Brydale day*: possibly also alluding to the Queen's accession day of 17 November, commemorating her 'marriage' to England. Cf. Norton (1944).

164-5 *Hesper . . . Bathed*: cf. Virgil, *Aeneid*, 8. 589-91 where Hesperus, the evening star, is called Lucifer. Spenser's alteration is tactful: Essex's enemies were later to dub him 'Lucifer'. Cf. *Epith*, 95 and note.

168 *goodly*: handsome.

169 *Two . . . Knights*: the prospective bridegrooms.

173-4 *twins . . . bright*: Castor and Pollux (cf. note to lines 42-3) were transformed into the constellation of Gemini. Cf. Ovid, *Fasti*, 5. 693-720.

173 *in sight*: in appearance.

174 *Bauldricke*: (baldric) a sword belt worn diagonally across the chest, here used figuratively of the Zodiac. Cf. *FQ*, 5. 1. 11. The constellation Cygnus (the Swan) might represent the ladies.

176 *Brides*: finally converting the signifier (birds) into the signified.

177 *tyde*: time or occasion (continuing the river imagery).

COMMENDATORY SONNETS

To Harvey

This sonnet was first published in Gabriel Harvey's *Foure Letters, and certaine Sonnets* (1592). For Harvey's relationship with Spenser cf. *SC*, 'Epistle', 8; *June*, 9-16; *September*, [176] and notes. The form of the sonnet is Spenserian (rhyming *ababbcbccdcdee*).

3 *critique*: critical, judicious.

4 *dislikes*: discontentments.

  condition: station, rank.

7 *reprehension*: censure.

9 *entreat*: handle, write about.

13 *doomefull*: in the dual sense of judgemental and determining the 'doom' or fate of those considered.

14 *endighting*: writing.

Prefixed to *Nennio*

This sonnet, along with three others by Samuel Daniel, George Chapman, and Angel Day, was prefixed to *Nennio, or A Treatise of Nobility: Wherein is discoursed what true Nobilitie is, with such qualities as are required in a perfect Gentleman* (1595). The work is a translation of Giovanni Battista Nenna's *Nennio* (1542) by Sir William Jones and is dedicated to the Earl of Essex. The form of the sonnet is Spenserian (rhyming *ababbcbccdcdee*).

2 *type*: pattern, summit.

5 *visnomy*: physiognomy (i.e. form or character).

7 *for . . . dignitie*: in terms of dignity, i.e. they both contest the supreme position. Nenna decides in favour of merit over birth.

9 *equall insight*: impartial or balanced perception.

11 *to thee*: for yourself.

12 *behight*: express, grant.

Prefixed to *The Historie of George Castriot*

This sonnet was prefixed to *The Historie of George Castriot, surnamed Scanderbeg, King of Albanie. Containing his famous actes, his noble deedes of Armes, and memorable victories against the Turkes, for the Faith of Christ. Comprised in twelue Bookes: By Iaques de Lavardin, Lord of Plessis Bourrot, a Nobleman of France. Newly translated out of French into English by Z. I. Gentleman* (1596). The translator is usually identified as Zachary Jones and the work is dedicated to Sir George Carey, later Lord Hunsdon, to whose wife Spenser dedicated *Muiop*. Scanderbeg was George Kastrioti (1403–67), the 'Dragon of Albania', widely credited with preserving Christianity from Turkish incursion. The form of the sonnet is English or Shakespearean (rhyming *ababcdcdefefgg*).

3 *daunt*: intimidate, put in awe.

6 *Colossoes:* for the Colossus of Rhodes cf. *RR*, 23–4 and note.

8 *threat:* threaten, menace. Cf. *RR*, 50.

11 *name:* repute, fame.

12 *meere*: wholly, totally.

Prefixed to *The Commonwealth of Venice*

This sonnet was prefixed to *The Commonwealth and Gouernment of Venice* (1599), a translation by Lewis Lewkenor of Cardinal Gasparo Contarini's *De Magistratibus et Republica Venetorum* (1543). The work is dedicated to Anne Russell, widow of Ambrose Dudley, Earl of Warwick, and one of the dedicatees of *FW*. The form of the sonnet is Spenserian (rhyming *ababbcbccdcdee*).

1 *antique Babel*: i.e. Babylon. Cf. *RR*, 15–16 and note.

2 *threatned skie*: cf. Genesis 11: 4; *RR*, 50.

3 *Second Babell*: Rome. Cf. *TW*, sonnet 13. 14 and note.

4. *ayry*: lofty.

6 *feare:* was afraid of, or terrify, i.e. either all the world feared Babylon and Rome or they terrified all the world.

10 *last worlds*: alluding to the belief that the world was in its last phase prior to the millennium. Cf. *VW*, 7 and note.

12 *policie of right*: political justice.

ATTRIBUTED VERSES

From *The Historie of Ireland*

Sir James Ware (1594–1666), antiquarian and auditor-general of Ireland, included the first edition of Spenser's *A Vewe of the Present State of Irelande* in his *Historie of Ireland* (1633). Richard Boyle (1566–1643), who arrived in Ireland in 1588, acquired Sir Walter Ralegh's estates at Youghal and became the first Earl of Cork. Cf. D. L. Miller (1996), 146–71.

From Fuller's *Worthies of England*

Fuller relates the following anecdote: 'There passeth a story commonly told and believed, that *Spencer* presenting his Poems to Queen *Elizabeth*: She highly affected therewith, commanded the Lord *Cecil* Her Treasurer, to give him an *hundred* pound; and when the Treasurer (a good Steward of the Queens money) alledged that sum was too much, then *give him* (quoth the Queen) *what is reason*; to which the Lord consented, but was so busied, belike, about matters of higher concernment, that *Spencer* received no reward; Whereupon he presented this petition in a small piece of paper to the Queen in her Progress . . . Hereupon the Queen gave strict order (not without some check to her Treasurer) for the present payment of the hundred pounds, she first intended unto him' [cf. *The History of the Worthies of England* (1662), 'London', 220]. For the earliest allusion to this alleged incident (1602), cf. *The Diary of John Manningham*, edited by John Bruce, Camden Society, vol. 99 (1868), 43. Manningham supplies a variant reading of the lines as follows:

> It pleased your Grace vpon a tyme
> To graunt me reason for my ryme,
> But from that tyme untill this season
> I heard of neither ryme nor reason.

GLOSSARY OF COMMON TERMS

abie, aby atone for, pay the penalty for, suffer, endure

abusion abuse, misdoing, deception

accord (vb) agree, harmonize, unite; (n) harmony, unity

accordance harmony, union

address prepare, make ready

admiration wonder

adrad afraid

advance extol, praise, lift up, raise up, promote

affect feeling, passion

affection desire, lust, passion

affray(e) (vb) frighten, terrify; (n) assault

albe(e) although

algate(s) at all events, anyway

als also

amaze (vb) astonish, stun, bewilder; (n) astonishment

amazement astonishment, distraction

annoy (vb) trouble, hurt; (n) annoyance, tribulation, distress

appall make pale, dismay, daunt, shock

arck arch

aread(e), areed(e) declare, tell, recite, counsel, adjudge, decide

array(e) clothe, dress

aslake assuage, lessen

aspect appearance, look, glance, perception

assay (vb) attempt, try, test; (n) trial, attempt, tribulation, assault

assoile, assoyle discharge, release, remove

assurance security (often excessive)

astonied stunned, astonished

aswage, asswage allay, abate, mitigate, slake

aswagement alleviation

at earst at once, already, at length

attonce, attones at the same time, all at once, together

avail(e) profit, benefit

availe, avale bring down, lower, abase, humble

awfull awesome, awe-inspiring, full of awe

aye ever

bale misery, suffering, mischief, evil

balefull noxious, deadly, grievous, wretched

balefulness anguish, distress

band bond, link, fetter

bandogs mastiffs, bloodhounds

bane destruction, destroyer, evil, mischief

banefull pernicious, injurious

base simple, lowly, plain

bedeawed, bedewed besprinkled, moistened

bedight adorned, bedecked, arrayed

befalls occurs, happens (to be)

beheast bidding, command

behight, *behote* named, called, decreed

behoves, *behooves* befits, is proper for

bene (*been*) are

beseme, *beseeme* befit, suit, become

besprent, *besprint* besprinkled

betided, *betyded* befell, occurred

bewray reveal, disclose, divulge, expose

bide abide, endure

blasted blighted

blaze, *blazon* proclaim, describe in heraldic terms

boot(*e*) avail, profit

borowe, *borrowe* surety, pledge

bowre chamber, esp. bedchamber

brackish salty

brave fine, excellent, handsome

braverie bravado, finery, ostentation, splendour

brent burnt

brunt blow, onslaught

brust burst

carefull anxious, full of cares, dutiful

carelesse carefree, uncaring, heedless, uncared for, untended

caroling singing

caroll sing

case predicament, plight

cast decide, resolve, consider, conceive

casualtye mischance, accident, mishap

caytive (n) caitiff, villain; (adj) base, abject

certes certainly

chaunce mischance, misfortune

chauncefull risky, perilous

cheare face, countenance, (cheerful) expression or disposition

close (adj) secret, hidden; (adv) secretly

closely secretly, covertly

clout rag, bandage

clownish rustic

colour(*e*) (vb) disguise, excuse; (n) pretence, disguise

colourable deceitful, specious, plausible

coloured, *colowred* disguised, fair-seeming, plausible

compas, *compasse* (vb) attain, achieve, plan, encompass; (n) expanse, extent, circumference

compast encircled, encompassed, surrounded, arched, circular

con(*ne*), *kon* learn, know

conceipt notion, understanding, intelligence, poetic image or device

confound overthrow, defeat, discomfit

confusion destruction, overthrow

conning, *cunning* (n) skill, craft; (adj) skilful, knowledgeable

conningly skilfully, deftly

concent, *consent* harmony, accord

conspire, *conspyre* contrive, collude, agree

constrainte distress, affliction, duress

corage courage, strength of heart

corpes, *corpse*, *corse* body (Latin *corpus*)

countenance appearance, façade

couth could, knew how (to)

crew(*e*) company, entourage

crudled curdled, congealed

culver dove

curious ingenious, intricate

curiously deftly, ingeniously

daintie, dainty delicate, refined

deck(e) attire, clothe, adorn

deem(e) judge, consider, comprehend

deface destroy, spoil, mar, defame (pret. defast)

degree rank, station, order, extent

depend hang down

deplore lament, grieve for

descry discover, disclose, perceive

despight malice, scorn, contempt, anger

detect divulge, uncover

devicefull ingenious, cunning

devise (vb) conceive, compose, fashion, invent; (n) composition, devising

dight (vb) order, adorn, fashion, compose, prepare, put on or don (of clothes); (adj) adorned, dressed, prepared, designed

dint (vb) strikes, dents; (n) blow, stroke

disaray, disarray strip, unclothe

dismay (vb) debilitate, weaken, rout, daunt; (n) discouragement, faint-heartedness

display spread out, unfold, expound, disclose

dispread spread out, display

dole, doole grief, sorrow

doom(e) judgment, sentence

dowre dowry

dreade, drede, dreed (n) fear, danger; (adj) dreaded, dreadful

dreadful terrible, fearsome

dreeriment, dreriment gloom, despondency

drent drowned

dreryhead, dryrihed sorrow, gloom, affliction

earne yearn

earst, erst formerly, recently, not long ago (cf. *at earst*)

eath(e) easily

edifide, edified built, constructed

eeke increase

eft moreover, further, afterwards, thereafter

eftsoones soon after, forthwith

eke also, too, moreover

eld(e) age

els otherwise, in other circumstances, else

embase humble, bring low, degrade, demean

embrew, embrue stain (esp. with blood)

empassion impassion, inflame

empassionate impassioned

emperished enfeebled, impaired

empierce, empierse pierce, penetrate

engrained dyed (in the grain)

ensample (vb) exemplify; (n) exemplar, example, instance

ensew, ensue follow, pursue

enure accustom

enured usual, customary

eyen, eyne eyes

faine (vb) wish; (adj) willing, eager; (adv) gladly, eagerly

faine, fayne, feyne feign, pretend, dissemble, delude, imagine

fained, fayned imagined, imaginary, false, delusive

faitor, faytour impostor, cheat

fancies fantasies

fantasies imaginings, delusions

fashion shape, mould

fay(e) faith

fell cruel, ruthless, fierce

fellie, felly fiercely, cruelly

felon, felonous wicked, mischievous
file defile
fit seizure, paroxysm
fon fool
fonde foolish
fondly, fonly foolishly
fondness foolishness
fone foes
for thy for this reason, therefore, on this account
forbeare leave off, discontinue
forlore, forlorne abandoned, forsaken, deserted, wretched
fraight, fraught laden, filled
frame (vb) fashion, compose, construct, tune (of a musical instrument); (n) structure, shape, form
franke free
fray frighten, intimidate
fro from
frorne frozen
froward adverse, unfavourable, contrary, refractory
funeral(l) (n) grave, monument; (adj) dismal, funereal
gage pledge
gaie, gay bright, brilliant, ostentatious, sportive, joyful
gan began
gang go
gastlie, ghastlie frightful, horrible
gate gait, bearing, carriage
geason uncommon, rare, extraordinary
gentle well-born, noble, elevated, well-bred, kind
ghost spirit, apparition
gin trap, snare (engine)
ginne, gynne begin
girland, gyrlond garland

greevance, grievance distress, injury, disease
grieslie, griesly (grisly) frightful, horrible, ghastly
guerdon reward
han have
hap fortune, chance
haplesse unfortunate
happely by chance, accidentally
happy fortunate
hardie, hardy bold, courageous, stout
hardie hedde, hardyhedde bold presumption, audacity
hardly with difficulty, scarcely
hartlesse timid, terrified, disheartened
haunt(en) frequent, live, dwell
haveour, haviour bearing, deportment, behaviour
heast, hest command, bidding, behest
heavily sadly, with heavy heart
heaviness(e) despondency, heaviness of heart, weariness
heavy sad, despondent
heben ebony
hem them
hend seize, grasp, take hold of (pret. hent)
her their
hew(e), hue appearance, beauty, sheen
hight, hote named, called
hire, hyre payment, recompense
hoarie, hoary grey
husband farmer, husbandman
impatient unbearable, intolerable, lacking patience, unable to endure
inly inwardly

jar (*iar, iarre*) quarrel, dispute, disagreement

javels (*iavels*) rascals, rogues

jolly (*iolly*) cheerful, sprightly, handsome, fine

joy (*ioy*) (vb) enjoy, rejoice

joyance (*ioyance*) pleasure, recreation

ken, kenst know, perceive, recognize

kind, kynd nature

kindly(e) (adj) natural, beneficent, according to one's nature or 'kind'; (adv) naturally

kon, con learn, know

lack want, need, fall short of

languor grief, distress, affliction

launch (vb) pierce, cut open; (n) piercing, cutting

lay(e) song, ditty

laye, lea, lee pastureland, grassland, meadow

leasing, lesing lie, falsehood

lere learn

lewd ignorant, artless, base, wanton

lewdly ignorantly, stupidly

liefe dear

liefest dearest

lig, ligge(n) lie

light (adj) wanton, fickle, capricious, facile; (adv) quickly, lightly

list, lyst desire, wish, choose

lorne lost, forlorne, left alone, forsaken

losel(l) scoundrel, good-for-nothing, rogue

lust wish (list)

lustihede, lusty head lustfulness, delight

madding frantic, frenzied

mard, marred spoiled, torn, damaged

maske(n) (vb) dance or act in a masque, wear a masque-like disguise; (n) masque, pageant

mate consort, spouse

maugre, maulgre despite, in spite of

mazed amazed, bewildered, dazed

mazefull bewildering

meade meadow

meane lowly, moderate, humble

meare (vb) mark the boundary or border; (n) boundary

measure rhythm, metre

meate food

medle mingle

meed(e) reward, payment

meet(e) suitable, fitting, proper

mickle, mochell much

mischance misfortune, calamity

misdeeme mistake, think evil of

misgovernaunce mishandling, misuse, mismanagement

mishap misfortune

moe more

molde, moulde soil, clay, earth

moniment memorial, monument, record

morion helmet

mote might, must

mought may, might (occasionally confused with *mote*, must)

nathelesse, naythles, nethelesse nevertheless, notwithstanding

nathemore never the more, none the more

ne not, nor

newfanglenesse modish novelty (esp. sartorial)

nie near

nigheth approaches, nears

nighing approaching

nill will not

nis, nys is not

note know not

nould would not

noursling, nursling child, charge, offspring

noyous noisome, vexatious, annoying

outrage grievous injury

outragious violent, frenzied, excessive

outworne worn out, worn away

overgo surpass, overcome, outdo

overgone surpassed

pain(e) difficulty, affliction, care

paragone equal, rival, analogy, exemplar, nonpareil

pass surpass, excel

passing surpassing, excelling

paynims pagans

peare, pere peer, equal, companion, lord

peerless(e) matchless, unrivalled, without equal

perdie (French *par dieu*) surely, truly, indeed

perforce, perforse of necessity, by force

pight fixed, planted, placed, pitched

pine, pyne (vb) languish, waste away, fret; (n) affliction, distress, pain

pineons, pyneons wings

plain(e) complain, lament, bewail

plaint complaint, lamentation

pleasaunce pleasure, delight, pleasant aspect or demeanour

plight state, condition, pledge

policie intrigue, statecraft

pray prey

prayd ravaged, spoiled

preeve, prove test, make trial of, experience, endure

preife, prief(e) proof, experience, trial

previly, privily secretly, stealthily

price prize, reward, value, worth

pricke spur

prime spring

prive, privie secret, private

proof(e) test, trial, ordeal

puissance power

puissant potent, powerful

quight, quite utterly, wholly, completely, entirely

quite, quitt(en) redeem, release, discharge, repay

race, rase raze, destroy, erase, obliterate

raced razed, destroyed

rancke lush, abundant, prolific, fecund

rare excellent, rarified, fine

raught reached, proffered

reade, rede, reede advise, account, declare, interpret, discover, comprehend, predict (of fortune)

record (vb) recollect, bear in mind, relate, sing; (n) memorial, document

recure cure, remedy, restore, recover

reft taken or torn away, carried off

regard glance, look, aspect

regardfull noteworthy, worthy of regard

rehearse recite, recount, perform

rend tear or break apart

renne run

renowmed renowned, celebrated

rent torn asunder

requite repay

rew, *rue* pity, lament, grieve for

rewth, *ruth* pity, compassion, sorrow

ribaudrie ribaldry

rife plentiful, abundant

rifelye abundantly, copiously

rive, *ryve* split, break apart

riven split, sundered

rude rustic, unskilful

rudely discourteously, ignorantly, roughly

rudeness(e) rusticity, lack of (literary) refinement, vulgarity

ruthfully dolefully, piteously

.s. namely, E. K.'s abbreviation for the Latin *scilicet*

sable black

sad (adj) serious, sober, solemn, melancholy, wearisome; (adv) mournfully, despondently

salvage savage, wild, untamed

salve remedy, cure

satietie satisfaction, gratification

sdeign disdain

sdeignfull, *sdeinfull* disdainful

seare, *sere* withered

seely, *silly* innocent, harmless, helpless, simple

semblant appearance, likeness, resemblance

shade shadow

sheene shining, resplendent

shend disgrace, put to shame

shield forbid (as in 'God shield')

shrike shriek

shrill (vb) sound or sing shrilly

shriving confession

shrouded concealed

sich, *sike* such

sicker, *syker* (adj) secure, certain; (adv) truly, certainly, indeed, at any rate

signe mark, token, emblem

sith since

sithence, *sithens* since, since then

sits, *sittes* is fitting, becoming, or proper

skill (vb) understand, comprehend; (n) art, craft, knowledge, ability

slake abate, assuage

slight sleight, trickery, dexterity

smart pain, suffering, affliction, grief

solein, *sollein* sullen, sad, brooding

somedele somewhat

somewhile at some time

soote sweet

sovenance remembrance

sperst dispersed

spill destroy, ruin, ravage, spoil

spoyle (vb) despoil, plunder, devastate; (n) devastation, destruction, plunder

sprent sprinkled

spright, *sprite* spirit

stayed steady, fixed, halted, detained

stead(e), *stede* place

sterve starve, die, perish

stie ascend, mount

still constantly, perpetually, continuously

store abundance, plenty, wealth, stock

stounde, *stownd* moment of pain or trial, fit, shock, pang, stroke

stoure, *stowre* distress, turmoil, (emotional) crisis, fit, onslaught

straight, *strayt*, *streight* (adj) strait, strict, tight, severe; (adv)

immediately, straightaway,
  tightly
strange foreign, exotic
surcease desist, forbear, cease
surquedrie arrogance, presumption,
  pride
survew(e) survey, overlook
swaine, swayne man, boy, rustic,
  servant, labourer
swerve stray, deviate
swink labour, struggle
teade torch
teene grief, woe
temper govern, control, moderate,
  balance
thilk, thilke this or that, these or
  those
tho, thoe then, those
thrall (vb) enslave; (n) slave
threat affliction, misery
thrill pierce, excite
throghly, throughly fully,
  thoroughly, wholly
timely (adj) seasonable, opportune,
  welcome, early; (adv)
  opportunely, quickly
tine, tyne sorrow, affliction
tort(e) injury, wrong
toy(e) trifle, whim, amorous sport
trace walk, tread, dance
traine, trayne snare, trap, deceit,
  sleight
traveiled, traveled travailed,
  wearied, troubled, laboured
travel travail, labour
treason trickery, treachery
tride, tried attempted, experienced,
  ascertained, tested
tromp, trump trumpet (emblematic
  of fame)
trophee spoils, memorials of victory
trow(e) believe

trustlesse untrustworthy,
  treacherous
tway two
tyde tied, bound
tynde set alight, burned (tinded)
tyne grief, affliction
tyre attire
uncase strip, unclothe
undersong refrain, burden
uneth, un(n)eath, unnethes scarcely,
  with difficulty, hardly
unfold(e) disclose, discover, reveal
unhappie unfortunate
unkend, unkent unknown
unkind(e) unnatural, villainous
unkindly unnatural
unmeet unfitting, unsuitable
unstayed, unstayd uncontrolled,
  unrestrained, unsupported
unwares (adj) unaware, unwitting;
  (adv) unintentionally,
  without warning, suddenly
unweeting unwitting,
  uncomprehending, unaware
vassal slave
vaunt boast, exult
vaunted celebrated, esteemed
vauntfull boastful
vaute, vawte (vb) vault, leap (on a
  vaulting horse); (n) vault
vauted vaulted
visnomie, visnomy physiognomy
vouchsafe deign, grant
want (vb) lack, miss; (n) lack,
  absence
wanton frolicsome, unruly, skittish,
  lewd
warbling melodious, tuneful
ward (vb) protect, guard, avert; (n)
  vigilance
wast (vb) decay, dissolve; (n)
  devastation

wasted decayed, exhausted, spent, devastated

wasteful wasting, desolating, desolate, barren

wayment (vb) lament; (n) lamentation, complaint

ween(e), *wene* think, believe, suppose

weet(e) know

weetingly knowingly, skilfully

welaway, *wellaway* alas!

weld wield, govern, manage, brandish

welked waned, dimmed

welkin sky, heavens

well-deemed well-regarded

wend go, travel, make one's way

wex(e), *wexen* grow, increase, become

whilome once upon a time, in the past, in former times

whot(e) hot

wight creature, being, person

wishfull desired, longed for

wist knew

wit intellect, understanding

wite(n), *wyte(n)* blame, impugn, censure

witless(e) senseless, stupid

wood(e) mad, frantic, reckless, wild

wonne, *woon* (vb) live, dwell; (n) home, dwelling

wont accustomed (to)

wonted usual, customary

wot(e) know

woxe grew, grown

woxen grown

wreake (vb) wreak vengeance upon, avenge; (n) harm, injury, damage

wreck ruin, overthrow, disaster

y- archaic prefix denoting past tense

yclad clothed

ycond learned

yead, *yede* go

yfere together, in company

ygirt girdled

ygoe ago, gone

ylike like, alike, similar, identical

ylke the same

yode went

younkers youngsters, young men

ypent penned in, imprisoned

ytost troubled, harassed

TEXTUAL APPARATUS

The text for the present edition has been established by systematically correcting that of Ernest de Sélincourt (Oxford University Press, 1910) against the first and subsequent Elizabethan and Jacobean editions of all of the works included. As a result it differs substantially from that of de Sélincourt in rejecting many of the emendations he adopted. De Sélincourt's text was used for the convenience of type-setting in view of the poor condition of many of the extant quartos and of their modern facsimiles. It was chosen for its general level of accuracy and its careful preservation of Tudor orthography in respect, for example, of the usage of 'u' and 'v', and of 'i' and 'j', although the modern 's' has been substituted for the older form and all contractions have been expanded. This is consistent with the practice adopted by Thomas P. Roche for the Penguin edition of *The Faerie Queene* (1978). Readings from first editions have been favoured wherever they offer clear and coherent sense, but the erratic nature of the earliest punctuation, particularly in the case of the *Amoretti*, has often necessitated correction from the folios. The textual apparatus records all variants from the first editions, all substantial variations between corrected and uncorrected sheets of such editions, and all variations from de Sélincourt other than minor variations of orthography or reversals of emendations which lack textual authority. The textual apparatus is therefore intended to be functional rather than exhaustive, and readers are directed to the Variorum Edition (vols. 7 and 8), *The Minor Poems*, for full textual information. The following abbreviations for the various collected editions are used throughout the textual notes:

F1	*Works*, first folio, 1611	Ch	Child edition, 1855
F2	*Works*, second folio, 1617	Co	Collier edition, 1862
F3	*Works*, third folio, 1679	M	Morris and Hales edition, 1869
F	agreement of folio editions	G	Grosart edition, 1882–4
Hu1	Hughes edition, 1715	D	Dodge edition, 1908
Hu2	Hughes edition, 1750	S	de Sélincourt edition, 1910
Hu	agreement of Hughes editions	R	Renwick editions, 1928–34
T	Todd edition, 1805	V	Variorum Edition, 1932–58

Abbreviations specific to particular texts are listed in the headnotes to the works concerned. In recording changes to punctuation, a swung dash ~ is used to denote the word which immediately precedes the punctuation in question.

FROM *A THEATRE FOR WORLDLINGS*

The text is established from the Bodleian copy, 1569 [Douce N. 36], denoted as Tw.

Sonnet 8

2 heauen] M; heaue Tw

Sonnet 11

1 length,] S; ~. Tw
4 great] S; ~. Tw
6 to] S; so Tw
10 backes] S; backe Tw

13 thunder,] S; ~. Tw

Sonnet 12

7 espie,] S; ~. Tw

Sonnet 14

13 traine,] T; ~. Tw

THE SHEPHEARDES CALENDER

The text is established from the Bodleian copy of the first quarto, 1597 [4° F 2 (11) Art. BS.] which has been checked against the Bodleian copies of the second quarto, 1581 [Mal. 338], the third quarto, 1586 [Wood C 17 (1)], the fourth quarto, 1591 [Douce S 187], the fifth quarto, 1597 [Mal. 617 (4)], and the folio editions of 1611, 1617 and 1679 listed above among the collected works. Bathurst's Latin translation of 1653 has also been consulted. The quartos are denoted as Q1–Q5. R denotes the W. L. Renwick edition of 1930.

Epistle

70 ofentimes] Q1; oftentimes Q2–5S
81 cleare] Q1; clean Q3–5S
91 not so] Q3; no so Q1
92 if them] R; if the Q1; if they S
109 though Q1; though it Q3–5S
147 habilities:] Q3–5; ~? Q1
156 scarce growen] Q2; scarcegrowen Q1
191 considerations] Q2;
    cousiderations Q1
195 learning.] Q2; ~.) Q1

214 darknesse,] Q1; ~. Other copies
    of Q1
221 and] Q2; aud Q1

General argument

9 more, then] Q5; most and Q1
12 Inuencion] Q2; Inuericion Q1
46 in] Q2; iu Q1
66 Abib] F; Abil Q1
70 of] Q2; of of Q1
101 Shepheard] Q2; Sepheard Q1

[120] Behight] F; Bedight Q1

Januarye

49 hower,] Q2; ~. Q1
53 such] Q2; snch Q1
[75] The gloss follows 'Embleme' in
 Q1–5, but is correctly positioned
 in F1.

Februarie

'Argument' purpose'] Q2; pnrpose Q1
 142 ouerawed] Q1; ouercrawed Q3S
 176 wounds] Q1; woundes Q2S
 [39] cold.] Q5; ~: Q1
 [135] encombreth] M; encombrerh Q1
 [166] worthiest.] Q2; ~ Q1
'Emblem' Erasmus] Q2; Erasimus Q1S

March

 4 nigheth] F; nighest Q1
 55 and] Q2; and Q1
 57 greene.] Q3; ~, Q1
 85 seeing I,] Q1; ~, ~ Q5S
 95 that] Q3; thast Q1
 [2] ouergone.] Q2; ~ Q1
 [23] pleasures] Q1; ~, Q5S
 [97] invulnerable] Q3; invnluerable Q1
 [97] loue.] Q2; ~ Q1

Aprill

 8 thristye] Q1; thriftye S
 34 *Elisa*] Q1; *Eliza* Q5S
 39 For sake] Q1; Forsake S
 113 not] Q3; not not Q1
 143 Cheuisaunce,] Q5; ~. Q1
 144 Delice.] F; ~, Q1
 [50] δὲ ὁ μητίετα] S; δέ ε μητίετα Q1

Maye

'Argument' fift] Q5; firste Q1
 7 Wods] Q1; Woods Q5S
 36 swinck?] M; ~. Q1
 54 great] Q5; gread Q1
 82 worldly] Q2; wordly Q1
 113 shepheards] Q2; shephears Q1
 170 hidde,] Q3; ~. Q1S
 177 reason,] F1; ~. Q1
 186 wreathed] Q1; wrethed Q5S
 192 iollitee.] Q5; ~ Q1
 214 stroke.] Q5; ~ Q1
 254 deceitfull] Q2; deceifull Q1S
 261 were.] Q5; ~, Q1
 [38] entirely.] Q2; ~ Q1
 [75] Algrind] Q5; Algrim Q1
 [142] who (] Q5; (~ Q1
 [142] imagination,] Q2; ~ Q1
 [145] worke.] Q2; ~: Q1
 [189] πάθος] Co; παφός Q1
 [247] Charitie.)] S; ~. Q1; ~, Q2–5
 [309] priest.] T; ~, Q1

June

 1 *Colin*] Q2; *Collni* Q1
 6 ground] Q2; gronnd Q1
 16 shroude] T; shouder Q1; shroud
 F
 18 doth thee] Q2; doth the Q1
 21 shepheards] Q2; shipheards Q1
 23 Rauens] F1; Rauene Q1
 38 steps:] F; ~. Q1
 46 but] Q2; bnt Q1
 [10] thereof.) Lying] Q1; ~) lying Q4S
 [57] is] Q2; is is Q1
 [103] vndermyne] Q5; vndermynde Q1

Julye

12 great] Q4; Great Q1
14 tickle] Q5; trickle Q1
100 strawe.]; ~, Q1; straw. Q5
116 which] Q2; Which Q1S
120 that] Q2; That Q1
177 gold,] Q4; ~. Q1
208 melling.] Q2; ~, Q1
215 gree,] Q3; ~. Q1
219 ill,] Q2; ~. Q1
230 bett] EK gloss; better Q1S
233 *Thomalins*] EK gloss; *Palinodes* Q
[12] Seneca] Q2; Sene-neca Q1
   (divided between lines)
[12] lapsu] Q3; lapsus Q1
[33] dread then] Q3; dread and Q1
[51] Synecdochen.] Q2; ~ Q1
[59] Titan.] Q3; ~: Q1S
[63] Adam)] D; ~ Q1
[79] both] Q2; borh Q1
[203] prowde.] Q2; ~ Q1
[213] Algrin)] V; ~ Q1
'Emblem' altissimus] Q3; allissimus Q1

August

16a PERIGOT] Q2; PERIGOR Q1
18 see.] Q2; ~, Q1
76 woode] S; Woode Q1; wood F
84 thy] F; my Q1
104 curelesse] Bathurst Co; carelesse QF
105 bought,] Q2; ~. Q1
124a CVDDYE.] Q2; ~, Q1
134 him] Q2; hm Q1
148 deede.] Q3; ~, Q1
154 a part] Q3; apart Q1
162 sleepe.] Q5; ~ Q1
[138] golden] Q2; goldden Q1

September

56 ah Hobbin] Q2; ah hobbin Q1S
59 hande] Q1; honde S
67a HOBBINOLL.] Q2; ~, Q1
132 thou] Q2; thon Q1
139 endured.] Q3; ~ Q1
145 yead] F; yeeld Q1
153 Christendome] Q2; Chrisiendome Q1
162 priue] Q1; priuie Q4S
165 theyr] Q2; thoyr Q1
169 They] Q5; The Q1
196 awaye,] S; away. Q1; away, Q3
201 thanck.] S; ~ Q1; thancke. Q5
207a HOBBINOLL.] Q2; DIGGON. Q1
255 can,] Q3; ~: Q1
257 her] Q1 Pforzheimer copy; his Q1 Bodley copy
[20] Thrise] V; These Q1; Thrice F1S
[45] stoutely.] Q2; ~ Q1
[57] lefte.] S; ~ Q1; left. Q2
[96] practises] Q2; pract-tises Q1
   (divided over two lines)
[124] Brace)] S; ~ Q1
[151] founde] Q2; sounde Q1
[162] Priue] V; Preuely Q1; Privy F1; Priuie S
[171] flock.] S; ~ Q1; flocke. Q2
[176] vnknown] Q2; vuknown Q1
'Emblem' looking] Q2; lookng Q1
'Emblem' poore.] Q1; ~, Q2S

October

'Argument' *which*] Q2; *whishe* Q1; *whiche* S
'Argument' euen] Q2; enen Q1
2 chace,] Q5; ~: Q1
6 dead.] S; ~? Q1; deade. Q5
18a PIERS] Q2; PIRES Q1S

39 giusts.] R; ~, Q1S
40 crowne,] R; ~. Q1S
79 thy] Q3; the Q1
90a PIERS] Q2; PIRES Q1S
96a CVDDIE] Q3; omitted in Q1–2
100 demaundes,] T; ~. Q1; demands, F
101 dwell:] F; ~, Q1; ~. S
113 buskin] EK gloss; bus-kin Q1S
118a PIERS] Q3; PIRES Q1S
[21] eyther] Q2; eythet Q1
[27] matters] Q2; mattes Q1
[27] Arabian] Q3; Aradian Q1
[32] Iuno] Q2; Inno Q1
[47] meaneth] Q2; meanerh Q1
[50] more] Q2; moro Q1
[57] Georgiques] Q3; Bucoliques Q1
[78] Sarcasmus] Q3; Sacrasmus Q1
[90] destinie.] Q2; ~ Q1
[93] Petrarchs.] Q3; Petrachs Q1
[113] as is] Q2; as it Q1

Nouember

4 misgouernaunce.] Q5; ~, Q1
14 taske,] F; ~: Q1
88 budde,] Co; ~. Q1; bud, Q3
128 mourne] Q3; morune Q1
129 tourne] Q3; torune Q1
132 carefull] Q2; carsefull Q1
147 seare:] Q5; ~, Q1S
[30] Castalias] Q3; Castlias Q1
[83] diminutiue] Q3; dimumtine Q1
[91] nomore] Q1; no more Q2S
[107] Tinct] Q3; Tuict Q1
[145] the signe of] Q3; the of Q1

[148] Atropos] Q3; Atropodas Q1
[148] daughters] Q3; ughters Q1
[148] is Atropos] Q3; ~ Atrhpos Q1
[165] night] Q3; might Q1S
[174] happened.] Q3; ~, Q1
[186] expresse] Q2; epresse Q1
'Emblem' desert.] Q2; ~) Q1

December

24 espyed.] Q2; ~, Q1
38 Muse,] Q1; ~ F2S
40 mirth,] T; ~. Q1S
43 doe] EK gloss; to Q1
64 playe:] V; ~. Q1 (light period); ~, S
69 see] Q2; se Q1
75 Also] Q1; All so Q3S
89 tenrage] Q3; to tenrage Q1; t'enrage S
106 before] Q4; ~. Q1
108 wipe.] Q2; the period is misplaced in Q1
113 *Rosalind*] Q2; *Rolalind* Q1
114 dight?] Q3; ~, Q1
139 your] Q2; yonr Q1
139 glee] Q2; final e inverted in Q1
[17–18] Cabinet] Q3; Eabinet Q1
[84] skill] Q3; still Q1
[87] inuented] Q1; niuented Q1
[97–8] Thus] T; This Q1
[109] fragrant] Q3; flagraunt Q1S
[139] Glee) mirth.] R; ~ ~) Q1; ~) ~ S
'Emblem' quod] Q3; quae Q1
'Emblem' ferrum] Q3; ferum Q

FROM *LETTERS* *(1580)*

The text is established from the Bodleian copy of *Three Proper, and wittie, familiar Letters. Two other very commendable Letters*, 1580 [Mal. 662], denoted as Q. This has been checked, in the case of 'Iambicum Trimetrum', against the version printed in the Bodleian copy of Abraham Fraunce, *The Arcadian Rhetorike*, 1588 [Mal. 514 (2)], denoted as Fr.

Iambicum Trimetrum

2–3 flying thought, / And] V;
     flying / Thought, and Q;
     flying / Thoughts, and Fr
21 if]; If Q
21 saye: *this was, Immerito?*] Q; say,
     this was ~? Fr

Ad Ornatissimum virum

16 diffissa] F3; diffessa Q
47 Nae] V; Næ Q
59 Pater] F3; Paeter Q
61 liquentia] F3; liquentio Q
65 Stultorum] V; Sultorum Q
72 oblatum] F3; ablatum Q
100 Clivosas] F3; Clibosas Q

COMPLAINTS

The text is established from the Bodleian copy of the quarto of 1591 [Mal. 617], denoted as Q. Like most other extant copies of the quarto this comprises both corrected and uncorrected sheets. The Variorum Edition supplies a detailed table of variants (vol. 8. 682–5). Corrected readings are denoted below as Qc, uncorrected readings as Qu. Occasional emendations are also recorded from BM Harleian MS 6910, denoted as H, and from John Jortin, *Remarks on Spenser's Poems*, 1734, denoted as J.

The Ruines of Time

'Dedication' 30 *handes*] F; *haudes* Q
    32 a while] F2; awhile QS
    84 Princesse.] F; ~, Q
    100 mee,] Q; variant copies of Q
      read ~;
    154 more.] F; ~, Q
    175 endure.] F; ~, Q
    259 giue.] F; ~, Q
    330 wretched] F; wetched Q

333 *Linus,*] Qc; ~ Qu
361 do] F; to QS
363 couetize] F; couertize Q
413 giue?] F2; ~. Q
414 *Mausolus*] F; *Mansolus* Q
447–8 For he that now welds all things
    at his will, / Scorns . . . his] Q;
    For such as now have most the
    world at will, / Scorne . . .
    their F
451 him, that first was] Q; such as
    first were F

453 him] Q; them F
454 O let the man] Q; O! let not
    those F
497 praid.] F; ~, Q
551 which] F; with Q
574 worlds] F; words Q
588 spide.] F; ~? Q
671 exceedingly] F; exceedtngly Q

The Teares of the Muses

'Dedication' 20 Sp.] F1; ~ Q
  1 nine,] F; ~: Q
  52 Can] Qc; Gan Qu
 136 mind] V; minds QFS
 171 answering,] F; anwering. Q
 197 vnhurtfull] F; vnhurtfnll Q
 256 night:] F; ~? QS
 310 wit;] F2; ~. Q; ~, S
 346 paine,] F; ~: Q
 347 distresse:] F; ~, Q
 399 defaced] F; defacd Q
 414 him . . . him] Qc; them . . . them
    Qu
 435 crime] Qc; raine Qu
 446 bredd] Qc; bred Qu
 447 Inachus,] Qc; ~? Qu
 448 dedd] Qc; ded Qu
 450 awake?] Qc; ~. Qu
 486 souenance] H; souerance QF
 517 they,] Qc; ~ Qu
 518 discipline;] Qc; ~, Qu
 520 diuine,] Qc; ~. Qu
 521 me,] Qc; mee Qu
 549 tunefull] QcF; fruitfull Qu
 566 bee] S; beee Q; be F
 568 mysterie;] F; ~. QS
 590 fed,] F; ~; Q
 591 food;] F; ~, QS
 598 mone,] F; ~: Q
 599 breake.] F; ~, Q

Virgils Gnat

122 heart] S; hear Q
126 reare] F; ~, Q
144 eate.] F; ~, Q
149 Ascræan] J; Astræan QF
150 life;] F; ~. QS
233 Shepheards] F; Speheards Q
308 creast-front tyre] F; creast front-
    tyre Q
368 relent.] F; ~, Q
387 throat] F; threat Q
406 fluttering] F; flattering Q
490 Hesione] J; Ixione QFS
536 slye] Q; subtile FS
575 billowes] H; billowe Q; billows F3

Prosopopoia. Or Mother Hubberds Tale

'Dedication' 10 euen] S; enen Q
  53 Gossip] F; Goship Q
  67 vp on high] Q; high S
  94 entice.] F; ~, Q
 121 or] F; ot Q
 160 a] Qc; our Qu
 169 anie.] Qc; ~ Qu; ~: S
 175 doubt,] Qc; ~ QuS
 177 cannot,] Qc; ~ QuS
 177 brother,] Qc; ~ QuS
 184 vndonne,] F; ~. Q
 251 t'afford,] F; ~. Q
 301 increce] Qc; increace QuS
 302 woolly] Qc; woolley QuS
 304 dog.] Qc; ~ QuS
 308 winges] Qc; wings Qu
 648 at all] HF; all Q
 713 eare,] F2; ~. Q
 732 himselfe] F; himfelfe Q
 745 needfull)] Q; variant copies of Q
    read ~);

804 shuttelcocks,] F; ~. Q
997 whether] F; whither Q
1019 Whither] F; Whether Q
1108 Conge] F; Couge Q
1231 The] S; And Q
1289 on] S; ~, Q
1301 him] Q; did S
1304 hart;] Q; ~, S
1363 abusion,] F; ~. Q

Ruines of Rome: by Bellay

21 *Mausolus*] F; *Mansolus* Q
21 glorie,] S; ~. Q
28 seuen] F; 7. QS
32 Palaces,] Hu; ~ Q
32 that] Hu; ~, Q
48 The old] Qc; Th'old Qu
49 seuen] F; 7. QS
56 *Viminal*] Qc; *Vimnial* Qu; *Viminall* S
56 *Auentine*] Qc; *Anentine* Qu; *Aven-
  tine* S
106 earth] F; ~, Q
143 hardiehead] Qc; hardie head QuS
145 heate,] T; ~; Q
146 fild,] Q; ~; S
210 Now to] F; To Q
243 ornaments] Hu; ornament Q
270 *Tethys*] Qc; *Tethis* Qu
271 came] Qc; come Qu
272 dimmed] Qc; dimned Qu
412 yeallow] Qc; yeolow Qc
414 stackes] F12; stalkes Q
420 scater] Qc; scatter Qu
435 verses] F; yerses Q

Mviopotmos: or the Fate of
the Butterflie

3 Betwixt two] F; Betwixttwo Q
34 yougth] V; yonght Q; youngth S

36 wast;] Hu; ~, QS
37 attire,] T; ~; QS
196 Dull Poppie] Qc; Poppie Qu
247 lay,] F; ~. Q
250 dispacing] Qc; displacing Qu
346 attempted,] Qc; ~. Qu
354 Enfestred] Qc; Enfested Qu
370 framde craftilie] Qc; did slily frame
  Qu
391 those] F; thoss Q

Visions of the Worlds Vanitie

110 natiue] Qc; natures Qu
152 much] Qc; soone Qu

The Visions of Bellay

12 inconstancies,] Hu; ~. Q
22 On] Ch; One Q
22 golds] Qc; gold Qu
43 pillours] F2; pillowes Q; pilloures
  S
61 addrest,] F; ~ Q
94 fold,]; ~; QS
98 arise] Qc; ariser Qu
101 couer'd] Qc; couered Qu
110 mew,] F1; ~ Q
113 astonied] Qu; astoined Qc
113 ghoast] Qc; ghost Qu
115 down] Qc; downe Qu
115 loast] Qc; lost Qu
117 pot,] F; ~. Q
140 rayse?] F; ~. Q

The Visions of Petrarch

27 moment] F; monent Q
29 Then] D; The Q

DAPHNAÏDA

The text is established from the British Museum copy of the first quarto, 1591 [G. 11538], denoted as Q1, which has been checked against the Bodleian copy of the second quarto, 1596 [Mal. 617 (2)], denoted as Q2. 'enotes the agreement of both quartos. The Huntington Library copy .ue first quarto (denoted as Qh) has also been consulted. The Q1 version of the dedication was unavailable to de Sélincourt. The present edition restores all of its readings.

100 keepe,] F; ~. Q		388 th'heauens] F; th'eauens Q
153 bend] Q2; ~: Q1		391 till] Hu; tell Q
208 faire,] Q2; ~ Q1		469 Inne] Q2; Innne Q1
212 womankinde,] M; ~; Q1		524 swaines,] Qh; ~; Q; ~ S
254 discontent,] Q2; ~ Q1		549 a sdeinfull] T; asdeinfull Q

COLIN CLOVTS COME HOME AGAINE

The text, together with that of *Astrophel*, and *Dolefull Lay of Clorinda*, is established from the Bodleian copy of the quarto of 1595 [Mal. 618 (1)]. This copy represents the revised state of the quarto, denoted below as Qc. The unrevised state is denoted as Qu, and the agreement of both as Q.

1 knowen] F; knowne Q	451 Paragone.] Qc; ~, Qu
44 delight,] F; ~. Q	457 told,] Qc; ~: Qu
128 Nath'lesse] Q; Nath lesse S	458 *Cynthia:*] Qc; ~, Qu
168 singulfs] Q; singults FS	460 sayd;] Qc; ~, Qu
193 fare:] F; ~, Q	467 serue;] Qc; ~. Qu
292 fon] Q; son S	469 chastitie,] Qc; ~: Qu
303 daies.] F; ~, Q	471 modestie:] Qc; ~, Qu
353 praise,] F3; ~: Q	475 sacrifice:] Qc; ~, Qu
354 mak'st] Qc; makest Qu	476 shee,] Qc; ~: Qu
359 enhanced,] Qc; ~: Qu	482 valleyes] Qc; ~, Qu
367 the] Qc; that Qu	482 made] Qc; ~, Qu
369 selfe,] Qc; ~ Qu	487 *Vrania*] F; *Vriana* Q
372 laesie,] Qc; ~? Qu	495 bright;] Qc; ~. Qu
373 applie?] Qc; ~, Qu	500 grace] Qc; ~, Qu
375 worthylie] Qc; worthilie Qu	502 worthie] Qc; worthie she Qu
376 nor so] Qc; ~ ~, Qu	502 place,] Qc; ~: Qu
378 blow] F; ~, Q	557 And] Q; (~ S
381 *Cynthia:*] Qc; ~, Qu	558 see,] T; ~. Q; ~) S
382 *Corydon*] Hu; a *Corydon* Q	567 she] Qc; he Qu
449 gone:] Qc; ~. Qu	570 see,] Qc; ~. Qu

571 hart.] Qc; ~, Qu
573 esteeme:] Qc; ~, Qu
577 commended:] Qc; ~, Qu
586 make,] Qc; ~. Qu
590 case] Qc; ~, Qu
593 bestowd,] Qc; ~; Qu
593 day;] Qc; ~, Qu
600 clusters] F; glusters Q
601 bunches] Q; braunches S
642 forgotten,] F; ~. QS
670 Darest] Q; Durst S
737 worthie] Co; worrhie Q
743 expound] F; ~, Q
757 fare] F; far Q
772 there?] F; ~, Q
774 here.] F; ~, Q
775 Paragraph indentation in F, not
    in Q
776 No paragraph indentation in F,
    indentation in Q
796 led,] F; ~: Q
805 growing, he] F; ~ ~, Q
846 agree?] F; ~. Q
861 life] F2; like Q
868 passion,] F; ~: Q
875 fynd] T; ~, QS
884 the] F; their Q

914 compell?] F; ~. Q
920 reuile,] F2; ~: QS
923 rimes,] F; ~: Q
924 praise:] F; ~, Q
954 skies] F2; ~, Q

Astrophel

16 breed,] FS; ~. Q
33 greet] F; ~, Q
50 often] F; oft Q
72 alas).] F2; ~) Q
89 needeth] F; need Q
91 fortuned,] F; ~ Q
91 he] F; ~, Q
116 brood] F2; ~: Q
122 flow:] Q; ~, F
154 adorned,] F; ~ Q
209 greene] F; ~, Q

Dolefull Lay of Clorinda] There is no title
in Q

3 vnfold] Q; enfold S
17 they like] V; ~, ~ S
17 wretched] V; wetched Q; ~, S
35 Great] F; Creat Q
35 him did see] F; him see Q

AMORETTI AND EPITHALAMION

The text is established from that of the British Museum copy of the octavo
of 1595 [G. 11184], denoted as O. The punctuation of O is erratic and has
frequently been corrected against the folio editions. Some sheets of O were
corrected in printing and uncorrected readings are denoted below as Ou.
For a full list of octavo variants see the Variorum Edition, vol. 7. 697–8.

'Darke is the day'

4 way:] F; ~, O
11 neighboures]; neighoures O;
   neighbors S

'Ah Colin'

1 *plaine,*] F; ~. O
2 *roundelaies*] Co; roudelaies O
4 *daies:*] F; ~. OS
6 *quill,*] F; ~. O
8 *skill,*] F2; ~. OS

Sonnets

III
13 write] F; ~, O

VI
1 mind] F; ~, O

VII
7 askew,] F; ~ O

VIII
5 guest] F; ~, OS

XI
3 addresse] F; ~, O
8 vnpittied] F1; vnpitteid O

XII
1 eies] F; ~, O

XIII
6 borne,] F; ~: O

XIIII
6 belay;] F; ~, O; ~: S

XVI
4 delight,] Co; ~. OS

XVII
6 guide,] F; ~: O
7 workmanship] F;
   wormanship O

XIX
9 rayse,] T; ~ OS

XXI
1 Art,] F; ~? O
2 face,] F; ~: O
4 grace?] F; ~. O

6 loue] F; loues O
8 impure.] F2; ~, O

XXIII
4 vnreaue:] F; ~, O; ~. S

XXIIII
8 see;] F1; ~. O

XXVIII
2 giues] F; guies O
8 attyre:] F3; ~ O

XXIX
1 damzell] O; damzoell Ou

XXX
12 deuyse?]; ~. O; deuise? F

XXXI
11 bath] F; ~, O

XXXII
9 fit,] F; ~: O

XXXIII
9 wit,] F2; ~: O

XXXIIII
2 way,] F; ~. O
3 guyde,] Co; ~. O
5 ray] V; ~, O
12 grief.] F; ~, O

XXXV
8 poore.] F; ~ O

XXXVI
4 release?] V; ~. OS
8 miseryes?] T; ~. OS

XXXVII
7 enfold] F; ~, OS

XXXVIII

4 allur'd] F; allu'rd OS
8 will,] O; ~. S

XXXIX

13 meat]; ~, OS

XL

3 appeare] F; ~, O
8 ray:] F; ~ O
10 fled,] F; ~: O; ~ S

XLI

2 foe?] F; ~: O

XLII

8 hart,] F; ~ O

XLIIII

7 arre,] F; ~. O

XLV

5 shew] F; ~, O

XLVI

5 obay?] T; ~, O
13 sustaine] F; ~, O

XLVII

5 guyde] F; ~, O

XLVIII

1 hand] F; ~, O
10 th'anguish] O; the anguish FS

XLIX

10 kill] F; ~, O

L

2 griefe:] V; greife: O; ~, S
5 priefe,] F; ~: O
8 please?] F; ~. OS
9 appease] F; ~, O

LII

2 field,] F; ~: O
9 vaine]; ~, OS
11 disdayne] T; ~, OS

LIII

1 hyde] Co; ~, O
6 hew,] F; ~: O; ~ S
10 ornament:] O; ~, S

LV

2 compare:] O; ~, S
14 rest.] F; ~: OS

LVII

10 stoures.] F; ~, O
13 grace,] F; ~. OS

LVIII

1 reposeth] F; ~, O
3 supposeth] F; ~, O
7 prayd] Co; ~, O
14 arre?] F2; ~. OS

LIX

9 spight] F; ~, O

LX

4 spheare.] F; ~ O
5 cleare]; ~, OS

LXI

11 scorne] F; ~, O

LXII

6 amend,] F; ~ O
9 send]; ~, OS

LXIII

4 sore:] F; ~. O
6 arryue,] O; ~; S
9 atchyue] T; ~, O

LXIIII
12 Iessemynes:] F1; ~, O; ~. S

LXV
1 vaine,] F; ~ O
12 wound:] F; ~ O

LXVI
8 state?] F; ~. O

LXVII
2 away,] F; ~: O
4 pray:] F; ~. O

LXVIII
3 away] F; ~, O
4 win:] F; ~. O
6 thou] F; tbou O

LXIX
8 chastity?] F2; ~. OS

LXX
2 displayd] F; ~, O

LXXI
3 lurke] F; ~, OS
13 see,] F; ~. O

LXXIII
2 tye,] Hu; ~: O

LXXV
2 away] F; a way O
6 immortalize,] F; ~. O
9 deuize] S; ~, O

LXXVII
3 entertayne] F; ~, O
4 roialty?] V; ~. OS
5 ly] F; ~, O
11 paradice] S; ~: O

12 By] O; by S (the line is not
indented in O)

LXXVIII
14 mee.] F; ~: O

LXXX
2 compile,] F; ~ O

LXXXI
9 display] F2; ~, OS
12 spright:] F; ~, O; ~. S

LXXXIII
4 complayne.] S; ~ O
14 shadowes] O; ~, FS

LXXXIIII
3 desyre] T; ~: O
6 sprites,] V; ~ OS

LXXXV
13 thunder,] F; ~ OS

LXXXVI
4 well;] F; ~. OS
13 reward,] F; ~. O

LXXXVII
3 moue] F; ~, O

LXXXIX
3 vow] F2; vew O
4 late;] F; ~. OS
8 doue:] S; ~ O
9 houe]; ~, OS

Anacreontics
1 old,] F; ~. O
18 shame] F; ~: O
20 other.] F1; ~, OS
30 withall?] F; ~. O

69 well,] F; ~ OS
72 blis?] F; ~. O
73 recured] F; ~, OS
75 enured] F; ~, OS
81 please] F; ~, O

Epithalamion

  6 prayse;] F; ~. OS
 11 dreriment:] F; ~. OS
 24 doue,] F; ~ O
 49 wrong,] F; ~ OS
 61 take,] F; ~. O
 67 deere] G; dore O
 70 neer,] V; ~ OS
109 ring.] F; ~ O
116 see.] F; ~ O
129 aloud] F; ~, O
158 Queene.] F; ~, O
168 before?] F; ~, OS
184 ring.] F; ~ O
209 you.] F; ~, O
214 faces;] F; ~ O; ~: S

215 may] F; ~, O
218 play] F2; ~; O
220 throates] F; ~. O
237 vnsownd.] F; ~, O
239 band?] F2; ~, O
240 Angels,] F; ~ O
241 ring.] F; ~ O
280 How] O; ~. Ou
290 nights] O; nightes S
300 Now] O; The Ou
304 couerlets.] F; ~, Q
310 brooke.] F; ~ O
314 ring.] F; ~ O
341 Pouke] Co; Ponke O
356 poure] Ou; ponre O (error in the
        corrected sheet)
356 your] O; the Ou
359 your] O; the Ou
373 bright?] F; ~, O
380 Latmian] O; Latinian Ou
385 thy] F; they O
401 delight] O; ~. O
        (Huntington copy)
411 clods] Hu; ~: O; ~, S

FOWRE HYMNES

The text is established from the Bodleian copy of the quarto of 1596 [Mal. 617 (2)], denoted as Q.

An Hymne in Honovr of Love

 83 hated] F; hate Q
120 perceiuing,] F1; ~ Q
120 boy] F2; ~, QS
221 aduenturous] S; aduenturons Q
242 aby:] F; ~, Q
274 endeere] F1; ~, QS

An Hymne in Honovr of Beavtie

 14 soule] F2; foule Q
 30 behold,] F; ~ Q
 32 mould] F; ~, Q

An Hymne of Heavenly Love

261 embrace:] F; ~, Q; ~; S

An Hymne of Heavenly Beavtie

23 to] F; ro Q
50 eye] Hu; ~, Q

80 behold] F; ~, Q
165 And] Hu; The dark & Q
170 more bright, more cleare] F; more
      cleare Q
180 found] F; ~, Q
270 paine.] Hu; ~, Q
294 on] F; no Q

PROTHALAMION

The text is established from the Bodleian copy of the quarto of 1596 [Mal.
617 (3)], denoted as Q.

72 softly,] F; ~ Q
75 yield] F; yeild QS
90 softly,] F; ~ Q
102 your] F; you Q
113 resound.] F; ~? Q
114 forth] F; ~, Q
116 tong,] F; ~ Q
129 gaue] F; ~, Q

130 take] Q; place (Wrenn copy of Q)
134 bowers,] F; ~ QS
143 daye,] S; ~ Q
144 softly,] F; ~ Q
147 thunder,] F; ~. Q
162 softly,] F; ~ Q
174 bright.] F; ~, Q

COMMENDATORY SONNETS

To Haruey
The text is established from the Bodleian copy of *Foure Letters, and certaine
Sonnets*, 1592 [Mal. 567].

3 this worldes]; thisworldes (1592)

Prefixed to *Nennio*
The text is established from the Bodleian copy of *Nennio, or A Treatise of
Nobility: Wherein is discovered what true Nobilitie is, with such qualities as
are required in a perfect Gentleman*, 1595 [Don. e. 2 (2)].

10 then] V; the (1595); them S

Prefixed to *The Historie of George Castriot*
The text is established from the Bodleian copy of *The Historie of George Castriot, surnamed Scanderbeg, King of Albanie*, 1596 [AA 37 Art. Seld].

Prefixed to *The Commonwealth of Venice*
The text is established from the Bodleian copy of *The Common-Wealth and Gouernment of Venice*, 1599 [Radcl. e. 19].
'Signature' Edm.]; Edw. (1599)

ATTRIBUTED VERSES

The texts are established from the Bodleian copies of *The Historie of Ireland*, 1633 [Douce. H subt. 13] and Thomas Fuller, *The History of the Worthies of England*, 1662 [H. 2. 17. Art].

FURTHER READING

(Where multiple items are cited for any author they are listed in chronological order. The dates supplied for the annual issues of *Spenser Studies* are the official dates appearing on the volumes' spines. Actual dates of publication are often considerably later.)

Adler, D., 'Imaginary Toads in Real Gardens', *ELR*, 11 (1981), 235–60.

Aesop, *The Complete Fables*, translated by Olivia and Robert Temple (Harmondsworth, 1998).

Alciati, Andreas, *Emblemata* (Antwerp, 1574).

Allen, D. C., 'On Spenser's Muiopotmos', *SP*, 53 (1956), 141–58.

—— *Image and Meaning: Metaphoric Traditions in Renaissance Poetry* (2nd edn; Baltimore, 1968).

Allman, E. J., '*Epithalamion*'s Bridegroom: Orpheus-Adam-Christ', *Renascence*, 32 (1980), 240–47.

Alpers, P., 'The Eclogue Tradition and the Nature of Pastoral', *College English*, 34 (1972), 352–71.

—— *What is Pastoral?* (Chicago, 1996).

Anderson, D., ' "Unto My Selfe Alone": Spenser's Plenary *Epithalamion*', *SSt*, 5 (1984), 149–68.

Anderson, J. H., 'The July Eclogue and the House of Holiness: Perspective in Spenser', *SEL*, 10 (1970), 17–32.

—— ' "Nat Worth a Boterflye": *Muiopotmos* and *The Nun's Priest's Tale*', *JMRS*, 1 (1971), 89–106.

—— ed. with D. Cheney and D. A. Richardson, *Spenser's Life and the Subject of Biography* (Amherst, Mass., 1996).

Atchity, K. J., 'Spenser's *Mother Hubberd's Tale*: Three Themes of Order', *PQ*, 52 (1973), 161–72.

Attridge, D., *Well-Weighed Syllables: Elizabethan Verse in Classical Metres* (Cambridge, 1974).

Baroway, I., 'The Imagery of Spenser and the Song of Songs', *JEGP*, 33 (1934), 23–45.

Bartholomaeus Anglicus, *Batman uppon Bartholome, his Booke De Proprietatibus Rerum* (London, 1582).

Bateman, Stephen, see Bartholomaeus Anglicus.

Bates, C., *The Rhetoric of Courtship in Elizabethan Language and Literature* (Cambridge, 1992).

Bath, M., 'Verse Form and Pictorial Space in Van der Noot's *Theatre for Worldlings*', in K. J. Höltgen et al., eds., *Word and Visual Imagination: Studies in the Interaction of English Literature and the Visual Arts* (Erlangen, 1988), 73–105.

Bender, J. B., *Spenser and Literary Pictorialism* (Princeton, 1972).

Bennett, J. W., 'The Theme of Spenser's *Fowre Hymnes*', *SP*, 28 (1931), 18–57.

—— 'Spenser's Muse', *JEGP*, 31 (1932), 200–219.

Berger, H., 'Spenser's *Prothalamion*: An Interpretation', *EIC*, 15 (1965), 363–80.

—— 'The Spenserian Dynamics', *SEL*, 8 (1968), 1–18.

—— 'Mode and Diction in *The Shepheardes Calender*', *MP*, 67 (1969), 140–49.

—— 'The Aging Boy: Paradise and Parricide in Spenser's *Shepheardes Calender*', in M. Mack and G. deForest Lord, eds., *Poetic Traditions of the English Renaissance* (New Haven, Conn., 1982), 25–46.

—— (a) 'The Mirror Stage of Colin Clout: A New Reading of Spenser's *Januarye* Eclogue', *Helios*, 10 (1983), 139–60.

—— (b) 'Orpheus, Pan, and the Poetics of Misogyny: Spenser's Critique of Pastoral Love and Art', *ELH*, 50 (1983), 27–60.

—— *Revisionary Play: Studies in the Spenserian Dynamics* (Berkeley, 1988).

Berlin, N., 'Chaucer's *The Book of the Duchess* and Spenser's *Daphnaïda*: A Contrast', *Studia Neophilologica*, 36 (1966), 282–9.

Bernard, J. D., 'Spenserian Pastoral and the *Amoretti*', *ELH*, 47 (1980), 419–32.

—— '*June* and the Structure of Spenser's *Shepheardes Calender*', *PQ*, 60 (1981), 305–22.

—— *Ceremonies of Innocence: Pastoralism in the Poetry of Edmund Spenser* (Cambridge, 1989).

Berry, H. and E. K. Timings, 'Spenser's Pension', *RES*, n.s. 11 (1960), 254–9.

Berry, P., *Of Chastity and Power: Elizabethan Literature and the Unmarried Queen* (London, 1989).

Bieman, E., ' "Sometimes I . . . mask in myrth lyke to a Comedy": Spenser's *Amoretti*', *SSt*, 4 (1983), 131–42.

—— *Plato Baptized: Towards the Interpretation of Spenser's Mimetic Fictions* (Toronto, 1988).

Bjorvand, E., 'Spenser's Defence of Poetry: Some Structural Aspects of the *Fowre Hymnes*', in Maren-Sofie Røstvig, ed., *Fair Forms: Essays in English Literature from Spenser to Jane Austen* (Cambridge, 1975), 13–53.

Blank, P., 'The Dialectic of *The Shepheardes Calender*', *SSt*, 10 (1989), 71–94.

Boccaccio, Giovanni, *De Genealogia Deorum* (i.e. *Genealogiae Joannis Bocatii*) (Venice, 1511).

Bond, R. B., '*Invidia* and the Allegory of Spenser's *Muiopotmos*', *English Studies in Canada*, 2 (1976), 144–55.

—— 'Supplantation in the Elizabethan Court: The Theme of Spenser's February Eclogue', *SSt*, 2 (1981), 55–65.

Bondanella, J. C., *Petrarch's Visions and their Renaissance Analogues* (Madrid, 1978).

Bondanella, P. E. and J. C. Bondanella, 'Two Kinds of Renaissance Love: Spenser's *Astrophel* and Ronsard's *Adonis*', *ES*, 52 (1971), 311–18.

Botting, R. A., 'A New Spenserian Rhyme Scheme?', *JEGP*, 36 (1937), 384–6.

Bradbrook, M., 'No Room at the Top: Spenser's Pursuit of Fame', in J. R. Brown and B. Harris, eds., *Elizabethan Poetry* (London, 1960), 91–109.

Bray, A., *Homosexuality in Renaissance England* (London, 1982).

Brennan, M. G., 'Foxes and Wolves in Elizabethan Episcopal Propaganda', *Cahiers Elisabéthains*, 29 (1986), 83–6.

Brink, J. R., 'Who Fashioned Edmund Spenser?: The Textual History of *Complaints*', *SP*, 88 (1991), 153–68.

—— ' "All his minde on honour fixed": The Preferment of Edmund Spenser', in J. H. Anderson, D. Cheney and D. A. Richardson, eds., *Spenser's Life and the Subject of Biography* (1996), 45–64.

Brinkley, R. A., 'Spenser's *Muiopotmos* and the Politics of Metamorphosis', *ELH*, 48 (1981), 668–76.

Brooks-Davies, D., ' "Shroude" versus "shoulder" in the *June* Eclogue of Spenser's *Shepheardes Calender*', *N&Q*, n.s. 39 (1992), 292–3.

—— ed., *Edmund Spenser: Selected Shorter Poems* (London, 1995).

Bryan, R. A., 'Poets, Poetry and Mercury in Spenser's *Prosopopoia: Mother Hubberd's Tale*', *Costerus*, 5 (1972), 27–33.

Burchmore, D. W., 'The Image of the Centre in *Colin Clouts Come Home Againe*', *RES*, n.s. 28 (1977), 393–406.

Byrom, H. J., 'Edmund Spenser's First Printer, Hugh Singleton', *The Library*, 4th series, 14 (1933), 121–56.

Cain, T. H., 'Spenser and the Renaissance Orpheus', *UTQ*, 41 (1971), 24–47.

—— *Praise in 'The Faerie Queene'* (Lincoln, Nebr., 1978).

Camden, William, *Britain, or a Chorographical Description of England, Scotland and Ireland*, translated by Philemon Holland (London, 1610).

—— *Remains Concerning Britain* (1674).

Campbell, G., '"The Crab Behind his Back": Astrology in Spenser's *Epithalamion*', *N&Q*, n.s. 34 (1987), 200–201.

Carpenter, F. I., *A Reference Guide to Edmund Spenser* (Chicago, 1923).

Cartmell, D., 'Beside the Shore of silver streaming Thamesis: Spenser's *Ruines of Time*', *SSt*, 6 (1985), 77–82.

Casady, E., 'The Neo-Platonic Ladder in Spenser's *Amoretti*', in *PQ*, 20 (1941), 284–95.

Castiglione, Baldesar, *The Book of the Courtier*, translated by George Bull (2nd edn; Harmondsworth, 1976).

Chaucer, Geoffrey, *The Riverside Chaucer*, edited by L. D. Benson et al. (Boston, 1987).

Cheney, D., 'Spenser's Fortieth Birthday and Related Fictions', *SSt*, 4 (1983), 3–31.

—— 'The Circular Argument of *The Shepheardes Calender*', in G. M. Logan and G. Teskey, eds., *Unfolded Tales: Essays on Renaissance Romance* (Ithaca, NY, 1989), 137–61.

Cheney, P., 'The Old Poet Presents Himself: *Prothalamion* as a Defence of Spenser's Career', *SSt*, 8 (1987), 211–38.

—— '"The Nightingale is Sovereigne of Song": The Bird as a Sign of the Virgilian Orphic Poet in *The Shepheardes Calender*', *JMRS*, 21 (1991), 29–57.

—— *Spenser's Famous Flight: A Renaissance Idea of a Literary Career* (Toronto, 1993).

Chinitz, D., 'The Poem as Sacrament: Spenser's *Epithalamion* and the Golden Mean', *JMRS*, 21 (1991), 251–68.

Cirillo, A. R., 'Spenser's *Epithalamion*: The Harmonious Universe of Love', *SEL*, 8 (1968), 19–34.

Clements, R. J., 'Iconography on the Nature and Inspiration of Poetry in Renaissance Emblem Literature', *PMLA*, 70 (1955), 781–804.

Collinson, P., *The Elizabethan Puritan Movement* (London, 1967).

—— *Archbishop Grindal 1519–1583: The Struggle for a Reformed Church* (London, 1979).

Comes, Natalis, *Mythologiae* (Venice, 1567; first published 1551).

Comito, T., 'The Lady in a Landscape and the Poetics of Elizabethan Pastoral', *UTQ*, 41 (1972), 200–218.

—— 'A Dialectic of Images in Spenser's *Fowre Hymnes*', *SP*, 74 (1977), 301–21.

Cooper, H., *Pastoral: Mediaeval into Renaissance* (Ipswich, 1977).

Copeland, T. A., 'Surrender of Power in *Epithalamion*', in *Selected Papers from the West Virginia Shakespeare and Renaissance Association*, 13 (1988), 58–65.

Court, F. E., 'The Theme and Structure of Spenser's *Muiopotmos*', *SEL*, 10 (1970), 1–15.

Cullen, P., *Spenser, Marvell and Renaissance Pastoral* (Cambridge, Mass., 1970).

Culpeper, Nicholas, *The Complete Herbal* (London, 1653).

Cummings, L., 'Spenser's *Amoretti* VIII: New Manuscript Versions', *SEL*, 4 (1964), 125–35.

Cummings, P. M., 'Spenser's *Amoretti* as an Allegory of Love', *TSLL*, 12 (1970), 163–79.

Cummings, R. M., *Spenser: the Critical Heritage* (London, 1971).

Dasenbrock, R. W., 'The Petrarchan Context of Spenser's *Amoretti*', *PMLA*, 100 (1985), 38–50.

Davies, H. N., 'Spenser's *Shepheardes Calender*: The Importance of November', *Cahiers Elisabéthains*, 20 (1981), 35–48.

DeNeef, L., '*The Ruins of Time*: Spenser's Apology for Poetry', *SP*, 76 (1979), 262–71.

—— *Spenser and the Motives of Metaphor* (Durham, NC, 1982).

Di Matteo, A., 'Spenser's Venus-Virgo: The Poetics and Interpretative History of a Dissembling Figure', *SSt*, 10 (1989), 37–70.

Du Bellay, Joachim, *Les Regrets et Autres Oeuvres Poëtiques suivis des Antiquitez de Rome. Plus un Songe au Vision sur le mesme subject*, edited by J. Jolliffe, introduced and annotated by M. A. Screech (Geneva, 1966).

Dubrow, H., *A Happier Eden: The Politics of Marriage in the Stuart Epithalamium* (Ithaca, NY, 1990).

—— *Echoes of Desire: English Petrarchism and Its Counterdiscourses* (Ithaca, NY, 1995).

Dundas, J., '*Muiopotmos*: A World of Art', *YES*, 5 (1975), 30–38.

—— '"The Heavens Ornament": Spenser's Tribute to Sidney', *EA*, 42 (1989), 129–39.

Dunlop, A., 'Calendar Symbolism in the *Amoretti*', *N&Q*, n.s. 16 (1969), 24–6.

—— 'The Unity of Spenser's *Amoretti*', in A. Fowler, ed., *Silent Poetry: Essays in Numerological Analysis* (London, 1970), 153–69.

—— 'The Drama of *Amoretti*', *SSt*, 1 (1980), 107–20.

Durr, R., 'Spenser's Calendar of Christian Time', *ELH*, 24 (1957), 269–95.

Eade, J. C., 'The Pattern in the Astronomy in Spenser's *Epithalamion*', *RES*, 23 (1972), 173–8.

Edwards, T. R., *Imagination and Power: A Study of Poetry on Public Themes* (New York, 1971).

Elcock, W. D., 'English Indifference to Du Bellay's *Regrets*', *MLR*, 46 (1951), 175–84.

Ellrodt, R., *Neoplatonism in the Poetry of Spenser* (Geneva, 1960).

Emerson, O. F., 'Spenser's *Virgil's Gnat*', *JEGP*, 17 (1918), 94–118.

Ericksen, R., 'Spenser's Mannerist Manoeuvres: *Prothalamion* (1596)', *SP*, 90 (1993), 143–75.

Ettin, A. V., *Literature and the Pastoral* (New Haven, Conn., 1984).

Falco, R., 'Instant Artifacts: Vernacular Elegies for Philip Sidney', *SP*, 89 (1992), 1–19.

—— 'Spenser's *Astrophel* and the Formation of Elizabethan Literary Genealogy', *MP*, 91 (1993), 1–25.

—— *Conceived Presences: Literary Genealogy in Renaissance England* (Amherst, Mass., 1994).

Ferguson, M. W., ' "The Afflatus of Ruin": Meditations on Rome by Du Bellay, Spenser, and Stevens', in A. Patterson, ed., *Roman Images*, Selected Papers from the English Institute, 8 (Baltimore, 1982), 23–50.

Fichter, A., ' "And nought of *Rome* in *Rome* perceiu'st at all": Spenser's *Ruines of Rome*', *SSt*, 2 (1981), 183–92.

Ficino, Marsilio, *Opera* (2 vols.; Basle, 1576).

—— *Marsilio Ficino's Commentary on Plato's Symposium*, edited and translated by S. R. Jayne, *University of Missouri Studies*, 19 (Columbia, 1944).

Fletcher, J. B., 'Benivieni's *Ode of Love* and Spenser's *Fowre Hymnes*', *MP*, 8 (1911), 545–60.

Forster L., (a) *Janus Gruter's English Years: Studies in the Continuity of Dutch Literature in Exile in Elizabethan England* (Leiden, 1967).

—— (b) 'The Translator of the *Theatre for Worldlings*', *ES*, 48 (1967), 27–34.

—— *The Icy Fire: Five Studies in European Petrarchanism* (Cambridge, 1969).

Fowler, A., *Spenser and the Numbers of Time* (London, 1964).

—— (a) *Triumphal Forms: Structural Patterns in Elizabethan Poetry* (Cambridge, 1970).

—— (b) ed., *Silent Poetry: Essays in Numerological Analysis* (London, 1970).

—— *Conceitful Thought: The Interpretation of English Renaissance Poems* (Edinburgh, 1975).

—— 'The Beginnings of English Georgic', in *Renaissance Genres: Essays on Theory, History and Interpretation*, ed. B. K. Lewalski (Cambridge, Mass., 1986), 105–25.

Fox, A., 'The Complaint of Poetry for the Death of Liberality: the Decline of Literary Patronage in the 1590s', in J. A. Guy, ed., *The Reign of Elizabeth I: Court and Culture in the Last Decade* (Cambridge, 1995), 229–57.

Friedland, L. S., 'A Source of Spenser's "The Oake and the Briar" ', *PQ*, 33 (1954), 222–4.

—— 'The Illustrations in *The Theatre for Worldlings*', *HLQ*, 19 (1956), 107–20.

Friedrich, W. G., 'The Stella of *Astrophel*', *ELH*, 3 (1936), 114–39.

Fukuda, S., 'A Numerological Reading of Spenser's *Daphnaïda*', *Kumamoto Studies in Language and Literature*, 29–30 (1987), 1–9.

—— 'The Numerological Patterning of *Amoretti and Epithalamion*', *SSt*, 9 (1988), 33–48.

Gerard, John, *The Herbal or General Historie of Plantes* (London, 1597).

Gibbs, D., *Spenser's 'Amoretti': A Critical Study* (Brookfield, 1990).

Gilman, E. B., '*A Theatre for Voluptuous Worldlings* (1569) and the Origins of Spenser's Iconoclastic Imagination', in J. Moller, ed., *Imagination on a Long Rein: English Literature Illustrated* (Marburg, 1988), 45–55.

Gleason, J. B., 'Opening Spenser's Wedding Present: the "Marriage Number" of Plato in the *Epithalamion*', *ELR*, 24 (1994), 620–37.

Gless, D., *Interpretation and Theology in Spenser* (Cambridge, 1994).

Goldberg, J., *Voice Terminal Echo: Postmodernism and English Renaissance Texts* (New York, 1986).

—— *Sodometries: Renaissance Texts, Modern Sexualities* (Stanford, 1992).

Gorges, Arthur, *The Poems of Sir Arthur Gorges*, edited by H. E. Sandison (Oxford, 1953).

Gottfried, R., 'Spenser and the Italian Myth of Locality', *SP*, 34 (1937), 107–265.

Grant, P., *Images and Ideas in Literature of the English Renaissance* (Amherst, Mass., 1979).

Graves, R. N., 'Two Newfound Poems by Edmund Spenser: The Buried Short-Line Runes in *Epithalamion* and *Prothalamion*', *SSt*, 7 (1986), 199–238.

Greco, N., 'Spenser's *Shepheardes Calender*, February Eclogue', *Explicator*, 41 (1982), 5–6.

Greene, R., '*The Shepheardes Calender*: Lyric, Dialogue, Periphrasis', *SSt*, 8 (1987), 1–33.

Greene, T. M., 'Spenser and the Epithalamic Tradition', *CL*, 9 (1957), 215–28.

—— *The Descent from Heaven: A Study in Epic Continuity* (New Haven, Conn., 1963).

—— *The Light in Troy: Imitation and Discovery in Renaissance Poetry* (New Haven, Conn., 1982).

Greenlaw, E., 'Spenser and the Earl of Leicester', *PMLA*, 25 (1910), 535–61.

—— *Studies in Spenser's Historical Allegory* (Baltimore, 1932).

Greville, Fulke, *The Prose Works of Fulke Greville*, edited by J. Gouws (Oxford, 1986).

768 FURTHER READING

Grimal, Pierre, *The Dictionary of Classical Mythology* (Oxford, 1986).

Grindal, Edmund, *The Remains of Archbishop Grindal*, edited by W. Nicholson (Cambridge, 1843).

Hamilton, A. C., 'The Argument of Spenser's *Shepheardes Calender*', *ELH*, 23 (1956), 171–82.

—— ed., *Essential Articles for the Study of Edmund Spenser* (Hamden, Conn., 1972).

—— ed., *The Faerie Queene* (London, 1977).

—— et al., eds., *The Spenser Encyclopedia* (Toronto, 1990).

Hammond, N. G. L. and H. H. Scullard, eds., *The Oxford Classical Dictionary* (Oxford, 1970).

Hannay, M. P., ' "My Sheep are Thoughts": Self-Reflexive Pastoral in *The Faerie Queene*, Book VI and the *New Arcadia*', *SSt*, 9 (1988), 137–59.

Hardin, R. F., 'The Resolved Debate of Spenser's *October*', *MP*, 73 (1976), 257–63.

Hardison, O. B., '*Amoretti* and the *Dolce Stil Novo*', *ELR*, 2 (1972), 208–16.

Harris, B., 'The Ape in *Mother Hubberd's Tale*', *HLQ*, 4 (1941), 191–203.

—— 'The Butterfly in Spenser's *Muiopotmos*', *JEGP*, 43 (1944), 302–16.

Harris, D. and N. L. Steffen, 'The Other Side of the Garden: An Interpretative Comparison of Chaucer's *Book of the Duchess* and Spenser's *Daphnaïda*', *JMRS*, 8 (1978), 17–36.

Harrison, T. P., Jr, 'Turner and Spenser's *Mother Hubberd's Tale*', *JEGP*, 49 (1950), 464–9.

Harvey, E. R., *The Inward Wits: Psychological Theory in the Middle Ages and the Renaissance* (London, 1975).

Harvey, Gabriel, *Works*, edited by A. B. Grosart (3 vols.; London, 1884–5).

—— *Marginalia*, edited by G. C. Moore Smith (Stratford-upon-Avon, 1913).

Helgerson, R., 'The New Poet Presents Himself: Spenser and the Idea of a Literary Career', *PMLA*, 93 (1978), 893–911.

—— *Self-Crowned Laureates: Spenser, Jonson, Milton, and the Literary System* (Berkeley, 1983).

—— *Forms of Nationhood: The Elizabethan Writing of England* (Chicago, 1992).

Heninger, S. K., Jr, 'The Renaissance Perversion of Pastoral', *JHI*, 22 (1961), 254–61.

—— 'The Implications of Form for *The Shepheardes Calender*', *SR*, 9 (1962), 309–21.

—— *Touches of Sweet Harmony: Pythagorean Cosmology and Renaissance Poetics* (San Marino, 1974).

—— *The Cosmographical Glass: Renaissance Diagrams of the Universe* (San Marino, 1977).

—— 'Spenser and Sidney at Leicester House', *SSt*, 8 (1987), 239–49.

—— 'The Typographical Layout of Spenser's *Shepheardes Calender*', in K. J. Höltgen et al., eds., *Word and Visual Imagination: Studies in the Interaction of English Literature and the Visual Arts* (Erlangen, 1988), 33–71.

—— *Sidney and Spenser: The Poet as Maker* (University Park, Pa., 1989).

Henley, P., *Spenser in Ireland* (Cork, 1928).

—— 'Galathea and Neaera', *TLS*, 32 (1933), 464.

Herendeen, W. H., 'Spenserian Specifics: Spenser's Appropriation of a Renaissance Topos', *Medievalia et Humanistica*, 10 (1981), 159–88.

Herman, P. C., '*The Shepheardes Calender* and Renaissance Antipoetic Sentiment', *SEL*, 32 (1992), 15–33.

Hester, M. T., ' "If thou regard the same": Spenser's Emblematic Centerfold', *American Notes and Queries*, n.s. 6 (1993), 183–9.

Hieatt, A. K., *Short Time's Endless Monument* (New York, 1960).

—— 'The Daughters of Horus: Order in the Stanzas of *Epithalamion*', in W. Nelson, ed., *Form and Convention in the Poetry of Edmund Spenser* (1961), 103–21.

—— 'The Genesis of Shakespeare's *Sonnets*: Spenser's *Ruines of Rome: by Bellay*', *PMLA*, 98 (1983), 800–814.

—— 'Cymbeline and the Intrusion of Lyric into Romance Narrative: *Sonnets, A Lover's Complaint*, Spenser's *Ruins of Rome*', in G. M. Logan and G. Teskey, eds., *Unfolded Tales: Essays on Renaissance Romance* (Ithaca, 1989), 98–118.

Hill, W. S., 'Order and Joy in Spenser's *Epithalamion*', *Southern Humanities Review*, 6 (1972), 81–90.

Hoffman, N. J., *Spenser's Pastorals: 'The Shepheardes Calender' and 'Colin Clout'* (Baltimore, 1977).

Holinshed, R., *Chronicles of England, Scotland and Ireland* (6 vols.; London, 1807–8).

Hollander, J., 'Spenser's Undersong', in M. Garber, ed., *Cannibals, Witches and Divorce: Estranging the Renaissance* (Baltimore, 1987), 1–20.

Hulse, C., *Metaphoric Verse: The Elizabethan Minor Epic* (Princeton, 1981).

Hume, A., 'Spenser, Puritanism, and the "Maye" Eclogue', *RES*, n.s. 20 (1969), 155–67.

—— *Edmund Spenser: Protestant Poet* (Cambridge, 1984).

Hutton, J., 'Cupid and the Bee', *PMLA*, 56 (1941), 1036–57.

Hyde, T., 'Vision, Poetry, and Authority in Spenser', *ELR*, 13 (1983), 127–45.

—— *The Poetic Theology of Love: Cupid in Renaissance Literature* (Newark, Del., 1986).

Hyman, L. W., 'Structure and Meaning in Spenser's *Epithalamion*', *Tennessee Studies in Literature*, 3 (1958), 37–41.

Janowitz, A., *England's Ruins: Poetic Purpose and the National Landscape* (Oxford, 1990).

Jayne, S., 'Ficino and the Platonism of the English Renaissance', *CL*, 4 (1952), 214–38.

Johnson, L. S., 'Elizabeth, Bride and Queen: A Study of Spenser's April Eclogue and the Metaphors of English Protestantism', *SSt*, 2 (1981), 75–91.

—— '"And taken up his ynne in fishes haske"', *SpN*, 18, no. 1 (1987), 14–15.

—— *'The Shepheardes Calender': An Introduction* (University Park, Pa., 1990).

Johnson, P., *Form and Transformation in Music and Poetry of the English Renaissance* (New Haven, Conn., 1972).

Johnson, W. C., 'Spenser's *Amoretti* and the Art of the Liturgy', *SEL*, 14 (1974), 47–61.

—— '"Sacred Rites" and Prayer-Book Echoes in Spenser's *Epithalamion*', *Renaissance and Reformation*, 12 (1976), 49–54.

—— *Spenser's 'Amoretti': Analogies of Love* (Lewisburg, Pa., 1990).

—— 'Spenser's "Greener" *Hymnes* and *Amoretti*: "Retractation" and "Reform"', *ES*, 73 (1992), 431–43.

—— 'Gender Fashioning and the Dynamics of Mutuality in Spenser's *Amoretti*', *ES*, 74 (1993), 503–19.

Jones, H. S. V., *A Spenser Handbook* (New York, 1930).

Jortin, John, *Remarks on Spenser's Poems* (London, 1734).

Judson, A. C., 'Mother Hubberd's Ape', *MLN*, 63 (1948), 145–9.

Kaske, C. V., 'Another Liturgical Dimension of *Amoretti* 68', *N&Q*, n.s. 24 (1977), 518–19.

—— 'Spenser's *Amoretti and Epithalamion* of 1595: Structure, Genre and Numerology', *ELR*, 8 (1978), 271–95.

—— 'Rethinking Loewenstein's "Viper Thoughts"', *SSt*, 8 (1987), 325–9.

Kastner, L. E., 'Spenser's *Amoretti* and Desportes', *MLR*, 4 (1908–9), 65–9.

Kay, D., *Melodious Tears: The English Funeral Elegy from Spenser to Milton* (Oxford, 1990).

Kennedy, J. M., 'The Final Emblem of *The Shepheardes Calender*', *SSt*, 1 (1980), 95–106.

Kennedy, J. M. and J. A. Reither, eds., *A Theatre for Spenserians* (Toronto, 1973).

Kerrigan, J., ed., *Motives of Woe: Shakespeare and 'Female Complaint'* (Oxford, 1991).

King, J. N., *English Reformation Literature: The Tudor Origins of the Protestant Tradition* (Princeton, 1982).

—— 'Was Spenser a Puritan?', *SSt*, 6 (1985), 1–31.

—— *Spenser's Poetry and the Reformation Tradition* (Princeton, 1990).

Kinsman, R. S., 'Skelton's Colyn Cloute: the Mask of Vox Poluli', in *Essays Critical and Historical Dedicated to Lily B. Campbell* (Berkeley, 1950), 17–26.

Klein, L. M., ' "Let us love, dear love, lyke as we ought": Protestant Marriage and the Revision of Petrarchan Loving in Spenser's *Amoretti*', *SSt*, 10 (1989), 109–38.

Knowlton, E. C., ' "Oricalche" and "Phoenice" in Spenser's *Muiopotmos*', *N&Q*, n.s. 27 (1980), 138–9.

Koller, K., 'Spenser and Raleigh', *ELH*, 1 (1934), 37–60.

—— 'Identifications in *Colin Clouts Come Home Againe*', *MLN*, 50 (1935), 155–8.

Kostic, V., 'Spenser's *Amoretti* and Tasso's Lyrical Poetry', *Renaissance and Modern Studies*, 3 (1959), 51–77.

Kuin, R., 'The Gaps and the Whites: Indeterminacy and Undecidability in the Sonnet Sequences of Sidney, Spenser, and Shakespeare', *SSt*, 8 (1987), 251–85.

Lambert, E. Z., *Placing Sorrow: A Study of the Pastoral Convention from Theocritus to Milton* (Chapel Hill, 1976).

Landrum, E., 'Spenser's Use of the Bible and his Alleged Puritanism', *PMLA*, 41 (1926), 517–34.

Lane, R., *Shepheards Devises: Edmund Spenser's 'Shepheardes Calender' and the Institutions of Elizabethan Society* (London, 1993).

Lerner, L., *The Uses of Nostalgia: Studies in Pastoral Poetry* (London, 1972).

Lewis, C. S., *English Literature in the Sixteenth Century excluding Drama* (Oxford, 1954).

—— *The Discarded Image: An Introduction to Medieval and Renaissance Literature* (Cambridge, 1964).

Lindheim, N., 'Spenser's Virgilian Pastoral: The Case for *September*', *SSt*, 11 (1990), 1–16.

Loewenstein, J. F., 'Echo's Ring: Orpheus and Spenser's Career', *ELR*, 16 (1986), 287–302.

—— 'A Note on the Structure of Spenser's *Amoretti*: Viper Thoughts', *SSt*, 8 (1987), 311–23.

Lotspeich, H. G., 'Spenser's *Virgil's Gnat* and its Latin Original', *ELH*, 2 (1935), 235–41.

—— *Classical Mythology in the Poetry of Edmund Spenser* (Princeton, 1942).

Low, A., *The Georgic Revolution* (Princeton, 1985).

Luborsky, R. S., 'The Allusive Presentation of *The Shepheardes Calender*', *SSt*, 1 (1980), 29–67.

—— 'The Illustrations to *The Shepheardes Calender*', *SSt*, 2 (1981), 3–53.

MacArthur, J. H., *Critical Contexts of Sidney's 'Astrophil and Stella' and Spenser's 'Amoretti'* (Victoria, BC, 1989).

McCabe, R. A., *The Pillars of Eternity: Time and Providence in 'The Faerie Queene'* (Dublin, 1989).

—— 'Edmund Spenser: Poet of Exile', 1991 Lectures and Memoirs, *Proceedings of the British Academy*, 80 (1993), 73–103.

—— ' "Little booke: thy selfe present": the Politics of Presentation in *The Shepheardes Calender*', in H. Erskine-Hill and R. A. McCabe, eds., *Presenting Poetry: Composition, Publication, Reception* (Cambridge, 1995), 15–40.

MacCaffrey, I. G., 'Allegory and Pastoral in *The Shepheardes Calender*', *ELH*, 36 (1969), 88–109.

McCanles, M., '*The Shepheardes Calender* as Document and Monument', *SEL*, 22 (1982), 5–19.

McCoy, R. C., 'Eulogies to Elegies: Poetic Distance in the April Eclogue', in P. E. Medine and J. Wittreich, eds., *Soundings of Things Done: Essays in Early Modern Literature in Honour of S. K. Heninger* (Newark, Del., 1997), 52–69.

McElderry, B. R., Jr, 'Archaism and Innovation in Spenser's Poetic Diction', *PMLA*, 47 (1932), 144–70.

Macfie, P. R., 'Text and *Textura*: Spenser's Arachnean Art', in D. G. Allen and R. A. White, eds., *Traditions and Innovations: Essays on British Literature of the Middle Ages and the Renaissance* (Newark, Del., 1990), 88–96.

McLane, P. E., *Spenser's 'Shepheardes Calender': A Study in Elizabethan Allegory* (Notre Dame, Ind., 1961).

Maclean, H., ' "Restlesse anguish and unquiet paine": Spenser and the Complaint, 1579–1590', in J. Campbell and J. Doyle, eds., *The Practical Vision: Essays in English Literature in Honour of Flora Roy* (Waterloo, Ont., 1978), 29–47.

MacLure, M., 'Spenser and the ruins of time', in J. M. Kennedy and J. A. Reither, eds., *A Theatre for Spenserians* (Toronto, 1973), 3–18.

Mallette, R., 'Spenser's Portrait of the Artist in *The Shepheardes Calender* and *Colin Clouts Come Home Again*', *SEL*, 19 (1979), 19–41.

—— *Spenser, Milton and Renaissance Pastoral* (London, 1981).

Manley, L., 'Spenser and the City: the Minor Poems', *MLQ*, 43 (1982), 203–27.

Mantuan, Baptista Spagnuoli, *The Eclogues of Baptista Mantuanus*, edited by W. P. Mustard (Baltimore, 1911).

Marot, Clément, *Œuvres*, edited by G. Guiffrey and J. Plattard (5 vols.; Geneva, 1969; first published 1911).

Marotti, A. F., '"Love is Not Love": Elizabethan Sonnet Sequences and the Social Order', *ELH*, 49 (1982), 396–428.

Martin, E. E., 'Spenser, Chaucer, and the Rhetoric of Elegy', *JMRS*, 17 (1987), 83–109.

Martz, L. L., 'The *Amoretti*: "Most Goodly Temperature"', in W. Nelson, ed., *Form and Convention in the Poetry of Edmund Spenser* (1961), 146–68.

Marx, S., '"Fortunate Senex": The Pastoral of Old Age', *SEL*, 25 (1985), 21–44.

Mazzola, E., 'Marrying Medusa: Spenser's *Epithalamion* and Renaissance Reconstructions of Female Privacy', *Genre*, 25 (1992), 193–210.

Meyer, S., *An Interpretation of Edmund Spenser's 'Colin Clout'* (Notre Dame, Ind., 1969).

Micros, M., '"Ryse up *Elisa*" – Woman Trapped in a Lay: Spenser's *Aprill*', *Renaissance and Reformation*, 17 (1993), 63–73.

Miller, D. L., 'Authorship, Authority and *The Shepheardes Calender*', *MLQ*, 40 (1979), 219–36.

—— 'Spenser's Vocation, Spenser's Career', *ELH*, 50 (1983), 197–231.

—— 'The Earl of Cork's Lute', in J. H. Anderson, ed., *Spenser's Life and the Subject of Biography* (1996), 146–71.

Miller, J. T., '"Love Doth Hold My Hand": Writing and Wooing in the Sonnets of Sidney and Spenser', *ELH*, 46 (1979), 541–58.

Miller, P. W., 'The Decline of the English Epithalamion', *TSLL*, 12 (1970), 405–16.

Millican, C. B., 'The Northern Dialect of *The Shepheardes Calender*', *ELH*, 6 (1939), 211–13.

Miola, R. S., 'Spenser's "Anacreontics": A Mythological Metaphor', *SP*, 77 (1980), 50–66.

Montrose, L. A., '"The perfect Paterne of a Poete": The Poetics of Courtship in *The Shepheardes Calender*', *TSLL*, 21 (1979), 34–67.

—— '"Eliza, Queene of Shepheardes", and the Pastoral of Power', *ELR*, 10 (1980), 153–82.

—— 'Interpreting Spenser's February Eclogue: Some Contexts and Implications', *SSt*, 2 (1981), 67–74.

—— 'Of Gentlemen and Shepherds: The Politics of Elizabethan Pastoral Form', *ELH*, 50 (1983), 415–59.

Moore, J. W., 'Colin Breaks his Pipe: A Reading of the *January* Eclogue', *ELR*, 5 (1975), 3–24.

Morey, J. H., 'Spenser's Mythic Adaptations in *Muiopotmos*', *SSt*, 9 (1988), 49–59.

—— 'Latimer's Sermon on the Plough and Spenser's *Muiopotmos*', *N&Q*, n.s. 42 (1995), 286–8.

Mounts, C. E., 'The Ralegh–Essex Rivalry and *Mother Hubberd's Tale*', *MLN*, 65 (1950), 509–13.

—— 'Spenser and the Countess of Leicester', *ELH*, 19 (1952), 191–202.

Mulryan, J., 'Spenser as Mythologist: A Study of the Nativities of Cupid and Christ in the *Fowre Hymnes*', *Modern Language Studies*, 1 (1971), 13–16.

—— 'Literary and Philosophical Interpretations of the Myth of Pan from the Classical Period through the Seventeenth Century', in Jean-Claude Margolin, ed., *Acta Conventus Neo-Latini Turonensis* (Paris, 1980), 209–18.

Nashe, Thomas, *Works*, edited by R. B. McKerrow (5 vols.; revd edn, Oxford, 1958).

Neely, C. T., 'The Structure of English Renaissance Sonnet Sequences', *ELH*, 45 (1978), 359–89.

Nelson, W., ed., *Form and Convention in the Poetry of Edmund Spenser* (New York, 1961).

—— *The Poetry of Edmund Spenser: A Study* (New York, 1963).

Neuse, R., 'The Triumph over Hasty Accidents: A Note on the Symbolic Mode of the *Epithalamion*', *MLR*, 61 (1966), 163–74.

Norbrook, D., *Poetry and Politics in the English Renaissance* (London, 1984).

Norton, D. S., 'Queen Elizabeth's "Brydale Day"', *MLQ*, 5 (1944), 149–54.

—— 'The Tradition of Prothalamia', in *English Studies in Honour of James Southall Wilson* (Charlottesville, Va., 1951), 223–41.

Oakeshott, W., 'Carew Ralegh's Copy of Spenser', *The Library*, 5th series, 26 (1971), 1–21.

Oates, M. I., '*Fowre Hymnes*: Spenser's Retractations of Paradise', *SSt*, 4 (1983), 143–69.

O'Connell, M., '*Astrophel*: Spenser's Double Elegy', *SEL*, 11 (1971), 27–35.

Oram, W. A., '*Daphnaïda* and Spenser's Later Poetry', *SSt*, 2 (1981), 141–58.

—— 'Elizabethan Fact and Spenserian Fiction', *SSt*, 4 (1983), 33–47.

—— 'Spenser's Raleghs', *SP*, 87 (1990), 341–62.

Oram, W. A., et al., eds., *The Yale Edition of the Shorter Poems of Edmund Spenser* (New Haven, Conn., 1989).

Orwen, W. R., 'Spenser and the Serpent of Division', *SP*, 38 (1941), 198–210.

—— 'Spenser's "Stemmata Dudleiana"', *N&Q*, 190 (1946), 9–11.

Osgood, C. G., *A Concordance to Spenser* (Philadelphia, 1915).

Panofsky, D. and E. Panofsky, *Pandora's Box: The Changing Aspects of a Mythical Symbol* (Princeton, 1962).

Parmenter, M., 'Spenser's "Twelve Aeglogves Proportionable to the Twelve Monethes"', *ELH*, 3 (1936), 190–217.

Patterson, A., 'Re-opening the Green Cabinet: Clément Marot and Edmund Spenser', *ELR*, 16 (1986), 44–70.

—— 'Still Reading Spenser After All These Years?', *ELR*, 25 (1995), 432–44.

Patterson, S. R., 'Spenser's *Prothalamion* and the Catullan Epithalamic Tradition', *Comitatus*, 10 (1979–80), 97–106.

Pearcy, L. T., 'A Case of Allusion: Stanza 18 of Spenser's *Epithalamion* and Catullus 5', *Classical and Modern Literature*, 1 (1981), 243–54.

Peter, J., *Complaint and Satire in Early English Literature* (Oxford, 1956).

Peterson, R. S., 'Spurting Forth upon Courtiers: New Light on the Risks Spenser Took in Publishing *Mother Hubberds Tale*', *TLS*, May 16 (1997), 14–15.

Petrarch, Francesco, *Petrarch's Lyric Poems: The 'Rime Sparse' and Other Lyrics*, translated and edited by R. M. Durling (Cambridge, Mass., 1976).

Pigman, G. W., *Grief and English Renaissance Elegy* (Cambridge, 1985).

Prager, C., 'Emblem and Motion in Spenser's *Prothalamion*', *Studies in Iconology*, 2 (1976), 114–20.

Prescott, A. L., *French Poets and the English Renaissance: Studies in Fame and Transformation* (New Haven, Conn., 1978).

—— '"The Thirsty Deer and the Lord of Life": Some Contexts for *Amoretti* 67–70', *SSt*, 6 (1985), 33–76.

—— 'Triumphing over Death and Sin', *SSt*, 11 (1990), 231–2.

Quint, D., *Origin and Originality in Renaissance Literature: Versions of the Source* (New Haven, Conn., 1983).

Quitslund, J. A., 'Spenser's Image of Sapience', *SR*, 16 (1969), 182–213.

—— 'Spenser and the Patronesses of the *Fowre Hymnes*: "Ornaments of all True Love and Beautie"', in M. P. Hannay, ed., *Silent But for the Word: Tudor Women as Patrons, Translators, and Writers of Religious Works* (Kent, Ohio, 1985), 184–202.

—— 'Questionable Evidence in the *Letters* of 1580 between Gabriel Harvey and Edmund Spenser', in J. H. Anderson et al., eds., *Spenser's Life and the Subject of Biography* (1996), 81–98.

Rambuss, R., *Spenser's Secret Career* (Cambridge, 1993).

Rasmussen, C. J., '"Quietnesse of Minde": *A Theatre for Worldlings* as a Protestant Poetics', *SSt*, 1 (1980), 3–27.

—— '"How Weak Be the Passions of Woefulness": Spenser's *Ruines of Time*', *SSt*, 2 (1981), 159–81.

Reamer, O. J., 'Spenser's Debt to Marot – Re-examined', *TSLL*, 10 (1969), 504–27.

Rebhorn, W. A., 'Du Bellay's Imperial Mistress: *Les Antiquitez de Rome* as

Petrarchist Sonnet Sequence', *Renaissance Quarterly*, 33 (1980), 609–22.

Rees, C., 'The Metamorphosis of Daphne in Sixteenth- and Seventeenth-Century English Poetry', *MLR*, 66 (1971), 251–63.

Renwick, W. R., ed., *Complaints* (London, 1928).

—— ed., *Daphnaïda and Other Poems* (London, 1929).

—— ed., *The Shepheardes Calender* (London, 1930).

Rice, E. F., *The Renaissance Idea of Wisdom* (Cambridge, Mass., 1958).

Richardson, J. M., *Astrological Symbolism in Spenser's 'The Shepheardes Calender'* (Lewiston, NY, 1989).

Ringler, W., 'Spenser and Thomas Watson', *MLN*, 69 (1954), 484–87.

Rix, H. D., *Rhetoric in Spenser's Poetry* (University Park, Pa., 1940).

Roche, T. P., Jr, ed., *The Faerie Queene* (Harmondsworth, 1978).

—— (a) *Petrarch and the English Sonnet Sequences* (New York, 1989).

—— (b) 'Spenser's Muse', in G. M. Logan and G. Teskey, eds., *Unfolded Tales: Essays on Renaissance Romance* (Ithaca, NY, 1989), 162–88.

Rogers, W. E., 'The *Carmina* of Horace in *Prothalamion*', *American Notes and Queries*, 15 (1977), 148–53.

—— '"Perfect Speculation" in Spenser's *Fowre Hymnes*', in *The Three Genres and the Interpretation of Lyric* (Princeton, 1983), 184–202.

Rollinson, P., 'The Renaissance of the Literary Hymn', *Renaissance Papers* (1968), 11–20.

—— 'A Generic View of Spenser's *Four Hymns*', *SP*, 68 (1971), 292–304.

Ronsard, Pierre, *Œuvres Complètes*, edited by H. Vaganay (7 vols.; Paris, 1923–4).

Rosenberg, D. M., *Oaten Reeds and Trumpets: Pastoral and Epic in Virgil, Spenser, and Milton* (Lewisburg, Pa., 1981).

Rosenberg, E., *Leicester: Patron of Letters* (New York, 1955).

Rosenmeyer, T. G., *The Green Cabinet: Theocritus and the European Pastoral Lyric* (Berkeley, 1969).

Røstvig, Maren-Sofie, *The Hidden Sense and Other Essays* (Oslo, 1963).

—— 'Images of Perfection', in E. Miner, ed., *Seventeenth-Century Imagery: Essays on the Use of Figurative Language from Donne to Farquhar* (Berkeley, 1971).

Russell, D., 'Du Bellay's Emblematic Vision of Rome', *Yale French Studies*, 47 (1972), 98–109.

Sacks, P. M., *The English Elegy: Studies in the Genre from Spenser to Yeats* (Baltimore, 1985).

Sagaser, E. H., 'Gathered in Time: Form, Meter (and Parenthesis) in *The Shepheardes Calender*', *SSt*, 10 (1989), 95–108.

Sandison, H. E., 'Spenser's "Lost" Works and their Probable Relation to *The Faerie Queene*', *PMLA*, 25 (1910), 134–51.

—— 'Arthur Gorges, Spenser's Alcyon and Ralegh's Friend', *PMLA*, 43 (1928), 645–74.

—— 'Spenser and Ralegh', *ELH*, 1 (1934), 37–60.

Satterthwaite, A. W., 'Moral Vision in Spenser, Du Bellay, and Ronsard', *CL*, 9 (1957), 136–49.

—— *Spenser, Ronsard and Du Bellay: a Renaissance Comparison* (Princeton, 1960).

Schleiner, L., 'Spenser and Sidney on the Vaticinium', *SSt*, 6 (1985), 129–45.

—— 'Spenser's "E. K." as Edmund Kent (Kenned / of Kent): Kyth (Couth), Kissed, and Kunning-Conning', *ELR*, 20 (1990), 374–407.

Servius Grammaticus, *Servii Grammatici qui feruntur in Vergilii Carmina Commentarii*, edited by G. Thilo and H. Hagen (3 vols.; Leipzig, 1878–87).

Shawcross, J. T., 'Probability as Requisite to Poetic Delight: A Re-view of the Intentionality of *The Shepheardes Calender*', *SP*, 87 (1990), 120–27.

Shepherd, S., *Spenser* (Atlantic Highlands, NJ, 1989).

Shire, H., *A Preface to Spenser* (London, 1978).

Shore, D. R., *Spenser and the Poetics of Pastoral: A Study of the World of Colin Clout* (Kingston, Ont., 1985).

Sinfield, A., *Literature in Protestant England, 1560–1660* (London, 1983).

Sjøgren, G., 'Helena, Marchioness of Northampton', *History Today*, 28 (1978), 596–604.

Smith, B. R., 'On Reading *The Shepheardes Calender*', *SSt*, 1 (1980), 69–93.

—— *Homosexual Desire in Shakespeare's England* (Chicago, 1991).

Smith, C. G., *Spenser's Proverb Lore: with Special Reference to his Use of the 'Sententiae' of Leonard Culman and Publilius Syrus* (Cambridge, Mass., 1970).

Smith, H., 'The Use of Conventions in Spenser's Minor Poems', in W. Nelson, ed., *Form and Convention in the Poetry of Edmund Spenser* (1961), 122–45.

Smith, J. N., 'Spenser's *Prothalamion*: A New Genre', *RES*, n.s. 10 (1959), 173–8.

Smith, R. M., 'Spenser's Irish River Stories', *PMLA*, 50 (1935), 1047–56.

Snare, G., 'The Muses on Poetry: Spenser's *The Teares of the Muses*', *Tulane Studies in English*, 17 (1969), 31–52.

Sowton, I., 'Hidden Persuaders as a Means of Literary Grace: Sixteenth-Century Poetics and Rhetoric in England', *UTQ*, 32 (1962), 55–69.

Spiller, M. R. G., *The Development of the Sonnet: An Introduction* (London, 1992).

Spitzer, L., 'Spenser, *Shepheardes Calender, March*, ll. 61–114, and the Variorum Edition', *SP*, 47 (1950), 494–505.

Stapleton, M. L., 'Spenser, the *Antiquitez de Rome*, and the Development of the English Sonnet Form', *Comparative Literary Studies*, 27 (1990), 259–74.

Starnes, De Witt T. and E. W. Talbert, *Classical Myth and Legend in Renaissance Dictionaries: A Study of Renaissance Dictionaries in their Relation to the Classical Learning of Contemporary English Writers* (Chapel Hill, 1955).

Steen, J., 'On Spenser's *Epithalamion*', *Spectrum*, 5 (1961), 31–7.

Stein, H., *Studies in Spenser's 'Complaints'* (New York, 1934).

Steinberg, T. L., 'Spenser, Sidney and the Myth of Astrophel', *SSt*, 9, 11 (1990), 187–202.

Stern, V. F., *Gabriel Harvey: A Study of his Life, Marginalia, and Library* (Oxford, 1979).

Stewart, J. T., 'Renaissance Psychology and the Ladder of Love in Castiglione and Spenser', *JEGP*, 56 (1957), 225–30.

Stewart, S., 'Spenser and the Judgement of Paris', *SSt*, 9 (1988), 161–209.

Strickland, R., 'Not So Idle Tears: Re-reading the Renaissance Funeral Elegy', *Review*, 14 (1992), 57–72.

Strong, R. C., *The Cult of Elizabeth: Elizabethan Portraiture and Pageantry* (London, 1977).

—— *Gloriana: The Portraits of Queen Elizabeth I* (London, 1987).

Stubbs, John, *John Stubbs's 'Gaping Gulf' with Letters and Other Relevant Documents*, edited by L. E. Berry (Charlottesville, 1968).

Tasso, Torquato, *Le Rime di Torquato Tasso*, edited by A. Solerti (4 vols.; Bologna, 1898–1902).

Thompson, C., 'Love in an Orderly Universe: A Unification of Spenser's *Amoretti*, "Anacreontics", and *Epithalamion*', *Viator*, 16 (1985), 277–335.

Thornton, B., 'Rural Dialectic: Pastoral, Georgic, and *The Shepheardes Calender*', *SSt*, 9 (1988), 1–20.

Tribble, E., 'Glozing the Gap: Authority, Glossing Traditions and *The Shepheardes Calender*', *Criticism*, 34 (1992), 155–72.

—— *Margins and Marginality: The Printed Page in Early Modern England* (Charlottesville, Va., 1993).

Tromly, F. B., 'Lodowick Bryskett's Elegies on Sidney in Spenser's *Astrophel* Volume', *RES*, n.s. 37 (1986), 384–8.

Tucker, G. H., *The Poet's Odyssey: Joachim Du Bellay and the 'Antiquitez De Rome'* (Oxford, 1990).

Tufte, V. J., *The Poetry of Marriage: The Epithalamium in Europe and its Development in England* (Los Angeles, 1970).

Turner, M., 'The Imagery of Spenser's *Amoretti*', *Neophilologus*, 72 (1988), 284–99.

Tuve, R., *Allegorical Imagery: Some Mediaeval Books and their Posterity* (Princeton, 1966).

Tylus, J., 'Spenser, Virgil and the Politics of Poetic Labour', *ELH*, 55 (1988), 53–77.

Van der Berg, K., 'The Counterfeit in Personation: Spenser's *Prosopopoia*', in L. Martz and A. Williams, eds., *The Author in his Work: Essays on a Problem in Criticism* (New Haven, Conn., 1978), 85–102.

Van Dorsten, J. A., *The Radical Arts: First Decade of an Elizabethan Renaissance* (Leiden, 1970).

—— 'Literary Patronage in Elizabethan England: The Early Phase', in G. F. Lytle and S. Orgel, eds., *Patronage in the Renaissance* (Princeton, 1981), 191–206.

Villeponteaux, M. A., ' "With her own will beguyld": The Captive Lady in Spenser's *Amoretti*', *Explorations in Renaissance Culture*, 14 (1988), 29–39.

Vink, J., 'A Concealed Figure in the Woodcut to the *Januarye* Eclogue', *SSt*, 7 (1986), 297–8.

Waldman, L., 'Spenser's Pseudonym "E. K." and Humanist Self-Naming', *SSt*, 9 (1988), 21–31.

Waller, M. R., *Petrarch's Poetics and Literary History* (Amherst, Mass., 1980).

Wallerstein, R. C., *Studies in Seventeenth-Century Poetic* (Madison, Wis., 1950).

Warkentin, G., 'Spenser at the Still Point: A Schematic Device in *Epithalamion*', in H. B. de Groot and A. Leggatt, eds., *Craft and Tradition: Essays in Honour of William Blissett* (Calgary, 1990), 47–57.

Warton, Thomas, *Observations on the Faerie Queene of Spenser* (London, 1754).

Waters, D. D., 'Spenser and Symbolic Witchcraft in *The Shepheardes Calender*', *SEL*, 14 (1974), 3–15.

Watkins, J., *The Specter of Dido: Spenser and Virgilian Epic* (New Haven, 1995).

Watson, E. L., ' "Sylvanus" Tree Emblems at Kenilworth and Spenser's *Februarie* Eclogue', *Explorations in Renaissance Culture*, 19 (1993), 115–33.

Webster, J., ' "The Methode of a Poete": An Inquiry into Tudor Conceptions of Poetic Sequence', *ELR*, 11 (1981), 22–43.

Weiner, A. D., 'Spenser's *Muiopotmos* and the Fates of Butterflies and Men', *JEGP*, 84 (1985), 203–20.

—— 'Spenser and the Myth of Pastoral', *SP*, 85 (1988), 390–406.

Weiner, S., 'Spenser's Study of English Syllables and its Completion by Thomas Campion', *SSt*, 3 (1982), 3–56.

Wells, R. H., 'Poetic Decorum in Spenser's *Amoretti*', *Cahiers Elisabéthains*, 25 (1984), 9–21.

Wells, W., ' "To Make a Mild Construction": The Significance of the Opening Stanzas of *Muiopotmos*', *SP*, 42 (1945), 544–54.

—— ed., *Spenser Allusions in the Sixteenth and Seventeenth Centuries*, *SP*, Texts and Studies, 68–9 (1971–2).

Welsford, E., *Spenser's 'Fowre Hymnes', 'Epithalamion': A Study of Edmund Spenser's Doctrine of Love* (Oxford, 1967).

West, M., 'Prothalamia in Propertius and Spenser', *CL*, 26 (1974), 346–53.

Whidden, M. B., 'Method and Value in *Amoretti* 15', *Explicator*, 51 (1993), 73–5.

Whipp, L. T., 'Spenser's *November* Eclogue', *SSt*, 11 (1990), 17–30.

Whitaker, V. K., *The Religious Basis of Spenser's Thought* (Stanford, 1950).

Wickert, M. A., 'Structure and Ceremony in Spenser's *Epithalamion*', *ELH*, 35 (1968), 135–57.

Wilkin, G., 'Spenser's Rehabilitation of the Templars', *SSt*, 11 (1990), 89–100.

Wind, E., *Pagan Mysteries in the Renaissance* (2nd edn; London, 1967).

Wine, M., 'Spenser's "Sweete Themmes": Of Time and the River', *SEL*, 2 (1962), 111–17.

Woodward, D. H., 'Some Themes in Spenser's *Prothalamion*', *ELH*, 29 (1962), 34–46.

Yates, F., *Astraea: The Imperial Theme in the Sixteenth Century* (London, 1975).

READ MORE IN PENGUIN

PENGUIN AUDIOBOOKS

A Quality of Writing That Speaks for Itself

Penguin Books has always led the field in quality publishing. Now you can listen at leisure to your favourite books, read to you by familiar voices from radio, stage and screen. Penguin Audiobooks are produced to an excellent standard, and abridgements are always faithful to the original texts. From thrillers to classic literature, biography to humour, with a wealth of titles in between, Penguin Audiobooks offer you quality, entertainment and the chance to rediscover the pleasure of listening.

You can order Penguin Audiobooks through Penguin Direct by telephoning (0181) 899 4036. The lines are open 24 hours every day. Ask for Penguin Direct, quoting your credit card details.

PENGUIN AUDIOBOOKS

The Man in the Iron Mask by Alexandre Dumas, read by Simon Ward

Adam Bede by George Eliot, read by Paul Copley

Joseph Andrews by Henry Fielding, read by Sean Barrett

The Great Gatsby by F. Scott Fitzgerald, read by Marcus D'Amico

North and South by Elizabeth Gaskell, read by Diana Quick

The Diary of a Nobody by George Grossmith, read by Terrence Hardiman

Jude the Obscure by Thomas Hardy, read by Samuel West

The Go-Between by L. P. Hartley, read by Tony Britton

Les Misérables by Victor Hugo, read by Nigel Anthony

A Passage to India by E. M. Forster, read by Tim Pigott-Smith

The Odyssey by Homer, read by Alex Jennings

The Portrait of a Lady by Henry James, read by Claire Bloom

On the Road by Jack Kerouac, read by David Carradine

Women in Love by D. H. Lawrence, read by Michael Maloney

Nineteen Eighty-Four by George Orwell, read by Timothy West

Ivanhoe by Sir Walter Scott, read by Ciaran Hinds

Frankenstein by Mary Shelley, read by Richard Pasco

Of Mice and Men by John Steinbeck, read by Gary Sinise

Dracula by Bram Stoker, read by Richard E. Grant

Gulliver's Travels by Jonathan Swift, read by Hugh Laurie

Vanity Fair by William Makepeace Thackeray, read by Robert Hardy

War and Peace by Leo Tolstoy, read by Bill Nighy

Barchester Towers by Anthony Trollope, read by David Timson

Tao Te Ching by Lao Tzu, read by Carole Boyd and John Rowe

Ethan Frome by Edith Wharton, read by Nathan Osgood

The Picture of Dorian Gray by Oscar Wilde, read by John Moffatt

Orlando by Virginia Woolf, read by Tilda Swinton

READ MORE IN PENGUIN

A CHOICE OF CLASSICS

Matthew Arnold	**Selected Prose**
Jane Austen	**Emma**
	Lady Susan/The Watsons/Sanditon
	Mansfield Park
	Northanger Abbey
	Persuasion
	Pride and Prejudice
	Sense and Sensibility
William Barnes	**Selected Poems**
Mary Braddon	**Lady Audley's Secret**
Anne Brontë	**Agnes Grey**
	The Tenant of Wildfell Hall
Charlotte Brontë	**Jane Eyre**
	Juvenilia: 1829–35
	The Professor
	Shirley
	Villette
Emily Brontë	**Complete Poems**
	Wuthering Heights
Samuel Butler	**Erewhon**
	The Way of All Flesh
Lord Byron	**Don Juan**
	Selected Poems
Lewis Carroll	**Alice's Adventures in Wonderland**
	The Hunting of the Snark
Thomas Carlyle	**Selected Writings**
Arthur Hugh Clough	**Selected Poems**
Wilkie Collins	**Armadale**
	The Law and the Lady
	The Moonstone
	No Name
	The Woman in White
Charles Darwin	**The Origin of Species**
	Voyage of the Beagle
Benjamin Disraeli	**Coningsby**
	Sybil

READ MORE IN PENGUIN

A CHOICE OF CLASSICS

Charles Dickens	**American Notes for General Circulation**
	Barnaby Rudge
	Bleak House
	The Christmas Books (in two volumes)
	David Copperfield
	Dombey and Son
	Great Expectations
	Hard Times
	Little Dorrit
	Martin Chuzzlewit
	The Mystery of Edwin Drood
	Nicholas Nickleby
	The Old Curiosity Shop
	Oliver Twist
	Our Mutual Friend
	The Pickwick Papers
	Pictures from Italy
	Selected Journalism 1850–1870
	Selected Short Fiction
	Sketches by Boz
	A Tale of Two Cities
George Eliot	**Adam Bede**
	Daniel Deronda
	Felix Holt
	Middlemarch
	The Mill on the Floss
	Romola
	Scenes of Clerical Life
	Silas Marner
Fanny Fern	**Ruth Hall**
Elizabeth Gaskell	**Cranford/Cousin Phillis**
	The Life of Charlotte Brontë
	Mary Barton
	North and South
	Ruth
	Sylvia's Lovers
	Wives and Daughters

READ MORE IN PENGUIN

A CHOICE OF CLASSICS

Edward Gibbon	**The Decline and Fall of the Roman Empire** (in three volumes)
	Memoirs of My Life
George Gissing	**New Grub Street**
	The Odd Women
William Godwin	**Caleb Williams**
	Concerning Political Justice
Thomas Hardy	**Desperate Remedies**
	The Distracted Preacher and Other Tales
	Far from the Madding Crowd
	Jude the Obscure
	The Hand of Ethelberta
	A Laodicean
	The Mayor of Casterbridge
	A Pair of Blue Eyes
	The Return of the Native
	Selected Poems
	Tess of the d'Urbervilles
	The Trumpet-Major
	Two on a Tower
	Under the Greenwood Tree
	The Well-Beloved
	The Woodlanders
George Lyell	**Principles of Geology**
Lord Macaulay	**The History of England**
Henry Mayhew	**London Labour and the London Poor**
George Meredith	**The Egoist**
	The Ordeal of Richard Feverel
John Stuart Mill	**The Autobiography**
	On Liberty
	Principles of Political Economy
William Morris	**News from Nowhere and Other Writings**
John Henry Newman	**Apologia Pro Vita Sua**
Margaret Oliphant	**Miss Marjoribanks**
Robert Owen	**A New View of Society and Other Writings**
Walter Pater	**Marius the Epicurean**
John Ruskin	**Unto This Last and Other Writings**

READ MORE IN PENGUIN

A CHOICE OF CLASSICS

Walter Scott	**The Antiquary**
	Heart of Mid-Lothian
	Ivanhoe
	Kenilworth
	The Tale of Old Mortality
	Rob Roy
	Waverley
Robert Louis Stevenson	**Kidnapped**
	Dr Jekyll and Mr Hyde and Other Stories
	In the South Seas
	The Master of Ballantrae
	Selected Poems
	Weir of Hermiston
William Makepeace Thackeray	**The History of Henry Esmond**
	The History of Pendennis
	The Newcomes
	Vanity Fair
Anthony Trollope	**Barchester Towers**
	Can You Forgive Her?
	Doctor Thorne
	The Eustace Diamonds
	Framley Parsonage
	He Knew He Was Right
	The Last Chronicle of Barset
	Phineas Finn
	The Prime Minister
	The Small House at Allington
	The Warden
	The Way We Live Now
Oscar Wilde	**Complete Short Fiction**
Mary Wollstonecraft	**A Vindication of the Rights of Woman**
	Mary and **Maria** (includes Mary Shelley's **Matilda**)
Dorothy and William Wordsworth	**Home at Grasmere**

READ MORE IN PENGUIN

A CHOICE OF CLASSICS

Leopoldo Alas	**La Regenta**
Leon B. Alberti	**On Painting**
Ludovico Ariosto	**Orlando Furioso** (in two volumes)
Giovanni Boccaccio	**The Decameron**
Baldassar Castiglione	**The Book of the Courtier**
Benvenuto Cellini	**Autobiography**
Miguel de Cervantes	**Don Quixote**
	Exemplary Stories
Dante	**The Divine Comedy** (in three volumes)
	La Vita Nuova
Machado de Assis	**Dom Casmurro**
Bernal Díaz	**The Conquest of New Spain**
Niccolò Machiavelli	**The Discourses**
	The Prince
Alessandro Manzoni	**The Betrothed**
Emilia Pardo Bazán	**The House of Ulloa**
Benito Pérez Galdós	**Fortunata and Jacinta**
Eça de Quierós	**The Maias**
Sor Juana Inés de la	
Cruz	**Poems, Protest and a Dream**
Giorgio Vasari	**Lives of the Artists** (in two volumes)

and

Five Italian Renaissance Comedies
(Machiavelli/**The Mandragola**; Ariosto/**Lena**; Aretino/**The Stablemaster**; Gl'Intronati/**The Deceived**; Guarini/**The Faithful Shepherd**)
The Poem of the Cid
Two Spanish Picaresque Novels
(Anon/**Lazarillo de Tormes**; de Quevedo/**The Swindler**)

READ MORE IN PENGUIN

A CHOICE OF CLASSICS

Basho	**The Narrow Road to the Deep North**
	On Love and Barley
Cao Xueqin	**The Story of the Stone** also known as **The Dream of The Red Chamber** (in five volumes)
Confucius	**The Analects**
Khayyam	**The Ruba'iyat of Omar Khayyam**
Lao Tzu	**Tao Te Ching**
Li Po/Tu Fu	**Poems**
Shikibu Murasaki	**The Tale of Genji**
Sarma	**The Pañcatantra**
Sei Shonagon	**The Pillow Book of Sei Shonagon**
Somadeva	**Tales from the Kathasaritsagara**
Wu Ch'Eng-En	**Monkey**

ANTHOLOGIES AND ANONYMOUS WORKS

The Bhagavad Gita
Buddhist Scriptures
Chinese Love Poetry
The Dhammapada
Hindu Myths
Japanese No Dramas
The Koran
The Laws of Manu
Poems from the Sanskrit
Poems of the Late T'Ang
The Rig Veda
Speaking of Siva
Tales from the Thousand and One Nights
The Upanishads

READ MORE IN PENGUIN

A CHOICE OF CLASSICS

ANTHOLOGIES AND ANONYMOUS WORKS

The Age of Bede
Alfred the Great
Beowulf
A Celtic Miscellany
The Cloud of Unknowing and Other Works
The Death of King Arthur
The Earliest English Poems
Early Christian Lives
Early Irish Myths and Sagas
Egil's Saga
English Mystery Plays
The Exeter Book of Riddles
Eyrbyggja Saga
Hrafnkel's Saga and Other Stories
The Letters of Abelard and Heloise
Medieval English Lyrics
Medieval English Verse
Njal's Saga
The Orkneyinga Saga
Roman Poets of the Early Empire
The Saga of King Hrolf Kraki
Seven Viking Romances
Sir Gawain and the Green Knight

READ MORE IN PENGUIN

A CHOICE OF CLASSICS

Francis Bacon	**The Essays**
Aphra Behn	**Love-Letters between a Nobleman and His Sister**
	Oroonoko, The Rover and Other Works
George Berkeley	**Principles of Human Knowledge/Three Dialogues between Hylas and Philonous**
James Boswell	**The Life of Samuel Johnson**
Sir Thomas Browne	**The Major Works**
John Bunyan	**Grace Abounding to The Chief of Sinners**
	The Pilgrim's Progress
Edmund Burke	**A Philosophical Enquiry into the Origin of our Ideas of the Sublime and Beautiful**
	Reflections on the Revolution in France
Frances Burney	**Evelina**
Margaret Cavendish	**The Blazing World and Other Writings**
William Cobbett	**Rural Rides**
William Congreve	**Comedies**
Cowley/Waller/Oldham	**Selected Poems**
Thomas de Quincey	**Confessions of an English Opium Eater**
	Recollections of the Lakes
Daniel Defoe	**A Journal of the Plague Year**
	Moll Flanders
	Robinson Crusoe
	Roxana
	A Tour Through the Whole Island of Great Britain
	The True-Born Englishman
John Donne	**Complete English Poems**
	Selected Prose
Henry Fielding	**Amelia**
	Jonathan Wild
	Joseph Andrews
	The Journal of a Voyage to Lisbon
	Tom Jones
George Fox	**The Journal**
John Gay	**The Beggar's Opera**

READ MORE IN PENGUIN

A CHOICE OF CLASSICS

Oliver Goldsmith	**The Vicar of Wakefield**
Gray/Churchill/Cowper	**Selected Poems**
William Hazlitt	**Selected Writings**
George Herbert	**The Complete English Poems**
Thomas Hobbes	**Leviathan**
Samuel Johnson	**Gabriel's Ladder**
	History of Rasselas, Prince of Abissinia
	Selected Writings
Samuel Johnson/	**A Journey to the Western Islands of**
James Boswell	**Scotland and The Journal of a Tour of**
	the Hebrides
Matthew Lewis	**The Monk**
John Locke	**An Essay Concerning Human**
	Understanding
Andrew Marvell	**Complete Poems**
Thomas Middleton	**Five Plays**
John Milton	**Complete Poems**
	Paradise Lost
Samuel Richardson	**Clarissa**
	Pamela
Earl of Rochester	**Complete Works**
Richard Brinsley	
Sheridan	**The School for Scandal and Other Plays**
Sir Philip Sidney	**Arcadia**
Christopher Smart	**Selected Poems**
Adam Smith	**The Wealth of Nations (Books I–III)**
Tobias Smollett	**Humphrey Clinker**
	Roderick Random
Edmund Spenser	**The Faerie Queene**
Laurence Sterne	**The Life and Opinions of Tristram Shandy**
	A Sentimental Journey Through France
	and Italy
Jonathan Swift	**Complete Poems**
	Gulliver's Travels
Thomas Traherne	**Selected Poems and Prose**
Henry Vaughan	**Complete Poems**